Wally Klah

Washington State Fishing Guide

Eighth Revised Edition

Terry W. Sheely, Editor

EDITOR AND PUBLISHER: Washington State Fishing Guide, 8th Revised Edition is published by TNScommunications, PO Box 86, Black Diamond, WA 98010. Phone 360-886-9798. FAX 360-886-9796. $19.95 US, $30.95 Canada. Email: tsheely@sosnet.net. Also publishes Pacific Northwest Seafood Cookery, $14.95.

Co Publishers: Terry W. Sheely and Natalie S. Sheely

Cover Photos: Front, David Freel with rainbow trout. By Terry W. Sheely.
    Back, Terry W. Sheely, ocean chinook salmon. By James Goerg.

Production: Charles B. Summers, Pacific Publication Services, PO Box H, South Bend, WA 98586.

Graphic Artist: James Goerg, Coordinating Services, PMB, A16, 621 SR 9, Lake Stevens, WA 98258.

Founding Publisher: Stanley N. Jones

Printed in the United States of America

ISBN 0-939936-05-4

Acknowledgments

A tremendous amount of expertise, experience, fishing time and research is required to produce this comprehensive guide covering more than 2400 fishing spots. We called on dozens of local experts and fisheries managers throughout the state to make every effort possible to assure the accuracy of every entry. It couldn't have been done without the generous and selfless assistance of dozens.

Special thanks to Jim Goerg, publisher of The Reel News, a fine fisherman and an outstanding friend for his unflagging enthusiasm and unlimited willingness to share his exceptional artistic talents in producing many of the quality illustrations.

To Julie Jones for her support and cooperation in advancing the book conceived, originated and published for 7 editions by her father and Publisher Emeritus Stanley N. Jones, to whom we forever will owe a debt of fishing gratitude.

To outdoor writers Wayne Kruse, *The Everett Herald;* Lenny Frasure, *The Lewiston Tribune*; Allen Thomas, *Vancouver Columbian*, and Rob Phillips, *Yakima Herald,* for fact-checking their regions and adding personal insights about lakes and streams. To Mike Meseberg of MarDon Resort at O'Sullivan Lake and Gordon Steinmetz of Big Wally's on Banks Lake for their considerable local know-how.

A statewide county-by-county fishing guide requires the cooperation of regional Washington Department of Fish and Wildlife (WDFW) fish managers, specialists and biologists to provide the latest stocking and management information.

Most WDFW regional staffers gave generously of their time and expertise. These regional authorities went above and beyond to provide the most accurate information possible and deserve the special thanks of every fisherman who benefits from their work. Jim Cummins, Region 3 fish biologist, Jeff Korth Region 2 fish biologist, Heather Bartlett, Region 2, Okanogan County Fish Biologist, John Whalen, Region 1 Fish Program Manager, Stacie Kelsey, Region 5 Fish Program Specialist, Jay Hunter and Tim Flint, Region 6 Fish Biologists

Thanks also to Jim Byrd, WDFW Olympia, Region 4 Chuck Phillips, Mark Downen and Jim Johnston; Region 5 Joe Hymer; Region 6 Dan Collins, Lorna Wargo, and Bill Freymond. National park information was provided by Reed Glesne, North Cascade National Park Aquatic Ecologist and Timothy R. Manns, NCNP Chief Interpreter.

And to Chuck Summers, without his technical skills production would not have been possible.

Bibliography

Washington Atlas and Gazetteer, DeLorme Mapping Company.

Olympic Mountains Fishing Guide Dave Shorett, LakeStream Publications.

Mt. Rainier & South Cascades Fishing Guide, Dave Shorett, LakeStream Publications.

Lakes of Washington, Vol. I and II, Ernest Wolcott, Washington DOE.

Reconnaissance Data On Lakes Of Washington, Vol. 1-7. Washington DOE.

Washington Saltwater Fishing Guide, Stan Jones Publishing.

Western Steelhead Fishing Guide, Milt Keizer, Amato Publishing.

Washington's Blue Ribbon Fly Fishing Guide, John Shewey, Amato Publishing.

Dedication

Especially to Natalie

For her amazing dedication, tireless assistance, faith and tolerance. You made this project possible.

And to every fisherman who generously and patiently shares valuable, finite days on the water with inexperienced anglers, and wide-eyed beginners; and to the hope that one day bureaucrats will listen to their biologists and good fishing will be measured not in terms of fish caught, but in fish that can be sought.

And smiles.

Table of Contents

Fish of Washington 6
    Cold-water Fish 6
    Warm-water Fish 10
    Marine Fish 13
    Anadromous Fish 18
    Freshwater Fish of Washington 22
Washington's Record Fish 23
    Freshwater Fish 23
    Saltwater Fish 24
Washington Fishing License Requirements 26
    Where to Call 27
Map of Counties and WDFW Regions 28
Adams County: WDFW Region 2 29
Asotin County: WDFW Region 1 33
Benton County: WDFW Region 3 36
Chelan County: WDFW Region 2 38
Clallam County: WDFW Region 6 47
Clark County: WDFW Region 5 56
Columbia County: WDFW Region 1 64
Cowlitz County: WDFW Region 5 67
Douglas County: WDFW Region 2 75
Ferry County: WDFW Region 1 78
Franklin County: WDFW Region 3 83
Garfield County: WDFW Region 1 85
Grant County: WDFW Region 2 87
Grays Harbor County: WDFW Region 6 101
Island County: WDFW Region 4 109
Jefferson County: WDFW Region 6 111
King County: WDFW Region 4 116
Kitsap County: Region 6 140
Kittitas County: Region 3 143
Klickitat County: WDFW Region 5 152
Lewis County: Region 5 156
Lincoln County: WDFW Region 1 167
Mason County: Region 6 170
Okanogan County: WDFW Region 2 178
Pacific County: WDFW Region 6 190
Pend Oreille County: WDFW Region 1 195
Pierce County: WDFW Region 6 201
San Juan County: WDFW Region 4 210
Skagit County: WDFW Region 4 212

Skamania County: WDFW Region 5 221
Snohomish County: WDFW Region 4 231
Spokane County: WDFW Region 1 248
Stevens County: WDFW Region 1 253
Thurston County: WDFW Region 6 259
Wahkiakum County: WDFW Region 5 265
Walla Walla County: WDFW Region 1 267
Whatcom County:WDFW Region 4 270
Whitman County: WDFW Region 1 280
Yakima County: WDFW Region 3 282
Mount Rainier National Park 292
North Cascades National Park 298
    North Unit 299
    South Unit 300
    Ross Lake N.R.A. 300
    Lake Chelan N.R.A. 301
Olympic National Park 303
Major Saltwater Salmon Fishing Areas 311
    Public Saltwater Fishing Piers 315
    Saltwater Fishing Rigs 317
Fishing With Kids 320
Steelhead Secrets 323
    Winter Steelhead 323
        Top Winter Rivers 325
    Summer Steelhead 325
        Use Light Gear 326
    Steelhead Drift Fishing Techniques 326
    Float Fishing 328
River Salmon Fishing 330
    River Salmon Species 330
    Locating Salmon 331
    Techniques & Tactics 331
    Locations & Seasons 332
Fishing With Eggs 334
    Rigging and Fishing Single Eggs 334
    Putting Up Bait Eggs 335
Specialty Fisheries 337
    Alpine Lakes 337
    Tiger Muskies 338
    Kokanee Come On in May 339
    Cutthroat Trout 341
    Warm Water Species 345
        Warm water lakes and streams 345
    Tackling Dinosaurs: Sturgeon 347
    Ice Fishing.. 348
        Top Ice Fishing Lakes 350
    Secret Sauce Fish Barbecue 351
    Where The Hatcheries Are 352
        WDFW Hatchery Locations 352
        National Fish Hatcheries 353
Appendix 354
    Lakes Of Washington 354
    Streams Of Washington 384
Index 398

Fish of Washington

We fish open-water every day of the year, or at least we could and that's a boast not too many states can make.

The diversity and challenge of Washington sport-fishing is as overwhelming as it is rare.

Few other places in the world allow fishermen, theoretically, to start the morning fishing for 5 species of salmon, plus rockfish, halibut and ling cod in saltwater, brunch with winter and summer steelhead, lowland rainbow trout, bass, panfish, tiger muskies, and beaver pond brookies, then lunch in a spectacular mile-high alpine meadow backpacking for high mountain cutthroat and goldens, switching in mid-afternoon to river rainbows, Lahontan cutthroat and walleye, then spend the evening watching mayflies hatch on a desert lake filled with challenging browns, rainbows, brookies and tiger trout.

Any fishing time left over can be used to chase blue water albacore tuna, 10-foot sturgeon, millions of shad, tough channel catfish, tasty perch, burbot and landlocked salmon.

Cold-water Fish

Cold-water fishermen tackling Washington's thousands of freshwater lakes, rivers, ponds and streams challenge seven species of trout and char, plus several subspecies, three species of landlocked salmon, plus a scattering of grayling and three species of whitefish.

Rainbow, cutthroat, brown and golden are true trout (Salmo). Dolly Varden, bull trout, brookies and mackinaw (AKA lake trout) are chars (*Salvelinus*), not trout. Chars are easily distinguished from trout by a white border on the leading edge of the pectoral, pelvic and anal fins. Chars also have very fine scales easily removed, and rarely jump when hooked, delivering a dogged, surging fight.

Trout and char are often found in the same water, have similar spawning characteristics, and are caught with similar fishing techniques and tackle.

Several subspecies of rainbow and cutthroat trout have been introduced, including Beardslee, Donaldson's, steelhead hybrids, and tiger rainbows. Cutthroat subspecies include, anadromous sea-runs, coastal, Crescenti (exclusively in Lake Crescent), West slope, Lahontan, Montana black spots, and possibly a few Yellowstone cutts.

There are three varieties of whitefish: pygmy, lake and mountain. Lake whitefish, an introduced species, are caught in only a few waters in any important numbers; Soda, Banks, and Moses lakes are the most prominent. The fishery usually takes place in spring when 2 to 4 pound adults are massing to spawn. River anglers target native mountain whitefish, 10 to 14 inches, which are rarely publicized but are fine light-tackle game fish especially in the winter when few other fishing options are open. Many Cascade Range rivers have special mid-winter openings specifically for whitefish.

Attempts to establish grayling (*Thymallus*) have pretty much failed. The few that may have survived are confined to a few remote high-elevation lakes deep in the north and central Cascade Range and are fully protected by a statewide WDFW fishing closure. Excluding brook trout, the two most prominent chars in Washington are land-locked Dolly Varden and its close cousin river-dwelling bull trout. Only a few waters (most in NW counties) are still open for dolly or bull trout fishing. Targeting these fish is illegal in most areas of the state, closed by federal Endangered Species Act (ESA) listing.

Several salmon species (*Oncorhynchus*) which by nature are anadromous fish, have been evolved to live year-round in freshwater and contribute significantly to the sport-fishery in all regions of the state.

Landlocked salmon include chinook, coho, sockeye, and kokanee. Kokanee are abundant and the most popular of the landlocked salmon species.

With the exception of mackinaw and brook trout which can spawn in lakes, most cold-water fish spawn in creeks and streams. Mackinaw and brookies spawn in lakes scattering eggs on rocky shelves usually 6 to 20 feet deep. Anadromous steelhead and cutthroat trout, sea-going salmon, bull trout and Dolly Varden char spawn in defined beds in freshwater rivers and streams. In lakes without tributary streams resident fish will sometime spawn at springs or gated inlets. In both tributary and spring sites, the female prepares a nest called a "redd," in a gravel bed by tail-fanning silt and debris away from a small area of the stream bottom. She exudes eggs at the top of the redd and as they drift downstream into the redd they are fertilized by a male releasing milt. Fertilized eggs settle between the redd stones , where they develop and hatch in 6 to 8 weeks.

The newly hatched fish, called alevins, stay in the gravel for 2 to 4 weeks. They are fed by absorbing the yolk sack which remains attached to the alevin's belly.

After the yolk has been absorbed young fish enter the fry stage and wiggle free of the gravel. It begins to feed on microscopic plant and animal organisms. Aquatic and terrestrial insects are added to the diet as the fry reach smolt stage. By the time they are several inches long and known as smolts, they are feeding on large insects, nymphs, freshwater shrimp, small fish, crayfish, snails, and plankton.

RAINBOW TROUT (*Oncorhynus mykiss*). Native to Washington, rainbow are the most

important fresh water fish in the state. Sea-run rainbow are called steelhead. Golden trout are the most colorful of all rainbow strains. Environment influences color of fish, but in general rainbow are bluish-green on the back with silver sides and belly. There are black spots along the back and on the dorsal, adipose and caudal fins. A red band sometimes extends along both sides. Rainbow have short heads. The lip bone on the upper jaw rarely extends past the hind margin of the eye. They do not have teeth on the back of the tongue. Sea-run rainbow (steelhead) have been taken to 36 pounds from Kispiox River in British Columbia. Lake varieties to 42 pounds have been recorded. A 10-12 inch female produces 800 to 1000 eggs. A rainbow over 24 inches may produce from 5000 to 9000 eggs. Most rainbow spawn in the spring. Subspecies include: goldens, Beardslee, Donaldson's, and steelhead hybrids.

CUTTHROAT TROUT (*O. clarki*). Another native, the cutthroat also may migrate to

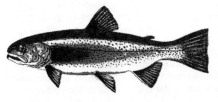

saltwater. It gets its name from red slash marks on both sides of the under jaw. Fish fresh from saltwater may not have these marks, but all have teeth at back of the tongue. Usual color for cutthroat is dark green backs with olive sides and silver belly. Numerous black spots are found on the back and sides, and on the caudal, adipose and dorsal fins. Eastern Washington or mountain cutthroat are more brilliantly colored. Montana black spots are a strain of inland cutthroat. One of largest cutthroat taken was a 41 pounder from a lake. Sea-run cutthroat are usually 1 to 3 pounds, with an occasional fish 4 pounds. The inland variety in streams is usually smaller. Cutthroat are spring spawners, spawning in headwaters of small creeks. Subspecies include: anadromous sea-runs, coastal, Crescenti (exclusively in Lake Crescent), West slope, Lahontan, Montana black spots, and possibly a few Yellowstone cutts.

BROOK TROUT (*Salvelinus fontinalis*). Brook trout, actually a char, were introduced

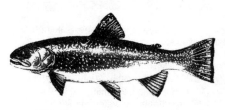

from the E. coast and have done well in Washington, particularly in alpine lakes and streams and in beaver ponds. Their general color is olive-green, darker on the back and lighter on sides. They have dark wavy markings on back and on dorsal fin. Small green spots appear on the sides, some with red centers bordered with blue. Lower fins often are edged with white along front portion. A brookie of 14.5 pounds has been recorded, but a 3 pounder is large for Washington waters. Spawning is in the fall in spring-fed tributaries or over patches of gravel in lakes. A female may deposit from 500 to 2500 eggs.

BROWN TROUT (*Salmo trutta Linnaeus*). Also called German brown and Loch Leven

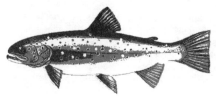

trout, the browns were introduced from Europe and are found in expanding numbers in Washington. Most of the expansion has been in low-elevation west slope lakes. Very rarely, a brown may migrate to saltwater. General color is golden brown, with large dark-brown or black spots. A distinguishing characteristic is the light halos around the large dark spots. Brown trout of 41 pounds have been reported. In Washington a brown of 5 pounds is a heavy fish. Spawning is ordinarily in the fall from October to January. The browns can adapt to warm and sluggish water, but prefer cold tributary streams for spawning.

TIGER TROUT. The first stockings of these sterile hybrids was made in 2001 in the

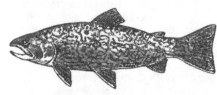

Columbia Basin. Tiger trout are the offspring of female brown trout and male brook trout char. WDFW stocked 40,000 of these exotic hybrids in the Columbia Basin lakes and streams, including Beda, Brookie, Upper Crab Cr. Dry Falls, Dusty, Gloyd Seeps, Harris, Homestead Lake, Spring, Creek Canyon, Index #1 and #2, Lenice, Magpie Beaver Pond, Merry, Nunnally, Sage East and Sage West, and Quail. Tigers are named for the striped body markings and their voracious appetites. Tigers are considered more aggressive than either parent species. Light brown, gold color with striking vermiculations on the upper back and side. Belly yellow-orange. Surface feeders, easily caught, and used for put and take fisheries. How big they grow in Washington is unknown at this printing.

KOKANEE SALMON (*Oncorhymchus nerka*) Sometimes erroneously called silver trout, kokanee are landlocked sockeye salmon (See Anadromous Fish) Like all Pacific salmon they die at sexual maturity, 3 or 4 years. Spawning takes place in inlet streams and the fish turn brilliant red with green heads. Kokanee are widespread and are stocked as fry by the millions. Many consider the red kokanee meat as the finest freshwater fish available for the table. Kokanee are similiar in appearance to trout but distinguished by a deeply forked tail, bright blue backs and silver sides. At maturity they range from 8 to 20 inches. Plankton feeders that often stratify at mid depths. Caught by stillfishing with maggots, small salmon eggs, bits of worm on No. 12 and smaller hooks. Trolling is the most popular technique with flashers to attract salmon to small spinners baited with maggots or bits of worm, and tiny thin spoons like hot pink Needlefish, Dick Nites or the classic Martin Red Magic.

GRAYLING (*Thymallus arcticus*). Only one lake in Washington, Big Granite in Skagit  County, is reported to successfully carry these exotic fish, although there have been limited plants in other high lakes. Easily distinguished by sail-like dorsal fin. Grayling have low tolerances for anything other than pristine habitat and they are unlikely to increase in Washington. In Canadian and Alaskan waters grayling reach 24 inches, but 12 to 15 inches is more common. Grayling spawn in streams during May and June. Do not build nests. Eat aquatic and terrestrial insects. The fish are spectacular when they rise to dry flies. The flesh has the taste of thyme, and the scientific name, "thymallus," refers to the odor of this seasoning, but you'll have to go north to sample it. WDFW prohibits grayling fishing statewide.

LAKE TROUT (*Salvelinus namaycush*). Another introduced char, lake trout, AKA 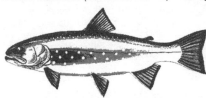 mackinaw, were introduced from the northern regions of Canada and Alaska. In general, lakers are colored greenish, brownish or grayish, with numerous gray or white irregular spots on back and sides. Dark and light markings on dorsal, adipose and caudal fins. Tail deeply forked. Lake trout of 60 pounds have been caught. Most are in the 5 to 25 pound range. The fish prefer deep, cold water lakes. Fall spawners, ordinarily over reefs in lakes.

DOLLY VARDEN (*Salvelinus malma*). Although native to Washington waters, the 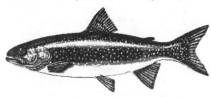 complete story on these char is not known. Some fish migrate to saltwater, while others are found in alpine streams. In recent years fish scientists have divided these chars into two subspecies: Dolly Varden and bull trout. Their general color is olive-green, with numerous round, light spots. The spots close to the lateral line are usually red or orange and larger than the rest. Pectoral, pelvic and anal fins are often bordered with white. Sea-run dollies known as **BULL TROUT** are more silvery and the spots are pale. A 32 pound Dolly Varden was taken from Pend Oreille lake in Idaho. Fish to 10 to 15 pounds are not unusual in Washington waters, but 1 to 3 pounders are more common. Spawning is in streams in the fall. Most Dolly Varden and bull trout are ESA protected, and fishing is allowed in only a few northwest counties.

WHITEFISH, Mountain (*Prosopium williamsoni*). Mountain whitefish are found in most 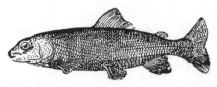 Washington streams. These fish are related to the salmonoids, differing in that they have small mouths and large scales similar to grayling. Silvery, sometimes with dark-bronze back, few spots on the head and adipose fins. Mouth is small with no teeth. Most mountain whitefish are under 12 inches, with an occasional fish to 15 inches. They are found chiefly in cold and swift streams where they feed on the bottom on aquatic insect larvae (Maggots and periwinkles are great bait). Whitefish are good eating, will take a fly and are generally under-rated by fishermen. Spawning takes place in the fall.

WHITEFISH, Lake (*Coregonus clupeaformis*). An introduced species, lake whitefish are much larger than their mountain cousins, will weigh several pounds and have a large mouth. Fall spawners on rocks and ledge, and often congregate near the mouths of rivers in the spring and fall. Feed mostly on insects. A strong, slab sided fighter. Popular smoked.

Warm-water Fish

These introduced warm-water fish are widespread statewide, and rapidly gaining popularity. Common in lakes, sloughs and large rivers.

Several species, in fact, are creating a lot of excitement, especially the rapid spread of large smallmouth bass, world-record size walleye, widespread introductions of channel catfish and increased distribution of tiger muskies on both sides of the state.

Like brook trout, panfish such as perch, pumpkinseeds and bluegill sometimes reproduce so rapidly that they can crowd out other species and stunt their own species. Perch fishing is really gaining ground on the west side of the state, while some of the east side's traditional panfish lakes seem to be sliding. While catch and release is a conservation-oriented goal for most fish, anglers are encouraged to keep all the perch, crappies, bluegills and pumpkinseeds they can eat. Except for catfish which are scaleless, warmwater fish have large scales, and fins that can stiffen. Scales should be removed or the fish skinned before eating. Three dominant warm-water families are present in Washington: Perch, Sunfish, and Catfish

YELLOW PERCH (*Perca flavescens*). The only freshwater perch in Washington,

perch are yellowish with green vertical stripes, orange tinged pectoral and lower fins, and 2 doral fins. Perch spawn in late winter or early spring, with females depositing flat, ribbon-like bands over weeds or sticks on sandy bottoms. A female may produce 10,000 to 40,000 eggs. Most yellow perch are under 12 inches, but a few 1 pounders are taken. Feed on larvae, insects, minnows and crustaceans. Found in large schools. Worms, perch eyes, bits of perch flesh are excellent bait.

WALLEYE (*Stizostedion vitreum***).** Generally restricted to Columbia River and

tributaries upstream from Vancouver, and Columbia Basin lakes. A member of the perch family, walleye are dark olive with mottled brassy specks and two dorsal fins. Vermiculations on the side of the head. The lower jaw is flesh colored and there is a large black spot at base of last dorsal fin. Walleye prefer cold lakes or rivers, spawn in early spring in tributary streams or on gravel bars in lakes. Minnows are primary food. Lower Columbia River walleye are among the largest in North America, pushing 20 pounds.

LARGEMOUTH BASS (*Micropterus salmoides*). Largemouth are probably the most

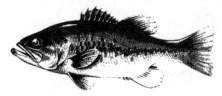

prized of the state's warm-water species. They are found in lakes in all sections of the state, and in the sloughs of most large rivers. Color is dark green over the back, with greenish-silver on sides. Distinguishing dark lateral line. Belly is whitish. Mouth extends beyond the eye.

Dorsal fins are sharply separated. During warm weather largemouth prefer shallow, weedy lakes or sloughs with weedy bottoms and 60 to 70 degree water temperatures. In winter they retreat to deep-water. Spawning from early May through June when water temperatures are 60 to 68 degrees. Males guard the eggs and young fish, eating some. Largemouth of 2 to 6 pounds are common in Washington. They eat minnows, crayfish, leeches, aquatic insects and frogs. Catching nesting fish leaves the nest vulnerable to predators.

SMALLMOUTH BASS (*Micropterus dolumiui*). Smallmouth are booming. Once found  mostly E. of the Cascades, many excellent fisheries have now been established in the colder waters of W. Washington lakes. Several rivers, including the Columbia above saltwater, Snake, lower Yakima, and Okanogan, offer outstanding fishing, especially in May-June. Smallmouth are dark green to pale olive-brown with gold flecking. Sides are usually either lightly mottled or have vertical bars. Smallmouth do not have the distinctive dark lateral line that distinguishes largemouth. Mouth is large but does not extend past the eye. Prefer clear water with gravel bottoms and rock gardens that support crayfish, a favorite food. Spawn late spring-early summer in shallow round gravel nests. Most smallmouth in the state are under 3 pounds, but have been caught at more than 8 pounds. Principal food insect larvae, minnows and crayfish. Males guards the nest, and will devour hatchlings, but if caught and even temporarily removed, predators will devastate the nest.

WHITE CRAPPIE (*Pomoxis annularis*). Thin, plate-shaped white crappie are on both sides of the Cascade Mountains. White's tolerate more turbid water than black crappie are silvery, with several dark vertical bands. Produce 2000 to 14,000 eggs in early summer. Most crappie are under 8 inches, but fish up to 16 inches have been taken in Washington. Feed on minnows, insects, worms, and crayfish. Prefer submerged brush and stick habitat, and live in large schools. Jig brush and sunk trees with 1/16 top 1/8 oz. small white or yellow plastic worms, or spinners that imitate minnows. May-June tops.

BLACK CRAPPIE (*Pomoxis nigro maculatus*). Thin, plate-shaped black crappie prefer 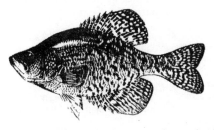 clear, weedy lakes and large streams. Not as widespread as whites. Blacks are silvery olive with olive-green mottling, dusky spot on gill cover. Blacks seldom exceed 12 inches, and feed mostly on minnows, crayfish and larvae. Spawn in early summer. Females produce 20,000 to 60,000 eggs. Colony nests in water of 3 to 8 foot depth. Jig inside sunken tree limbs and brush with 1/16 top 1/8 oz. small white or yellow plastic worms, or spinners that imitate minnows. May-June tops.

SUNFISH. Bluegill (*Lepomis macrochirus*) and Pumpkinseeds (*Lepomis gibbosus*) are 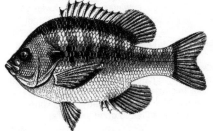 the most important of the sunfish in Washington. Bluegill identified by a light bluish-green body color, blue-black gill flap, and bluish tint on gill cover, flat-sided and may reach 9 inches. Most are less than 6 inches. A cousin, pumpkinseeds are smaller and brightly colored, with dark bluish olive sides spotted with orange. Cheeks are orange with blue streaks. A bright red spot is on lower edge of gill cover.

Bluegills and pumkinseeds build round-shaped nests 12 to 40 inches deep fanning slight depressions in gravel or sand bottoms. spawning begins in May and may extend into September. Multiple spawns. Males guard nest. Feed on larvae and flying insects, small crustaceans, snails and fry. Good lures are worms, grasshoppers, surface poppers, wet flies.

ROCK BASS (*Ambloplites rupestris*) and WARMOUTH (*Lepomis gulosus*).

Uncommon in most waters, these darkly-colored panfish are most plentiful in lowland lakes in Thurston, Pierce and S. King counties and Skookumchuck River. Both have large scales, mottled dark bronze bodies. Average 7 to 10 inches. Rockies prefer rocky or gravel areas and have bright red eyes. Warmouth are less plentiful than rock bass and distinguished by the 3 spines on anal fin and teeth on the tongue. They have yellowish bellies, and rock bass are uniformly dark. Rock bass favor rocks, warmouth favor mud bottoms and dense weedbeds. Both feed on minnows, insects and crayfish and are tasty on the table.

CHANNEL CATFISH (*Ictalurus puncta tus*) and BLUE CATFISH (*Ictalurus furca tus*).

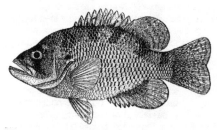

Channel catfish are found in established numbers in eastern Washington especially in Yakima and Snake river sloughs and are being stocked in increasing numbers statewide, especially in Western Washington lakes. Sharp spine at front of dorsal and pectoral fins. Channels are slate-gray with dark freckles over their body. Spots may disappear on large adults. Tail deeply forked. Blues are fairly rare, slate-gray above and white below. Tail deeply forked. No freckles. Large channel catfish are smaller than large blues. Most channel cats are 12 to 16 inches although fish to 32 pounds have been caught. Spawn in late spring or summer. Bottomfish with worms, chicken or beef liver. Channels often feed heavily on mayflies and can be caught on dry fly patterns.

BULLHEAD CATFISH.

Brown bullhead catfish (*Ameiurus natalis*), black bullhead catfish (*Ameiurus melas*), and a few yellow bullhead catfish (*Ameiurus natalis*) are in lakes throughout the state. Flat head, large mouth, smooth, scaleless bodies and barbels or "whiskers" on chin and head. Sharp spine at front of dorsal and pectoral fins. Bullheads to 4 pounds are taken, but in most lakes are about 10 inches. Spawn in early summer, with females depositing a gelatinous mass of eggs totaling from 2,000 to 10,000. Bullhead catfish herd schools of young. Good eating. Skin and fillet. Best fishing at night with nightcrawlers, sliding sinkers on bottom.

BURBOT (*Lota lota*).

Sometimes called freshwater ling this is the only member of the

codfish family found in freshwater. Bottom dwellers that are usually caught in winter on nightcrawler or sucker meat baited setlines through the ice. The body is elongated with a rounded head and tail fin that somewhat resembles a catfish. Dark olive colored with chain-like black or yellow markings along side. May reach 30 pounds, but most are less than 18 inches long, and averaging around 1.5 pounds. Washington has produced burbot in the 17 pound range. Top lakes are Palmer, Chelan and Sullivan. Spawns under the ice over sand and gravel in shallow water. Feed voraciously on crayfish, whitefish, minnows. It's considered fair to good tablefare.

TIGER MUSKIE (*Esox m. immaculatus*). One of Washington's most recently introduced fish, tiger muskellunge are a sterile hybrid of muskellunge and northern pike. They have been introduced into numerous lakes, primarily as a predator to thin high numbers of suckers, northern pikeminnows and other undesirable infestations that upset the food chain balance. Tigers were first introduced at Mayfield Lake in 1988 and have since been planted in Newman, Merwin, Redrock, Evergreen, Curlew, South Lewis County Park Pond, Tapps and Seattle's Green Lake. Grass colored, long, slender bodied with rows of inward pointing razor sharp teeth, tigers are shallow-water predators that feed best during the heat of summer. Washington's are expected to reach 30 pounds. Most are caught by anglers casting large bucktail spinners or plugs (6 inches are about right) at logs, grassy beds and shallow reefs where the big fish hide and hunt. Tiger muskies are being raised at the Columbia Basin Hatchery in Moses Lake (See Tiger Muskie feature, page 338) .

NORTHERN PIKE (*Esox lucius*), and a few **GRASS PICKEREL** (*Esox americanus vermiculatus*) have been in Washington waters for about 30 years, exclusively in the eastern counties. The first confirmed reports of northerns came from Long Lake on the lower Spokane River, in the 1970s. Biologists believe the predators, which can weigh 20 pounds easily, drifted downstream from Idaho where they are numerous. According to WDFW there is no evidence that northerns are expanding their range, although the Spokane River is a major tributary to the Columbia River. Grass pickerel are small, rarely exceeding a foot, and have been reported in Cow and Finnel lakes and tributaries into the Palouse River. Both fish are caught on minnow-imitating lures, spinners, wobbling plugs, spoons with pork rind.

NORTHERN PIKEMINNOW (*Ptychocheilus oregonensis.*). Formerly called "squawfish" northern pikeminnows are a voracious predator common to all major rivers and many lakes throughout the state. They have been taken weighing 10 pounds, but most are around a foot long. They have little sport-fishing value, except for a bounty program that has paid rewards for dead squawfish caught on the lower Columbia River where it's believed they severely impact schools of salmon and steelhead smolts headed downstream. Caught mostly on meat baits in slow current. Dusky green along back, silvery white along sides and belly. Mouth trout-like, meat bony and lacks flavor.

Marine Fish

Dozens of prime game fish fall under the marine label and can be caught from boats, piers and beaches on the Washington coast, Puget Sound, Hood Canal and San Juan Islands. In most cases you can get a hint from their name on where to fish for them. Flatfish on flat bottoms, rockfish around rocks, kelp greenling around kelp, and surf perch in the surf, pile perch around pilings, etc.

The catch includes seven flatfish ranging from halibut and skates that can weigh several hundred pounds through flounders and soles that rarely crack a pound. A half-dozen rockfish, most notably blacks, coppers, canaries, quillbacks and yellow-eyes, several greenlings including ling cod, plus true cod, walleye pollock, three types of perch and more than enough sharks.

Fishing is as simple as a handline with a bell sinker and a No. 6 hook sweetened with shrimp dangled off a pier, or as sophisticated as a modern boat bulging with electronics. Our saltwater offers something for everybody.

For top marine areas see, Major Saltwater Fishing Areas, Public Saltwater Fishing Piers, and Artificial Reef Locations.

HALIBUT (*Hippoglossus stenolepis*). The heavyweight champ of Northwest saltwater fish is the Pacific halibut, which may grow to 400 pounds. Halibut populations boomed in the early 1980s, and is gaining popularity. Halibut feed on and around underwater mountains and plateaus. The state's most well-known halibut grounds are at Swiftsure Bank on the Canadian border near the entrance to the Strait of Juan de Fuca, about 20 miles north of Neah Bay. Other productive halibut-fishing areas are off the northern

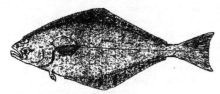

Washington coast, around Neah Bay and Sekiu, Port Angeles and on several underwater humps near the east end of the Strait of Juan de Fuca. Best fishing is during the spring. Halibut will take octopus, herring, squid, salmon heads, greenling and other baits. Deep-water anglers often bounce heavy leadhead jigs with large, plastic grub bodies, pipe jigs, or baitfish-imitating metal jigs along the bottom.

STARRY FLOUNDERS (*Platichthys stellatus)*. Found in many of Washington's marine

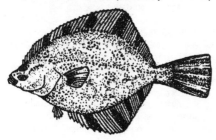

areas, and are most commonly caught from shallow-water estuaries such as Grays Harbor, Willapa Bay and some of Puget Sound's larger river mouths. Occasionally stray into fresh water, and have been caught up the Columbia River as far as Bonneville Dam. They're good-eating and not too choosy about the baits. Starry's average 14 but can reach 36 inches. Easily identified by striking alternating orange and dark bars on fins and large rough scales.

SOLES. Washington has a range of small flatfish, including arrowtooth flounder, sand

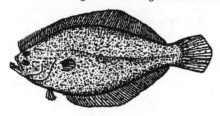

sole, English sole, petrale sole, rock sole and Pacific sanddab. Soles and dabs are common in most shallow areas of Puget Sound and sometimes taken from surprisingly deep water. Nearly always on the bottom, but sometimes found at mid-depths feeding on small shrimp or crab spawn. Most average about 12 inches in length but may reach 24 inches. Prefer small chunks of meat baits, but occasionally taken on small jigs. Petrale sole are taken almost exclusively from deeper water, and can weigh several pounds. Distinguished by a mouth full of pointed teeth.

SKATES (*Raja)*. The big skate might be considered a sort of halibut look-alike,

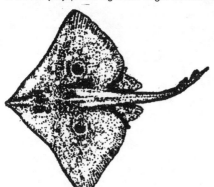

although it's much more closely related to sharks than to halibut. Sometimes growing to 8 feet and100 pounds, the solid white meat in the "wings" are highly prized table fare, sometimes passed off as "scallops." Common in Puget Sound, especially in bays

BLUE SHARKS *(Prionace glauca)*. Grow to fairly large size in Washington, often 7 to

12 feet, and are pursued by some anglers along the coast. Fair fighters and provide fair eating. Mostly in open ocean.

SPINY DOGFISH (*Squalus acanthias)*. Considered a pest, dogfish sharks are

commonly caught by Washington anglers when salmon fishing with slow moving bait near the bottom in all saltwater areas. They travel in huge schools and their fight is not spectacular. Popular as food in Europe, they are not often eaten here. The forward edges of dorsal fins have sharp spines capable of inflicting slightly venomous wounds. Rarely exceed 10 pounds.

OTHER SHARKS. Other sharks frequently swim Washington's coastal and inland

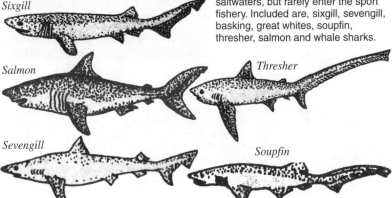

saltwaters, but rarely enter the sport fishery. Included are, sixgill, sevengill, basking, great whites, soupfin, thresher, salmon and whale sharks.

Sixgill

Salmon

Thresher

Sevengill

Soupfin

YELLOWEYE ROCKFISH *(Sebastodes ruberrimus)*. A bright orange with prominent

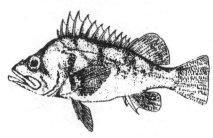

yellow eye, this is one of the biggest and most colorful of Washington's many rockfish species. Yelloweyes often weigh over 10 pounds, and sometimes top the 20-pound mark. They can live to be several decades old. Yelloweyes are a deep-water denizen, usually caught near bottom in at least 150 feet of water, and sometimes at depths of several hundred feet. As their name implies, rockfish like hard, rocky bottoms, and those are the best places to fish for yelloweyes. They'll take herring and all jig-type artificials quite readily. Often erroneously called "red snapper."

CANARY ROCKFISH *(Sebastodes pinniger)*. Another orange inhabitant of Washington's deep-water marine areas. Black peppering along back. Although not as large as yelloweyes, they are caught in many of the same places and by the same fishing methods. Usually 2 to 5 pounds, found in large schools.

OTHER ROCKFISH *(Sebastes)*. Although commonly lumped under the label of "bottomfish," many rockfish species may be found well off the bottom, sometimes on the surface. Black rockfish are one of the most common and most popular rockfish, providing fast action for coastal charter anglers as well as small-boat fishermen in places like Neah Bay and Sekiu. Lots of fun on spinning gear and fly rods. Small plastic worm/jig combos are very productive wiggled through kelp beds. Averaging 1 to 6 pounds, black rockfish are excellent light-tackle fighter and can be found at virtually any depth. Schools often feed in shallow-water kelp beds and frequently thrash the surface in open water and along breakwaters—especially at night. When swarming near surface, they'll take anything from herring and small jigs to streamer flies and surface plugs. Excellent food value. Blue rockfish closely resemble blacks, and the two are often caught together. Blues tend to run a little smaller, and have smaller mouths. Copper rockfish are common especially near shore and around shallow-water rock piles and other hard structure. They're cooperative and fun to catch on light tackle. Puget Sound coppers are recovering from intense overfishing. Many other rockfish species are available to Evergreen State saltwater anglers. Tiger rockfish are the most brightly colored example. Boccaccio are one of the bigger rockfish, often topping 20 pounds, and is usually caught from fairly deep water. China rockfish can be identified by distinctive yellow-on-black coloration. Yellowtails and widows, both a golden brown, are common in the ocean.

LING COD (*Ophiodon elongatus*). As prized by Washington anglers as they are feared by

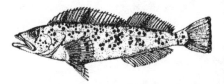

smaller fish. Everything from herring, anchovies and crabs to other ling cod are considered fair game when a big ling gets hungry. Playing on its hearty appetite, anglers often use live bait to catch a big ling, sometimes more than 60 pounds, but leadhead jigs, metal jigs and other artificials also will fool them.

All large lings are females and should be released. Meat is usually white but may be greenish blue which turns white when cooked. Both are delicious. Ling cod habitat is a hard, rocky bottom with lots of steep drops and jagged pinnacles. In the spring they often come into rocky breakwaters and revetments. Ling cod are slow-growing fish that have been terribly overfished by commercial draggers. Conservative seasons and creation of bottomfish sanctuaries and artificial reefs is showing some success in recovering ling cod populations in the Strait of Juan de Fuca and Puget Sound.

CABEZON (*Scorpaenichthys marmoratus).* Largest member of the sculpin family,

sometimes growing to over 20 pounds. Tough fighters, especially when hooked in fairly shallow water or on light tackle. Cabezon feed primarily on crustaceans, especially crabs, using powerful jaws to crush prey. Small fish, however, are also included in their diet, so herring and baitfish-imitating metal jigs bounced along the

bottom will take them too. Orange plastic jigs are favorites. Although the large head, fins and heavy bones are not edible, cabezons provide a pair of thick, tasty, white-meat fillets for seafood gourmets. Cabezon eggs are reported to be poisonous.In recent years cab numbers have plummeted east of Sekiu.

KELP GREENLING (*Hexagrammos decagrammus).* Smaller relatives of (and a fine bait

for) ling cod, common throughout Washington's marine waters. Kelp beds and shallow, rocky areas are the best places to look. Easily caught on small baits and jigs. Greenling are among the fish commonly used for live ling cod bait, but they're very good table fare in

their own right, providing firm, white-meat fillets. Females are bright copper colored, and males are greenish purple. Whitespotted greenling are occasionally caught in Puget Sound and Juan de Fuca Strait.

SCULPINS. Most sculpins hold little angler interest, including the red Irish lord, great sculpin, staghorn sculpin and buffalo sculpin.

PACIFIC COD (*Gadus macrocephalus*). A true codfish, which explains its most

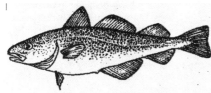

common nickname, "true cod." Cod fillets are white, flaky and excellent on the dinner table, making true cod popular among anglers even though they are not tough fighters. Baits such as whole or plug-cut herring will take cod, as will pipe jigs and other artificials. Whatever you use, fish it close to the bottom. Until about 15 years ago Puget Sound literally swarmed with massive schools of true cod which supported an enthusiastic winter jig fishery. Devastating commercial drag net fisheries and environmental changes have all but eliminated the fish. It is now illegal to catch more than one true cod in much of its traditional range.

WALLEYE POLLOCK (*Theragra chalcogrammus*), Another good-eating

bottomfish closely related to Pacific cod, although somewhat smaller. Meat is a little on the soft side. Pollock are often found over the same sand and gravel bottoms where Pacific cod are found, usually at least 100 feet deep, and can be caught with the same baits and lures. Unfortunately, like true cod, pollock numbers are disastrously low in Puget Sound. Pollock have been caught to 3 feet, but most are around 15 inches.

PERCH. Four subspecies of sea perch are widely available in shallow marine waters and great light tackle sport. The three most popular perches are pile, striped and red-tailed surf perch. Shiner perch are too small to interest anglers, averging about 4 inches. The 3 other marine perch average about 12 inches and can grow to 17 inches. Casting into the breakers along virtually any coastal beach, with clam necks, shrimp, sand worms or other bait will take red-tailed surf perch, an amazingly strong fighter. Redtails are also a very good eating fish, which, like other sea perch species, bear live young rather than laying eggs. Striped sea perch and pile perch are more common in Puget Sound, where they're often caught around docks,

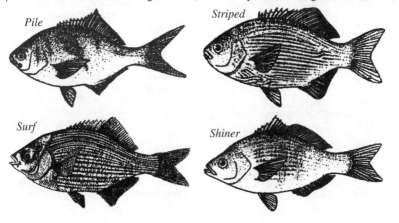

Pile

Striped

Surf

Shiner

floats and piers on an incoming tide. Use small pieces of shrimp, pile worms, or crab bait on No. 6 hooks.

SABLEFISH (*Anoplopoma fimbria*). Sometimes called black cod, sablefish are 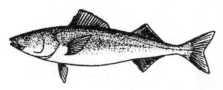 deep-water fish that until a few years ago were very common throughout central and northern Puget Sound. Numbers have declined in recent years. Usually caught in winter 200 to 400 feet deep. They have slender, elongated bodies with 2 dorsal fins,1 anal fin and are slate gray with green or blue tint sides, average 17 inches growing to 40. Herring bait. Oily meat, very good for smoking.

ALBACORE TUNA (*Thunnus alalunga*). Albacore are semi-tropical blue-water fish 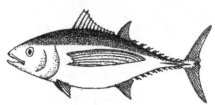 that follow the warm 60 to 66 degree (F) Japanese Current northward each summer to spawn in North Pacific waters. Most years the off-shore current flows like a warm river through the 45 degree North Pacific ocean. In August, the near-tropical stream comes within 100 miles of the Washington coast within reach of charter boats from Westport and Ilwaco. During El Niño years, albacore may swim within 20 miles of the coast. Because of the long open ocean run to tuna grounds, most of this fishery is dependent upon ocean-worthy charter boats. Albacore, sometimes called longfin tuna, are prime tablefare, some consider it the best tasting tuna. May weigh up to 90 pounds, but average 15 to 20 pounds. Powerful, never jump, but will battle far beyond their weight with long, strong, high speed runs. Nearly always hooked near surface. Typically, skippers troll feathered or plastic jigs to locate schools then chum live herring or anchovies to hold schools near the boat while fishermen free-spool unweighted, bait fish into the frenzy. Caught in international waters, no limit.

Anadromous Fish

Anadromous fish are hatched in freshwater where most spend much of their first year, before migrating to saltwater where they grow to maturity, returning to freshwater to spawn. In Washington, anadromous includes all of the 5 species of Pacific salmon (excluding landlocked subspecies), summer and winter steelhead trout, sea-run cutthroat trout, and bull trout/Dolly Varden char. It also includes American shad, green and white sturgeon and smelt. All Pacific salmon die after spawning. Trout and char may spawn several times, but stress and predation take a heavy toll. Sturgeon can live more than 75 years, spawning repeatedly, and frequently range into distant coastal river systems.

STEELHEAD (*Salmo gairdneri*). Sea-going rainbow trout/steelhead start their lives in 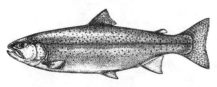 freshwater rivers and creeks, migrate to sea, where they spend one to six years feeding then returning to home streams to spawn and repeat the cycle. Unlike salmon, steelhead may spawn several times. Steelhead are not specifically school fish, generally filter upstream a few dozen at a time, and are widely scattered between tidewater and spawning areas. We have two subspecies, winter-runs and summer-runs, and both spawn from mid-winter to late-spring. Adult winter-run steelhead return to more than 100 Washington streams from Nov. through

Apr. A few streams still have wild steelhead runs that provide a self-sustaining population, but cumulative losses of clean spawning gravel through siltation and erosion, suitable rearing habitat, warming water temperatures, overharvests and a host of other problems, has greatly depleted the wild steelhead runs in many river systems. Most hatchery winter steelhead typically return in Dec. and Jan. Wild fish return Feb.-Apr. Summer-run steelhead slide upstream in freshwater from Apr. to Oct. Anglers catch summer fish in good numbers from about three dozen Washington rivers and creeks. Most adult winter and summer steelhead return from the Pacific after two or three growing seasons, and weigh from 5 to 14 pounds. Those coveted, once-in-a-lifetime 20-to-30-pounders are fish that stay at sea four to six years. WDFW plants hatchery winter steelhead in some 75 streams and summer-runs in about 45 streams. Regardless of WDFW sanctioned limits, wild steelhead should be released on all streams.

CHINOOK SALMON (*Oncorhynchus tshawytscha*). Chinook are the largest Pacific

salmon, averaging 15 to 20 pounds and occasionally growing to over 100 pounds. Sometimes called king salmon. Immature chinook, especially those in Puget Sound, are commonly referred to as "blackmouth," because of a distinctive black gum line. In summer (July) into early fall mature salmon move into inland saltwater areas, filtering into freshwater spawning grounds in moderate-sized schools. Washington has the potential to offer saltwater chinook fishing all year long, although ESA listings have forced closures in recent years. In addition to saltwater fisheries on the coast, Strait of Juan de Fuca, San Juan Islands and Puget Sound, chinook also provide freshwater angling action mostly in rivers. A subspecies, spring-run chinook (springers) return in Mar.-June. Except for the mainstem Columbia River run, and marginal returns to southwest rivers, spring chinook fishing is in trouble. Once great returns in the Skagit system are now fully protected. Landlocked resident chinook may be found in some lake systems such as Lakes Chelan and Cushman. In the ocean chinook are often in the top 50 feet of water, but once inside they head for the bottom typically 100 to 200 feet down.

COHO SALMON (*Oncorhynchus kisutch*). Coho salmon are about half the size of a

mature chinook, more abundant, rarely deeper than 50 feet and their acrobatic surface fighting style endears them to anglers. Adult hatchery coho mature at 3 years, weigh four to 10 pounds, but wild fish have been caught weighing in the mid 20s. Coho return later than chinook, in small schools, to spawn in small creeks and streams, not major rivers. They usually hit spawning streams in September and continue to filter upstream into December in some rivers. Young coho spend their first year in freshwater rivers. Large, late returning coho are called "hooknoses" for the distinctive beaked snouts. Most hooknoses come in after mid-September. Natural production is supplemented by state and federal hatcheries that produce millions of coho. Coho are also a favorite of freshwater anglers when the adult salmon return to spawning streams in fall. Surplus hatchery coho are also sometimes stocked in some year-round western Washington lakes.

PINK SALMON ((*Oncorhynchus gorbuscha*). Pinks return to Washington only during

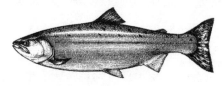

odd-numbered years, migrating and spawning in large schools. With a two-year life cycle, they are a small fish averaging three or four pounds at maturity and seldom topping 10-pounds. Commonly called "humpies" because of the large camel-like hump that spawning males develop. Both genders can be identified by the large, oblong or oval spots on the upper and lower portion of the tail and by very small scales. Meat is somewhat soft and less desirable than coho or chinook. It's oily, however, and smokes well. Trolling with herring or any of the standard salmon offerings will take pinks from salt water, but hot colors (pink for pinks is a good rule) work best in salt and fresh water. Saltwater anglers add flashers. Most pink rivers are in the north part of the state, Skagit, Snohomish, Stillaguamish, systems, although there are runs in the Puyallup and Nisqually rivers. Pinks enter the Straits and Puget Sound in Aug. and enter rivers in Sept. to spawn in Oct. In saltwater they often swim just under the surface. In rivers, they free leap and roll often and congregate in deep holes.

CHUM SALMON (*Oncorhynchus keta*). Nicknamed "dog salmon" (for its large canine

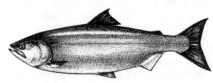

teeth and the fact that it was often used as dog food), chums are strong, aggressive fish in both salt and freshwater. They are the second-largest Pacific salmon with many in the high-teens and low-20-pound range. They travel in large schools, are the last spawning salmon to return each fall, arriving as 3 to 5 years olds at most natal streams from Nov. to Jan. Chums move rapidly from the ocean into rivers, barely hesitating at Puget Sound, which affords saltwater anglers only a quick shot before they're into freshwater. Spawning usually occurs within a few miles of saltwater, and the young migrate immediately to sea. Spawning colors are distinctive with olive backs and tiger striped bars of red and yellow. Chums are tough, explosive, acrobatic fighters and an outstanding river challenge on light tackle. Chums seem to prefer green lures. Bright fish are excellent on the table, and make a great smoke.

SOCKEYE SALMON (*Oncorhynchus nerka*). Considered by many to be the best-

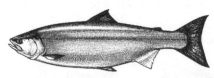

eating salmon, but anglers catch relatively few of them on sport gear especially in saltwater. The most notable sport fishery occurs on Lakes Wenatchee and Washington during years of abundant returns. A saltwater fishery on British Columbia's Fraser River stocks is developing in the San Juan Islands. Sockeye travel in huge schools and are small salmon, averaging 5 to 7 pounds with a rare fish to 15. Largely plankton feeders, sockeye are notoriously difficult to entice, especially in saltwater. In lakes they are often caught with flashers swinging short leaders and unbaited colored hooks at a dead slow troll. They are unique in that sockeye spawn (at 3 to 5 years old) in freshwater rivers, but the young require a lake in which to mature for a year before migrating to sea. They are an early summer returning fish, often entering freshwater from early July-Sept. Mature spawners in freshwater are brilliant red with green heads.

ATLANTIC SALMON (*Salmo salar*). Atlantic salmon have only recently entered the

Washington fishery, mostly into Puget Sound as escapees from net pen salmon farms in British Columbia and Puget Sound. There is evidence that Atlantics, which unlike Pacific salmon, can spawn multiple times, are spawning in Puget Sound streams, particularly the Green and Puyallup rivers. The body of an Atlantic is 5 times as long as it is deep. The body is brownish olive with small red spots on the sides and 2 or 3 black spots on the jaws. Atlantics have been caught in their native water weighing upwards of 100 pounds. Here they rarely exceed 12 pounds and most are around 7.

They fight well, more like a steelhead than a Pacific salmon, are fine tablefare. Biologists are warily watching to see the long-range impact that these immigrants will have on Pacific salmon and steelhead.

STURGEON. Greens *(Acipenser medirostris)* and **Whites** *(Acipenser*

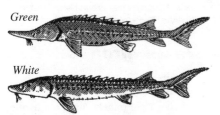

Green

White

transmontanus). The largest anadromous species Washington anglers will encounter. This prehistoric fish is available in the Columbia, Snake, Chehalis, Naselle, Snohomish and several other large Northwest streams year-round. They are also caught in Grays Harbor, Willapa Bay, Port Gardner and occasionally in other Puget Sound estuaries. Greens are

the smaller of the two, and less numerous. White sturgeon are the most common and largest. Both are anadromous, but most greens are caught within a few miles of saltwater. Whites are common in all Columbia and Snake River impoundments upstream into Canada and Idaho. Whites are certainly the largest, sometimes measuring over eight feet and weighing several hundred pounds. The largest Washington sturgeon reported was 1,285 pounds caught in 1912 near Vancouver. To be kept for the table, sturgeon must fit within a slot limit of between 42 and 60 inches. Sturgeon feed on the bottom, cruising along and picking up tasty morsels with their sucker-like mouth. Anglers usually fish for them with smelt, shad, shrimp, lampreys, salmon eggs and other fresh baits rigged on sliding sinkers anchored on bottom. Hooked sturgeon, especially larger ones, often jump completely out of the water, providing a spectacular show. Popularity of this fishery is exploding on the Columbia and Chehalis rivers.

AMERICAN SHAD *(Alosa sapidissima).* American shad are a large member of the

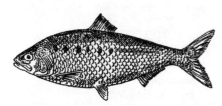

herring family that hatch in freshwater, migrate to sea, then return to freshwater to spawn. Shad are not native, and were imported from the East Coast in the late 19th century. Washington's most important shad fishery involves millions of shad swarming into the Columbia River and concentrating a hugely popular sport

fishery immediately below Bonneville Dam. Shad roam upstream into the Snake River. Smaller runs enter a few other southwest streams like the Chehalis. The height of the run is from mid-May to mid-June. Adult shad range in size from males averaging about 1-1/2 or two pounds to females that weigh four pounds or more. All are tough fighters and make a strong showing for anglers using light tackle. There is no daily catch limit and although they are "bony," the flesh had a good flavor, especially when smoked. The roe is a delicacy. Brightly colored mini-jigs, spinners, even a couple of red beads above a bare hook will take shad.

SMELTS (*Osmeridae*). Comprised of a family of schooling fishes with marine,

anadromous and freshwater members. Eulachon are an anadromous smelt primarily in the lower Columbia tributaries, most notably the Cowlitz River, which once provided good eulachon-dipping action, using long-handled dip nets in Feb.-Mar. Runs

there have plummeted in recent years, though. Surf and longfin smelt are popular marine fish, and one of the most common beach fish inside Puget Sound, along the Strait of Juan de Fuca, and the coast. Fisheries occur on both spawning and non-spawning congregations of adults and juveniles. Spawning fish are best harvested from shore on early morning or late evening high slack tides using a dip bag or smelt rake. Best beach raking is usually from 1 hour before to 1 hour after high tide. Non-spawning fish are commonly taken with ganglions of small, bright No. 8-12 hooks jigged from piers or boats. A popular surf smelt fishery occurs at LaConner, which throws an annual smelt-jigging festival the first week of February. Other smelts in Washington include whitebait, night, and capelin. Longfin smelt are in Lake Washington. Most fishermen smoke or deep fry smelt whole. Average 6 to 10 inches.

Freshwater Fish of Washington

Bass
- Largemouth
- Rock
- Smallmouth

Bluegill

Bullheads
- Yellow
- Brown
- Black

Burbot

Carp
- Buffao,
- Goldfish,

Catfish
- Blue
- Channel
- Flathead

Char, Arctic(see trout)

Chub
- Tui
- Lake,
- Peamouth

Chiselmouth

Crappie
- Black
- White

Dace
- Longnose
- Leopard
- Speckled

Flounder,
- Pacific Sanddab
- Starry
- Rock Sole
- English Sole
- Sand Sole
- Petrale Sole
- Dover Sole

Grayling, Arctic

Lamprey
- River
- Pacific
- Western Brook

Madtom

Mosquitofish

Mudminnow, Olympic

Musky, Tiger (muskie/northern hybrid)

Perch,
- Shiner
- Pile
- Striped
- Redtail Surf
- Yellow

Pike,
- Northern
- Grass Pickerel

Pikeminnow, Northern

Salmon,
- Atlantic
- Tule Chinook
- Spring Chinook
- Summer Chinook
- Chum
- Coho
- Kokanee
- Pink
- Sockeye

Sandroller

Shad, American

Sculpin
- Coastrange
- Margined
- Mottled
- Pacific Staghorn
- Piute
- Prickly
- Reticulate
- Riffle
- Shorthead
- Slimy
- Torrent

Smelt,
- Longfin
- Surf
- Eulachon

Steelhead,
- Summer-Run
- Winter-Run

Stickleback, Three-Spine

Sturgeon,
Green
White

Sucker
Bridgelip
Largescale
Longnose
Mountain

Sunfish,
Green
Pumpkinseed

Tench

Trout,
Brown
Cutthroat Crescenti
Cutthroat Coastal Resident
Cutthroat Coastal Searun
Cutthroat Lahontan
Cutthroat West Slope
Bull Trout (Char)

Dolly Varden (Char)
Brook Trout (Char)
Golden
Lake (Mackinaw, Char)

Trout, Rainbow
Resident
Beardslee
Donaldson
Kamloops
Triploid
Diploid
Tiger (Brookie/Brown Hybrid)
Walleye
Warmouth
White Amur (Grass Carp)
Diploid
Triploid
Whitefish,
Lake
Mountain
Pygmy

Washington's Record Fish

Freshwater Fish

FISH RECORD	ANGLER	WHERE CAUGHT	DATE
Largemouth-11 lbs. 9 oz.	Carl Pruitt	Banks Lake	4/9/77
Smallmouth-8 lbs. 12 oz.	Ray Wonacott	Columbia River/Hanford Reach	4/23/66
Burbot -17.01 lbs.	Patrick Bloomer	Palmer Lake, .	1/15/93
Carp-41 lbs 4 oz.	Kevin Wolf	Long Lake, Thurston Co.	6/21/80
Brown bullhead-3.90 lbs.	Joe Ochota	Ludlow Lake,	6/26/97
Black bullhead-1.75 lbs.	John E. Moore	Mud Lake, Skagit Co.	6/29/98
Yellow bullhead-1.63 lbs.	Mike Schlueter	Banks Lake,	5/22/94
Blue catfish-17 lbs. 12 oz.	Rangle Hawthorne	Columbia River	7/9/75
Channel catfish-36.20 lbs.	Ross Kincaid	I-82 Pond #6,	9/6/99
Flathead catfish-22.8 lbs.	C. L. McCary	Snake River	6/28/81
Black crappie-4 lbs. 8 oz.	John W. Smart	Lake Washington	5/19/56
White crappie -2.8 lbs.	Don J. Benson	Columbia R. Burbank Slough	7/21/88
Arctic grayling	No state record– season closed		
Pikeminnow-7 lbs. 4oz.	Louis A. Picard	Snake River, Whitman Co.	6/4/96
Yellow perch-2 lbs. 12 oz.	Larry Benthien	Snelson's Slough, Skagit Co.	6/22/69
Northern pike-32.2 lbs.	Fred R. Ruetsch	Long Lake, Spokane Co.	4/15/95
Tiger musky 31.25 lbs.	John Bays	Mayfield Lake, Lewis Co.	9/22/01
Shad-3.44 lbs.	Pete Green	Columbia River, Clark Co.	6/19/99
Bluegill-2 lbs. 5.3 oz.	Ron Hinote	Tampico Park Pond,	6/10/84
Green sunfish-.79 lbs.	Mickey Hough	Bailey Lake, Spokane Co.	5/29/94
Pumpkinseed-12 oz.	Doug Molohon	Hicks Lake	8/3 /77
Rock bass-1 lb. 6 oz.	William Jackson	Steilacoom Lake	6/28/81
Warmouth-53 lbs.	Linda Hatlelid	Silver Lake, Cowlitz Co.	5/27 /96
Atlantic salmon-8.96 lbs.	Gregory Lepping	Goat Lake, Jefferson Co.	9/13 /92
Atlantic salmon(sr)-14.38 lbs.	Ron Howard	Green River, King Co.	9/22 /99
Brown trout-22 lbs.	R. L. Henry	Sullivan Lake	5/22 /65
Bull trout-22 lbs. 8 oz.	Louis Schott	Tieton River	4/23/61
Chinook-68.26 lbs.	Mark Salmon	Elochoman River	10/5/92
Chum-27.97 lbs.	Johnny Wilson	Satsop River	10/19/97

FISH RECORD	ANGLER	WHERE CAUGHT	DATE
Coho-23 lbs. 8 oz.	David Bailey	Satsop River	1/12/86
Cutthroat sea-run-6 lbs	Bud Johnson	Carr Inlet, Pierce Co.	5 /43
Cutthroat-12 lbs.	W. Welsh	Lake Crescent	7/61
Cutthroat Lahontan-18.04 lbs.	Dan Beardslee	Omak Lake	7/1 /93
Cutthroat-westslope No state record			
Dolly Varden-10 lbs. 15 oz.	Leroy Thompson	Whitechuck River	8/5 /99
Brook trout-9 lbs.	George G. Weekes	Wobbly Lake, Lewis Co.	5/7/88
Golden trout-3.81 lbs.	Mark S. Morris	Unnamed, Okanogan Co.	8/06 /91
Kokanee -5.47 lbs.	Don Growt	Lake Roosevelt	6/4/93
Mackinaw-33 lbs. 6.50 oz.	Lyle Smith	Lake Chelan	8/9/01
Pink salmon 14.49 lbs.	Avis Pearson	Skykomish River	9/22/01
Rainbow trout 25.45 lbs.	Robert Halverson	Rufus Woods Lake	2/23 /98
Rainbow Beardslee 16 lbs. 5 oz.	Richard L. Bates	Lake Crescent,	9/7/89
Sockeye 10 lbs. 10 oz	Gary Krasselt	Lake Washington	7/20/82
Steelhead(sum) 35 lbs. 1 oz.	Gilbert Pierson	Snake River	11/23/73
Steelhead(win) 32 lbs. 12 oz.	Gene Maygra	E.F. Lewis River	4/14/80
Walleye 18.76 lbs.	Mike Jones	Columbia River (below McNary)	4/9/90
Lake whitefish 6.63 lbs.	Jerry Hamilton	Lk. Roosevelt,	3/31/97
Mt. whitefish 5 lbs. 2 oz.	Steven Becken	Columbia River	11/30/83

Saltwater Fish

FISH RECORD	ANGLER	WHERE CAUGHT	DATE
Ratfish 3.9 lbs.	William J. Denning	Hein Bank	7/19/96
Hake No state record			
True cod 19 lbs. 10 oz.	Ralph Bay	Ediz Hook	3/6/84
Tomcod No state record			
Pollock No state record			
Sanddab No state record			
Arrowtooth flounder No state record			
English sole-No state record			
Halibut -288 lbs.	Vic Stevens	Swiftsure Bank	9/9/89
Petrale sole-7 lbs. 9 oz.	John Stone	Jefferson Head	6/11/80
Rock sole-4 lbs. 3 oz.	Alan Schram	Hein Bank	7/9/89
Sand sole No state record			
Starry flounder-8.57 lbs	Danny Patterson	Sekiu	7/6/97
Greenling-3 lbs. 8 oz.	Diana Kottkey	San Juan Islands	8/3/93
Lingcod-61 lbs.	Tom Nelson	San Juan Islands	7/30/86
Black rockfish-10 lbs. 4 oz.	Joseph Eberling	Tacoma Narrows	5/20/80
Blue rockfish 3.91 lbs.	Erik M. Herbig	Westport	6/22/96
Bocaccio 23 lbs. 10 oz.	Carson Kendall	Swiftsure Bank	8/8/87
Brown rockfish No state record			
Canary rockfish 10 lbs. 9 oz.	Ben Phillips	Neah Bay	8/30/86
China rockfish 4 lbs. 3 oz.	Steven Ripley	Duncan Rock	7/11/89
Copper rockfish 10 lbs.	David Northington	Point Roberts Reef	8/6/89
Greenstripe rockfish-1 lb.10 oz.	David Wedeking	Possession Bar	1/19/85
Quillback rockfish 7 lbs. 3 oz.	Bror Hultgren	Middle Bank	10/29/87
Tiger rockfish 7 lbs. 8 oz.	James Wenban	Middle Bank	11/30/89
Vermillion rockfish 6.55 lbs.	James S. Duffy	Makaw Bay	5/23/98
Yelloweye rockfish-27 lbs.12 oz.	Jan Tavis	Dallas Bank	4/15/89
Yellowtail rockfish-7 lbs. 6 oz.	Ken Culver	Westport	9/15/92
Sablefish-30 lb.	Jeff Rudolph	Westport	6/28/94
Chinook (salt)-70 lbs. 8 oz.	Chet Gausta	Sekiu	9/6/64
Chum (salt)-25.26 pounds	Fred Dockendorf,	Westport	8/6/01
Coho salmon-22 lbs. 8 oz.	James Veselovec	Sekiu	9/19/01

FISH RECORD	ANGLER	WHERE CAUGHT	DATE
Pink (salt)-6.38 lbs.	Rodney M. Hansen	Mukilteo	8/25 /97
Sockeye (salt) No state record			
Cabezon-23 lbs.	Wesley S. Hunter	Dungeness Spit	8/4/90
Blue shark No state record			
Sixgill shark-220 lbs.	Jim Haines	Gedney Island	1/30/91
Spiny dogfish-20 lbs. 4 oz.	Roger Petersen	Middle Bank	5/22/98
Skate-130 lbs.	Dan Cartwright	Double Bluff	5/18/86
Pile perch-3 lbs. 9 oz.	Steve Urban	Quartermaster Harbor	3/14/81
Redtail surfperch-4.05 lbs.	Chris Maynard	Kalaloch	8/4/96
Striped seaperch-2 lbs. 1 oz.	Chris Urban	Quartermaster Harbor	6/2/80
Albacore tuna-52 lbs.	Kurt Strickland	Pacific Ocean-Westport.	10/1/97
Wolf eel No state record			

Skykomish River angler Avis Pearson caught this state and IGFA world record pink salmon on a Dick Nite spoon, Sept. 22, 2001. It was one of several fresh and salt water records smashed that exceptional year.

Washington Fishing License Requirements

Annual licenses run from April 1 through March 31
WDFW licenses are required for both residents and non-residents 15 years of
    age and older. Reduced-fee licenses are available for qualified disabled
    persons, disabled veterans, youths age 15, and resident seniors age 70+.
WDFW licenses are not required in Mount Rainier or Olympic National Parks. A
    license is required in North Cascades National Park.
License requirements summarized here may change

Annual Saltwater License

A saltwater license is required to fish for most marine and anadromous species in
    saltwater. $18 for residents 16-69 years
$5 for residents age 70 and older,
$36 for non-residents 16 and older.
Resident shellfish/seaweed license $7 and $5 for residents age 70 and older, and
    $20 for non-residents 16 and older.

Annual Freshwater License

Annual freshwater license is required to fish for most freshwater species
$20 annually for residents 16-69 years of age
$5 for residents age 70 and older
$40 annually for non-residents ages 16 and older.

Combination License

Required for freshwater/saltwater and shellfish/seaweed.
$36 for residents
$72 for non-residents and to disabled anglers
$5 for and resident and non-resident youth (under age 15)
$6 for 2-day combination freshwater/saltwater and shellfish/seaweed license for
    both residents and non-residents
A free combination catch record card is required to fish for or retain steelhead,
    salmon, sturgeon, halibut or Dungeness crab.

Kids and Seniors

Juvenile anglers are residents or non-residents 14 years and under. Juveniles
    can fish for free, no licenses required, for all legal species, in all open
    waters during open seasons. A free catch record card is still required for
    steelhead, salmon, sturgeon, halibut and Dungeness crab.
Resident seniors, 70 years of age or older, can buy reduced-fee freshwater,
    saltwater, or shellfish/seaweed licenses for $5 each. Non-resident seniors
    pay the standard non-resident fee.

Disabled Licenses

A $5 combination freshwater, saltwater and shellfish/seaweed license is available
    to residents who are physically handicapped and confined to a wheelchair,
    legally blind, developmentally disabled, or a qualified disabled veteran.
    Disability license applications may be obtained by writing to the
    department's License Division at the Olympia or at WDFW regional offices.

Tribal and Military Reservations

Fishing permits are required to fish on designated tribal and military reservation waters. Available at stores or tribal headquarters offices, and on base.

National Parks

Mount Rainier: no fishing license required, back country permits for overnight stays. Admission fee.

North Cascades: Washington state fishing licenses, no admission fee, USFS permit required at some trailheads.

Olympic: no fishing license required. Admission fee.

National Forests

No federal fishing license. Washington State fishing license required and regulations apply. Parking fees required at many trailheads in all national forests.

Where to Call

Washington Department Fish and Wildlife

WDFW Main Office, Olympia: 360-902-2700

Fishing Hotline: 360-902-2500

Shellfish Hotline: 360-796-3215

WDFW Regional Offices: Spokane 509-456-4082; Ephrata 509-754-4624; Yakima 509-575-2740; Wenatchee 509-662-0452; Mill Creek 425-775-1311; Vancouver 360-696-6211; Montesano 360-249-4628; Point Whitney 360-796-4601; Willapa Bay 360-665-4166.

Washington State Parks 1-800-233-0321

National Parks

Olympic NP 360-452-4501

Mount Rainier NP 360-569-2211

North Cascades NP 360-856-5700

National Forests

Mount Baker-Snoqualmie 1-800-627-0062 or 425-775-9702; Wenatchee 509-662-4335; Olympic 360-956-2400;

Okanogan 509-826-3275; Colville 509-684-7000; Gifford Pinchot 360-891-5000; Umatilla 503-276-3811.

Tribal, Military Reservations

Quinault Nation 360-276-8211; Colville Confederated Tribes 509-634-4711; Yakama Nation 509-865-5121; Lummi Tribe 360-384-1489; Swinomish Tribe 360-466-7228; Makah Tribe 360-645-2201.

Fort Lewis Military Reservation 253-967-6263.

US Fish and Wildlife, 360-753-9467

Mount St. Helens National Vocanic Monument 360-247-3900

Bureau of Land Management 509-536-1200

Columbia River Gorge National Scenic Area 541-386-2333

Map of Counties and WDFW Regions

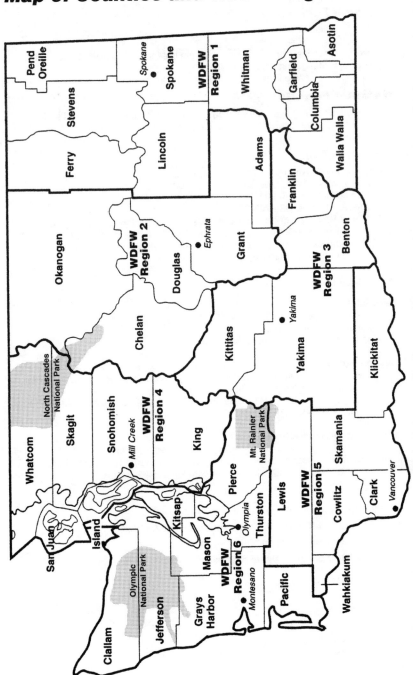

Adams County

WDFW Region 2

Washington Department of Fish and Wildlife, 1550 Alder St. NW, Ephrata, WA 98823-9699. Phone 509-754-4624

Rolling across semiarid sagebrush plains, rocky coulees and wheat farms on the southeast edge of the Columbia Basin, Adams County is one of Washington's largest and driest regions with few lakes and even fewer streams. The western edge of the county, does however, ease into the wetlands of the Columbia National Wildlife Refuge (CNWR) and includes several of the productive "seep lakes" below the dam impounding O'Sullivan (Potholes) Reservoir. The county's largest lake is Sprague Lake, a major fishing resource which is visible from the south side of I-90 northeast of Ritzville. Approximately 1203 acres of Sprague Lake are in Adams and 638 acres in Lincoln County.

Much of the eastern county drains to Cow and Rock Creeks, tributaries to the Palouse River. Most of the west county drains to Crab Creek which is impounded to form both Moses Lake and O'Sullivan Reservoir. Near Othello Crab Creek swings W. to the Columbia River merging south of Beverly. Adams covers 1900 square miles making it the state's 16th largest. The high point is NE of Ritzville at 2100 feet, but much of the central and W. county is less than 800 feet. The county is mostly semiarid. Annual precipitation at Ritzville is 11.47 inches. Midsummer temperatures are in the high 80s and 90s, with winter lows 20 to 40 degrees. Best access routes are I-90, US 395 and WA 26.

BLACK LAKES. Two small, rarely fished hike-in lakes in the CNWR. Big Black covers 19 acres, Little Black 6 acres. Both have largemouth bass, black crappie, bluegill, perch, and are fed by an irrigation wasteway from Lower Goose Lake. Located 8 miles NW of Othello. From McMannaman Road go N. on H-SE, then E. on gravel road to Lower Goose Lake, then hike S. .05 mile to the lakes.

BUTTE LAKES. Three warm water species lakes with largemouth bass, black crappie, bluegill, perch, covering 30 acres, 7.3 miles NW of Othello on S. side of Crab Creek on CNWR. Formed by seepage.

CAMPBELL LAKE. A 115-acre private lake 9 miles N. of Othello, bordered on the E. side by E. Potholes Canal. Carp.

COW CREEK. Drains from Sprague, Middle, (Hallin) Cow and Finell lakes into Palouse River at Hooper Junction. Few crossing lateral roads. Supports a few brookies, browns and rainbow. Spring best. Extremely low water in summer.

COW LAKE. Warm water species and rainbow share this 226-acre enlargement of Cow Creek. Lots of waterfowl. Holds perch, walleye, brown bullhead, channel catfish, pickerels, bluegills and largemouth bass. Dam at outlet. Public access. Located 9.5 miles E. of Ritzville. From I-90 go S on Wellsandt Road to Cow Lake Rd.

CRAB CREEK (Lower). A large, soft-bottom stream that flows S. from Potholes Reservoir through CNWR/Seep Lakes for about 6 miles before entering Grant County and turning west to spill into the Columbia River near Beverly. Minimal fishing opportunities. Best in May and June. Holds scatterings of rainbow, a few brown trout, and brookies from plantings above Moses Lake and Seep Lakes. Some warm water species, lots of carp. Excellent carp bow-fishing April-June. In the early spring large numbers of spawn-run rainbow, bass and walleye concentrate in the creek below the Potholes Dam, but in recent years this fishery has been closed. Check annual WDFW regulations. Multiple diversion dams make boating through CNWR difficult. From E side of Potholes Reservoir dam turn S. on Soda Lake Rd. Multiple access points in CNWR. To access lower section from Hwy. 26, just east of Royal City turn S. on Red Rock Rd., to Lower Crab Creek Rd, and continue W. mostly along the south side of the creek to Beverly. WDFW access to quality fishing lakes, Lenice, Nunnally and Merry is N. of the creek, just E. of Beverly.

CRANE LAKE. Also known as Mallard or Long. About 15 miles E. of Ritzville drains into Palouse River. Holds warm water variety. Primarily a waterfowl nesting lake.

DEADMAN LAKE. Private. No access. Largemouth bass and bluegill lake of 12.4 acres about 5 miles NW of Othello and 300 feet S. of Halfmoon Lake. Drains to Crab Creek.

FINNEL LAKE. Private, no access. 30.9 acre lake with largemouth bass, bluegills, pickerels, and brown bullheads 7 miles E. from Ritzville and 3 miles SW of Cow Lake.

FOURTH OF JULY LAKE. Ice fishing for rainbows is popular and productive in this 110 acre lake, which is managed as a winter-only lake open Dec.-Mar (74 acres in Adams County, 36 acres in Lincoln County). Heavily stocked with catchables and fry. Go S. from Sprague on Hwy. 23 for 1 miles, turn W. on dirt road at Milepost I. Continue about 1 mile to cattle guard, turn right and take left fork of road 1 mile to lake.

GREEN LAKE. Weedy 4.5 acres, in NE county, rarely fished but has largemouth bass.

HALFMOON, MORGAN, SHINER and **HUTCHINSON.** Chain of shallow lakes located adjacent to the McMannaman Road 6 miles NW of Othello on CNWR. Gas outboards not allowed. **Morgan** and **Halfmoon** have rainbow and Lahontan cutthroat. Morgan is mostly on private land, accessible by going past Halfmoon Lake. **Shiner** and **Hutchinson** are managed for bass and bluegill, possibly a few stray trout. Rough boat launch at Hutchinson. Lakes drain into Crab Creek. Easy access to all the lakes.

HALLIN LAKE. A 33.3 acre enlargement of Cow Creek 11 miles E. of Ritzville. Largemouth bass, bluegills and brown bullheads.

HAYS CREEK. Outlet of Halfmoon Lake.

It holds some rainbow and warm water species.

HERMAN LAKE. A 33 acre rainbow lake 5 miles N. of Othello on private land. A trail leads from Pit Lake parking area past Quail Lake to E. end of Herman. Fed by Teal Creek. Private access will remain open as long as anglers keep it clean. Pick up all litter! Stocked in Apr. with 5000 catchable rainbows

LINDA LAKE. Fed by irrigation water, Linda covers 99.2 acres and has largemouth bass, bluegill, pumpkinseeds, perch and brown bullheads. It's 5.3 miles SW of Othello draining to Scooteney Lake.

LUGENBEAL SPRINGS CREEK. Few rainbow trout in this stream which flows into N. end of Hallin Lake. Creek is about 4 miles long and heads at Lugenbeal Springs.

LYLE LAKE. 22 acres, stocked with 2000 catchable rainbows in Apr. Good bow fishing for carp in spring. Public access area. 5 miles N. of Othello and 1200 feet SW of Herman Lake. Take McMannaman Road W. from Othello for 4.5 miles, then NE on gravel road into CNWR. Turnoff is marked.

McMANNAMAN LAKE. Rainbow and cutthroat, 7-acres, 6 miles NW of Othello. Turn N. at E. end of Halfmoon Lake about 1.5 miles. Drive past field headquarters of CNWR There is a short walk in. Best in spring and early summer. Follow the inlet to Para Lake, (see Grant County) and the outlet into Morgan Lake.

PALOUSE RIVER. A shallow, easily waded river with good smallmouth bass fishing in April, May and June. Also, channel catfish. The river is the S. border of Adams County, flows S. along the E. border of Franklin County into Snake River.

PINES LAKE. Narrow, 120 acre lake planted occasionally with rainbow. It's 2000 feet S. of Fourth of July Lake and 3.5 miles S. of Sprague. Waterfowl nesting. Drains to Palouse River.

QUAIL LAKE. A year-round, fly-fishing only, catch and release rainbow lake of 12 acres just E. of Herman Lake in Seep Lakes on CNWR Best fished from float tubes. 1 mile walk to lake from S. end of Herman Lake. This can be an exceptional fishery for large trout, possibly tiger trout.

ROCK CREEK. Only 2.5 miles of this outlet stream from Rock Lake are in Adams County, but this stretch offers enjoyable stream fishing for rainbows, browns and smallmouth bass. Best in July, August and September. A county road crosses the creek .05 miles from the Whitman County line near Paxton Station. Camping and drinking water at Weaver Springs.

ROYAL LAKE. Largemouth bass, black crappie, pumpkinseeds, yellow perch and brown bullheads. A narrow, 102 acre lake 3 miles N. of Highway 26 on Adams-Grant County line. County road adjacent to N. shore. Heavily used by waterfowl.

SPRAGUE LAKE. Largest lake and one of the best fishing bets in Adams County. This 1840-acre lake, (1203 acres in Adams County, 637 in Lincoln) is a good prospect for warm water fish, and a fair bet for trout. It is lightly stocked in late winter with about 5000 catchable rainbow, and holds a few carryover brown trout. Good spring early summer prospect for walleyes, largemouth and smallmouth bass, perch, black crappie, bluegill, and channel catfish. May to September usually best. Some winter ice fishing. Located at an elev. of 1841' in the NE corner of the county about 2 miles SW of Sprague, adjacent to I-90. New WDFW

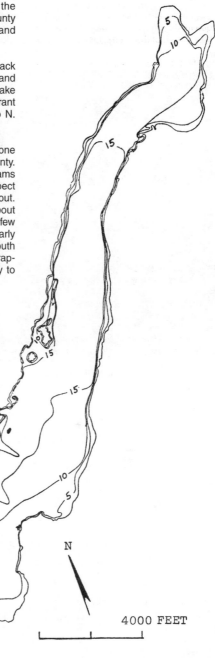

Sprague Lake
1840 acres
Adams County
©Washington State Fishing Guide

N

4000 FEET

access on SW end. A private fee launch is on SE side. Two resorts one N. and the other S. ends of lake.

THREAD LAKE. A slim, shallow, 1.4 mile long 29.4 acre lake adjacent to McMannaman Road 3 miles N. of Othello. Inlet from Lyle Lake. Stocked with bluegills and perch. Poor for rainbow. Public access area.

WALL LAKE. Planted with hardy Lahontan cutthroat, but infrequently winter and summer kills. 15 acres, 19 miles SE of Ritzville and 1 mile SE of Paxton Station. Follow private road S. from Paxto.

Adams County Resorts

Sprague Lake: Sprague Lake Resort, 509-257-2864; Four Seasons Campground, 509-257-2332.

Mike Crow fly-fishing sagebrush lake.

Asotin County

WDFW Region 1

Washington Department of Fish and Wildlife, 8702 N. Division St., Spokane, WA 99218. Phone, 509-456-4082.

Located in the extreme SW corner of Washington tiny Asotin County's 637 mountainous square miles are wedged between the Snake River and Idaho on the E, Oregon on the S, the Blue Mountains on the W, and the edge of the Palouse on the N.

Its two major fishing assets are the Snake and Grande Ronde rivers. Not counting Snake River impoundments, there are only 36 acres of water in 10 small lakes in the entire county, and most of these are in the Blues above 2500 feet elev. Small streams in the Blue Mountains, while no longer stocked by WDFW still offer some of the finest fishing in the county, mostly for small wild rainbows.

As the 35th largest county (out of 39) the topography of Asotin is mostly open, gently mountainous with steep canyons. Only 7 percent is classed as forest, all in the Blue Mountains. The northern two-thirds of the county drain east through Alpowa and Asotin creeks, both decent trout streams, and the southern county falls into the beautiful Grande Ronde as it winds NE from Oregon into the Snake River at a steelhead and smallmouth bass hot spot south of Asotin. The major city, with full traveler services and tackle shops, is Clarkston (pop. 6810) on the Snake River in the NE corner of the county.

Summer fishing temperatures can range from blistering in the Snake River canyons to comfortable in the mountains. At the small community of Anatone, elev. 3790 ft., summer temperatures rarely exceed the low 80s, and drop to about 20 degrees in the winter. The record low, though, is -30. The climate is fairly dry, especially at lower elevations. Anatone gets about 23 inches of rain a year, but snowfall often reaches 95 inches. Elevations range from 842 feet at Asotin on the Snake River to 6191 feet on Ray Ridge in the Blues.

Major access into the county is via US 12 across the NE edge of the county to Clarkston. State Hwy. 128, a lonely two-lane, runs EW across the N. county. Hwy. 129 in E. county, is the main NS road going through Asotin and Anatone crossing the Grande Ronde and connecting with OR Hwy. 3 to Enterprise and Joseph. Roads, some paved, follow creeks up major canyons. Much of the W. county N. of the Blues is dry and fairly roadless.

ALPOWA CREEK. Small Snake River tributary that dips into N. Asotin County from Garfield County and eases into the Snake R. W. of Clarkston at Silcott near Chief Timothy State Park. The creek is followed by US 12 but is bordered by private lands. Small wild rainbows are available if you can get permission to fish. Smallmouth bass near the mouth.

ASOTIN CREEK. Most of the stream is open only during the summer. Trout plants have been discontinued. One of the longest streams in the county, this was once one of the finest trout streams in the state. Now its restrictively managed to protect wild steelhead. Selective gear rules often apply. Read the regs before dropping a line in Asotin Creek. The stream offers wild rainbows, whitefish and some steelhead but most ironheads return in winter after the creek closes. Aug.-Oct. try for wild rainbows above Lick Creek. Most tributaries are closed to protect spawning steelhead. Asotin Creek Road follows the creek upstream from Asotin to and beyond the Asotin Wildlife Area.

CHARLIE FORK CREEK. An Asotin Creek tributary that supports wild rainbow. Closed to fishing.

COTTONWOOD CREEK. A tributary of the Grande Ronde, accessible from Grande Ronde Rd., 2 miles W. of Hwy. 129 bridge. Primitive road follows upstream. Small pockets of native rainbow. Fishes best in spring right after runoff.

EVANS, GOLF COURSE, SILCOTT PONDS, small heavily stocked impoundments in the extreme N. side of county near the Snake River below Alpowa grade Accessible from US 12 near Alpowai Interpretive Center. Evans and Golf Course ponds are most heavily stocked, each getting upwards of 20,000 catchable rainbows to 2 pounds every spring. Silcott is stocked with about 4000 rainbows. Public access, year-round season, heavy pressure in spring.

GRANDE RONDE RIVER. The heart of Asotin County fishing, this is a popular and very productive fishery for summer steelhead (in the winter), smallmouth bass and in the lower reaches channel catfish and a scattering of panfish. Chinook salmon are found here, but fishing for them is not allowed. The Grande Ronde heads as a trout stream, deep in Oregon's Wallowa Mtns. and flows NE through SE Asotin County into the Snake River. The mouth is a popular steelhead hole beginning in Sept. and is good for smallmouth bass most of the summer and fall. In fall and early winter steelheading in the lower 2.5 miles of the Grande Ronde is catch-and-release only. Good sometimes excellent steelheading holds up all winter upstream to the Oregon border. Peak months are Feb.-Mar. In cold weather concentrate on deep holes. From Asotin drive S. on Hwy. 129. Where the highway bridges the river turn W. on Grande Ronde Rd., which continues upstream along the N. bank. A few primitive roads make their way into the lower river, but much of this belongs to drift boat and raft fishermen. A good road runs S. from Asotin along the Snake River to the mouth and a short distance upstream. Boat ramps at the mouth and at the end of the paved road, and upstream at Bogans Oasis.

HEADGATE POND. This Asotin Creek impoundment is open to juveniles and seniors only. Usually planted with 2000 catchable rainbows in April.

JOSEPH CREEK. About 4 miles of this Grande Ronde tributary are in Washington. Follow Joseph Creek Rd. upstream from the mouth of the Grande Ronde for about 5 miles along the creek which goes through the Chief Joseph Wildlife Area. Small wild rainbows best in late summer. Watch for rattlesnakes.

Grande Ronde River (Lenny Frasure photo).

RATTLESNAKE CREEK. A fast-falling rainbow stream that follows the W. side of Hwy. 129 from near Fields Spring State Park S. to the Grande Ronde. Best fished in late spring after runoff.

SNAKE RIVER. Forms the NE and E. border of the county, and is closely paralleled by good paved roads above and below Clarkston to mouth of the Grande Ronde River. Several boat launches. Good seasonal fishing for steelhead, sturgeon (catch and release), smallmouth bass, channel catfish, crappie. Major fishing areas near Silcott below Alpowa Creek mouth, at Chief Timothy State Park, Evans Road, Clarkston waterfront, mouth of Asotin Creek at Asotin, and especially at the mouth of Grande Ronde. Lots of bank access from adjacent roads.

TENMILE CREEK. A small stream running NE along Weissenfels Ridge and dumping into the Snake River about 7 miles S. of Asotin. Some rainbow trout.

WENATCHEE CREEK. A small Grande Ronde tributary, running S. from the Blue Mtns. and into the 'Ronde about 1 mile from Oregon border. Tough hike-in access from Ranger Creek trailhead near Blue Mtns. Wenatchee Guard Station . From where the stream crosses the Grande Ronde River Rd., walk upstream for fair wild rainbow trout fishing. Some private ground.

Smallmouth bass are plentiful in Asotin County.

Benton County

WDFW Region 3

Washington Department of Fish and Wildlife, 1701 S. 24th Ave., Yakima, WA 98902. Phone 509-575-2740.

Most of the fishable water in Benton County is moving, either in the Columbia River which flanks it on three sides or the lower Yakima River which divides it in the middle. Take away these two major flows and there are only 229 acres of lake water in the entire county. Ironically, though, some of the best chinook salmon and walleye fishing in Washington takes place here.

Benton covers 1767 square miles west of Tri-Cities, and is one of the driest areas in the state. Annual precipitation is only 7.49 inches measured along the Columbia River at Kennewick. Either the land is irrigated agriculture or it's sandy and desertlike. The Rattlesnake Hills dominate an almost uninhabited region in the NW part of the county ending in the breaks of the Yakima near Benton City. NE of the Rattlesnake Hills the land is flat, gently sloping toward the Columbia, with sparse vegetation, dry creek beds and basalt outcroppings. Not one spot in the county qualifies as forest. The highest elevation in the county is 3629 feet in the Rattlesnake Hills near Grandview. Most of the county, however is between 250 and 340 feet.

The Columbia River borders the county on the S., E., and N. The lower Yakima River cuts W. to E. through the central plain nearly dividing the county equally. The Department of Energy's sprawling Hanford Site occupies most of the NE county. South of the Yakima River the Horse Heaven Hills and Plateau divide the Yakima and Columbia river drainage's.

Summer's can be brutally hot, with mid-day temperatures frequently climbing into the high 90s. Winter temperatures are in the range of 25 to 30 degrees.

The Yakima and Columbia rivers hold the most potential for fishermen. Major highways cut through the county from just about every direction following and crossing the rivers at several well-developed recreation sites. On the S., Hwy. 14 parallels productive walleye areas of the Columbia R. to US 12 then N. into the Tri-Cities. US 12 crosses the middle of the county south of the Yakima River's prime smallmouth areas to connect Yakima and Tri-Cities. On the N. side of the county, Hwy. 24 goes from Yakima to Vernita Bridge, jumpoff point for summer upriver bright chinook fishing in the last free-flowing section of the Columbia River.

COLUMBIA PARK FAMILY FISHING POND. This 7-acre pond in Kennewick at the end of the US 395 bridge is Washington's first, "family fishing pond", opened to juveniles and licensed adults who are accompanying juveniles. Stocked annually with catchable and large Triploid rainbow trout, and has a good population of smallmouth and largemouth bass, crappie, bluegills and channel catfish.

COLUMBIA RIVER. The most important fishery in the county. The Columbia River borders Benton County on the N., E. and S. and offers just about every freshwater fish found in the state. In July and August the upriver bright chinook fishery is outstanding. Best spots are from the Vernita Bridge downstream to White Bluffs. These fish are typically 20 to 45 pounds and hit trolled plugs. Fall chinook return to the Hanford Reach from Sept. through Nov. Steelheading is a maybe proposition. The National Marine Fisheries Service has listed upper Columbia River steelhead as endangered closing the river to steelhead from US 395 bridge at Pasco upstream. WDFW is working to open an Oct.-Mar. hatchery steelhead fishery in the Tri-Cities from the Hwy. 395 bridge to Hanford Townsite.

Bank fishing is allowed at Ringold Hatchery and it can be very good. There is often good steelhead fishing July through Mar. in the Richland-Ringold area, immediately above McNary Dam, at Devil's Bend and Alder Creek. Whitefish angling in the Priest Rapids Dam-Vernita area is best from in Dec. and Jan., with smallmouth bass fishing May to Sept.

Best bass fishing is from Hanford downstream, especially near the mouth of the Yakima, Paterson Slough and at Crow Butte State Park. There is often good summer steelhead angling in the Richland-Ringold area, as well as in the Devil's Bend and Alder Creek drifts below McNary Dam. Good fishing for steelhead from McNary Dam through the Wallula area in Oct. and Nov. This same area is a popular sturgeon spot. In addition smallmouth bass, channel catfish (to 10 pounds in McNary Pool), bluegill, pumpkinseed, crappie and brown bullhead provide fishing opportunities especially in the sloughs and backwaters.

The southern border of the county supports some of the finest walleye fishing in Washington. Walleyes are caught throughout McNary and John Day Pools, below McNary and John Day Dams. Excellent walleye areas can be reached by launching at Crow Butte, Paterson, and Plymouth. Good to outstanding smallmouth bass fishing takes place in the sloughs at Paterson. Largemouth and smallmouth are in the Hanford area and near the mouth of the Yakima River. Good largemouth bass fishing, as well as some fair crappie, perch, and brown bullhead action can be found in the Finley area. Columbia Park, which has 4.5 miles of river bank, is located at Kennewick. There are overnight camping facilities plus 4 boat ramps and boat docks at the park. While it's possible to bank fish, especially near the dams and hatcheries, this is big water and a trailerable boat is advised.

MITCHELL POND. A 3.7 acre pond located 13.5 miles SE of Kennewick and adjacent to the W. side of Lake Wallula. Formed by a railroad fill. Contains large and smallmouth bass, perch, crappie and catfish. Drains into Wallula. Only access is by boat from the Columbia R.

MOUND POND. Formed by railroad fill adjacent to NW shore of Lake Wallula. Situated about 14.5 miles SE of Kennewick. Holds small and largemouth bass, perch, catfish and crappie. It is 34 acres.

PIT PONDS. Ponds formed by a railroad fill. Both ponds hold small and largemouth bass, perch, crappie and catfish, as do **PALMER** and **WALL PONDS** in the same vicinity. Only access is by boat from the Columbia R.

SWITCH POND. Another "side lake" formed by a railroad fill along Lake Wallula. Located about 15.5 miles SE of Kennewick and 0.4 miles S. of **YELLEPIT POND**, which was also formed by a railroad fill. Both ponds hold small and largemouth bass, perch, crappie and catfish. Only access is by boat from the Columbia R.

WALLULA LAKE. The massive Columbia River reservoir behind McNary Dam. About 40% of the reservoir's 38,800 acres are in Benton County. Best fishing is for warm water species, including channel catfish and possibly a few blues during summer. Most, but not all of the Columbia River entry is within Wallula Lake.

YAKIMA RIVER. Benton County is divided about evenly by the Yakima River. Good roads run down both sides of the river offering access. Smallmouth bass fishing good below Prosser in spring and summer. Below Benton City, smallmouthing is excellent in May and June when large Columbia R. fish enter the Yakima to spawn. Smallmouth are generally under 1.5 pounds, but fish to 3 pounds and more are caught. Whitefish angling during winter. Best from Prosser to W. Richland and in vicinity of Horn Rapids dam where there is a boat launch. Whitefish angling is often good during October and November. Channel catfishing excellent in the lower Yakima River. The Richland area is a favorite area for catfish 2 to 8 pounds. Fair largemouth bass and crappie fishing can also be found on the lower Yakima near Richland. The entire river is closed to steelhead fishing. Spring and fall chinook and coho seasons are sometimes opened.

YELLEPIT POND. A 36-acre pond formed by a railroad. fill 15.4 miles SE of Kennewick. Connected by culvert to Lake Wallula. Holds warm water species.

Chelan County
WDFW Region 2

Washington Department of Fish and Wildlife, Region 2, 1550 Alder St. NW, Ephrata, WA 98823-9699. Phone 509-754-4624

This is high lake and backpacking country. Only 38 of Chelan's hundreds of lakes are located below 2500 feet elevation. This mountainous county includes some of the most spectacular and remote alpine lake areas in the central and north Cascades nearly all reached by hiking on maintained trails in the Wenatchee and Okanogan national forests.

The county offers miles of remote fishing for backpacking anglers. It include all or portions of Glacier Peak, Lake Chelan-Sawtooth, Henry M. Jackson and Alpine Lakes wilderness areas, and the Lake Chelan National Recreation Area segment of North Cascades National Park.

Trout dominate the region's waters, although a handful of lowland lakes have large and smallmouth bass and panfish. Recent Endangered Species Act protections for summer steelhead and bull trout have had an impact on stream fishing. Rivers and streams that are open are tightly regulated, many with selective gear and minimal bag limits. It's good advice to dig out the current WDFW regs before dropping a line into any moving water.

Chelan is the third largest in the state. Four major rivers—-the Stehekin, Chelan, Entiat and Wenatchee—-drain the county running east from the Cascade Range into the Columbia River. Bonanza Peak, at 9511 feet, is the most lofty point in Chelan, although there are many peaks over 8000 feet. Lake Chelan, is the largest natural lake in the state covering 33,104 acres and 1605 feet deep. Most lakes in the 50 to 300 acre range, easily fished from small boats or float tubes.

Only about 22 percent of the county is in ranch or cropland and the rest, generally everything W. of the Columbia River, is vertical. Nearly all of the mountain area is public ground, most managed by Wenatchee National Forest. Lands near the Columbia River are mostly private, except for specific access areas managed by WDFW.

The climate is marked by extremes but is generally very dry, and the farther east you get from the mountains the drier it gets. The Cascades get about 94 inches of precipitation a year, mostly snow, while at Wenatchee most years get only 8.56 inches. Excellent camping all summer.

Wenatchee, at the confluence of the Columbia and Wenatchee rivers is the largest city in the county. Both major highways run through this city of 24,180. US 2 cuts E-W across the southern county, and US 97 Alt. rolls N-S along the west bank of the Columbia leading to several Columbia River camping areas.

AIRPLANE LAKE. A 10 acre rainbow planted lake at 5350 feet 32 miles NW from Leavenworth on E. side of Mt. Saul. Drains to Indian Creek and White River.

AUGUSTA LAKE. Cutthroat inhabit this 25.7 acre lake on Icicle Ridge 8.8 miles NW from Leavenworth. Open shoreline. Elev. is 6750 feet. Augusta drains to Cabin Creek and Wenatchee River.

ANTILON LAKE. Originally a natural lake of about 20 acres, Antilon was dammed to create a 96 acre, 57-feet deep reservoir (Including Long Jim Reservoir.) It is about 5 miles N. of Manson on Grade Creek Road past Roses and Wapato Lakes. Planted with brown trout fry, largemouth, crappie, bluegills and pumpkinseed panfish.

BATTALION LAKE. This rainbow planted

lake of 6.4 acres is at 5334 feet 3.4 miles SE from High Bridge Guard Station. Drains to Stehekin River.

BEEHIVE RESERVOIR. An 11.5 acre impoundment formed by a dam on upper Squilchuck Creek. Planted with 18,000 catchable rainbows and brook trout fry. Best in May. In mid summer the lake switches to catch-and-release, selective gear rules. Beehive is 8 miles SW of Wenatchee. Route is up Squilchuck Creek Road from South Wenatchee about 10 miles to Squilchuck State Park, then NW 1.5 miles to the reservoir.

BIG JIM LAKES. Alpine rainbow lakes of 4.3 and 4.5 acres at 6400 and 7000 feet on NE side of Big Jim Mountain, and 3300 feet NE from Augusta Lake. Drain to Wenatchee River.

BLACK LAKE (Wheeler Reservoir). Spring planted with 2000 pan-size brookies and 6000 fry. Located 8.5 miles S. of Wenatchee on Wheeler Hill at 3425 feet. Covers about 28 acres. May-June is best fishing. Private land and fishing may be restricted.

BOULDER CREEK. Wild rainbow are in this Stehekin River tributary about 1 mile above Lake Chelan. Trail leads up W. side of creek, touching the stream about 1 mile from mouth, then continuing to headwaters. Regular boat service from town of Chelan serves the community of Stehekin at end of Lake Chelan in North Cascade National Park.

BRIDGE CREEK. Enters Stehekin River at end of road leading from N. end of Lake Chelan. Rough road follows creek 4 miles to Bridge Creek Campground, then Cascade Crest Trail continues up creek to forks at Fireweed Campground. Also reached by following Twisp River Rd. from Twisp to end of road where there is a campground, then hiking about 5 miles over Twisp Pass and down E. fork of Bridge Creek. Rainbow and cutthroat in July and August. Trout are in the 8-10 inch range. Creek is in North Cascade National Park.

CANAAN LAKE. A 2.5 acre lake at 5500 feet at head of Royal Creek on SW side of Mt. Mastiff. Holds cutthroat. Drains to Nason Creek.

CAROLINE LAKES. Big Caroline Lake is at 5400 feet, 10.3 miles SW from Leavenworth in headwaters of Pioneer Creek. Little Caroline Lake is 3.5 acres at 5900 feet and 2000 feet NW from Big Caroline. Both lakes have been cutthroat planted. Drain to Wenatchee River.

CHELAN LAKE. Largest natural lake in Washington State, Chelan extends over 50 miles and 33,104 acres from Chelan to Stehekin at upper end. It averages about 1 mile in width, and maximum depth, off mouth of Big Goat Creek, is over 1500 feet. Notoriously windy. Mail boat service from Chelan calls at various points along the lake. Road up W. shoreline reaches as far as **TWENTY-FIVE MILE CREEK.** where there is a popular state park, before turning S. to wind through the mountains to Shady Pass and to drop down to the Entiat RiverRoad. Chelan has strikingly beautiful mountains rising steeply from the lake shore. It is not uncommon to spot mountain goats from boats. Most popular fish in Chelan are kokanee, although the huge lake also contains chinook salmon, rainbow, cutthroat, Dolly Varden, lake trout, burbot (freshwater ling), smallmouth bass. Kokanee fishing starts as early as April, and holds up all summer, supported by annual fry plants of 330,000. Stocked in the S. end with 75,000 catchable rainbows and 16,000 cutthroat in July and Aug. Another 88,000 mackinaw fry are stocked annually. Dolly Varden are present especially in the upper lake, but are ESA protected. Trophy anglers troll for landlocked chinook. These big fish are tough to come by. Best bet is to line up a guide who's familiar with the specialized techniques. Good for large mackinaw (holds state record) picked up by trollers with downriggers. Very limited smallmouth bass fishery along the rocky shoreline of the S. end. Burbot are taken by bait fishing on the bottom from Feb.-Apr., and with baited jigs off Wapato and Manson points. These strange fish fit a frying pan very nicely. Most of this massive lake is open year-round. However, upper reaches and tributary mouths may be seasonally closed. Tough lake to bank fish. Ramps at Chelan, Lake Chelan State Park, Manson, 25 Mile Creek, Granite Falls Marina and the Cove Marina. Resort facilities at Stehekin, with saddle and pack horses, taxi and rental cars. Stehekin is reached only by boat, air or by hiking.

CHIWAUKUM CREEK. Drains into Wenatchee River above Tumwater Canyon 1 mile N. of Tumwater Campground on the

Stevens Pass Hwy. Road follows creek about 2 miles upstream from mouth, then trail continues to Chiwaukum Lake. Series of beaver ponds in the creek below the lake cover about 10 acres. Creek and ponds support brook and rainbow trout.

CHIWAUKUM LAKE. Mountain lake at 4950 feet, the 66 acre lake fed by Larch and Cup lakes. Holds a few cutthroat, but mostly brookies. Trail follows Chiwaukum Creek from campgrounds at end of road for about 8 miles to lake. **JASON LAKES** are located about 0.5 miles S. of Chiwaukum. Hold 7 to 9 inch cutthroat. No trail.

CHIWAWA RIVER. May be ESA closed. Consult regs. Empties into Wenatchee River 6 miles below Lake Wenatchee on US 2 about 15 miles W. of Leavenworth. FS Road 62 parallels river approximately 25 miles upstream. Late June to Sept. rainbow. Supports summer steelhead, rainbow and cutthroat. Larger tributaries include Buck, Chickamin, Meadow, Marble, Phelps and Rock creeks. Road ends at Trinity, and trail 1513 continues into Glacier Peak Wilderness to Buck Creek Pass. Excellent roadside campgrounds along the river.

CHORAL LAKE. Golden trout have been stocked in Choral, a 1.5 acre lake at 7200 feet about 35.5 miles NW of Entiat at head of Choral Creek. Drains to Entiat River. May freeze out.

CLEAR LAKE. A 4.8 acre, heavily stocked trout lake about 9 miles S. of Wenatchee at 3000 feet. Stocked with 25,000 catchable cutthroat and brookies after road opens in spring. Catch and release rules after July 5. WDFW access. Drains to Semilt Creek.

COLCHUCK LAKE. A deep 88 acre alpine lake at 5570 feet elev. at the head of Mountaineer Creek 10.5 miles SW of Leavenworth. Cutthroat planted, and rainbow are self-sustaining. Icicle Creek Rd W. from Leavenworth for 5 miles, then up Eight Mile Road for 3 miles to Stuart Lake trailhead, then 2.5 miles to junction with Colchuck Trail, then 1.5 miles to lake. A trail follows Eight Mile Creek from about 4 miles to 72 acre **EIGHT MILE LAKE** at 4450 feet, which has rainbow, cutthroat and mackinaw, and FS campground.

COLUMBIA RIVER. The broad, impounded flow of the Columbia River forms the boundary with Douglas County. From Wenatchee N to Okanogan County Old US 97 follows the W. bank and provides excellent river access points. To follow the river S. of Wenatchee follow Malaga-Alcoa Hwy. to Colockum Rd. then Dillville Rd. to Colockum Wildlife Area at Whitson Canyon and Kittitas County border. Starting on the S. county border and moving upstream, the Columbia impoundments are Wanapum Lake, Rock Island Lake, Lake Entitat in Rocky Reach, and Lake Pateros above Wells Dam. Fish ladders at the dams have visitor observation areas. Fair walleye fishing in power dam tailraces below Wells, Rocky Reach and rock Island dams, especially Feb.-Apr. when large spawners stage. White sturgeon occasionally caught in catch-and-release fishery. Sloughs and backwaters have largemouth and smallmouth bass, perch, sunfish and a few channel catfish. Summer steelhead and spring and fall chinook salmon swim these waters and collect at mouths of Wenatchee, Entitat, and Methow rivers. Salmon and steelhead fisheries are heavily restricted and subject to ESA protections. Late summer sockeye salmon bound for Lake Wenatchee concentrate at Wenatchee River mouth. Winter whitefishing at shallow gravel bars near most tributary mouths. Boat ramps and parks at dam complexes and sporadically along the highway. The river also touches or nears 4 WDFW wildlife areas offering public fishing and hunting, including, from the S. upstream, Colockum, Swakane, Entitat, and Chelan Butte.

COMPANY CREEK. Joins Stehekin River from the W. above Lake Chelan near a primitive airstrip. Trail 1243 follows this brushy creek for about 6 miles into Glacier Peak Wilderness before turning S. up Hilgard Creek. Company Creek supports wild cutthroat, rainbow and brookies.

DOMKE LAKE. A 271 acre lake 2 easy miles on Trail 1280 SW from Lucerne on NW shore of Lake Chelan. Rainbow are self-sustaining, cutthroat have been planted. Cabins, boats and camping sites. Reached by float plane or passenger ferry boat from Chelan to Lucerne. Best fishing from mid-June to mid-July, and recovers again in fall. Fed by **EMERALD PARK CREEK** which has cutthroat and rainbow.

DONALD LAKE. Rainbow lake, 12.4 acres at 5800 feet, 14.4 miles NW from Leavenworth. Drains to Wenatchee River.

DRY LAKE (Grass). A shallow 76.8 acre lake with some hefty largemouth bass. Lots of small perch, sunfish, crappie and some large brown bullhead catfish. Good fishing in Mar. Apr. but it's only 11 feet deep and weeds rapidly. 1.6 miles N. of Manson. Fed by Roses Lake and drains to Stink Creek to Lake Chelan.

EDNA LAKE. A 3.5 acre mountain lake planted with golden trout 12.2 miles N. of Leavenworth at 6500 feet in headwaters of Index Creek. Drains to Wenatchee River.

EIGHT MILE LAKE. A 71.6 acre rainbow lake at 4450 feet in Alpine Lakes Wilderness 10.5 miles SW of Leavenworth. Drains to Eight Mile Creek to Icicle Creek. Icicle Creek Rd./FS 7600 to Bridge Creek Campground, S. on FS 7601 to Trail 1552.

EILEEN LAKE (Loch Eileen). Fall fishing is most productive in this 24 acre lake about 9 miles E. of Stevens Pass at 5200 feet. Stocked with rainbow and cutthroat which attain good size. Lake lies in semi-open meadow country. Reached by trail 1 mile above Julius Lake (See Julius Lake).

ELSEY LAKE. Golden trout have been planted in this 16.4 acre lake at 6200 feet, 18.7 miles NE of Stevens Pass and 11.5 miles NW from Lake Wenatchee. Drains to Napeequa River.

ENCHANTMENT LAKES. Group of remote cutthroat and golden trout lakes of 4.6, 18.2, ll.8 and 23.3 acres at elevations of 6700 to 7060 feet, about 10 miles SW from Leavenworth in Alpine Lakes Wilderness in the spectacular Stuart Range. Drain to Icicle Creek. From Icicle Creek Rd. 7600 at Snow Creek Wall, hike SW on Trail 1553.

ENTIAT RIVER. A large tributary flowing into the Columbia River at Entiat. Supports wild rainbow and summer steelhead. River and tributaries may be closed to protect ESA listed steelhead. When allowed, trout fishing is best between July and Sept. Fall best for summer-run steelhead. No closures above Entitat Falls, a barrier to anadromous fish, which offers wild rainbows. Winter whitefishing from Hwy. 97 bridge to falls. FS Rd. 371 parallels the Entiat about 40 miles to road-end at Cottonwood Campground. Trail 1400 continues past Myrtle Lake to headwaters in Glacier Peak Wilderness. The Entiat is snow-fed and sometimes colored during hot weather. Trout tributaries include Choral, Anthem, Snow Brushy, Cool and Ice creeks.

ETHEL LAKE. Rainbow in 15.6 acres at 5400 feet on end of Chiwaukum Mountains in Alpine Lakes Wilderness, 9.3 miles E. of Stevens Pass. From US 2, Trail 1585 up Gill Creek.

FISH CREEK. Enters Lake Chelan at Moore Point. Lower stretches heavily tapped for irrigation water. Upper reaches of this small creek are paralleled by trails up both N. and E. forks, yield cutthroat and rainbow of moderate size from June through August.

FISH LAKE. A heavily-stocked and excellent year-round multi-species producer 1 mile NE of Lake Wenatchee. Lake level fluctuates between 500 to about 600 acres. Deep spot is 135 feet. Very popular spring and summer and gaining popularity as an ice fishing destination. Numerous small inlets and about 150 acres of marsh at W. end. Planted with 50,000 rainbow, brown trout and brookies. Some very large browns for fishermen who enjoy a challenge. Try night fishing for browns, trolling blade strings and bait for rainbows. Also holds big perch which are targeted summer and winter, plus a fishable number of smallmouth and largemouth bass. Resort has launch and rental boats. From US 2, 16 miles NW of Leavenworth, turn N. at Coles Corners on Hwy. 207 past Lake Wenatchee outlet.

FLORA LAKE. Cutthroat in a 10.7 acre Alpine Lakes Wilderness lake at 5900 feet, NW from Leavenworth off Trail 1571 in headwaters of S. Fork Chiwaukum Creek.

HEATHER LAKE. One of several lakes clustered in Henry M. Jackson Wilderness, Heather covers 89 acres at 3890 feet 8 miles N. of Stevens Pass. From Hwy. 207 N. of Lake Wenatchee turn S onto 6500/6701 Rds. and continue up Lake Creek on S. side of Little Wenatchee River, then up Heather Lake Road 400 to Trail 1526. Rough, steep climb for the last 1.5 miles. Total distance about 3 miles. Planted with rainbow and cutthroat. Shoreline brushy, but good campsites along lake. **DONALD LAKE** 2500 feet W. of Julius at 5800 feet planted with cutthroat. No trail to Donald. **GLASSES LAKE**, 0.5 mile S. of Heather at 4750 feet,

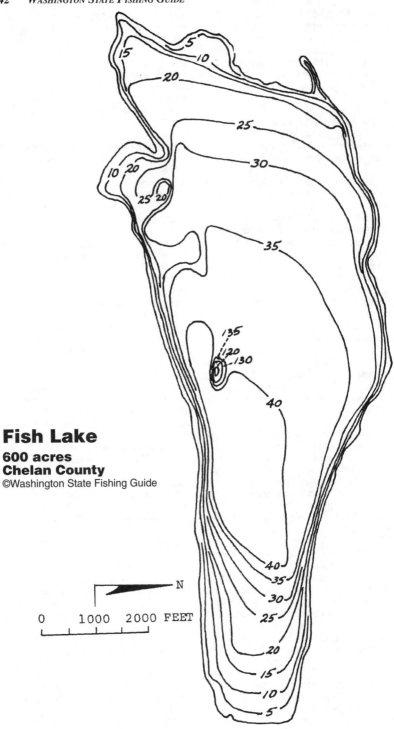

Fish Lake

600 acres
Chelan County
©Washington State Fishing Guide

N

0   1000   2000 FEET

has been planted with cutthroat. It covers 24.5 acres, and is reached via PCT 2000 by way of Smithbrook. Fly fishermen do well at Glasses in Aug. and Sept.

HOPE LAKE A small lake at 4400 feet at head of Basin Creek on PCT 2000 S. of Stevens Pass. Planted with cutthroat, but brookies reported.

ICICLE CREEK. A large heavily-fished stream offering poor catches of wild summer rainbow and cutthroat, and some years a congested fishery for spring chinook near hatchery in May-June. Summer steelhead are in the stream, but fishing is not allowed. Once heavily stocked with rainbows by WDFW at popular campsites, this pretty, tumbling freestone stream now relies on wild fish to handle the considerable pressure. Sadly, the waters near most campground areas rapidly fish out after the June opener, forcing anglers to head into remote and distant upstream reaches for small native trout. Selective gear rules and special closures. From US 2 at Leavenworth turn S. and W. up Icicle Road 7600. Several popular streamside campgrounds for about 20 miles. Trailheads to alpine trout lakes lead from Icicle Road into E. side of Alpine Lakes Wilderness.

KING LAKE. 6000 feet elev. in Glacier Peak Wilderness, this 12.2 acre lake has been planted with golden trout. Fed by glacier melt on NE side of Buck Mt. From Lake Wenatchee go N. on FS 62 up Chiwawa River to Trinity then hike NW on Trail 1513 to bushwhack up Buck Creek the King Lake outlet.

KLONAQUA LAKES. A pretty pair of 66 and 67 acre lakes at 5450 feet (Lower Klonaqua) and at 5500 feet (Upper Klonaque) on French Ridge in Alpine Lakes Wilderness. Drain into Icicle Creek. Both planted with cutthroat. From end of Icicle Creek Road at Rock Island CG to trail 1551 up the Icicle about 2 miles to French Creek. Turn SW up French Creek on Trail 1595 about 6 miles, then W. on Trail 1563 for 2 tough miles to lakes. Dam at outlet of lower lake impounds water once used for irrigation. Aug. and Sept. best fishing. Log rafts and primitive camps.

LAKE CREEK. Drains Heather Lake into Little Wenatchee River at Lake Creek Campground. Road 400 follows the creek for about 2 miles, to the trail upstream to Heather Lake. Aug. best for the small rainbow and cutthroat.

LICHTENWASSER LAKE. A mountain lake at 4754 feet 3.3 miles north of Stevens Pass. Reached by 2.5 mile trail from E. end of old railroad tunnel. Or continue from end of Smith Brook/6700 Rd. N. from US 2 for 1 mile then a 1.5 mile scramble SW up the lake's outlet. Brushy shoreline. This 22 acre lake produces cutthroat from mid-July on.

VALHALLA LAKE at 5050 feet covers 29 acres in a very scenic setting under a rocky pinnacle about 1 mile W. of Lichtenwasser. Trail from Smith Brook/6700 Rd. Valhalla holds cutthroat, some large. Good campsites at N. end of lake.

LILY LAKE. Heavily stocked with 60,000 trout this 15-acre lake 9 miles S. of Wenatchee was originally used for irrigation but now gets regular plants of rainbow and brookies and has a reputation for hiding large carry-overs. Summer catch-and-release. From Malaga-Alcoa Rd., turn SW up Stemilt Creek Rd. along Jumpoff Ridge to 3100 elev. then S. on dirt road to lake.

LITTLE WENATCHEE RIVER. A beautiful trout stream that could have been tailor-made for wading spin and fly casters, but this tributary flowing into SW end of Lake Wenatchee has the bad luck to also support ESA listed steelhead, chinook and bull trout which for several years has resulted in the river's closure to fishermen below the falls. Above the falls, the stream is small and fast but open for wild rainbows, cutthroat and a few brookies. From US 2 turn N. onto Hwy. 207 and continue about 12 miles around Lake Wenatchee, then turn S. across White River onto FS Rd. 6500 which parallels river about 18 miles to road end at Little Wenatchee Ford Campground where trails continue into Henry M. Jackson Wilderness and PCT 2000. Several roadside campgrounds along the river. Beaver ponds provide fishing for rainbow, cutthroat, and brookies. Major tributaries of the Little Wenatchee, include Rainy, Lake, Falls, Fish and Cady Creeks, which when open offer fair fishing.

MAD RIVER. Merges into Entiat River about 10 miles W. of Entiat below Tyee Ridge. From Ardenvoir follow FS 5700 up Mad River to Pine Flat campgrounds. Trail 1409 parallels river to headwaters. No longer planted with trout. Besides wild 'bows, there are bull trout and cutthroat. May be closed by ESA.

MEADOW CREEK. An Alpine Lakes Wilderness rainbow tributary to Jack Creek which joins Icicle Creek at Chatter Creek Campground. Follow Icicle Creek Rd. W. 15 miles to Chatter Creek CG then S. on Trail 1558 from campground for about 6 miles to confluence of Jack and Meadow Creeks then upstream on Trail 1559. Trail 1558 continues up Jack Creek to the icy glaciers on the slopes of Mt. Stuart. Meadow Creek heads E. below Paddy Go Easy Pass which crosses Wenatchee Mtns. into upper Cle Elum drainage.

MEADOW LAKE (Galler Res.). A county right of way allows access to this 36 acre irrigation, bass and panfish lake 1 mile SW of Malaga on the Columbia River. Roiled much of the summer by irrigation.

MERRITT LAKE. A shallow 7 acres at 5000 feet on Nason Ridge at the head of Mahar Creek. Brookies are self-sustaining. From US 2 just W. of Merritt, bushwhack up Mahar Creek to Trail 1583 to lake. **LOST LAKE** is 2900 feet N. of Merritt at 4900 feet. This 31 acre lake gets periodical cutthroat plants.

MIRROR LAKE. A 26 acre lake at 5490 feet about 4 miles SW of Lucerne on Lake Chelan in Glacier Peak Wilderness. Route from Lucerne is via Emerald Park and Mirror Lake trails for 11 miles. Cutthroat and is reported to hold some lunker rainbow.

MISSION CREEK. A small Wenatchee River tributary with wild rainbow entering at Cashmere. A road parallels the popular creek S. for 15 miles below Tronsen Ridge. N. segment is paved giving way to rough gravel that connects with **Beehive Lake** S. of Wenatchee. Popular drive for wildlife watching.

MYRTLE LAKE. A 4 mile hike from end of Entiat River Road to this 19 acre lake at 3750 feet. Brookies. Campsites and easy access to the lake.

NASON CREEK. US 2 follows this creek from its headwaters near Stevens Pass to where it joins Lake Wenatchee's outlet. Easily reached and fished in extreme upper reaches for small wild rainbow and cutthroat. In recent years the long, beautiful roadside section from the mouth up-

stream to Smith Brook has been closed because of ESA summer steelhead, and is no longer stocked with WDFW trout.

PESHASTIN CREEK. ESA closed below Ruby Creek in recent years. US 97 parallels this fast-falling, rocky, brushy creek from the Wenatchee River just above Dryden S. to Tronsen Creek confluence. Highway 97 continues up Tronsen Creek to Swauk Pass. Paved FS 7320 turns SW and follows Peshastin Creek upstream to Blewett Pass. FS 7320 rejoins US 97 a little over 2 miles N. of Mineral Springs. Lower stretches below Ingalls Creek support small rainbow and summer steelhead. Feeder streams, including the Scotty, Tronsen, Negro, Shasher and Ingalls have small wild trout. Very low water in late summer.

PRINCE CREEK. Enters N. side of Lake Chelan about two-thirds up the lake. Accessible by plane or boat only. Forest service campground at mouth. Trail follows creek upstream to headwaters. Small rainbow in lower section, with cutthroat in top stretches.

RAINBOW CREEK. Enters Stehekin River about 1 mile above head of Lake Chelan. Campground where Stehekin River Road crosses Rainbow Creek near Rainbow Falls, a large creek which is often discolored by snow melt. Trail takes off road about 1 mile past Rainbow Falls, then swings back to parallel stream to head waters. Primarily a cutthroat show, but rainbow are taken also.

ROCK LAKE. Golden trout have been stocked in Rock at 5600 feet. The lake covers 3.5 acres 7 miles NE from Stevens Pass on E. side of Rock Mountain. Drains to Nason Creek.

ROSES LAKE (Alkali). One of the best icefishing lakes in the region. Stocked in fall with 15,000 rainbows 11 to 20 inches. Also has largemouth bass, crappie and channel catfish. Roses covers 131 acres, and has been previously stocked with brown trout. Open year-round, WDFW access and ramp, resort. 1 mile N. of Manson on Lake Chelan adjacent to Wapato Lake. From US 97 at Chelan, go NW to Manson.

SCHAEFER LAKE. An 83 acre mountain lake 8.5 miles at 5050 feet. Cutthroat and small brookies. Chiwawa River Road/FS 62 leads upstream from US 2 about 12 miles to Finner Creek Campground where Trail 1519 heads NW 6 miles to the lake at edge of Glacier Peak Wilderness.

SQUILCHUCK CREEK. A small rainbow stream which heads above Squilchuck State Park and flows NE approximately 12 miles to the Columbia River at South Wenatchee. A road from South Wenatchee follows the creek upstream to the park.

STEHEKIN RIVER. A fast, pool-pocked river filled with the North Cascade Mountains. Stehekin is the largest tributary to Lake Chelan, flowing into the remote N. end of the lake through Stehekin after draining a large glacier and mountain region of Glacier Peak Wilderness and North Cascades National Park. An all-weather road follows the river about 12 miles from town to High Bridge, providing access for anglers who rent cars, book shuttles or enjoy long walks. A rough road continues upstream for another 10 miles to Cottonwood Campground in NCNP where a trail leads upstream into the spectacular glacier and spire region around Boston Glacier and Cascade Pass. Passenger ferry or private boat, charter float plane or a long hike are the only ways to reach Stehekin. Once you get there, taxi, resort and horse service is available. The river is often colored with snow melt during summer, but holds very nice wild rainbows to several pounds, plus large bull trout, and some cutthroat. Bull trout hit best Mar-June catch-and-release season. From July-Oct. anglers are allowed 2 trout, 15 inch minimum.

SWIMMING DEER LAKE. A 3-acre rainbow lake on E. side of PCT 2000 at 2800 feet, S. of Josephine Lake. Drains to Icicle Creek.

THREE LAKE (Mud). Private 33 acres reservoir 5.5 miles SE of Wenatchee. Fed by Stemilt Creek and drainage from Meadow Lake. Panfish and catfish.

TOP LAKE (Summit). 10 miles N. of Stevens Pass on just E. of PCT 2000 covering 7 acres, at 4700 feet in Henry M. Jackson Wilderness. Planted with cutthroat. From end of FS Rd. 6701 S. of Lake Creek Campground to Trail 1506 over Shoofly Mt. 5-mile hike.

TRAP LAKE. 11 acres at 5150 feet, planted with cutthroat, and reported to contain a few lunker 'bows. About 6 miles S. of Stevens Pass, adjacent to PCT 2000. **TRAPPER LAKE**. An exceptionally beautiful, deep mountain lake covering 146 acres at 4165 feet in a dramatic basin under spectacular peaks and glaciers 3 miles SE of Cascade Pass in North Cascade National Park. Drains via Cottonwood Creek into upper Stehekin River. Holds cutthroat. Tough, steep bushwhack climb of about 1 mile up the outlet S. from Cottonwood Campground at end of Stehekin River Rd.

TROUT LAKE. 17 acres at 4850 elev. 5 miles S. of Chatter Creek CG on Icicle Creek Rd. Rainbow and cutthroat and is located in a basin which offers good tent sites. Drains to Icicle Creek. Best route is SE from Rock Creek CG up Trail 1558 to Trail 1555.

TWENTY-FIVE MILE CREEK. A popular state park and recreation area where this stream enters Lake Chelan at the end of the road on the SW side of the lake 18 miles NW of Chelan. This large creek drains a sweeping basin shoulder of the Chelan Mts. E. of Devils Backbone Ridge. Rd. 5900 goes S. from the lake about 2 miles to Ramona Park CG where the creek and road forks. The N. fork continues Rd. 5900 around Grouse Mt., with viewpoints, above the North Fork of 25-Mile Creek to Handy Springs. Trail 1265 roughly follows the N. Fork from Ramona CG. The S. fork road, a rough route, becomes Rd. 8410 climbing up Slide Ridge above 25-Mile Creek to headwaters on Devils Backbone. Trail 1266 follows the creek from Ramona. Twenty-Five Mile Creek has rainbow, cutts and brookies and is a kokanee spawning stream. State park at mouth has 75 sites, ramp, and dock moorage.

WAPATO LAKE. Often rated by WDFW as "the best" spring trout lake in Chelan County, this 216 acre lake is in the rolling, dry hills just above Lake Chelan 2 miles N. of Manson, and adjacent to Roses Lake. Wapato is planted with brookies and rainbow 10 to 16 inches, including a generous helping of large triploids. It's stocked three times a year, twice with catchables in Mar. and Apr. and then heavily (19,000 catchable trout) in Nov. after the lake closes for the season. An additional 65,000 rainbow fry are planted each fall to go into the next spring's fishery. From Aug.-Oct. the lake goes to selective gear, catch and release regs. Also offers some exceptionally large largemouth bass (5 to 9 pounders not unusual), bluegill, and stunted crappie and pumpkinseeds. Best fishing from opener through June. No WDFW access. Fee ramp and private campgrounds on both ends of lake. Road from Manson parallels S. side of lake. From Chelan take Hwy. 150 toward Manson, then NW on Swartout Rd.

WENATCHEE LAKE. A much better camping and boating destination than a fishing spot. Lake Wenatchee is a natural, 5-mile long lake covering 2445 acres at the head of Wenatchee River 15 miles N. of Leavenworth. In recent years, despite its size and potential, the fishery has steadily declined with ESA protections for Dolly Varden/bull trout, and a bare bones rainbow trout fishery. The headliner now is small kokanee salmon and the limit on these marginal fish has fallen to 5 a day. The lake is the primary rearing area for Dolly Varden/bull trout in the Wenatchee Basin, and there are 10 pound dollies to catch: and carefully release. The lake is also a nursery for sea-going sockeye salmon and very rarely during years of bumper crop sockeye, WDFW will authorize an August sport fishery. The best resident kokanee fishing is in late summer and early fall. Lake is open year-round. Anglers often camp here for the aesthetics, but head to nearby **FISH LAKE** for their angling fix. From US 2 at Cole's Corner turn N. on Hwy. 207 about 3 miles to E. end of lake and Wenatchee State Park. Road up S. side of lake leads 3 miles to Glacier View Campground. North shore road wraps around the lake and forks at NW end. Left fork Rd. 6500 runs along **LITTLE WENATCHEE RIVER** about 16 miles to Little Wenatchee Ford CG, a trailhead into Henry M. Jackson Wilderness. Right hand fork FS 6400 parallels **WHITE RIVER** 12 miles to end of road at White River Falls CG and trailhead into Glacier Peak Wilderness. Resorts along Lake Wenatchee N. shore, state park and FS campsites.

WENATCHEE RIVER. Hold that rod. This large, beautiful stream heads in Lake Wenatchee and flows 60 miles along US 2 to join the Columbia River at Wenatchee. Great roadside access, but probably no fishing. The Wenatchee is one of the most problem plagued rivers in the state. The big pools and broad tailouts in the upper stretches support good resident rainbow trout, and Dolly Varden/bull trout and the middle and lower sections were once famous for summer-run steelhead and chinook salmon. However, the river has been closed to all fishing (except winter whitefish), a closure that may continue yet. Check this year's regs. The river was closed to protect ESA listed chinook salmon, bull trout and summer steelhead. The closure may extend to many of the tributaries such as Chiwaukum, Nason, Peshastin, Chumstick, Beaver, Mission, Icicle creeks plus the Chiwawa River. The ESA closures and an end to WDFW stocking plan has eliminated one of the best trout streams in the state.

WHITE RIVER. Milky glacial water holds down summer fishing pressure on this major tributary to Lake Wenatchee. A major sockeye salmon spawning river. Fished above the North Fork for wild rainbow and cutthroat. No longer stocked by WDFW. Dolly Varden/bull trout may be caught, but must be released. FS Rd. 6400 follows the river upstream for 12 miles from the NW end of **LAKE WENATCHEE** at **LITTLE WENATCHEE RIVER** confluence, ending at trailheads into Glacier Peak Wilderness. Three FS campgrounds are located along the road. Major tributaries with wild trout are Boulder, Panther, Indian and Napeequa creeks.

Chelan County Resorts

Chelan Lake: 25-Mile Creek State Park, 509-687-3610. Graybill Guide Service, 509-682-4294. The Cove Marina, Chelan, WA 98816. 509-687-3789. North Cascades Stehekin Lodge, 509-682-4494. Silver Bay Inn Stehekin, 509-682-2212. Campbell's Resort, 509-682-2561. Wapato Point Resort, 509-687-9511

Fish Lake: The Cove Resort, 509-763-3130. Cascade Hideaway, 509-763-5104.

Roses Lake: Kamei Resort, 509-687-3690. Paradise Lake Resort.

Wenatchee Lake: Lake Wenatchee State Park, 509-763-3101. USFS Lake Wenatchee 509-763-3103.

Clallam County

WDFW Region 6

Washington Department of Fish and Wildlife, 48 Devonshire Rd. Montesano, WA 98563-9618. Phone 360-249-4628

Clallam is timber, rain and fishing country and what it lacks in freshwater trout and bass water it makes up for with anadromous salmon, steelhead, sea-run cutthroat, and fish boxes that can still bulge with saltwater ling cod, halibut, rockfish and more. The lion's share of western Olympic Peninsula's legendary steelhead rivers flow through Clallam County .

A lightly populated region, Clallam County spreads across the N. side of Olympic Peninsula much of it squeezed between the mile-high fame of Olympic National Park (ONP) and the sea-level fog of the Strait of Juan de Fuca. On the E. is the shoulder of Sequim Bay and on the W. the ocean and Forks a community synonymous with a handful of the most productive steelhead rivers left in the western part of the state. The only significant city is Port Angeles, which with 18,540 residents is the largest town on the Peninsula. The next largest is Sequim with 4200.

The county is a patchwork of blackberry edged pastures, private mostly clear-cut timber lands, national forest, national park, national wildlife refuges and tribal reservations linked by US 101. It includes a wide swath of Olympic National Forest, 497 square miles of Olympic National Park including spectacular Hurricane Ridge, Quillayute Needles National Wildlife Refuge (NWR), Flattery Rocks NWR, Dungeness NWR and Protection Island NWR. The coastline is pocked with tribal reservations including, Quileute Indian Reservation (IR), Ozette IR, Makah IR, Lower Elwha IR, and Jamestown S'Klallam IR.

Covering 1787 square miles Clallam ranks 20th in size among the state's counties, and includes Cape Alava which is the westerly most point in the lower 48 states and Lake Ozette at 7787 acres the third largest natural lake in the state. It is home to several saltwater sport-fishing ports facing the Strait of Juan de Fuca including Sequim Bay, Port Angeles, Sekiu, Pillar Point and Neah Bay. On the ocean side a modern newer marina at LaPush provides access to some prime bottomfish and salmon water and is a stepping of spot to miles of undeveloped public beach managed by Olympic NPS.

Fishermen who are not coming for the saltwater fun are probably headed for steelhead, which is the Peninsula's biggest claim to fame. Although just a shadow of the magnificent rivers they once were, steelhead continue to call fishermen to the Bogachiel, Sol Duc, and Quillayute which still offer the best odds in the state of catching a 20-pound plus native. While WDFW stubbornly continues to allow anglers to keep wild steelhead, we strongly encourage 100% release of all wild fish as a conservation investment that will pay off for our grandchildren.

Smaller but also sometimes productive steelhead rivers include the Dickey, Calawah, Hoko, Clallam, Sekiu, Lyre, Elwha, and Dungeness. These smaller rivers can offer good sea-run cutthroat fishing in late summer and fall when the cutts follow upstream behind spawning chinook.

Most of the peninsula rivers are at their best during the winter but some, like the Sol Duc, get a minor return of summer-runs. Nearly all are also good producers of chinook and coho salmon in season. Bull trout are numerous, tough fighters, but fully protected by Endangered Species Act (ESA) listing.

The major access highway is US 101 which traces the northern and western edges. The few other state routes important to fishermen flow off of US 101. These include Hwy. 112 a scenic route which runs along the edge of the Straits from the outskirts of Port Angeles to Sekiu and Neah Bay. Hwy. 113 is a connector route linking US 101 and Hwy. 112 roughly between Sekiu and Sappho. Hwy. 110 is an asphalt squib between Forks and LaPush. Except for a couple of short sections of US 101 all the routes are two-lane roads with infamous reputations for sharp curves and logging trucks

The climate is maritime but it's far from typical. On the ocean side monsoon rains drop more than 200 inches of water a year nurturing spectacular world-famous rain forests. Near Sequim, protected by the dry shadow of the Olympic Mountains, rainfall is often less than 15 inches a year and cactus grows wild.

Within a few miles elevations may vary from sea-level to 7,218 feet the high point at the N. end of Gray Wolf Ridge only 15 miles S. of Sequim. ONP and ONF dominate the south-center county, tapering rapidly to a narrow apron that skirts the saltwater.

AGENCY CREEK. A short-run winter steelhead stream on the Makah IR. The creek flows into the E. side of Neah Bay.

ALDWELL LAKE. Impounded by a power. dam on the lower Elwha River, Aldwell covers 320 acres 6 miles W. of Port Angeles, and S. of US 101. It will be drained with the future demolition of Elwha Dam The lake supports wild rainbow, brook trout, kokanee and some bull trout. Fall fishing is often surprisingly good for brook trout. WDFW access ramp.

BEAVER LAKE. Year-round lake adjacent to Hwy. 112 about 3 miles NE of Sappho. The 36 acre lake is brushy along shorelines, delivers small cutthroat in April and May, then slows. Trout anglers are restricted to 1 fish and selective gear. Summer offers perch, largemouth bass, crappie, and a few kokanee. Car top boats may be launched from highway shoulder.

BIG RIVER. A small river that heads under Sekiu Mt., and drains into Lake Ozette at Swan Bay. Comes on in fall for sea-run cutthroat. Hoko-Ozette Road to Lake Ozette parallels 5 miles of the river.

BLAKES PONDS. Three small brook trout ponds totaling about 1 acre, 0.7 miles E. of Sequim on Bell Creek. May not be open to public fishing.

BOGACHIEL RIVER. One of the legendary steelhead and salmon rivers of the Olympic Peninsula, flowing W. from Seven Lakes Basin on the crown of ONP, through the towering, moss swaged rain forest trees, under US 101, through Forks, picking up the Calawah River about 3 miles below Forks, before flowing into the Sol Duc River to form the Quillayute River.

In the park, the upper river is a quick boulder and rapid flow that can be a real tackle eater and tough to fish. The further upstream you fish, the fewer fish there are to catch. The upper stretches are followed E. beyond Bogachiel State Park by a heavily-used hiking trail into ONP. Below ONP the Bogey is big, wide water best fished from drift boats but with respectable bank access at several spots. The water, especially in summer, is often chalky green with snow melt and runoff. The river annually produces about 1700 steelhead including a Mar/Apr fishery that delivers more than 400 wild steelhead many in the 15 to 25 pound range (WDFW allows the retention of wild Bogey steelhead, but responsible, conservation-minded anglers release all wild fish.) Most hatchery steelhead are caught in Dec. and Jan. There is usually a lull in February before action picks up again in Mar. and April when wild steelhead arrive.

A hatchery rearing pond complex SW of Forks and W. of US 101 is the centerpoint during the hatchery steelhead run. The most intensive fishing pressure is from the rearing ponds downstream to LaPush Road (Hwy. 113) access and boat ramp at the confluence of the Sol Duc.

US 101 parallels several miles of the Bogachiel. E. of US 101 side roads extend up both banks for 6 miles. South Bogachiel Road ends at a launch popular with drift boaters taking out at the state park. Going W. from Forks on Hwy. 113, the LaPush Road comes within striking range of the river at a number of points, crossing the Bogachiel just above the jct. with the Sol Duc. The Bogey supports fishable runs of spring and fall chinook and fall coho salmon. A very few summer steelhead are taken (probably misguided winter-runs) and there is a decent fishery for sea-run cutthroat from Aug.-Oct. Best summer-run fishing is at the mouth of the Sol Duc which supports a good summer fishery. Public access and boat launch at confluence of Bogachiel and Sol Duc Rivers, Bogachiel Rearing Ponds, and at Bogachiel State Park which has campsites where US 101 crosses Bogachiel. Motels and river guides in Forks.

CALAWAH RIVER. In many respects this major tributary to Bogachiel River, is a sleeper that offers exceptional catches of winter and summer steelhead, plus has runs of chinook and coho salmon and sea-run cutthroat. Salmon fishing has been tough in recent years. The stretch below US 101 is difficult to fish because of lack of roads. A good road leaves US 101 about 1.5 miles N. of Forks and parallels N. side of the Calawah 3.5 miles to where the N. and S. forks join. A rough road follows the Calawah's North Fork about 12 miles over Schutz Pass. This road drops down to hit the Sol Duc River near Sappho. The Calawah and its South Fork deliver about 200 summer-run steelhead, and 1100 winter-runs every year mostly hatchery fish. Best summer fishing takes place in June and October when there's plenty of water to fish. In mid-summer, the Calwawah is pretty skinny and fishing is tough. Winter steelheading gets off to a fast start in Nov. peaks in Dec. runs solidly through Jan. then falls off sharply in Feb. This is a top stream for wade fishing, and although drift boats can get down it—in winter—they'll be banging through some pretty tough spots. Scout this one before kicking off.

CLALLAM RIVER. A small, pretty, brushy stream which enters Strait of Juan de Fuca at Clallam Bay E. of Sekiu. Hwy. 112 roughly parallels the lower 5 miles. Anglers, in a good year, will land a dozen winter steelhead. This winding, tree-canopied stream is best known for sea-run cutthroat in the fall. Nice light tackle and fly water.

CLINE SPIT. A WDFW access on the S. shore of Dungeness Bay, the spit beach provides crabbing, oysters and some surf smelt dipping from Oct. through Jan. WDFW launch ramp.

CRESCENT LAKE. See Olympic National Park.

DEEP CREEK-WEST TWIN RIVERS. Public access to Strait of Juan de Fuca beach E. of the mouth of Deep Creek at the E. and W. Twin Rivers. Sea-run cutthroat sometimes prowl shallows on incoming tides in fall. Surf smelt dipping from May-Sept., and surf perch fishing most of the year. Black rockfish and greenling may be coaxed out of kelp beds in spring and summer.

DICKEY RIVER. Best for light-tackle fall sea-run cutthroat, the Dickey runs about 20 miles from Dickey Lake SW to the Quillayute River about 1 mile from the ocean at Mora. Produces about a dozen wild steelhead a year, mostly in Mar. Mina-Smith Road from Hwy. 113 at Quillayute extends to the forks, where a trail leads up the West Fork to Dickey Lake.

DUNGENESS RIVER. Once one of the best N. peninsula rivers for late-run winter steelhead, the Dungeness River is now a poster-river for bad habitat management. Irrigation diversions and channelization of the lower river has created major habitat problems that have taken a serious toll on anadromous fish. the once-coveted spring and summer chinook run is now listed as "threatened" under the ESA protections, summer pink salmon are depressed, fall pinks are critical and winter steelhead and coho are listed as depressed by WDFW and bull trout are federal listed as threatened. The braided, lower Dungeness is crossed by US 101 about 1.5 miles W. of Sequim. Taylor Cut-Off Road up W. side runs about 5 miles to WDFW hatchery. The Happy Valley Road touches the E. side of the river 1 mile below the hatchery. Palo Alto Road from US 101 about 3 miles E. of Sequim leads about 8 miles to Dungeness Forks FS Campground where Graywolf River joins the Dungeness. Forest service road continues up the Dungeness from the forks for about 10 miles. Watch for elk.

DUNGENESS SPIT. Extending into Strait of Juan de Fuca, this long, sandy finger wraps around Dungeness Bay which is a good spot for crab potting, diving and salmon fishing in the fall. Salmon best from boats on the outside of the spit, but some energetic anglers cast from the end of the spit, but it's a monster hike. Better to launch into bay at Old Town off Sequim-Dungeness Way and boat fish. Some sea-run cutthroat fishing Aug.-Oct. at mouth of Dungeness River. NWR and state wildlife areas at the foot of the spit. Directional signs from US 101 in Sequim.

EDUCKET CREEK. Small tributary to Waatch River on the Makah IR, joining that river one mile S. of village of Neah Bay. Some winter steelhead.

ELWHA RIVER. The Elwha heads high in Olympic National Park on the slopes of Mt. Olympus, draining a tremendous territory before entering the Strait of Juan de Fuca at Angeles Point, a few miles W. of Port Angeles. Before it was dammed, the Elwha supported what was estimated to be the greatest migratory fish runs on the Olympic Peninsula. It was one of three rivers supporting all five Pacific salmon species, plus winter and summer steelhead, sea-run cutthroat and Dolly Varden char. The run included a race of chinook salmon that sometimes weighed 100 pounds. The salmon and steelhead were decimated when the two dams were built without fish ladders in 1912 and 1920. The first dam impounding Lake Aldwell restricts anadromous steelhead and salmon runs to just 4.8 miles of river, and impounds **Lake Aldwell.** Hatchery steelhead furnish fishermen with about 150 winter-runs and 50 summer-runs. Nov-Jan. produces best, and June and October deliver the most summer-runs, but summer-run smolt planting was stopped in 2000. Winter fish are netted by tribes. Hatchery runs of coho and chinook, replacing 100 pound native kings with 20 pound hatchery fish. In recent years only coho have been legal. The Elwha's best offering now is trout. Sea-run cutthroat provide a good fall fishery from the dam downstream. The Glines Canyon Dam impounds 451-acre **Lake Mills** above US 101, which offers challenging fishing for brookies, rainbows and cutthroat. Best stream fishing found by hiking upstream into the park, especially from Mary's Falls (9.7 miles in) upstream. Excellent streamside trail from the end of Elwha River Road at Whiskey Bend above Lake Mills. The pool and riffle upper stretches of the Elwha (See Olympic Nat. Park) offer very good light tackle and fly fishing for wild rainbows 14 to 20 inches, and Dolly Varden that are weighed by the pound. From US 101 turn S. on Elwha River Road at bridge, continue past Lake Mills to trailhead. Efforts to remove the lower dams are plodding through the bureaucracy. This fishery is heavily restricted, check current WDFW regs before making the hike.

GRAYWOLF RIVER. A brawling mountain stream that enters the Dungeness River at Dungeness Forks Campground. A trail follows the river into the park. The Graywolf holds steelhead, 18-inch Dolly Varden, pan-size rainbow, pink salmon and brook trout, with July, August and September best. Pocket water with a few deep runs and pools. Selective tackle rules, 14 inch minimum. Follow FS 2880 to FS 2870 to

bridge. Closed below bridge. Undulating trail follows the river upstream. Try tributaries for some surprisingly nice rainbows and dollies.

HOKO RIVER. A small, rain-fed stream which heads on the N. side of the Dickey-Hoko summit. Hwy. 112 and Hoko-Ozette Road follow the lower river past Hoko Falls, then a rough logging road turns SE along another 2 miles. Lower river provides decent winter steelheading in December and January. Sea-run cutthroat after first heavy fall rains. Extremely low in late summer. Fly-fishing only Sept.-Oct. Upper river above concrete bridge is always catch and release fly-fishing for trout.

JOHN WAYNE MARINA. This Sequim Bay facility provides an excellent ramp for accessing Strait of Juan de Fuca and attracts dense concentrations of surf smelt during the winter. Jigging from the docks can be very good.

LAPUSH. Located on the Quileute IR W. of Forks at the mouth of the Quillayute River. A modern marina provides small boat access to excellent bottomfish sea stacks and reefs and salmon areas on the outside. Can be hazardous. Tribal permits required. This was once one of the great bottomfish ports in Washington, but was closed to non-Indians for years and has not recovered its pre-closure popularity since the marina was rebuilt and opened to the public on a permit/fee basis. From US 101 N. of Forks turn W. on Highway 110.

LIZARD LAKE. A 2-acre cutthroat pond 6 miles S. of Sekiu.

LYRE RIVER. The outlet to Lake Crescent, (see Olympic Nat. Park) the Lyre is crossed by Hwy. 112, 4 miles W. of Joyce. Produces about 450 winter-runs, best in December and January. A trickle of summer steelhead. This rocky, fast stream is usually fishable when other Peninsula streams are out of shape. Trails follow the river upstream from Hwy. 112. Crossed near the lake by the Piedmont Road. Hit it right and this river can ring up huge memories. Bring lots of tackle.

MILL CREEK. Tributary to Bogachiel River, this 5-mile-long stream contains fall sea-run cutthroat. Joins the Bogey about 1.5 miles above the Calawah Confluence.

MORSE CREEK. A small stream which has received winter steelhead plants. Crossed by US 101 2 miles E. of Port Angeles. Deer Park Road roughly parallels the stream on the E., S. of US 101.

NEAH BAY. A small community with a large modern marina and ramp on the Makah IR that provides trailerable boat access to confluence of Strait of Juan de Fuca and Pacific Ocean off NW tip of Olympic Peninsula. Popular saltwater fishing areas include Waada, Tatoosh, Sail, Seal islands, sea stacks on outside south of Tatoosh, Red Buoy, Slab Rock and others. Excellent March-June for light tackle flies and plastic worm jigs casting for black rockfish, cabezon and ling cod near shore in kelp beds, jetty, rock piles. Once a major charter boat fishing port, but in recent years, because of fractured salmon seasons, the charters only work from here during halibut season when they run to Swiftsure Bank. Excellent launch, tackle shop, moorage, boat gas, motels, camping, grocery, restaurant. Very busy during halibut season. Excellent coho, chinook and pink salmon area July-September when open. A good spot to troll surface flies in rips for coho.

OZETTE LAKE. The third largest natural lake in the state, Ozette is 8.5 miles long and averages 2 miles wide, covering 7,787 acres between logging clear cuts and the ocean edge of Olympic NP. Ozette holds cutthroat, with fall months best for this species, plus steelhead, largemouth bass, northern pikeminnows and perch. Ozette's sockeye salmon are on the federal ESA threatened list. No sockeye fishing. Fishing is best described as challenging. This is big water, far from the beaten path and not much is known about it. The South end of the big lake produces most of the large fish. Trolling gang trolls with worms or eggs is effective technique. Primary tributaries are Big River and Umbrella Creek. The lake drains 4 miles via Ozette River into the Pacific Ocean. Road ends at a camping area, boat launch and store at Ozette. Trails start at this point into Olympic National Park to remote ocean beaches including the 3.5 mile hike to Cape Alava, the most westerly point in the contiguous United States. There is also a boat ramp at Swan Bay on the NE side. Ozette is 15 miles S. of Neah Bay, a 21 mile drive via Hoko-Ozette Road from the Hwy. 112 just W. of Sekiu. Turn S. at Swan Bay Road to reach this ramp. Winds can lash this big lake.

PILLAR POINT. The point juts into Juan de Fuca Strait 8 miles E. of Sekiu and protects a small, shallow bay with boat launch, RV park and small camping area. Low tides will leave the bay high and dry. Good base for fishing migrating pink, coho and chinook salmon in late summer. Small boats can cover most of the same water being fished from Sekiu. Rip fishing for pinks and coho (sometimes out to the shipping lanes) and near shore mooching for kings. Try the coal mine area for July-August kings and Mar.-June blackmouth, when open. For decades Pillar Point was a honey hole for big chinook fanatics but popularity tumbled with the contemporary salmon restrictions. Halibut in spring, especially 7 miles E. on the shelf off Twin Rivers. Some rockfishing and ling cod. Follow Hwy. 112 W. from Port Angeles.

PLEASANT LAKE (Tyee). This 486 acre year-round lake visible from US 101 holds rainbow, cutthroat and kokanee in addition to salmon and steelhead that migrate up the outlet into Sol Duc River. April and May for cutthroat and rainbow, try June for kokanee. Slot limit on kokanee of between 8 and 20 inches to protect a remnant run of look-alike sockeye which still come into the lake. Most trout and kokanee anglers troll with attractor blades and bait. Turn off US 101 about 5 miles W. of Sappho on W. Lake Pleasant Road to rough boat ramp.

PORT ANGELES. The largest city on the Olympic Peninsula and once a major sportfishing port for late summer anglers challenging Juan de Fuca Strait migrating coho, pinks and chinook. Excellent marina, ramps, hoists and facilities for trailered boats. Charter boats have pretty well given up on this port because of wildly fluctuating salmon seasons. When WDFW opens the area for summer salmon, though, action can still be excellent for coho and kings headed toward Hood Canal and Puget sound. PA is also an odd-year hot spot where huge schools of pinks concentrate before heading into Puget Sound. Good winter blackmouth fishery at The Ediz Hook Humps and Green Point. Spring halibut 20 to 50 pounds, at Green Point and offshore on Coyote Bank. A few well known rock piles can produce marginal rockfish and ling cod fishing. Good crabbing inside hook. Follow US 101 W. to harbor and Ediz Hook turnoff.

PYSHT MILL POND. A 1-acre brook trout pond draining into Deep Creek, 4.5 miles

S. of Pysht. From Hwy. 112 follow road up Jim Creek to the pond.

PYSHT RIVER. A small stream fished mostly for fall cutthroat, although it has been planted with winter steelhead producing 100 or so fish in December and early January. Hwy. 112 parallels the river for approximately 5 miles from the mouth at Pillar Point State Recreation area to Hwy. 112 to jct. of Burnt Mt. Road (Sappho cutoff).

QUILLAYUTE RIVER. The largest river on the ocean side of the Olympic Peninsula, the Quillayute is formed by the merging of the Bogachiel, Calawah, Sol Duc and Dickey rivers. It's less than 5 miles long and enters the ocean at LaPush. Roads to LaPush and to Mora follow both sides of the river, although bank access is difficult. The lower river is on the Quileute IR and is intensely netted for steelhead and salmon . The Quillayute carries large numbers of wild and hatchery steelhead and salmon as well as sea-run cutthroat, most bound for the big upriver tributaries. The river does provide anglers with 200 to 300 winter steelhead most in Dec.-Feb. Summer steelhead are rare and most are headed for the Sol Duc. Excellent fishing potential at confluence of Bogachiel and Sol Duc rivers, especially during low water. There is a public boat launch site and resort at this spot. Boating is the best way to fish the river.

RIALTO-RUBY BEACHES. Ocean beaches offering surf dipping for spawning surf smelt from May through September. Rialto Beach is just N. of LaPush. Ruby Beach is N. or Kalaloch off US 101 and of the two is the best dipping spot. Also try surf casting with pyramid sinkers and clam neck or shrimp baits for surf perch.

SAIL RIVER. 5 mile long winter steelhead planted river flowing into Strait of Juan De Fuca E. of Kiachopis Point on Makah IR. Tribal fishing license required.

SEKIU (CLALLAM BAY). Probably the most popular coho and chinook port on Strait of Juan de Fuca, but like most strait ports this community about 50 miles W. of Port Angeles has fallen on hard times because of unpredictable salmon seasons. When WDFW approves summer salmon seasons, action can still be very good for small boat anglers. Charter boats are rare here now. One of the reasons that Sekiu is so popular with small boaters is because you can be fishing prime chinook water at the edge of the bay just a couple of hundred yards from harbor safety. Coho and

Sol Duc River.

odd-year pinks travel in schools just under the surface in the rip lines from August deep into September anywhere from a hundred yards offshore to the middle of the shipping channel. Kings are usually sought in July and August near kelp beds along the shore. Popular mooching spots for kings are The Caves, Mussolini Rock, Coal Mines and mouth of the Hoko. Ramps and protected moorage at Sekiu and Clallam Bay adjacent to Hwy. 112. All services, including bait, ice, restaurants, motels, campgrounds, available during summer seasons. March-June can be good for blackmouth chinook, but services are limited. Some rockfishing, halibut (try the Hoko River flats area) and ling cod.

SEKIU RIVER. A small stream entering Strait of Juan de Fuca 5 miles W. of Sekiu. Hwy. 112 crosses at the mouth at a primitive campsite. Supports a few wild winter steelhead and salmon. May provide good fall sea-run cutthroat fishing.

SEQUIM BAY. A large placid bay off the Strait of Juan de Fuca E. of Sequim with some crabbing, winter surf smelt dipping, flounder and sole fishing and occasionally salmon near the mouth. Popular jump-off to Hein Bank halibut, rockfish and salmon. The bay is protected from Strait's winds by a narrow neck between Gibson and Travis spits. Stay between the buoys. Launches at John Wayne Marina (land donated by 'The Duke'), Sequim Bay State Park (camping) and Port Williams at Marilyn Nelson County Park.

SOL DUC. Sol Duck, Sol Duc, Solduc or Soleduck—anyway you spell it, and it seems that every map maker picks a different way, it still spells FISH. The Sol Duc is one of the best migratory fish rivers on the coast, supporting wild and hatchery runs of winter and summer steelhead, coho, chinook, sockeye, chums and pink salmon, cutthroat and bull trout. The sockeye, chum and pink runs are minimal, and bull trout are protected by ESA listing. Almost two thirds of the steelhead catch is wild fish. Most 'Duc anglers concentrate on winter steelhead and fall salmon. The river has a spring and fall chinook run and an exceptional Aug.-Nov. run of coho. Anglers take about 1000 winter steelhead from December through April. Best action begins in January and peaks in March carried mostly by wild fish many in the 15 to 25 pound range. The once productive na-

tive summer-run fishery has dropped to less than 100 fish a summer, most caught in July and October skirting the low water mid-summer months. Some really energized sea-run cutthroat arrive with the summer and fall salmon. This is an excellent, but challenging river for drift boats in winter and a couple of large boulder gardens will test the best boatmen. I recommend floating with an experienced boatman or checking at Forks sporting good stores. Summer flows are low and warm-weather drift boating is a bang and drag adventure. US 101 follows and frequently crosses the river from 4 miles W. of Lake Crescent for approximately 25 miles. About 2 miles N. of Forks. Hwy. 110 and the river turn W. toward LaPush. At a fork a right turn onto Mora Road will cross the Sol Duc near the Quilayute River confluence about 2 miles E. of the Quileute IR. Turn left at the Fork onto the LaPush Road and you cross the Bogachiel River. The upper Sol Duc continues to Sol Duc Hot Springs Road and parallels the river into Olympic National Park where an old road continues about 7 miles to headwaters under Pine Mt.

SOOES CREEK. Begins in the hills N. of Lake Ozette, and flows mostly through Makah IR. Reached by road from Neah Bay. Enters the ocean at Makah Bay. Heavily planted with steelhead and salmon. Fair for sea-run cutthroat.

SOOES RIVER. Rises below Wahburn Hill on Makah IR 10 miles S. of Neah Bay. Planted with winter steelhead and salmon. A tribal fish hatchery with trap two miles upstream from Makah Bay.

SUTHERLAND LAKE. A year-round 370-acre lake on US 101 with a deserved but aging reputation for producing large cutthroat. Also stocked in March and May with 10,000 catchable rainbows. Good kokanee salmon trolling and stillfishing. The lunker cutthroat are few and far between now, but trollers till manage to ring up a few in the 2 to 5 pound class each year. Small wobbling plugs are often effective for the biggest cutts. Spring and fall months are most productive trout fishing and kokanee hold through the summer. Kokanee trollers often use attractor blades towing small jeweled spinners baited with worm or white corn. Stillfishermen find it productive to chum (still legal here) with corn or feed eggs. Sutherland may once been connected to Lake Crescent before a slide

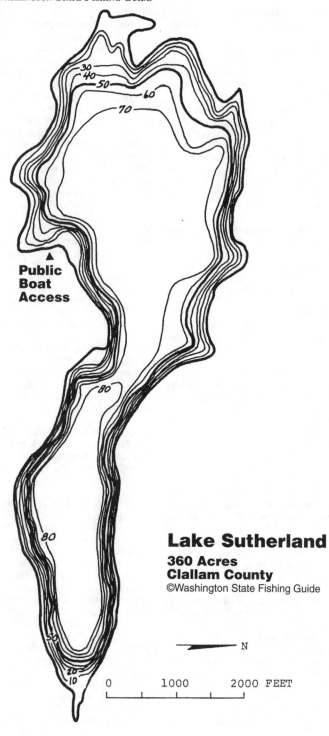

**Public
Boat
Access**

30
40
50
60
70
80
80
50
20
10

Lake Sutherland
**360 Acres
Clallam County**
©Washington State Fishing Guide

N

| 0 | 1000 | 2000 FEET |

blocked it. The lake is 12 miles W. of Port Angeles along US 101. WDFW access, ramp.

TWIN RIVERS. East and West Twin Rivers cross Hwy. 112 within a short distance of where they flow into the Strait of Juan de Fuca 23 miles W. of Port Angeles. Produces a dozen or so wild winter steelhead, and is fair for fall sea-run cutthroat. Surf smelt spawn on the fine gravel beach between the two streams. Spring halibut fishing in deep water well offshore. Primitive beach-side campsites. FS Rd. 3040 leaves Hwy. 112 and goes S. up East Twin. Follow FS 3034 up West Twin.

UNDI LAKE. A 15 acre lake 5 miles SE of Forks. Drains to Bogachiel River. Turn right at N. end of US 101 bridge over Bogachiel and follow road short distance to lake. Poor for cutthroat.

VILLAGE CREEK. Short run creek on Makah IR that flows into Strait of Juan De Fuca at Neah Bay. Planted with winter steelhead. Tribal license required.

WAATCH RIVER. Short-run winter steelhead planted stream on Makah IR. Joins Makah Bay at Waatch Point. Tribal permit required.

WENTWORTH LAKE. 53 Acres 7.7 miles NW of Forks off Dickey River Road. Drains to West Fork Dickey. Open year-round, stocked with 3500 catchable rainbows in April. Surplus adult steelhead and juvenile coho are sometimes stocked.

WHISKEY CREEK RECREATION AREA. Good summer dipping for spawning surf smelt in May-Sept. Creek enters Juan de Fuca Strait between Crescent Bay and Lyre River. From Hwy. 112 turn N. on Gossett Road.

Clallam County Resorts

Clallam Bay: Coho Resort, 360-963-2333.

Crescent Lake: See Olympic National Park.

Neah Bay: Big Salmon Resort, 360-645-2374.

Pillar Point: Silver King Resort, 360-963-2800.

Port Angeles: Thunderbird Boathouse, 360-457-4274. Swain's 360-452-2357. Straitside Resort, 360-963-2100.

Quillayute, Sol Duc, Bogachiel Rivers: Three Rivers Resort, 360-374-5300.

Sekiu: Olson's Resort, 360-963-2311.

Happy halibut anglers at Dungeness spit (Vence Malernee photo).

Clark County
WDFW Region 5
Washington Department of Fish and Wildlife, 2108 Grand Blvd. Vancouver, WA 98661-4624 Phone 360-696-6211.

This small southwest county is surrounded by and splattered with surprising year-round fishing potential despite the urban shadow of Oregon's population center.

Crossed N-S by I-5, Clark County is bordered on the south and west by the broad swirl of the Columbia River, on the east by nationally-acclaimed Columbia River Gorge National Scenic Area, and on the north by the salmon and steelhead that swim the North Fork Lewis River and a tiger musky lake.

Covering only 65 square miles, Clark County ranks 34th in size, but there's nothing small about its fishing potential. The Columbia River is the main focus for regional fishermen, a broad, tidal-affected river, speckled with uninhabited sandy islands and pocked with white sturgeon holes, and prominent hot spots for migratory chinook, coho, steelhead and shad. The Big C also offers plenty of northern pike-minnows, and spots to catch smallmouth, largemouth bass, walleye, perch, bullhead and channel catfish. On the south and west the river winds around the shoreline of the county creating a scattering of sloughs, beaches and sand islands that invite summer boat camping and fishing.

Lakes are few but an aggressive stocking program by the regional WDFW has created one of the best year-round fishing areas on the West Side. Lakes in and around Vancouver, Woodland, Battle Ground and Camas are frequently stocked with thousands of browns, rainbows, triploid rainbows, plus seasonal releases of surplus hatchery steelhead and salmon. One of the most popular trout lakes, Battle Ground Lake, is in the crater of an extinct volcano. Vancouver, Lacamas and adjacent Round lakes and river sloughs also support panfish and bass. The north county line follows the North Fork Lewis River upstream and continues through the center of two large reservoirs. Lakes Merwin and Yale offer trout and kokanee salmon. Lake Merwin is one of only a handful of Washington lakes planted with tiger muskies. The eastern-most impoundment in the Lewis River chain, Swift Reservoir, is in Skamania County.

Summer and winter steelheaders and salmon fishermen are familiar with the green holes and runs on the North Fork Lewis, East Fork Lewis and Washougal rivers. The East Fork produced the state record winter-run steelhead, 32-pound, 12-ounce, caught in 1980. Except for the lower East Fork Lewis, these rivers are closely followed by paved highways with lots of roadside access.

The E. quarter of the county is rural, heavily logged foothills with few lakes and ponds. Some streams hold small wild trout, but are extremely brushy and difficult to fish. Many of the upper watersheds are closed to protect wild steelhead and salmon. Most of the E. county highlands belongs to timber companies or the Washington Department of Natural Resources and the DNR lands are clear-cut or planted with reprod. The highest point in the county is at 4,000 feet on the E. shoulder of Silver Star Mt. 390 feet short of the summit, which is in Skamania county.-

The county's W. side is flat, river-bottom agricultural and residential areas, densely roaded with little public land.

WDFW operates a trout hatchery in SE Vancouver, and manages the Shillapoo/ Vancouver Lake wildlife area W. of Vancouver. Ridgefield National Wildlife Refuge, a waterfowl Mecca that also includes some under fished pothole lakes, is at the NW corner of the county. Gifford Pinchot National Forest touches the E. side of the county. The forest headquarters and information center is adjacent to Hwy. 500/Fourth Plain Ave., in Orchards E. of Vancouver.

Winter temperatures are mild enough for pleasant open water fishing, and lack the maritime influence felt closer to Puget Sound. Most winter trout and steelhead days hover in the high 30s and 40s—good fishing weather. Summer temperatures can edge into the 80s and low 90s but are usually somewhere in the comfortable 70s.

Average annual precipitation at Vancouver, just 100 feet above sea level, is 39.03 inches about five inches more than Seattle. Several feet of snow will fall in the upper foothills on the E. side of the county.

The main fishing routes into Clark County are I-5 running N-S between Woodland and Vancouver. Hwy. 14 crosses E-W following the N. bank of the Columbia River. Hwy. 503 follows the North Fork Lewis E-W from Woodland before turning N-S circling back the center of the county, crossing the East Fork Lewis River at Lewisville County Park, north of Battle Ground.

BACHELOR SLOUGH. A narrow, shallow 3 mile long side channel of the Columbia River near Ridgefield that isolates Bachelor Island, a popular summer boat camping area on the Columbia River side. The upper slough flows into Lake River just N. of Ridgefield City Marina and joins the Columbia River at Ridgefield NWR. The lower slough swings SW around Bachelor Island and returns to the Columbia River. Lake River continues S. from the Bachelor Slough confluence into Vancouver Lake. Both sloughs are lightly fished for largemouth bass, perch and bullhead catfish from May to October. A few sea-run cutthroat are also taken in late summer and fall. Good pot spot for crayfish. Bachelor can be navigated by shallow-draft boats but can be extremely shallow in late summer on S. end. A fee ramp and public fishing dock at Ridgefield City Marina a mile downstream from the forks. From I-5 Exit 14 W. onto Hwy. 501 to marina

BATTLE GROUND LAKE. This wooded, bowl-shaped 28-acre lake fills an extinct volcano crater in a state park NE of Battle Ground. Its deep, clear water and supplemental trout stockings offer good year-round fishing. WDFW frequently plants rainbow, brood stock rainbows, triploids 20 to 26 inches, surplus hatchery steelhead and brook trout. A few largemouth bass. Trail circles the lake, provides bank fishing to all areas. Can be very good in April and May. State park (360-687-4621) camping, swim beach, fishing dock and boat launch. No gasoline motors. From Battle Ground at jct. of Hwys. 502 and 503 turn E. on Main Street to E. side of town, then N. on N. Grace Ave., then E. on NE 229/Heisson Rd. 3 miles to lake.

BIG TREE CREEK. A small stream flowing into E. Fork Lewis at Moulton about 14 miles upstream from Battle Ground. Reported to hold cutthroat early in the season. Tough access. Crossed by Yacolt/Sunset road.

BURNT BRIDGE CREEK. Urban tributary to Vancouver Lake, this small polluted creek flows through northern Vancouver. Poor for carp and perch in lower reaches.

CAMPBELL LAKE. No public access to this 247 acre island lake between Lake River and Columbia River 2.5 miles S. of Ridgefield. Has largemouth bass, perch, crappie and catfish.

CANYON CREEK. A long, picturesque stocked trout stream that provides rainbow and cutthroat fishing in June and July. Planted with 8500 catchable rainbows before June 1 opener. Canyon Creek flows into the county from the Tatoosh Hills below Cougar Rock at Zig Zag Lake and flows NW through mostly DNR and Forest Service lands to enter the thin neck of North Fork Lewis River between Merwin and Yale Reservoirs. Sometimes stocked with rainbows. Lower section is popular with white water kayakers. Upper section followed by good gravel road most of the length in Clark County. A web of FS roads provides access to upper river and tributaries. Frequent washouts. From Hwy. 503 at Chelatchie Prairie turn NE on Healy Road around Tumtum Mt. then bear E. up Canyon Creek on FS 54. Campground closed, some primitive sites.

CANVASBACK LAKE. No public access to this 167-acre Bachelor Island lake 1 mile W. of Ridgefield. Holds largemouth bass, perch, channel catfish and brown bullhead, crappies and bluegills..

CARTY LAKE. No public access to this 42 acre lake on Ridgefield NWR adjacent to NW side of Ridgefield. Brown bullhead and yellow perch.

CEDAR CREEK. A small pastoral stream which joins the North Fork Lewis River at the big river's most popular salmon and steelhead hole 3 miles below Lake Merwin. Cedar Creek is paralleled from Woodland to near Amboy at a short distance by Cedar Creek Road. It is bordered by mostly private lands. The flow powers a flour grist mill on upper end and passes through Amboy heading near Yacolt. Above the North Fork Lewis the stream supports a few steelhead.

CHELATCHIE CREEK. A small, short-run creek fishable for approximately 4 miles from Chelatchie on Hwy. 503 to Amboy where it enters Cedar Creek. Fair in spring for rainbow.

COLUMBIA RIVER. The Columbia forms the S. and W. borders of Clark County where it is easily fished by bank and boat anglers for white sturgeon, shad, winter and summer steelhead, sea-run cutthroat, salmon, largemouth bass, panfish, northern pike minnows and catfish. All wild steelhead and sea-run cutthroat trout must be released in this area. The Vancouver area is perhaps best fished for white sturgeon and walleye near Ough Reef at Washougal, Lady, Reed, and Government island and I-205 bridge; smallmouth upstream from Government Island, shad and other seasonal anadromous steelhead and salmon near the mouths of the Washougal and Lewis rivers. Most sloughs downstream of Camas, especially those near Ridgefield, offer perch, crappie and largemouth bass. Bullhead catfish are popular with bank fishermen in the slough forming Caterpillar Island at WDFW Shillapoo/Vancouver Lake recreation area and Ridgefield NWR. Good bank fishing opportunities for sturgeon and salmon along Lower River Road, and from Frenchmen's Park in Vancouver. A public fishing dock extends into the river at Steamboat Landing on the S. side of Hwy. 14 at the E. side of Washougal near Cottonwood Beach. A 2-lane boat ramp at Ridgefield City Marina goes into Lake River a short run above the main Columbia. A small rough WDFW ramp at Caterpillar Island off Lower River Road. Excellent multi-lane ramps/docks at Marine Park just E. of the I-5 Bridge, and at the Port of Camas/Washougal. Both Marine Park and the Camas/Washougal facility are accessed from Hwy. 14.

COPPER CREEK. Only 1 mile of this Skamania County stream flows into Clark County through a steep, wooded area S. of Sunset Falls. June best for wild cutthroat. From East Fork Lewis River Rd. to Sunset Falls Rd. at Sunset Falls campground cross river on FS 41 along stream.

DEAD LAKE. No public access to this 15-acre lake on NW Lake Rd., on N. side of Camas near Lacamas Lake, and just W of Hwy. 500. Has bass, panfish.

FARGHER POND A 3 acre lake planted with brown trout 3.5 miles W. of Amboy, adjacent to dry bed of Fargher Lake.

FIFTH PLAIN CREEK. A small stream with a few wild trout. From Hwy. 500 in Orchards turn NE onto Ward Road then E. on Davis Road which bridges the creek.

FLY CREEK. Drains into Canyon Creek above Chelatchie. Contains native cutthroat. Easily fished by following banks. Fly fishing is effective June, July and August.

GEE CREEK. Small stream heading in farm and ranch lands E. of Ridgefield NWR entering refuge about 1 mile N. of Ridgefield then flowing NW through a series of lakes to enter Columbia River. Very little access. Some largemouth bass, crappie, perch and catfish. Inquire at refuge headquarters in Ridgefield for map and regulations.

GREEN LAKE. No public access to this 127 acre lake adjacent to E. side of Lake River. Supports largemouth bass, perch, channel catfish and brown bullhead, pumpkinseeds, crappie and bluegills..

KLINELINE POND. A large public park and heavy stocking efforts have developed this little I-5 pond into a great year-round fishing opportunity, especially for children. The former gravel pond is a wide spot on Salmon Creek adjacent to I-5 north of Hazel Dell and is planted with more than 36,000 catchable rainbows, triploids, and another 4500 brown trout, plus surplus broodstock up to 26 inches, cutthroat and steelhead. Plant numbers vary annually. Excellent bank fishing for bobber watchers at Salmon Creek Park. No boat access. From Hwy. 99 turn W. on 117th Ave. to park.

LACAMAS CREEK. Heads under Elkhorn Mt. then meanders through farmland in lower reaches, flowing through Proebstel

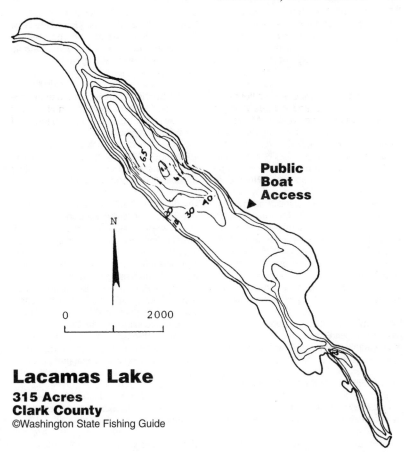

Public
Boat
Access

N

0   2000

Lacamas Lake
315 Acres
Clark County
©Washington State Fishing Guide

on Hwy. 500 E. of Orchards through Lacamas and Round lakes into the Washougal River. Fair June and July for rainbow and some cutthroat. A sleeper portion of the creek is the short section that flows out of Round Lake through Lacamas Lake Park to drop down into the Washougal River.

LACAMAS LAKE. Formed by a dam on Lacamas Creek, this 315 acre, 65-foot deep lake produces fair fishing for more than 33,000 planted browns to 14 inches, 29,000 rainbows, a few cutthroat, plus largemouth bass, perch, bluegill, pumpkinseeds and brown bullhead and channel catfish. Most trout are taken by trollers working the heart of the lake N. of the boat launch, while bass and panfish are found in the lily pad beds and shallows at both ends of the main lake and from brushy shallows around the shoreline. Lots of weed

growth in the shallows. The extreme E. end plunges into a deep-water bowl and is reached from the main lake by crossing through a shallow channel. Watch for stumps. The cool water is away from ski action, and is a good spot for late summer bass and perch. Open year-round. Good bank fishing access from Hwy. 500 in Camas, NW Lake Rd. on the SW side, and from Leadbetter Rd. which follows the entire NE bank. A small, difficult WDFW boat ramp is on the N. side along Leadbetter Road W. of Hwy. 500. The launch-preparation and parking area is on the opposite side of the road from the launch. **ROUND LAKE** is connected to Lacamas by a narrow channel that crosses under Hwy. 500 at the entrance to Lacamas Lake Park. Grocery store has bait. Round covers 32 acres and offers the same species of fish as Lacamas. Shore trails offer excellent bank fishing.

LAKE RIVER. The outlet to Vancouver Lake, Lake River flows N. about 12 miles separated from the Columbia River by a series of large, low islands before merging into the Columbia River at the N. end of Bachelor's Island. It's a slow, mud-bottom stream that can be power boated its entire length. Much of the river flows through the S. and N. units of Ridgefield NWR, and is crossed by a bridge to the S. Unit. Brushy shorelines. Great bird watching, fair fishing for largemouth bass, perch, crappie, brown bullheads, carp, bluegills, some sea-run cutthroat and a rare steelhead. Good canoe water and access to N. end of Vancouver Lake. Public ramp at Ridgefield City Marina and a private fee ramp in Felida at the end of NW 122nd. W. of NW 36th Ave. Can also be entered by boats launched into Vancouver Lake. **SALMON CREEK**, which is planted with winter steelhead, and attracts sea-run cutthroat, enters Lake River about 3 miles below Vancouver Lake and is a good spot to try in late fall.

LANCASTER LAKE. No public access to this 97 acre lake located on the NE border of Ridgefield NWR. Perch and brown bullhead present.

LEWIS RIVER EAST FORK. Still one of the best winter and summer steelhead rivers in SW Washington, although not nearly as productive as it was a few years ago. Smallest of the two Lewis River forks. The East Fork's claim to fame is a 32-pound, 12 ounce steelhead caught near Lucia Falls that still holds the state record for winter-runs. The years have not been any kinder to this wonderful little river than to other western Washington steelhead rivers. For comparison, in 1985 anglers caught 2161 summer-runs and 2541 winter-runs. By 1999 the catch was 331 summer and 573 winter-runs. Salmon are completely protected and all sea-run cutthroat must be released. Winter steelheading is best Dec.-Jan. and falls off rapidly on both sides of those months. Summer steelheaders do best in May, June and early July. Late summer usually means extremely low clear water. The river is closed to fishing above Horseshoe Falls which is downstream from the Sunset Falls campground.

For steelheaders, the East Fork divides into two sections. The upper section, paralleled by Lucia Falls/County Rd. 12, from Heisson Bridge upstream to the deadline 400 feet below Horseshoe Falls. Don't boat this section. The lower section from Lewisville County Park on Hwy. 503 N. of Battle Ground downstream. The heart of this lower section is a drift-boat floatable stretch between Lewisville and Daybreak County parks. There's a ramp at the upper end of Lewisville Park, a steep skid-launch on the SE side of Hwy. 503 bridge, and a developed ramp at Daybreak Park bridge. Gates into the parks are often locked during off hours. Not suitable for jet boats.

Good roadside bank access along the entire upper section and at Lewisville and Daybreak parks. For drift boaters floating downstream from Daybreak the next takeout is a primitive road end slide on Pollock Road S. of LaCenter or at Paradise State Park adjacent to the I-5 bridge near the mouth. Above Lewisville Park the East Fork is fast falling, with boulder bed pools, deep runs and fast chutes. Lucia Falls, previously a private fee fishing area, is now a county park, with no fishing or swimming. Below Lewisville Park, the lower section drops more gradually and develops more classic pocket, deep pool, riffle and tail-out fisheries. Below Daybreak Park the river broadens, slows through pastures and develops a lot of eddies, clay banks and frog water. It's a good place to boondoggle shrimp or eggs from a drifting boat.

LEWIS RIVER MAIN STEM. The main stem is a short, dike-walled section between I-5 and the Columbia River S. of Woodland that produces spring and fall chinook and coho, summer and winter steelhead and sea-run cutthroat. Bank access along the dike. Several public and private boat launches, including a WDFW launch on the dike just below the confluence. The N. bank is reached through W. Woodland by turning S. on S. Pekin Rd., or continuing W. to Kuhns Rd. which becomes Dike Road and follows the lower third of the river. It can be tricky finding a direct route to the S. bank. From I-5 Exit 17, W. on 319th, then N. on NW 41st. Ave. to the East Fork confluence, where there is a launch. A private launch is just W (downstream) on NW Pekin-Ferry Rd. Private fee campground at mouth. Most fishing effort is concentrated at the mouth during the peak of salmon and steelhead runs. Suitable for prop boats with caution.

LEWIS RIVER NORTH FORK. The largest of the two Lewis River forks, the lower North Fork Lewis is one of the best known and heavily fished salmon and steelhead rivers in SW Washington. The middle river is the impounded arterial feeding the chain of Merwin, Yale and Swift reservoirs, and the upper river is a pretty, lightly fished catch-and-release wild trout stream in Gifford Pinchot NF.

Anadromous fish do not get above Merwin Dam, the lowest of the three, although suplus hatchery salmon and steelhead are sometimes trucked upstream and released into the lakes. The river forms the boundary between Cowlitz and Clark counties.

Primary access is from I-5 Exit 21 at Woodland onto Hwy. 503 which follows the N. bank upstream before turning S. between Merwin and Yale resevoirs. Where Hwy. 503 turns S., FS 90 continues E. along N. shore of Yale and Swift reservoirs swings S. across the inlet to Swift then E. to continue about 40 miles into Skamania County. Above Swift Reservoir the North Fork Lewis is a lightly fished fair to good wild cutthroat rainbow stream, punctuated by a series of three impressive waterfalls. There's some very large dollies between Swift Reservoir and Lower Falls, but fishing for them is not allowed. An alternate route to continuing upstream, is to turn N. at the upper end of Swift Reservoir onto FS 25 which leads backroad explorers N. on paved road through Gifford Pinchot NF, along the E. side of Mt. St. Helens National Volcanic Monument across the **Cispus and Cowlitz** rivers to intersect with US 12 at Randle.

The S. bank of the lower river is reached from Woodland, by turning S. across the river then E. on Cedar Creek Road which follows the south bank upstream. Most boat ramps (for both drift boats and jet sleds) are on the N. bank off Hwy. 503. The Cedar Creek Road, however, leads to several major south bank fishing sites, including the legendary Cedar Creek Hole, the most popular spot on the river.

The lower river is best known as a summer-steelhead and salmon producer with spring chinook from April into June and fall chinook and coho from August into November. Coho usually deliver the most action. There is a salmon hatchery (with launch) on the N. bank. Sea-run cutthroat were once plentiful, but hatchery stockings have been stopped and there is a 20-inch minimum on trout kept, and all wild trout, including steelhead, must be released. A winter steelhead run enters the river from December into April. Winter-fishing peaks in December when anglers catch around 100 steelhead. The total winter-run catch in 1999 was 198 fish compared to 1294 in 1986. About 3 times as many summer-run steelhead are caught from May-Oct. Best months are July and August each delivering more than 100 summer-steelhead. The total summer-run catch in 1999 was 333, compared to 2764 caught in 1986. There is a boat launch at the base of Merwin Dam, another at the salmon hatchery above Cedar Creek, a third several miles downstream, and ramps in Woodland.

LOST LAKE. No longer planted, but may have remnant populations of brown trout. Lost is 2 acres, 7.5 miles NE of Yacolt and 2.5 miles E. from Tumtum Mountain. Drains to Canyon Creek.

MERWIN RESERVOIR. This 12-mile long, 4089 acre, 190-feet deep lake is the lowest of three North Fork Lewis River impoundments. It begins 10 miles E. of Woodland on the S. side of Hwy. 503. Merwin delivers several species of fish, but is best known for 10 to 16 inch kokanee salmon and tiger muskies. It also holds wild cutthroat, rainbow trout, perch, some coho, northern pikeminnows. The reservoir produces best kokanee trolling in April and May, but catches hold up into October. Tiger muskies were planted in 1995, and there is a 36-inch minimum. Best muskie fishing is in August, especially in shallow Speelyai Bay where there is a boat launch. A larger ramp and dock is available at the E. end of the lake in the Cresap Bay Park W. of Hwy. 503. Merwin Park on the W. end of the lake provides access for bank fishing, but no boat ramp. Below the dam is a ramp for river craft. Most reservoir play boat traffic, and much of the fishing effort is concentrated near the ramps in the E. end of the lake, which leaves lots of room for explorers.

MUD LAKE. Not open to public access. This swampy 92 acre lake is 1 mile SW of Paradise Point State Park W. of I-5 and S. of the North Fork Lewis at the edge of Ridgefield NWR Fish species include largemouth bass, crappie, pumpkinseeds, brown bullheads and bluegills.

POST OFFICE LAKE. 77 acres on an island between Columbia and Lake rivers SW of Ridgefield. No public access. Mostly used for waterfowl nesting and hunting. Holds perch, yellow and brown bullheads and bluegills.

ROCK CREEK. A small, tributary flowing into the East Fork Lewis River about 1 mile upstream from Lewisville Park NW of Heisson . Best fishing in June for wild rainbow and some cutthroat.

ROCK CREEK. A large trout stream flowing from the slopes of Silver Star Mt. W. along a good gravel road through the community of Dole into the East Fork Lewis about 5 miles W. of Sunset Campground. Wild rainbows and cutthroat, best in June and July, but deep pools keep it productive most of the summer. From Hwy. 503 turn S. on Dole Valley Rd., then continue E on DNR Rd.1200/Rock Creek Rd., past Rock Creek Campground. From Dole Valley upstream the creek is a tumbling freestone stream. Below Dole Valley it enters a large marshy area.

ROUND LAKE. No public access to this 16-acre island lake between Columbia and Lake rivers SW of Ridgefiled. Holds a variety of fish including crappie, bluegill and channel catfish

SALMON CREEK. A lengthy tributary to Lake River, Salmon Creek is crossed by I-5 just S. of I-205 jct. in Hazel Dell. **KLINELINE POND** is impounded on the stream just W. of I-5. The lower reaches are slow and produce a mix of trout, bass and panfish. E. of I-5 it's a quick, shaded trout stream planted with winter steelhead and sea-run cutthroat and supports a fair population of wild rainbows. Runs E-W across much of the county. E. of I-205 it's paralleled by Salmon Creek Road almost to Brush Prairie. E. of Battle Ground the creek is followed into the foothills by NE Risto Rd. and NE 209th St. Bridge accesses.

SHANGHAI CREEK. A small, grassy, unstocked tributary of Fifth Plain Creek. Reported fishless.

SIOUXON CREEK. Tough to reach this stream which empties into E. side of Yale Lake at the head of a pretty mile long inlet, about 2 miles above Yale Dam. Boat camping on inlet. Belvins Road, sometimes gated, leaves **CANYON CREEK**, heads N. along the E. shore of Yale bridging the inlet. A very rough trail heads upstream. Private logging roads to upper creek often gated. Lightly fished for wild rainbow, cutthroat. Bull trout are protected.

VANCOUVER LAKE. A large, shallow and lightly fished lake on the W. side of Vancouver. The lake is 3 miles long and 2 miles wide, covers 2858 acres and surprisingly is not surrounded by residential areas. The big, brush-shouldered lake sits in a pocket of land owned by city and county parks, WDFW, federal refuge and railroad right of way. WDFW's Shillapoo/Vancouver Wildlife Recreation Area and a poor boat launch is on the S. shore. Most of the W. shore is a large county park. Lake River flows from the N. end. Fish include largemouth bass, perch, crappie, brown and yellow bullhead and channel catfish and carp. Open year-round. May-July and early fall are top fishing periods. Decent May fishing for crappie and maybe largemouth in the forest of flooded willows that ring the lake. Some bank fishing from park area, but most bank anglers stake out forked sticks on the SW corner at the mouth of Flushing Channel and stillfish for bullheads. Also some roadside fishing in WDFW site. Good bow-fishing for carp in May. A low boat speed limit eliminates play boat disruptions. From I-5 Exit 1D W onto Fourth Plain Blvd. and continue W. to Lower River Road, park and lake. To reach the WDFW launch, at the S. end of the lake turn N. from Fourth Plain onto Fruit Valley Road, then W. on Laframbois Rd. to launch. Also reached from Ridgefield Marina by boating S. on Lake River.

WASHOUGAL RIVER. Once one of the state's top streams, the Washougal enters the Columbia River through Camas Slough under the Hwy. 14 bridge. Steelhead and salmon hatcheries produce small runs of coho, chinook, winter and summer steelhead. Sea-run cutthroat planting program has been discontinued and all wild cutthroat and steelhead must be released. A May-June shad fishery develops upstream from the mouth in the Columbia River at upper end of Lady Island. The Washougal system includes the mainstem, West Fork Washougal which enters in Skamania County below the steelhead hatchery, and the Little Washougal River which enters at Blair Road. The main river is followed by paved Hwy. 140/Washougal River Road from Hwy. 14 in Washougal NE to WDFW salmon hatchery and Dougan Falls. A gravel road continues upstream from the falls into DNR timber lands, but this section of river has been closed to fishing. It was smolts from the Skamania steelhead hatchery on the West Fork that were sent east to launch the Great Lakes steelhead fishery that continues today. Years have not been as kind to the Washougal, however. The 1999 summer-run catch for the entire system was just 66 steelhead most in June and July. In 1985 it was producing more than 3000 summer-runs, fish that were nationally heralded for their aggressiveness. Recent winter-run steelhead catches have been just 112, most in January, compared to the mid 1980s when winter anglers were catching 2000 steelhead a season. Annual fall salmon fisheries have collapsed and only occasionally is a river salmon season opened. Fall salmon fishing is still popular off the mouth at the head of Lady Island. **LITTLE WASHOUGAL** enters the main river from the W. about 4 miles above mouth and is paralleled by Blair Road upstream through dairy farms and back yards. Minimal steelhead and wild trout fishing. **WEST (NORTH) FORK OF WASHOUGAL** joins the Washougal river near the Clark-Skamania County line and is the outlet from the WDFW steelhead hatchery. Fishing is not allowed between main river and hatchery.

WIDGEON LAKE. Located on Bachelor Island 1 mile W. of Ridgefield, the 38 acre lake holds perch and brown bullhead. No public access.

WHIPPLE CREEK. A few leftover brown trout from since discontinued stockings may still be in this small Lake River tributary. The creek is crossed by NW 41st Ave., Vancouver.

YALE RESERVOIR. An impounded Lewis River power-generating reservoir 20 miles E. of Woodland on Hwy. 503, Yale is 8 miles long and covers 3801 acres. Open year-round, but extreme draw downs in winter inhibit boat launching. Fished mostly for kokanee salmon beginning in mid-May through Labor Day. Abundant kokanee from natural production in Cougar Creek. Lots of northern pikeminnows, a few rainbow and cutthroat and some very large, but protected Dolly Varden. The big reservoir is impounded by an earthen dam on the Lewis River creating depths of up to 190 feet. Because of cold water temperatures Yale is usually a slow starter, but comes on strong in May and June for trollers with blade strings and bait. Good day use fee boat ramps at Saddle Dam, Yale, Cougar Camp and Beaver Bay which also has power company camping. Several areas on the E. and S. shores are used by boat campers, especially in the Siouxon Creek arm. A huge shallow sandbar extends almost to midlake on the SE side and is both a boating hazard and a fine swimming area with camping on the peninsula. Lots of mid summer play boat activity. All boat ramps are accessed from FS Rd. 90, which is the paved eastward extension from Hwy. 503 following the W. shore. Small town of Cougar, at mid lake, has all services, bait and some tackle. Lots of blacktailed deer and elk to watch. For updated reservoir levels call 1-800-547-1501.

Columbia County
WDFW Region 1
Washington Department of Fish and Wildlife, 8702 N. Division St., Spokane, WA 99218. Phone, 509-456-4082.

Columbia County is mostly rolling, semi-arid wheat fields at the edge of the Palouse, then climbing to the mountain peaks of the Blue Mountains and Wenaha-Tucannon Wilderness. Fishing is primarily in small streams, with the exception of the Snake River, which forms the county's N. boundary.

The 16 lakes listed for the county cover only 41 acres. Most stream fishing is for wild or native trout. The state has discontinued stocking streams with catchable trout. Many streams support endangered bull trout, which are federally protected and must be released unharmed.

The county covers 862 square miles and rates 31st in size in the state. Highest point is 6401 feet at Oregon Butte SE of Dayton in Blue Mountains. Most of the county drains into the Touchet River system and then into the Walla Walla River, both offering fishing promise. The N. county drains into the Tucannon and Snake rivers. The Blue Mountains dominate the S. part of Columbia.

Best access into the county is via US 12 W from Clarkston or NE from Walla Walla. Summer fishing is usually warm, dry and sunny with temperatures in the high 80s, low 90s and low winter temperatures in the 20s. Annual precipitation is less than 20 inches.

BURNT FORK CREEK. Limited fishing for small wild trout. Release bull trout. The stream joins the S. Fork Touchet River at end of the S. Fork Road. A trail continues upstream to its headwaters under Griffin Mtn. S. Fork Road is rough. From Dayton drive E. on 4th Street right across bridge at Signal Junction. S. Fork Road is just E. of town. Lower creek is on private ground.

BUTTE CREEK. Butte provides rainbow fishing. Bull trout and spring chinook are present, but protected. Snow melt runoff typically lasts until July 4 . A highly scenic area. All but 2 miles of this tributary to Oregon's Wenaha River are in Washington. Upper reaches may be fished by taking trail from end of Godman Springs Road at Teepee FS campground, and hiking about 4 miles down the E. Fork to junction with the main creek. .

CROOKED CREEK. Headwaters and most of the creek are in Washington's Columbia and Garfield Counties, draining to Oregon's Wenaha River. It is reached from Pomeroy via Pomeroy Grouse Road 40,

or from Troy, OR, through Grouse Flat and past the abandoned Hunt School to end of road. Three Forks Trail leads 3 miles to creek. Trails parallel creek. Snow often lingers until July. Holds rainbow and bull trout. Release bull trout. Best in August, September and October.

CUMMINGS CREEK. Enters Tucannon River from the E. about 10 miles above Marengo. A side road (may be closed to vehicles) closely follows Cummings for 7 miles. The creek offers rainbow and a few steelhead. Best fishing is inside the Wooten W.R.A. in May and June.

DAM POND. Good in spring for approximately 2000 planted rainbows. This small pond is just above Little Goose Dam on Snake River. From SR 261, W. of Starbuck, turn N. onto Little Goose Dam Road and continue NE to dam.

DAYTON JUVENILE POND. Small, easily bank fished kids pond in Dayton. Receives 3000 rainbow catchables in Feb., Mar., April. Open year-round.

GRIFFIN FORK. Limited fishing opportunities for wild rainbow in this tributary to Touchet River S. Fork. Follow Robinette Mtn. Road up S. Fork of Touchet to Griffin Fork and hike the trail upstream. Can also be reached by hiking downstream from Burnt Fork.

JIM CREEK. Rated fair for rainbow during May and June. A small tributary of the E. Fork of the Touchet River, flowing in about 10 miles upstream from Dayton. A rough road leaves E. Fork road at Greiner Ranch and parallels the creek for 4 miles. Lower creek is on private property.

LEWIS CREEK. Another E. Fork Touchet River tributary entering 3 miles upstream from Jim Creek. E. Fork Road crosses the creek at its mouth and rough trails lead upstream. To fish downstream strike the trail at Patrick Springs, 3 miles N. of Godman Springs FS campground. Best fishing is for rainbows in June. Good population of bull trout which must be released.

ORCHARD POND. Small Snake River impoundment near Lyons Marina. Stocked in Feb. with 2000 rainbows 8 to 14 inches. Spring fishing best.

PATIT CREEK. Small creek flowing into Touchet River at Dayton. Patit Road follows the creek upstream for about 8 miles. N. Patit Rd. continues up the N. Fork. Marginal native trout angling, extreme low water in summer.

RAINBOW CREEK. Tributary of Butte Creek's W. Fork. Best rainbow fishing from June on. Reached by a 3-mile trail from Godman guard station. Trail follows SW slope of Godman Peak. Low flows in late summer.

ROBINSON CREEK. A native rainbow stream that joins Wolf Fork of the Touchet River near Mountain Home Camp, and flows into the E. Fork of the Touchet River 5 miles SE of Dayton. From Dayton follow N. Fk. Touchet River Road upstream 3 miles then S. on Wolf Fork Rd. bearing right at forks up Robinson Creek 2.5 miles. Wolf Creek Rd., parallels **WOLF FORK** 6 miles to road end. A trail follows Wolf Fork through mostly private property.

SNAKE RIVER. Good steelhead, excellent smallmouth bass, fair channel catfish and occasional crappie and sturgeon action available in this major year-around fish producer. Substantial plants of steelhead are made by hatcheries in Washington, Oregon and Idaho. Top steelhead months are Sept. through Dec. Very few steelhead during the rest of the year and all trout—including steelhead—are usually closed from April through mid June to protect downstream migrants. Popular steelheading spots include the mouth of the Tucannon River, Choke Cherry Canyon (2 miles upstream on Little Goose Dam access road), below Little Goose Dam and Lyons Ferry area. This stretch of the Snake delivers excellent smallmouth fishing mid April through October. Some of the top bass areas are in Lake Bryan, at Lyons Ferry, mouth of Tucannon River, and sloughs and coves above Little Goose Dam. Rip rap rock area just below Little Goose Dam is good also. Channel catfish in this section. Best catfish bite is in Mar. Apr. and again from July into Oct. in the same areas as smallmouth and steelhead. Some white and black crappie, bluegill and perch. Good numbers of sturgeon and salmon but they must be released. This is big water with difficult bank access. Boat fishing is most productive. Prop boats OK. Boat launches at Lyons Ferry, above Little Goose Dam and at mouth of Tucannon River. Ramps, campsites and picnic areas are provided at the dams. The Snake is the boundary between Columbia and Whitman counties.

TOUCHET RIVER. This small mountain river supports browns, whitefish, summer steelhead and a few rainbows. Best fishing June through Sept. The S. and N. Forks merge about 2 miles SE of Dayton creating the main stem Touchet which joins the Walla Walla River near Touchet. There is beautiful, scenic territory along both forks with roads paralleling both streams to their upper reaches and the Wenah-Tucannon Wilderness Area. If supplemental hatchery plants occur it will be below the forks. Follow the Ski-Bluewood signs SE from Dayton.

TUCANNON LAKES. Eight heavily-stocked artificial lakes on the Wooten W.R.A., 10 miles S. of Pomeroy along Tucannon River. The lakes, and their usual hatchery allotment of rainbow trout, include **SPRING**, 10,300; **BLUE**, 21,300; **RAINBOW**, 22,300; **DEER**, 3000; **WATSON**, 15,300; **BEAVER**, 1500; **BIG FOUR** 2300 and **CURL** 15,300. These lakes provide some of the most productive trout fishing in Columbia County especially early in the season. Pressure is heavy.

TUCANNON RIVER. River is in fishable shape from June on. Best rainbow trout fishing downstream of Marengo, about 10 miles upstream of US 12. Also whitefish, summer steelhead, chinook salmon and bull trout. No fishing for chinook or bull trout. Large rainbows move into the lower river below Merengo in the fall. Stocked with steelhead and the lower river offers very good steelhead fishing from Sept. through Jan. This small river starts in the Blue Mtns. and flows 50 miles N. and W to join the Snake River 5 miles below Starbuck. A good road follows the Tucannon from Columbia County for 28 miles. A trail continues from road end. Tucannon Campground at Hixon Canyon, 17 miles S. of Marengo.

WHITNEY CREEK. Limited population of wild trout. Joins Wolf Creek 2 miles from end of the Wolf Creek Rd. Creek trail follows upstream 3 miles.

Fish dislike human smell

Do fishermen really stink? There is evidence that migratory steelhead and salmon not only don't appreciate the smell of humans, but will leave the scene if possible when subjected to that smell.

Fish biologists at Bonneville Dam on the Columbia River noted this aversion of fish to man smell while working around the fishways. While both salmon and steelhead would swim and jump around men, when someone would put a bare hand in the water, all fish movement would stop for at least 30 minutes. Fish workers put this B.O. factor to work on several occasions when zestful spring Chinook salmon were ascending the fish ladders. The energy-packed springs were jumping so high in the low-ceilinged ladders that they were breaking the expensive overhead lights. A hand in the water at top of the ladder put the salmon down .

British Columbia fish biologists, work ing on silver salmon counts on the Stamp River, had a similar experience. The silvers were going over a counting ladder at a steady clip until one of the biologists waded bare footed into the river above the ladder. All fish movement immediately stopped. Intrigued, the men made some tests. A ten minute check of salmon over the ladder came up with 34 fish. They then immersed bare hands in the water for one minute, following this with another ten minute check. Only four fish passed them during this period.

The biologists tested a number of solu tions to determine whether foreign organic substances spooked the fish. After several months of such tests they concluded that with the exception of hand rinses, no solution showed suffi cient effect on the migratory rate.

Biologists have figured for years that it is the olfactory organs of salmon and steelhead which enable them to "home" to the stream where they spent their pre-ocean years. Evidently this same highly developed sense of smell comes into play with fish's aversion to human smell.

In view of these findings, fishermen might consider pulling on gloves before baiting. It could be the considerate thing to do.

Cowlitz County

WDFW Region 5

Washington Department of Fish and Wildlife, 2108 Grand Blvd. Vancouver, WA 98661-4624 Phone 360-696-6211.

If you're a fisherman, ya gotta love Cowlitz County. The heart of the county pours down the Cowlitz River, a wide, deep, powerful flow that drops from glaciers on the upper rim of Mount Rainier and pours into the Columbia River at Longview. While the Cowlitz is a far cry from the monster fishing river it was in the 1980s, it is still one of the top year-round steelhead and salmon prospects in the state. On the far side of adjoining ridges creeks flow into the Toutle, Coweeman, and Kalama rivers, all steelhead, salmon, and cutthroat waters. The Toutle River, devastated by the eruption of Mount Saint Helens, is showing surprising recovery, and in fact is delivering some excellent summer-run steelhead fishing.

On the upper slopes under the still-steaming maw of Mount Saint Helens in the National Volcanic Monument (NVM) Coldwater Lake is earning a reputation for producing extraordinarily large rainbows and cutthroat, and a nearby lake is delivering 10-pound rainbows. Silver Lake, east of I-5, is one of the most praised largemouth bass and panfish lakes in western Washington, and at Merrill Lake fly-fishermen turn out in droves when giant Hexagenia yellow may flies are being slurped by browns, rainbows and cutthroat. The W. county line is outlined by well-known salmon, steelhead and sturgeon holes on Columbia River. In recent years, WDFW has instituted a year-round trout stocking program, including some lunker size plants, that is invigorating lowland lake fishing. If the county has a piscatorial shortcoming it's the lack of alpine lakes. Only 9 lakes, less than 75 total acres, are higher than 2500 feet elevation. The only really large lakes in the county, Merwin Reservoir and Yale Reservoir, are shared with and listed in Clark County.

Cowlitz County covers 1171 square miles, ranks 28th in the state in size, and the highest spot is Goat Mountain at 4965 feet 8 miles N. of Cougar at the W. edge of the Mount Saint Helens National Volcanic Area. The low spot is 5 feet above sea level at the edge of Wahkiakum County and the Columbia River.

It's largely a rural county, except for the urban center surrounding Longview-Kelso at I-5 where three major rivers converge—the Cowlitz, Coweeman and Columbia. Most of the county E. of I-5 is intensively logged, rolling foothills leading into the Cascades. The I-5 corridor is pastoral lowlands and river bottoms, and the W. County near Ryderwood is rumpled with low mountains rising to 2577 feet. Clear-cut logging has been devastating in the foothills E. and W. of I-5 and most small waters are recovering from heavy siltation, erosion, increased water temperatures, and brush encroachment. Forests have been replaced with fields of reprod plantings, and the impact of the 1980 eruption is also still visible in the Toutle River drainage.

Most creeks are followed by roads and while unstocked, support some small wild cutthroat and rainbows.

The climate is maritime and temperate with an annual precipitation at Longview of 45 inches, mostly rain. Annual temperature averages a fish-friendly 52 degrees with summers nudging into the low 80s and lots of 60 to 70 degree weather. Steelhead rivers, with rare exception, are ice and snow free all winter.

Main access roads connect with the N-S I-5 corridor along the W side of the county. Hwy. 504 runs E. along Silver Lake and continues up the Toutle River drainage to Mount Saint Helens. Hwy. 4 runs W. from Longview along the Columbia River toward the Willapa Hills and the ocean. Hwy. 503 runs E. from Woodland along the S.

border of the county to Merwin and Yale reservoirs. Paved roads are rare in most of the E. county which is crisscrossed by a maze of gravel and dirt logging roads, some of which are gated. The extreme E. side of the county edges into the Mount Saint Helens National Volcanic Monument (NVM) and access permits are required for trail, lake and stream use.

ABERNATHY CREEK. Late summer and fall best for catch-and-release sea-run cutthroat. WDFW has stopped trout plants and all wild trout, steelhead and salmon must be released. The creek enters the Columbia River 12 miles W. of Longview at the jct. of Abernathy Road and Hwy. 4 . The road follows upstream for about 10 miles. Mouth of the creek offers winter steelhead, boat ramp.

ALDER CREEK. Enters the North Fork Toutle River 22 miles E. of Castle Rock on Hwy. 504. Park at mouth of stream, and follow a dirt road/trail upstream. No longer stocked, closed to all fishing.

ARKANSAS CREEK. A meandering stream which joins the Cowlitz River from the W. opposite town of Castle Rock. Hwy. 411 crosses the creek 0.4 miles above its mouth, and county roads roughly follow Arkansas Creek and its N. Fork up Arkansas Valley. Early season fishing for rainbow is fair, sea-run cutthroats from September on. Tributaries to Arkansas Creek include **DELAMETER** and **MONOHAN**. They offer fair early season rainbow fishing and some cutthroating later in year.

BLUE LAKE. A popular 8 acre hike-in cutthroat lake in the NVM NE of Merrill Lake. Not stocked. From Cougar turn N. on FS Road 8100 past Merrill Lake, then E. at Kalama Horse Camp. At a fork turn NE on FS Road 8123 which continues to trailhead parking lot. Hike .04 miles to lake.

CASTLE CREEK. Heading in Skamania County, Castle Creek joins the Toutle's N. Fork about 7 miles below Spirit Lake. Weyerhaeuser logging road 3500 crosses the creek at its mouth, and a rough road follows Castle up W. side for 2 miles. A cutthroat creek, Castle is brushy and snow-fed.

CASTLE LAKE. Tough to reach, but can be worth the effort, this 200 acre lake was created by the mud flow triggered by the 1980 eruption of Mt. St. Helens down Toutle River Valley. The lake has never been stocked but now provides good fishing for wild, self-sustaining rainbows up to 10 pounds. Selective gear, 1-fish 16 inch minimum. The lake, located within the NVM, is open year-round but snow generally blocks logging road access until May. From Hwy. 504 turn S. cross North Fork Toutle and follow Weyerhaeuser Roads 4100, 5600 and 3000 E. into Toutle Mt. Range past Spotted Buck and Spud mtns. to gate at edge of NVM. Lake is visible below and it's a steep downhill hike to get there.

COAL CREEK. A tributary to Coal Creek Slough which is crossed at its mouth by Hwy. 4 about 7 miles NW of Longview. Road parallels stream for about 4 miles. Coal Creek provides fair fly fishing for wild cutthroat early, and sea-run cutthroat in Sept./Oct. No longer planted with steelhead. Boat launch at mouth at old county dump site.

COAL CREEK SLOUGHS. One of several Columbia River sloughs on Hwy. 4 W. of Longview. Boat launch at old garbage dump site where Coal Creek enters the slough. Early spring can be productive for crappie, perch and catfish. March and April are best for largemouth bass. In late May and early June spring freshets in the Columbia River back up water and flood these and other sloughs adjacent to the river.

COLDWATER CREEK. Closed to fishing. This natural spawning stream is the inlet and outlet of Coldwater Lake In NVM. Drains into the North Fork Toutle on Hwy. 504 about 42 miles E. of Castle Rock.

COLDWATER LAKE. Created when mud slides from the eruption of Mount St. Helens May 18, 1980, blocked Coldwater Creek transforming a steep-walled valley into a 750-acre cold, ultra-clear lake that is becoming one of the best big trout lakes in western Washington. Planted with rainbow fingerlings in the late 1980s, Coldwater Lake now delivers self-sustaining rainbows in the 15 to 25 inch range, plus wild cutthroat. A lakeside trail provides bank access to 2 fishing spots. Elsewhere it's not legal to walk off trail even to fish. Best fishing is from tubes or small boats. The lake is almost 2 miles long and few anglers invest fishing time rowing or kicking to the

Spring Chinook, Cowlitz River.

and spring and fall salmon fishing for chinook and coho is best (when run-size justifies season openings) in April-May and late August into October. Sloughs at the mouth of the Coweeman and Cowlitz, and W. of Longview can be good for warm water fishermen who have the time to unravel the puzzle, usually kicking off in late May and June and running strong into the summer. Some of the best, and most ignored, action is available during the low water of early fall. Boat ramps are at the mouth of Abernathy Creek on Hwy. 4, in the Cowlitz River at Hwy. 432 bridge, on the Oregon side NW of the Lewis and Clark Bridge, at Kalama, and just S. of the mouth of the Lewis River in Lake River at the Ridgefield City Marina.

COUGAR CREEK. A short-run stream which empties into Yale Reservoir from the N. about .04 miles E. of Cougar. Poor for small wild rainbow and cutthroat. Trail along lower reaches. The creek is a major spawning stream for Yale's kokanee salmon and is closed to fishing after August. Great spot to watch this bright red fish spawn in late fall. Pacific Corp. campground near mouth.

COWEEMAN LAKE. A cutthroat lake at 2750 feet at head of Coweeman River 21.5 miles E. from Kelso and .05 miles N. of Elk Mt. Lookout. Logging road access.

COWEEMAN RIVER. Once an excellent steelhead, salmon and cutthroat river which now offers a marginal fishery for winter-steelhead and catch and release for wild cutthroat. The Coweeman joins the Cowlitz River just above the Columbia. No longer planted with sea-run cutts, but still offers a promising catch and release fishery for wild sea-runs August into late fall. Fair c&r for wild cutts in upper reaches after June. Closed to salmon fishing. The river gives up about 40 winter steelhead a year, nearly all in January. Lower river above Hwy. 5 reached via road at end of Allen Street E. for about 4 miles on N. side of river. The Rose Valley Road which heads E. from I-5 Exit 36 picks up Coweeman on the S. side and follows it for 13 miles. Major tributaries include Gobie, Mulholland, Baird and Skipper Creeks. A road follows Gobie Creek about 2.5 miles providing access to rainbow and cutthroat. Most Coweeman River tributaries are cutthroat streams.

COWLITZ RIVER. Only the lower, south-flowing 25 miles of this monster year-round

N. end, which concentrates almost all of the fishing effort in the S. Gas outboards are not allowed, electric okay. Excellent small boat launch and paved-road access on S. end by continuing from Hwy. 504 past the Coldwater Ridge Visitor's Center which sits above the lake. Mount St. Helens fills the horizon S. of the lake. Permits can be purchased at the NVM visitor centers to park and use boat launch. For NVM and fishing information call 360-274-2131. This 2490-foot elev. lake is open year-round, but access road sometimes snow closed. Selective gear regs., 1-fish, 16-inch minimum. Lots of fly fishing opportunity (bring a black leech), and light tackle casting or jigging. Many small boat anglers row-troll small barbless spoons and spinners. Although the fish are large, success can be slow.

COLUMBIA RIVER BARS. Columbia River fishermen divide into two camps in the Longview area. Main river fishermen target the bars and holes for salmon, steelhead and sturgeon, and the bass, crappie, perch, and catfish anglers slide into the network of sloughs S. and W. of Longview. Popular bar fishing areas include the mouth of the Cowlitz River (a hog line site), Kalama, N. Fork Lewis at Woodland, Willow Grove, Johnson's Beach and the County Line Bar on the Cowlitz-Wahkiakum line. Summer fishermen, after mid-May, catch steelhead headed for upper Columbia tributaries, and also tap winter and spring steelhead, along with salmon. Sea-run cutthroat hit from August into October steelhead, salmon and cutthroat river are in Cowlitz County. This segment is wide with subtlety defined holding water, and the banks, below the Toutle River confluence, still show the scars and debris left by the Mount St. Helens mud flow. The Cowlitz County reach is paralleled on the E. bank by I-5 and along the W. side by Hwy. 411 (For water upstream of I-5 refer to Lewis County). It's a rare year when this big river is not at the top of west slope steelhead production, and during years of healthy salmon runs it produces spring and fall chinook and September-December coho. There's also been a healthy resurgence of sea-run cutthroat fishing in late summer and early fall.

Banks on both sides are accessible to shore fishermen, mostly plunkers, and the depth allows both jet and prop boats to hogline or troll. Wind and a mellow current can make this section a long, tough row for drift boaters.

All anadromous fish in the Cowlitz River system move through the Cowlitz County segment, and that can be a lot of fish. In 1999 steelheaders caught almost 3300 summer and 2300 winter steelhead. In recent years the emphasis has changed from winter to summer steelheading For comparison, in 1986 the summer-run catch was almost 1300 and the winter-run was almost 11,000.

The Cowlitz River enters Cowlitz County S. of Vader and flows into the Columbia on the S. side of Longview at a popular hogline bar. This is wide, often rip-rapped water that invites bank plunking and back-trolling lures and baits from anchored boats or trolling along the shoreline drops. Hot spots: the graveled mouth of the Toutle River, the Olequa area on the W. side near the Cowlitz-Lewis County line 1 mile SE of Vader and the mouth of the river S. of Longview. This is truly a year-round fishing hole. Winter steelheading starts in November and continues into April when spring and summer steelhead move in and provide action into fall when the first winter-runs show. March, April and May bring a run of spring chinook, in late July the first fall chinook, September for silvers and jack salmon of both species. This is also a popular smelt dipping spot in February and March especially in the Kelso and Castle Rock areas. Sea-run cutthroat will arrive with the salmon runs from July into December. Sturgeon are occasionally taken from Castle Rock downstream, especially in the Kelso area. Boat launches in Longview just

NW of Hwy. 432 bridge, near Rocky Point, Castle Rock Fairgrounds, Olequa, N. of the county line at the I-5 bridge and Mission Bar.

DEER CREEK. A small wild cutthroat stream joining North Fork Toutle from the S. side about 27 miles E. of Castle Rock on Hwy. 504. Tough to reach. Rated fair in fall. Camping at Hoffstadt Creek Park.

ELK CREEK. Enters Kalama River from the N. Drive E. up Kalama River Road past Camp Kalama (about 20 miles) then NE on DNR Rd. 6000, when gates are open, about 8 miles where road crosses Elk Creek. Fish upstream from here or drive another 1.5 miles to strike Elk Creek at higher point. Fair to good for wild rainbow and cutthroat.

FAWN LAKE. A 23 acre mountain lake at 3700 feet elev. NW of Coldwater Lake at headwaters of Shultz Creek, a tributary to Green River. Access is from Coldwater Ridge Visitor Center on gravel roads. May be closed to vehicles. Brookies and cutthroat.

GERMANY CREEK. A long, large creek that begins the Willapa Hills and flows under Hwy. 4 into the Columbia River 11 miles W. of Longview. A road follows upstream about 6 miles. Lower mile produces a few winter steelhead and fall sea-run cutthroat. WDFW has stopped planting sea-run cutts. Best fishing on a freshet.

GOBAR CREEK. A pretty wild rainbow and cutthroat tributary with a few summer steelhead, that flows into the N. side of Kalama River E. of Pigeon Springs. A DNR road turns N. from Kalama River Road and follows the creek about 5 miles upstream. June and September best fishing.

GREEN RIVER. A large tributary flowing into the North Fork Toutle at Maple Flat 20 miles E. of Castle Rock on Hwy. 504. Railroad bridge crosses the Toutle near mouth of the Green. Follow rough trail on S. side of Green River, or drive on Weyerhaeuser Roads that parallel most of the river. Logging roads may be gated. The Green River was spared much of the devastation that hit the Toutle River during the 1980 eruption and has recovered exceptionally well. It now offers good fishing for hatchery summer and fair fishing for winter steelhead. Most years there's seasons for fall coho and sometimes spring chinook. Summer steelheading is the best, and June and July and top months. A few winter-runs are caught in November and when the season is allowed to run a couple of dozen are caught in January. Very clear, shallow river, best fished with light tackle and fly gear. Check the regs carefully on this one. Release all wild steelhead, and trout fishing is not allowed. From Hwy. 504 at 19 Mile Camp, turn N. on Rd. 1000 to 2500 which runs upstream.

HOFFSTADT CREEK. Enters North Fork Toutle on N. side at St. Helens on Hwy. 504 about 24 miles from Castle Rock. A tributary, **BEAR CREEK**, is paralleled by a road. A few small wild trout.

HORSESHOE LAKE. A trout and warm water fishery with park access in Woodland. Great spot to take the kids. Lots of bank fishing area and potential for 10 pound trout. This year-round lake covers 79 acres in what was once a channel of the nearby North Fork Lewis River. Heavily planted with catchable browns and rainbows, some broodstock and triploid rainbows up to 26 inches, plus hatchery steelhead and sea-run cutthroat. WDFW stocks the lake several times of the year including winter. Fair fishing in April, May and early June. Summer anglers target largemouth bass, yellow perch, brown bullhead and yellow bullhead, bluegills, pumpkinseeds and warmouth. Boat launch in park. I-5 Exit 30 onto Frontage Rd and continue W. of I-5 to park.

HATCHERY CREEK. A Kalama River tributary joining at lower Kalama hatchery. Good steelheading near the mouth.

KALAMA RIVER. A small, quick, winding heavily fished year-round steelhead and salmon river. Although now just a shadow of the river that earned fame in the 1980s, there's not a month of the year when there's not some kind of fish with big shoulders to challenge, including an occasional sturgeon caught at the mouth. Excellent access for both bank and drift boat fishermen. This is one of the finest drift boat rivers in western Washington. Boat access on the W. side of I-5 at WDFW site, at Camp Kalama, S. side of Modrow Bridge, Beginners Hole, Sink Hole, Prichard's Western Fly Shop, the Red Barn Hole, Kalama Falls Salmon Hatchery, and several kick and rope launches in small water above the hatchery. Impassable Kalama Falls and the "canyon" is downstream from the hatchery and boaters need to take out, not launch at the hatchery access. Bank fishermen have lots of room to fish from the paved Kalama River Road which parallels the river's N. side. Upper section from Summer's Creek to Kalama Falls is usu-

Camp Kalama River fall salmon fishing.

ally reserved for fly fishing. Summer steelies readily take a fly in this river in July and August.

Fishermen target summer and winter steelhead, spring and fall chinook, early and late stock coho and sea-run cutthroat although cutthroat action has diminished since WDFW stopped stocking them and made it illegal to keep wild sea-runs. The river produces about 400 summer runs (half of those in June and early July) and 250 winter-runs most in December and January. Compare those catches to 1985 when the Kalama produced 4300 summer-runs and 2400 winter-runs, plus big runs of spring and fall salmon. There are spring and fall runs of chinook and fall runs of coho that can be fished when runs are big enough to allow it. Trail No. 238 starts from trailhead at Kalama Horse Camp 8 miles N. of Cougar on FS Road 81. and follows the river upstream to the outlet of Merrill Lake. Main tributaries include **LITTLE KALAMA**, **GOBAR** and **ELK CREEKS**. They furnish limited fishing during June and July. The Kalama enters the Columbia River a short distance N and W of Kalama. From I-5 Exit 32. Go W. to a very rough WDFW ramp and bank fishing access in frog water, or continue to road-end access to the Columbia. Turn E. and follow Kalama River Road along the N. bank of the river all the way to its headwaters in Merrill and McBride lakes N. of Cougar. The folks at Camp Kalama and Prichard's keep close tabs on runs, and may steer you in the right direction plus arrange drift boat shuttles.

KNOWLTON CREEK. Joins Kalama River from the S. below Pigeon Springs.

KRESS LAKE. A popular, kid-friendly 30 acre spring-fed lake near I-5 Exit 32 and Kalama River Road. A former gravel pit, now heavily stocked in spring with 8000 foot-long brown trout, and in January, April and May with upwards of 17,000 catchable rainbows, broodstock, triploids, cutthroat to 18 inches and steelhead. Best trout fishing is from fall through late spring. Also offers largemouth bass, channel catfish, black crappie, bluegill, pumpkinseed, and yellow perch. Open year-round, carry-in boat access, no internal combustion outboards. Lots of bank access for kids. From I-5 for .03 mile E. on Kalama River Road then N. .04 miles to lake.

LAKEVIEW PEAK LAKE. A 3 acre cutthroat lake 10.5 miles E. of Pigeon Springs on E. side of Lakeview Peak. Drains to Kalama River.

Lake Merwin.

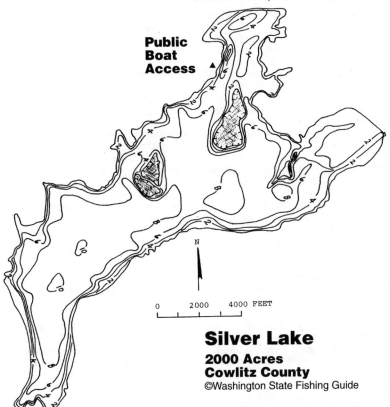

**Public
Boat
Access** ▲

N

0   2000   4000 FEET

Silver Lake
**2000 Acres
Cowlitz County**
©Washington State Fishing Guide

LEWIS RIVER (East Fork, North Fork, Main stem). See Clark County.

McBRIDE LAKE (Snowshoe Lake). Headwaters of the Kalama River, 6 miles NE of Lake Merrill at 2700 feet in NVM. Lake covers 9 acres holds brookies and cutthroat and is adjacent to FS Road 8100 NW of Ape Cave entrance.

MERRILL LAKE (Trout). A large, deep flyfishing only lake in a mountain bowl N. of Cougar. Small boat ramp, and carry-in boat access, almost no residential development and a ban on gasoline motors makes this a favorite with float tubers and canoers. This is one of the must-try lakes for most western Washington fly fishermen, especially in late July and August when there are tremendous evening hatches of Hexagenias, those succulent giant yellow mayflies that drive these fish nuts. Slurping in those 2-inch plus flies are coastal cutthroat, browns and rainbows to several pounds. Special regs on this one, read carefully.

Best route from I-5 is through Woodland on Hwy. 503 continuing E. on FS 90 to a N. turn onto FS 81 about .07 miles W. of Cougar. Follow FS 81 uphill 3 miles to the 344 acre lake at 1541 feet. Drains NW into the Kalama River. Most fishermen launch from DNR boat access or skid roads from FS 81 along E. side of lake. A rough road comes into the W. side of the lake from Kalama Falls, and a steep trail leads to the S. end.

MILL CREEK. Enters Columbia River 12 miles west of Longview under Hwy. 4. Closed to angling.

OSTRANDER CREEK. A small Cowlitz River tributary which crosses I-5 near Ostrander. Produces wild 'bows early in the year, and sea-run cutthroat in the fall. Paralleled for .05 miles by a road heading NE from top of hill in Ostrander.

SACAJAWEA LAKE. A heavily-stocked year-round park-lake in Longview at jct. of

Hwy. 4 and 432. Covers 48 acres and is planted in Jan., Mar., April, and June with 12,000 catchable browns and 14,000 rainbows and several hundred triploids, plus fall and winter plants of excess hatchery coho and steelhead. Has a self-sustaining population of channel catfish and largemouth bass, crappie, pumpkinseed, warmouth, perch, and yellow and brown bullhead catfish. Drains to Columbia River. Lots of bank fishing and row boat access. Good lake for kids.

SILVER LAKE. The arms, bays, points and pad beds of this shallow, 3000 acre, year-round lake are sometimes hailed as the best big bass lake in Western Washington. A WDFW planting of grass carp to control rampant millfoil has been wildly successful, and the vast seas of impenetrable growth that crippled fishermen in the early 90s have disappeared. The 14-inch minimum size limit on largemouth bass, along with habitat improvements paint a rosy picture for this big lake. In addition to largemouth bass that often zip past 5 pounds (8 pounders are possible), Silver offers crappie, perch, bluegills, brown bullhead catfish, warmouth, pumpkinseeds and in 2001 was stocked with 10,000 catchable rainbows. The deepest spot in this sprawling, lily pad ringed lake is 10 feet, which allows it to warm quickly in the season, kicking off good bass catches as early as February, long before other west slope lakes. Most largemouth as taken from the vast brush, logs, trees, channels and pad beds that surround the shoreline. These lunker largemouth get pounded pretty seriously by lots of bass specialists, club and tournament fishermen. It's not a lake for those who prefer lonesome water, but there's enough of it that you can always find solitude and structure to your liking. Perch are available to worm dunkers in late summer and May through July are prime for crappie and bluegill. June, July and August are best for catfish. Most trout are caught by trollers near midlake. Bank fishermen stake out spots along the shoulder of Hwy. 504 and there's limited fishing room at the boat launch. The many channels, islands and pad beds near the launch are ideal for small boat fishing, but it's a loooong row to the "far end" of the lake. A small WDFW boat ramp and short pier are on the N. shore off Hwy. 504. Rental boats, bait, tackle, cabins and resort facilities are available at three resorts on the lake, all accessible from Hwy. 504. Mount Saint Helens National Volcanic Monument Information Center and Seaquest State Park is at the NW end of Silver Lake. From I-5, Exit 49 eastbound onto Hwy. 504 for about 6 miles to the WDFW site.

SPIRIT LAKE. Fishing is prohibited in this infamous lake since the 1980 eruption of Mount Saint Helens doubled its size and moved it several hundred feet up the mountain. Once thought barren but in 2001 biologists reported catching and netting dozens of large rainbow trout with steelhead genetics. These trophy trout, however, are just tantalizing teasers since there are no plans to ever allow angling in Spirit's 2500 acres, at least while volcanologists and fish biologists are using it as a test tube to study natural post-eruption recovery. The lake is directly below the Windy Ridge Observation Area. From US 12 at Randle, go S. on FS 25 and follow signs to NVM.

TOUTLE RIVER (Main). One of the state's best steelhead rivers before being devastated by Mount Saint Helens' 1980 eruption, the Toutle is now responding well to post-eruption plants of summer steelhead, and providing a fair winter catch and release fishery. There are signs the river may soon return as a top producer of sea-run cutthroat, coho, fall chinook and steelhead. Both forks begin in the NVM. The NORTH FORK TOUTLE, the most productive arm, begins in Spirit Lake in NVM and is paralleled for most of its length by Hwy. 504 which provides roadside and spur road access. The SOUTH FORK TOUTLE flows south of the low Toutle Mountain range and is followed by logging roads. The South Fork is emerging as a very good summer steelhead river, and catch and release winter steelhead fishery. The North and South forks meet at Toutle and create the main Toutle which crosses under I-5 about 2 miles N. of Castle Rock and flows into the Cowlitz River. There can be good fishing for moving steelhead and salmon at the mouth. Both forks should dramatically improve as habitat recovers.

Cowlitz County Resorts

Cowlitz River: Barrier Dam Campground Salkum, 360-985-2495.

Kalama River: Camp Kalama, 360-673-2456.

Silver Lake: Silver Lake Motel And Resort, 360-274-6141. Streeter's Resort, 360-274-6112.

Douglas County
WDFW Region 2
Washington Department of Fish and Wildlife, 1550 Alder St. NW, Ephrata, WA 98823-9699. Phone 509-754-4624

With a couple of exceptional exceptions, Douglas County is a tough place to find a wet spot and an even tougher place to find a fish.

Most of the 1862 square miles (Washington's 18th largest) are on a vast, fairly flat, semi-arid plateau. Land not cultivated into miles of wheat fields is mostly scabland on the high plateau E. of the Columbia River. The SE border drops sharply over high basalt cliffs into the Grand Coulee channel. Moses Coulee, created by torrents pouring from melting ice-age glaciers, runs SW to the Columbia.

The high point is 4240 feet about 6 miles SW of Waterville. Badger Mountain cuts the skyline E. of Wenatchee.

Overall the region has no major streams, fewer year-round creeks and few lakes. The largest natural lake, Jameson Lake, at 332 acres, is an outstanding exception to the county's fishless rule, and one of the most productive trout lakes in the state. Nearby Grimes Lake is an oasis of huge Lahontan cutthroat.

Douglas is hot in the summer (averaging in the low 80s), cold in the winter (it once hit 30 below) and dry. The average annual precipitation at Waterville, is 11.28 inches.

The Columbia River impoundments which form the W. boundary with Chelan County, provide walleye and smallmouth bass, especially near the dams, and Rufus Woods Reservoir has turned into one of the big trout places in the state during late winter and early spring. It's also a good walleye bet. The E. side of the county is framed by Grand Coulee an ice-age trough that now holds Banks Lake, the Sun Lakes chain (including the trout-fat Park, Blue and Dry Falls) and Lake Lenore, another premium Lahontan Cutthroat water. Unfortunately, for Douglas County's piscatorial repertoire, these famous fisheries are just E. of the border in Grant County (**See Grant County**)

Public land is almost nonexistent. Squares of BLM and BOR land are scattered between vast tracts of mostly private agricultural ground. State parks and public campgrounds are spaced along Columbia River highways.

Major routes through the county are: US 2 which crosses the Columbia River at N. Wenatchee, swings N. along the E. bank of the river, then cuts E. for the slow climb up Waterville (Pine) Canyon to the plateau at Waterville, the county's population center with a population of 1115 (East Wenatchee is actually the largest city with 4850). US 97 follows the W. side of the county N-S along the Columbia River and Hwy. 17 (173) angles N-S between Coulee City and Brewster.Hwy. 172 runs a right angle course through the center of the county connecting US 2 at Farmer with Mansfield and Hwy. 17.

COLUMBIA RIVER (See Chelan County). Walleye fishing is popular near the dam afterbays between Wenatchee and Pateros. Spring walleye and trout fishing is especially good below Grand Coulee Dam and Wells Dam. **Rufus Woods Reservoir** which forms the N. county line E. of Bridgeport is an excellent walleye producer and exceptional Feb.-Mar. target for very large rainbows. This section produced the state record rainbow, 24.45, pounds in Feb. 1998. The reservoir gained regional fame in the late 1990s when a net pen ripped at a private fish rearing facility and sent thousands of large triploid trout into the lake. Many are still there and growing. There's also a good number of rainbows (and walleye) in the upper lake below Grand Cou-

Jameson Lake

500 Acres
Douglas County
©Washington State Fishing Guide

N

0   2000   4000 FEET

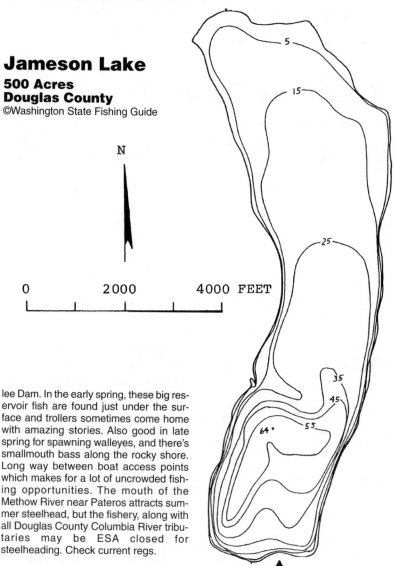

lee Dam. In the early spring, these big reservoir fish are found just under the surface and trollers sometimes come home with amazing stories. Also good in late spring for spawning walleyes, and there's smallmouth bass along the rocky shore. Long way between boat access points which makes for a lot of uncrowded fishing opportunities. The mouth of the Methow River near Pateros attracts summer steelhead, but the fishery, along with all Douglas County Columbia River tributaries may be ESA closed for steelheading. Check current regs.

Public Boat Access

DOUGLAS CREEK. Spotty fishing opportunities. This small stream heads above Douglas and meanders about 15 miles SE to Moses Coulee, then SW about 13 miles to join the Columbia River near the Chelan-Kittitas County line. A few rainbow are caught before July.

FOSTER CREEK. Marginal fishing. Enters the Columbia River just below Chief Joseph Dam at Bridgeport. Hwy. 17 follows the creek 2 miles S. from Bridgeport, then swings E. to parallel East Fork to Leahy. A

road heads S. up the W. Fork of Foster for about 10 miles to the headwaters. Some rainbows and brown trout.

GRIMES LAKE. If you love tackling big, challenging trout for the fun of it, not the skillet, you'll love this 150 acres of sun drenched Alkali water. Lahontan cutthroat 3 to 5 pounds are plentiful, and there's a frightening number of bigger cutts. An 11.5

fish was weighed (and released) by WDFW in 1999. The lake is undeveloped except for a Spartan WDFW access/ramp area and lies in coulee flanked by low hills of open sage. Much of the shoreline is crowded with cattails. Grimes has traditionally not opened for fishing until June and closes the end of Aug. Usually crowded on the opener. Selective tackle regs, and a 1 fish daily limit (but I wouldn't advise eating one. These fish live in Alkali water and generally hit most folks taste buds a bit sideways.) No gas motors (electrics ok). A resort on nearby Jameson Lake sometimes has rental boats on Grimes. Excellent for cartoppers, float tubes (when the wind doesn't blow) and rafts. US 2 to Hwy. 172 N. and E. to Mansfield, then S. on Mansfield Rd (becoming Wittig Rd.) about 5.5 miles. Turnoff is about 2 miles N. of Jameson Lake.

JAMESON LAKE. Usually one of the top rainbow trout lakes in the state, Jameson covers 332 acres in the treeless sage and ledge rock at the head of Moses Coulee about 8 miles S. of Mansfield. Expect big crowds on openers. Heavily stocked with almost 170,000 fry rainbow each year which grow quickly in the lake's fertile waters. Yearling rainbows average about 11 inches, and there's always a high number of carryovers 12 to 14 inches. Typically managed on a split season basis, opening in the spring and early summer, closing July-Sept. then re-opening in fall. The schedule is good for the fish and okay with fishermen who have seen the thick midsummer algae bloom or ever survived a blistering Basin summer sun in an open boat. Best fishing at Jameson is from the opener through May, and again in October. Foot-long trout are common, and 'bows of 3 to 5 pounds are not uncommon. A few Lahontan cutthroat may be present riding high water downstream from Grimes Lake. Oddly, the big lake is not encircled by a road. Resorts with rental boats, bait, cabins and camping are at both N. and S. ends and a WDFW access site, ramp and primitive camping at the S. end. From US 2 about 10 miles E. of Farmer turn N. onto Jameson Lake Road up Moses Coulee 6 miles to lake's S. end. To continue to the N. end bear E. on Jameson Lake East Access Road which cuts inland about 1 mile and continues to N. end resort. Also accessible on N. end by turning S. from Hwy. 172 at Mansfield onto Mansfield Rd./Wittig Rd. for 8 miles.

ROCK ISLAND PONDS. Three small Douglas County ponds adjacent to Rock Island Dam on the Columbia River are stocked with about 13,000 catchable rainbow trout in March for the opening day fishery, and just before Free Fishing Weekend in June. Ponds also support small largemouth bass and bluegill.

RUFUS WOODS RESERVOIR (See Columbia River).

Douglas Count Resorts

Jameson Lake: Jack's Resort,
    509-683-1095.

Ferry County

WDFW Region 1

Washington Department of Fish and Wildlife, 8702 N. Division St., Spokane, WA 99218. Phone, 509-456-4082.

Small to medium size trout lakes, massive Lake Roosevelt, and three major river systems provide promising fishing opportunities in the mostly wooded low mountains of this large NE Washington county.

Much of of the county is on the Colville Indian Reservation, and a tribal permit is required to fish reservation waters. Canada forms the northern border and the Columbia River the south. On the west and east are Okanogan and Stevens counties. Ferry County covers 2259 square miles and is the 9th largest county in the state. Major rivers are the Kettle, San Poil and Columbia including a long stretch of Lake Roosevelt, the impoundment behind Grand Coulee Dam. Highest point is Cooper Butte, 7135 feet. About half of the lakes in the county are above 2500 feet elevation.

Ferry County mountains are foothills to the Rockies and are mostly rounded, wooded and easy to access. Less than 12 percent of the county is range, pasture or cropland. Summer fishing is usually pleasant with temperatures in the 80s. Winter lows average about 15 degrees, and with less than 15 inches of annual precipitation trails and roads to mountain lakes are generally snow free by late March. Major access is from Hwys. 20 and 21.

BARNABY CREEK. Small stream on west side of Lake Roosevelt that produces small brookies and rainbow in spring. Heads under White Mtn. and flows into Lake Roosevelt opposite Rice in Stevens County. From Inchelium go W. along shore of Roosevelt Lake for 10 miles to where the creek enters the lake. Turn NW onto Barnaby Creek Road toward Lake Ellen. Road follows 3 miles of the creek.

BOULDER CREEK. A fair size valley stream that can produce small brookies and rainbows after runoff. Enters Kettle River 10 miles upstream from Lake Roosevelt. From US 395 about 3 miles S of Orient, turn W. onto Boulder Creek Road. After 2 miles the road forks to parallel both N. and S. forks. Improved FS campground near the headwaters of N. Fork.

BOURGEA LAKE. Rainbow populate this 21.9 acre lake 4.6 miles S. of Inchelium on Colville Indian Reservation. It drains to Roosevelt Lake. From Inchelium go W on Twin Lakes Rd., S. on Silver Creek Rd. then SW (right) on Covada Rd. to Bourgea Lake in Stray Dog Canyon.

CADY LAKE (Cody). Six acres on the Colville Indian Reservation 22 miles S. of Republic. Sometimes planted with brookies.

CURLEW LAKE. One of the most popular and productive year-round fishing, camping and resort lakes in eastern WA, Curlew covers 869 acres in wooded hills at an elev. of 2333 feet. Plants of about 22,000 rainbow fry and more than quarter million pen-reared trout. One of the few lakes in this region to be stocked with tiger muskies, a sterile hybrid introduced to thin abundant northern pikeminnows. Earning a reputation for good largemouth bass fishing, but the fish are typically small. Most anglers catch rainbows, but brookies are also available. Curlew provides good fishing the entire season. It's a nutrient rich lake and trout gain weight rapidly. In the spring most trout are about 12 inches, with a lot of 14 to 16 inchers, and more than an average number of 20 to 25 inchers. The tiger muskies were first stocked in 1998. Muskies and bass are in the shallows. Most trout fishing is from boats, although dock and bank fishing is available. Some areas of the lake are more than 130

Curlew Lake

869 Acres
Ferry County
©Washington State Fishing Guide

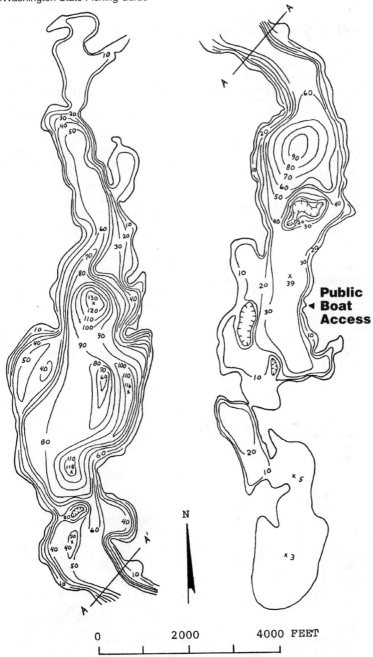

Public
◄ Boat
Access

N

| 0 | 2000 | 4000 FEET |

feet deep. Lots of competition in midsummer from pleasure boat recreation. 5 resorts, a large state park (87 campsites) on E. shore, multiple boat ramps, rental boats, fishing docks, store supplies available. Hwy. 21 follows the E. side of lake. Hwy. 21 is 2 miles E. of Republic. To reach the W. side turn W on W. Curlew Lake Road about 6 miles N. of Republic.

DAVIS LAKE. Cutthroat trout lake covering 17 acres NW of Boyds on the E. flank of Thompson Ridge. A fair trout producer all season. Accessible by road from Hwy. 395 at Boyds. Has a campground.

DEADMAN CREEK. Small brookies and rainbow. It is paralleled by Deadman Creek Rd. from Hwy. 395 just S. of Boyds and heads W. upstream for more than 15 miles into Colville National Forest.

ELBOW LAKE. Hook-shaped Colville Indian Reservation brook trout lake, 51.2 acres, 13.5 miles N. of Inchelium on Elbow Lake Rd. Fed by Onion Creek, drains to Roosevelt Lake.

ELLEN LAKE.Planted with rainbow, and usually holds up all season. Covers 77 acres 14 miles N. of Inchelium at an elevation of 2300 feet. An improved FS campground on E. end of lake. From Hwy. 395 follow road up Barnaby Creek.

EMERALD LAKES. Pair of small lakes in Hoodoo Canyon 22 miles E. of Republic and 4200 feet SE from Lily Lake. May hold brookies.

EMPIRE LAKES. Three tiny lakes of 4, .06 and 1.5 acres at 3600 feet ll miles N. of Republic. Planted with brookies. Drains to Curlew Lake. From Hwy. 21 follow North Empire Creek Rd. 7 miles to lake.

FERRY LAKE. Popular 34-acre mountain lake that produces catchable rainbow trout which are planted regularly to offset winterkill. Fair fishing especially spring and fall. Lake is located in Colville National Forest at 3329 feet. Drains down Scatter Creek to San Poil River. FS campground. From Republic, head S. 9 miles on Hwy. 21, then W. up FS 53 (Swan Lake Rd.) along Scatter Creek 7 miles to marked lake turnoff.

FISH LAKE. Planted with rainbows, 4 -acre mountain lake at 3300 feet, 1 mile S. of Ferry Lake. Accessible by road. .

FROSTY MEADOW CREEK. Colville Indian Reservation stream that produces small brookies.

KETTLE RIVER. A large, picturesque trout and whitefish river which enters Ferry County from Canada at Ferry, flows SE to Curlew, and then swings N. re-entering Canada at Danville before looping back into the U.S. at Laurier and flowing south to Lake Roosevelt across from Kettle Falls. The river forms the E. boundary of Ferry County and is paralleled by US 395 to its mouth on the west side of Lake Roosevelt N. of Kettle Falls bridge. Fall is the best fishing time for the river's rainbow, while February whitefishing can be excellent with maggots bounced on bottom. Rainbow fishery is bolstered by some surprisingly good brown trout action in lower river and upper loop. Stray walleye are taken by trollers just above the confluence with Lake Roosevelt. This is a tightly regulated river with WDFW conservation rules in effect to protect wild rainbow, which grow to several pounds. Most of the river is followed by and accessible from US 395 which parallels the west bank. Developed and primitive campsites are numerous. Good bank fishing areas as well as river boats, canoes and kickboats.

LA FLEUR LAKE. Located on the Colville Indian Reservation 9 miles N. of Inchelium at 2250 elevation, La Fleur is 24 acres and has been planted with brookies and rainbow.

LAMBERT CREEK. Entering Curlew Creek at Karamin just above Curlew Lake, Lambert produces small brookies and rainbow.

LONG LAKE. A narrow 24 acre, fly-only lake situated at 3250 feet elevation 11 miles S. of Republic. Route is S. from Republic 9 miles on Hwy. 21, then W. up Scatter Creek 7 miles to lake shore. Good late fall cutthroat fishing. No gas motors.

LONG ALEC CREEK. Joins the Kettle River at Curlew. A road follows the stream for several miles from the town. Contains small brookies and rainbow.

LYNX CREEK. The stream enters Roosevelt Lake 1 mile N. of Inchelium. A road from that town follows the creek N. and W. about 5 miles to Seylor Valley where Hall and Spring Creeks join Lynx. The road continues 2 miles W. up Lynx. It is considered a fair bet for small brookies .

MUD LAKE. A shallow lake located about 1.5 miles NW of Republic. Winterkills and is not stocked.

RENNER LAKE. A small, deep lake of 9.6 acres located I.8 miles W. from Barstow. Stocked with browns and brook trout. Drains to Kettle River. From US 395 go S on Hodson-Price and Lakin roads to a trail that leads .25 mile to lake. Elevation is 2525 feet.

ROUND LAKE. A brook trout lake of 52.1 acres, at 2275 feet on the N. side of Moon Mtn. about 5.5 miles W. of Inchelium. Round is on the Colville Indian Reservation. Reached by taking the Cornstalk Creek Road from Inchelium through Impach.

SAN POIL RIVER. This may very well be one of the best kept secrets in the state. While it rarely makes headlines outside of the local area, this scenic, remote river delivers good catches of rainbow (some to several pounds), brookies, whitefish and even the occasional walleye. The size of the trout have increased under catch-and-release, barbless hook regulations that apply to non-reservation waters. The San Poil is a steady producer all season with peaks in spring after runoff and early fall. Hwy. 21 parallels most of its length from Republic for about 58 miles to its junction with the Columbia. The lower river is on the Colville Indian Reservation. Much of this river is wadeable during summer and fall and numerous log jams create deep pools and cover for trout to 3 pounds or more. Most trout, of course are 6 to 10 inches. Near the confluence, anglers sometimes catch walleye straying upstream from Lake Roosevelt. The W. Fork, which joins the main river from the W. about 16 miles S. of Republic, is a good producer during spring and summer.

SHERMAN CREEK. A rainbow stream and kokanee spawning area for Lake Roosevelt, Sherman produces small trout throughout much of the season. The creek enters Roosevelt Lake on the Columbia River 9 miles S. of the Kettle Falls bridge. Hwy. 30 follows the main stem of Sherman Creek from its mouth to its headwaters under Sherman Creek Pass. Beaver ponds on the S. Fork hold brook trout.

SHERMAN LAKE (Summit). A 3 acre lake at 5900 feet elev. 1700 feet S. of Sherman

Early morning lake fishing from a dock.

Pass on the S. side. The lake winter kills and is not stocked.

SIMPSON LAKES, lakes of 21.9 and 9.6 acres at 2250 feet which lie just S. and E. of La Fleur, have brookies.

SWAN LAKE. A popular mountain lake located at 3641 feet elevation in Colville National Forest a few miles E. of the Okanogan County line. Swan covers 52 acres and is 95 feet deep. There is an improved FS Campground on the E. shore. About 15,000 rainbow fry are planted annually, and there are holdover brookies, some to several pounds. Largemouth bass have been illegally stocked and are not growing very fast in the cold water and short growing season. Swan Lake is reached via Hwy. 21, 9 miles S. of Republic, then W. on FS 53 along Scatter Creek, past Ferry Lake, about 8 miles to the lake shore.

TONATA CREEK. A small Kettle River tributary, entering that stream 7 miles E. of Curlew on the Kettle River highway. A road leads upstream from a point 1 mile SE of the creek's mouth and continues upstream about 10 miles to headwaters near Kelly Mtn. Hosts rainbow and brookies .

TORODA CREEK. This stream offers good fishing for 'bows and brookies . It is paralleled by a road from its confluence with the Kettle River at community of Toroda to upper reaches in Okanogan County.

TROUT LAKE. A narrow, 8 acre lake 8.5 miles W. of Kettle Falls at SE end of Hoodoo Canyon. Elevation is 3000 feet. It is annually stocked with about 5000 rainbow fry. From Hwy. 20, 2 miles W. of Sherman Creek Campground, turn N. on Trout Lake Road to the lake. There is a small FS campground and ramp.

TWIN LAKES. Two of Ferry County's largest and best known rainbow and brook trout lakes. Both are on the Colville Indian Reservation and require tribal permits to fish. North Twin covers 884 acres. South Twin is about 978 acres. A channel connects the lakes which lie at 2572 feet elevation. Both lakes are rich in nutrients that produce fast fish growth and deep-bodied trout. Both of these rich, shallow bowl-shaped lakes also have largemouth bass lurking in the lily pads. The lakes are reached by good road from Inchelium on Lake Roosevelt. Drive about 8 miles W. on Twin Lakes Rd. up Cornstalk Creek. Boat ramps, resorts, rental boats on both lakes.

WARD LAKES. Two brook trout lakes of 3 and 4 acres at 3625 feet 9.4 miles N. from Republic. Drainage is into Curlew Lake. These lakes sometimes winter kill.

Ferry County Resorts

Curlew Lake: Pine Point Resort, 509-775-3643. Tiffany's Resort, 509-775-3152. Black Beach Resort, 509-775-3989. Fisherman's Cove, 509-775-3641.

North Twin Lake: Rainbow Beach Resort, 509-722-5901.

South Twin Lake: Log Cabin Resort, 509-722-3543. South Twin Lake Resort, 509-1722-3935.

Franklin County

WDFW Region 3

Washington Department of Fish and Wildlife, 1701 So. 24th Ave., Yakima, WA 98902. Phone 509-575-2740.

One of the driest and hottest places in Washington, much of Franklin County offers limited fishing opportunities, especially for trout. Streams are almost nonexistent. Most ponds and small lakes, however, hold fair to good numbers of warm water species and often get very light fishing pressure. The county also has one of the most productive and remote sections of the Columbia River which forms much of the W. border.

Franklin County is in S. central Washington roughly between Tri Cities on the S. and Hwy. 26 near Othello on the N., an almost treeless, arid, scab lands area that gets between 7 and 10 inches of precipitation annually. The White Bluffs free-flowing section of the Columbia River forms most of the W. boundary at the edge of the DOE Hanford site. The E. county follows the Palouse and Snake rivers. The arid and lightly roaded Wahluke Wildlife Area. The Esquatzel Coulee, a geologic wonder, is one of the most prominent landmarks. It's a steep-walled gouge in the topography near Connell. Much of the county is flat or gently rolling, marked by steep coulees, basalt walls, sage brush, sand dunes, and irrigated crop lands. The Saddle Mtns. taper into the county along the gentle inclination of the Wahluke Slope on the NW border. High point is a 1,636-foot lump N. of Kahlotus near the county line. In most places the elevation is less than 500 feet. Most summer fishing is squeezed into early mornings, late evenings or at night. Mid-day summer temperatures can soar into the upper 90s and the only shade is what they bring. Winter lows average in the upper 20s.

Most of the county's lakes are man-made, created by seepage from drainage or by dams forming reservoirs. With 1276 square miles, Franklin is 27th in size among the state's 39 counties. The main roads into the county are N-S US 395 and E-W Hwy. 260 which intersect at Connell. Hwy. 17 from Othello intersects with US 395 S. of Connell.

CAMP LAKE. A private 25 acre lake formed by seepage. Camp is 5.5 miles N. of Mesa. From Hwy. 17 at the S. end of Scooteney Reservoir turn W. on Hendricks Rd., then S. on Canal Bank Rd. Mixed species of bass and panfish.

CHARLENE LAKE. Warm water panfish and bass are in this 14 acre lake 1 mile down the Snake River from Levey. Walk-in public access, good for smallmouth bass.

CLARK POND The middle pond in a string of 3 small ponds 5 miles SW of Mesa on Ironwood Road. Clark covers 49 acres and has bass (a few very large largemouth), perch, bluegill and carp. Open year-round, best in spring. Public fishing area.

DALTON LAKE. Narrow 30 acre lake 11 miles N. of Pasco on Kahlotus Road. Re-ceives spring plant of 20,000 catchable rainbows. Trout plant is fished out by end of March. Also supports largemouth bass, smallmouth bass, yellow perch, black crappie and brown bullhead. Bass can be excellent in spring and summer.

EMMA LAKE. A 20 acre lake formed by a railroad fill adjacent to backwaters of Ice Harbor Dam. Contains large and smallmouth bass, black crappie, yellow perch and brown bullhead. About 7 miles NE of Ice Harbor Dam.

KAHLOTUS LAKE (Washtucna). Originally a 321 acre lake, Kahlotus is a water source for the community and water levels fluctuate widely. It has shrunk in recent years, and actually dried up in the late 1980s. In 1999 it was stocked with largemouth bass and bluegill. Located in

Kahlotus Lake.

Kahlotus on Hwy. 260. Open year-round, public access area.

MARMES POND. 3-acre put-and-take fishery near Lyons Ferry Hatchery at confluence of Palouse and Snake rivers. Open year-round, stocked with 1500 rainbows in March.

MESA LAKE. A 50 acre lake fed by irrigation water overflow 1 mile W. of Mesa. Public access on W. shore. Stocked with walleye, largemouth bass, black crappie, yellow perch and brown bullhead. Can be very good for perch in summer.

POWERLINE LAKE. A 22-acre warm water species lake on the WDFW Windmill Ranch, 8 miles NW of Mesa. Good fishing for largemouth bass, perch, crappie and brown bullheads. There is a 2.5 mile walk-in access trail.

RAILROAD POND. 10 acres, 2 miles NE of Mesa. Stocked with catchable and triploid rainbows up to several pounds. Managed as a selective fishery, artificial lures only, catch and release encouraged.

SCOOTENEY RESERVOIR (Eagle Lake). A 685 acre enlargement of Potholes Canal. There is a variety of warm water fish including walleye, perch, bluegill, sunfish, crappie, small and largemouth bass. Open year-round, good in spring and summer and a popular ice-fishing lake. There are two sections in the reservoir of 425 and 260 acres connected by a canal. Campground and boat launches. Lake is 13 miles SE of Othello adjacent to Hwy. 17.

SNAKE RIVER (Sacajawea Lake). Forms the SE boundary with Walla Walla County. 32-mile-pool named Sacajawea Lake is formed by Ice Harbor Dam about 10 miles E. of Pasco. Sacajawea backs up to the foot of Lower Monumental Dam. There is a great variety of fish in the Snake River including smallmouth and largemouth bass, walleye, crappie, channel and bullhead catfish, steelhead and salmon plus sturgeon. Can be excellent in late spring for smallmouth and channel cats. Steelhead, salmon and sturgeon fisheries are tightly regulated with emergency closures. Always consult regs before fishing for anadromous species in the Snake. Boat launch at Sacajawea State Park at mouth of the Snake and at Levey Park approximately 10 miles from Pasco on the Kahlotus Road. Generally, the best fishing is in summer.

WORTH LAKE. 10 acre lake 7 miles W. of Mesa. From Hwy. 17 go W. on County Rd. 170. Offers largemouth bass and yellow perch.

Garfield County
WDFW Region 1

Washington Department of Fish and Wildlife, Region 1, 8702 N. Division St., Spokane, WA 99218. Phone, 509-456-4082.

This small, wind-washed chunk of rolling Palouse is a tough place for fishermen. There are no natural lakes in Garfield County and if it wasn't for a couple of fair trout streams, the Snake River and two of its productive impoundments the only reasons to visit would be to buy wheat, flush pheasants, chase chukars and drive Hwy. 128 south up Pataha Creek and on into the northern edge of the Blue Mountains and Umatilla National Forest.

About seventy-five percent of the county's 717 square miles are essentially treeless, made up of pastures, range lands and crops, mostly horizon-to-horizon wheat fields. The only forested land in the county is in the extreme south where Pataha Creek slips out of the Blue Mountains with a spider web of small tributaries, most only marginally fishable.

Garfield is 33rd in size in the state. Most of the county is at an elevation of approximately 2700 feet and the highest point is Diamond Peak 6379 feet. The climate is dry, 16 inches of precipitation at Pomeroy increasing to 50 inches in the Blues. Summer temperatures run in the high 80s to low 90s, and winter temperatures average in the mid 20s.

Major access is via US 12 which crosses E.-W. near the center of the county through Pomeroy.

ALPOWA CREEK. Hwy. 12 picks up the creek's N. Fork about 18 miles E. of Pomeroy, and follows it 5 miles to the Asotin County line. Two miles W. of the county line a road heads SW up the Alpowa's S. Fork for about 5 miles. The small, clear stream supports native rainbows. Stocking has been discontinued. Fish early in spring. Alpowa Creek gets extremely low during summer.

BAKER POND. This 2 acre farm pond has public access through cooperation with the landowner, and is stocked with 1500 catchable rainbow in May or June. It drains via Pataha Creek into the Tucannon River. Reached via Hwy. 128 and the Mountain Road.

BEAR CREEK. Located in Grouse Flat territory, Bear is reached via Troy, Oregon, or Mt. View road via Big Butte Clearwater Guard Station road. Contains rainbow. Limited water.

CROOKED CREEK. About 5 miles of this mountain stream are in Garfield County, and the remainder is in Columbia County and Oregon. The area is within Wenaha-Tucannon Wilderness and no mechanized vehicles are permitted. The stretch in Garfield is reached by taking the road through Grouse Flat SW of Mt. View, W. past the abandoned Hunt school and the Evans and Neal ranches to road end. Continue on Three Forks trail to Crooked Creek Trail which follows that stream both up and downstream. There can be good rainbow fishing in the creek. Bull trout are also present, but must be released.

DEADMAN CREEK. Heads E. of Gould City 10 miles N. of Pomeroy, and flows W. to join the Snake River at Central Ferry. The creek is followed by good roads for over 15 miles, with another road paralleling N. Deadman Creek. Rainbow trout, and juvenile steelhead. Occasionally a trout of a pound or more is taken.

PATAHA CREEK. A large, fishy creek that flows from the edge of the Blue Mountains north into Pomeroy, then west into Columbia County followed closely by US 12. Best fishing, however, is south of Pomeroy in the upper reaches above Columbia Center. Follow Hwy. 128 S. Good for native rainbow plus small brook trout. Stocking has been discontinued. Muddy roads during early part of the season often makes upper stretches of the Pataha tough to reach.

SNAKE RIVER. Snake River impoundments are Garfield County's most promising fishing bets. The large Columbia River tributary forms the northern and eastern border of Garfield County with Asotin, Columbia and Walla Walla counties. From September through December the Snake is an excellent summer run steelhead river. Most steelheaders troll diving plugs. It also offers good to excellent fishing for smallmouth bass and channel catfish. Early July when water temperatures nudge 60 degrees, and on into early November is the best time for these warmwater fish, although diehards will begin to hit smallmouth as early as March. Lake Bryan and Lower Granite Lake are very good bass producers. The reservoirs also hold crappies, perch, bluegills and walleye. There also have been reports of blue catfish in this area, but most of the cats are channels. Salmon run the Snake most of the summer, but all species are protected. There is also some good white sturgeon fishing in the summer, especially near the dams. Hot spots vary weekly, especially where anadromous steelhead are concerned.

Some of the better fishing areas include upper end in Garfield County via Silcott; lower end via Central Ferry; mid-reaches via Wawawai Grade Road, Casey Creek Road and Rice's Hill road. Some bank fishing available, especially in the dam afterbay areas, but a boat is a huge asset on this big river. There are good boat ramps at Central Ferry State Park, Hastings Bar, Almota Ferry, Boyer Park, Lower Granite Dam, on the north bank at Crum, Wawawa River Road, Nisqually John Canyon and just east of the Asotin County border at Chief Timothy State Park.

TUCANNON RIVER. Only the extreme upper section of this river runs through Garfield County, but this thin-water section, much of it hike-in, offers some good light-tackle water for wild rainbows. It also holds whitefish and bull trout. Bull trout must be released. This river is heavily regulated by WDFW with barbless hook and selective gear rules and varied opening and closing dates depending on the stretch. Consult current regulations before tackling this stream. The best trout water is south of Pomeroy. Go S. on Hwy. 128 from Pomeroy about 25 miles past Rose Springs to Teal Springs where a trail of about 2 miles continues S. to the Tucannon. There is a FS campground at Teal Springs, and the trail to the river takes off 1.5 miles E. of the campground. In the lower river near the Snake River, an excellent steelhead fishery takes place all winter. Steelhead action usually begins in late September. Several small ponds in Garfield County are planted with rainbow. The best are Baker's and Casey's ponds.

Grant County

WDFW Region 2

Washington Department of Fish and Wildlife, Region 2, 1550 Alder St. NW, Ephrata, WA 98823-9699. Phone 509-754-4624

There's a staggering amount of quality trout, bass and pan fishing water available in this semi-arid county where rain is rarer than state record fish.

Warm weather fishing seasons in Grant County are washed in perpetual sunshine and dusty blue skies. The county gets only about 8 inches of precipitation a year—mostly snow, hardly the kind of environment you'd expect to find a wet wealth of fishing water. But year after year this giant county kicks out some of the finest fishing memories in the state.

The credit for goes to an extensive network of dams, impoundments, seeps, and leaks from irrigation projects built to subsidize the county's vast agricultural economy. The process of turning desert into farmland has created pockets of some of the most fertile water in the state, including such famed reservoirs as O'Sullivan (Potholes) Lake, Moses Lake and Banks Lake: big year-round lakes with big reputations for rainbows, walleye, large and smallmouth bass, perch, crappie, and other panfish.

It includes a large slice of the popular Seep Lake system below O'Sullivan Dam, an area famous for Mar.-May trout fishing, and early summer largemouth bass, walleye and panfish. For many anglers, the new fishing year traditionally starts in March with a trip to the Seep Lakes, where dozens of potholes and mini-lakes fill coulees and sage brush with trout.

Grant County supports some of the most famous fly fishing destinations in the state: Dry Falls, Lenice, Nunnally, and that rare frigid spring creek that grows lunker rainbows in the desert-Rocky Ford Creek.

Clusters of popular trout lakes are in the Columbia National Wildlife Refuge (CNWR), scattered along Crab Creek and in the Caliche Lakes and Quincy Wildlife Area along I-90. The Desert Wildlife Area, a jigsaw complex of sand dunes, bass and panfish ponds extends for miles north and west of Potholes Reservoir.

The Grand Coulee, a 50-mile long trench that once held the Columbia River now holds a chain of fine cold water fishing including lunker Lahontan cutthroat in Lake Lenore, the trout, kokanee and warm-water fish in the hugely popular Sun Lakes chain, Banks Lake and a finger that touches the walleye, rainbow, kokanee and smallmouth bass water above Grand Coulee Dam in Lake Roosevelt.

Most of the trout lakes peak in March, April and May and again in September and October when the sun is less intense and daytime temperatures slip out of the 80s and 90s that are common in mid summer. The county has the dubious distinction of breaking the state high temperature record twice—the last time at 118 degrees on the harsh, treeless Wahluke Slope in the south county. But it is, as they say, "a dry heat."

Ice fishing is also gaining a toehold in the county following the WDFW trend to manage an increasing number of lakes on a year-round basis.

Grant covers 2807 square miles, making it the 4th largest county in the state. It's 102 miles from the northeast corner at Grand Coulee Dam to the southwest corner at Priest Rapids Dam. The county's terrain is fairly flat or rolling. The high point is 2800 feet elev. 6.5 miles northeast of Quincy. There are no forest or woodlands—just sagebrush, irrigated fields, scablands and grass.

Most of the county is privately owned, however, nearly all of the waterways are surrounded by or included in state wildlife areas, national refuges, BLM or BOR tracts or state parks. WDFW manages numerous Wildlife Areas in the county, and nearly all of them are built around standing water with good fishing. The vast tracts of private property rarely pose a problem to fishermen, except for the few creeks and streams that follow basalt walled channels across croplands.

I-90 is the route of choice to most of Grant County's fishing fortunes, crossing the Columbia River at Vantage and running E-W between the Caliche Lakes and Quincy Wildlife Area lakes, just N. of O'Sullivan and across Moses lakes. From I-90 near George Hwys. 28 and 283 angle NE-SW connecting with Hwy. 17 which runs N-S along through the Grand Coulee along Lake Lenore and the Sun Lakes chain. US 2 crosses the N. county past the south end of Banks Lake. Hwy. 26 from Vantage to Othello is a major route to O'Sullivan Lake, the Seep Lakes and Lower Crab Creek lakes.

ALKALI LAKE. A 308 acre year-round lake in the Grand Coulee between Blue and Lenore lakes 9 miles N. of Soap Lake on Hwy. 17. Alkali was originally a part of Lenore. A highway and dam now separate the lakes. Alkali is managed for largemouth bass, bluegill, and catfish and also holds perch, crappie and a few rainbow. Offers winter ice fishing. WDFW access and ramp.

ANCIENT LAKES. A group of 4 small walk-in lakes totaling about 15 acres that vary in size due to seepage. Drive W. of Quincy on Hwy. 28 for 4 miles, then S. on Road T N.W. for 1 mile, then right on road though breaks of Columbia. About 2 mile hike from gate. The south most lake has rainbows, the rest offer largemouth bass, bluegill, brown bullhead and perch.

BANKS LAKE. A very popular and productive year-round lake, 32-miles-long covering 27,000 surface acres with rainbow, kokanee salmon, walleye, smallmouth and largemouth bass, perch, crappie, carp and lake (in winter) whitefish, and minor fisheries for burbot and bullhead catfish. Banks was formed by dams across Grand Coulee pumping water from Lake Roosevelt on the Columbia River. It's a fertile lake and typically produces fish far above state average weights. Perch in the 1 pound class (open water and through the ice), are fewer than in past years, but showing signs of rebounding; rainbows (winter and summer) from a cooperative net pen rearing project that often hit 5 pounds, lots of smallmouth in the 4 pound range, and what many consider the finest walleye fishing in the state. Because it is so productive, despite the considerable distance from population centers, Banks is on the tournament circuit of most state walleye and bass clubs. Best bass fishing is along the rocky shoreline; largemouth in the N. end, smallmouth in the S. A good, but lightly fished, winter fishery has developed on the S. end near the

net pen rearing project for oversize rainbows cruising just below the surface. It's cold fishing, but many of the trout flirt with the 5 pound mark. Banks was once famous for growing fat, delicious kokanee salmon of 1 to 3 pounds, but this fishery has plummeted in recent years. WDFW is attempting to rebuild the salmon population and is stocking more than 1 million fry a year. Success has been marginal. Because of its size, fishing is best from boats, but there is plenty of shore access from Hwy. 155 which follows the E. bank from Coulee to Electric cities. There are 5 public boat launch and fishing sites along the giant reservoir, along with several resorts. Coulee City park, WDFW launches on SW corner, Million Dollar Mile at mid lake, Steamboat Rock State Park (509) 633-1304, Sun Banks Resort, Coulee Playland and Barker Canyon. Steamboat Rock State Park, at midlake about 12 miles S. of Grand Coulee, has excellent camping (200 sites) and is one of the most popular boating, camping and water play destinations in the state. For fishing conditions or fishing guide service contact Big Wally's (509) 632-5504.

BEDA LAKE. 45 acre lake with rainbow, tiger, and brown trout, E. of Dodson Road just S. of Winchester Wasteway. Difficult to fish from shore. Selective gear rules, 1 fish limit.

BILLY CLAPP LAKE . It would seem difficult to keep a 1010 acre, 110 foot deep lake a secret, especially in an area of scarce water, but for most anglers Billy Clapp Lake is the secret they haven't heard about. It's part of WDFW's North Columbia Basin Wildlife Area, and is famous for waterfowl hunting. What's not so well known is that it's also a good producer of walleye, largemouth and smallmouth bass, crappie, perch, and pumpkinseeds and is a fair promise, especially early and late in the season for large rainbows and lots of kokanee. Waterfowl hunting and nesting has a priority here and has produced a special Feb.-Sept. season. There is a good WDFW boat launch.

BLUE LAKE. One of the most popular trout lakes in the Sun Lakes chain, 11 miles N. of Soap Lake on Hwy. 17 which runs along the NW shore of the 536 acre lake. A natural lake that is stocked with a quarter million fry rainbow and browns. Yearling trout are 10 to 11 inches and with lots of 14 to 16 inch holdovers. Crowded on opening weekend. Good shore access, WDFW boat launch plus 3 resorts. 180 camp sites are at nearby Sun Lakes State Park on **PARK LAKE** a few hundred yards NE.

BLYTHE, CORRAL and **CHUKAR LAKES.** Trio of large seep lakes below Potholes Reservoir. Turn S. on gravel road at W. end of O'Sullivan Dam across from Mar Don Resort. Boat launch sites on Corral, an 80 acre lake, and on 30 acre Blythe. Blythe and Chukar, also 30 acres, are on CNWR. All are heavily stocked with rainbow and provide excellent spring fishing. Corral often holds up into early summer.

BROOK LAKE (AKA STRATFORD). A 427-acre waterfowl and warm water fish lake off the S. end of Billy Clapp Lake. Stocked with largemouth, smallmouth bass, crappie, perch, bluegills and pumpkinseeds. Open season Feb.-Sept. Located .05 mile N. of Hwy. 28 at Stratford. See Billy Clapp driving directions.

BURKE LAKE. One of several lakes on Quincy W.R.A. 7.5 miles SW of Quincy, and about 3 miles NW of I-90. The 57 acre lake is planted annually with 15,000 catchable rainbow, and has 2 boat launches. Dusty stocked with rainbows and browns, Quincy with rainbows, and the bass and panfish waters of Stan Coffin Lake and Evergreen Reservoir which also has walleye and tiger musky, are grouped with Burke. To reach the recreation area drive S. from Quincy to county road 5 NW, and then turn W. 2.5 miles. From I-90 turn N. on Hwy. 281, then W. on 3 NW to launches at Burke and Evergreen lakes.

CALICHE LAKES. A trio of early producing trout lakes. The most popular are Upper and Lower Caliche which total 30 acres and are adjacent to SE side of I-90 about 5.5 miles SW of George. Exit 143, then NE on Frontage Road 1.4 miles. Both lakes are good

rainbow producers for the first few weeks after the Mar. 1 opening. Lower receives 12,000 rainbow fry, Upper 6,000 and West about 1000. WDFW access. Ramp on Upper. Lower is good for float tubes and carry-in boats. Excellent bank fishing. Most anglers soak bait or troll. Lower is excellent for wind drifting wet flies from float tubes.

CANAL, HEART and **WINDMILL.** A connected chain of three well-stocked and popular rainbow lakes in the heart of the Seep Lakes S. of Potholes Reservoir. All 3 can provide excellent spring and early summer rainbow fishing for trout 10 to 16 inches. Canal is annually stocked with about 35,000 rainbow fry, Heart 10,000 fry plus triploids, and Windmill about 14,000. Canal and Windmill have handicap access. Free boat ramps on each. Primitive camping in vicinity. Canal is 76 acres, while Heart covers 20 acres, and Windmill, 33. From O'Sullivan Dam Road E. of dam turn S. at the 2nd right (opposite Lind Coulee) onto gravel road and continue 4 miles to Heart Lake. Windmill and Canal Lakes are adjacent.

CASCADE, CLIFF, CUP, DOT, SPRING and **CRYSTAL LAKES.** A group of small lakes on the Quincy WRA, a little W. of Burke Lake. Rainbow.

CASTLE LAKE. 1 mile SW of Coulee City this 12 acre lake drains into Deep Lake which is 1.5 miles S. Hike of 0.5 miles, then down steel ladder over a cliff. Holds rainbows and brook trout. Fry planted with about 2000 trout.

CHUKAR LAKE (See Blythe lake).

CLEMENTINE LAKE. A 4 acre largemouth bass and channel catfish lake on Crab Creek W.R.A.

COLUMBIA RIVER. Wanapum Pool above and below the I-90 Vantage Bridge offers challenging fishing for smallmouth bass and walleyes. This area is closed to steelhead and trout fishing. Some May-June smallmouth bass action near mouth of Crab Creek. 2 boat launches on Kittitas County side at Vantage. Rough launches on Grant County side along Hwys. 26/243 and a good ramp at Wanapum Dam. Some bank fishing opportunities S. of Vantage Bridge, but N. of the bridge the river runs far below high cliffs. Best fishing is usually from boats in the rocks and reef areas above Priest Rapids Dam.

CORRAL LAKE (See Blythe lake).

CRAB CREEK. Enters North Grant County from Lincoln County at Marlin then meanders W. and S. to join Moses Lake, emerges in the Crab Creek Channel of O'Sullivan Lake (where it's the primary access into the Sand Dunes area and a good walleye bet). Below O'Sullivan Dam it flows through the seep lakes' area into Adams County, re-enters Grant County near the Hwy. 26 bridge and heads almost due W. along Crab Creek Road to the Columbia River. Has browns, brookies and rainbow trout, but fishing success is spotty. Most trout are in the Seep Lake area or above Moses Lake. In the Boating is difficult in the Seep Lake segment where the creek is often choked with cattail mats, and blocked by numerous diversion dams. The lower few miles run through WDFW's Crab Creek Wildlife Area and supports lots of carp (bring the bow) and a few smallmouth bass. This segment is easily canoed between the mouth at the Columbia River and the bridge at Red Rock Coulee Road which connects Crab Creek Road to Hwy. 26 just E. of Royal City. Several WDFW access spots along lower Crab Creek Road between Smyrna and Hwy. 243 at Beverly near the Columbia confluence. The three quality fly-fishing (selective tackle) lakes of **Lenice, Nunnally** and **Merry** are reached from lower Crab Creek Road just E. of Beverly.

CRATER LAKE. A 25 acre, 35 foot deep lake 4 miles W. of Quincy. Black crappie, pumpkinseed, perch and yellow and brown bullhead. Private access.

CRATER SLOUGH. 3 miles W. of Quincy on Hwy. 28. The 15 acre slough offers perch, crappie and largemouth bass.

CRESCENT BAY LAKE. A 90-acre impounded lake formed by a dike on an arm of Lake Roosevelt about 0.5 miles E. of Grand Coulee. Holds perch, crappie, walleye, large and smallmouth bass and whitefish. Public access.

DEEP LAKE. The top kokanee lake in the chain of popular lakes in Sun Lakes State Park. Road to (fee) ramp at W. end of lake. Deep is 1.5 miles long, covers 104 acres and produces well for kokanee salmon that average about 12 inches, and a few lake trout (mackinaw). Poor rainbow fishery from a plant of 4000 catchables and 10,000 fry. Gets more than 40,000 kokanee fry each year. The park is on Hwy. 17 about 5 miles SW of Coulee City.

DRY FALLS LAKE. A beautiful lake lying at the base of vaulting cliffs in the N. part of Sun Lakes State Park, and one of the most productive and popular fly-fishing (actually selective tackle rules) destinations in the state. The lake gets its oxymoronic name from a wall of rock where in prehistoric times a waterfall flowed over cliffs. Covering 99 acres Dry Falls is planted with thousands of rainbow and tiger trout and 2000 catchable brown trout in early spring, sweetening a pot already heavy with large numbers of large carry-overs possible because of the 1-fish daily limit. Browns make up less than 10 percent of the catch and are usually taken by fly fishermen at night. Very popular with float tubes and carryable car-top boats. No developed ramp. An aerial view of the lake is available from a lookout at Dry Falls Interpretive Center on

Dry Falls Lake.

Hwy. 17. The lake is open from April-Nov. and some of the best brown trout fishing occurs when the snow flies and the lunker spawners are cruising the shallows. There are some trout in here that will tow small boats, but they can be finicky. Crowded on opener.

DUSTY LAKE. A "pocket" lake of 30 acres, surrounded on 3 sides by basalt cliffs, on the Quincy Wildlife Area N. of I-90 and 7 miles SW of Quincy. Trail leads from Burke Lake about 0.5 miles to Dusty. Planted annually with about 10,000 rainbow fry and 2000 catchable browns and tiger trout. From Hwy. 28, 2 miles W. of Quincy, turn S. on T NW for 6 miles to trail at Burke Lake. Open Mar. 1-July 31, and peaks early.

EPHRATA LAKE. A barren 25 acre lake formed by irrigation seepage 4 miles NE of Ephrata. Drains to Rocky Ford Creek and Moses Lake.

EPHRATA PARK POND. A small kids-only pond in Ephrata stocked with about 1000 catchable rainbows.

EVERGREEN RESERVOIR. Recent introduction of tiger muskies has put an element of mystery in every strike at this popular Quincy WRA lake. Located a few hundred yards S. of Burke Lake, the reservoir covers 235 acres and is 1.5 miles long. It has 3 boat ramp sites and also supports walleye, largemouth bass, bluegill, perch, crappie and a few rainbow trout. Tiger muskies must be 36 inches to be kept. Winter ice fishermen target perch. Disabled access, WDFW ramp and year-round season.

FALCON LAKES. 5 small cattail ringed lakes immediately below O'Sullivan Dam covering about 15 acres. They are on the CNWR and accessible by scrambling down rip rap rocks or a steep hillside from access near W. end of O'Sullivan Dam. Planted with catchable rainbows and brook trout. Because of the difficult access these lakes sometimes escape the fishing pressure that hits the other seep lakes in March. A trail along an old roadbed connects the lakes on the E. side.

FLAT LAKE. A 98.2 acre irrigation-runoff lake about 6.5 miles S. from Quincy with largemouth bass.

GOLDENEYE LAKE. A CNWR rainbow

lake 0.5 mile S. of O'Sullivan Dam fed by Falcon Creek.

GLOYD SEEPS CREEK. In the past, plants of browns, brookies and rainbow have been made in this meandering, marshy stream. Planted only when WDFW has excess trout to stock. May have tiger trout.

GOOSE LAKES. A pair of large warm-water species lakes in the Seep Lakes S. of O'Sullivan Dam. **UPPER GOOSE,** 112 acres, is stocked with walleye, perch, large-mouth bass, brown bullhead and crappie and may support an occasional rainbow. An experimental Lahontan cutthroat stocking has been discontinued. There is a boat launch. Upper Goose is reached from O'Sullivan Dam Road, turning S. at E. end of dam. **LOWER GOOSE,** 50 acres, is separate but adjacent to Upper Goose. It also has a boat launch and is managed for largemouth bass and bluegills, but also supports black crappie, brown bullhead, perch and a few rainbow. Lower lake is accessed from McMannaman Road in Adams County.

"H" LAKE. A 7.2 acre lake 6.7 miles SW of Quincy on the Quincy WRA west of outlet to Stan Coffin Lake. Bass and bluegill. See Burke Lake for route.

HAMPTON LAKES. A pair of popular Mar. 1 opening trout lakes in the Seep Lakes. **UPPER HAMPTON LAKE,** 53 acres, and **LOWER HAMPTON,** 19 acres, plus a series of 6 smaller lakes covering 12 acres referred to as Hampton Sloughs. All are on CNWR and contain rainbow. The road from the E. end of the O'Sullivan dam leads to Upper Hampton. Fertile lakes where yearling plants grow to more than 13 inches by opener and carry-overs average 18 inches. Lower Hampton gets the lion's share of stocked trout, about 10,000 rainbows. In 1998 Upper produced a 10-pound, 13-oz. rainbow. No gasoline motors on either lake. Usually close July 31.

HATCHERY CREEK. A small creek at the Columbia Basin Hatchery near Moses Lakes planted with rainbow and brook trout. Open year round. From the hatchery to the confluence, open to juvenile and disabled license holders only. The rest of the stream, beginning May 1, is open under family fishing rules.

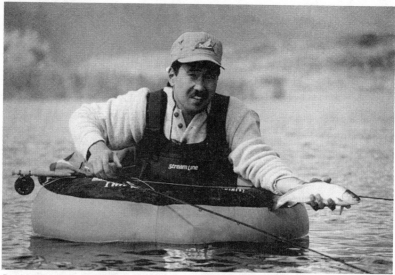

Lenice Lake.

HEART LAKE (See Canal Lake).

HERRON LAKES. Two small lakes adjacent to S. side of O'Sullivan Dam, 2000 feet N. of Goldeneye Lake. Each lake is planted with 200 brookies and 200 rainbows.

HOURGLASS LAKE. A 2 acre rainbow planted seep lake between Cattail and Sage Lakes on E. Canal Road below O'Sullivan Dam. Difficult access.

JUNE LAKE. A small, early season rainbow lake just N. of the CNWR Windmill Lake group.

LEMNA LAKE. Rainbow are stocked in this 3 acre lake in Pillar-Widgeon group. A Lahontan cutthroat program has been discontinued. 8.5 miles N. of Othello adjacent to W. shore of Shoveler Lake.

LENICE LAKE. The heart of a 3-lake walk-in group managed for quality fishing on lower Crab Creek just E. of the Columbia River town of Beverly. **MERRY** and **NUNNALLY** lakes are nearby. All open Mar-Oct, restricted to selective gear, and are among the state's most popular destinations for fly-fishing. Lenice covers 100-acres, Merry 40 and Nunnally 120, with a 40-acre arm sometimes called **BOBBY LAKE**. All are heavily stocked with rainbow, tiger and brown trout. These desert lakes are shallow and exception-

ally fertile, promoting quick growth and large trout with lots of carry-overs in the 15 to 20 inch range thanks to the selective tackle regulations. Fish to 6 pounds are not uncommon. All 3 were chemically rehabilitated in 2000 to eradicate an infestation of stunted sunfish and restocked with larger than average catchables and triploids. Much of the shoreline is encrusted with tule and cattail reeds, limiting shore casting. Best to bring a float tube, inflatable raft or carryable boat. The Crab Creek valley is a low, treeless furrow between Royal Slope and Saddle Mountains that connects the flat sun seared fields near Othello with the Columbia River S. of Vantage which can turn the valley (and lakes) into a wind tunnel. Expect lots of anglers early in the season, and lonesome tubing at the end which is when the biggest browns are usually caught. It's about 0.5 mile walk to Lenice from WDFW parking access on Crab Creek Beverly-Smyrna Rd. Lenice and Merry share a trailhead. The trail into Nunnally is 0.5 mile E.

LENORE LAKE. The state's first and still one of the best Lahontan cutthroat waters. Lenore is almost 5-miles long, narrow, covering 1670 acres between high basalt cliffs 4 miles N. of Soap Lake in the Grand Coulee chain of lakes. Its heavily alkaline waters support only Lahontans, originally imported from Pyramid Lake, NV which grow to trophy proportions. 10 pounders are caught, most average between 2 and 5 pounds. Season is Mar-Nov., but best action is nearly always early during the catch-and-release season Mar-May and late fall when the big trout are cruising the shoreline and near surface. Selective gear rules. Best from boats, but good catches are made casting from shore. The shallow S. end is a well known spring and fall bank fishing, and wading area. Good wade and cast or boat spots on N. end, too. Be aware of posted closures at the N. and S. ends. 4 WDFW access sites, 3 with rough boat launches. Hwy. 17 runs along the E. side of Lenore and provides roadside access. Wind can be a problem. There's a spawning channel at midlake on E. side if you want a close-up look at a big Lahontan that's not on your barbless hook.

LIND COULEE WASTEWAY. A long, rocky arm on the SE side of Potholes (O'Sullivan) Reservoir paralleled on the S. side by O'Sullivan Dam Road. A very good winter spot for large rainbows, some spring walleye, plus crappie, smallmouth bass and carp. Open year around. 2 WDFW launch sites off dam road. Accessible by boat from Potholes Reservoir. Lots of bank fishing from the rip rap rock road foundation, but limited parking.

LONG LAKE. A 75-acre seep lake on the irrigation canal adjacent to Soda Lake with fair fishing for walleye, large and smallmouth bass, perch, bluegill, crappie, lake whitefish and early season rainbow trout.

MALLARD LAKE. 8 acre CNWR lake with a few large and smallmouth bass, black

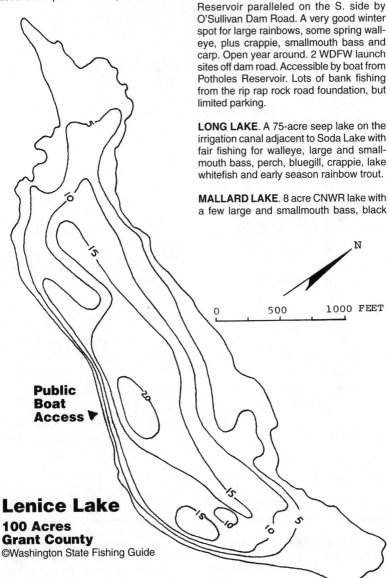

N

0   500   1000 FEET

**Public
Boat
Access ▼**

Lenice Lake
**100 Acres
Grant County**
©Washington State Fishing Guide

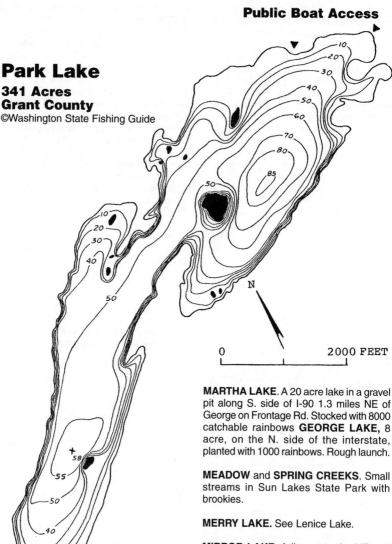

Public Boat Access

Park Lake
341 Acres
Grant County
©Washington State Fishing Guide

N

0   2000 FEET

MARTHA LAKE. A 20 acre lake in a gravel pit along S. side of I-90 1.3 miles NE of George on Frontage Rd. Stocked with 8000 catchable rainbows **GEORGE LAKE**, 8 acre, on the N. side of the interstate, planted with 1000 rainbows. Rough launch.

MEADOW and **SPRING CREEKS**. Small streams in Sun Lakes State Park with brookies.

MERRY LAKE. See Lenice Lake.

MIRROR LAKE. Adjacent to the NE end of Park Lake in Sun Lakes State Park. Mirror is a 4.5 acre lake lightly planted with rainbows and brookies.

MOSES LAKE. Covering 6815 acres, 38 feet deep in a long, narrow channel, crossed twice by I-90. Moses Lake is regaining some of its previous luster with a net-pen trout rearing project that sweetens the waters with thousands of fat rainbows, a very good April-June walleye fishery (some say the best around,) and recently a surge in 8 to 12 inch perch, partially offsetting a steady decline in largemouth and

crappie, bluegill, pumpkinseed, perch and brown bullhead. Drains to Crab Creek.

MARCO POLO LAKE. A 10-acre seep lake about 0.5 miles N. of North Windmill Lake in a rock-walled coulee. Planted with rainbow.

smallmouth bass, bluegills, and crappies. WDFW hopes to slow the drop with restrictive panfish limits.(see current regs.) Bass fishing is best in spring. The lake has a very large, and pretty well ignored, population of 2 to 3 pound lake whitefish that stage in huge spawning schools in spring. The city of Moses Lake is adjacent to Lewis Horn and Parker Horn arms of the lake and provides multiple ramps and parks that offer bank fishing and picnics. Access is available at countless city and state parks, and roadsides, marina and a resort. Winter fishing, especially for perch, is gaining popularity through the ice and from boats. S. of I-90 the lake filters through a puzzle of sand dunes into Crab Creek Channel of Potholes Reservoir on WDFW's Potholes Wildlife Area which is reached by going S. from Moses Lake on Potato Hill Rd. then W. on Sand Dunes Rd. The upper end of Moses Lake is fed by **ROCKY FORD CREEK**, a classic spring creek and the most productive big trout stream in the Columbia Basin. Follow Hwy. 17 N. to N. reaches or West Shore Road.

NORTHRUP LAKE. A heavily planted 3 acre rainbow lake 2.9 miles S. of Electric City in a coulee. Drains S. to Northrup Creek and Banks Lake. Walk-in access. Can be surprisingly good for its size.

NUNNALLY LAKE. See Lenice Lake.

PARA-JUVENILE LAKE. Southern tip of Para is in Adams County. The narrow, 12 acre lake is fed by the Hampton Lakes and has been planted with rainbow and Lahontan cutthroat. The Grant County portions are in the CNWR.

PARK LAKE. A very popular and productive natural lake covering 341 acres in the Sun Lakes chain in Grand Coulee about 6 miles SW of Coulee City. Hwy. 17 runs along the W. side The NE third of Park is within Sun Lakes State Park, and a road from the park follows the E. shore. Resort, camping, boat launch at park. Park Lake is heavily stocked with rainbow and brown trout fry that often reach 10 to 11 inches by opening day, plus catchable browns and lots of carryovers in the 14 to 16 inch range. Produces best in spring and early summer. Big opening weekend crowds but fishing holds up well because of the sheer number of stocked trout.

PERCH LAKE. A classic put-and-take lake on NE end of Sun Lakes State Park. 15 acre lake heavily planted with about 10,000 rainbows. Most planters are fished out within the first month of season. Boats must be carried in. Lots of good bank access. Nice spot to bring the kids.

PILLAR LAKE. A 9 acre seep lake on the CNWR, annually stocked with about 2000 rainbows. No longer stocked with Lahontan cutthroat. Lies just below Soda Lake on the E. Canal Road.

PIT LAKE. 40 acre rainbow lake below O'Sullivan Dam adjacent to the S. side of Potholes Canal opposite Canal Lake.

POTHOLES RESERVOIR (AKA O'SULLIVAN RESERVOIR) For most anglers, this 28,200-acre multi-species lake is the anchor for Columbia Basin fishing. Located between Moses Lake on the N. and Othello on the S. at the edge of the CNWR and popular Seep Lakes, Potholes supports large and smallmouth bass, perch, bluegill, black crappie, pumpkinseed, walleyes, carp and is planted with thousands of net-pen reared rainbows. Some of the 'bows caught here will hit 10 pounds, and there are an awful lot of 2 to 5 pounders. Trout fishing is good year-round. A fine winter fishery takes place off the shore at Medicare Beach along the reservoir's E. bank. For years this huge lake was famous for panfish, producing buckets of crappie and perch. These fisheries have deteriorated, and WDFW has put size and number restrictions in place to help recovery. Smallmouth and largemouth bass are doing well, and the net-pen project, in cooperation with Mar Don Resort, has breathed a lot of new life into this lake. The reservoir is impounded behind the rip-rap rock of O'Sullivan Dam (a good spot for crappie and smallmouth) impounding Crab Creek. Seepage through this dam is what creates the Seep Lakes. The N. side of the reservoir filters into ever-changing channels between thousands of Sand Dunes, flooding willows which are excellent habitat for largemouth bass and crappie in the spring. The reservoir in the circuit for many walleye and bass tournaments. The dunes are in WDFW's South Columbia Basin Wildlife Area and make a good place to base a boat camp. Crab Creek Channel is a great spot for spring walleyes. Unfortunately, by late summer many of these channels are dry or too low for boats and the lake may have a few weeks of algae bloom. All facilities are on the S. side of the lake. MarDon Resort is at the W. end of O'Sullivan Dam, Potholes State Park have camping and boat ramps. More boat ramps at Lind Coulee, at both ends of the dam and rough launches at Medicare Beach. MarDon Resort (509-346-2651) is the information and facility center for Potholes Reservoir and includes a store, restaurant, boat rentals and a very popular fishing dock.

PRIEST RAPIDS RESERVOIR. Created by Priest Rapids Dam across the Columbia River S. of the I-90/Vantage bridge. Hwy. 243 follows the E. bank and provides access. Hatchery at the dam and WDFW wildlife areas. Good ramp at the end of Road 26 SW between Desert Aire and Mattawa W. of Hwy. 243. About 59 percent of the 7700 acre pool is in Grant County, with 27% in Kittitas and 14% in Yakima County. It backs up to the foot of Wanapum Dam. The pool contains whitefish and migratory steelhead, salmon and warm water species including smallmouth bass (try the Crab Creek mouth in May-June) and a few walleye. Not one of the hottest Columbia River impoundments for fishermen.

QUINCY LAKE. 62 acres on the Quincy WRA area 7 miles S. of Quincy between Stan Coffin and Burke lakes. Stocked with about 15,000 catchable rainbow in February for the Mar. 1 opener, plus fry plant. Notoriously cold water, slow starter, with better fishing in Apr. WDFW ramp.

RAINBOW LAKE (Vic Myers). A man-made lake of 8 acres in Sun Lakes State Park, fed by seepage from Dry Falls Lake. Planted with brookies and rainbow. Best fishing in spring.

RED ROCK LAKE. A little-known 180-acre seep lake SE of Royal City that holds tiger muskies, largemouth bass, perch, pumpkinseeds, crappie and carp. Light fishing pressure. From Hwy. 26 turn S. on Red Rock Canyon Rd. toward Smyrna for 1.3 miles, then E. on rough road. Primitive boat launch and camping area. Outlet follows canyon road S. to Crab Creek.

ROCKY FORD CREEK. Washington's premier, if not most intensely fished, fly-fishing only spring creek. Open year-round, and widely known for its large, finicky rainbows. I doubt there's a day of the year when somebody isn't fishing this small

Rocky Ford Creek.

stream, flowing between basalt walls in a coulee E. of Ephrata. Only the upper mile is on WDFW land with unlimited streamside access (no boats or wading allowed). The middle 3 miles flow through private ranches and the lower 2 miles are barely marginal fishing before the creek flows into the N. end of Moses Lake. Fed by a cold spring the WDFW upper access is a magical mile where 24-inch rainbows fin in mossy runs. These fish get pounded by the best fly fishermen in the Northwest and are extremely selective. Some of the best fishing takes place while the snow is flying. Mid summer temperatures will broil anything wearing neoprene. Rocky Ford Creek leaped into statewide prominence in 1994 when 20,000 rainbow trout were donated by Trout Lodge, which operates a hatchery facility at the springs. Because of catch-and-release management many of those trout are still here and getting bigger. Handicap access, dock. From Hwy. 17 about 3.5 miles N. of Hwy. 282 turn E. on Road C NE.

ROUND LAKE. Private 110 acres 2 miles SW of Stratford. Largemouth bass and crappie.

SAGE LAKES. Two 5-acre lakes, one sometimes called Sago, in the seep lakes below O'Sullivan Dam located 200 feet apart and 500 feet NE of Long Lake. On the CNWR and planted annually with about 1000 rainbows, brown trout, and tiger trout.

SAND LAKE. Largemouth bass and bluegill are in this 28.4 acre lake in the sand dunes adjacent to N. side of Frenchman Hills Wasteway in WDFW Desert Wildlife

Areas. From the Hwy. 26 E. of Royal City, turn N. on Dodson Road to DWA.

SEEP LAKES. The Columbia Basin Seep Lakes area is one of the most intriguing, productive and unusual fishing areas in Washington. More than 50 lakes, ranging from less than one to more than 155 acres, are scattered across a rocky treeless plain, punctuated by basalt buttes in a maze of coulees, depressions, marshes and impoundments N. of Othello and S. of Potholes (O'Sullivan) Reservoir.

Almost all of this vast area is public land managed either as part of the Columbia National Wildlife Refuge (CNWR) or WDFW's Seep Lakes Wildlife Area. A few of the lakes in the extreme S. end near Hwy. 26 have private access. The lakes are connected by a network of dirt and gravel roads, trails and channels. There is primitive camping, boat launches at the larger lakes and not much else in the way of services. Many of the lakes open March 1 and are the traditional fishing season kick-off for hundreds of fishing families. Spring comes early to the Seep Lakes, and

dropping flies, lures and bait to willing trout and warmwater fish, then sleeping under the stars, wrapped in the scent of blooming sagebrush, listening to coyotes howl at the night, is not a bad way to start the year.

Some lakes are strictly trout, mostly rainbows, but others—especially the largest—carry a mixed bag of trout (some to 10 pounds), largemouth, smallmouth, walleyes and panfish. One of the most unusual fisheries is at the N. end of Soda Lake in March for spawning lake whitefish that can weigh several pounds.

The lakes are filled with seep water draining through the porous rip rap rocks impounding Potholes (O'Sullivan) Reservoirs and from Crab Creek which flows from Potholes through the center of the seep lake area before turning W. to the Columbia River. As a rule, most of the smaller lakes offer their best catches from Mar.- May and by early June are either too warm, weeded, or sunburned. The larger, deeper, mixed species lakes, however, will produce fish all summer. Fall is one of the best periods to fish. Crowds are down and

Seep Lake Directory

The following directory was prepared by Mike Meseberg of Mar-Don Resort, (509-346-2651) the major fishing supply, information, fishing report and accommodation center for the Seep Lakes. Mar-Don is at the W. side of Potholes Dam Road which is the primary access road to the Seep Lakes from the north. From the south use Hwy. 26 and McMannaman Road.

[Key: Handicapped access to Upper and Lower Teal, Long, North Corral, Upper Goose, Lyle, Thread, Herman, Windmill, Canal, Soda and Dike 1 (*) Drive-in access, (**) Walk-in access, *** Open year-round]

Seep Lakes

BLACK***(**) – walleye, bass, perch, crappie.
BLYTHE***(*) – rainbows, rough boat launch.
CAMPBELL – private lake, not open to public fishing
CANAL***(*) – rainbows, launch, handicapped fishing access and handicap toilet.
CATTAIL(**) – (in Pillar-Widgeon group) rainbows, open Mar. 1–March 31 and Sept. 1–Sept. 30
CHUKAR***(**) – (connected to Scaup) rainbows
CORRAL***(*) – rainbows, boat launch on north end with handicapped access.
CRESCENT***(*) – (on irrigation canal next to Long Lake) walleye, large and smallmouth bass, crappie, perch, rainbow, whitefish, bluegill. Rough boat launch.
DABBLER(**) – rainbow, open Mar. 1–July 31 (**)
FALCON***(**) – (3 lakes just below O'Sullivan Dam) rainbow (**)
GADWALL(**) – (in Pillar-Widgeon group) trout, open Mar. 1–31 and Sept. 1–30.
GOOSE, LOWER***(*) – largemouth bass, walleye, perch, crappie, rainbow, bluegill and cutthroat.

GOOSE, UPPER*(*)** – Rainbows, walleye, large and smallmouth bass, perch, bluegill and crappie.

HALFMOON(**) – rainbow and cutthroat trout open Mar. 1–Sept. 30.

HAMPTON, LOWER(*) – rainbows, no gasoline motors, open Mar. 1–July 31

HAMPTON, UPPER(**) – rainbows up to 26", no gasoline powered motors allowed, open Mar. 1–July 31.

HEART*(*)** – rainbows, triploids planted in 1998.

HERMAN*(**)** – rainbows, great lake to archery fish for carp.

HOURGLASS(**) – in Pillar-Widgeon group, trout, open Mar. 1–31 and Sept. 1–30.

HUTCHINSON(*) – all game fish, no gas motors, open Mar. 1–Sept. 30, rough launch.

JANET*(**)** – rainbow.

JUNE*(**)** – rainbow.

JUVENILE(**) – trout, anglers under 15 years only. Mar. 1–July 31

KATY*(**)** – rainbow.

LEMNA(**) – in Pillar-Widgeon group, rainbow, open Mar. 1–31-Sept. 30.

LOIS*(**)** – rainbow.

LONG*(*)** – (on irrigation canal) rainbows, walleye, large and smallmouth bass, crappie, perch, bluegill, whitefish.

LYLE*(*)** – rainbow and good bow and arrow fishing for carp.

MARCO POLO*(*)**–rainbow.

MARIE(**) – (AKA Hampton Sloughs) rainbow, open Mar 1–July 31.

MARSH UNIT 1 & 2 – Closed.

McMANNAMON*(**)** – rainbow and cutthroat, short walk.

MORGAN(**) – rainbow, cutthroat open Mar. 1–Sept. 30,

PARA(**) – trout, juvenile anglers under 15 years only, open Mar. 1–July 31.

PILLAR(**) – rainbow, open Mar. 1– 31 and Sept. 1–30

PIT*(**)** – rainbows.

POACHER(**) – in Pillar-Widgeon group, rainbow, open Mar. 1–31 and Sept. 1–30.

QUAIL*(**)** – rainbow, tiger trout, catch and release, fly fishing – artificial flies with a single barbless hook only, no motors.

SAGE*(**)** – rainbow, browns, tiger trout.

SAGO(**) – in Pillar-Widgeon group, rainbow, open Mar. 1–31 and Sept. 1–30.

SCAUP*(**)** – connected to Chukar, rainbow.

SHINER(*) – connected to Hutchinson, largemouth bass, bluegill, no gas motors, open Mar. 1–Sept. 30.

SHOOFLY*(**)** – largemouth bass, bluegill, perch but has tendency to winter kill.)

SHOVELER(**) – in Pillar-Widgeon group, rainbows, open Mar. 1–31 and Sept. 1 – 30.

SNIPE(**) – in Pillar-Widgeon group, rainbow, open Mar. 1–31 and Sept. 1–30.

SODA*(*)** – walleye, large and smallmouth bass, crappie, bluegill, perch, whitefish, large rainbows.

SUSAN*(*)** – rainbow, rough boat launch.

TEAL*(*)** – rainbows, small panfish.

THREAD*(*)** – (outlet of Lyle Lake) largemouth bass, perch, poor fishing for rainbows.

VIRGIN*(**)** – rainbows.

WARDEN & SOUTH WARDEN(*) – rainbows and browns. Open Mar. 1–July 31

WIDGEON(**) – rainbow, open Mar. 1–31 and Sept. 1–30.

WINDMILL*(*)** – rainbow, handicapped fishing access (*)

NORTH AND NORTH NORTH WINDMILL(**) - rainbow in both.

fish are active. Some of the approximately 30 year-round lakes are attracting ice fishermen. Quail Lake , a walk-in, is set aside for fly-fishing.

Miles of excellent bank fishing opportunities and small waters, especially those with walk-in access, are perfect for float tubes and other portable craft. Rough launches for trailerable boats at many of the larger lakes. Check current WDFW regs for tackle and outboard motor restrictions and season changes.

SHOVELER LAKE. A 6 acre rainbow planted seep lake in CNWR 400 feet NW of Widgeon Lake.

SODA LAKE. Largest and one of the most diverse of the seep lakes below O'Sullivan Dam, connected to Potholes Canal. Soda covers 180 acres, and supports crappie, walleye, lake whitefish, large and smallmouth bass, bluegill, perch, brown bullhead catfish, a few brookies, and quite a few rainbow, some to 8 pounds. Very good for 1 to 3 pound lake whitefish early spring-fall. Turn S. 1 mile from E. end of O'Sullivan Dam. Road parallels W. shoreline. Lots of open bank fishing access, but best catches usually go to those with small boats or float tubes. Wind can be a factor. Two access areas, primitive camping, rough launches, year-round season. Adjacent **LONG LAKE**, 75 acres, supports the same species.

STAN COFFIN LAKE. 41 acres on West Potholes WRA. Holds largemouth bass, black crappie, bluegill, perch, walleye, and brown bullhead. Boat launch.

SPRING LAKES. Two small private rainbow lakes 100 feet apart about 500 feet W. of Crystal Lake. No access.

STRATFORD LAKE. See Brook Lake.

SUSAN LAKE. A 20 acre seep lake in a rocky-coulee, Susan is annually planted with rainbows that reach 8 top 12 inches on Mar. opener. Turn S. from O'Sullivan Dam Road 3 miles from E. end of dam, and drive 2 dusty miles to marked right turn. Primitive camping on bluff above lake, rough road to lakeside. Lots of bank access, best fished from small boats.

TEAL LAKES. North 22.5 acres and South Teal 28 acres lakes are on CNWR. Planted with rainbows. The lower reach of South Teal is in Adams County.

THOMPSON LAKE. 13.6 acres near the center of Steamboat Rock peninsula jutting into the E. side of Banks Lake. Supports largemouth bass, black crappie and perch. Turn W. from Hwy. 155 to Steamboat Rock State Park.

TICK LAKE. A small pond annually stocked with about 300 rainbows.

TRAIL LAKE. This 6 acre lake is actually a somewhat hazardous wide spot in Main Canal, holds crappie, perch and walleye. About 3 miles S. of Coulee City.

VIRGIN LAKE. 20 acre seep lake 0.5 mile E. of North Windmill Lake. Rainbow.

WANAPUM RESERVOIR. A 14,680 acre impounded Columbia River pool behind Wanapum Dam 28 miles E. of Ellensburg. Crossed by I-90 bridge at Vantage. Marginal fishing value. Migratory steelhead and salmon are off limits here. Fair white sturgeon fishing near Rock Island Dam, some smallmouth and walleye. Excellent boat ramps at Vantage, rough launch on E. side of bridge, at Crescent Bar. Because of the sheer canyon walls which sometimes fall more than 100 feet to the water, there is a little bank fishing opportunity, and little boat pressure because of the marginal rewards. It is, however, a great place for lonesome boat camping on the Colockum WRA. Be prepared for stiff winds.

WARDEN LAKE. Two large trout lakes on the NE side of the seep lakes area SE of O'Sullivan Dam. Both lakes are heavily stocked with rainbow and brown trout, a mix of fry and catchables, that provide 10-inch fish on the Mar. 1 opener. Cold air temperatures, historically, slow the opening bite and extend the productive season into spring. Warden covers 211 acres, and South Warden 24 acres. Just E. of the end of Lind Coulee, O'Sullivan Dam Road passes near the N. end of Warden Lake. Boat ramp on N. side of Warden. Several dirt access roads.

WIDGEON LAKE. 10 acres between Sago and Upper Hampton Lakes below O'Sullivan dam. Rainbows.

WILLIAMS LAKE. 11-acre lake at the head of Dry Coulee about 8 miles SW of Coulee City. No public access when water level is low. Largemouth bass, bluegill.

WILLOW LAKES. An enlargement of Crab Creek, South Willow is 39.4 acres and offers black crappie, pumpkinseed, perch, brown bullhead and is sometimes planted with rainbow trout. About 6.5 miles SE of Soap Lake. **NORTH WILLOW** holds the same species as Willow.

WINCHESTER WASTEWAY RESERVOIR. An enlargement of Winchester Wasteway in WDFW's North Columbia Basin Wildlife Area. Poor for largemouth bass, possibly a few crappie, bluegill and perch. Two access areas on Winchester WRA. Drive N. from George on Hwy. 283 to Road 5 NW, then E. for 4 miles. Outlet flows SE through Desert WRA and series of ponds which empty into SW side of Potholes Reservoir near state park. The Wasteway is crossed by Dodson Road and is gaining favor as a canoe route from I-90 SE through the South Columbia Basin Wildlife Area to the reservoir.

WINDMILL LAKES. A chain of 3 rainbow seep lakes in the CNWR near Heart and Canal lakes. Windmill, 33 acres, **NORTH WINDMILL**, 20 acres, and **NORTH NORTH WINDMILL**, 4 acres. All are fry planted. Windmill has handicap access, others are walk-in (See Canal Lake).

Grant County Resorts

Banks Lake: Coulee Playland, 509-633-2671. Steamboat Rock State Park, 509-633-2325. Big Wally's, 509-632-5504.

Blue Lake: Coulee Lodge, 509-632-5565. Blue Lake Resort, 509-632-5364. Laurent's Sun Village Resort, 509-632-5664.

Moses Lake: Perch Point Resort & Store, 509-766-9447. Big Sun RV Resort, 509-765-8294. Moses Lake Tourism, 1-800-992-6234

Potholes (O'Sullivan) Reservoir: Mar-Don Resort, 509-765-5061. O'Sullivan Sportsman Resort, 509-346-2447.

Chad Sheely fly fishing for Susan Lake rainbows (Sheely photo).

Grays Harbor County
WDFW Region 6
Washington Department of Fish and Wildlife, 48 Devonshire Rd. Montesano, WA 98563-9618. Phone 360-249-4628

Divided by the broad Chehalis River Valley and wedged between the Pacific Ocean and rolling mounds of heavily clear-cut foothills, Grays Harbor County offers a mix of salt and fresh water fishing ranging from beaver pond cutthroat to backwater bass, sturgeon to salmon, rockfish to halibut, surf perch to several respectable steelhead rivers.

The county is home to Washington's largest commercial charter boat fleet at Westport, a bony shadow of its heyday when dozens of 6 and 12 man boats competed for dock space. Only a few of the big charters boats are berthed here now, but it's still a fine place to start a memorable fishing trip. Westport boats work the top chinook salmon spots on the coast, and deliver excellent coho fishing when seasons are opened. Boats also run for halibut, rockfish, ling cod and albacore tuna. The boat basin and adjoining 85 square miles of Grays Harbor have their own lists of fishing and crabbing opportunities, and miles of ocean beaches offer highly coveted razor clams and wildly ignored surf fishing. Unfortunately, WDFW has abandoned a sport-fishing program that saw dozens of small ponds in the county stocked with cutthroat.

The county covers 1921 square miles. The north county is foothills rising into the Olympic Mountains. The south county slopes into the Willapa Hills, and the east county runs into the Black Hills outside of Olympia. Highest elevation is 4965 feet near the headwaters of the Wynoochee River. The ocean reaches the coastline in long roller waves that break over gradually declining shallows leading to sandy beaches that vary from narrow strips to large flats humped with low grassy dunes. Beach driving is allowed in some areas.

Of the 122 lakes officially listed for the county few are large, but there are some excellent beaver ponds for bushwhackers willing to explore small streams. The folds and ridges in Duck Lake just a long cast from the ocean are almost a big bass secret, and with the decline of salmon and steelhead runs, WDFW has put more effort into stocking trout lakes periodically throughout the season.

Anadromous winter and summer steelhead, coho, chinook and chum salmon, and sea-run cutthroat may be caught in the Chehalis, (along with some prime white sturgeon), Satsop, Wynoochee, Humptulips, Wishkah, Hoquiam, Quinault and North rivers. Small streams draining directly into the ocean often attract fall sea-run cutthroat.

With a few exceptional days, temperatures are moderate, (you can fish every day of the year) the climate is maritime and wet (between 85 and 128 inches of rain), although late summer days can be spectacularly blue and sunny.

South of Olympic National Forest there is little public-owned land, but huge tracts owned by timber companies are generally open to the public, although fees may be required in some areas. Intensive logging efforts have left the back country with a spider web complex of gravel road access. Except for along the major highway arterials, the county is lightly populated. Aberdeen is the largest city with 16,700 residents plus 9000 in adjoining Hoquiam, 3500 in Montesano and 2055 in Westport.

Major highways into the county almost all point to Aberdeen and include US 101 which arrives from the N. and continues through the western part of the county to Raymond on Willapa Bay. The major route from Washington's population centers is Hwy. 8, a fairly straight multi-lane route between US 101 at Aberdeen and I-5 at

Olympia. This limited access freeway crosses nearly all of the county's major steelhead and salmon rivers. US 12 joins Hwy. 8 at Elma and continues jointly to Aberdeen. Hwy. 105 winds along the S. shore of Grays Harbor through Westport and on down the coast to Willapa Bay. Hwy. 109 runs from Hoquiam N. along a chain of ocean beaches, a popular road with razor clam diggers. US 12 cuts across the SE corner of the county following the upper Chehalis River between I-5 and Hwy. 8.

ABERDEEN LAKE. A stocked and popular 64 acre lake on the outskirts of Aberdeen formed by Van Winkle Creek and water piped from the Wynoochee River. Planted with 14,000 rainbows, 10 to 14 inches, in April and May for the general opener, plus holds cutthroat. Always crowded on opening day. Best in late April, early May and October. City of Aberdeen has a park on the lake. 2 miles E. of Aberdeen and W. of Central Park turn N. from US 12/Hwy. 8 at hatchery sign and continue .05 mile to lake. Park boat launch.

BEAVER CREEK. Cutthroat have been planted in beaver ponds along this small stream which joins Joe Creek 0.5 miles from Pacific Ocean at Pacific Beach State Park. Ocean Beach Road follows lower stretches.

BLACK CREEK. A marshy stream with difficult access that enters Wynoochee River 2.5 miles upstream from US 12/Hwy./ 8 bridge. Turn NE from Wynoochee Valley Road to follow creek upstream. Holds native cutthroat.

BLACK RIVER (See Thurston County).

CARLISLE LAKES. Group of 5 cutthroat lakes in marshy area ranging from 0.7 to 4 acres. They are 2.5 miles N. of Copalis Crossing.

CEDAR CREEK. A Chehalis River tributary, joining 3 miles NW of Oakville. The small creek produces cutthroat in May and June. A road leads E. from US 12 upstream for about 2 miles.

CHEHALIS RIVER. A broad, deep powerful flow the Chehalis is the county's largest river and the arterial that anadromous fish travel from the ocean to dozens of inland rivers and streams. The Chehalis provides the second largest spawning system in the state behind the Columbia, with 1400 rivers and creeks in its drainage. It supports a tantalizing variety of sport fish including chinook, coho and chum salmon, winter and summer steelhead, sea-run cutthroat, largemouth bass, panfish, white sturgeon and even a few American shad. The Chehalis forms near I-5 in Lewis County flows through the Chehalis Valley to empty into Grays Harbor at Aberdeen. Along the way it collects the Wynoochee, Satsop, Wishkah, Black and Newaukum rivers. Nearly the entire river is followed by good roads that provides easy bank fishing and boat accesses. In the Oakville vicinity there river is stream-like, wadeable in many areas with lots of riffles and pools. From Elma downstream the river is tidal influenced and below Montesano the river is fat with tributary drainage, wide, sullen, deep, murky and the shores are pocked with pilings from old log rafts.

The river is open year-round and there's nearly always a game fish to challenge. The slough-like mouth of the Chehalis between Cosmopolis and the mouth of the Wynoochee produces sturgeon which hit best in July, February and March. Concentrate on the deeper slots at sweeping bends or creek mouths, using smelt, sand shrimp or shad for bait. Night fishing is very popular in summer. There

Chehalis River chinook and coho.

are a few Columbia River style "oversizers" in the 8 foot range, but most of the Chehalis sturgeon run smaller and the chances of catching a legal slot fish are pretty good.

Sloughs and eddies in this lower section also hold a little-fished population of large largemouth bass that bite well from June through September. June and July is when shad spawn in the shallow, easily waded upper river above Oakville. Starting in mid-August through early September a large run of fall chinook salmon moves into the lower river. A run of spring chinook hits in March and April. In mid-September and October coho return some headed for a net pen rearing site at 28th St. Landing just west of the Port of Grays Harbor Dock and others headed upstream to the Wynoochee and Satsop. Coho are in the river beginning in mid-September sometimes into January. The late return is mostly Satsop River fish, a late run of larger than average coho that in 1986 included the 23 lb., 8 oz. state record. The Nov./Dec. coho run takes place at about the same time as a chum salmon run, also headed for the Satsop which delivered the state record 25 lb., 10 oz. chum in 1988. Both record breakers came up the Chehalis. The chum run in fact, is earning a lot of attention during these years of low coho and chinook returns. Troll or cast green plugs or green yarn drift gear for dog salmon especially near the mouth of the Satsop. Once a fair steelhead river, the Chehalis steelhead run has hit hard times, now delivering as few as 200 winter-runs and a dozen or so summer-runs. The Chehalis River system produces upwards of 1500 winter and 1300 summer steelhead, but almost all are caught in the tributaries. Chehalis plunkers take most of the river's fish and most of those in March, with a few in December and January. Plunking is popular from Elma downstream.

Aberdeen fishermen have been getting a shot in the arm from a WDFW program of planting sea-run cutthroat in the extreme low intertidal area where fishing can be very good on an incoming tide near the sloughs and creek mouths. Sea-run cutthroat fishing often starts in July at mouth of Satsop River and downstream and remains good into fall. Trolling spinners and worms close to the Chehalis River's brushy banks is effective. The Chehalis also lends itself to drift hunting for ducks. Lots of ramps. Some of the most popular are at the US 101 bridge, in Cosmopolis, near mouth of Wynoochee,

from Satsop River Brady Loop access just S. of US 12/Hwy. 8 bridge, and in the skinny water at Porter, Cedarville, and bank skids near Oakville. Prop boats okay below Montesano.

CHEHALIS RIVER POTHOLES, PONDS. The banks of the lower Chehalis often flood, leaving potholes on private property that hold a mix of trout, largemouth bass, and perch. Ponds on the WDFW Chehalis Wildlife Area off Schouweiler Road near Elma offer largemouth bass, crappie and perch along with a few trout. Gravel walking paths follow the bank of the Elma ponds making it a good place to take the kids.

CHENOIS CREEK. A cutthroat stream entering North Bay at Chenois Creek settlement. Crossed by Powell Road near mouth. Beaver ponds along the creek hold cutthroat.

CLOQUALLUM CREEK. A small stream with steelhead and cutthroat joining the Chehalis River 1 mile upstream from South Elma. US 12 crosses Cloquallum at Elma's S. city limits, and a road, with shoulder access, parallels the creek upstream. Fall best for cutthroat, December and January top steelheading.

COPALIS RIVER. A small stream flowing across the sand into the Pacific Ocean at Copalis Beach. Access is tough upstream from the ocean. Can be fair for cutthroat from July through October. Holds a few winter steelhead.

COOK CREEK. Tributary to East Fork Satsop. Adjacent beaver ponds receive some trout plants. East Satsop Road crosses creek about 6 miles above US 12/Hwy. 8.

DAMON LAKE. A cutthroat planted lake of 15.7 acres 2 miles E. of Copalis Crossing. Drains to Humptulips River.

DECKER CREEK. Enters East Fork Satsop just below Schafer Park.

DELAZINE CREEK. A small, brushy tributary to the Chehalis River which provides good cutthroat fishing from July into October. Road to Weikswood leaves Chehalis River 2 miles E. of South Elma and follows creek about 8 miles. Difficult to fish.

DISCOVERY LAKES (Klone Lakes). Series of 3 cutthroat lakes of 2 to 5 acres on

Discovery Creek 8.7 miles NE of Grisdale. Drains to Wynoochee River. Elev. 3200 feet.

DUCK LAKE (Oyhut). A surprisingly under-recognized warmwater and trout fishery on the spit at Ocean Shores. Lake covers 3.5 miles, 450 acres on N. side of entrance to Grays Harbor. Fair for 3000 April-planted cutthroat and rainbow, and very good sum-mer fishery for largemouth bass to 7 pounds, black crappie and bluegill. Lots of brush and tree cover and this lake rarely gets the fishing pressure it deserves. Per-fect for cartop boats. Open year-round. Two public access areas.

ELK RIVER. A sea-run cutthroat stream that comes on early in the summer and again in fall. The stream is about 1.5 miles W. of Ocosta. Also has received winter steelhead plants. The river flows into a large saltwater bay that flows under Hwy. 105 into Grays Harbor near Westport. Turn S. from Hwy. 105 at Park's Store, drive about 0.5 miles to a point adjacent to the South Bay duck club. Boat fish for bay sea-runs on incoming tide.

FAILOR LAKE. A stocked, popular artificial lake, 60 acres, formed by a dam on Deep Creek. Stocked with about 10,000 rainbows in April, including large Triploids. Very popu-lar on opening weekend. Failor is 13 miles N. of Hoquiam on US 101 and then about 3 miles W. on a gravel road. Watch for sign on US 101. Produces primarily in April and May. Public boat launch site.

GRAYS HARBOR. A large, protected bay, shallow outside of the dredged shipping channel. The bay extends from the ocean jetties at Westport to Aberdeen. Most fishiermen target salmon during special seasons opened near Westport and near Aberdeen's 28th Street Landing to harvest net-pen reared salmon. When a season is opened, there can be some very excit-ing September and October herring troll-ing for chinook and coho just inside the Westport bar. Launch ramps in Westport at US Coast Guard Station, John's River mouth of Hwy. 105 and in Aberdeen near US 101 bridge. The mile-long South Jetty near Westport and shorter North Jetty near Ocean Shores also offer some great fish-ing experiences. Many anglers hike out on the broken rocks (or run their boats close) to cast plastic worms and leadhead jigs for black rockfish and ling cod. Lings

are best in spring when they move inshore to spawn. **South Jetty** is best for rockfish and salmon. Clamber out on the broken rocks and fish the inside. The ocean side gets pounded with powerful waves that have floated jetty fishermen. Smart fish-ermen are off the jetty by dark. Walking these angled broken slabs of granite at night is a good way to disappear. Salmon fishermen ease out onto the jetties to sus-pend plug cut or whole herring beneath grapefruit size bobbers, weighted with a few ounces of banana sinker. The rig is cast into the white froth line that parallels the jetty. They are surprisingly success-ful. The harbor is shallower inside the **North Jetty** where anglers may catch some exceptionally large starry sole, floun-ders, surf perch, greenling and a stray salmon. Rocks on the jetty hold ling cod, greenling and black rockfish that are suck-ers for plastic worm/jig rigs. The perch and flatfish prefer small baits like sand shrimp, clam necks, or bits of crab on an incom-ing or high slack tide. Net pen salmon rear-ing projects in the boat basins at Ocean Shores and Westport have developed popular Sept.-Nov. coho and chinook fish-eries in the boat basins. Some of the smaller streams feeding into the mid-bay through the grassy hummocks off Hwy. 105 offer sea-run cutthroat on incoming tides, especially in spring and fall. Check the regs for wild cutthroat release rules or minimum size and possession limits.

GRISDALE POND. A small cutthroat pond 5.4 miles from former Camp Grisdale logging community on the upper Wynoochee River.

HOQUIAM RIVER. Flows into Grays Har-bor at Hoquiam. US 101 follows much of the West Fork and main stem, and E. Hoquiam Road goes up the East Fork about 15 miles to headwaters in Olympic Wildlife Area. A WDFW boat launch is near the head of East Fork tide water. The Hoquiam produces a couple of dozen hatchery winter steelhead in December and January, fall chinook, coho and chums and sea-run cutthroat from July into Nov. WDFW stocks sea-run cutts which are fin clipped and legal. Wild cutts and steelhead must be released. Lots of slow tidal water, perfect for canoes or small outboard boats. Try tiny bits of sand shrimp or clam necks around the piling rows near the mouth for saltwater perch and flounders.

Humptulips River.

HUMPTULIPS RIVER. Once a top steelhead river producing a thousand or more winter fish the Hump now produces less than 200 steelhead and is best known for salmon and sea-run cutthroat. June is best for hatchery summer-run steelhead and Dec. and Jan. for winter-runs. Jan. is best steelhead month in the forks. A hatchery ensures good to excellent salmon fishing. Gets runs of hatchery fall chinook (many in the 40-plus range) , coho, chum salmon and sea-run cutthroat between Sept. and Dec. Hatchery at Stevens Creek. Slab kings just a few miles from saltwater test tackle into Nov. which is also the peak of the coho and chum action. The Hump enters North Bay in Grays Harbor NW of Hoquiam and is crossed near mouth by Hwy. 109. A road from the bridge heads upstream along E. bank. Copalis Crossing Road follows W. bank to US 101 at Humptulips. Excellent sea-run cutthroat angling from July into October in both East and West Forks. Several rough boat launches above US 101 and off Copalis Crossing Road. Bank fishing, too.

JOE CREEK. Flows into ocean at Pacific Beach State Park on Hwy. 109. Fall fishing for stocked sea-run cutts and salmon.

JOHNS RIVER. A wide, marshy tidal area on Hwy. 105 between Westport and Aberdeen marks where this fragmented stream pours into Grays Harbor. Primarily a sea-run cutthroat stream, but stocked with a very few winter steelhead and coho salmon. Johns River Road parallels the W. bank about 7 miles. A WDFW waterfowl hunting area offers a boat launch 400 feet upstream from Hwy. 105 bridge where small boat fishermen can launch and troll in late summer and fall for planted sea-run cutthroat. Limited cutthroat fishing in stream above tide water.

KLONES LAKES. Three small lakes at 3200 feet elev. above Wynoochee Reservoir, ranging from 2 to 9 acres. Occasionally planted with trout. Open year-round. Bring the hiking boots.

MILL CREEK POND. A juvenile-only pond in Cosmopolis. Stocked with trout and open year-round.

MOCLIPS RIVER. A fall sea-run cutthroat stream flowing into the ocean at Moclips. Roads follow at varying distances but access is not easy. Ocean beach is an outstanding razor clam area.

NORTH RIVER. Begins and ends in Pacific County, but makes a big swing into Grays Harbor County. North is stocked with steelhead but returns are poor. Steelheaders annually take less than 50 fish mostly in Dec. and Jan. Best known for sea-run cutthroat and jack salmon fishing. Lots of logs and brush in logged upper reaches. Crossed by US 101 at Artic about 15 crow-miles from its mouth. In Pacific County, Hwy. 105 skirts the N. shore of Willapa Bay, and crosses the mouth where there is a WDFW boat launch. North is best fished for cutts and salmon late July through Oct. by boating upstream from mouth about 4 miles to falls.

OCEAN SHORES BEACH, NORTH JETTY. Sand drift has formed long gradually deepening shallow beaches with marginal fishing opportunities on this spit that separates the NW side of Grays Harbor from the ocean. Bayside boat access at Marine View Dr. near WDFW Oyhut Wildlife Area. Beach casting for redtail surf perch, starry flounders, sole on both sides. Best bet is to fish N. jetty rocks in the spring and summer for ling cod, black rockfish, cabezon and several varieties of sea perch. Sept. and Oct. brings coho and chinook salmon opportunities. Trollers work inside Buoy 13. Jetty fishermen cast herring suspended below floats, Buzz Bombs or bright salmon jigs. Fair Aug. through Jan. coho fishery in the boat basin for fish returning to net pen release areas. Although Ocean Shores is surrounded by salt water possibly the best fishing bet is in the freshwater of **DUCK LAKE.**

PACIFIC BEACHES. Excellent razor clam digging and surf perch fishing from Ocean Shores N. to Moclips. Beach casting into incoming tides with pyramid sinkers and small baits (sand shrimp, clam neck pieces) is very productive for redtail surf perch, but few anglers take advantage of it. Dungeness and red rock crabbing and light-tackle fishing for pile and striped perch in lagoons along NW shore of Grays Harbor in late spring and summer.

POPE LAKES. Lakes of 3 and 7 acres 4 miles SW of US 101 bridge across Quinault Lake outlet. Drains to Quinault River.

PORTER CREEK. Sea-run cutthroat are in this upper Chehalis River tributary which enters at Porter NW of Oakville on Hwy. 12.

PRAIRIE CREEK. Crossed by US 10l about 1 mile W. of Lake Quinault. It heads under Higley Peak on the Grays Harbor-Jefferson County line. Possibly a few winter steelhead, some sea-run cutts.

QUINAULT LAKE. A beautiful, horribly under fished, 3729 acre natural lake surrounded by rain forest on the Quinault Nation Reservation 37 miles N. of Aberdeen and about 0.5 miles E. of US 101. Encircled by a paved road (watch for elk) and serviced by a stately lodge, plus two FS campgrounds, the lake offers cutthroat (some very large), Dolly Varden (they are legal here and very large), kokanee salmon and even a stray steelhead, and a special run

of sockeye salmon. For my money, the best bet is in the spring and fall trolling large greenish spoons or minnow-shaped plugs for Dollies that can reach 10 pounds. Most cutthroat are less than 2 pounds and fall to trollers using small wobbling spoons like Dick Nites, McMahons, and Needlefish. Kokanee salmon tend to collect in dense deep schools and locating them (bring a good depth finder) is 90 percent of the battle. Fishing is regulated by the tribe, and tribal fishing permits are available at nearby stores in Amanda Park and along S. shore. Two FS campgrounds on S. shore. Much of N. shore is in Olympic National Park, with campground at July Creek near E. end of lake.

QUINAULT RIVER. Flowing out of Olympic National Park (where it's managed by ONP), through national forest (where it's managed by WDFW) into and out of Lake Quinault (where it's managed by the Quinault Indian Nation), this is a complicated river with excellent access and better than average steelhead and wild trout fishing potential. The lower river is heavily stocked with winter steelhead by the Quinaults and is famous for delivering huge steelhead (15 to 25 pounders). Most steelhead are caught in Dec. and Jan. but the biggest fish arrive in Feb. and Mar. This excellent steelhead fishery however, requires that non-tribal anglers hire and fish with tribal guides. The upper river is a trout stream that flows into the E. end of Lake Quinault and is followed upstream by South Shore Road to Graves Creek Campground. A really hazardous section to boat, with bank fishing access. A few native summer and winter steelhead are caught between the lake and ONP boundary, but most anglers are after trout—many of which are feisty young native steelhead. Rainbows from 7 to 15 inches, Dolly Varden and whitefish are available by poking through the woods from the S. Shore Road. July through September is tops for summer steelhead around Graves Creek. Trails lead upstream from Graves Creek Camp along river into ONP Enchanted Valley, and up North Fork to ONP Low Divide from North Fork Campground. The upper stream is ultra clear, fast and tough to fish.

RAFT RIVER. Creek size where US 10l crosses the upper river, but gains volume in lower reaches through Quinault Indian Nation. Supports steelhead, cutthroat and several species of salmon. Rough Road

1700 heads W. 1.4 miles S. of Queets River on US 10l. It's 5.9 miles through reservation to end of road which dead ends at derelict logging bridge. The Raft enters ocean at Tunnel Island. Tribal fishing permit required on reservation.

SATSOP LAKES. A cluster of 5 lakes (2 are prominent) varying from 2 to 4 acres at 2500 feet elev. about 6 miles NE of Grisdale. Numerous logging roads in this area. From FS 22 at Wynoochee Lake turn NE on FS 2222 a forest trail leads 0.4 mile to lakes which are stocked with brookies, rainbow and cutthroat. Bring a raft.

SATSOP RIVER. This small but drift boatable river has it all: winter steelhead, state record coho and chum salmon, chinook, and sea-run cutthroats. The river flows under US 12 into the Chehalis River about 3 miles S. of Satsop. Both banks are followed upstream by East Satsop and Middle Satsop roads. In the last few years the Satsop steelhead run has crashed, and winter steelheaders now catch only about 50 fish a year, most in Feb. Salmon fishermen still flock here in good numbers in early winter to load the freezer with hatchery cohos and chums. Satsop supports a good run of coho salmon from early Oct. into Feb. with anglers trying to break the 23-lb., 8-oz. record set in 1986. The biggest silvers arrive after Christmas. The river also has a good and popular chum salmon run in Dec. and Jan. and holds that state record, too, with a 25-lb., 10-oz. caught in 1988. Most salmon fishermen hit the East Fork from Schafer State Park downstream. The West Fork is often colored during winter concentrating most fishing pressure on the East Fork and main river. Roadside skid launches at several spots and a good and popular launch at Schafer State Park. Many floaters take out at Brady Loop Road access at US 12 bridge. Brady is also a good access for drifting 1-mile down and into the nearby Chehalis River. This is a very nice river for drift boaters. Sea-run cutts usually come in with salmon runs and can be a lot of fun for light tackle anglers casting to troughs with overhanging brush or in the first mile or so above the Chehalis. Special regulations may be in effect.

SHYE LAKE. 9 acres 12 miles NW of Hoquiam and a short distance S. from Copalis Crossing. Holds cutthroat. Drains to Humptulips River.

STUMP LAKE. Brushy 23.2 acres 7.5 miles E. of Elma in old creek channel. The lake is filled with wood debris. Holds rainbow and cutthroat. Stocked with 3000 rainbows, some 14 inches or larger, in Mar. and Apr. Drains into Cloquallum Creek.

SYLVIA LAKE. A popular heavily stocked 32 acre, 45-foot deep lake 1 mile N. of Montesano, formed by a dam on Sylvia Creek. Annually planted with 5500 catchable rainbow and cutthroat. Produces best in April and May, restocked for June's free fishing weekend, and comes on again in Sept. Surplus winter steelhead and largemouth bass occasionally spice the fishery. State park camping, boat launch. Open year-round.

VANCE CREEK LAKE AKA ELMA PONDS. Three narrow lakes covering 9 acres 1.5 miles SW of Elma in lower Vance Creek. Stocked with rainbows and largemouth bass. Pond 1 (reserved for juveniles) is sometimes stocked with adult coho salmon in late fall. Developed, handicap access, WDFW and park areas. Beaver ponds along the stream have wild rainbows.

WILLABY CREEK. A trickle of winter steelhead stream flowing into **LAKE QUINAULT** at Willaby Campground on Quinault Shore Road.

WESTPORT. Home of Washington's largest ocean charter boat fleet for spring and summer rockfish, ling cod, spring halibut, late summer salmon and albacore tuna. Tuna come within charter boat range (50 to 150 miles) in late Aug. and early Sept. No limits on tuna and it can be a red hot memory maker. Boat basin ramp provides trailerable boat access to sometimes excellent Sept./Oct. coho salmon fishery inside mouth of Grays Harbor. Net pen rearing project in boat basin supports a popular, but concentrated and sometimes congested dock and bank coho fishery Oct.-Jan. Productive perch fishing, crabbing (star traps popular) from boat basin docks and pilings. Long public fishing pier extends from end of Revetment Drive into Grays Harbor. Rock revetments protecting boat basin are good places to throw plastic worms for black rockfish and ling cod, and dangle baited hooks for striped and pile perch. Rockfishing is sometimes best after dark, especially on an incoming tide. Halfmoon Bay, a sandy curve of beach between the tourists district and mile-long

South Jetty is a good place to beach cast stillfish rigs for redtail surf perch. Use flat or pyramid sinkers, No. 6 bait hooks and small shrimp baits (For **South Jetty** fishing see **Grays Harbor**). Excellent boat launch into protected boat basin at US Coast Guard Station. During the heyday of April-Sept. salmon fishing, Westport billed itself as "The Salmon Capitol Of The World," and was a buzzing hub with a marina packed with 50-foot charter boats and a waiting list for available slips. Collapse of the coastal salmon fishery has whittled the fleet down to less than a couple of dozen boats, but it's still a great place to fish and spend a weekend fishing, crabbing, boating and beach fun. Mar-Sept. charter bottomfishing for rockfish and ling cod is nearly always outstanding and limits are common, and when a summer salmon season is approved, this is the best place on the coast to find lots of chinook and limits of coho. This is also the most northerly port for boats running to blue water in the Japanese Current for albacore tuna in late summer. Westport Charter Boat Assoc. can provide lists of charter services. Some motels offer graveled RV camping, and nearby Grayland Beach and Twin Harbors state parks for tents. Lots of motels, resort services.

WISHKAH RIVER. A fair coho salmon, sea-run cutthroat and poor winter steelhead river that joins the Chehalis River at Aberdeen. Roads from Aberdeen go up both banks, and W. side road hugs the river and continues to headwaters. Best for hatchery sea-run cutthroat (wild cutt release) from late July through Nov. Winter steelhead catches have fallen to about 50 fish a winter, most in Dec. and Jan. Coho and jack fishery can be good in fall. Some sea perch in lower tidal area. Lower river is fairly placid and can be canoed. WDFW access and launch.

WORKMAN CREEK. Primarily a cutthroat stream. Beaver ponds along upper reaches often provide excellent spring and fall fishing. The small, brushy creek enters the Chehalis River 1.5 miles downstream from the South Elma bridge. A road from S. end of Chehalis River bridge follows 5 miles S. up the creek.

WYNOOCHEE RESERVOIR. A dammed section of upper Wynoochee River 39 miles N. of Montesano. Impoundment covers 1,120 acres, 4.4 mile long. Drive 1 mile W. of Montesano on US 12, then N. up Wynoochee River Rd., following signs to dam. Several campgrounds, boat launch. Supports cutthroat, rainbow and whitefish. June through Oct. season with special regs.

WYNOOCHEE RIVER. One of several rivers flowing from the south slopes of Olympic Mountains under US 12 and into the Chehalis River. A good bet for winter and summer steelhead, fall coho, chinook and chums and sea-run cutthroat. This tributary enters the Chehalis River 1.5 miles SW of Montesano. Roads from US. 12 about 1 mile W. of Montesano parallel both sides of the Wynoochee upstream. The E. side road continues to the headwaters and **Wynoochee Reservoir**. Touches the river in several spots and fishermen trails reach most stretches. The Wynoochee is one of the very few rivers where steelheaders still take about as many fish a year as they did 20 years ago. Most years they catch about 800 winter fish (best Jan.-Mar.) and 500 summer fish tops in June and July. Good sea-run cutthroat angling in late summer and fall behind chinook, coho and chum salmon. Salmon fishing, while it usually takes a back seat to the nearby **Satsop River**, can be very productive, especially for drift boat fishermen who can prospect a lot of river in a day. Best for coho in late Sept-Oct. This is a beautiful, almost placid drift boat float. Developed boat launches on E. bank at Black Creek 3 miles N. of US 12 and another 12 miles upstream from US 12.

ZIEGLER CREEK. Winter steelhead have been planted in this small stream which is crossed by Shore Road 0.5 mile S. of Lake Quinault into which it drains.

Grays Harbor County Resorts

Lake Quinault: Rain Forest Resort, 800-562-0948. Lake Quinault Resort, 800-650-2362. Lake Quinault Lodge,360-1288-2571.

Grays Harbor: Westport Charter Boat Assoc., 800-562-0173, Westport/ Grayland Chamber, 800-345-6223.

Island County
WDFW Region 4
Washington Department of Fish and Wildlife, 16018 Mill Creek Blvd., Mill Creek, WA 98012. Phone 425-775-1311.

The smallest county in Washington is six freshwater-poor salt-water islands in north Puget Sound. Island County barely covers 225 square miles of Washington, and 170 square miles of that total is on Whidbey Island. Camano Island adds 40 square miles, and the remaining 15 square miles are split between Smith, Strawberry, Ben Uhr and Hackney (Baby) Islands which do not have road access to mainland highways.

There's not a major stream in the county and relatively few lakes—although a couple are fishing standouts. The largest lake is Cranberry Lake, 128 acres at the N. end of Whidbey Island at Deception Pass State Park, and Lone Lake on SE Whidbey Island is well known as one of the best big trout lakes in the region. Most Island County lakes are stocked with rainbows, a few with cutthroat and Triploids, the sterile oversize rainbows that grow to several pounds each year. Brook trout stockings have been discontinued in the county. Six state parks with camping are available on Whidbey and Camano islands.

What it lacks in size and freshwater fishing potential, Island County makes up for with spectacular scenery mostly saltwater views from the low rolling terrain that typifies the islands. High spot is a 580-foot lump on Camano Island. It is also the site of one of Washington's most popular state parks. Deception Pass State Park, on the N. end of Whidbey Island, has 241 sites, the largest lake in the county, and a beach with sunset views across North Puget Sound to Vancouver Island and the San Juans.

The climate has produced one of the most uniformly mild and dry regions in the U. S., with an average annual temperature at Coupeville of 49.5 degrees, dropping to 38 in the winter and rising to 61 in the summer. The rain shadow cast by the Olympic Mountains holds annual rainfall to 17.60 inches about the same as Spokane. Everett, just 28 miles away, gets twice that amount.

Saltwater fishing, crabbing and shellfishing are the dominate angling sports in this area. The west side of Whidbey Island is well-known for salmon, rockfish and halibut. Even steelhead trout are a salt water game here. With no rivers to work, steelheaders have devised a productive beach-casting technique that produces upwards of 200 steelhead a year. The most popular beaches are at Fort Casey State Park beach, Bush and Lagoon points on the SW side of Whidbey. Steelheaders tie large Spin-n-Glo drift bobbers ahead of plastic squids and bounce the rig along the gravel bottom near shore.

Deception Pass can be very good for salmon and ling cod, and a sea-run cutthroat, Dolly Varden fishery is gaining popularity on the quiet gravel beaches along the protected inside (east shore) of the island .

Public piers and docks offering saltwater access are found at Cornet State Park, Coupeville, Kayak Point, Keystone, Langley and Oak Harbor's Flintstone Park.

Routes from I-5 to Island County fishing are from I-5 via Hwys. 20 and 525 down the heart of Whidbey Island, and Hwy. 532 to Camano Island.

ADMIRALTY BAY POND. A rainbow planted pond located adjacent to Admiralty Bay on W. side of Whidbey Island.

CAMP GRANDE. Surf smelt can be raked ashore during their spawning run from June through October. Camp is on the N. end of Camano Island, public access through Maple Grove County Park.

CAVELERO'S BEACH. Surf smelt raking on the eastern shore between Triangle

Cove and Camano Head, June through October. Some sea-run cutthroat action.

CORNET BAY STATE PARK. A state dock provides jigging for smelt and herring just east of the Deception Pass bridge. Sea-run cutthroat move through here.

COUPEVILLE WATERFRONT. Surf smelt raking June through October along the downtown waterfront and shoreline beaches east and west. Sea-run cutthroat run these beaches especially in the spring and fall.

CRANBERRY LAKE. The largest lake in Island County at 128 acres is located at the N. end of Whidbey Island on Deception Pass State Park, within the sound of saltwater waves crashing on the beach. Cranberry is a very popular fishing lake for vacationers and residents. Planted in May with almost 13,000 rainbows, and occasionally brown trout, plus largemouth bass, yellow perch and brown bullhead catfish. The lake drains into Rosario Strait. Offers carry-over rainbows to 18 inches and browns to 8 pounds. May and June are top months. The lake is rarely planted before May 1 to reduce bird predation. Boat ramp on N. shore, fishing pier on E. side. State Park has camp and RV sites, picnic areas, kitchens and boat ramps.

DEER LAKE. 82 acre rainbow and cutthroat lake with brown bullhead catfish 1 mile W. of Clinton on Whidbey Island. Deer has a good population of trout to 15 inches, some larger, and usually offers good May-June fishing. Planted with 19,000 fry, 8000 catchables and several hundred triploids. Public boat launch site on E. shore. Resort facilities.

DUGUALLA BAY LAKE. A 50 acre seep lake well known for producing exceptionally large rainbow trout. Lake is adjacent to Dugualla Dike Rd. N. of Oak Harbor and is stocked with rainbow. Fishes best in spring. The pond is rich with freshwater shrimp a fertile food that grows 'bows to 5 pounds. Drive N. from Oak Harbor on Hwy. 525, 3.7 miles to Frostad Rd. then E. 2.6 miles to lake on Dugualla Dike Rd.

GOSS LAKE (Camp). a deep 55 acre rainbow and cutthroat lake draining into Holmes Harbor in central Whidbey Island. Goss is stocked annually with pansize 'bows 8-11 inches, with holdover rainbows and cutthroat to 18 inches. Brown bullheads. Best in May, June and July. 3 miles W. of Langley. Public boat launch NE end.

GRAVEL PIT PONDS. Three small cutthroat ponds. One is 0.5 mile N. of Hwy. 113 on Keystone Rd. Other two are along Hwy. 113 just W. of the Keystone Rd. intersection.

HOLMES LAKE. A small rainbow planted pond near Freeland.

LONE LAKE. The best big trout lake in the county, Whidbey Island's 92 acre Lone Lake is 2.5 miles SW of Langley. Managed as a year-round quality fishery, the lake produces lots of 8 -10 inch catchable rainbows, 12-14 inch yearlings and some carry-overs 2 pounds and up. Triploid rainbows are also planted and an additional plant of catchables is often made after May 1 to reduce bird depredation. Daily limit is 1 fish, 18-inch minimum length. Lake is shallow, warms quickly and summer fishing can be tough. Best in spring and fall. This can be a good winter lake in February and early March. Try blood worm fly patterns. Large WDFW fishing access and boat launch on E. shore.

OLIVER LAKE. A 13 acre lake on SW side of Whidbey Island, 1.5 miles NE of Double Bluff about 900 feet from the beach. Can be good for largemouth bass. Drains into Useless Bay.

ORR'S POND (Martin Orr). 1 acre pond SW of Whidbey Island's Columbia Beach. Planted with catchable rainbows, may have some remnant brook trout. Considered poor to fair in late April and May.

PONDILLA LAKE. A 3.7 acre warm-water species lake offering catfish, perch, largemouth bass and crappie. It's 1200 feet N. of Partridge Point on the W. flank of Whidbey Island. Pondilla produces from May into August. Access is difficult. Best route is on Libby Rd. to West Beach parking lot and then up a short trail to lake.

SILVER LAKE. A 15 acre lake 5.4 miles E. of Oak Harbor. Silver holds bass and crappie, and may produce a rare remnant brookie. Drains into Saratoga Passage. The lake is tough to reach. Easiest route is over private logging roads from Mariner's Cove. Public access is questionable.

Island County Resorts

Lone Lake: Lone Lake Cottages, Langley, WA 98260. 360-321-5325.

Deception Pass State Park: 360-675-2417.

Jefferson County
WDFW Region 6

Washington Department of Fish and Wildlife, 48 Devonshire Rd., Montesano, WA 98563-9618. Phone 360-249-4628

Covering a wide topographically odd and largely unsettled region that swings from glaciers to cactus, rain forests to seasonal creeks Jefferson County stretches from Hood Canal on the E. to the Pacific Ocean on the W. touching saltwater on both east and west ends roughly 90 miles apart. Almost 830 of the county's 1879 square miles are isolated inside Olympic National Park (ONP), much of it roadless and encased in ice and snow for half the year.

The high point is 7,965 feet at the west summit of Mount Olympus and the low point is at sea level. If you're not on either the extreme west or east ends of the county, you probably are living out of a backpack.

The county ranks 17th in relative size in the state. The only noticeable settlements are on both ends and the center includes some of the most difficult, and rarely used terrain in the state. There are still relatively unknown lakes and small streams in some parts of this rugged county especially inside the national park and Olympic National Forest. Not surprisingly in such vertical, lush country, most recreationists stick to improved trails and rarely venture cross-country on bushwhacking expeditions to the myriad of small streams, ponds and isolated lakes.

Most of the fishing can be divided into two segments: those you backpack to and those that can be reached from US 101 which crosses the E. and W. ends between the saltwater and the mountains. The county's northern border follows an imaginary line through ONP, and the S. border is lost in a no man's land of logging clearcuts, wilderness areas, ONP, Olympic NF and Quinault Indian Nation Reservation.

Best fishing is for migratory steelhead, salmon and sea-run cutthroat streams. The Elwha and Dungeness Rivers drain a small portion of the N. part through Clallam County into the Strait of Juan de Fuca. The rest flows either into the ocean or Hood Canal. On the ocean side are the steelhead legends: Hoh, Queets and Quinault river systems. On the E. the Duckabush, Dosewallips and Quilcene drain the majority of the E. part of Jefferson into Hood Canal. The canal offers prime spot shrimp (prawn) trapping, crabbing, oysters, clams, plus gravel beaches and oyster beds where sea-run cutthroat feed, and all 5 salmon species.

Freshwater lowland lakes are in short supply. The largest is Leland Lake, covering only 99.3 acres just W. of US 101 near Quilcene which is a lot better known for its oysters than for Leland's trout and bass.

Like the other counties under the spires of the Olympic Mountains, the climate is extremely diverse. Annual precipitation at Port Townsend NE of the mountains is only 18.19 inches. On the ocean side in the Hoh River Valley annual rainfall averages 126.73 inches. Daily temperatures, excluding the ONP peaks area, are seasonally moderate and you can fish every day of the year. The largest city is Port Townsend, which is located on a dogleg of the county extending N. to touch the Strait of Juan de Fuca. US 101 is the road that leads to all the fishing in Jefferson County.

ANDERSON LAKE. An exceptionally productive trout lake 8 miles S. of Port Townsend. This 59-acre lake is stocked with 30,000 rainbow fry and another 5000 catchables in May. It's a combination that delivers a lot of foot-long, plus trout from opening day into July and a healthy number of carryovers, some in the 3 pound range. This is a fertile lake and the fry grow quickly. Sept. and Oct. are restricted to catch-and-release months to protect next year's crop of growing fry. The C&R season is becoming very popular with fly fishermen because of the large number of hefty holdovers that go on the prowl in fall. From US 101 on S. end of Discovery Bay turn E. onto Hwy. 20, to Anderson Lake Road, to state park boat launch. No camping.

BROWN'S LAKE. Private. No public access. Cutthroat are in this 3 acre lake 7.5 miles W. of Port Ludlow and 1 mile NE from Tarboo Lake.

CHIMICUM CREEK. A small brookie and cutthroat stream. Turn N. from Hwy. 104 on the Center Valley Road. The creek follows W. side of road about 5 miles, then continues N. to drain into Port Townsend Bay just N. of Irondale.

CLEARWATER RIVER. A short-run tributary flowing into the Queets River from the N. just W. of US 101/Queets River bridge. The Clearwater delivers a couple of hundred winter steelhead, nearly all wild fish, Jan.-Apr. Best in Mar. and Apr. Sea-run cutthroat from July through September. Also hosts marginal returns of summer and fall chinook and fall coho. Good road access. About 5 miles SE of the Queets River/US 101 bridge, turn N. from US 101 cross the Queets and follow the Clearwater for 10 miles before dropping into the Hoh Valley. Can be drift boated from a primitive launch on upper river to a ramp at the confluence.

CROCKER LAKE. Once a very popular trout, bass and panfish lake, Crocker is now closed to public fishing. It is 3.5 miles S. of Discovery Bay adjacent to US 101. The lake covers 65 acres and holds rainbow, perch, largemouth bass, and brown bullhead.

DEVIL'S LAKE. Linger Longer). An 11 acre lake surrounded by timber 2 miles S. of Quilcene at 844 feet elev. overlooking Quilcene Bay. Good cutthroat fishing. Route is S. from Quilcene on Bonneville Road, then short trail hike to lake.

DOSEWALLIPS RIVER. A sad shadow of what was once a productive Hood Canal winter steelhead river, now best known for wild sea-run cutthroat and fall coho and chum salmon runs. Not so long ago the Dosey, a small clear stream, kicked out a couple of hundred steelhead a year. If two dozen fish hit the bank this winter it will have been exceptional. Sea-run cutthroat move upstream in late summer and fall with the salmon runs, and when salmon sea-

Clearwater River.

sons are open, can deliver a lot of fun on light tackle. State park at mouth where the river enters Hood Canal. Sea-runs can be picked out of the saltwater year round near the mouth. A paved FS road follows the Dosey's N. bank approximately 13 miles, 3 miles deep into ONP. FS campground along the river and another at end of road in park. During warm weather the river is often milky with snow melt.

DUCKABUSH RIVER. Another tumbling Hood Canal summer and winter steelhead river with a lot more memories than present fish. If it wasn't for a trickle of fall sea-run cutthroat and a brief spurt of late fall chum salmon the Duck would be out of luck. It has suffered a rapid and horrible decline in steelhead fishing similar to the Dosewallips. WDFW's 1999 steelhead summary showed anglers catching 3 winter and 3 summer steelhead. Just 10 years earlier the Duck produced more than 200 winter steelhead. It flows into Hood Canal about 3 miles S. of Brinnon. A road from US 101 follows N. side of the river, roughly paralleling the stream for about 7 miles. FS campground at the 5 mile point. Access to the Duck is difficult and requires bucking brush in most spots. The Duckabush heads high in Olympic National Park (see park section) and usually is fishable quicker after high water than other Hood Canal rivers.

FULTON CREEK BEAVER PONDS. Bushwhacking is required to fish these ponds. Turn NW from US 101 about 1 mile N. of Triton Cove on Hood Canal. Road crosses creek at approximately the 2 mile mark. Go upstream and down to locate ponds which hold cutthroat.

GIBBS LAKE. Year-round, spring-planted with 3000 catchable rainbows, this 37 acre lake restricted to catch and release trout fishing with selective gear. Lake is 7 miles NW from Port Ludlow and 3.5 miles SW from Chimacum. Also contains cutthroat, largemouth bass (keepable) and coho. Drains to Chimacum Creek.

GOODMAN CREEK. Enters the Ocean 6 miles N. of Hoh River's mouth. Furnishes sea-run cutthroat June through Sept. Follow Goodman Mainline Road from Oil City Road on N. side of Hoh River N. to cross Goodman Creek. The stream receives winter steelhead plants.

HOH RIVER. Top winter steelhead and salmon river on the Olympic Peninsula. The Hoh is a wide, deep, sullen river that heads high on the slopes of Mt. Olympus in Olympic National Park (see park section) and flows W. into the ocean 15 miles S. of Forks. The upper stream is fast, rocky and tough to fish in ONP. The lower river along US 101 carries summer and winter steelhead, cutthroat, protected Dolly Varden, spring, summer and fall chinook, coho and jack chinook salmon. Because of super heavy smolt plants, most years anglers will catch 1000 to 1500 winter-runs and 300 to 500 summer-run steelhead, despite heavy downstream netting during the peak of the run. Hatchery steelhead peak in Jan., taper through Feb. then steelheading booms in Mar. and Apr. when natives return. Some of these will bottom out 25-lb. scales.

Summer-run fishing is best in Aug. and Sept. but there's some fish in the river all summer and catches would likely be much higher if the Hoh wasn't colored with glacial melt most of the summer. Late summer and fall months are prime for sea-run cutthroat, chinook, coho and tons of 2-to 5-pound fall chinook jacks. Spring chinook are taken in May through August overlapping with incoming runs of summer and fall chinook. In August break out the spinning rods, spinners and nightcrawlers and enjoy one of the best sea-run cutthroat fisheries in the state.

US 101 follows the Hoh often within sight for about 8 miles along the lower river's S. bank, then bridges the river. One-half mile N. of the bridge the N. side road leads down river to Oil City on the ocean. Two miles N. of US 101 bridge a paved road heads upstream about 20 miles to end of road in rain forest of ONP. Approximately 10 miles SW of US 101 bridge a road leaves the highway and follows the S. side of the river to the Hoh Indian Reservation at the river's mouth. The river is popular with drift and jet boats but there's lots of bank access, too.

HORSESHOE LAKE. A one-fish, selective gear limit keeps this 13 acre lake producing fair fishing for about 1000 stocked rainbow and cutthroat well into early summer when largemouth bass begin to bite. Located 4 miles SW of Port Ludlow. Follow Hwy. 104 from NW end of Hood Canal bridge to within 0.4 mile of Horseshoe's S. tip.

HOWE CREEK. Plants of cutthroat have been made in Howe, primarily in beaver ponds along its 5 mile length. The creek drains into Little Quilcene River. Drive N. from Quilcene on US 101 for 2 miles, then NW on FS 2909 for 3 miles over Ripley Creek. Fish upstream from bridge, or drive 1 mile more to road junction, then turn N. on road which crosses upper portion of creek within 1.5 miles.

JUPITER LAKES. Four small lakes on NE side of Mt. Jupiter 11 miles SW of Quilcene. Lake sizes are 0.5, 1.5, 3 and 6 acres. Cutthroat. Drains to Dosewallips River.

KALALOCH CREEK. A brushy sea-run cutthroat stream that crosses US 101 between the Queets and the Hoh rivers and enters the ocean at Kalaloch. July through September best. Rough trails up and downstream from the highway.

LELAND CREEK. Outlet of Leland Lake, the 4-mile-long creek heads S. from the lake, paralleling the W. side of US 101 for about 3 miles before joining the Little Quilcene River 1 mile NW of Quilcene. Wild cutthroat.

LELAND LAKE (Hooker). The largest lake in Jefferson County, 99-acre Leland is adjacent to US 101 about 4.5 miles N. of Quilcene on the E. side of the county. Heavily stocked with 13,000 rainbows sporadically Mar-May. Lots of 12-inch plus trout and an exceptional number of carryovers to several pounds. Also hosts warm water species including some big largemouth bass, bluegills and brown bullhead. Open year-round. WDFW access and a county park.

LENA LAKE (Lower). A 55 acre lake in the headwaters of the Hamma Hamma River 15 miles N. of Hoodsport. Follow Hamma Hamma River Road about 7 miles to Lena Creek campground, then hike 3.5 miles by trail to the lake. Holds rainbows and brook trout. Campground on lake.

LOST LAKE. Closed to public fishing. A private 7-acre rainbow lake 2.5 miles NW of South Point W. of Hood Canal bridge on Hwy. 104.

LUDLOW CREEK. Drains E. from Ludlow Lake about 5 miles to enter Port Ludlow Harbor about 1 mile S. of town. Ponds along the creek have received both cutthroat and brook trout plants. Largest pond lies 1 mile E. of Ludlow Lake (See Ludlow lake for route).

LUDLOW LAKE. This 15-acre rainbow and largemouth bass lake is 4.5 miles W. of Port Ludlow. Stocked with 1000 catchable rainbows in Mar. and Apr. Drive W. on Hwy. 104 from W. end of Hood Canal bridge for 8 miles, then turn N. about 0.4 miles where road passes within a few hundred yards of the lake's W. shore.

MOSQUITO CREEK. A few steelhead and sea-run cutthroat are in this small stream which enters the ocean N. of Hoh River. Follow Oil City Road along N. side of the Hoh to Goodman Mainline Road N. about five miles to cross the creek. This road continues to Bogachiel River.

PENNY CREEK AND PONDS. Cutthroat ponds along a 4-mile-long creek which heads in a marsh 4 miles NW of Quilcene. Creek enters the Big Quilcene River at the U.S. Fish Hatchery about 2 miles SW of Quilcene. FS Road 2823 leads N. from hatchery 4 miles, closely following the stream.

QUEETS RIVER. See Olympic National Park section.

QUILCENE RIVER. A poor Dec.-Jan. steelhead stream. Sea-run cutts from July to October. Enters Hood Canal at the N. tip of Quilcene Bay. Crossed by US 101 about 2.5 miles above mouth, paralleled by the highway for 3 miles S. of the bridge. A road heads W. from Quilcene 1 mile, then S. to follow the river about 2 miles.

QUINAULT RIVER (See Grays Harbor County).

RIPLEY CREEK. Cutthroat plants have been made in beaver ponds along this stream which is 2.5 miles long. It drains into the Little Quilcene River. Drive N. from Quilcene 2 miles on US 101, then NW on FS Road 2909 for 1.5 miles where road crosses creek. Work up stream to locate ponds, watching for beaver sign or patches of dead trees which indicate ponds.

SALMON RIVER. A major tributary of the Queets River heavily planted with steelhead by the Quinault Indian Nation. Produces about 300 winter-runs a year, most in Jan. Crossed by the Upper Queets Road near mouth about 1.5 miles N. of US 101. The river heads on the Quinault Indian Reservation and flows W. and then N. a short distance to enter Jefferson

County, then joins the Queets River in ONP.

SANDY SHORE LAKE. This 36 acre private lake has been planted with rainbow and is reported to also host brook trout and largemouth bass. 8 miles W. of W. end of Hood Canal Bridge, then S. for 1.5 miles on road which touches the lake's W. shore. Carry boat access.

SHINE CREEK. Cutthroat in beaver ponds along the stream which is 3 miles long. Flows into Squamish Harbor 1 mile W. of Shine at W. end of Hood Canal Bridge. Explorers may find trout by walking upstream and down from bridges crossing the creek twice on the South Point-Port Ludlow road which leaves Hwy. 104 and heads N. about 2 miles from Shine.

SILENT LAKE. Rainbow, cutthroat and brook trout in this 11.9 acre lake 5.3 miles SE of Quilcene on E. side of Dabob Bay. Drains to Hood Canal.

SILVER LAKES. Cutthroat lakes of 1 and 2 acres at head of Silver Creek 9 miles W. of Quilcene. Drain to Dungeness River.

SNOW CREEK. Closed to fishing. Supports winter steelhead and sea-run cutts. Flows into S. tip of Discovery Bay.

TARBOO CREEK. Cutthroat stream flowing from Tarboo Lake 7 miles S. to Tarboo Bay on Hood Canal 4 miles NE of Quilcene. Upper reaches reached from Tarboo Lake Road. Lower stretch is reached by turning left from Chimacum-Quilcene Road on a parallel road 0.5 miles S. of Hwy. 104. This road closely follows the last 3 miles of creek.

TARBOO LAKE (Cord). Stocked with 3000 catchable rainbows and cutthroat and another 6000 fry, this 21 acre lake is usually fair for 9 to 11 inch trout early in the season, plus some carry-overs. Take the Chimacum-Quilcene Road S. from Hwy. 104 at W. end of Hood Canal bridge for 3 miles, then button hook right and continue 3 miles to lake. WDFW access.

TEAL LAKE. 2 miles S. of Port Ludlow off Teal Lake Road. Covers 15.3 acres and supports largemouth bass and panfish Rough boat launch. Drains to Port Ludlow Harbor.

THORNDYKE CREEK. Brook trout are the colorful attraction in this small stream that heads in Sandy Shore Lake and flows 6 miles S. to enter Hood Canal at Thorndyke Bay. Go W. from Hood Canal Bridge 4 miles, turn onto South Point Road for 1.5 miles, to Thorndyke Road for about 4 miles to crossing of Thorndyke Creek at large culvert. Brushy going down stream.

TOWNSEND CREEK. Lower 2 miles of this 7 mile long brook trout stream spills across many falls and cascades, but upper reaches may be fished. Enters Big Quilcene River 5 miles W. of Quilcene. Heads on the SE flank of Mt. Townsend. Drive W. from center of Quilcene to U.S. fish hatchery, then NW for 1 mile, then S. on FS 2812 which winds W. and N. to follow E. side of the creek.

TWIN LAKE, UPPER (Deep). 4.6 acre lake at 860 ft., elev. that supports largemouth bass. 4.5 miles SW from Port Ludlow. Drains to Port Ludlow Harbor.

YAHOO LAKE. One of the few western Olympic Peninsula lakes. Rainbow planted 8.3 acres at 2350 feet elev. on logged DNR land. Drains to Clearwater River. From US 101 near Hoh River Bridge, go NE on Clearwater River Road. 2 miles NE of Copper Mines Bottom Campground, turn E at signed jct. and continue for 10.l miles to DNR campground at lake.

Jefferson County Resorts

Hoh River: Hoh River 101 Resort, 360-1374-5566. Westward Hoh Resort, 360-374-6657.

King County
WDFW Region 4
Washington Department of Fish and Wildlife, 16018 Mill Creek Blvd., Mill Creek, WA 98012. Phone 425-775-1311.

Few counties anywhere in America, certainly no urban counties, offer the fishing promise, potential and problems found in the sea-to-mountain diversity of King County. Fishing is a multiple choice decision beginning on the west at sea level boat ramps and ending on the east in unbelievably spectacular lakes tucked into top-of-the-world alpine basins.

Within an hour's travel King County anglers may try saltwater for flounder, rockfish, sea-run trout and salmon; cast into cold-water rivers for steelhead and salmon; fish hundreds of lakes stocked with mixed bags of trout and warm-water fish, then backpack to trout in remote alpine lakes that are strung like cyan jewels on a chain of hiking trails along the crest of the Cascades.

The diversity of King County's fishery is truly amazing; tiger muskies and salmon in downtown Seattle, cutthroat, rainbow, bass, crappie, whopper perch and seasonal salmon in urban rimmed lakes; piers for saltwater fish, squid and shrimp and the occasional stray sturgeon.

Unprecedented Northwest population growth is centered in King County, tremendously impacting the quality of this natural quantity, and forcing a right-angle shift in traditional recreational fishing management. Still, in many instances WDFW is scrambling to catch up.

The historically-famous blue ribbon anadromous winter and summer-run steelhead and fall salmon fisheries have suffered tremendously in recent years. Puget Sound salmon fishing has gone from a year-round opportunity to window openings with minimal limits, emergency closures and tackle restrictions. Rockfish, pollock and cod are depleted to the point that catch limits have fallen from 15 a day to 1. True cod—measured by the millions less than 20 years ago—are few and fully protected. A thriving Seattle charter boat fishing fleet has collapsed.

As steelhead and salmon fisheries dropped, there have been gains in lowland lake fishing. WDFW's long-standing put-and-take, spring and summer rainbow trout program has shifted to stocking programs geared to year-round fishing seasons beefed up with brown trout and fast-growing triploid rainbows which add the entice-ment of possibly connecting with a trophy-size fish. An increase is continuing in the number of lakes allowed to support warm-water fish, especially large and smallmouth bass, perch and channel catfish. Several lakes are emerging as hot spots for big smallmouth bass, and huge yellow perch in Lake Washington are a major fishery waiting to happen.

WDFW has stopped stocking catchable trout into streams in this region, although most of the creeks support resident cutthroat and some rainbows. These wild trout provide mostly catch-and-release opportunities because of 2 fish daily limits and 12 to 14 inch minimum sizes on many streams. Few wild creek trout top 10 inches.

King County is Washington's 10th largest covering 2206 square miles. Elevations vary from sea level where Puget Sound laps the shoreline to 7936 feet at the glaciated summit of Mount Daniels in the Wenatchee Mountains N. of Snoqualmie Pass. The E. boundary generally follows the crest of the Cascade Mountains.

The county has more than 750 lakes, 377 of these are mountain lakes over 2500 feet elev. Major drainages are the Green, Cedar, Raging, Tolt and Snoqualmie Rivers. The Skykomish River drains the NE edge and the White (Stuck) River the extreme S border with Pierce County. Lowland lakes hold trout, mostly rainbow, plus kokanee salmon. Brook trout, once heavily stocked in the county, are no longer planted, but many lakes—especially in the foothills and mountains have thriving reproducing brook trout populations. Many one-time, trout-only lowland lakes now also offer warm-water species including large and smallmouth bass, perch, crappie, brown bullhead and channel catfish, rockbass, and warmouth.

The Green and Snoqualmie rivers support winter and summer steelhead, chinook, coho and chum salmon. The Snoqualmie also gets a small run of pinks. The smaller Tolt and Raging rivers offer steelheading. Cedar River, once a popular winter steelhead water, is now closed to sport fishing and serves primarily as a nursery for sockeye salmon to fuel commercial gillnet and recreational hook and line fisheries in Lake Washington.

North and Middle Forks of the Snoqualmie River are trout streams that reach into the mountains paralleled by gravel roads. The South Fork Snoqualmie flows along I-90 from North Bend almost to Snoqualmie Pass, but is a poor fishing prospect. WDFW has stopped planting county streams and rivers with catchable trout, depending on natural reproduction and catch-and-release no-bait regulations to meet sport fishing pressure. The result is that most small streams and rivers have a poor to fair population of small native trout—few over 14 inches and most 6 to 8. Some rivers and creeks, however, attract surprisingly large sea-run cutthroat.

The low foothills between I-90 at North Bend and Hwy. 2 at Gold Bar have many remote lakes, beaver ponds and streams that support largemouth bass, rainbow, cutthroat and brook trout. Most are on clear-cut tree farms owned by the Weyerhaeuser/Plum Creek timber companies. The company allows free access to these lands for anglers on bicycle, foot and horseback. A fee is charged for permits allowing vehicle access, however. For information phone, 1-800-433-3911.

Snow accumulation in the high Cascades is measured in yards and during average snowfall years mountain lake fishing doesn't begin until June . Lower lakes in the 2500 to 4000 foot range may be ice free in mid May. Extremely high lakes are often frozen until July. Snow is possible every month in the high mountains.

Climate is maritime mild with lowland temperatures averaging 52 degrees allowing year-round open-water fishing in saltwater and lowland lakes and rivers. Summer temperatures rarely climb into the 90s and most days are in the high 70s and low 80s—comfortable fishing weather. Lowland precipitation averages 35 inches which produces lush brush jungles that shroud many trouty beaver ponds, lakes, creeks and streams in impenetrable tangles.

The county's major access roads are I-5 N-S through the Puget Sound metro area, I-90 E-W across Snoqualmie Pass, Hwy. 18 NE-SW across the Green, Raging and Cedar rivers, Hwys. 169/410 E-W to Mount Rainier NP, and Hwy. 203 N-S along the Snoqualmie River.

ALICE LAKE (Mud). A 33-acre year-round mixed species lake at 875 feet elev. 2.5 miles S. of Fall City off Preston-Fall City Road. Alice gets annual plants of about 4000 rainbows bolstering reproducing populations of cutthroat and brook trout, largemouth bass and panfish. Heavily fished in spring. WDFW public access, ramp on E. shore. Lake Alice Rd. leads SE from Fall City to the lake.

AMES LAKE. No public access to this 80 acre lake 2 miles W. of Carnation. It's ringed with private homes. Mixed species. Route is via Carnation Farm Rd. N. from Carnation to Ames Lake Rd. then S. to lake.

ANGLE LAKE. Spring plants of 8000 legal rainbow, 25,000 kokanee fry and 1000 Triploids create a good fishery for trout, kokanee salmon, perch, largemouth bass, carp and catfish. Usually planted in March, year-round season. Boat launch at county park. Angle covers 102 acres at Hwy. 99 S. and S. 194th near SeaTac airport.

BASS LAKE (AKA Carlson). A few remnant cutthroat and rainbow still swim in this year-round 24 acre cattail-encircled lake, but most anglers target largemouth bass, crappie, pumpkinseed and perch. Lots of lily pads. Rough, brushy WDFW launch for small boats. Lake is 3.5 miles N. of Enumclaw on W. side of Hwy. 169.

BEAVER LAKE, a 13 acres private lake is 1700 feet SE of Bass Lake holds rainbow, bass and panfish. No public access

BEAVER LAKES. A connected chain of three lakes totaling 82 acres with large-mouth bass, yellow perch, brown bullhead, and spring planted with 5000 rainbow trout. Open year round. Public fishing area, ramp on E. shore of 62.5 acre lake. The other lakes in the chain cover 11.6 and 5.9 acres. From Front St. in Issaquah go NE. on Issaquah-Fall City Rd., N. on 264th Pl. SE, then W. on Issaquah-Beaver Lake Rd then N. on East Beaver Lake Rd.

BEAR CREEK (Big Bear). Closed to fishing. A small, Sammamish River tributary which heads near Ring Hill and flows SW about 6 miles. Woodinville-Duvall highway roughly parallels the stream.

BEAR LAKE. A 49-acre rainbow lake at 3670 feet elev. in the headwaters of Taylor River, Alpine Lakes Wilderness Area. From North Bend drive NE on FS 56 up Middle Fork Snoqualmie River for 11 miles to trailhead at Taylor River confluence. Walk the old road bed up Taylor River for 5 miles to Trail 1002 which continues 1.5 miles past Snoqualmie Lake to Bear.

BECKLER RIVER. Small river fishing for 6 to 10 inch wild rainbow and cutthroat trout and mountain whitefish. The river enters King County from Snohomish County 5 miles N. of Skykomish and joins the Skykomish River at Skykomish. FS Rd. 65 follows the river upstream providing easy access. Developed and primitive camping areas.

BENGSTON LAKE. Covering only 2.7 acres this cranberry bog has amazing big fish potential. WDFW reports rainbow trout to several pounds, brook trout and resident coho salmon. It's open year round. Lake is on Weyerhaeuser's Snoqualmie Tree Farm and to drive into the lake requires a fee permit. Located at 2600 feet elev. 7 miles S. of Startup on county line. A logging road comes within 250 feet of the east shore and a brushy spur road leads to the south shore.

BIG CREEK. Small tributary to the Snoqualmie River's N. Fork. The creek produces small rainbows into fall months. Heads NW of Philippa Lake. From North Bend follow the rough gravel of North Fork County Road 12 miles N. to where it crosses the mouth of the creek.

BITTER LAKE. A 19 acre Seattle lake at Greenwood Avenue and N. 133rd. Holds largemouth bass, black crappie, yellow perch and brown bullhead. County park access, but no ramp.

BLACK LAKE. 7000 stocked rainbow fry and a few large cutthroat are in this 26 acre lake in Weyerhaeuser's Snoqualmie Tree Farm N. of North Bend. Vehicle permit required. Black is at 1213 elev. on the Main Line Rd. 6 miles N. of Spur 10 jct. Black starts slow, then picks up as water warms. **MUD LAKE** is 1 mile N. on the main line. It covers 16 acres and holds bass and rainbow.

BLACK DIAMOND LAKE (Chub Lake). A 9 acre pond with a few rainbow, cutthroat and bullhead catfish. Located 1 mile SW of Black Diamond at end of 248th Ave. SE. Access is difficult.

BOREN LAKE. A 15.3 acre, 47-foot deep lake 4 miles N. of Renton on Coal Creek Pkwy. Largemouth bass, yellow perch, brown bullhead and some rainbow trout. Public park has access, fishing pier. WDFW boat ramp.

BOYLE LAKE. Located on Weyerhaeuser's Snoqualmie Tree Farm 5 miles N. of North Bend, this 34-acre lake is one of three lakes (see Klause and Bridges lks) in a chain planted with largemouth bass, perch and managed for native cutthroat. Lake can be reached by hiking from Spur 10 on the County Road or by vehicle with a Weyerhaeuser permit.

BREWSTER LAKE (Kerrs). A private 3 acre rainbow pond 3.5 miles S. of North Bend. Go S. from Hwy. 90 at Exit 32 on Cedar Falls Rd., then W. about 1 mile. No access.

BRIDGES LAKE. The upper lake in a series of three warm-water species lakes located about 6 miles NE of Snoqualmie. Bridges covers 34 acres and adjacent **KLAUS** is 62 acres. Hold largemouth bass and perch. No longer stocked with trout and no known reproduction. Drains to Ten and Tokul Creeks to Snoqualmie River. Follow North Fork County Road N. from North Bend for 6 miles to Spur 10 then W. onto Weyerhaeuser property for 1 mile to Road 3710, then N. for about 1 mile to Klaus Lake. Primitive trails to **BOYLE** and **BRIDGES** lakes.

BURIEN LAKE. Private property surrounds this 44 acre lake located on the SW outskirts of Burien near SW 154th St.

BURTON ACRES COUNTY PARK. Located at Quartermaster Harbor on Vashon Island. Offers good surf smelt raking on the north side from October through February.

CALLIGAN LAKE. Wild rainbow, brookies and cutthroat are in this remote 361 acre lake 9 miles NE of North Bend at 2222 feet elev. Best fished from cartop boats or float tubes. It's on the Weyerhaeuser Snoqualmie Tree Farm and requires a vehicle access permit. From North Bend go N. on North Fork County Road for 6 miles to Spur 10 intersection. Turn E. on Spur 10 for 3 miles and follow main logging road E. about 2 miles to NW tip of the lake.

CALLIGAN CREEK. A fast-dropping waterfall of a small stream that drains Calligan Lake into the Snoqualmie's N. Fork. Tough, brushy rainbow fishing. Good access just below lake, but this area is closed to fishing.

CAROLINE LAKE. A deep, 59.6 acre lake in a large open basin at 4740 feet elev. in Alpine Lakes Wilderness S. of Preacher Mt. and about 6 miles NW of Snoqualmie Pass. Rainbows. Drains N. to Middle Fork Snoqualmie River.

CEDAR RIVER. A major S. King County river with no fishing opportunities. Until the 1980s this was a significant winter steelhead river. The Cedar is now closed to sport fishing and serves primarily as a nursery for commercially-important sockeye salmon for tribal gillnetters in Lake Washington. When sockeye returns are exceptionally heavy a sport-fishery is sometimes opened in Lake Washington. The Cedar begins under Yakima Pass on the Cascade Crest. The headwaters are impounded south of North Bend behind a Seattle water department dam creating 1682 acre **CHESTER MORSE LAKE** (Cedar Lake). The reservoir is used as a water supply for Seattle, and is closed to public entry. The Seattle watershed ends at Landsburg Dam on 276th Ave. between Hobart and Ravensdale. The river turns N. through Maple Valley along Hwy. 169 to Renton where it enters Lake Washington. **ROCK CREEK**, a tributary of the Cedar, holds rainbow. It joins the river about 2.5 miles E. of Maple Valley

CHERRY CREEK. The creek heads in Cherry Lake near the King-Snohomish County line and flows W. to enter the Snoqualmie River 2 miles N. of Duvall. A brushy creek with brookies and cutthroat in beaver ponds along upper reaches. From Hwy. 203 S. of Duvall turn E. on Cherry Valley Road to creek.

CHERRY LAKE. Source of Cherry Creek, this brushy 3 acre pond offers brook trout for float tubers. From Hwy. 203 at Stillwater turn N. up Stossel Creek Rd. for about 8 miles. Where the road crosses upper Cherry Creek a trail goes upstream about 1 mile to the lake.

CHARLIE LAKES. String of four mountain rainbow trout lakes 8.5 miles S. of Skykomish on SW side of Camp Robber Valley. Lakes are at 3800 to 4200 feet elev. Acreage's are 2, 1.5, 3.5 and 4.5 acres. From US 2 go S. on Miller River Rd./FS 6410 then FS 6412. Trailhead at road's end.

CHETWOOD LAKE. A 113 acre lake at 5200 feet elev. 10.8 miles S. of Skykomish and 1800 feet S. from **ANGELINE LAKE.** Holds rainbow. This is the headwater of the W. Fork Foss River. From US 2 go S. on FS 68 along Foss River to FS 6835. Continue on Trail 1064 to lakes.

CLEVELAND LAKE. A 2.5 acre rainbow lake at 4300 feet elev. located 3.4 miles SW of Skykomish on N. side of Cleveland Mt. Drains to Miller River. Outlet crosses FS Rd. 6410 just N. of Miller River Campground.

COAL CREEK. A small tributary of the Snoqualmie River at town of Snoqualmie. **KIMBALL CREEK** joins Coal Creek 0.4 miles S. of Snoqualmie. Tough fishing for wild rainbow and cutthroat.

COTTAGE LAKE. A popular 63 acre multi-species lake on the Woodinville-Duvall Rd., 3 miles E. of Woodinville. A large county park on the N. shore has a fishing pier and carry-in boat access. Offers good fishing in May and June for 10 to 12 inch stocked rainbow trout, plus cutthroat and all summer for a variety of warm-water fish including large perch, largemouth bass, crappie and bullhead catfish. Gets a plant of 20,000 trout fry.

COUGAR LAKE (Big). A remote 19.7 acre lake at 4123 feet 14 miles NE of North

Chetwood Lake.

Bend. Once planted with golden trout. **LITTLE COUGAR** lies 4900 NW from Big Cougar. Drain to Lennox Creek at the E. end of North Fork Snoqualmie River Rd. Follow primitive trail S. up Cougar Creek.

COVINGTON CREEK. Flows from Lake Sawyer SW to enter Soos Creek above WDFW salmon hatchery. The creek gets its water from the lake and from small springs. Upper sections sometimes go dry during low water years. Hosts native cutthroat, a few rainbow. A run of coho salmon and sea-run cutthroat enter the stream in late November-December and climb the fish ladder into Lake Sawyer.

CRATER LAKE. Cutthroat, rainbow, and possibly goldens are reported in this 17 acre lake at 3500 feet in headwaters of South Fork Tolt River. From Hwy. 2 take Money Creek Rd./FS 6420 past Elizabeth Lake to road end. Follow Trail 1071 for 1 mile to lake's outlet stream, then bushwhack .08 miles upstream to lake.

CRAWFORD LAKE. A 19.8 acre golden trout lake at 5350 elev. in Alpine Lakes Wilderness. It lies 1600 feet SE of **CHETWOOD LAKE** and drains into Middle Fork Snoqualmie. From the end of Middle Fork Rd. take trail 1030 to outlet on shoulder of Iron Cap Mt. then bushwhack up outlet to lake.

DEEP CREEK. A small stream draining into North Fork Snoqualmie River. It has rainbow, brookies and cutthroat and fair summer fishing into October. Drive up North Fork County Road from North Bend to Lennox mine.

DEEP LAKE. A popular state park lake with year-round fishing located at 770-feet elev., 0.8 miles SW of Cumberland and 6.5 miles N. of Enumclaw on Veazie-Cumberland Rd. Deep covers 39 acres is 76 feet deep, and offers rainbow, (planted with 4000 trout in April), cutthroat, kokanee salmon, bullhead catfish, perch and crappie. Nolte State Park (360-825-4646) has picnicing, swim beach and small fishing dock. Bank fishing from trail that encircles lake. Carry-in boat launch.

DENNY CREEK. A pretty, forested tributary to South Fork Snoqualmie River. FS campground at mouth about 18 miles E. of North Bend at marked I-90 exit. Poor to fair for summer and fall cutthroat. FS Trail 1014 leads from the campground upstream along the creek for 4 miles to headwaters in **MELAKWA LAKE**.

DERRY LAKE (Dairy). 5 acre brook trout lake SE of North Bend. Exit I-90 at Edgewick and drive S. about 1.5 miles, crossing South Fork Snoqualmie River. Lake is 0.5 mile E. of Edgewick.

DESIRE LAKE (Echo). Residentially-developed 72 acre year-round lake SE of Renton. Stocked with 7000 rainbows in April, some hold-over trout. Good for trout April-June. Also offers largemouth bass, black crappie and perch which hold up well through summer. Slot limit on bass. Large WDFW access, boat launch, fishing dock on N. shore, but limited bank fishing. To reach the lake drive S. from Renton on Petrovitsky Road to SE 184th St., then N. along West Lake Desire Dr. to access.

DOLLOFF LAKE. A 21-acre year-round neighborhood lake in Federal Way adjacent to I-5. Stocked with 1600 catchable rainbows in March, but best for largemouth bass, perch, pumpkinseed, brown bullhead and rockbass. Some very large bass in this little lake. Lunkers over 10 pounds are documented. WDFW access, ramp on SE shore. Military Road parallels the W. shore, and 310th St. leads to access.

DOROTHY LAKE. A huge and popular hike-in lake on the W. wall above Camp Robber Valley in Alpine Lakes Wilderness. Rainbow, coastal cutthroat and naturally reproducing brook trout. Dorothy is 1.5 miles long, covers 290 acres, and is 152 feet deep. A cluster of islands at the S. end provide isolated camp sites for hikers toting rafts. Elev. is 3052 feet. Located 7.8 miles S. of Skykomish. Drains to East Fork Miller River. From Hwy. 2 go S. on Miller River Rd./FS Rd. 6410, bear left on FS 6412 and continue to road's end. Trail 1072 continues about 0.70 mile to Dorothy Lake.

DREAM LAKE. 35 acre rainbow lake 17.5 miles NE North Bend. Drains to Taylor River. Go N on Middle Fork Snoqualmie Rd./57 to Taylor River confluence. Continue on Trail 1002. for several miles to where Big Creek outlet crosses trail. Dream is about 1 mile upstream.

DRUNKEN CHARLIE LAKE. A 3-acre sphagnum moss-lined year-round lake in logged area 9 miles NE of Duvall. Stocked with rainbow fry that average 8 inches in summer, but holdovers to several pounds are available. Bring a raft. A puzzle of logging roads leads to the lake.

DUWAMISH RIVER (See Green River).

ECHO LAKE. An 11 acre lake adjacent to Hwy. 99 just inside the King-Snohomish County line. Stocked with rainbow and supports a few hold-overs to 12 inches. Access is from power line road through county park.

ECHO LAKE. A 20 acre lake adjacent to S. side of I-90 about 2.5 miles SW of Snoqualmie, just E of Hwy. 18. Rainbow, cutthroat and largemouth bass. No public access.

EDDS LAKE. Golden trout are planted in this pretty 10 acre lake at 4300 feet on E. side of Mt. Thompson N. of Snoqualmie Pass. Lake is on PCT 2000 on N. side of Alaska Mt. about 4.5 miles NE of trailhead at Snoqualmie Pass West Summit Exit. Drains to Burntboot Creek and Middle Fork Snoqualmie River.

FENWICK LAKE. A pleasant 18 acre year-round mixed species lake on Kent West Hill. Stocked in March with about 3000 catchable rainbows, supplementing a good population of largemouth bass, pumpkinseed panfish, perch and brown bullhead. Lots of wood structure. No outboards. WDFW access and ramp and city park with fishing dock. From I-5 Exit 147 E. on Hwy. 516/272nd St. to Reith Rd., turn W. on Reith then S. on Lake Fenwick Rd. for 05 mile.

FISH LAKE. Wild rainbow, cutthroat and largemouth bass are in this 17 acre lake 1 mile SW of Nolte Lake State Park. WDFW access and small boat launch. Brushy shoreline. From Veazie-Cumberland Rd. N. of Enumclaw take first W. turn S. of entrance to Nolte State Park then next right on gravel road and continue .05 mile to lake at road end. **DEEP LAKE** is 1 mile NE.

FIVE MILE LAKE. Public access through county park, boat ramp, to this 38 acre lake. Stocked with rainbow in the spring and largemouth bass. Best March-June. Military Road skirts E. side of lake where the park is located. Lake is about 1.5 miles NE of Milton. From I-5 use Exit 143 to 320th St. E. to Military Rd., then S. 3 miles to lake.

FOSS LAKES (W. FK.) Several large, beautiful hike-in trout lakes in the headwaters of the West Fork Foss River in Alpine Lakes Wilderness. Shortest access is from Hwy. 2. Drive E. from Skykomish for 1.5 miles, then S. on Foss River Rd./FS 68 to FS 6835 and continue S. to road end trailhead. Trail 1064 continues to lakes in the headwaters of the E. Fork Foss River. **ANGELINE LAKE** is a 198-acre cutthroat lake at 5100 feet. Other nearby lakes are: **TROUT LAKE** (17 acres) rainbow, 2012 feet elev. at the 1.5 mile mark. **MALACHITE** (80 acres) rainbow, cutthroat, 4200 feet elev., lies a short distance to the right 3.5 miles in from road end, while **COPPER** (148 acres) rainbow, cutthroat, brookies, 4000 feet elevation, is another 0.5 mile along the main trail. **LITTLE HEART** (29 acres) rainbow, cutthroat, 4250 feet elevation, and **BIG HEART** (191 acres) rainbow, cutthroat, 5100 feet elevation, are 6 and 8 miles in from road end. **CHETWOOD** (113 acres) rainbow, 5200 feet elevation, is located 1800 feet S. of Angeline. **AZURITE** (41 acres) cutthroat, is at 5100 feet elevation, **OTTER** (183 acres) cutthroat, 4400 feet elevation, and DELTA (47 acres) rainbow, cutthroat, 3500 feet elevation, are situated approximately 1 mile or less E. and N. of Angeline. Rough trails to these four lakes.

FOSS RIVER. A tumbling mountain stream heading in NE King County under the Cascade Crest, the Foss flows N. to junction with the Tye River 2 miles E. of Skykomish. The Beckler River joins these streams 1.5 miles W. of their junction and these three rivers then form the South Fork Skykomish River. From Hwy. 2 at Skykomish, Foss River Road heads SE 2 miles becomes FS 68 which swings S. to follow the Foss River 4 miles to junction of W. and E. Forks, then continues as FS 6835 about 2 miles up the W. Fork. FS Trail 1064 continues S. to Foss Lakes in Alpine Lakes Wilderness Area. The Foss River supports small native rainbow, some whitefish and bull trout char. Bull trout fishing is illegal under ESA conservation rules. Fair small rainbow fishing from June into October.

GENEVA LAKE. Anglers working this 29 acre lake are surprised occasionally by large triploid rainbow. Geneva is planted in March with 3500 catchable 'bows and 300 triploids avageraging 1.5 pounds. Fades fast after opening day. Some largemouth bass fishing. Public access on SW shore. From I-5 Exit 143 onto 320th E. to Military Rd., then S. over Hwy. 18 to 342nd St. at Lake Geneva Park.. **LAKE KILLARNEY** is located across the street.

GRANITE CREEK. A tributary of Middle Fork Snoqualmie River, Granite provides fair to good native cutthroat fishing in late summer and fall. The creek drains **GRANITE LAKES** of 9 and 14 acres located 8.8 miles SE of North Bend at 3660 and 2950 feet. Stocked with rainbow fry. From I-90 E. of North Bend turn N. at Edgewick Exit onto Middle Fork Snoqualmie Rd. In about 3 miles a gated logging road comes in from the E. This road parallels creek to Trail 1009A which continues below Granite Lakes to Thompson Lakes. Granite Creek enters Middle Fork at the bridge where road crosses to N. side of river.

GREEN LAKE. A shallow, weedy 255-acre lake in N. Seattle near the intersection of Aurora Ave (Hwy. 99) and 60th St. N. Stocked with tiger muskies, bullhead and channel catfish, largemouth and rock bass, rainbow and brown trout, perch, carp and goldfish. Open to fishing year-round and usually stocked with trout several times between mid March and mid June. Annual catchable trout plant averages 12,000 This big urban lake provides good to fair angling through much of the year. Surrounded by park, this is a good place for kids and bobber-worm rigs. Lake is ringed by a paved pathway with total bank access. Rental boats are available at NE corner and small boats may be carried in from various access points. No ramp.

GREEN (DUWAMISH) RIVER. Once a great steelhead and salmon river, the Green is barely a shadow of its former productive self, but is still the most popular river in South King County.

The Green begins on Blowout Mt. just below the crest of the Cascades S. of Stampede Pass and ends as the renamed industrialized Duwamish River flowing into Elliott Bay in S. Seattle. Some stretches still resemble a classic steelhead flow especially the miles of undeveloped gorge with plunging pools, white water, towering cliffs and almost no easy access. Until recent years the Green was one of the state's top 10 winter steelhead rivers. In the late 1980s sport fishermen were catching between 4500 and 7000 winter-runs and 1200 summer-runs a year. By 1999 those healthy catch counts were reduced to less than 800 winter-runs and 460 summer runs. The river is used as water supply by the city of Tacoma, and the lower river is netted for steelhead and salmon by treaty-empowered tribes. WDFW has a salmon hatchery at Soos Creek/Hwy. 18 and a steelhead rearing facility at Palmer at the upper edge of the gorge.

The river can be divided into four sections. The extreme upper reaches near the abandoned railroad town of Lester are reached from I-90 by turning S. at Stampede Pass. This area has native rainbow trout in a small, shallow flow that winds W. into Tacoma's watershed and collects behind the dam impounding Howard Hanson Reservoir. The watershed is closed to public entry. Below the watershed the river enters the rugged, practically unboatable Green River Gorge at Palmer and emerges at Flaming Geyser State Park where there is excellent bank fishing. The gorge is hazardous and should only be boated by skilled kayakers or small rafts. The few drift boats launched into the gorge have come out in small pieces, if they came out at all. The most popular drift boat float is the "middle river" putting in below Flaming Geyser Park at Whitney Bridge (just W. of the park entrance) and float downstream to a primitive ramp just above Hwy. 18. This is classic pool-run water with limited public access. Walk-in access is available at Metzler and O'Grady county parks, a trail on the south bank below Hwy. 18, and at several unmarked spots. From Hwy. 18 through Auburn and Kent the river flows slowly through a flat, urbanized valley. Bike and walking paths provide walk-in access in most areas. From the Renton Junction downstream to Elliott Bay the river is known as the Duwamish and is considered tide water.

A few trout, mostly sea-run cutthroat and young steelhead, are caught below Flaming Geyser State Park, but the Green is primarily a steelhead and salmon river. Peak winter steelheading is in December and January for hatchery fish and late February-early March for wild fish. Summer-run fishing is best in July and Aug. and again in Oct. when the first fall rains pull in fish. Salmon openings vary annually. Chinook and coho are found mostly downstream from the Hwy. 18/Soos Creek hatchery, and bright chums as far up as Flaming Geyser Park. September and October are peak salmon months.

To reach the middle river from I-5 Exit 142B E. on Hwy. 18 through Auburn to Green Valley Rd. which parallels the river upstream to Hwy. 169 passing Soos Creek access, Metzler Park, Whitney Bridge and Flaming Geyser State Park. Gorge sections are accessed through WDFW's Palmer Rearing facility, Kanasket State Park, Hwy. 169/Kummer Bridge S. of Black Diamond. Just S of Hwy. 169 bridge the Franklin-Enumclaw Rd. follows several miles of the river, at a distance. Old logging roads go to the edge of the gorge.

GREENWATER RIVER. A medium sized, heavily fished valley stream managed as a wild trout fishery. Flows into the White River at the community of Greenwater on Hwy. 410 about 17 miles E. of Enumclaw. No longer stocked by WDFW. Few small, wild rainbow, cutthroat and occasional brookie. No bait, selective gear restrictions, 2-fish, 12-inch minimum. Many primitive camp sites. A popular area with mushroomers and deer/elk hunters. From end of pavement FS Trail 1176 continues along the now creek-size river SE 2 miles to **GREENWATER LAKES** on the King-Pierce county line at 2780 feet elev. These 4 and 6 acre lakes hold cutthroat, rainbow and brookies. From Hwy. 410 about 2 miles SE of Greenwater turn E. on FS 70, a paved road, which leads upstream through logging areas for approximately 10 miles offering easy river access. When snow free FS 70 continues to headwaters of Little Naches River.

GROTTO LAKE. A deep, 4 acre rainbow lake at 3900 feet on NE side of Grotto Mt.. Drains to S. Fork Skykomish.

HALLER LAKE. A 15 acre N. Seattle neighborhood lake at Meridian and N. 125th. Largemouth bass, perch and brown bullhead. Public access from street ends at W. and N. ends of the lake.

HANCOCK LAKE. 236 acre mountain lake at 2172 feet elevation above North Fork Snoqualmie River near Calligan Lake. Hancock has wild rainbow, brookies and cutthroat and is on Weyerhaeuser Snoqualmie Tree Farm requiring vehicle access permit. Best from boat, steep brushy shoreline. Drive N. of North Bend on the North Fork County Road 6 miles to Spur 10 gate, then E. on Spur 10 for 0.5 miles to Spur 13 which leads approximately 2 miles to the lake's W. tip. Best fishing late summer, fall. All tributary streams closed.

HANSEN CREEK. A wild cutthroat stream near I-90, Hansen fishes best in summer and fall. Drains Scout Lake to South Fork Snoqualmie River at Bandera airstrip on I-90 about 7 miles W. of Snoqualmie Pass. Bandera Road leaves I-90 and FS Rd. continues up Hansen Creek. At switchbacks, park and bushwhack hike 1.5 miles to **SCOUT LAKE** at 3850 feet. It holds cutthroat and 'bows.

Many King County year-round lakes offer bluegills like this one caught by Natalie Sheely.

HEART LAKES. Alpine Lakes Wilderness lakes in head of W. Fork Foss River. Big Heart at 5100 feet elev. covers 190.7 acres 9 miles S. of Skykomish. **LITTLE HEART** is at 4250 feet and covers 28.6 acres. Both have rainbow.

HESTER LAKES. Big Hester is a mountain rainbow lake of 66.6 acres, on Mt. Price at 4050 feet, on Middle Fork Snoqualmie River Rd. **LITTLE HESTER** once planted with golden trout, is a 9.5 acre lake at 4200 feet, 700 feet W. of Big Hester. From Middle Fork Rd. follow Dingford Cr. Trail 1005 NE then S. on Trail 1005A to Big Hester.

HOLM LAKE (Nielson). Year-round lake lightly planted with 1200 catchable rainbow and largemouth bass. A 19-acre lake 4 miles E. of Auburn. Small WDFW access, launch. From Hwy. 18 exit onto Auburn-Black Diamond Road cross the Green River and immediately turn E. onto Lake Holm Road for 2 miles.

HOLOMAN LAKE. 6 acre mountain pothole with rainbows, 4.8 miles SW of Index at 3650 feet. Drains to North Fork Tolt River.

HORSESHOE SLOUGH. 7.1 acre Snoqualmie River backwater with largemouth bass and perch. Drive 4.5 miles N. of Fall City on Hwy. 203 then S. on Neal Rd. adjacent to river.

HULL LAKE. A 5.7 year-round lowland cutthroat pond on Weyerhaeuser's Snoqualmie Tree Farm, 9.5 miles N. of Snoqualmie in East Fork Griffin Creek drainage to Snoqualmie River. Brushy, bring a float tube.

ISLAND LAKE. Popular day-hike mountain Lake covering 17.4 acres on Bandera Mt. N. of I-90. Holds rainbows. Lake is at 4200 feet 13 miles SE from North Bend. Drains to Talapus Lake. Take Talapus Lake exit N. of I-90 to FS Rd. 9030 to trailhead.

ISSAQUAH CREEK. Closed to fishing, this wild cutthroat spawning and salmon hatchery stream passes through Issaquah under I-90 to enter S. end of Lake Sammamish at state park. Heads NE of Hobart and flows N. along Issaquah-Hobart Rd. about 10 miles to Issaquah. WDFW Issaquah salmon hatchery has excellent observation decks and underwater instream views of returning fall salmon beginning in late August.

JANICKE SLOUGH. A "U" shaped 10.2 acre Snoqualmie River backwater 2 miles N. of Fall City on Hwy. 203. Holds largemouth bass, yellow perch.

JENKINS CREEK. A spring creek flowing from the city of Kent watershed near Lake Sawyer SW into Big Soos Creek. Much of the stream roughly follows a railroad track that provides brushy access to deep shaded pools and log jams that hold surprisingly large resident cutthroat. Some coho spawning.

JONES LAKE (Fourteen). Cattail encircled 23 acre lake with rainbow, bass, crappie, catfish and perch. No public access. Adjacent to Hwy. 169 on S. side of Black Diamond.

JOY LAKE. 105 acres, with rainbow, cutthroat and perch. Up to 50 feet deep this is an excellent fish-growing lake with poor, often unmarked public access on NW shore. Most trout are self sustaining. Access disagreements with residents have lead to sporadic trout stocking. There are some very large trout, here, however. Drive 2 miles N. of Carnation on Hwy. 203 to Stillwater turn N. up Stillwater Hill Rd for 1 mile, then NE. onto Lake Joy Road which encircles the lake. Small boats or tubes needed.

JUANITA LAKE (Wittenmeyer, Mud). 3 acre pond with bass and crappie, at Firloch about 1.5 miles NE of Juanita. Good fishing lake for kids.

KATHLEEN LAKE (Meadow). 39 acre suburb lake 4 miles E. of Renton, Kathleen has rainbow, bass and perch. From Renton go E. on NE 4th St./SE 128th St. about 3 miles to Lake Kathleen Road, then S. 0.5 mile to lake. Drains to May Creek. Access is restricted.

KERRS LAKE (Brewster). Cutthroat are in this 3 acre lake 3.4 miles S. of North Bend W. off Cedar Falls Rd. Drains into South Fork Snoqualmie River.

KILLARNEY LAKE. A year-round largemouth bass, perch, sunfish and brown bullhead lake just S. of Hwy. 18. 31 acres with small WDFW access on the NE shore. Military Road to 342nd street, then W. 0.5 miles to intersection of S. 38th and S. 344th. Low water will make late summer boat launching difficult. **LAKE GENEVA** is across the street.

KINGS LAKE. A 3 acre brook trout lake up North Fork Snoqualmie River surrounded by 50 acres of peat bog swamp on Tokul Creek. It lies 1 mile W. of **BOYLE LAKE**. Fishing is best in spring and fall (See Bridges Lake for route). Vehicle access requires Weyerhaeuser permit.

KLAUS LAKE. A 62 acre lake in logged area of Weyerhaeuser Snoqualmie Tree Farm connected to Boyle and Bridges lakes. Has fair to good fishing for cutthroat to 16 inches, largemouth bass to several pounds and perch. Rough boat access on SE corner. Requires Weyerhaeuser vehicle access.

KULLA KULLA LAKE. 60-acre mountain lake with small brook trout at 3765 feet elev. in a timbered bowl on E. slope of Mt. Defiance. Cutthroat and rainbow. Follow Pratt Lake trail system from I-90 Exit 45 to FS Rd. 9030 about 0.8 miles W. of the Asahel Curtis FS picnic area. Stay N. on FS Rd. 9030 to trailhead for **TALAPUS LAKE** at 3780 feet. Drains to Pratt River.

OLALLIE LAKE. One of several scenic ridge-top trout lakes just N. of I-90's Exit 45 at the SW edge of Alpine Lakes Wilderness Area. Lakes drain to Pratt River. Olallie Lake, 17 acres, at 3780 elev., is 2400 feet NE of Talapus Lk. Has rainbow and cutthroat. Reached from Talapus Lk. on trail 1009. Trail 1007 forks N. from Olallie Lake about 2 miles to **PRATT LAKE** at 3385 feet. Pratt has brookies. Trail 1009 continues W. from Olallie for 1.5 miles to pass between **RAINBOW LAKE**, a rainbow lake at 4270 feet, and **BLAZER LAKE** which holds rainbow. Both are about 6 acres. Blazer elev. is 4060 feet. Approximately 0.8 miles farther W. a side trail leads 0.4 miles S. to **MASON LAKE**, 33 acres at 4180 feet elev. Mason and Little Mason have rainbow. **LITTLE MASON** is just over the ridge line from Mason at 4260 feet off FS Trail 1009. Ice-free in mid-June. Sept.-Oct. often excellent. Short, but steep route to Mason Lakes from I-90 Exit 45 turn N. on FS Road 9030 and continue W. on 9031 to road end at Trailhead 1036. Trail begins as an overgrown logging road crosses outlet then turns sharply uphill and climbs steeply through forest, boulder field and root-and-rock wall to lake.

LANGENDORFER LAKE.(Stossel Lake) One of two adjacent ponds at head of Stossel Cr., 6 miles NE of Hwy. 203 jct. with Stillwater Hill Rd. Stocked with fat coastal cutthroat. Best in spring, from float tube or raft. Open year-round. From Hwy. 203 follow Stillwater Hill Rd. to Kelly Rd. then NE on Stossel Creek Rd. to lake.

LANGLOIS LAKE. A very popular quiet, undeveloped lowland lake 1.5 miles S. of Carnation. Stocked in mid-April with 6000 rainbows, some large carry-overs and largemouth bass. Heavily fished in early May for stockers, but by late summer and early fall the crowds are gone and Langlois (pronounced Lang-Loy) is a great place to try for husky holdovers. Good fly lake. The lake is 98 feet deep, and covers 40 acres. Private shoreline is rimmed with timber and fallen tree structure. Large WDFW access and ramp on SE shore. Disabled paved access. Go S. from Carnation on Hwy. 203 then E. on Langlois Lake Rd./NE 24th to lake.

LARSEN LAKE. A 7.3 acre peat bog pond in Belleuve Park. Cutthroat, largemouth bass, bullhead catfish, and perch. Trail access, public fishing pier, best from float tube. Open year-round. Drains to Lake Washington.

LENNOX CREEK. A cold, tumbling pool and riffle major tributary to North Fork

Snoqualmie River. Best in late summer and fall for small wild rainbow and cutthroat. Lennox Creek joins the North Fork Snoqualmie in Snoqualmie National Forest about 18 miles NE of North Bend. Follow North Fork County Road/FS 57 from North Bend past confluence and upstream on FS 5740 along Lennox Cr. for 7 miles. Several trails lead from creek to mountain lakes.

LEOTA LAKE (Summit). A 10.1 acre lake 2 miles E. of Woodinville adjacent to Woodinville-Duvall Rd. It has rainbow, largemouth bass, bluegill, black crappie, perch and brown bullhead. Access is difficult.

LODGE LAKE. Rainbow trout lake, 9.3 acres, 1.5 miles SW of Snoqualmie Pass. Drains into Lodge Creek to South Fork Snoqualmie River at Denny Creek.

LOOP LAKE. A 35.7 acre brook trout lake on Weyerhaeuser Snoqualmie Tree Farm. Vehicle access permit required. Loop is encircled in dense brush and you'll need a small boat or float tube to fish it effectively for brookies that reach two pounds. Most are smaller. Lake is up gated Griffin Creek Rd. which runs E. from Hwy. 203 S. of Carnation. Drains to Tolt River.

LUCERNE-PIPE LAKES. Pair of deep connected lakes in Covington off Hwy. 516/Kent-Kangley Rd. Lucerne is 16 acres and Pipe covers 52 acres. Decent rainbow fishing in spring, but best for perch and largemouth bass. A few cutthroat and bullhead catfish. Drive 7 miles E. of Kent on Hwy. 516, to 213th Pl. then N. 0.4 miles to lakes. Access is from street end located between the lakes.

LYNCH LAKE. Wild cutthroat lake in a logging area on Weyerhaeuser's Snoqualmie Tree Farm, vehicle permit required. Lynch covers 23 acres, N. of Tolt Pipeline Rd. Open year-round.

MALACHITE LAKE. A large cutthroat and rainbow lake of l79.7 acres in a large rocky bowl at 4200 feet, in Alpine Lakes Wilderness 7.4 miles S. Skykomish. Drains to W. Fork Foss River. From Foss River Rd./FS 68/6835 to Trail 1064.

MALONEY LAKES. Group of three small lakes at 4000 feet on crest of Maloney Ridge 2.8 miles S. of Skykomish. Planted with rainbow and cutthroat fry. Drain to S.

Fork Skykomish. From Hwy. 2 go S. on FS 68 to FS 6846.

MARGARET LAKE (Marion). Planted with catchable rainbow and cutthroat. Notoriously slow starter but picks up in summer and fall. Cutts of 9-12 inches are common in this 44 acre lake. Some largemouth bass. Drains to Snoqualmie River. Drive 3.5 miles E. from Duvall, then N. 2 miles to the lake's W. shore WDFW access, ramp.

MARIE LAKE. A cutthroat lake, Marie is 10 acres, produces fair in spring, but is best in late summer and fall. Drive 2 miles E. of Fall City on Hwy. 202, then N. on 365th for 1 mile to W. end of the lake. Boggy shore.

MARMOT LAKE. A 135 acre mountain cutthroat lake reached by trail from the end of the Cle Elum River Road 33 miles N. of Cle Elum. Follow Trail 1376 NW for 5 miles, passing Hyas Lake to PCT 2000 at Deception Pass. Follow Trail 1066 NW 3.5 miles to Marmot Lake at 4900 feet elev. **CLARICE LAKE** a 41 acre brookie lake lies at 4500 feet about .75 mile N. of Marmot.

MARTEN LAKE. Rainbow are in this remote 40 acre lake which sits in a rocky bowl and drains into the Taylor River NE of North Bend. Marten is at an elev. of 2959 feet, accessible by tough hike from Taylor River Trail 1002. **DREAM LAKE** is reached by continuing 2 miles past Marten's outlet to Big Creek, then toughing it up the creek 1.5 miles to Dream at 3800 feet. This rainbow lake covers 35 acres. Leave I-90 at Exit 34/Edgewick Rd 3.2 miles E. of North Bend and drive Middle Fork Snoqualmie River Rd./FS 56 for 15 miles. At Garfield Mt. road branches N. to Taylor River trailhead. Hike 3.5 miles on Trail 1002, cross Marten Lake outlet, and scramble 1 mile upstream to lake.

MARTIN CREEK. Rainbow and cutthroat are taken from this Tye River tributary. Access is difficult via an abandoned trail upstream from mouth at Tye Canyon FS campground located 7 miles E. of Skykomish on the N. side of the Tye.

MASON LAKE. Big Mason covers 32.6 acres and lies at 4180 feet l2 miles SE of North Bend. **LITTLE MASON**, 4.3 acres, is just NW. Both have rainbow plants and drain to S. Fork Snoqualmie. See Olallie Lake for directions.

MAUD LAKE. Very good fishing for 14-inch coastal cutthroat planted in this 2.1 acre lake adjacent to E. side of North Fork County Road/FS 57 about 8 miles N. from North Bend at 1140 feet. Drains to North Fork Snoqualmie. Short bushwhack. Raft or float tube essential.

McDONALD LAKE. A poor largemouth bass lake of 18 acres 6 miles E. of Renton and 0.5 miles SE of Kathleen Lake. Drains into Issaquah Creek. Drive E. from Renton on SE 128th St. for 4 miles then S. on 196th Ave. SE for 1 mile to W. side of lake.

McLEOD LAKE. A brushy, short hike-in lake covering 13 acres with fair to good fishing for rainbow, brookies and a few cutthroat. Tough, limited bank access, best from rafts, float tubes. McLeod lies at 1006 feet elev. 5 miles N. of North Bend. It drains into Tate Creek and North Fork Snoqualmie River. From North Bend follow North Fork County Road/FS 57 N. for about 4.5 miles to a sharp curve where Spur Road H-10 intersects. Park at barricade and walk old road 0.4 miles E. to a primitive trail to lake shore.

MEADOWBROOK SLOUGH. Three connected segments make up this 13.9 acre slough in E. Snoqualmie. Holds largemouth bass and perch. Drains to Snoqualmie River.

MELAKWA LAKES. A pair of small Alpine Lakes Wilderness waters on N. side of I-90 about 3 miles W. of Snoqualmie Pass. Lower Melakwa is at 4490 feet and covers 7.9 acres. It is fed by **UPPER MELAKWA**, a 1.8 acre lake 300 feet N. Both hold rainbow and drain to Pratt River. From I-90, Exit 47 to Denny Creek camp to FS Trail 1014 N. to lakes near Hemlock Pass.

MERIDIAN LAKE. A popular year-round lake stocked with 9000 catchable rainbows early in spring with anglers switching to kokanee that matured from plants of 30,000 fry and warm water species in mid-summer. The rainbow plant is usually in early May. Good numbers of large and smallmouth bass, (5 pounders are caught) pumpkinseed, perch and brown bullhead catfish. Lake is adjacent to busy Hwy. 516 in a residential area E. of Kent, covers 150 acres and is 90 feet deep. Small WDFW access and ramp on NE. shore. Large county park with long public fishing pier is accessed from Hwy. 516/Kent-Kangley Rd. Drains to Soos Creek.

METCALF SLOUGH. A series of marshy ponds covering about 5 acres at base of Fuller Mt. Supports mostly stocked cutthroat and small brookies. Slough is 6.7 miles N. of North Bend just N. of Spur 10 jct. where it connects North Fork County Road/FS 57 and Weyerhaeuser's mainline mill road. Walk-in access through a thin band of brush dividing Weyerhaeuser and

Moolock Lakes.

North Fork County Roads or drive-in with Weyerhaeuser vehicle access permit. Drains to **METCALF LAKE**, a 6 acre pond with the same species.

MILLER RIVER. A tributary of South Fork Skykomish River 2 miles W. of Skykomish and Hwy. 2. Pools in the Miller provide fair rainbow and cutthroat fishing in summer and early fall. Money Creek FS campground is just W. of mouth. From Hwy. 2 FS road 6410 and 6412 track the river upstream 9 miles to Camp Robber Valley where FS Trail 1072 climbs 1.5 miles to **DOROTHY LAKE** in Alpine Lakes Wilderness.

MONEYSMITH LAKE. A long, shallow, narrow weedy lake with largemouth bass, perch, crappie and catfish. Covers 22 acres 4 miles E. of Auburn and 0.5 miles S. of Lake Holm. Exceptionally large perch have been taken. Go E. of Auburn on Auburn-Black Diamond Road, cross Green River and turn E. on Lake Holm road (336th) about 2 miles to Moneysmith Road, then S. to lake.

MOOLOCK LAKES. A cluster of 3 mountain lakes N. of North Bend's Mt. Si between N. and Middle Forks Snoqualmie river. The largest is Moolock Lake, a 45 acre rainbow and cutthroat lake at 3903 feet about 1.5 miles SE and 1700 feet higher than **HANCOCK LAKE'S** E. tip. Nearby are **SMC**, 40 acres at 3702 elev. and **NADEAU** 18.9 acres, at 3722 elev. Lakes are on E. side of Weyerhaeuser Snoqualmie Tree Farm, vehicle access permit required. From North Bend drive North Fork County Road/ FS 57 N. to Spur 10, go E. through gate then turn S. on logging road and climb to trail near crest. A decent trail links the logging road and all 3 lakes.

MORTON LAKE. A year-round 66-acre rainbow planted lake near Covington. WDFW access and ramp on NW shore. Good in April and early May for 8600 planted catchable rainbows. A few largemouth bass are present. From Hwy. 18, at Covington turn SE on Hwy. 516/272nd to stoplight at Wax Road, then S. on Wax to Covington Way SE. Turn left on Covington for 2.5 miles, then right on 188th Ave. SE to lake.

MOSS LAKE. A 6.5 acre year-round wild cutthroat lake 3 miles N. of Carnation off Stillwater Hill Road. Good for float tubes, small boats, some shore access.

MUD LAKE. A tough to reach 11 acre lake in the foothills 4 miles S. of US 2 at Index. Wild brook trout 9 to 11 inches, some to 14 inches. Best in spring. No trail. Follow N. branch of Index Creek. Logging roads come close to lake.

MURPHY LAKES. Remote, seldom fished mountain lakes near Scenic on US 2. Lower Murphy, 4300 feet elev. and 3.5 acres; Upper Murphy, 4500 feet, 7 acres, lie at head of Murphy Creek 1.5 miles S. of Scenic The lakes hold rainbow and cutthroat. Best route is to follow the ridge on W. side of Murphy Creek S. to the lakes. No formal trail.

MYRTLE LAKE. Rainbow planted lake of 18 acres at 3950 feet elev. north of Middle Fork Snoqualmie River. Fed by **LITTLE MYRTLE** LAKE 2800 feet S. of Big Myrtle. Lakes drain to Middle Fork Snoqualmie River. Follow Middle Fork County Road/FS 56 NE to Dingford Creek Trail 1005 to reach lakes in Alpine Lakes Wilderness.

NEWAUKUM CREEK. A Green River tributary heading under Enumclaw Mt. and flowing W. across Enumclaw Plateau under Hwy. 169 for approximately 15 miles entering the Green River below Whitney Bridge. Creek has wild rainbow, cutthroat and a few spawning steelhead and coho salmon. Little public access.

NORDRUM BASIN LAKES. Several high mountain cutthroat and rainbow lakes in a basin in Taylor River drainage of Alpine Lakes Wilderness. Cutthroat are in Nordrum a 60 acre alpine lake at 3800 feet elev. 17 miles NE of North Bend in the headwaters of the Taylor River's S. Fork. **JUDY LAKE**, 1500 feet W. of Nordrum, covers 10 acres and is fed by underground outlet from Nordrum. **CAROLE LAKE**, 11 acres is 3000 feet W. of Nordrum. **ROCK LAKE** and **LUNKER LAKES,** 9 and 3 acres, are in the same group. These lakes contain cutts and rainbow. From North Bend at I-90 Exit 34 to Middle Fork Snoqualmie River Rd. for 15 miles to mouth of Taylor River. Hike NE up Taylor River Trail/FS 1002 for 10 miles to Nordrum Lake Trail 1004 and continue 4 tough miles to Nordrum. Rough trails lead to other lakes in the basin.

NORTH LAKE. A 55 acre rainbow and largemouth bass lake with a large developed WDFW access on its W. shore.

Stocked in April with about 7000 catchable rainbows. North is 3 miles W. of Auburn and drains into Commencement Bay through Hylebos Creek. From I-5, Exit 143 onto 320th E. to a S. turn onto 32nd. Ave. S., to N. shore of lake.

PANTHER LAKE. A poor to fair bet for perch, largemouth bass, bullheads and other warm water species. This 33 acre, residential area lake is on Kent's East Hill. From Hwy. 515/Benson Rd., turn E. on 204th St. for 0.5 miles to S. end of lake.

PARADISE LAKE. An 18 acre private lake 5 miles NE of Woodinville with cutthroat and rainbow. Drains into Bear Creek to Sammamish Slough. Route is E. from Woodinville 4.5 miles, passing Cottage Lake, then N. on Paradise Lake Road 1.5 miles to S. side of lake.

PETERSON LAKE. A cattail-encircled 10 acre year-round lake E. of Renton adjacent to Petrovitsky Rd. at 196th Ave. SE. Holds rainbow, cutthroat, bass, perch, catfish. Drains to Cedar River. Difficult access, no bank fishing, bring float tube. Take Hwy. 169 S. to Maple Valley/Hwy. 18 overpass. Turn S. over Hwy. 18 then immediately NW. onto 220th Ave. SE, then N. onto Petrovitsky and continue to lake.

PHANTOM LAKE. 3.5 miles SE of Bellevue this 63.2 acre lake has largemouth bass, black crappie, pumpkinseed, yellow perch and brown bullhead. Public park access on W. side. A launch permit is required from Bellevue City Park Dept. A small float offers limited shore fishing. Drains to Lake Sammamish. SE Phantom Way follows the N. shore. Open year round. Take 156th Ave. SE to an E. turn onto 16th St. to lake.

PHILLIPA LAKE. A tough to reach, rarely fished 121-acre, 76 feet deep mountain lake at 3346 feet elev. at the headwaters of Phillipa Creek which spills down cliff face to North Fork Snoqualmie River 11 miles NE of North Bend. Phillipa is the westernmost lake in Alpine Lakes Wilderness and has rainbow trout. Nearby **ISABELLA LAKE** covers 12 acres 700 feet E. of Phillipa. It has cutthroat. The lakes are reached by driving N. from North Bend on North Fork County Road to Spur 16 which leads E. and S. up Brannon Creek for about 1.5 miles. Phillipa is a brushy, steep 2 miles up Phillapa Creek. No trail.

PINE LAKE. Rainbow, large triploids, browns (to several pounds), cutthroat, largemouth and smallmouth bass and pumpkinseeds are in Pine, an 88 acre lake 4 miles N. of Issaquah. About 12,000 catchable 'bows and 2000 triploids are planted in April. Also stocked with 10,000 rainbow and 6000 brown trout fry. Starts slow, but often holds up well all season. King County Park access on E. shore with picnic area, small boat ramp and large fishing pier. N. from Issaquah onto Issaquah-Fall City Rd., then NW onto Issaquah-Pine Lake Rd. and continue to lake.

PRATT RIVER. If you crave lonely, challenging fishing for wild trout this is your stream. The Pratt is a large, remote tributary of the Middle Fork Snoqualmie River flowing along the N. side of the ridge that towers above the N. side of I-90 between North Bend and Denny Creek. The Pratt is a turbulent mountain stream best fished from mid- summer into fall after snow runoff. Supports small wild rainbow, cutthroat and a few brook trout. The river is followed by FS Trail 1035 from the mouth upstream through a steeply walled valley into Snoqualmie National Forest. This trail connects, on the E. near Pratt Mt., with trails leading to the I-90 trailheads at Talapus Lake and Denny Creek. Primitive campsites along stream. Best access is at the mouth where the Pratt joins Middle Fork Snoqualmie River. From I-90 Exit 34 go N. on Middle Fork Road for about 9.5 miles to a small unsigned pullover at the edge of the river. The spot is marked by large chunks of concrete remaining from a long-gone bridge. Wade across the Middle Fork to start of Trail 1035.

PRESTON MILL PONDS. A pair of 2 acre ponds which drain into Raging River at the community of Preston off I-90 Exit 22. Sometimes stocked with catchable rainbows.

PTARMIGAN LAKE (Upper). Golden trout have been planted in this deep 12.8 acre mountain lake at 5000 feet elev. near the S. end of Tonga Ridge. Drains for 800 feet into **LOWER PTARMIGAN**, 28 acres, a rainbow lake, 7.8 miles SE of Skykomish. Lakes drain NE to Fisher Creek which spills into Deception Creek at trailhead end of FS Rd. 6830. From US 2 at Foss River turn S. on FS 68, then E. on FS 6830 up and over Tonga Ridge ending at Fisher Creek outlets from Ptarmigan Lakes.

PUGET SOUND. Several public fishing piers and docks provide non-boating fishing access to Puget Sound. Marine fishing areas include Dash Point pier, Des Moines pier, Dockton Park dock on Vashon Island, Elliot Bay fishing pier, Maury Island dock at Tramp Harbor, North Shilshole pier, Redondo pier and Seacrest pier in West Seattle. Artificial reefs have been built near some of the piers attracting a variety of rockfish, flounder, salmon, popcorn shrimp and crabs. The lighted piers provide good night snagging for winter squid.

RAGING RIVER. A small fast-flowing winter steelhead stream that heads E. of Hwy. 18, and rumbles W. crossing under I-90 at Exit 22 through the small community of Preston then flowing N. 4 miles along the winding Preston-Fall City Rd. to enter Snoqualmie River at a large WDFW access site in Fall City. A small stream that clears quickly and is often fishable when larger rivers flood. Snaggy. Bring lots of tackle. Mostly wild steelhead in Nov., Dec. and Jan. between Preston and Fall City.

RATTLESNAKE LAKE. A fishy, fertile, stumpy lake S. of North Bend. Stocked in April with 12,000 rainbows. A large park with small boat ramp on E. shore. Electric motors allowed, but not gasoline powered engines. Great for float tubes, but often lashed with high winds. Rattlesnake is managed as a selective tackle fishery, producing fish in the 10 to 15 inch range. Tops in spring, but produces all summer as long as there's water. At full pool the lake is around 100 acres but can fluctuate to 50 acres. Rattlesnake lies at 911 feet elev. at the edge of Cedar River Watershed. From North Bend I-90 Exit 32 S. onto 436th SE/Cedar Falls Rd. 4 miles to lake.

RAVENSDALE CREEK. Spring and summer for wild cutthroat and rainbow. A brushy, shallow tough-fishing creek that meanders about 3 miles through overgrown clear cuts SW from Ravensdale Lake, crossing under Hwy. 169 to enter the SE end of Lake Sawyer.

RAVENSDALE LAKE (AKA Beaver). A tree and brush encircled 18-acres with some surprisingly good wild cutthroat angling in spring and fall. Abandoned railway skirts SE shore. From Hwy. 169 at Four Corners, go E. on Hwy. 516/Kent Kangley Rd. to Ravensdale then SE on Ravensdale-Black Diamond Rd. to lake. No developed

access, but some bank fishing areas, and places where car-top boats and tubes may be carried to the water. Selective tackle, no bait, 12-inch trout minimum.

RED CREEK. May produce small brookies, wild cutthroat. A tributary of the White River. Drive 6 miles E. of Enumclaw on Hwy. 410 which crosses the stream at Mud Mountain Dam turnoff

REID SLOUGH. Covering 3.4 acres, 1.4 miles N. of North Bend just S. of North Fork County Rd bridge across Middle Fork Snoqualmie River. Largemouth bass and yellow perch. Drains to Snoqualmie River.

RETREAT LAKE (AKA Thirty-Two and Fish). No public access. Rainbow, cutthroat, kokanee salmon, perch and crappie are in this 53 acre lake 2 miles E. of Ravensdale. From Hwy. 169 at Four Corners turn E. on Hwy. 516/Kent-Kangley Rd. through Ravensdale then S. on Kanasket Rd. to SE 276th which nearly encircles the lake.

ROCK CREEK. Cedar River tributary closed to fishing. Wild rainbow, cutthroat, spawning sockeye salmon are present in this pastoral stream flowing from Taylor Mt. to the Cedar River below Landsburg Dam.

ROCK CREEK. A short, brush-canopied, spring creek flowing from springs S. of Black Diamond N. under Auburn/Black Diamond Rd. to enter the S. end of Lake Sawyer. Tough, brushy fishing for wild rainbow and cutthroat. May have spawning coho.

ROCK LAKE. 23 acre mountain lake with brown and rainbow trout. Elevation is 4400 feet. Location is 5 miles S. from Skykomish off FS Rd. 6846. Drains to W. Fork Foss River.

ROUND LAKE. A 2.6 acre pond with largemouth bass about 2 miles E. of Issaquah, draining to Issaquah Creek.

RUTHERFORD SLOUGH (AKA Fall City Slough) A shallow, swampy oxbow covering 18 acres 0.5 mile N. of Fall City adjacent to Hwy. 203. Excellent producer of largemouth bass in spring, early summer. Access from highway shoulder. Raft or small boat necessary.

SAMMAMISH LAKE. Very popular, residentially-encircled 8 mile long, 4897 acre

Jerry Olson with Lake Sammamish smallmouth.

lake between I-90 and Redmond E. of Bellevue. Open year-round and offers a variety of cold and warm water fishing, some of it very good. Some lake veterans troll for big (20 inchers are taken) cutthroat in winter and spring, and shoreline fishing is above average for largemouth and smallmouth bass spring into summer, plus perch, catfish, rainbow, several species of salmon and steelhead. Fishing is closed for the lake's ESA protected kokanee salmon which only a few years ago were the lake's leading fishery. Sammamish is deep, 100 feet maximum, with steep shorelines. Both ends, however, are shallow and good fishing for bass. The N. end near Marymoor Park is marshy and supports cattails, lily pads and pilings that offer good early morning and evening casting for largemouth bass in mid-summer. The E. shoreline is steep, rip rapped with large rocks and often has a gravel bottom that attracts smallmouth to docks, rock piles and drop-offs. Sammamish is an excellent lake in May and June for very large smallmouth. Submerged forest at elbow on SW shore is a favorite smallmouth spot. The piling-studded, gravel bottom near the boat launch and mouth of Issaquah Creek at the S. end of lake is especially hot for smallmouth in spring when salmon smolts are pouring into the lake from the WDFW Issaquah Salmon Hatchery. Occasionally WDFW will open a fall coho or chinook fishery for returning hatchery adults. Summer fishermen compete with heavy play boat congestion. Access can be a problem. The lake is rimmed with private homes and except for a small bank fishing area at the state park all access is from boats. The only decent public ramp, however, is a deluxe state park facility, open daylight hours only, at the S. end off East Lake Sammamish Pkwy. Almost every boater launching onto this 8-mile long lake in the heart of a major population center is jammed into this one overworked, part-time ramp. Expect long lines and congestive chaos on summer weekends. A ramp is very much needed at Marymoor County Park on Sammamish's N. end. Park goers may dodge the ramp lines by carrying portable boats to the lake. Private resorts have ramps from West Lake Sammamish Pky. To reach the large state park from I-90 Exit 17 N. to park entrance. To reach the boat launch continue N. then NW on East Lake Sammamish Pky. to marked launch. For state park information call 425-455-7010. No camping.

SAMMAMISH (SLOUGH) RIVER. The slough is the sluggish connection between Lakes Sammamish and Washington. It flows NW from Marymoor County Park at the N. end of Lake Sammamish to enter Lake Washington at Kenmore where a public boat launch site is located at the Kenmore bridge. The ditch-like stream still has a fair run of winter steelhead, and sea-run cutthroat in spring and fall. However, there are few if any steelhead in the slough during the brief angling season June 1-Aug. 31 between 68th Ave. NE bridge and Lake Sammamish. Much of the slough is followed by a paved pathway.

SAWYER LAKE. Third largest lake in King County this 279 acre natural lake has long been a top multi-species lake. Open year-round it offers chunky rainbow and cutthroat trout (10 to 14 inchers are typical), kokanee salmon, smallmouth and largemouth bass, crappie, perch, bullhead catfish and a few bluegills. Very popular with bass clubs, especially early in the season. Boat speeds in excess of 8 mph are allowed only at mid-day, limiting play boat activity and reserving morning and evenings for fishermen. In recent years Sawyer has developed into a smallmouth bass honey hole. Bronzebacks (5 pounders are not unheard of) are best April-June, large-mouth (to 7 pounds) tops May-July. This lake is a challenge and doesn't part with its fish easily, but some nice fish are at the end of the puzzle. March to June and September to December are good for trout. Kokanee hit trolled pop gear or still-fished maggots from May into mid-summer. Chumming is legal. Most trout fishermen troll mid lake. Worm fishing for perch in the many lily pad and weed bed areas can be good, especially from late summer into early September. Mid lake depths to 60 feet, yet the depth is about 15 feet inside the water ski buoy line that circles the lake 100 feet offshore. This is a good depth for bass and panfish and off limits for ski boats. A private membership-only resort on the W. shore is not open to the public. Small boat ramp with limited parking and shore fishing access in the park on the NW side. The S. end of the lake is undeveloped King County park property with no parking and marginal bank fishing. From Hwy. 18 turn E. on Hwy. 516/Kent-Kangley Rd. to 216th Ave. SE, then S. for 1.5 miles past Lake

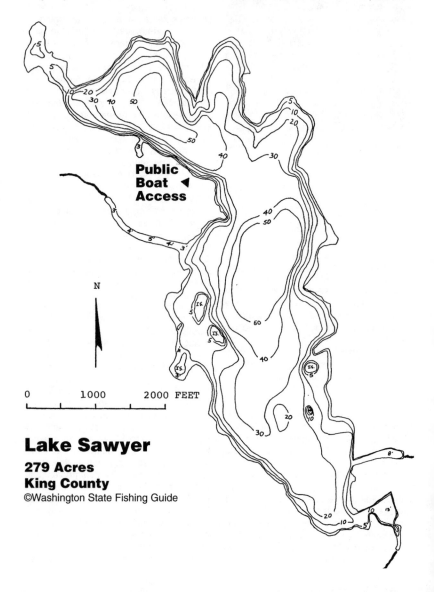

Public Boat ◀ Access

N

0   1000   2000 FEET

Lake Sawyer
279 Acres
King County
©Washington State Fishing Guide

Sawyer Grocery (coffee, bait & tackle) to SE 296th St. and marked boat launch. Fish ladder and outlet to Covington Creek is just past boat launch turnoff.

SECOND LAKE. A 2.5 acre rainbow and cutthroat pothole E. of Enumclaw. From Hwy. 410 walk-in access by going N. on gated logging road at Weyerhaeuser White River mill along Boise Ridge. Drains to White River.

SHADOW LAKE. A year-round 50 acres multi-species lake 5 miles from Hwy. 169. Shadow gets a plant of 3000 rainbows in March. Also offers largemouth bass, black crappie, pumpkinseed and perch. Small WDFW access, ramp on narrow arm leading to the main lake from N. shore. Very limited bank fishing. From Renton SE on Hwy. 169 then S. on 196th Ave. SE 4 miles to lake.

SHADY LAKE (AKA Hostak & Mud). Restrictive regulations are developing a quality fishery at this 21 acre lake 5 miles SE of Renton. In mid-May, Shady is stocked with 2500 catchable rainbows, adding to a self-sustaining population of largemouth bass, sunfish and perch. Season is from June 1 to Oct. 31 with one trout over 14 inches allowed in the 5 trout limit. WDFW access, ramp, disabled access on S. shore. From Benson Rd./Hwy.515 turn E. onto 176th/ Petrovitsky Road for 5 miles then N. on SE 192nd Dr. which circles lake.

SIKES LAKE. A 14 acre private lake with brook trout and brown bullheads on Carnation Farm, N. of Carnation. Drains to Snoqualmie River.

SKYLINE LAKE. 2 acre rainbow lake at 4950 feet elev. 1 mile N. from Stevens Pass. Drains to Tye River.

SKYKOMISH RIVER SOUTH FORK. The South Fork Sky edges across the extreme N. side of the county and is formed by the Foss, Tye and Beckler Rivers which meet 1 to 2 miles E. of town of Skykomish. Miller River and Money Creek enter the South Fork about 2 miles W. of Skykomish. WDFW no longer stocks catchable trout. Fishing is for small wild rainbows, a few cutthroat and rare brookie from June into September. Anadromous salmon and trout are excluded from the upper river by Sunset Falls 2 miles upstream from North Fork confluence near Index. During fall and early winter sea-run salmon, steelhead and cutthroat stack below the falls. US 2 follows the South Fork from Index SE to Skykomish, then continues to Steven Pass along the Tye River. The North Fork and main Skykomish are listed in Snohomish County.

SNOQUALMIE LAKE. One of several large low mountain lakes at the head of the Taylor River NE of North Bend in the W. Alpine Lakes Wilderness Area. Snoqualmie Lake covers 126 acres at 3225 feet elev. and has rainbow, cutthroat and brookies. Taylor River Trail to Snoqualmie Lake continues 1 mile to **DEER LAKE**, a 46 acre rainbow and cutthroat lake at 3630 feet where there are campsites, and **BEAR LAKE** 49 acres at 3670 feet elevation which is adjacent to E. side of Deer. Bear holds rainbow and cutthroat. One mile E. by trail is **DOROTHY LAKE** at 3052 feet, 290 acres with cutthroat and brookies. Dorothy drains N. into the East Fork Miller River. The other lakes empty W. into Taylor River. These are among the earliest high lakes to shed winter ice and are sometimes fishable by late May. From I-90 Exit 34 turn N. onto Middle Fork Road/FS 56 for 12.7 miles to Taylor River confluence. Hike NE on Trail 1002 up Taylor River 9.5 miles to the lake.

SNOQUALMIE RIVER MAIN. A shadow of what it was in the 1980s but still one of Puget Sound's most productive and popular steelhead, sea-run cutthroat and salmon rivers, the mainstem Snoqualmie River forms at North Bend in the confluences of the North, Middle and South Forks swirls through a flat mile of dry fly cutthroat and rainbow trout water (18 inchers are taken here) for about 1 mile then plunges 268 feet over Snoqualmie Falls. The falls are a natural barrier to anadromous fish, allowing an exclusive trout fishery in the forks. Trout only rivers are rare in King County where most flows support sea-going trout and salmon. Below the falls the river flows N. through good winter and fair summer steelheading areas through the Snoqualmie Valley to join the Skykomish River and form the Snohomish River W. of Monroe. Summer steelheading is best from July-October with an annual catch of about 700 fish and winter-runs peak in December and January at about 1000 fish. Both are the results of liberal smolt plants from a WDFW hatchery on **TOKUL CREEK** just downstream from the falls on Hwy. 202.

The bank immediately below Tokul Cr. is a popular fishing area with lots of access. A boat ramp at Plum's Landing feeds drift and jet boaters downstream through the most productive section of hatchery steelhead water to a ramp at the mouth of the Raging River in Fall City. Other WDFW ramps are below Fall City at Nielsen's along Hwy. 203 at Neal Rd., at the mouth of the Tolt River and in Duvall. Winter and summer steelhead are also planted in the Raging and Tolt. Sea-run cutthroat are caught from mid-July into fall. The river is excellent for bank fishing. Hwys. 202, 203 follow its E. side for most of its length. Just N. of Fall City, Neal Road SE loops W. from Hwy. 203 and closely follows the river to several access points before looping back into Hwy. 203 at the Nielsen's ramp. Just below the **TOLT RIVER** mouth in McDonald Park in Carnation is also a popular steelheading area. From Carnation downstream is lots of deep, snaggy, sluggish frog water. From June 1-Nov. 30 selective gear rules are in place and bait is prohibited. The Snoqualmie gets fall runs of coho, chinook and a few pinks. Salmon fishing is opened only during years of exceptional returns but can be excellent on the lower end for coho and pinks.

SNOQUALMIE RIVER MIDDLE FORK. Catch and release fishing for wild trout and whitefish, plus selective gear, and no bait restrictions make this an excellent bet for fly and light spin tackle anglers. This rumbling freestone river rolls through a broad mountain valley from the high country N. of Snoqualmie Pass to I-90 at North Bend. Snoqualmie Falls prevents anadromous fish from diluting the population of resident wild trout in the forks. No longer stocked by WDFW. According to WDFW surveys, cutthroat to 16 inches are in the lower few miles where the river is a broad mix of gradually dropping riffles, boulder beds, and large pools. The Middle and Upper reaches are stairstep pool and chute water with a mix of cutts and rainbow 7 to 10 inches. The river is paralleled for 26 miles by rough gravel road to the edge of the Alpine Lakes Wilderness, where trail 1030 continue upstream to Dutch Miller Gap. From I-90 Exit 34 N. to Middle Fork Road/56. No developed campgrounds, but many river-side primitive sites on forest service land. **TAYLOR RIVER** enters the Middle Fork at milepost 15. Dingford Creek trailhead is at milepost 20. Last few miles can be very rough for passenger cars. No developed boat access.

SNOQUALMIE RIVER NORTH FORK. A wide, often deep, but wadeable gin clear freestone wild trout river draining much of the Weyerhaeuser Snoqualmie Tree Farm and the west front of the Cascade Range N. of North Bend. No longer stocked by WDFW. The North Fork is topographically divided into three sections. The lower river is a deep, cliff-walled chute and pool stairstep section known as Black Canyon. This gorge extends from the mouth upstream 2.5 miles. Access is extremely difficult, often hazardous, and can require a cliff scramble greatly reducing fishing pressure and allowing wild rainbow and cutthroat to reach respectable size. Most trout are 7 to 10 inches but there are a few in this section that will be measured by the pound. The middle section is 4 miles between Calligan Creek and Spur 10 bridge includes many large deep pools cut through sandstone and deep troughs. The upper section includes more shallow riffles, pools and logjam eddies. A few 6 to 9 inch brook trout and ESA protected bull trout join the wild rainbow and cutthroat menu in the upper river. The North Fork is paralleled, often at a distance, for 15 miles by North Fork County/FS 57 from North Bend to its headwaters at the confluence of **LENNOX CREEK** and **ILLINOIS CREEK** at the edge of Snoqualmie National Forest. Rough roads continue about 4 miles up these tributaries, offering creek fishing and trailheads to high lakes. Despite the nearby road, access to some of the better areas can require a difficult scramble through overgrown clear-cuts. Fishing is best after snow melt from mid June to October. Excellent fly and light spin water. There is a 10-inch minimum size and 2 fish limit with selective gear rules, no bait. No developed boat access.

SNOQUALMIE RIVER SOUTH FORK. The best known fork of the Snoqualmie River paralleled by I-90 from North Bend to Snoqualmie Pass. Heads at Source Lake. South Fork is a fast-falling, shallow, braided stream with some pockets and pools that hold mostly small cutthroat, rainbows and whitefish. Much of the lower river is channelized and diked and heavily fished for 6 to 9 inch rainbows. Larger trout, some to 14 inches, are in the less-fished areas between Twin Falls at Olallie State Park and 436th Ave. SE. Most of the upper stream supports cutthroat and whitefish. Best access to the middle section is from paved roads on the S. side of the river.

Snow Lake.

Leave I-90 at Exit 36 and rejoin at Exit 38 or leave at Exit 42 and rejoin at Exit 47. These roads also connect with forest roads leading to high lake trailheads. Camping at Denny Creek and Tinkham Rd. No camping at Olallie S. P. There is a 10-inch minimum size and 2 fish limit with selective gear rules, no bait. An extended catch-and-release season is allowed from Nov. 1-May 31. No developed boat access.

SNOW CREEK. Small tributary of the upper Green River, flowing into the Green 5 miles NE of the old railroad town of Lester. Produces a few small cutthroat during summer. From I-90 Exit 62 head S. on FS 54 over Stampede Pass.

SNOW LAKE. Very popular hike-in 160 acre rainbow and cutthroat lake at 4016 feet elev., NW of Snoqualmie Pass. From Alpental ski area follow Trail 1013 about 4 miles to lake. At Snow Lake the trail forks. Trail 1013 drops 7 miles into the Middle Fork Snoqualmie River to Goldmeyer Hot Springs. Trail 1012 fork continues 0.5 mile to **GEM LAKE** at 4857 feet on Wright Mt. Gem has rainbow. This trail continues to Wildcat Lks.

SOOS CREEK (AKA BIG SOOS). A major tributary to the Green River entering at Hwy. 18 bridge. Soos supports a WDFW salmon hatchery just above the confluence. The short stretch of creek between hatchery and river is a good summer sea-run cutthroat producer (special restrictions), and is sometimes opened in fall for children to catch surplus coho or chinook salmon. Deep

pools above the hatchery hold 6- to 14-inch native cutthroat and rainbow.

SOUPHOLE LAKE. Cutthroat lake of 3.4 acres at 820 feet on the King-Snohomish County line 4.5 miles NE of Duvall. Drains to Lake Margaret.

SOURCE LAKE. Cutthroat planted lake. Headwaters of South Fork Snoqualmie. Lies at 3750 feet 2.7 miles NW from Snoqualmie Pass on NE side of Bryant Peak. Trail is just S. of Snow Lake off Trail 1013.

SPOOK LAKE. A marshy 19.5 acre brook trout lake 2.5 miles SE from Carnation. in Weyerhaeuser Snoqualmie Tree Farm. Vehicle access permit required. Drains to Tolt River.

SPRING LAKE (Otter). Planted with 4500 rainbows in late March. Also has largemouth bass, perch and brown bullhead catfish. The 68 acre lake drains via Peterson Creek into Cedar River. WDFW access, narrow ramp on W. shore. Limited bank fishing. Hwy. 169 S. to Hwy. 18 access. Cross Hwy. 18, turn right onto Petrovitsky Rd., then N. on 196th SE then W. on SE 183rd to lake.

STAR LAKE. April and May are peak months for Star Lake's 2000 stocked rainbow. Summer fishing for largemouth bass, perch and brown bullhead catfish. The lake covers 34 acres. Public access, primitive boat ramp from S. 277th on the S. shore. On Kent's West Hill take Military Road to a E. turn onto Star Lake Rd /277th, for l.5 miles to lake.

STEEL LAKE. Popular 46 acre Federal Way lake with large public park, and fair to good fishing. Large shore and boat access at south shore county park. Largemouth bass and perch dominate. Trout fishermen get a boost each spring when WDFW plants 5000 catchable rainbows and occasionally large triploids. From Hwy. 99 turn E. on S. 312th to Steel Lake Park. Drains to Hylebos Creek.

STICKNEY SLOUGH. An old river channel 3 miles NW of Fall City covering 5.6 acres, offering largemouth bass and perch. Drains to Snoqualmie River.

STOSSEL CREEK. Small wild cutthroat and rainbow in this brushy stream which flows into the Tolt River 5 miles NE of Carnation. Upper reaches of creek best reached by driving Hwy. 203 N. of Carnation, then E. on Stillwater Hill Rd. for 5 miles to the creek's headwater in 5-acre **STOSSEL LAKE**, (AKA Langendorfer). The lake is reported to hold cutthroat.

SUNDAY CREEK. High mountain tributary to the upper Green River which offers rainbows early summer and fall. It enters the Green 2 miles E. of Lester. and is paralleled by FS road 54 from near the summit of Stampede Pass for about 5 miles.

SUNDAY CREEK. Tributary to North Fork Snoqualmie River, that drains Sunday and Loch Katrine lakes. Difficult to fish. A few small rainbows, cutts. Creek crosses North Fork County Road/FS 57 13 miles N. of North Bend. Overgrown trail along creek to Sunday Lake.

SUNDAY LAKE. A 21 acre hike-in lake in Snoqualmie Tree Farm reported to have large cutthroat, and a few brookies and rainbow. Located 13 miles NE from North Bend at 1865 feet elev. at head of Sunday Creek. Brushy shoreline, best fished from float tubes or rafts. From North Fork County Rd/FS 57 follow overgrown trail up Sunday Creek about 2 miles to lake. Lower or **LITTLE SUNDAY** is a 2 acre pond with cutts and bows. Campsites on the lakes. **LOCH KATRINE** is a brushy, remote, seldom fished 51 acre rainbow lake 1 mile NW and 2000 steep feet above Sunday Lake. No trail. Campsite at outlet. Best from July-Sept. An overgrown logging road runs close to the lake's outlet. Obtain a tree farm map. **UPPER LOCH KATRINE LAKE** is at 4250 feet elev. about 4500 feet S. of Loch Katrine. It is 24 acres and holds cutthroat and rainbow. No trail. Bushwhack W from S. end of Sunday Lake about 1.5 miles. It's a rough, steep trek but you'll never have to share the water.

SURPRISE LAKE. A hike-in lake S. of Hwy. 2, with brook trout. Surprise covers 28 acres at 4600 feet and is fed by the outlet of **GLACIER LAKE**, 1 mile S. a 60-acre brookie lake at an elev. of 4900 feet. From Scenic take FS Rd. 6088 a short distance to Trail 1060 which follows Surprise Creek to lake. PCT 2000 runs along E. side of lakes. Campsites on both lakes.

SURVEYORS LAKE. A rainbow stocked 5.1 acre lake on the crest at 3980 feet elev.

2 miles S. of Snoqualmie Pass. Drains to Rockdale Creek.

SWANS MILL POND. A 5 acre pond in logging clear cuts 1.5 miles NE of Lake Joy with brookies and cutthroat. Drains into Stossel Creek.

SYLVIA LAKE (AKA Boundary Lake). A shallow, marshy lake 7 miles SE of Sultan at 2310 feet elev. with large brook trout, Best fished from raft or tube. Open year-round.

T'AHL LAKE. Golden trout have been stocked in this high 6.5 acre mountain lake. It lies at 5200 feet about 10 miles SE from Skykomish. Drains to Necklace Valley and E. Fork Foss River at Trail 1062.

TALAPUS LAKE. Easy hike to brown trout that have been stocked in this popular lake at 3270 feet elev. The lake covers 17.8 acres and is 4.7 miles W. from Snoqualmie Pass. Drains to South Fork Snoqualmie River. From I-90 Exit 45 go N. on FS 9030 to road end trailhead.

TATE CREEK. Tributary to North Fork Snoqualmie River with small rainbow and brookies. Fair from spring into fall. Flows into North Fork about 1 mile from the mouth off North Fork County Rd./FS 57..

TAYLOR RIVER. A major tributary of the Middle Fork Snoqualmie River that provides fair to good rainbow and cutthroat angling from July into fall months. Most fish are 6 to 8 inches. Lots of hikers, few fishermen in upper reaches. From North Bend I-90 Exit 34 N. to Middle Fork Rd./FS 56 and continue N. along Middle Fork for 12.5 miles to Garfield Mt. Middle Fork Rd. turns sharply E. Large pullover at trail head to Trail 1002 which continues up Taylor River, below the imposing cliff face of Garfield Mt. first as an abandoned road, and then as a good hiking trail to Snoqualmie Lake, the river's source.

TERRACE LAKES. High lakes of 2 and 1.8 acres which offer rainbow. They lie at 5200 and 5300 feet 7 miles S. of Scenic on SW side of Terrace Mt. Drain to Tye River.

THOMPSON LAKE (Horseshoe). A 47-acre hike-in rainbow lake at 3650 feet elev. on the W. end of Mt. Defiance Ridge. Drains to Pratt River. Shortest route is by driving

Fly fishing North Fork Snoqualmie River gorge.

up Middle Fork Snoqualmie River Rd./FS 56 for 3.5 miles to gated road up Granite Creek. Hike or mountain bike up this gravel road to Trail 1009A which continues to the lake. At the head of Granite Creek are **LOWER GRANITE LAKE**, a 9 acre lake at 2950 feet elev. and **UPPER GRANITE**, 15 acres at 3060 feet. The lakes are close together and planted with rainbow. Granite Creek road passes within 0.4 miles of E. side of the lakes at the 2.5 mile mark.

TOKUL CREEK. Lower end drains into Snoqualmie River below falls and is usually a no-fishing zone leading to WDFW steelhead hatchery. In years of abundant winter-steelhead returns, a section below the hatchery may be opened and fishing is very good. Above Hwy. 202 Tokul Creek is a major drainage in Weyerhaeuser's Snoqualmie Tree Farm with many beaver ponds and a good population of wild cutthroat, brookies and rainbow. Lightly fished but fair to good during early summer and fall. Tokul Creek Road heads N. up the creek from Hwy. 202 at Snoqualmie Falls. Locked gate blocks vehicle traffic at entrance to tree farm. **BEAVER** and **TEN CREEKS** are small, brushy tributaries of Tokul Creek that offer beaver pond fishing for cutthroat with some brookies. Vehicle access requires Weyerhaeuser permit.

TOLT RIVER. Winter and summer steelhead, coho salmon, and whitefish swim the fast, snaggy Tolt from the mouth at McDonald Park on the Snoqualmie River 0.5 miles SW of Carnation upstream beyond the road end. Best steelheading is in lower 6 miles. Tolt River Road NE follows upstream from the center of Carnation to road end. There are a few roadside access points and a WDFW access. The S. side of the river above Carnation is undeveloped logging land, but tough to walk through. December and January are best for winter-runs. Summer-run fishing is poor but there are some fish in the river July into October. Salmon seasons are rare. No boat fishing. The North and South Forks have some steelhead, plus some 12 to 14 inch, tough to reach resident rainbows and cutthroat. The forks are not accessible from Tolt River Rd., and require entrance, and a permit, from Weyerhaeuser's Snoqualmie Tree Farm. City of Seattle has a large reservoir and watershed on the South Fork.

TOP LAKE. A hike-in 5 acre lake at 4500 feet on Maloney Ridge 3.8 miles S. of Skykomish. Planted with rainbow and cutthroat. A small deep pothole below Top has large cutthroat. Drains to Evans Lake and Foss River. From Skykomish head S and W on FS 68, then S. on 6846 to Trail 1069.

TRADITION LAKE. A 19-acre largemouth bass and perch lake along the popular Tiger Mt. Trail 1.4 miles E. of Issaquah. Drains to Issaquah Creek. Trailhead is 2 miles E. of Issaquah. The lake is under the power line.

TROUT LAKE (Jovita). An 18 acre multi-species lake 2 miles NE of Milton. It has been stocked with about 1000 triploid rainbows, some catchables, plus largemouth bass and bullhead catfish. Public access from a county road end on the S. shore. From Military Road, turn E. on 369th Pl. Trout is 0.4 miles S. of **TROUT LAKE**. A 21-acre mountain lake at 2012 feet elev. in the W. Fork Foss river drainage about 7 miles S. of Skykomish. A popular hiking destination, heavily fished for small rainbows. From Skykomish drive S. on FS 68 then 6835 to road's end trailhead. Trail 1064 leads about 1.25 mile to lake.

TWELVE LAKE (Cow). A year-round, 43 acre lake 1.5 miles NE of Black Diamond, Lake Twelve is lightly planted with about 1200 catchable rainbows, and occasionally cutthroat in April, but most fishing is for small largemouth bass, pumpkinseed, perch and foot-long brown bullhead catfish. Trout fishing tails off by June. WDFW access and small-boat ramp on S. shore off Green River Gorge Road. Residences on W. end, marsh on E. end. Weeds can be a problem in summer. No gas motors. From Hwy. 169 in center of Black Diamond, turn E. on Green River Gorge Road.

TYE RIVER. A wadeable, sometimes brushy wild-trout tributary entering the Foss River at outskirts of Skykomish. US 2 follows the Tye to its headwaters on Stevens Pass. Anadromous fish are blocked from the upper river by Alpine Falls, leaving a Tye River population of 6 to 9 inch rainbow, cutthroat and brook trout. Above Alpine Falls small wild trout are available and bait is allowed. Below the falls, bait is only OK during the special whitefish only season Nov. 1 through Feb. Otherwise, no bait, selective gear rules and a 14-inch trout minimum are in effect. Best fishing in mid summer to fall.

UNION LAKE. A 598 acre year-round lake in the heart of Seattle, pooled between Ballard Locks saltwater and Lake Washington. It offers a mishmash of usually poor fishing opportunities, and severe pollution problems. Saltwater dominates the lower lake, and freshwater fish usually concentrate on the E. and N. shores. There are flounders and sole, some very large largemouth and smallmouth bass, perch, crappie, sunfish, brown bullhead catfish and good populations of crayfish. Anadromous cutthroat, steelhead, and salmon use the lake as a conduit between the locks and Lake Washington spawning tributaries. Chumming is allowed E. of Fremont Bridge. Many private marina and moorage ramps and hoists. Paved public ramps on N. shore. Seattle Parks Dept. ramps on Lake Washington Ship Canal at end of 14th St. and on N.W. Northlake Way near Sunnyside Ave. just E. of Gas Works Park. Deep water boat access from Lake Washington through Lake Washington Ship Canal.

WALKER LAKE (Crow). A 54-foot deep, 12 acre residential lake below Enumclaw Mt. stocked in mid March with 2000 rainbows and cutthroat. Also has pumpkinseed panfish. Fishes out rapidly after April opener. Cumberland-Veazie Rd., 0.5 miles SW of Cumberland then E. 1 mile to the lake which is circled by a road. WDFW access area on SW shore.

WASHINGTON LAKE. The glistening showpiece and freshwater recreation center for Seattle's greater metro area. Lake Washington is a natural lake covering 22,138 acres, 20 miles long, 209 feet deep, between Seattle and the East Side cities of Renton, Bellevue, Kirkland and Bothell I-405 follows the E. side of the lake, at a distance. Major tributaries are Cedar and Sammamish Rivers, along with a host of small streams. Drains to Lake Union from midlake outlet N. of Hwy. 520 bridge. Open year-round, and generally underfished, despite its proximity to population centers.

Lake Washington offers large resident rainbow and cutthroat (5 pounders are not surprising), kokanee salmon (any sockeye under 15" is considered a kokanee here,), largemouth and smallmouth bass, bullhead catfish, crappie, exceptionally large perch, plus seasonal migrations of steelhead and salmon. Annual plants of 22,000 rainbow fry. Reports of mackinaw and white sturgeon. Trout fishing is best October through April with a very good troll fishery developing near the floating bridges in mid winter. Other trout spots are the shoreline around Mercer Island, East Channel, Rainier Beach, flats off Kenmore, Mercer Slough, Waverly Park, Houghton Beach and Chism Park. In mid-summer most trout go deep, but are willing biters for anglers willing to seek them out. Off Seward Park and the mouth of the Cedar are always good trout bets when open. Kokanee numbers are falling but there is still some fishing in May.

Bass fishing is good to very good May through August and again in late fall if you know the lake. It can be horribly frustrating if you don't. There are a lot of bass in Lake Washington, but they are spread out, and the secret is to learn the big lake's structure. Five pound smallmouth and largemouth to 7 pounds. Above average bass areas, along with crappie, in Union Bay near the U. of W. Stadium, inlets of the arboretum, E. shoreline S. of I-90, Juanita pilings. The lake is famous for producing huge yellow perch. Twelve inchers are not uncommon and some weigh 2 pounds. Perch school on the bottom in 30 to 50 feet of water. Best in late summer and early fall. Searun cutthroat follow coho, chinook and sockeye salmon to the mouths of Sammamish and Cedar Rivers from September into November. Check state fishing regs for closed areas. Generally, salmon fishing is closed but occasionally there are emergency openings for sockeye—a staggeringly popular summer fishery—in the S. end and coho and chinook in the N. end. Contemporary salmon concerns have produced a stack of special fishing regulations, zone closures and restrictions. Check the regs carefully, especially when trout or salmon fishing. Excellent bank, pier, dock and boat fishing opportunities. Almost all city parks have pier, dock and shoreline fishing. Public ramps at Kirkland's Moss Bay, Kenmore, Magnuson Park, Sand Point, Gene Coulon Park in Renton (very congested during summer weekends), Rainier Beach, Atlantic City, Sweyolocken Park, and Newport Shores.

WILDCAT LAKES. A pair of Alpine Lakes Wilderness lakes 5.4 miles NW of Snoqualmie Pass on N. side of Lake Roosevelt. Upper Wildcat Lake covers 54 acres and holds rainbow and cutthroat at 4218 feet elev. **LOWER WILDCAT** is 19 acres at 3880 feet about 1500 feet E. of the upper lake. Holds rainbow and cutthroat. Shortest route is a bushwhack from Middle Fork Snoqualmie River SW up Wildcat Creek 2 miles to the lower lake and another 0.4 mile to Upper Wildcat. No trail from Middle Fork. A longer route, but on maintained trail from Snoqualmie Pass at Alpental trailhead is Trail 1012 continuing past Snow Lake to Lower Wildcat.

WILDERNESS LAKE. A large county park with lots of bank fishing access and heavy annual plants of catchable and triploid rainbows make this one of the most popular trout lakes in SE King County. A few largemouth bass. The lake produces best for trout in late April and May when anglers target 12,000 planted rainbows, including 1-1/2 lb. and up triploids. In May and June there is some trolling (electric motors) for kokanee. Wilderness covers 67 acres 2.5 miles S. of Hwy. 169 at Wilderness in Maple Valley. Public access is through county park. From Hwy. 169 turn S. on Witte Rd. for 1.5 miles then E. on 248th to county park and WDFW boat ramp. No gas motors.

WISE CREEK. Tributary to Middle Fork Snoqualmie River, Wise produces small rainbow and cutthroat from mid-summer into fall. Enters the Middle Fork 1.5 miles downstream from the mouth of Taylor River.

WITTENMEYER LAKE. 3 acre pond with largemouth bass and perch 1.5 miles NE of Juanita. Drains to Lake Washington.

WINDY LAKE. A remote, rarely fished 5.7 acre rainbow lake in Alpine Lakes Wilderness at 4186 feet elev. about 5 miles NW of Snoqualmie Pass. Drains to Kaleetan Lake and Pratt River. Steep switchback hike on Trail 1010. N. on Denny Creek Trail 1014 to Hemlock Pass then W. on Trail 1011 to Trail 1010.

King County Resorts

Green Lake: Green Lake Rentals 206-527-0171.

Puget Sound: Edmond's Bud's Baits, 425-774-1921. Des Moines Pier, 206-824-4773.

Sammamish Lake: Vasa Park Bellevue, 425-746-3260.

Kitsap County
WDFW Region 6

Washington Department of Fish and Wildlife, 48 Devonshire Rd. Montesano, WA 98563-9618. Phone 360-249-4628

A small, water-oriented county west of Seattle most of Kitsap's 469 square miles are bordered by Puget Sound or Hood Canal. The upland county is relatively flat, a terrain that produces countless beaver ponds and marshes many of which have been planted over the years with cutthroat and brook trout, plus some rainbow.

Most of the fishing is directed at saltwater and reads like a who's who of the most productive water in central Puget Sound: Jefferson Head, Point Monroe, Agate Pass, Point No Point, Presidents' Point, Blake Island, Appletree Cove, Rich Pass.........

The largest freshwater lake is Long Lake near Port Orchard which covers 314 acres. Bainbridge and Blake Islands are both in Kitsap County. The county ranks 36th in the state and the highest elevation is 7 miles W. of Bremerton, the major city, at the 1761 summit of Gold Mountain. Public recreation land is at a premium, with no forest service or national park tracts. Most beach areas are privately owned and posted against trespass. Four state and several county and city parks and a couple of WDFW ramps provide small beach and boat access at key points. Some of the brushy, thinly timbered uplands are owned by logging companies that may allow access. Three small Indian Tribal Reservations are spaced along the water at Suquamish, Port Madison and Port Gamble.

The Puget Sound population boom has pushed residential development into the farthest reaches of the county, draining, closing or privatizing many once-favored fishing spots.

The county's irregular shaped shoreline winds around inlets, bays and beaches that offer shallow-water sea-run cutthroat, flounders, clams, and crabs, but watch out for private beach problems. Fishermen enjoy a climate that is mild, maritime with an annual rainfall of just under 37 inches. Salt and freshwater fishing is a year-round opportunity.

The major routes to the county are Hwy. 16 from Tacoma across the Narrows Bridge to Bremerton, which joins Hwy. 3 which bisects the center of the county north-south between Belfair and Hood Canal Bridge. State ferry service connects Fauntelroy (south of Seattle) and Vashon Island to Point Southworth, downtown Seattle to downtown Bremerton, and Edmonds to Kingston.

BAINBRIDGE ISLAND POND. A juvenile only pond, stocked in April with about 500 rainbows.

BEAR LAKE. Private. Now closed. Marshy shore lines surround this 12 acre bass lake 3.8 miles E. of Belfair. Road from S. border of Bremerton Airport leads 1 mile to lake's W. shore. No public access.

BIG BEEF CREEK. Can be good for sea-run cutthroat from July to Oct., the creek also holds limited numbers of winter steelhead in Dec.-Feb. Heads near Tahuya Lake and flows N. to Hood Canal at Big Beef Harbor, 2 miles NE of Seabeck. A road from the mouth heads upstream for about 0.5 mile.

BAINBRIDGE ISLAND LAKE (Grazzam). Closed. Located on W. side of Bainbridge Island, the 12.7 acre lake is planted with rainbow. Drainage is to Port Orchard.

BUCK LAKE. 20 acres near tip of Kitsap Peninsula approximately 1.5 miles SW of Hansville. Stocked with 2000 catchable rainbows in Apr. plus largemouth bass. Public access on E. shore. Access road runs W. from Hansville Road NE between Hansville and Point No Point.

BURLEY CREEK. Flows into Burley Lagoon at head of Henderson Bay. A short run stream of about 5 miles flanked on the E. side for most of its length by Hwy. 16. A few winter steelhead and sea-run cutthroat.

COULTER CREEK. Heads E. of Bremerton Airport and is fed in part by Kriegler Lake. Flows SW into Mason County, and yields fair cutthroat angling from July into Oct. Road from mouth follows creek for about 2.5 miles.

CURLEY CREEK. Outlet of Long Lake, Curley flows NE for 2.5 miles to join Puget Sound at South Colby. The small stream produces sea-run cutthroat in spring and fall months, and has been planted with winter steelhead. Road from South Colby, located between Port Orchard and Harper on Hwy. 160 follows Curley Creek upstream to Long Lake.

FAIRVIEW LAKE (Theresa). Closed. A private lake of 7.5 acres with largemouth bass and brown bullhead plus some rainbow 6.7 miles SW of Port Orchard. Drains to Case Inlet.

FLORA LAKE. Closed. Privately owned 6.5 acres and holds rainbow, largemouth bass and brown bullhead. 5 miles SW of Port Orchard.

GLUD PONDS. Closed. Three small ponds 3.8 miles S. of Keyport on Steel Creek. Previously stocked with rainbow and cutthroat.

HORSESHOE LAKE. A 40 acre lake planted with 3000 7-to 9-inch rainbow in April, and sometimes with adult coho salmon in the fall. Also holds brown bullhead catfish. Horseshoe is best immediately after opening day. From Port Orchard go S. on Hwy. 16 for 7 miles, then W. 2 miles through Burley, and S. again 1 mile to the W. shore and a public access site.

ISLAND LAKE. Located 2 miles SW of Keyport on Hwy. 303, Island is nearly encircled by county roads. Covers 43 acres and receives plants of 4500 catchable rainbow before opening day and also supports largemouth bass and brown bullhead catfish. County boat launch on E. side. Drains to Barker Creek.

KITSAP LAKE. A heavily stocked and popular 238.4 acre multi species lake, Kitsap produces year-round and has a reputation for delivering large carryover trout in early spring. In Mar-Apr.-May Kitsap is stocked with about 9000 catchable rainbows, plus 2000 triploids from 14 inches to several pounds. It also produces cutthroat through much of the year, and holds largemouth bass, bluegill, pumpkinseeds, crappie and brown bullhead catfish. Drains to Kitsap Creek. Public access and small county park with dock on the W. shore. Kitsap is 1 mile W. of Bremerton. Hwy. 3 runs close to the lake's N. tip and county roads encircle the lake.

KOENEMAN LAKE. A 19 acre lake with largemouth bass, and a few state planted triploid rainbow trout.

LONG LAKE. A narrow 2 mile long, 314 acre lake with cutthroat, a small plant of triploid rainbows, largemouth bass, catfish, crappie, bluegill steelhead and salmon. Inlet is Salmonberry Creek, and outlet is Curley Creek. There is a public access on lake's W. shore. Fishing is best May through Sept. 3.5 miles SE of Port Orchard, with county roads from East Port Orchard leading to and around lake.

LUDVICK LAKE. A private 2 acre lake located in headwaters of Dewatto River 2 miles S. of Holly. Largemouth bass and wild cutthroat.

MISSION LAKE. A reputation for delivering large hold-over trout in the spring, contributes to the popularity of this 88 acre, 25-feet deep lake just N. of Mason County line. In mid April receives a plant of about 8000 catchable rainbows. Brown bullhead catfish. Public access on N. shore. Go S. from Gorst on Hwy. 3 to Belfair, then NW on Old Belfair Hwy. along Union River to Mission Lake Road.

MISSION POND, 4 acres, 2000 feet SE of Mission Lake. Cutthroat and catfish and drains into Union River via Bear Creek.

PANTHER LAKE (AKA No Fish). Despite its nickname, this 104 acre lake really does have fish; about 6000 planted rainbow arrive in Apr. and there are brown bullhead catfish. Best spring and fall. The lake is 10 miles W. of Bremerton on the Mason County line and drains into Panther Creek to Tahuya River. From Gorst, drive S. on

Old Belfair Hwy. to Bear Creek Corner, then right on Bear Creek Rd. to lake. Public access on S. shore.

POULSBO. Spawning surf smelt may be raked at the S. edge of Liberty Bay Oct.-Feb.

ROSS POINT. A WDFW owned beach on the south shore of Sinclair Inlet, one mile W. of Port Orchard. Offers some surf smelt raking Oct.-Feb., some sea-run cutthroat. Carry-in boat access, poor parking.

SCOUT LAKE (Tin Mine). Private, no public access. Rainbow, cutthroat and brook trout in 3 acre pond 2 miles SW of Wildcat Lake.

SQUARE LAKE. Private, no public access to this 8 acre rainbow and bass pond 4.5 miles SW of Port Orchard.

TAHUYA LAKE. A 17.9 acre peat bog lake with largemouth bass 5 miles S. of Seabeck. Drains to Tahuya River.

THREE FINGER CHAIN BEAVER PONDS. Cutthroat planted ponds W. of Hintzville cut-off. Drive W. on Bear Creek road across Tahuya River about 0.8 miles, then right on Hintzville Rd. Roads and trails from this road touch the ponds along their several miles of length. Roads may not be open to vehicles. Large cutthroat have been taken from these ponds.

TIGER LAKE. Only 6 of Tiger's 109 acres are in Kitsap County, with the rest in Mason County. Heavily planted in mid April with 10,000 rainbows, including some triploids and 250 cutthroat. Does very well from spring opener into summer. Road from S. end of Mission Lake leads 0.5 miles to N. tip of Tiger. Public access on N. side.

WILDCAT LAKE. Good fishing for April plant of 9000, 8-to 10-inch rainbows, cutthroat and late spring, summer for largemouth bass and brown bullhead catfish. Public access on N. shore and a county campground on E. shore. Covers 117 acres. Delivers best in the spring, and then comes on strong during the fall. Outlet is Wildcat Creek to Dyes Inlet. The lake is 6 miles NW of Bremerton. Follow Hwy. 3 NW of Bremerton for 3 miles then W. and N. on Seabeck Hwy. NW up Wildcat Creek for 2.5 miles, then S. for .5 mile to the lake which is ringed by a road.

WYE LAKE (Y). A year-round 38 acre lake stocked with about 3000 rainbows and 500 cutthroat in Apr. and May. Largemouth bass and brown bullhead catfish turn on in summer. Lake is 3.5 miles SE of Belfair. Public access on S. shore. Turn S. from Hwy. 3 about 2 miles W. of Gorst at head of Sinclair Inlet, drive 3 miles S. through Sunnyslope, then W. 0.5 miles, and S. again 2.5 miles to Wye, passing Bear Lake. Drains to Case Inlet.

Kitsap County Resorts

Hood Canal: Seabeck Marina, 360-830-5179

Kittitas County
WDFW Region 3
Washington Department of Fish and Wildlife, 1701 S. 24th Ave., Yakima, WA 98902. Phone 509-575-2740.

This is one of the most diversified freshwater fishing counties in Washington, and the cradle of outstanding high lake fishing. Kittitas County is the geographic center of the state, a unique positioning that includes much of the Alpine Lakes Wilderness Area and some of the most popular and spectacular high-Cascade backpacking destination lakes. One of the greatest concentrations of high mountain trout lakes in the entire Cascade Range is along the common border of Kittitas, King and Snohomish counties. From this craggy backbone along the Cascade crest the county rolls E. descending across a splattering of stocked lowland trout lakes and ponds, along the banks of what is arguably Washington's best trout river, through miles of big sky sage brush and finally falls into the Columbia River at Wanapum State Park, 3 miles S. of Vantage.

Much of the county's 2341 square miles is a mountainous transition zone that begins at the Cascade Crest where the Pacific Ocean's warm moist air collides with the semi-arid climate of central and eastern Washington.

It's a county of staggering climatic and topographic contrasts. At Snoqualmie Pass precipitation averages 108 inches a year, mostly snow. Just 50 miles E. in Ellensburg annual rain and snow add up to less than 9 inches. The impact on the landscape and fishermen is huge.

In the moist high Cascades N and S of Snoqualmie Pass, the county is lung-searing steep and thick with dense, brushy forests of mixed fir, larch, pine, and vine maple. Alpine lakes, most supporting rainbow, cutthroat or brook trout are cradled in stoney, heather-lined basins between the peaks. Most are connected by a stitchwork of maintained forest service hiking trails.

In the drier lower mountains the Douglas fir, hemlock and juniper forests give way to thick stands of lodgepole and open ponderosa pine. Lakes are larger, but fewer and farther apart. River and creek valleys are lined with cottonwoods and quaking aspen. From Ellensburg E. the horizon widens forming a flat agricultural region near the community of Kittitas. From Kittitas E. the county is nearly arid and filled mostly with scabrock and sage brush. Sand blows across alkali, and it's hard to find a tree tall enough to shade the camp dog. Fishing water is almost non existent.

Mt. Daniel, a striking heavily glaciated peak in the Wenatchee Mountains visible from I-90, is the highest point at 7986 feet. The low elevation mark is only 490 feet along the Coumbia River near Priest Rapids Dam. The trout-productive Yakima River and its tributaries drain most of the W. county, roughly paralleling I-90 from Snoqualmie Pass to Ellensburg where the river turns S. into the rugged Ellensburg Canyon along the edge of WDFW's L. T. Murray Wildlife Area, cutting through Manastash and Umptanum ridges and flowing into Yakima County north of Selah. The Yak is a popular float-fishing river, especially in fall and early spring.

WDFW no long stocks trout in most of the county's rivers and creeks but most have wild trout populations.

Of the 200-plus lakes in the county, over 150 are at elevations of more than 2500 feet. Largest natural lake is 246-acre Waptus, elev. 2,980'. Best trout fishing in most of the high lakes takes place between late June and mid September. Some of the trails and lower lakes, in the 3000 to 4000 foot elevation zone, are sometimes free of snow and ice by early June.

Kittitas is the 7th largest county in the state. Summer temperatures in the mountains are usually in the upper 60s, while E of Ellensburg summer days often hit the low 90s.

The main access routes are I-90 which cross E-W from Seattle, and US. 97 and I-84 which cross the county N-S connecting Yakima and Wenatchee. All three highways intersect at Ellensburg. A network of good, mostly gravel roads are maintained by either the Snoqualmie-Mount Baker or Wenatchee national forests lead to mountain trailheads, a few lakes and many streams. Trail maps are available from regional FS offices. The trout rich Ellensburg Canyon section of the Yakima River is paralleled by and accessible from paved Hwy. 821/Canyon Road between Ellensburg and Selah. In the Ellensburg-Cle Elum stretch the river is smaller, shallower, but just as productive. It's accessible from Hwy. 10 which follows the N. bank.

Many of the streams and rivers in Kittitas County support native populations of bull trout (formerly Dolly Varden), which at this printing are federally protected under Endangered Species Act conservation closures, and may not be fished for. Fishing regulations and trout stocking programs change annually in this area . Always consult current WDFW regulations.

ALASKA LAKE. A 35 acre hike-in lake 3.8 miles NE of Snoqualmie Pass at an elevation of 4230 feet. It is fed by Ridge Lake and drains into upper Gold Creek and Keechelus Lake. Holds cutthroat. Reached by exiting I-90 at Exit 52 on Snoqulmie Pass. Trailhead parking to Pacific Crest Trail 2000 on N. side of I-90 leads to the lake. Can also be reached by trail off Gold Creek Valley Road.

BAKER LAKE (Thetis). 5 acres, holds rainbow and small brook trout, at 4220 feet in headwaters of Thetis Creek. Drains to Kachess Res. From I-90 E. of Snoqulmie Pass turn N. on Lake Kachess Road and continue for 3 miles to microwave sign, then left, park at tower. Bushwhack 0.5 miles down hill to lake. Primitive campsites.

BOX CANYON LAKE. 1.6 acres, may have cutthroat. Elevation 4500 feet, 6.5 miles E. of Snoqualmie Pass. Drains to Kachess River.

BULLFROG POND. A rainbow planted 2.9 acre pond adjacent to W. side of Bullfrog cutoff Rd. on E. side of Cle Elum River.

CABIN CREEK. Supports brook trout and rainbow. June and July normally best fishing months for this small tributary to the upper Yakima River. From Easton, take Cabin Creek Rd./FS 41 upstream for several miles.

CARIBOU CREEK. June-Aug. are top fishing months for this small rainbow stream E. of Ellensburg. The creek bisects an irrigated valley before emptying into the Yakima River. Drive E. on I-90 about 6 miles from Ellensburg to Caribou Rd. which follows the creek for a few miles.

CHIKAMIN LAKE. A picturesque rainbow lake of 18.3 acres 6.5 miles NE of Snoqualmie Pass on PCT 2000. Elev. 5785 feet. Drains to Cooper River.

CLE ELUM LAKE. A large natural, year-round fishing lake that has been enlarged by dam on Cle Elum River to cover 4810 acres. Holds rainbow, cutthroat, kokanee, bull trout, brook trout, mackinaw, whitefish and burbot. Best known for 8-12 inch kokanee. Fair trolling after June 1. An occasional mackinaw is caught by trollers just after ice out. Most anglers troll for all game fish. The lanky reservoir stretches for nearly 8 miles and is touched at several points on E. shore by FS Rd. 903 from I-90 to Salmon La Sac via Roslyn. Launches at Wish-Poosh FS campground, Bell, Morgan and Dry Creeks. Launch sites often dry after mid-summer's extreme drawdowns which keep this pretty lake from becoming a quality fishery. Lake elev. 2223 feet, 7.3 miles NE of Cle Elum on the Salmon La Sac Rd.

CLE ELUM RIVER. Easy access from FS 903 and FS 4330 which parallel the upper section from Cle Elum Lake upstream to road's end about 2 miles SE of the river's source at Hyas Lake. Fishable in July after snow run-off for excellent population of wild rainbow, a few brookies and whitefish. Most trout 8-10 inches. Additional fishing in large tributaries, including Cooper and Waptus rivers and Fortune Creek. Best trout fishing July, Aug. early Sept. Good winter whitefishing below dam. Camping at Fish Lake and Salmon La Sac FS campgrounds. Lower sections are rated good for native rainbow July-Sept. Trails near the upper end of FS 4330 continue into Alpine Lakes Wilderness Area and connect with

PCT 2000: NW to Hyas Lake and Cathedral Rock, NE to Paddy Go Easy Pass and S. to Squaw Lake.

COLE CREEK. Brook trout in June and Aug. A tributary of Cabin Creek, accessible about 5 miles SW of Easton going S. on Cabin Creek Rd.

COLEMAN CREEK. June-Aug. is the most productive period for this small stream, a tributary to Naneum Creek. About 4 miles E. of Ellensburg follow Fairview Rd. to creek.

COOKE CREEK. A small Colockum stream ranked "good" for wild rainbows June-Aug. Best stretch is on N. edge of valley adjacent to irrigated fields. Drains into Wipple Wasteway near S. end of Kittitas Valley. Drive up the Cooke Canyon Rd. 8 miles E. and 7 miles N. of Ellensburg.

COOPER LAKE. A 120-acre mountain lake, accessible by car, that offers big browns, rainbow, cutthroat and kokanee. Campground, boat launch. Prime fishing June, July and October. Origin of the brown trout is unknown, but they are reproducing and have grown to several pounds. Elev. 2788 feet, 3.5 miles NW of Salmon La Sac. Several campsites on the shores. To reach Cooper, 1 mile S. of Salmon La Sac on Cle Elum River Rd., turn W. onto FS Rd. 46.

COTTONWOOD LAKES. Easily reached mountain lakes S. of Snoqualmie Pass. Upper lake is 1.5 acres. and the lower lake covers 8.3 acres, at an elev. of 3900 feet Outlets into Lost Lake. Planted with cutthroat, brookies and rainbow. From I-90, Exit 62 Stampede Pass Road, to Lost Lake Rd. and continue about 1 mile past Lost to Mirror Lake trail. Trail to lower Cottonwood is about 0.5 mile long. Bring a raft of float tube. The lakes are brushy and difficult to fish from shore. **MIRROR LAKE** lies 0.5 miles W. of Cottonwood at 4195 feet. It holds chunky rainbow and cutthroat. From Mirror Lake follow PCT 2000 for 0.5 mile to **TWILIGHT LAKE** which holds cutthroat.

DEEP LAKE. A 52 acre lake at 4450 feet elev., 9.5 miles N. of Salmon La Sac. Follow Cle Elum River Rd. FS 903/4330 for 2 miles past Fish Lake Guard Station/campsites. Trail crosses river and continues 2.5 miles S. past Squitch Lake to PCT 2000, then down to the lake. Total distance 7.5 miles. Lake has open shores and fine campsites. Planted with rainbow. Best fishing is from mid-August through fall. A good base for short hikes to another 6 nearby lakes **PEGGY'S POND,** elev. 5600 feet, lies 2700 feet N. of Deep at base of Cathedral Rock. The 5 acre pond is planted with cutthroat. **DEER LAKES,** 1 and 4 acres, are 2400 feet S. of Deep at 4600 feet elev. They hold rainbow. **CIRCLE LAKE** at 6100 feet is 0.8 mile W. of Deep cradled in a deep bowl. It covers 48 acres, and has excellent fishing for 7-12 inch cutthroat, but is often frozen until late August. **VINCENTE LAKE,** An 11-acre cutthroat lake at elev. 5700 feet, 1.4 miles SW of Deep.

DENMARK POND. A small, weedy borrow pit E. of Ellensburg at the corner of Kittitas Road (Broadview) and Denmark Rd. Stocked in April with several hundred catchable, and triploid rainbow. Good kids pond.

DIAMOND LAKE. Cutthroat are in this 5.1 acre lake, at 4950 feet 4 miles NW of Salmon La Sac on Polallie Ridge. Outlet to Hour Creek.

EASTON LAKE. May and June are the most productive fishing months at this 237-acre reservoir 0.5 miles NW of Easton, adjacent to I-90. It is formed by a dam on the Yakima River, and fed by Kachess River. No longer stocked by WDFW, but supports rainbow, cutthroat, and a few brook trout. Usually a fair fishery at best. Lake Easton State Park is on the N. shore, with 50 sites, boat launch, moorage.

EASTON PONDS. Several former gravel pits adjacent to I-90 on the NE. side of Easton S. of Yakima River. Some ponds are now used a rearing facilities for Yakima River coho salmon. Stocked with catchable and jumbo rainbows in May or June after the coho are released. Drain to Yakima River.

FIO RITO LAKES NORTH AND SOUTH. Popular 54 acres of year-round lakes 5 miles S. of Ellensburg on E. side of I-82. Good fishing for 8 to 14-inch rainbows. Also planted with lunker triploid and jumbo rainbows, and in late fall gets a shot of 6 to 12-pound surplus broodstock. Also hold brown trout, black crappie, brown bullhead and pumpkinseed. Large large public access, disabled access and paved trails; shelters. No gasoline motors. Popular in early spring and during winter ice season.

FISH LAKE (Tucquala). Roadside 63 acre marshy lake 7.5 miles N. of Salmon La Sac on the upper Cle Elum River. FS 4330 follows shoreline. A narrow, shallow and weedy lake, open year-round, best fished from small boats or float tubes. Rainbow and brook trout. Small boats may be launched from the Rd. Good camping spots. Seasonally nasty mosquitos. Nearby meadows can provide good huckleberry picking in late August and September. A popular base camp for hikers going into nearby Alpine Lake Wilderness Area.

FRENCH CABIN CREEK. Fished for rainbow in July and August. Drains into upper Cle Elum River 0.4 miles N. of Cle Elum Lake. Drive N. on Salmon La Sac Rd./FS 903 to N. end of Cle Elum Lake, turn W. cross Cle Elum River to French Cabin Creek Rd. 4308.

GLACIER LAKE. A 2.8 acre Rampart Ridge hike-in lake in Alpine Lakes Wilderness Area, stocked with golden trout. Lake elev. 4780 feet. It lies 2800 feet NW of **LILLIAN LAKE.** Outlet to Gold Creek.

GOLD CREEK. Creek is closed to fishing to protect ESA listed spawning bull trout. FS Trail 1314 continues up the creek for another 5 miles to headwaters in 30-acre **JOE LAKE**, at 4624 feet. Joe produces cutthroat and rainbow. Last 1.5 miles to lake are tough, and most anglers come in from PCT 2000 off Snoqualmie Pass. For

the creek route, however, take I-90 to Exit 54 at Hyak, exit to FS Rd. then N. upstream to end of road and FS Trail 1314.

GOLD LAKE. Rampart Ridge rainbow lake of 2.8 acres at 4780 feet, 2800 feet NW of **LILLIAN LAKE.** Outlets to Gold Creek.

HANSON'S PONDS. A pair of rainbow and brown trout planted ponds at Cle Elum just S. of I-90. Public access.

HUDSON CREEK. Small brook trout are in this Yakima River tributary. Mid-summer fishing best. From I-90 Exit 63 about 5 miles W. of Easton and follow Cabin Creek Rd.

HYAS LAKE. Brook trout, some to 14 inches with a reputation for being difficult, inhabit this 124-acre mountain lake. Open year-round and best fishing is from late July through Sept. Some winter ice fishing. The trail is a comfortable 1.5 mile hike along upper Cle Elum River from NW end of FS Rd. 4330, about 11 miles N. of Salmon La Sac. Lake is at 3550 feet elevation.

KACHESS LAKE. A very popular camping and fishing destination just N. of I-90 at Snoqualmie Pass. Reservoir supports kokanee salmon, rainbow, cutthroat, ESA protected bull trout, mackinaw and a few burbot sometimes called freshwater ling. The huge impoundment extends more than 10 miles N. into the Wenatchee National Forest and covers 4540 acres at full pool be-

Hanson's Pond.

hind a dam on Kachess River. By early June, Kachess starts to deliver 8-9 inch kokanee. This could be an exceptional fishing lake but seasonal irrigation drawdowns severely impact habitat and natural reproduction. Open year-round. Exit I-90 at Exit 62 about 2 miles E. of lower end of Keechelus Lake and follow paved road N. to W. shore of Kachess where a resort and several FS campgrounds are located. Good primitive boat camping sites in upper lake. Excellent boat launches. Lots of summer play boats. Expect crowds during peak season. A gravel road which follows some of the E. shore can be reached by continuing E. on I-90 to Exit 71 W. of Easton. There is also a trail on W. side of lake that parallels **LITTLE KACHESS** which is connected to the main lake by a narrow neck. Tough, brushy route NW up **MINERAL CREEK** to **PARK LAKES,** about 5 miles from N. end of Kachess. Logging Rd. and trail heads W. from Lake Kachess forest camp 4 miles to **SWAN LAKE** at 4040 feet. The 7 acre lake has been planted with cutthroat and rainbow. Several good camp areas. **ROCK RABBIT LAKES**are 2 small ponds located 1300 and 1800 feet S. and SW of Swan. **STONES THROW LAKE** is another pond 1800 feet NW of Swan. Fishing in these tiny lakes is for small cutthroat. Best fishing after June.

KACHESS RIVER. Connects Kachess Lake with Lake Easton. Minimal fishing value. Produces a few rainbow and cutthroat early in the season.

KEECHELUS LAKE. A huge irrigation reservoir on the S. shoulder of I-90, 3 miles SE of Snoqualmie Pass. Full pool covers 2560 acres behind a dam on the upper Yakima River. Open year-round, and can be fair to good in June for kokanee salmon 8 to 12 inches. Also available are rainbow, cutthroat, ESA protected bull trout, and a few burbot. Fishing and boating pressure is extremely light. Marginal fishery because of extreme habitat impact during irrigation drawdowns. A FS campground is on Yakima River, and a poor boat launch, unusable during drawdown periods, is on the N. end of the lake just SE of Hyak. Use I-90 exit 62 to boat launch. The SE end of the lake is followed at a distance by FS 5480. To reach this area continue 2 miles E. of the lake on I-90 to Stampede Pass/Lake Kachess Exit 62, turn S. then bear NW on FS 5480/Lost Lake Rd.

KENDALL PEAK LAKES. 3 small rainbow lakes of 2.1, 3.8 and 6.6 acres at head of Coal Creek about 1.8 miles NE of Snoqualmie Pass at elevations that range from 4380 to 4780 feet.

LAURA and **LILLIAN LAKES**. A pair of Rampart Ridge hike-in lakes 2.5 miles up Rocky Run Creek from Rocky Run guard station NE of I-90 and Keehelus Lake on Snoqualmie Pass. Exit I-90 at Hyak, turn N. across interstate then parallel the highway on FS 4832 which will switchback N. Trail 1332 leaves the road at 2517-ft. elev., and climbs to 4410 feet at 3-acre Laura, continuing to 4800 feet at Lillian, a 17 acre lake offering rainbow, cutthroat.

LAVENDER LAKE. A 20 acre freeway pond heavily stocked with catchable and tripolid rainbow trout and open year-round. Lake is 2 miles E. of Easton at East Nelson interchange. Disabled access.

LEMAH LAKE. Golden trout have been stocked in this small (0.5 acre) lake 8 miles NE from Snoqualmie Pass at 3900 feet. No recent reports. Drains to Pete Lake and Cooper River.

LOST LAKE. A 144 acre Snoqualmie Pass mountain lake accesible by good gravel road on the W. side of Keechelus Lake. Unimproved campsites and rough boat launch. Lost has cutthroat, brook trout, and small kokanee. Elevation is 3089 feet. Reached by leaving I-90 2 miles S. of Keechelus at the Kachess Lake/Stampede Pass exit. Go S. 1 mile to Lost Lake Rd./FS 5480 and W. 4 miles to lake. Road continues along W. side of lake for about 1.5 miles to trailhead for **MIRROR** and **COTTONWOOD LAKES**.

LOST LAKE. A hike-in trout lake on the N. side of Manastash Ridge S. of Cle Elum. From I-90 about 4 miles NW of Thorp, take Exit 93 and continue W. up Taneum Creek Rd/FS 33 for 11 miles to FS Rd. 3330, then S. 8 miles to FS Rd. 3111, then 4 miles to Buck Meadows. From SW side of Ellensburg, FS 31/Manastash Creek Rd. goes W. 19 miles to Buck Meadows. Nine-acre Lost Lake is 1.5 miles SW of the meadow on Trail 1350, at an elevation of 4820 feet. Brookies and cutthroat best in summer. Trail 1350 continues SE 1.4 miles to **MANASTASH LAKE** which is also accessible by rough four-wheel drive road from Bald Mountain. Manastash Lake is at

5000 feet, covers 23 acres and lies in a timbered bowl. It offers 8 to 14-inch brook trout, some larger. Heavy algae growth in late summer. Pleasant primitive camping.

MATTOON LAKE. A heavily stocked, heavily fished year-round lake on the outskirts of Ellensburg along I-90. Annually planted with approx. 12,000 catchable rainbows 8 to 14 inches, surplus brood stock to 12 pounds, 1100 triploids and 1000 browns. Some sunfish. Excellent bank access.

MCCABE POND. Small pond, SE of Ellensburg at jct. of Thrall and Canyon Rds. Go S. from I-90 Exit 109. Planted with 8 to 11 inch rainbows and cahnnel catfish to 8 pounds. No boats, 5 fish limit. Trout best in early spring, catfish in summer.

MERCER CREEK. A juvenile-only creek in Ellensburg that is stocked with catchable rainbows. Open June-Oct. 31.

MICHAEL LAKE (Round). Follow Salmon La Sac Rd./FS 903 to trailhead 1 mile N. of town at China Point. Trail 1324 goes N. past Davis Peak and Terrence Lake to Michael Lake, elev. 5100 feet. The 17 acre lake has been planted with rainbow fishing from open shoreline. **LAKE TERRENCE,** 14 acres, is 0.8 miles SW of Michael at 5550 feet and holds rainbows.

MILK CREEK. A lengthy, narrow, fast falling, brushy stream on S. side of Manastash Ridge, 28 miles W. of Naches on Hwy. 410/Chinook Pass. Flows into Naches River on Hwy. 410 at Halfway Flat FS Campground. Turn N. on FS 1708/Milk Creek Rd. Fair in July and August for small wild cutthroat and brook trout. Gravel roads follow most of the creek upstream to source at Milk Lake.

MILK CREEK POND. A small oval pond stocked with catchable rainbows and sometimes large Triploids. On Milk Creek Road/FS 1708 about 1.5 miles NE of Hwy. 410 turnoff at Halfway Flat FS Campground.

MILK LAKE. A pretty little 3-acre rainbow and brook trout lake on S. side of Manastash Ridge above the Naches River. From Hwy. 410/Chinook Pass Hwy., about 0.5 miles S. of Little Naches Rd. junction turn N. on Milk Creek Rd./FS 1708 and drive NE past Milk Pond to the lake. Last mile can be rough. The lake is at 4700 feet, and has primitive camping. Watch for elk, deer, mountain goats.

MIRROR LAKE. A deep, hike-in rainbow lake of 29 acres at 4195 feet, 5.8 miles S. of Snoqualmie Pass and 1400 feet SW of **COTTONWOOD LAKE.** It drains to Lost Lake and Roaring Creek. From I-90 take Stampede Pass Exit S. turning W. onto FS 5480 and continuing past Lost Lake to Trail 1302.

NANEUM CREEK. A Colockum trout stream N. of Ellensburg that heads near Table Mountain. Upper stretches produce native cutthroat 7-10 inches, while rainbow furnish action in lower reaches. Most productive June-Aug. Best rainbow fishing from city of Ellensburg intake downstream. Above intake, small cutthroat and rainbow are available. Naneum Creek drains to Yakima River and is reached by Naneum Canyon Rd. N. from Ellensburg.

NANEUM POND. A rainbow planted 1.5 acre pond about 4 miles E. of Ellensburg and 0.2 miles N. of Old Hwy. 10, adjacent to E. side of Naneum Rd.

PETE LAKE. Cooper Lake Rd./FS 46 and 4616 from Salmon La Sac comes within 3 miles of the lake which covers 37 acres at 2980 feet. It is a beautiful, hike-in mountain lake that holds a few rainbow and lots of brook trout. Primitive camping around lake. From upper end of Cooper Lake follow Trail 1323 upstream along Cooper Creek to Pete.

PARK LAKES. In the Alpine Lakes Wilderness Area these rainbow lakes of 9.8 and 10.8 acres, are 6 miles NE of Snoqualmie Pass on SW side of Chikamin Ridge. Elev. 4510 and 4700 feet. Upper Mineral Creek outlet drains from N. end of Lake Kachess. FS Trail 1331 follows outlet to the lakes from the end of Cooper River Rd./FS 4600

RACHEL LAKE. A popular 27.3 acre hike-in cutthroat lake 4 miles NE of Snoqualmie Pass on Rampart Ridge. Drains to Box Canyon Creek. Drive FS Rds 49/4930 N. along the W side of Lake Kachess, then up Box Canyon Creek to Trail 1313.

RIDGE LAKE. A 2.3 acre hike-in lake once stocked with golden trout. Elev. 5220 feet, 3.5 miles NE of Snoqualmie Pass and 1700 feet W. from **ALASKA LAKE** to which it drains. Follow PCT 2000 N. from Snoqualmie Pass trailhead.

SPADE LAKE. A hike-in lake, Spade cov-

Spade Lake.

ers 122 acres and holds cutthroat. From Salmon La Sac, take Trail 1319 to **WAPTUS LAKE** 8.5 miles. On the N. side of Waptus Lake turn N. onto Trail 1337 and continue to Spade Lake. It's a steep switchback hike gaining 2247 feet from Waptus to Spade at 5210.

SQUAW LAKE. A 12.4 acre rainbow lake at 4850 feet, 9 miles N. of Salmon La Sac. Drains to Cle Elum River.

STIRRUP LAKE. It's a short hike to this 9.1 acre rainbow and brookie lake at elev. 3550 S. of I-90. Is 3.5 miles W. from Stampede Pass on E. side of Cascade Crest at Meadow Pass. Drains to Meadow Creek. From Stampede Pass Exit of I-90, bear W. on FS 5480, then S. on FS 5483 to Trail 1338 near where lake outlet joins Meadow Cr. A spur road to Meadow Pass is just W. of this trailhead comes within a few hundred yards of Stirrup and passes tiny Meadow Lake which may have brook trout.

SUMMIT CHIEF LAKE. Golden trout have been stocked in this 6.5 acre lake at 6500 feet, 10.5 miles NW of Salmon La Sac and about 0.8 miles S. from Summit Chief Mtn. Drains is to Waptus River. From PCT 2000 above Waptus Lake, turn NW on Trail 1362 to outlets of lake. Rough hike.

SWAN LAKE. Cutthroat in this 7.4 acre lake at 4640 feet. It lies 5.8 miles SE from Snoqualmie Pass in headwaters of Gate Creek. From the NW end of Keechleus Lake follow FS 4832 E. past Rocky Run then E. on 4934, N. on 4948 for 2 miles, then left on spur road 120 to Swan, Rock Rabbit and Stonesthrow lks.

SWAUK CREEK. A fast-falling mountain stream that flows S. adjacent to Hwy. 97 from Swauk (Blewett) Pass for about 15 miles to Yakima River. Holds native rainbow, cutthroat and a few brook trout. Best fishing immediatley after runoff. Extremely low water in fall. Selective gear restrictions.

TANEUM CREEK. Joins Yakima River 2 miles N. of Thorp at I-90. Produces native rainbow and cutthroat June through August. Followed for about 12 miles by FS 33/Taneum Creek Rd. to its headwaters on Manastash Ridge. Taneum produces rainbow in May, June and July. Many nice primitive campsites. Selective gear restrictions.

TANEUM LAKE. A 3.1-acre rainbow lake near the top of Manastash Ridge, between Frost and Quartz Mtns. Elevation is 5266 feet. Drains to Taneum Creek. From FS 31 through Buck Meadows turn W. on FS 3100 and continue bearing left for about 1.7 miles W. of Frost Meadows. A short trail leads to the lake.

TEANAWAY RIVER. A shallow, picturesque stream that enters Yakima River 1 mile E. of of Hwy. 97/I-90 jct. The Teanaway offers small wild rainbow and cutthroat. It also has bull trout which are ESA protected. No bait, selective gear restricitons. Best fished after snow runoff (June) through early Aug. By mid-Aug. water levels are usually too low for good fishing. Wadeable, too shallow to boat. Much of the lower river passes through private ground. Three miles N. of the jct. paved Teanaway Road turns W. from Hwy. 97 and follows the river upstream to Casland where it splits into 3 forks. Cutthroat dominate the forks. Road up Middle Fork continues for 3 miles then trail takes off to headwaters near Jolly Mtn. Road up W. Fork climbs over the ridge and drops to Lake Cle Elum. Road follows N. Fork for 16 miles with branch Rds. offering access to tributaries including **INDIAN**, **JACK** and **STAFFORD CREEKS**. Other major N. Fork tributaries are **JUNGLE, BEVERLY** and **DE ROUX CREEKS. THREE QUEENS LAKE**. A golden trout planted lake of 1.5 acres at 5390 feet near SE end of Chikamin Ridge about 7 miles W. from Salmon La Sac. Outlets to Kachess River. Follow Cooper River Rd., FS 46/4600 W. past Cooper Lake to outlet. Bushwhack trail.

TERRACE LAKE. Terrace receives rainbow plants and is located 4 miles N. from Salmon La Sac at 5550 feet, on W. side of Davis Mtn. Drains to Waptus River.

THORP LAKE. A 4.4 acre rainbow and cutthroat stocked lake, 1.1 miles N. of Thorp at I-90 Exit 101. Outlet to Yakima River. Another Thorp Lake is on Kachess Ridge below Thorp Mtn. From N. end of Cle Elum Lake, turn W. on FS 4308 to 4312. Lake is 1.5 m. up trail at jct. of FS Trail 1315

TUCQUALA LAKE (Fish). Brook trout and a few cutthroat are in this popular 63 acre lake at 3225 feet. It lies in a narrow valley 7.5 miles N. of Salmon La Sac on the Cle Elum River. FS Rd. borders the N. side of the lake.

TWIN LAKES. A pair of hike-in lakes, 4.2 and 1.6 acres 4.8 miles S. of Snoqualmie Pass in headwaters of Cold Creek. They contain rainbow and outlet via Cold Creek to Lake Keechelus.

VENUS LAKE. Situated 1900 feet N. of

SPADE at 5600 feet. It covers 56 acres and holds cutthroat in the 8-12 inch range. From N end of Lake Keechelus go S. on FS Rd. 9070. No trail.

WAPTUS LAKE. An exceptionally popular hike and horse desitnation near the head of Waptus River. Trail 1310 heads N. from Salmon La Sac for 9.5 miles gradually climbing to the lake at 2980 feet. Waptus is a deep lake of 246 acres containing rainbow, brook trout and ESA protected bull trout. Trail follows N. shore. Primitive camping sites along both sides of the lake. Waptus is often used as a base camp for day hikes to other nearby mountain lakes.

WAPTUS RIVER. A beautiful mountain stream flowing 9.5 miles from the outlet of Waptus Lake to Cle Elum River entering 1.5 miles above Salmon La Sac. Holds fair numbers of wild rainbow and brook trout, and in 1997 WDFW biologists found brown trout although they've not been planted in this river. Trail 1310 to **WAPTUS LAKE** runs close to the river for the last 5 miles where the best fishing is found. August is top angling month.

WILSON CREEK. Lower section in Ellensburg is stocked with catchable rainbows and open only to juvenile anglers. The upper reaches are open to everyone and produce some decent wild rainbow fishing in June-Aug. Two branches of this year-round stream flow from Table Mountain on the S. side of the Colockum through Ellensburg. The 1.5 miles of stream in the city limits are stocked with about 4000 trout for kids in June or July. The upper public reaches are not supplemented with stocked trout. Accessible by Rd. along much of its length.

WOODHOUSE PONDS. Four small ponds off Woodhouse Rd., SE of Ellensburg. Planted with 8 to 11 inch rainbows. Best in early spring before stockers are fished out. Some largemouth bass, yellow perch and sunfish. Open year-round, walk-in access.

YAKIMA RIVER. Great trout fishing upstream, underfished smallmouth bass and channel catfish downstream—that pretty well defines this diverse 215 mile fishery. The upper and lower Yakima River fisheries are divided by Roza Dam on the lower Ellensburg/Yakima Canyon just north of Selah. Above the dam, and for a short distance below it, is 75 miles of quality trout water, including a 50 mile section downstream from Cle Elum that is arguably the prettiest and best large rainbow trout river in the state. This section is one of the few managed by WDFW for quality trout fishing (check the regs) catch-and-release rules, bait and boating restrictions. The result is nearly 500 trout per mile (95% rainbow, plus cutthroat, a very few browns and a rare brookie). Many of the 'bows are 12 to 16 inches long and there is a respectable number of 20-inch plus fish. Biologists estimate there are also 2000 whitefish per mile in this area which provide good winter fishing. Downstream of the dam the lower section, is slower water, heavily compromised by irrigation and polluted by agricultural and urban runoff. There is decent trout fishing in the first couple of miles below Roza, but not much further down. The extreme lower river near Tri-Cities, however, can be excellent for smallmouth bass, channel catfish, and some largemouth, panfish and other warm water species, especially in spring.

The Yakima begins as braids of cold water trickling from the Cascade Crest above Snoqualmie Pass. On the S. side of I-90 it collects in Keechelus Reservoir and squirts through the dam as a full grown river that ends as a broad warm-water tributary to the Snake River S. of Richland. Nearly all of the river, especially the upper section, is followed by paved roads and easily reached at countless points. The extreme upper river is a large creek between the dam impounding Keechelus Reservoir and Easton. This stretch is brushy, quick and generally difficult to fish. Logging roads access some pools and summer fishing is marginal for small wild rainbow, cutthroat and brookies.

The 27 miles from Cle Elum to Ellensburg are paralleled on the N. by Old Highway 10 and can be waded or boated with drift boats or rafts (no motors). There is a WDFW boat access site just E. of Cle Elum near the jct. of Hwy. 10 and US 97. Takeouts at Thorp and at the diversion dam below Thorp. Most boaters float from Cle Elum E. to Thorp takeouts (Driveway into DOT boat access at Thorp bridge is now cabled) or from Ellensburg at Ringer Rd.

WDFW access S. through the ruggedly scenic Ellensburg Canyon (watch for bighorn sheep) to Roza Dam. Highway access allows this 20-mile drift to be broken into several short floats. The E. bank is followed by Hwy. 821/Canyon River Road. From I-90 use Exit 109. Several boat and walk-in accesses.

Good to excellent rainbow trout fishing in the early spring (Mar.-Apr.) beginning in the Canyon Section and progressing upstream through fall. From mid-Sept. to mid-Oct. the Cle Elum-Ellensburg reach is excellent. During mid summer when irrigation is at its peak this valuable trout river is used as a mountain-to-valley conduit for irrigation water and runs high and slightly turbid. Summer fishing can be tough. By mid-September the river is in beautiful shape for float and wade fishing. The Canyon section is wider and deeper than the Cle Elum-Thorp section and not as easily waded. Winter trout fishing can be surprisingly good. The Yak is famous for edge fishing. Most trout, especially in the Canyon, hold within a few inches of the bank.

Excellent whitefish angling in winter from Cle Elum to Yakima County line.

Below Roza Dam, fishing is marginal through the Yakima area. From Prosser downstream very good spring boat and bank fishery for smallmouth bass and big channel catfish. In May and June big smallmouth migrate upstream from the Snake River to spawn and action can be memorable. For channel cats June and July are top months to stillfish chicken livers, nightcrawlers and shrimp baits.

The Yak's anadromous salmon run is being rebuilt and occasionally coho and spring chinook fisheries are opened in the late summer and fall. The confluence of the Naches River can be a good salmon area.

A few primitive camping areas at Roza Dam and scattered upstream to Cle Elum. FS and primitive camps between Easton and Lake Keechelus. Shuttles for boat trailers are sometimes available. Check with sport shops in Ellensburg and Yakima.

Kittitas County Resorts

Lake Easton: Lake Easton State Park, 509-656-2230.

Klickitat County

WDFW Region 5

Washington Department of Fish and Wildlife, 2108 Grand Blvd. Vancouver, WA 98661-4624 Phone 360-696-6211.

This long, narrow, sparsely populated Columbia River county has the characteristics of both east and western Washington. Summers are warm, sometimes hot and always dry. Winters are moderate and fishable.

The south border falls into an impounded area of the Columbia River well known for salmon, steelhead, smallmouth, walleye and sturgeon. The north border pushes against the Yakama Indian Reservation and the Simcoe Mountains. The west side is green with conifers and oaks and rolls through low mountains from the Indian Heaven Wilderness in neighboring Skamania County around hard carpets of vast lava beds and attractive trout and salmon rivers. The west side includes parts of the Gifford Pinchot National Forest, WDFW's Klickitat Wildlife Area, and Conboy Lake National Wildlife Refuge East of the Klickitat River there is little public land, mostly given over to high prairies, treeless hills, basalt formations and eroded coulees falling into seasonal streams, many of which go dry in the summer. Further east beyond US 97 the county is an open, sunburned region of dry land farming starved for water. The skies are so clear that the county was selected as the site for one of the nation's leading astronomy observatories near Goldendale. Summer temperatures often hit the 80s and frequently climb past 100. Little rain falls from June to mid September and annual precipitation at Goldendale is only 17.41 inches.

Klickitat County is our 14th largest at 1,932 square miles. The high point is 5,823 feet at Indian Rock, 12 miles north of Goldendale and west of Satus Pass on the summit ridge of the Simcoe Mountains. The lowest point is barely 160 feet above sea level at Spearfish Lake, a backwater of the Columbia. Most of the county angles between these two extremes.

The west county drains into the White Salmon and Klickitat rivers. The Little Klickitat River cuts southwest across the county and is becoming a favorite stream for fly fishermen. Nine creeks and streams are still stocked with catchable trout, more than in any other county.

Lakes are few and widely scattered. Most of the best for fishing are part of or adjacent to the Columbia River. Two mountain lakes, Porthole and Carp are located in extinct volcanic craters. For fishermen, the extreme south and west areas of the county hold the most appeal, and for many the county's fishing potential is limited to the Columbia River—its backwaters—and the rocky plunge of the Klickitat River.

The east-west highway is Highway 14 along the north bank of the Columbia River. North-South routes are winding two lanes that follow major rivers. State Hwy. 141 runs along the White Salmon River which becomes, on its north end, a Forest Service Road. State Hwy. 142 follows the Klickitat River before bending east to intersect with US 97 at Goldendale. US 97 is the county's main north-south highway, entering from Oregon at Maryhill State Park passing Goldendale and entering the Yakama Indian Reservation at Satus Pass, elev. 3,107.

BIRD CREEK. A small stream stocked in May with about 1,000 catchable size rainbows.

BLOCKHOUSE CREEK. In May a small plant of rainbows is made in this spring-fed creek which crosses Hwy. 141 at Blockhouse west of Goldendale. It flows through farm lands 8 miles W. of Goldendale and enters the Little Klickitat River.

BLOODGOOD CREEK A short-run creek which flows S. through Goldendale golf course and enters Little Klickitat River at W. city limits of Goldendale. It receives legal-sized rainbow plants.

BOWMAN CREEK. Headwaters of Bowman are in the Simcoe Mts. N. of Goldendale. Lightly planted with rainbows. Flows SW to the Little Klickitat River. Drive W. from Goldendale on Hwy. 142 for 16 miles. It also crosses the Goldendale—Glenwood Road. There are two campgrounds on the creek in the mountains N. of Goldendale.

CHAMBERLAIN LAKE. A shallow 80 acre lake formed by a railroad fill 0.5 miles W. of Lyle adjacent to the Columbia River. Offers smallmouth and largemouth bass, black crappie and brown bullhead. Best along highway.

COLUMBIA RIVER. This section of the Columbia is impounded behind The Dalles Dam as Lake Celilo and John Day Dam as Lake Umatilla and includes some of the finest smallmouth, salmon and walleye fishing available. Most salmon and steelhead fishermen aim for the mouths of the White Salmon and Klickitat rivers in Washington and Deschutes and John Day rivers on the Oregon side. Fall salmon and summer-steelhead begin to show up in catchable numbers in August. In season, the mouths of these rivers can become congested with small boats. Walleye fishing is very popular with boaters, especially in the Maryhill State Park/Biggs, OR region. Some of the largest walleye in North America, many above 15 pounds, come from this area of the Columbia. Smallmouth bass are plentiful in the rocky shores and reefs, especially near the mouth of the John Day River on the Oregon side. Many roadside pullovers on Hwy. 14 are at good smallmouth spots. The sloughs between the railroad and highway are good bets for June smallmouth and for panfish. There is a minimal sturgeon fishery, mostly catch and release, although in recent years one sturgeon has been allowed daily above The Dalles Dam. Check current regs for slot limits and retention seasons.

This area of the Columbia is swept almost daily by exceptionally strong winds and boating can be very hazardous especially in early afternoon. Most of the major access points offer trailerable boat launches including Maryhill State Park,

Bingen, Lyle, Biggs, near both dams, Rock Creek, Sandal and Roosevelt. Both shores of the river can be fished, from boats, with either Washington or Oregon licenses. Most convenient camping is at Maryhill State Park at US 97 bridge.

HORSETHIEF LAKE. A back-water of Lake Celilo on the Columbia River, Horsethief is popular with campers and fishermen. The 60-foot deep lake covers 92-acres in a rocky, open bowl and is stocked with more than 20,000 catchable and hatchery surplus brood stock rainbows in the spring and early summer. Good numbers of smallmouth bass, bluegill, crappie, and a few walleye. It is connected to the Columbia by a culvert. Adjacent state park offers fee boat launch, picnic tables, and 10 sites for camping. Ancient petroglyphs visible. The lake is 6 miles E. Lyle on Hwy. 14, 2.5 miles E of The Dalles Dam.

JEWITT CREEK. A small stream flowing through White Salmon into the Columbia. Planted with about 1000 catchable rainbows in June. There's a popular kids fishing derby on this small stream..

KLICKITAT RIVER. While the steelhead runs in most Washington rivers are mere shadows of what they offered 10 years ago, the Klickitat is an exception. From late June-Oct. it produces almost 700 summer steelhead, and in the fall it offers a good shot at chinook and coho salmon. The river gets runs of spring and fall chinook and coho fishing is often good near the mouth. Chinook fishing usually opens in August. The Klickitat is a very picturesque river, wide enough to be drift boated, rolling through a steep canyon of basalt and oak groves. There is primitive camping along the river, and many places to drop in a boat. The problem is summer snow melt from the glaciers on Mount Adams, which during the heat of summer will turn this beautiful flow a gray brown. When night-time temperatures are low enough to freeze the glaciers the river will often remain fishably clear until about noon. A few cutthroat and rainbow are caught along with whitefish in the upper section around the state wildlife area. Hwy. 142 follows the river upstream from Lyle through the town of Klickitat and on past Wahkiacus, offering easy access for 20 miles. Turn N. on Glenwood Road which continues several more miles along the river. A few miles above Lyle the Klickitat pours through a narrow, rockwalled gorge

Klickitat River.

that is not advisable for boaters. Indian fishing platforms overhang the gorge. Best access to Hwy. 142 along the Klickitat is from Hwy. 14 on the S. and US 97 at Goldendale on the NE.

LITTLE KLICKITAT. A large, trout-stocked stream flowing mostly E-W across much of the central W. county. It is stocked with about 2000 rainbows above Goldendale, and flows into main river from the E. about 2.5 miles NE of Wahkiacus. The Little Klickitat, especially the section N. and E. of Goldendale is popular for light tackle and fly fishing. The creek flows S. below the E. side of US 97 between Brooks Memorial State Park and Goldendale where it turns W. through farm land to join the main river along Hwy. 142.

LOCKE LAKE. A shallow warm-water species lake that fluctuates from 15 to 20 acres 3 miles E. of Bingen. The lake is bisected by Hwy. 14. It contains some rainbow, but is best for largemouth and smallmouth bass, black crappie and brown bullhead. Roadside access.

MAJOR CREEK. Flows into the Columbia 5 miles E. of Bingen, Major has a few native rainbow. Fish early, the lower section of this stream often dries up in late summer.

MARYHILL POND. In June this small pond at Maryhill State Park is stocked with about 600 catchable rainbows.

MILL CREEK. A long, brushy tributary to the Little Klickitat River. It flows parallel to and between Blockhouse and Bowman creeks. It is reached via Hwy. 142 about 11 miles W. of Goldendale, or 12 miles N. of Goldendale on the Cedar Valley road. Mill gets May plants of about 600 catchable rainbows.

MOUNT ADAMS POND. Stocked with about 600 rainbows in June.

NORTHWESTERN LAKE. A popular, tree shaded 97 acre trout lake on the Skamania County line formed by Condit Dam on the White Salmon River 3 miles N. of White Salmon. Northwestern produces rainbow in late April, May and June, as well as some cutthroat. Public launch/picnic area on the NW shore, small park at the north end. Planted with 20,000 rainbow fingerlings and generally produces foot-long trout. This lake will be drained with the removal of Condit Dam tentatively scheduled for 2006.

OUTLET CREEK. Stocked in May with about 900 catchable rainbows.

POTHOLE LAKE. One of two lakes cradled in neighboring extinct craters, Pothole covers 8 acres at 2300 feet elev. 6 miles N. of Goldendale. It offers rainbow, browns, and brookies. Fair in April and May. Another crater lake, **CARP LAKE**, 21 acres is 1 mile NW of Pothole Lake and 7 miles N. of Goldendale. The lake supports warm water fish. From Goldendale Observatory State Park go NW on Bloodgood Road, then N. on Pothole Road to that lake. Continue N. to Carp.

RATTLESNAKE CREEK. A tributary to the White Salmon River, joining at Husum on Hwy. 141. Easy access along the W. side for about 5 miles upstream. Primarily an early season show for small wild rainbow and brookies. Intermittent water in late summer.

ROCK CREEK. A small stream in the arid prairie 20 miles E. of Goldendale on the Bickleton Road. Sections dry up in summer, but in June it provides fair rainbow fishing in the upper stretches and good warm water fishing near the Columbia. The mouth is a 5-acre, cattail shouldered slough-like enlargement at Hwy. 14 with a small boat launch and fair to good smallmouth bass fishing some crappie, and bluegills. Rock Creek Road parallels it N. from Hwy. 14 for 12 miles. Some primitive camping. Above the Goldendale-Bickleton Rd. switchback bridge, the creek is small, difficult to reach with few public roads.

ROWLAND LAKE (DuBois). Heavily planted with catchables, brood stock and Triploid rainbows, plus brookies, this popular fishing area is adjacent to Bonneville Pool 4 miles E. of Bingen, about 1 mile E. of Locke Lake. It is divided by Hwy. 14 and covers 84 acres. Planted with about 20,000 'bows, 3000 brookies and 1500 Triploids from April into June. Also has a solid population of large and smallmouth bass, black crappie, bluegill, perch and brown bullhead. Public access on N. shore.

SPEARFISH LAKE. Size of this Columbia River seepage lake ranges from about 10 to 20 acres. It is 1 mile N. from The Dalles Dam and is fed by Five Mile Creek. It is stocked with about 11,000 rainbow and brown trout, a mix of catchables and brood stock. Also offers smallmouth, largemouth bass and crappie. Light boats may be launched along the shore. Lots of shore access for bank fishing. Season usually runs from April opener through February.

SPRING CREEK. A heavily-stocked spring creek which starts at Goldendale fish hatchery 4 miles W. of Goldendale and flows 8 miles SW to the Little Klickitat River. Stocked with upwards of 2000 rainbow before the June opener. Heavy fishing pressure.

TROUT LAKE. Once a large lake now reduced to a few shallow marshy acres. It lies 0.5 mile NW of the community of Trout Lake off Hwy. 141. Holds a few rainbows but there's more elk and deer than fish in this marsh. Wet, muddy access.

TROUT LAKE CREEK. Heading in Skamania County, Trout Lake Creek flows SE to Trout Lake. A paved road from Trout Lake follows the creek NW to a FS campground at the county line. Brushy fishing. Slow water near campground offers brook trout. Faster water upstream supports rainbow.

WHITE SALMON RIVER. A small river joining the Columbia 1.5 miles W. of White Salmon. Paved Hwy. 141 follows the river 35 miles upstream to the headwaters near Swampy Meadows. Fair wade fishing for wild rainbows in upper reaches. The lower 3 miles below Condit Dam impounding Northwestern Lake, has spring and fall chinook and September coho salmon. Produces about 1,100 steelhead a year, and is best from July-Sept. Also receives winter steelhead plants with a minor fishery peaking in January. Boat launch at mouth controlled by Indians. Small boats may be bank launched on east shore. Most larger boats launch at Hood River, OR and run across the Columbia into the White Salmon, or lauch at Bingen and run downstream.

Klickitat County Resorts

Horsethief Lake: Horsethief Lake State Park. 509-767-1159.

Lewis County
WDFW Region 5
Washington Department of Fish and Wildlife, 2108 Grand Blvd. Vancouver, WA 98661-4624 Phone 360-696-6211.

The largest county in western Washington and the 6th largest in the state, Lewis is a rural, heavily forested region that covers 2447 square miles and includes the top steelhead and salmon river some of the west side's best trout and kokanee fishing, Washington's finest tiger musky lake and a couple of real sleeper bass waters.

Lewis is an unusually long county touching both the Willapa Hills coastal mountain range, and the crest of the Cascade Mountains east of Mount Rainier. The far east county rises dramatically into the Cascade Mountains, brushes the south side of Mount Rainier NP, wraps around the picket crests of the Tatoosh Range to peak at the high point on Old Snowy Mountain at 7950 feet in the Goat Rocks Wilderness almost overlooking Yakima County's Rimrock Lake.

While a lot of the mountain areas are fairly roadless or a tangle of old logging roads, many gated, several major highways lead to the best fishing. The two main routes are I-5 which cuts N-S across the county through the Centralia-Chehalis flats, and US 12 which runs E-W from the interstate upstream along the Cowlitz River, across the tiger muskies in Mayfield Lake, past 23 miles of Riffe Lake, through the mountain town of Packwood to White Pass mountain lakes and the edge of Yakima County. On the W. side of I-5, Hwy. 6 rolls along the Chehalis River into the Willapa Hills. East of I-5, Hwy. 7 rolls N-S connecting US 12 and Elbe, along the way passing rich Mineral Lake, one of the most productive trout lakes in the state. More than 50 square miles of Lewis County are within Mt. Rainier National Park, and vast wilderness tracts are in the Tatoosh Range and Goat Rocks Wilderness. Forested chunks of the east county are in Mount Baker-Snoqualmie and Gifford Pinchot national forests. The south edge includes a large swath of Mount St. Helens National Volcanic Area (NVA).

Most of the county drains to either the Cowlitz or Chehalis river systems both productive and well known for chinook and coho salmon, winter and summer steelhead and sea-run cutthroat. Of the more than 200 lakes in the county, 142 are above 2500 feet elev. Many of these high lakes lie on an unusual high mountain plateau north of White Pass. The county also has a fair complement of fishable trout streams including three that are still heavily stocked with catchable trout.

The climate could be described as compromised maritime. Weather is influenced by South Puget Sound, but is also protected by the rain shadow extending W. from the Willapa Hills. This betwixt-and-between location means the county is wetter than Clark County to the south, and drier than Thurston County to the north. For fishermen, the result is moderate, fishable, often pleasant summer and winter temperatures except in the high mountains where winter snowfall is extreme.

Chehalis averages 45 inches of rain, a lot less than it would be if it weren't for the Willapa Hills which form a barrier that holds back much of the moisture coming from the Pacific. In the high Cascades east of Chehalis up to 100 inches of precipitation falls annually. There are a lot of areas in the state that claim, if you don't like the weather wait five minutes and it'll change. In the Cowlitz River Valley it's true.

ALDER LAKE (See Pierce county).

ART LAKE. A 1.5 acre mountain lake at

4000 feet 3 miles E. of Packwood. Planted with cutthroat, drains to Lake Creek and Cowlitz River.

BEE TREE LAKE. A broken dam has greatly reduced this one-time 10 acre lake S. of Randle and the Cowlitz River.

BIG CREEK. A large stream which enters the Nisqually River about 1.5 miles SE of National. FS 52 leaves Hwy. 706 0.5 miles E. of National and follows creek 9.4 miles to a point just short of Cora Lake, the source of Big Creek. Big Creek has wild rainbow, cutthroat and some brook trout. Produces best in June and July. Several FS camping spots.

BERTHA MAY LAKES. A pair of mountain lakes. Upper lake covers 30 acres at 4000 feet. Lower lake is 6 acres at 3700 feet 7 miles SE from National on NE side of Sawtooth Ridge and 1000 feet NE from Big Bertha May. Both lakes offer rainbow and drain to Pothole Lake and Teeley Creek.

BLUE LAKE. A large, pretty brook trout and rainbow lake of 127.9 acres, at 4050 feet. Follow FS 23 from Randle SE for 15.5 miles to Blue Lake FS campground, and hike either FS Trail 274 or 271 about 3 miles up Blue Lake Ridge to lake.

BLUFF LAKE. Cutthroat have been stocked in Bluff at 3900 feet, 7 miles NE of Packwood near N. end of Coal Creek Mt. Drains via Purcell Creek to Cowlitz River.

BORST LAKE (AKA Fort Borst Pond) An artificial lake and designated family fishing water, covering 5 acres at Fort Borst Park in Centralia. Stocked with more than 3000 catchable and Triploid rainbows.

BUCK CREEK BEAVER PONDS. Fair cutthroat fishing in May and June. Ponds are 2 miles above East Canyon along the Cispus River Road, and drain into Cispus River.

BUTTER CREEK. Cross Cowlitz River at Packwood N. on FS Rd. 52 and continuing about 2.5 miles to FS 5270 which leads E. and N. upstream more than 7 miles. Holds wild rainbow, brookies and cutthroat. Selective gear rules in effect.

CANYON CREEK. Stocked in May with about 9000 catchable size rainbows..

CARLISLE LAKE. A heavily-stocked 20.3 acre lake near Onalaska, popular with anglers targeting spring plants of 4000 browns and 15,000 rainbow, catchable and brood stock up to 26 inches long. Also good for largemouth bass and some bluegill. Very popular opening day lake. Closes Feb. 28. Public access and small ramp. No internal combustion outboards. Located 0.4 miles west of Onalaska off Hwy. 508.

CARLTON CREEK. A remote wild rainbow and cutthroat stream just outside Mount Rainier NP. Follow Hwy. 12 NE of Packwood 9 miles. Just 0.5 mile from the national park, turn E. on FS 44 and follow the creek upstream 8 miles to end of road. An overgrown trail continues up creek to Carlton Pass in William O. Douglas Wilderness Area.

CHAMBERS LAKE. A drive-in mountain lake 11.5 miles SE of Packwood, Chambers holds rainbows, browns, and brookies. Several small beaver ponds crowd the inlet. Feeds Chambers Creek and Cispus River. Chambers covers 14.4 acres, at an elev. of 4525 feet. Best after July 1. From Hwy. 12 about 2.5 miles SE of Packwood turn SE onto FS 21 up Johnson Creek. About 1 mile S. of Hugo Lake turn N. up FS 2150 and continue to campground on the lake.

CHEHALIS RIVER (Upper). Fair for rainbow and cutthroat in June. Sometimes decent for winter steelhead in Pe Ell area. Quick to flood. From Chehalis Hwy. 6 leads to and follows the river W. past Rainbow Falls State Park.

CISPUS RIVER. A pretty mountain stream, but lackluster fishery that produces small wild rainbow and cutthroat from June to August. At Randle on US 12 cross the Cowlitz River and take FS 25 to lower Cispus. FS 23 leads to upper Cispus via FS 21 and 2160 to Walupt Lake, a total distance of about 40 miles. FS campgrounds located at Tower Rock, North Fork, Cat Creek and Walupt Lake. Road leads up N. fork of the Cispus about 10 miles, with roads also up such major tributaries as Quartz Creek, Iron Creek and Yellow Jacket Creek, all decent prospects for wild trout. Watch for mountain goats.

CLEAR FORK (Cowlitz River tributary). A fast, lightly fished high elevation stream that supports wild rainbow, cutthroat and possibly brookies. Best fished after mid-summer. To reach the SE side leave Hwy. 12 about 4.5 miles E. of Packwood onto FS 46 and continue along Clear Fork

8 miles to the trailhead to **LILY LAKE.** Trail continues up Little Lava Creek 2 miles from road end to lake. US 12 roughly follows the N and W side toward White Pass.

COAL CREEK. A small mountain stream which enters the Cowlitz River 4 miles NE of Packwood. Wild cutthroat and rainbow are taken in early summer. Rough trail follows the creek to **BEAVER** and **LOST LAKES.** FS Road 4610 follows some of the creek near the middle.

CORA LAKE. Rainbow inhabit this deep, 28 acre lake at 3900 feet, 9.4 miles SE of National and 0.5 miles NW from High Rock on end of Sawtooth Ridge. Drains to Big Creek and Nisqually River. Follow FS 84 and 8430 to lake.

COWLITZ RIVER. From a glacial trickle at the edge of Paradise on the SE side of Mount Rainier, the Cowlitz River flows south and west collecting dozens of tumbling wild trout tributaries, dams, and reservoirs and eventually easing into the Columbia River as one of—if not the—hottest steelhead and salmon rivers in Washington.

For fishermen, the Cowlitz is five rivers in one long, winding bed.

The Lower Cowlitz from I-5 downstream is a wide, sluggish, channelized flow favored by hoglines, trollers and bank plunkers(See Cowlitz County entry).

The Middle Cowlitz downstream from Salkum Salmon Hatchery barrier dam past the WDFW trout hatchery at Blue Creek to I-5, is a wide, pool pocked, powerful flow and the heart of the river's famous steelhead and salmon fishery.

The Impounded Cowlitz is a reservoir segment that begins at Salkum at the hatchery's low barrier dam which stops the natural migration of anadromous fish. Surplus hatchery fish are sometimes trucked upstream and released. A few miles above the hatchery dam towering Mayfield Dam impounds Mayfield Reservoir (the state's first tiger musky lake). Water impounded for the lake backs into an arm of the old river bed at the bottom of steep-walled and treacherous Cowlitz Canyon. At the head of Cowlitz Canyon towers Mossyrock Dam, an imposing wall of concrete creating 15 mile-long Riffe Lake.

The Big Bottom segment is a wide, braided trout river draining a pastoral valley from the upper end of Riffe Lake upstream to just beyond the little mountain town of Packwood. In this section the wa-

Cowlitz River chinook.

ter is quick, a hundred feet or so wide in many places, and falls gradually between long stretches of riffles and pools. At first glance it appears to have all the ingredients for a super trout river. Unfortunately, it is exceptionally cold, nutritionally poor and often clouded by glacial silt; adverse conditions that greatly limit trout growing potential. There are, however, scattered numbers of rainbow, cutthroat and Dolly Varden char.

Upper Cowlitz is a wild, free-falling section of white water, rock beds and plunge pools rocketing from the slopes of Mount Rainier through the roadless Tatoosh Wilderness. There are a very few wild trout in this narrow, creek-like segment and those that are here are usually small. Access involves a difficult hike.

The Middle Cowlitz below Salkum is the most popular and productive fishing section for anglers targeting winter and summer steelhead, spring, summer and fall chinook, fall coho, sea-run cutthroat, and in the lower end dip netting for March smelt. The river is wide, deep and powerful, shoreline access is limited and it's easiest to fish from jet or drift boats. There are good ramps at the salmon and trout hatcheries (a good day's drift), at Massey Bar and I-5.

Shore anglers congregate, sometimes in incredible numbers, at the few accessible areas. The hatcheries are the two most popular bank fishing sites. As a rule, with many exceptions, salmon fishermen line up below the barrier dam, and steelheaders wedge into open spots at Blue Creek which is the outlet for the trout hatchery. There is excellent opportunities for both above and below, however. It's common for barrier dam anglers to cross the river in small boats and fish the less congested south side.

The Cowlitz nearly always ranks at the top of the winter steelhead ranking and is second only to the Columbia River in summer-runs. In 1999 steelheaders caught almost 3300 summer and 2300 winter steelhead. In recent years the emphasis has changed from winter to summer steelheading. For comparison, in 1986 the summer-run catch was almost 1300 and the winter-run catch was almost 11,000. In year's past this big river has delivered as many as 30,000 steelhead a year, twice the contemporary catch.

Salmon fishing can be outstanding, especially for boaters. Cowlitz spring chinook are one of the most prized fish anywhere, when enough spring chinook are available to allow a sport season in April, May or June.

Fall chinook and coho fishing is still very good. Chinook action begins in mid summer, peaks in September, and coho arrive in late September, October and November. From Blue Creek downstream past Toledo the river offers respectable sea-run cutthroat fishing in August and September.

The Cowlitz is truly a year-round fishing hole. Winter steelheading starts in November, peaks in December and January and continues into April when spring and summer steelhead move in. Best summer-run fishing is July, August and September. March, April and May bring a run of spring chinook, in late July the first fall chinook, September-December for silvers and jack salmon of both species. Smelt dipping in March in the Kelso and Castle Rock areas.

The river is roughly followed by, and accessible from, US 12 between I-5 Exit 68 and the junction of the Ohanapecosh River west of White Pass. For river flow/level updates call Tacoma City Light fishing hot line, 1-888-502-8690.

CORTRIGHT CREEK. Joins Clear Fork of the Cowlitz 1 mile NE of La Wis Wis campground on US 12 N. of Packwood. About 1 mile E. of Ohanapecosh Junction, turn onto graveled FS 45 which parallels the creek for 3.5 miles. Holds small wild cutthroat, brook and rainbow.

DAVIS LAKE. 18 acres of rainbow, cutthroat, largemouth bass and bluegill 1.5 miles SE of Morton just N. of US 12. Road from center of Morton runs E. along both N. and S. sides of the lake. Drains to Tilton River. Spring is best fishing

DECEPTION CREEK. From US 12 about 2.5 miles S. of Packwood Turn onto FS 21 and follow Johnson Creek 6 miles SE to FS road 2130 turning sharply NW up Deception Creek 2.5 miles. A small rainbow and cutthroat stream.

DUMBBELL LAKE. A 41.6 acre mountain cutthroat lake at 5200 feet 3.8 miles N. of White Pass on Cascade Crest Trail PCT 2000. Drains to **BUESCH LAKE**.

ELK CREEK. A small June producer of cutthroat that enters the Chehalis River at Doty.

FRYING PAN LAKE. A mountain lake on the high plateau of the Cascade crest along PCT 2000 at 4850 feet, 6.5 miles N. of White Pass. The 23 acre lake holds rainbow, cutthroat and brookies. Adjacent **LITTLE SNOW LAKE** has brookies. Lots of summer mosquitoes.

GLACIER CREEK. Outlet of **GLACIER LAKE** The small stream enters Johnson Creek 4.5 miles upstream from FS 21 which leaves Hwy. 12 about 2.5 miles SW of Packwood. Trail up N. bank continues 2 miles to Glacier Lake. The creek has wild cutthroat, a few rainbow and brook trout.

GLACIER LAKE. 19-acre headwaters of Glacier Creek and reached via a 2 mile hike. Lake lies at 3000 feet and has cutthroat and brookies.

GOAT CREEK. Begins in Goat Lake high in the Goat Rocks Wilderness Area on the Cascade Crest. Much of this beautiful creek flows through meadows. Cutthroat are colorful 10-12 inches. Some rainbow. Best from mid-July through September. Route from US 12 W. of Packwood, up Johnson Creek on FS 21 about 11 miles to FS 2150 to Chambers Lake campground. Trail 95 heads NE up Goat Ridge to Goat Lake. Creek flows below the ridge.

GOAT LAKE. 10 acres at 6900 feet at head

of Goat Creek. No report of fish. Frozen almost all year.

GRIMM CREEK. Crossed by US 12, S. of Mary's Corner, produces a few cutthroat in June.

HANNAFORD CREEK. Enters Skookumchuck River 1.5 miles N. of Centralia. Best cutthroat fishing in June. Road turns E. from Hwy. 507 at creek's mouth and follows upstream about 10 miles.

HORSESHOE LAKE. 1.5 miles SW of Centralia, this 4 acre lake holds catfish, panfish some bass. It's close to W. bank of Chehalis River.

HUGO LAKE. 1.5 acre, adjacent to E. side of FS 21 Johnson Creek about 11 miles from US 12. Some rainbow and cutthroat.

IRON CREEK. Wild rainbow are in this Cispus River tributary. From Cispus River Road, to FS road 2510 which leads up the creek for 5 miles. FS campground at mouth.

JACKPOT LAKE. 5.5 acre cutthroat lake at 4450 feet 9.8 miles S. of Packwood. Drains to Jackpot Creek and N. F. Cispus River.

JESS LAKE (Pipe). 8.5 acre cutthroat lake just W. of PCT 2000 on the high plateau 4.4 miles N. of White Pass, 2000 feet NW of **DUMBBELL LAKE.** Elev. 5175 feet .

JOHNSON CREEK. Major trout fishing tributary joining the upper Cowlitz 3 miles SW of Packwood. FS 21 follows upstream 12 miles to headwaters, and continues into Cispus River drainage. Fair fishing for wild rainbow, brook and cutthroat from mid-summer into fall. Tributaries include Glacier, Deception, Middle Fork, Jordan and Mission Creeks. All may be fished upstream from Johnson Creek and accessed from FS 21. Selective gear rules.

JUG LAKE. Lots of brook trout in this 28 acre hike-in lake 2.5 miles NE of Soda Springs Campground. Best July-Sept. Elevation 4550 feet. From US 12, turn N. on FS 45 and immediately left onto 4510, continue up Summit Creek, past falls, to Soda Springs Camp and continue on Trail 44 and 43 to lake.

KNUPPENBURG LAKE (Kuppenheimer). A pretty, but easily accessed and heavily fished 4-acre brown trout lake, at 4200 feet 1.5 miles S. of White Pass beside US 12. Drains to Cowlitz River. Picnic site.

LACAMAS CREEK. Enters the Cowlitz River 1 mile E. of Vader. Hwy. 506 crosses the creek's mouth, and Telegraph Road follows the NW side 3 miles upstream where Hwy. 5 crosses the creek. Contains rainbow and cutthroat, but all cutts must be released.

LAKE CREEK. Outlet of big Packwood Lake, flows NW 5 miles emptying into Cowlitz River 2 miles NE of Packwood where US 12 crosses Lake Creek. Rough trails lead upstream to good rainbow fly water. Also fished downstream from Packwood Lake but can be rough going.

LILY LAKE. Large brookies and rainbow in this 25 acre hike-in lake at 3750 feet 3.8 miles W. of White Pass and S. of US 12 in Goat Rocks Wilderness. From US 12 N. of Packwood, turn E. onto FS 46 and continue to road end. Hike 2 miles SE on Trail 61 to lake. Drains to Clear Fork Cowlitz River.

LINCOLN CREEK. A fishy, tributary joining the Chehalis River near Galvin. A deep, brushy creek with wild cutthroat, rainbow and a few steelhead. From I-5 N. of Centralia, turn W. on Hwy. 12 toward Oakville, then W. at Fords Prairie through Galvin and continue upstream on Lincoln Creek Rd. paralleling creek 15 miles. Good duck jump shooting. Lots of private, pasture land.

LITTLE NISQUALLY RIVER. Flows into S. arm of **ALDER LAKE** near Thurston County border. From Hwy. 7 about 2 miles N. of Mineral, turn NW on FS 147 through Pleasant Valley along S. shore of Alder Lake to river mouth. The road continues up Little Nisqually past **DUCK** and **GOOSE LAKES** to complete a loop back to Hwy. 7 near Mineral. Mid-June through September best for wild rainbow and cutthroat. West Fork Little Nisqually may offer good cutthroat angling in top reaches.

LONE TREE LAKE. A 2.5 acre cutthroat lake at 3500 feet, 6.8 miles SE of Randle on N. side of Lone Tree Mt. Drains to Camp Creek and Cispus River. Follow FS 55, S. on FS 5505 and left on spur 012 to lake.

LONG LAKE. Brown trout are in this 6 acre road-side lake at 4000 feet, 6.5 miles W. of Packwood. Drains to Cowlitz River. W. on FS 47 then S. on 4740 about 2 miles to lake.

LOST HAT LAKE. 3 acre cutthroat lake at 4500 feet, 3.4 miles NE of Packwood Lake outlet. Drains to Lava Creek and Clear Fork Cowlitz River.

MAYFIELD LAKE. A 13 mile-long, 2200 acre reservoir on the Cowlitz River 13 miles NE of Toledo. US 12 crosses near mid lake. A popular fishing and play boat lake and has the distinction of being the first lake in Washington to be stocked with tiger muskies. It produced the $28^{1/4}$ pound state record in 1995, and is the likely can-

didate to produce the next several records. Anglers also target rainbow, cutthroat, coho, perch, a few crappie, smallmouth and largemouth bass and brown bullhead. Try rocky areas for the smallmouth especially on the north bank and the logs and weedbeds for the largemouth. There are boat launch facilities, camping and picnicking at Kinswa State Park. Another ramp at the small county park on the NE shore. The lake is enjoying a resurrection of its rainbow fishery with lots of trout in the 1 to 2 pound class. In recent years WDFW has planted more than 25,000 rainbows, some to $1^{1/2}$ pounds, in March. Trolling blade strings with worms, small Flatfish, flies, spoons or spinners is a popular trout tactic. Muskies bite best in late summer, often in the early evening of a hot day. Tigers

Mineral Lake

277 Acres
Lewis County
©Washington State Fishing Guide

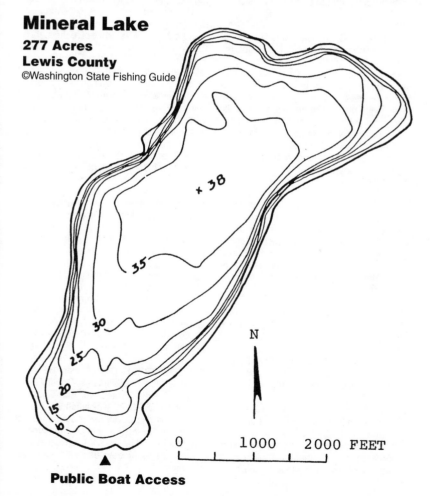

x 38

35

30

25

20

15

10

N

0   1000   2000 FEET

▲
Public Boat Access

like hot weather, and they like shallow weedy water where they can ambush bait fish. Try casting noisy spinners or surface plugs in the Tilton and Winston Creek arms, and weedbeds and floating logs, around the shoreline. Both ends of the US 12 bridge are good places to throw large, noisy lures. For more info on this exciting fishery read the Tiger Muskie Fishing feature

MINERAL CREEK. Good in lower reaches for rainbow and cutthroat in June. Bite improves in upper reaches in mid summer. This large creek enters Nisqually River 2 miles E. of Alder Lake and NE of Mineral Lake. From Hwy. 7 turn E. on Mineral Rd., go through town to Mineral Creek Road, which follows the stream upstream into logging areas. A railroad track follows the creek from the mouth upstream 3 miles to Mineral.

MINERAL LAKE. Massive plants (100,000 plus) of rainbow fry, topped off with annual spring plants of 15,000 net-pen raised catchable rainbows, a generous load of large Triploids and brood stock and 5000 browns keeps this pretty 277-acre lake close to the hearts of many fishermen. It is always one of the state's leading trout producers on opening day. Located 3 miles S. of Elbe at town of Mineral. Best for rainbows in May and June and generally enjoys a flurry of action just before the Sept. 30 closure. Brown trout help the summer fishery, especially at night. Good stillfishing with baits and trolling. Public access, small WDFW ramp (bring lots of patience, it's a circus of congestion on opening day), wheelchair accessible public fishing dock, and resort facilities with rental boats and fishing docks. Spectacular reflected views of Mount Rainier. Great place to bring kids.

MOSS LAKE. 3.5 acre cutthroat lake 1000 feet SW of **NEWAUKUM LAKES** at 3024 feet elevation. Drain to South Fork Newaukum River.

MUD LAKE. A 7.5 acre lake at 4850 feet on NW side of Hamilton Buttes 3.8 miles E. of Blue Lake. It offers cutthroat.

NEWAUKUM LAKE. Brown trout have been planted in this 17 acre lake in a logging area at 3000 feet 13 miles NE of Onalaska at head of S. Fork Newaukum River. From US 12 about 1.3 miles E. of Cinebar, turn N. and continue N. on Rd. 71

NEWAUKUM RIVER. A small river that furnishes wild rainbow and cutthroat, a few hatchery steelhead, and is generally a tough fishing prospect. The steelhead run is in tough shape, catches are down to about 60 fish a year the majority in March. For trout anglers, it's mostly a fish for fun stream because few of these wild fish exceed the 14 inch minimum. Fun on the fly, though. The Newaukum enters Chehalis River at Chehalis. To fish the North Fork follow Centralia-Alpha Rd. SE to North Fork Road. To hit the South Fork follow Hwy. 508 E. from I-5. The lower river can be picked up off the I-5 Rush Road exit.

NISQUALLY RIVER (See Pierce county).

PACKWOOD LAKE. A popular 452 acre mountain lake widely known for foot-long and larger wild rainbows, and the pleasant 3.5 forest walk to get there. Can also be reached on ATVs up powerline trail. Packwood Lake lies at 2858 feet 8.5 miles E. of Packwood. Some large rainbows are taken from mid-June through September. Selective gear rules ban bait fishing. Bring a raft or float tube. From US 12 about 1.5 miles NE of Packwood, turn E. onto FS 1266, bearing right onto 041 to scenic, and gentle lake trail. Route is marked. Primitive FS campgrounds at N. end.. Trail 78 from N. end of Packwood Lake leads 4 miles E. to **LOST LAKE** at 5100 feet. This 21 acre lake offers rainbow. Packwood is a popular destination for fishing families, and on midsummer weekends and holidays you can expect lots of company.

PLUMMER LAKE. This former gravel pit is now a 12-acre lake stocked in April with about 4000 catchable-size rainbows, supplementing a self-sustaining population of largemouth bass, perch and bluegills. A few browns may survive from earlier plants. The 36 foot deep lake is on W. side of Centralia adjacent to I-5. Open from end of April through February. Carry-in boat launch.

QUARTZ CREEK. Drive S. from US 12 at Randle on FS 25 across Cowlitz and Cispus rivers. At Iron Creek campground, turn W. onto FS 26 which follows the E. bank of Quartz Creek for about 8 miles to its source at Strawberry Mt. on the edge of the Mount St. Helens NVA. Supports wild cutthroat and rainbow, best mid-June into September.

Riffe Lake and Mossyrock Dam.

RIFFE LAKE. A 23-mile-long, lightly fished reservoir behind Mossyrock Dam on the Cowlitz River. Riffe is a huge, 11,830 acre reservoir winding between steep hills— unfortunately mostly brushy clear-cut logging areas—below US 12 which follows high up on the N. bank. The lake has no residential or commercial development and nearly all of the fishing pressure is concentrated within a mile or so of the two boat launches on the W. and E. ends. That leaves most of the 52 miles of shoreline available for boat camping and overnight exploration, although finding a flat tent spot on the steep banks can be a challenge. Fishing is allowed year-round, but seasonal draw downs and weather can make winter fishing tough. The fishing in Riffe is in many ways a local and reasonably well kept secret. That it's far from population centers helps.

Riffe is stocked with landlocked chinook and coho salmon, rainbow, brown, cutthroat trout, smallmouth and largemouth bass, crappie, bullhead and bluegill. The landlocked salmon are the biggest draw beginning in early spring when 12 to 15 inch fish are schooling near the surface. Both stillfishermen and trollers hit the salmon using worms, scented marshmallows, corn and small shrimp. Trollers nearly always use flasher blade attractors, and because of the lake's plunging depths, still fishermen often suspend their offerings below bobbers. The dam area on the W end is a very popular salmon fishing spot. A steep trail from the US 12 overlook leads to a popular bank fishing area. The E. end near 108 Bridge and Taidnapam Park is also a popular with stillfishermen in the spring. Anglers sometimes fish from the bridge, hoisting their catch 50 feet up from the water. The E. end also has the shallowest water and that's where bullhead catfish and smallmouth bass fishermen concentrate. Spring bass anglers also target the mouths of inlet creeks. Another good bass area is Swofford Cove near the islands on the SW end not far from the excellent boat ramp at Mossyrock Park Campground. Bass fishing just seems to get better here every year, despite the cold water. Fees are required to use the groomed campsites, play lawns and launch at Mossyrock Park. Facilities on the E. end are more primitive, including rough camping, a steep boat launch, and fewer people. Newer facilities are at Taidnapam Park (360-497-7707) at the mouth of the Cowlitz about 4 miles beyond the WDFW access. The E. end is reached from US 12 by turning S. on Kosmos Rd. between Morton and Randle. The W. end is reached by continuing through the community of Mossyrock. Route is well marked. For updated reports on reservoir levels, call 1-888-502-8690.

SALMON CREEK. A large tributary merging into the Cowlitz River 1 mile SW of Toledo where it's crossed by the Jackson Highway. Produces wild rainbow early in the season, some sea-run cutts in late summer and fall. East of Toledo Hwy. 505 crosses middle portions of the Salmon, and a road from SE end of Mayfield Lake turns S. at Winston to headwaters.

SCANEWA LAKE. One of the newest lakes in Washington, and an emerging trout hot spot thanks to stocking of catchable size rainbow trout, including an original plant of acrobatic Kamloops strain rainbows. The lake, SW of Randle, was impounded in 1994 behind Cowlitz Falls Dam and offers two parks managed by the utility district, (one with summer tent and RV camping), picnicking, two small boat ramps and small docks. Wheelchair accessible. Popular for small boat fishing. From US 12 W. of Randle, turn S. on Savio Rd. to Kiona Rd. and 2 miles to Falls Road for 3.7 miles to a left turn onto logging road 240. Take the next left to the lake. Route is marked. Scanewa, sometimes called Cowlitz Falls Lake, may be closed from March through May to protect out-migration of juvenile salmon and steelhead. Worms are a favorite bait, good place for kids to watch bobbers.

SILER CREEK. A small stream offering pocket picking for wild rainbow and cutthroat, south of US 12 at Randle. Creek is crossed by and paralleled by FS 23. Just S. of the Squire Creek confluence, FS 55 heads N. and crosses the creek following drainage to headwaters at Lone Tree Mt. **SILER POND** is stocked with about 1000 catchable rainbows before the April opener.

SILVER CREEK. This Cowlitz River tributary N. of US 12 can offer good wild rainbow fishing for anglers willing to walk and work for their seclusion. Selective gear rules (no bait) apply from the mouth to FS 4778. July and August are the most productive months. The creek is crossed by US 12 at Kehoe Mt. on the E. side of Randle. There are two routes. From US 12 at Randle, N. on FS 75 from ranger station about 4 miles on the creek's W. side dropping within 0.4 mile of the creek. A second route goes up the E. bank and begins one mile E. of the ranger station where FS 47 leaves US 12 and heads N. bypassing a tough canyon.

SKATE CREEK. One of the few West side streams still stocked with catchable rainbows, Skate Creek heads in N. Lewis County at Bear Prairie and flows S. to join the Cowlitz River at Packwood. Ten miles of the creek are followed closely by FS 52 which leaves US 12 in Packwood and continues NW to headwater. Lots of access, and bait fishing is allowed. A large creek with numerous tributaries, Skate also supports wild cutthroat. It's intermittently stocked from May-Sept. with up to 21,000 rainbows, plus another 3,000 14-inch plus Triploids. Bring light tackle, hip boots and the kids. Beaver ponds at Bear Prairie have cutthroat.

SKOOKUMCHUCK RIVER. A small, quick to flood, winter steelhead stream that peaks in March and April. The Skook' joins the Chehalis River at W. city limits of Centralia, but the best steelheading is nearly always just below the dam near the hatchery. When the winter steelhead arrive, expect lots of elbows around your ears. The lower river is paralleled by Hwy. 507 N. from Centralia to Bucoda. To continue upstream turn E. one mile N. of Bucoda onto Skookumchuck Road which leads E. upstream along the river to a steelhead hatchery and Skookumchuck Reservoir dam (See **Skookumchuck Reservoir** Thurston County) In the creek-like water above the reservoir, there is a possibility of hooking small wild trout in summer. Selective gear rules, a14-inch minimum, and maze of logging road access from Vail discourages most anglers. The lower reaches sometimes produce good runs of sea-run cutthroat starting in October.

SMITH CREEK. About 3 miles SW of Packwood FS 21 leaves Hwy. 12 to follow Smith Creek for 9 miles. This Cowlitz River tributary holds small wild rainbow and cutthroat during summer.

SNOW LAKE. A mountain cutthroat lake of 8 acres at 4975 feet adjacent to PCT 2000 in the William O. Douglas Wilderness 6 miles N. of White Pass. Drains to Summit Creek and Ohanapecosh River. Snow is one of dozens of small brook, cutthroat and rainbow lakes on this plateau. Shortest hike to Snow Lake vicinity is from Deep Creek Camp at the end of Bumping River Road on Trail 980 past Twin Sisters, then S. on PCT 2000. **LITTLE SNOW LAKE** is about 1 mile NW on Trail 43 between Frying Pan and Jug lakes.

SOUTH LEWIS COUNTY PARK POND.
Grab the kids, fishing rod and picnic basket when you head for this heavily stocked 17-acre pond SE of Toledo. Planted in March with 10,000 rainbows, 4000 browns 8 to 14 inches, plus largemouth bass and bluegills, and in 1999 tiger muskies were planted that will jump into the fishery in about 5 years. Open year-round.

ST. JOHN LAKE. Golden trout have been stocked in this deep, 3-acre lake 9.5 miles S. of Packwood. Drains to St. John Creek to North Fork Cispus River. From US 12 SW of Packwood, go S. on FS 21, then SW on FS 22 to Trail 568 hiking up Stonewall Ridge. Adventurous fishermen may bushwhack up St. John Creek where it crosses FS 22 just N. of FS 2212 jct.

SUMMIT CREEK. A tumbling, white-water creek that heads just under the Cascade Crest and flows W. to the Ohanapecosh River 2 miles S. of Mt. Rainier National Park, crossing Hwy. 123. Holds wild rainbow and fishes best from July into October. Two pleasant FS campgrounds in upper reaches. Best access is from US 12, one mile NE of Hwy. 123, turning NE on FS 4510. About 2 miles to Summit Creek Campground and another 3 miles to Soda Springs Campground at road end where Trail 44 continues E. up the creek into William O. Douglas Wilderness to Jug and Frying Pan Lakes and PCT 2000.

SWOFFORD POND. An outstanding multi-species fishery has been developed in this heavily stocked 240 acre pond formerly used for rearing steelhead. The pond is near the SW shore of Riffe Lake east of Mossyrock. Open year-round, it provides largemouth bass in the 3 to 7 pound range, bluegill, rainbow, brown trout, crappie, bullheads and channel catfish that may push 20 pounds. Stocked in March with 10,000 rainbows and 4000 browns. WDFW reports hold-over browns in excess of 10 pounds. Lots of bank access, a boat launch, but no internal combustion outboards. From US 12 head into Mossyrock, go SE on Aljune Road to Swofford Road and continue to lake.

TATOOSH LAKES. Remote alpine lakes of 2.5 and 10 acres 7.5 miles N. of Packwood at 5000 feet on NE side of spectacular Tatoosh Ridge near the center of Tatoosh Wilderness. Stocked with rainbow. Follow Trail 161. From Packwood head NE on FS 5290 which switchbacks to S. end

of Trail 161 near Hinkle-Tinkle Creek. To reach Trail 161 on the N. end, from Packwood follow FS 52 to FS 5270 upstream along Butter Creek to trailhead.

TILTON RIVER. One of the few western Washington streams still stocked with catchable trout, the Tilton is planted with 24,000 rainbows including about 3000 Triploids 14-inches and up. It also receives tanker truckloads of surplus coho and hatchery steelhead. The hatchery truck shows up with trout just before the June opener and again several times during the summer. The stream is a good producer in June, July and August. The river feeds Mayfield Lake. Best route is to take US 12 to Morton, N. on Hwy. 7 through town, then downstream on Hwy. 508 which follows the river. The Tilton offers some of the best West Slope stream fishing for trout, and can be good for truck-and-release coho in late November and December.

WALUPT LAKE. An extremely popular road-accessible mountain lake in a timbered bowl in Gifford Pinchot NF surrounded on three sides by Goat Rock Wilderness. It offers small boat fishermen, and float tubers a decent shot at rainbow and cutthroat. Walupt covers 384 acres, 200 feet deep at 3927 feet elev. 3 miles W. of the Cascade Crest. It produces rainbow and some cutthroat as soon as ice goes off in early summer and continues to offer action into fall months. Selective gear rules, no bait. Walupt also has a reputation for growing large, plentiful crayfish, which are popular—especially when boiled, shucked, slathered in butter and splattered with lemon juice. Walupt is a popular destination for a lot of recreationists as soon as snow lifts off the roads. Large FS camp at the NW end and a good boat ramp. From US 12 SW of Packwood, turn S. onto FS 21, drive about 14 miles S. to FS 2160 then E. 4.5 miles to lake. Trails 98 and 101 lead from campground into the surrounding wilderness area. Keep an eye peeled for elk.

WILLAME CREEK. Enters Cowlitz River 4 miles SW of Packwood. The rainbow stream is reached by crossing the Cowlitz at Packwood and driving N. for 4 miles on FS 52 to FS 42 which follows the stream about 1 mile. FS 4730 then leads SW for about 2.5 miles along the creek almost to **WILLAME LAKE** at 3650 feet. FS 4740 continues to **LONG LAKE** at 4000 feet. Long, a rainbow lake, covers 6 acres.

WINSTON CREEK. A long trouty foothills stream that flows into the S. tip of Mayfield Lake S. of US 12. Once heavily stocked by WDFW but in recent years only wild rainbow and cutthroat have been available. Still, it's a pleasant fishery experience with good potential for hooking trout, largely because of selective gear (no bait) restrictions and a 10-inch, 2-fish minimum. Cutthroat to 16 inches lurk in the brushy sections. Fishing is allowed June through Oct. From Hwy. 12 at the E. side of the Mayfield Lake Bridge, turn S. and continue past state park on Winston Creek Road which follows the stream about 5 miles.

WOBBLY LAKE. An 8-acre cutthroat and brookie lake 13 miles S. of Randle. Reached by driving FS 22 up North Fork Cispus River about 10 miles to FS 2208 then hike 2 miles on trail 273 up Wobbly Creek to lake. Wobbly produced a state record 9 pound brook in 1988.

WRIGHT LAKE (Little Fritzie). A 3 acre lake holding cutthroat and rainbow 9 miles SE of Packwood at 3100 feet at edge of Goat Rocks Wilderness. Drains into Johnson Creek. From US 12 SW of Packwood, turn SE on FS 21 and follow Johnson Creek to the lake.

Lewis County Resorts

Mayfield Lake: Lake Mayfield Marina Resort, 360-985-2357.

Mineral Lake: Mineral Lake Resort, 360-492-5367.

Riffe Lake: Riffe Lake Campground, 360-983-8122.

Lincoln County
WDFW Region 1
Washington Department of Fish and Wildlife, 8702 N. Division St., Spokane, WA 99218. Phone, 509-456-4082.

This is a big eastern Washington county, 8th largest in the state, with vast landscapes, sweeping horizons, and a relatively small fishing potential with a couple of very notable, heavily stocked exceptions, including miles of Lake Roosevelt, the state's largest lake. Lincoln County covers 2335 square miles and most of them are fairly flat, creased with scabland channels and coulees, or planted with irrigated grain crops. Summers are hot and dry—the annual precipitation at Davenport is only 16.72 inches. Temperatures average in the 80s, may climb above 100, and in winter have dropped as low as -27. The average elevation is about 1700 feet.

When you look for fishing action here you're looking at stocked trout lakes. Many small lakes and ponds in the county hold water only in the spring and early summer, evaporating by July. Almost all of the county tapers S. draining into the vast Crab Creek watershed, and Moses Lake.

Most of Lincoln County is north of I-90. The best east-west access is via US 2 which crosses near the center of the county through Davenport. Major north-south highways connecting with I-90 are Hwy. 21 on the W. and Hwy. 23 on the E. The two hottest fishing spots are Coffeepot and Fourth of July lakes.

COFFEE POT LAKE. One of the top mixed species lakes in the region offering stocked rainbow trout, largemouth bass, crappie, yellow perch, catfish, bluegills and sunfish. Coffee Pot covers 316.8 acres, and is an enlargement of Lake Creek. The creek continues below the lake and includes a series of small lakes, most of which offer limited fishing for warmwater species and some trout. Until 1998 Coffee Pot was closed to the public. It is tightly managed by WDFW to provide quality fishing. Selective gear and special limit rules are in effect. Fishing is allowed from Mar. through Aug. In March it's usually stocked with about 5,000 catchable rainbow trout. There are some very large holdovers in this fertile lake, however. Fly fishermen, especially, do well here. The lake is essentially divided into two lakes. The lower end is deep and wide and the upper is shallow and narrow. A marsh separates the two. Much of the lower West Lake is 65 feet deep, with steep edges. A shallow neck at the far west end near the outlet is favored by fly fishermen. The upper east lake is 5 to 25 feet deep, dotted with islands and many shallow areas. This area is heavily used by waterfowl. The lake is about 3 miles long. It is located 12 miles NE of Odessa and 14 miles due W of Harrington on the Coffee Pot Road. From Odessa follow Hwy. 21 N. to Coffee Pot Rd and turn E. continuing to the lake. A scrabble of dirt, private and county roads north of Odessa can provide access to some of the small lakes below Coffee Pot.

UPPER CRAB CREEK. The major drainage for Lincoln County, upper Crab Creek heads in NE Lincoln County, and crosses the county diagonally steadily enlarging with water from ground seepage and numerous small creeks. It flows SW to within 2 miles of the Adams County line, then swings W. to enter Grant County, picking up volume as it goes. The creek offers quite a few browns, tiger trout, some rainbow, a few panfish and carp. Trout fishing is best during the spring and early summer and again in late fall when the browns begin to spawn. About 1500 rainbow are usually stocked in Mar. or Apr. The creek is open year-round, but flows mostly through private property. Fishermen need landowner permission.

COTTONWOOD CREEK. A small stream which flows E. from Davenport for about 5 miles to join Hawk Creek, a major tributary into Lake Roosevelt. Sometimes lightly planted with rainbow.

DEER LAKE (Deer Springs). An enlargement in Lake Creek located ll miles NE from Odessa and 1 mile below **COFFEE POT LAKE** along Lake Creek. The lake covers 60 acres and in March is planted with about 500 8-to 14-inch rainbow. It also holds largemouth bass and panfish. Rough campsites along N. end. Deer produces best during the early part of the season.

DOWNS LAKE (See Spokane County).

FISHTRAP LAKE. A heavily stocked, exceptionally productive, narrow, 3-mile-long lake of 195 acres (22 acres in Spokane County) situated 6.5 miles E. of Sprague. This lake is very popular on the opening weekend often giving out limit catches. Best fishing is from the opener through May. Fishtrap is planted with rainbow fry, supplemented with catchables and occasionally large brood stock. It has a public boat launch access area and a resort. Drive NE from Sprague on I-90 to Fishtrap Exit, turn S. on Old State Highway, then E. on Scroggie Rd. to north end of lake. Drainage is to Negro Creek and Palouse River.

HAWK CREEK. Rises near Davenport and flows W. and N. about 20 miles to empty into Lake Roosevelt below Hawk Creek Falls. Roads NW from Davenport follow most of the creek's course. Hawk Creek is open year-round and is a good May and June bet for planted rainbow and a few brookies. It is stocked with about 2000 rainbows in Mar. or Apr. Just above Lake Roosevelt, the creek widens and in early spring and fall can be a hot spot for very large trout and walleye moving in from the lake. Good bank access in most areas.

INDIAN CREEK. Joins Hawk Creek 1.5 miles S. of Hawk Creek Falls. The Indian Creek Road follows the rainbow planted stream E. and S. upstream for about 10 miles.

PACIFIC LAKE. An enlargement in Lake Creek's channel below Coffee Pot Lake, Pacific is 1.8 miles long and covers 129 acres. It is reached via US 2 N. from Odessa 2.5 miles, then W. and N. 5 miles on county road which crosses W. end of

Houseboats are great fishing platforms for exploring Lake Roosevelt.

lake. Public boat launch site near W. end. It is very heavily stocked with rainbow fry, and there is good fishing for most warm water species. Another lake in the chain, **TULE LAKE**, 126 acres, lies 0.4 of a mile S. of Pacific. The two mile-long lake has warm water species.

SHERMAN CREEK. Road from Hwy. 2, 4 miles E. of Wilbur heads N. up Sherman Creek for about 6 miles to Sherman. The stream sometimes gets rainbow plants.

FRANKLIN D. ROOSEVELT LAKE (LOWER). The largest lake in the state at 79,000 acres, 151 miles long, created by Grand Coulee Dam on Columbia River 28 miles NE of Coulee City. The reservoir stretches across the northcentral part of the state, and forms the north border of Lincoln County continuing E. into Ferry and Steven County nudging into British Columbia. It is located in a relatively remote, semi-arid, low mountain region. The lower lake is in the Columbia Basin, a dry region of hot summers framed by rolling, rocky hills, sagebrush, willows, basalt columns and coulees. Lake Roosevelt supports one of the widest varieties of freshwater fish in the state. Species include cutthroat, rainbow, brookies , Dolly Varden, whitefish, lake whitefish, kokanee, kamloops, sturgeon, large and smallmouth bass, crappie, perch, sunfish, walleyes, carp, suckers, tench, shiners, chub, and an assortment of other rough fish. Best game fishing is at mouths of countless inlets along both shores of huge reservoir. Fishing success in the lower reservoir rises and falls dramatically, seasonally and often by species. One time rainbows—some to 6 pounds—will be the hot ticket, next will be kokanee or walleye and when that's not working some anglers enjoy huge success casting to shoreline rocks for bass. One of the most enjoyable ways to fish this big lake is by boat camping, or renting a houseboat and towing a fishing boat. The 660 miles of lake shore and 35 recreational areas in Coulee Dam RA are administered by National Park Service. All recreational areas may be reached by boat. Facilities include house boats rentals, 8 full service campgrounds, many primitive lakeshore camp sites accessible by boat, multiple concrete boat ramps, docks, picnic areas, swimming spots. Information center for the recreational areas is at the W. end of Coulee Dam at Colulee Dam National Recreation Area headquarters where maps and service directories are available. Call: 509-633-0881. Hwy. 25 parallels much of the S. shore. Grand Coulee Dam is accessible from Hwy. 155 N. from Coulee City and Hwy. 174 N.W from Wilbur on US 2. Fishing regulations and bag limits vary and should be read carefully before fishing this massive year-round reservoir.

SPRAGUE LAKE. Most of this sprawling multi-species lake is in Adams County, (see Adams County) but 637 acres are within Lincoln County. The N. end of the lake is only 1.5 miles SW of town of Sprague, and I-90 follows the E. shore. Sprague offers largemouth and smallmouth bass, walleye, bluegill, perch, rainbow, crappie, bullheads and channel catfish. Fishing is best from May to September. Ice fishermen also find it good for perch, crappie and bluegill during the winter. Resorts and public boat launches.

TWIN LAKES. About 500 feet apart, Lower Twin with 45 surface acres is the larger of this pair of enlargements on Lake Creek. Upper Twin covers 39 acres and is stocked with about 5000 catchable rainbows in Mar./Apr. The lakes are 15 miles NE of Odessa and about 2 miles up Lake Creek from **COFFEE POT LAKE**. County road passes 0.5 miles W. of Lower Twin. Both lakes provide largemouth bass, crappie and perch. Upper Twin has BLM access.

WALL LAKE (Big). A 32.2 acre lake located 10.5 miles NW of Harrington. It contains large and smallmouth bass, black crappie, pumpkinseed and yellow perch.

WEDERSPAHN LAKE. A 13.8 acre lake about 5.4 miles N. from Odessa in Lake Creek channel. Anglers will find large and smallmouth bass, black crappie, yellow perch and pumpkinseed.

WILSON CREEK. A large creek that flows from Wilbur on US 2 southwest to Crab Creek mostly through private farm ground. It's crossed by numerous county roads between Wilbur and Grant County offering bridge easement fishing holes. Occasionally planted with rainbow. Can deliver fair fishing in the spring.

Lincoln County Resorts

Roosevelt Lake: Seven Bays Resort, 509-725-1676.

Sprague Lake: Sprague Lake Campground, 257-2864. Four Seasons Campground, 509-257-2332.

Fish Trap Lake: Fish Trap Lake Resort, 509-235-2284.

Mason County
WDFW Region 6

Washington Department of Fish and Wildlife, 48 Devonshire Rd. Montesano, WA 98563-9618. Phone 360-249-4628

If you like fishing you'll want to spend a weekend or two exploring the fresh and salt water diversity of this largely rural, lightly settled county just NW of the state capitol. Protected inlet and passage reaches of South Puget Sound and the south end of Hood Canal are in the 1052 square miles encased by Mason County, offering year-round sea-run cutthroat, sole and flounder, shellfish and seasonal salmon fishing. Unfortunately many of the rivers are closed to steelhead and salmon fishing, but still offer decent sea-run cutthroat action.

The Skokomish, Hamma Hamma and Tahuya Rivers attract winter steelhead, fall sea- run cutthroat and several species of salmon.

The E. county drains into Hood Canal and the W. drains through tributary fingers of the Satsop River from intensely clear-cut logging areas into the Chehalis River.

More than 200 lakes offer a mix of planted and native trout, bass and panfish, landlocked salmon, and some of the county's best fishing is reserved for tough fishermen willing to buck thick brush up small streams to wet a line in countless, rarely fished beaver ponds. The county has an unusually high concentration of beautiful lowland trout ponds, comfortably small enough for float tubes and small cartop boats.

Mason County rates 29th in size in the state. Highest point is 6612 feet on Mt. Stone. The SE corner of Olympic National Forest dips into the county near Lake Cushman, the largest lake in the county, and includes the little known Wonder Mountain and Mount Skokomish wilderness areas. The forest service land spreads outward from the upper Skokomish River basin and blends on the S. with a wide swath of timber-company land that dominates the W. county from the S. slopes of the Olympic Mountains to US 12. This area is heavily roaded and made up of many small drainages, reprod tree farms and miles of stumps. In addition to trout ponds and creeks, the logging areas support Roosevelt elk, blacktailed deer, black bears, cougars and ruffed grouse.

Tribes have two reservations in the county. The largest is the Skokomish Indian Reservation which occupies the mouth of the Skokomish River at the outside of the Great Bend of Hood Canal, and is crossed by US 101. Squaxin Indian Reservation on the N. end of Squaxin Island in Pickering Pass off the W. side of Hartstene Island. Squaxin Island State Park, on the S. end of the island, is a popular base for boaters ambushing coho, chinook and chum salmon headed back to the Skokomish River and Squaxin net pen rearing areas. The gravel beaches near the park are well known sea-run cutthroat areas.

The county's terrain varies extremely from sheltered saltwater to flat prairie areas to low rounded hills that rise to the sharp peaks of the Olympic Mountains in the NW corner of the county. Mountain streams in the N. county are fast and drop quickly from the Olympics through steep-walled canyons into Hood Canal.

The E. side falls between fingers of saltwater passes and inlets reaching inland from the head of Puget Sound. The E. county line runs through the center of Case Inlet. Several state parks front the saltwater.

The climate is mild and mostly maritime in the lowlands. Winter's are wet. Annual precipitation is almost 64 inches at Shelton. At Cushman Dam, just 15 miles N. rainfall hits more than 100 inches a year. The Skokomish is always one of the first rivers in the state to flood.

Main route into the county is US 101 from Olympia at I-5 heading N-S through Shelton, the largest town, along the W. shore of Hood Canal. Hwy. 3 connects Shelton to the Bremerton area. Two secondary state hwys., Hwy. 102 and 108 lead W. from US 101 into the Satsop logging areas N. of US 12 and Hwy. 8. State Hwy. 119 leaves US 101 near Hoodsport and follows the N. shore of Lake Cushman to Mount Skokomish Wilderness Area at Staircase, a popular trailhead leading into the Olympic National Park.

ALDRIDGE LAKE. 9-acres lightly planted with catchable rainbows for opening day fishermen. Located 1.5 miles S. of Dewatto overlooking Hood Canal. Road W. at top of hill above Dewatto leads 1 mile to lake. Public access, poor ramp and DNR campground. Drains to Hood Canal.

ARMSTRONG LAKE. Private, no public access. 4 acres 2.8 miles NE of Eldon. Has trout.

BATHTUB LAKE. A 2 acre brook trout pond 4 miles S. of Union. Drive S. from Union up hill for 4 miles, then turn E. and N. for 0.5 miles to lake.

BENSON LAKE. Fair to good for cutthroat, kokanee and rainbow in the spring and fall. Stocked with 8000 catchable rainbows, including about 1000 triploids in April, and 4000 cutthroat fry. Also offers largemouth bass. Covers 81 acres. WDFW access, launch, no gas motors. Hwy. 3 NE from Shelton 11.5 miles, then N. on county road 2.2 miles. Drains to Oakland Bay.

BINGHAM CREEK. Tributary to Satsop River's E. Fork. Crossed by Matlock-Shelton Rd. 1.5 miles E. of Matlock. Roads parallel both Bingham and Outlet Creeks for about 5 miles. Bingham is tough to reach but provides good cutthroat fishing in mid-summer and fall.

BISER POND. Stocked annually with about 2000 cutthroat fry.

BLACKSLOUGH POND. Stocked with 1000 cutthroat fry annually.

BLACKSMITH LAKE. Largemouth bass are the attraction in this 18.3 acre lake 5.5 miles NW of Belfair. Drains to Tahuya River.

BUCK LAKE (See Wildberry).

CADY LAKE. Good bet for larger than average cutthroat. This cutthroat planted 15 acre, fly-fishing only lake, is 2 miles SE of Dewatto adjacent to S. side of road. Open year-round, lightly stocked in April, catch and release, no gas motors. WDFW access. Drains to Dewatto River.

CAMP POND. A 6 acre largemouth bass and rainbow trout lake 4 miles NW of Belfair. DNR campground. N. from Hood Canal on El Fendahl Rd. past Oak Patch Lake.

CARSON LAKE. Private, no public access. An 8 acre lake with brook trout 3 miles SE of Union.

CLARA LAKE (Don). 1200 planted rainbows provide fair to good spring fishing for 7 to 9 inch trout. 17 acres 1.5 mile S. of Dewatto and 0.5 miles W. of road up the hill out of Dewatto. Good WDFW access. Drains to Hood Canal.

COLLINS LAKE. A 4 acre private lake with brook trout and rainbow, largemouth bass and brown bullhead. Collins is 0.5 mile S. of Erdman Lake 5 miles NE of Tahuya. Loop road from Tahuya N. and E. down Stimson Creek passes between Erdman and Collins. **HOWELL LAKE**, 10 acres, is located 0.5 miles S. of Collins and is rainbow planted. It has a DNR campground. Both lakes drain into Tahuya River.

COULTER CREEK. Flows into North Bay at head of Case Inlet 3 miles S. of Belfair. Good cutthroat fishing. A road extends N. from Hwy. 3 up the creek.

CRATER LAKE (Haven). 2 miles W. of former Camp Govey above the S. Fork of the Skokomish River. Network of logging roads lace this area, and roads pass along both N. and S. shores of Crater Lake. Kokanee and brook trout are present.

CUSHMAN LAKE. The largest lake in the county, formed by a Tacoma dam on the Skokomish River's N. Fork, Cushman is 8.5 miles long and covers 4003 acres. Several other lakes are in the Cushman complex. Cushman's beautiful gin-clear water drops into depths that plunge more than 100 feet below 4000-foot high, emerald forested hills that rise into the hacksaw peaks of the

Lake Cushman.

Olympic Mountains. In some areas the table-size stumps of ancient cedars and Douglas fir trees logged before the lake was impounded, are visible far below the surface. The head of the lake, near Staircase, is a popular jump off point for hikers backpacking into ONP. The reservoir is open to fishing year-round and offers a variety including rainbow, cutthroat, brook trout, largemouth bass, kokanee and land-locked chinook salmon. It has quite a few ESA protected Dolly Varden/bull trout (many in the 5 to 10 pound range)which must be released unharmed. Lots of bank fishing access, but the plunging shoreline make bank fishing tough. Best to launch a trailerable boat at one of the 3 ramps. Cushman is best known for kokanee salmon from annual fry plants of 165,000. Annual plants of 21,000 rainbow fry support the trout fishery. Kokanee anglers troll flasher blades and worms from mid-June into Sept. Resort at the S. end of the lake with full facilities, a large state park with 80 campsites (30 with hookups) and boat launch facilities 2.5 miles N. on Cushman's E. shore. Keep an eye out for Roosevelt elk near the campground. **STANDBY LAKE** is adjacent to the SE end of Cushman. The 15 acre man-made lake contains cutthroat. Another reservoir, **KO-KANEE LAKE (LOWER CUSHMAN)**160-feet deep, covers 150 acres below Cushman Dam and behind a lower Tacoma dam. Planted with 6000 catchable rainbows

in April plus cutthroat and kokanee. Drains to North Fork Skokomish River. Open year-round. No fish passage facilities on either dam. To reach Lake Cushman from US 101 turn W. at Hoodsport onto State Hwy. 119/County Rd. 44 to FS 24 which runs along the shoreline. FS 24 also connects directly with US 101 just S. of Eldon. Cushman Lake is unique in that chinook salmon, which were trapped when the Tacoma dams were built in the 1920's, have survived and spawned in the Skokomish River feeding the lake. Adult, 5-year fish estimated at 20 pounds, have been observed while spawning and scale-checked for age.

DECKER CREEK. Tributary to the East Fork Satsop River, joining in Grays Harbor County just below Schafer State Park. Upper reaches are crossed by road coming NW from Matlock. Some cutthroat.

DEER LAKE (Seymour). Stocked with 700 rainbows in the spring, Deer covers 12 acres 10.8 miles NE of Shelton and 2 miles S. of Benson Lake, about 0.4 miles E. of Hwy. 3. Some rainbows in the 13-inch range. Drains into Pickering Passage.

DEVEREAUX LAKE (Trout, Deborah, Lakewood). Fair to good fishing for 6000 spring planted catchable rainbows, and a few hundred cutthroat, and there are reports every year of 5-pound plus carry-overs. Devereaux is a good summer row troll for kokanee salmon. A ban on gas outboards means that most kokanee anglers stillfish with bait. Lake covers 100 acres, public access, launch 1.5 miles NW of Allyn and 3 miles S. of Belfair. Hwy. 3 runs S. from Belfair and adjacent to NE shore of the lake.

DEWATTO RIVER. A small stream on the E. side of Hood Canal offering sea-run cutthroat, and too few winter steelhead to count. Sea-run cutts best at mouth and in lower reaches from summer through fall. Some years from October into December, coho salmon school at mouth in Dewatto Bay. Heads in Kitsap County and flows SW about 8 miles in Mason County to enter Hood Canal at Dewatto N. of the Great Bend. From Hwy. 300 at Tahuya turn N. on Dewatto Road to the mouth. Dewatto-Holly Road follows the river upstream from Hood Canal.

DRYBED LAKES. Upper lake covers 4.5 acres; lower lake 7 acres. They carry planted rainbow and brook trout. Head N. from Matlock, keeping right at first forks, and drive about 4 miles. Turn left (W.) for 1 mile, then right for 2.5 miles on Road 2255 to S. end of lower lake.

ELK LAKES. Formed by a natural obstruction in Jefferson Creek, Upper Elk is 3 acres, while Lower Elk covers 6 acres. Primarily brook trout with a few 'bow and cutthroat. Road up Jorsted Creek leaves US 101 approximately 4 miles N. of Lilliwaup, swings N. to follow Hamma Hamma River, then a branch turns W. 2.5 miles up Jefferson Creek to **JEFFERSON LAKES**. Lower Jefferson covers 10 acres. Upper Jefferson is 3 acres 800 feet SW from the larger lake. Rainbow, brook trout and cutthroat have been planted .

ERICKSON LAKE. A narrow 15 acres with cutthroat. Route is N. from Belfair 4 miles up Union River, then W. and N. for 8 miles, then S. for 0.4 miles on road along Erickson's E. shore.

FORBES LAKE. Largemouth bass are in this 38.4 acre lake 6 miles E. of Shelton. Drains to Mill Creek.

FUDGE POINT STATE PARK, DNR beach 24 on the E. shore of Hartstene Island is a good bet for oysters and sea-run cutthroat.

GOAT RANCH LAKE. A marshy 20 acres

3.5 miles NW of Belfair. Has rainbow and cutthroat. Locked DNR gate restricts access to foot and bicycle.

GOLDSBOROUGH CREEK. Small stream flowing through Shelton. May have remnant runs of winter steelhead and sea-run cutthroat.

GRASS LAKE. A 2.5 acre lake with some rainbow, cutthroat and brookies, 3 miles NE of Tahuya.

HAMMA HAMMA RIVER. A tough fishing prospect. Gets a good run of fall chum salmon, but there hasn't been a catch-and-keep chum season in memory, no plants of winter steelhead (although a trickle of natives make it back). Best bet is catch and release sea-run cutthroat in the lower 3 miles above Hood Canal where a falls blocks migratory fish just above Blue Hole. Access is limited in lower reaches. Top stretches above falls have fair fishing in June-July for resident rainbows. A road 1.5 miles N. of Eldon leaves US 101 to meet the Hamma Hamma 3.5 miles upstream from its mouth, and then parallels the river for about 8 miles. FS campgrounds are located at mouths of Cabin and Lena Creeks.

HANKS LAKE. At 27 acres, and 8 feet deep, the largest in a series of small lakes, holding rainbow and largemouth bass. From Shelton go 3 miles N. on US 101, then W. on Matlock Road 6 miles, then N. 1 mile to W. side of lake. **LITTLE HANK** Lake lies 500 feet S. Bass and catfish in little Hanks.

HATCHERY LAKE. Both rainbow and cutthroat have been planted in this peat bog lake of 10.7 acres 6.5 miles N. of Shelton. Drains to Skokomish River.

HAVEN LAKE (Carstairs, Call). WDFW rates this 70 acre lake good to excellent for 7000 spring planted catchable rainbows plus foot-long holdover rainbows and cutthroat and kokanee. WDFW access. Produces well in the spring and fall. Located 7.5 miles W. of Belfair between Wooten and Erdman Lakes. Hwy. 300 leads SW from Belfair 4 miles then heads N. and W. up Stimson creek about 6 miles to the lake.

ISABELLA LAKE. A 208 acre year-round lake with a good reputation for late winter, spring and fall trout in the 12-inch range and a summer filled with bass and panfishing. Planted in Mar. with 4000 catchable rainbows to boost spring prospects. In early fall sea-run cutthroat climb Mill Creek into the lake from Hammersley Inlet. Other species include a few kokanee, and good fishing for largemouth bass and brown bullhead. 2.5 miles S. of Shelton and 1 mile W. of US 101. WDFW access

ISLAND LAKE. Annually planted with 31,000 cutthroat fry and 4000 catchable rainbows adding to a year-round fishery built on smallmouth and largemouth bass, bullhead catfish and perch—some very large. Also has a few large rainbows. Island is a clear, 109 acre lake 2.5 miles N. of Shelton. About 1.5 miles N. of Shelton on US 101, turn E. at the airport and continue 1 mile to lake. WDFW access on E. shore.

JIGGS LAKE. A 8.8 acre largemouth bass and perch lake 1.5 miles NE from Tahuya. Drains to Tahuya River.

KOKANEE LAKE. See Cushman Lake.

LENA CREEK. The outlet of Lena Lakes entering the Hamma Hamma River 8 miles W. of US 101 on Hamma Hamma Rd. Produces wild rainbow in mid-summer. Trail upstream from mouth 4 miles to Lower Lena Lake in Jefferson County. FS campground at mouth.

LILLIWAUP CREEK. High falls block the stream 1 mile above mouth, Fair sea-run cutthroat fishing in this stretch. Upper reaches flow through a series of beaver ponds (See Lilliwaup Swamp). Lilliwaup State Park on the west shore of Hood Canal and US 101 just north of Lilliwaup has public oyster beds and offers some sporadic sea-run cutthroat fishing along the beach.

LILLIWAUP SWAMP. A series of beaver ponds sprawled over a large area in the headwaters of Lilliwaup Creek 6 miles N. of Hoodsport. Estimated at 25 acres total. Fishing these ponds requires tough bushwhacking. Easiest route is W. and N. up Hwy. 119/Lake Cushman Road from Hoodsport past Price Lake turnoff (about 7 miles) another 1.4 miles and head NE on good gravel road 2 miles where overgrown roads spoke S. into the brush. Fair fishing for wild brookies and cutthroat.

LIMERICK LAKE. An 80 acre lake created by a dam on Cranberry Creek with a reputation for providing fair rainbow fishing (stocked with 5000 catchables in spring), and great perch action in late summer. There's also a pretty good fishery for largemouth bass and brown bullhead catfish. Located about 4 miles N. of Shelton. Drive NE of Shelton on Hwy. 3, then W. from highway at Bayshore and follow signs. WDFW access, ramp.

LOST LAKE. This 121 acre lake gets about 8000 catchable rainbows before the opener and kokanee fry plants and offers brown bullhead catfish. From US 101 turn W. on Lost Lake Rd. and continue 8 miles SW of Shelton then N. for 0.5 miles to WDFW access, ramp.

MAGGIE LAKE. Spring plants of about 3000 catchable rainbows and cutthroat, plus a few hundred 14 inchers, keep this 22 acre lake well up on the opening day calendar for many local anglers. Tapers quickly. Also occasionally planted with adult coho salmon in Oct.-Nov. WDFW access, ramp. A road from Tahuya heads N. for 2.4 miles to W. shore.

MASON LAKE. One of the county's largest lakes, Mason covers 996 acres, and has year-round fishing for rainbow, cutthroat, kokanee, largemouth bass, yellow perch and brown catfish. Fishing is best during the summer and early fall for kokanee salmon, bass and panfish. WDFW access. From Shelton drive NE on Hwy. 3 for 11.5 miles then W. for 3.5 miles. Also 8 miles SW of Belfair. County park.

MELBOURNE LAKE. Covers 35 acres about 2.5 miles N. of Lilliwaup and provides pretty good fishing for cutthroat up to 14 inches. Best in fall.

MILLER MARSH. A beaver pond type lake of 15 acres carrying cutthroat at head of Eagle Creek. Drains into Hood Canal. It lies .08 miles E. of **OSBORN LAKE** and is reached by road up Jorsted Creek from US 101 about 4.5 miles N. of Lilliwaup.

NAHWATZEL LAKE. A popular Shelton-area lake stocked with catchable (about 8000 stocked in Mar. and May) rainbows, supplementing carry-overs to several pounds and largemouth bass. Also holds a few large cutthroat. Covers 268 acres, 25 feet deep with lots of shoreline shallows and docks to hide bass. Lake is 11 miles W. of

Shelton on Shelton-Matlock Road. Open year-round and produces both trout for trollers and still-fishermen early and late in the season, and a decent bass prospect all summer. WDFW access, ramp and resort.

NORTH BAY. Located at the N. end of Case Inlet, between a line drawn from Rocky Point to Reach Island and the mainland. Closed to clams and oysters year-round, except for state owned tidelands on the E. side of North Bay N. of power lines where it has been legal to pick oysters.

PANHANDLE LAKE. About 1200 catchable rainbows are annually stocked in Panhandle's 14.4 acres, 8 miles SW of Shelton. Drain to Goldsborough Creek and Oakland Bay. 4-H camp activity sometimes limits fishing opportunity.

PANTHER LAKE. See Kitsap County. The lake covers 103 acres with 30 acres in Mason County and the remainder in Kitsap.

Offers rainbow and has a WDFW access. Lake is 10 miles W. of Bremerton.

PHILLIPS LAKE. This 112 acre lake usually starts fast, delivering most of its 4000 planted rainbows shortly after the opener. WDFW access. Reached via Hwy. 3, 7.7 miles NE of Shelton, then E. 1.5 miles past **SPENCER LAKE** to Phillips Lake Road which leads 1.5 miles to the lake.

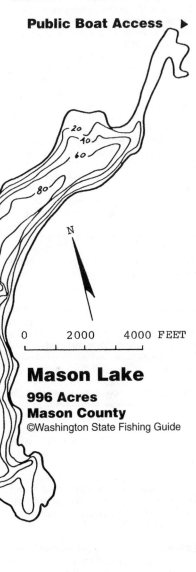

Public Boat Access ▶

20
10
60
80
90

N

0   2000   4000 FEET

Mason Lake
**996 Acres
Mason County**
©Washington State Fishing Guide

PINE LAKE. A mountain lake in headwaters of Pine Creek at 2250 feet elev. Pine covers 7 acres and hosts rainbow. Fair to good during summer. Drive up South Fork Skokomish River past the former Camp Govey and Brown Creek campground, 5 more miles NW, then 3.5 miles W. up Pine Creek to lake.

PRICE LAKE. An outstanding spring and fall prospect for large rainbows, cutthroat and brookies, thanks mostly to catch-and-release management and selective gear restrictions. Not a bad bet on quiet summer mornings and evenings, either. Has produced some very large brook trout along with rainbow in the 2-foot range. Price is a shallow, weedy lake, full of stumps, trees and brush—perfect for float tubes, canoes, small boats. Covers 61 acres. From US 101 at Hoodsport turn NW on Hwy. 119 (Cushman Lake Road). Just past state park turn E. on gravel road, bear left at fork to trail. It's about 0.2 mile walk to lake. Bring a portable boat. Outlet drains into Lilliwaup Creek, and beaver ponds along its 1 mile length may furnish good spring and fall fishing for brook trout and some cutthroat.

RENDSLAND CREEK. Located on E. shore of Hood Canal at the Great Bend, the beach at the mouth of the creek offers Pacific oysters, and casting for sea-run cutthroat on incoming tide.

ROBBINS LAKE (Robinson). A 16 acre lake stocked with 1500 catchable rainbows in April for opener. Quickly fished out. Lake is 1.5 miles S. of Dewatto in the "Oak Patch". DNR picnic and boat launch on E. bank.

ROSE LAKE. Rainbow and cutthroat are in this 8.5 acre lake 4 miles SW of Potlatch. Leave US 101 about 1.4 miles S. of Potlatch and turn W. for 1.5 miles, then S. for about 4 miles passing **STEVENS LAKE** (Steve's), an 8.5 acre rainbow lake, en route.

SHOE LAKE. Just 6 acres but a fair spring fishery for brookies and rainbow. The lake lies 8.5 miles W. of Belfair between **TEE** and **HAVEN LAKES**.

SIMPSON LAKE. Largemouth bass and brown bullhead catfish are present in this shallow 29.4 acre lake 9.5 miles N. of Elma. Drains to E. Fork Satsop River.

SKOKOMISH RIVER. Largest river feeding Hood Canal, and a monument to short-sighted river management that has crippled what should be an excellent steelhead and salmon fishery. Fish-ladderless Tacoma power dams at Lakes Kokanee and Cushman destroyed miles of prime spawning area that heavy hatchery plants have never been able to overcome. How sad is it...in 1999 WDFW recorded only 3 steelhead caught. Add a tribal netting program and....... The Skok produces probably best for sea-run cutthroat(wild fish release, and no hatchery plants are made). Try fishing the tidal water on incoming tides. There are runs of fall coho chinook and chum salmon. In early winter (Thanksgiving is prime) there's a big wad of bright chums jammed in the lower river reservation water below US 101. It's a catch-and-release fishery, but it's fun especially with a fly rod, and green yarn fly. The upper South Fork offer a limited wild trout fishery, good in spots, for rainbows and cutts. Upper stretches of the S. Fork may be fished by turning W. before crossing the river on US 101 and continuing upstream past the former Camp Govey on logging roads. FS campground at mouth of Brown Creek above Camp Govey.

The Skokomish enters Hood Canal in Annas Bay at the Great Bend about 10 miles N. of Shelton. The Skokomish Indian Reservation reaches from the mouth to 0.4 miles above US 101.

SPENCER LAKE. Plants of 8000 rainbow and cutthroat in Apr.-May make this year-round, 220-acre lake a fine spring/summer trout bet. Larger carry-over trout are fairly common and fishing holds up well through the summer. There is good, some would call it excellent summer largemouth bass fishing. The lake is 7.7 miles NE of Shelton on Hwy. 3, then .03 mile to right on county road, then right 1.2 miles to public access.

SPIDER LAKE. A narrow, 23 acre cutthroat and brook trout lake in the Skokomish River's headwaters. Reached by logging road N. from former Camp Govey on Skokomish River South Fork, past FS campground at Brown's Creek, then due W. about 6 miles to lake at an elev. of 1290 feet.

STANDBY LAKE (See Cushman Lake).

STUMP LAKE. 23 acres, 13 miles SW of Shelton and 3 miles S. of the Shelton-Elma

Road along Cloquallam Creek. A snag-filled lake with rainbows, and a few cutthroat and brook trout, and largemouth bass. Good for float tubes and small boats may be launched along the shore.

TAHUYA RIVER. A short-run, brushy stream that rises in the "Oak Patch" maze of lakes 10 miles NW of Belfair. Best known as a fall sea-run cutthroat river but occasionally attracts a handful of winter steelhead. Drops into fishable shape quickly after heavy rains, and drains into Hood Canal from E. side of Great Bend. From Tahuya follow River Road.

TEE LAKE. This 38 acre lake is quickly fished out for the 2500 catchable rainbows planted in March, but develops a fair to good perch and largemouth bass fishery in summer. Open year-round, Tee has a WDFW, access, ramp and is 2.5 miles SE of Dewatto between **SHOE** and **CADY LAKES**.

TIGER LAKE. A 109 acre lake straddling the Kitsap County line. Heavily planted in mid April with 10,000 8-10-inch rainbows, including some 14-inch triploids and 250 cutthroat. Does very well from spring opener into summer. Drive up Union River Road from Belfair for 4 miles, then turn left 2 miles to S. end of lake.

TRAILS END LAKE (AKA PRICKETT). Stocked with about 6000 catchable rainbows in Apr. and May, this 68 acre lake is 6 miles SW of Belfair. Brown bullhead present. Open year-round. WDFW access, primitive ramp. Drive SW for 5 miles from Belfair on Hwy. 106, then S. 1.5 miles to lake.

TRASK LAKE. A private lake that produces rainbow at start of season. Covers 13 acres 10 miles NE of Shelton and 1 mile N. of **MASON LAKE**

TWANOH STATE PARK. Located on the S. shore of the lower Hood Canal instep, Twanoh State Park provides public access in an area heavily given to no trespassing signs. Beach is a decent prospect for sea-run cutthroat. Troll or cast with small spoons, spinners, or herring strips on incoming tide near beach. Not much coho or chinook action. Park beach has been seeded with oysters. Drive Hwy. 106 between Belfair and Union. 36 campsites, launch ramp, mooring.

TWIN LAKES (Spider). Big Twin is 15 acres and adjoining Little Twin is 5 acres. The lakes are lightly planted with catchable rainbows in April. Located in the "Oak Patch" cluster of lakes 7 miles NW of Belfair and 1.5 miles NE of Wooten Lake. Big Twin has a launch and DNR campground.

UNION RIVER. Principally a sea-run cutthroat stream in the spring and early fall, with an extremely poor winter steelhead run. Flows into the toe at the extreme end of Hood Canal boot near Belfair. Paralleled by Old Belfair Hwy. upstream from mouth for several miles.

WEST LAKE. A marshy 16.5 acre lake with brown bullhead catfish 13 miles NW of Shelton.

WILDBERRY LAKE (AKA Buck) Located on Great Bend of Hood Canal 1.5 miles NW of Tahuya. This 8.1 acres lake receives about 800 catchable rainbows April. Maze of roads in this area termed the "Oak Patch." Watch for signs. Drains is to Hood Canal.

WOOD LAKE. Lightly planted with catchable rainbows this 10 acre lake is 2 miles N. of Tahuya and 0.5 miles NE of **BUCK LAKE**. Watch for signs.

WOOTEN LAKE. This 69 acre lake has a reputation for producing large, hold-over rainbow and often comes on strong in the fall. It gets Apr. and May plants of 7000 'bows including a few hundred large triploids, and cutthroat. WDFW access. Drive SW from Belfair on Hwy. 300 about 5 miles, then N. 2 miles up Stinson Creek, and W. about 5 miles to lake between **HAVEN** and **BENNETTSEN LAKES** in the "Oak Patch".

Mason County Resorts

Cushman Lake: Lake Cushman Resort,1-800-588-9630.

Hood Canal: Belfair State Park 360-275-0668. Mike's Hoodsport Beach Resort, 360-877-5324.

Nahwatzel Lake: Lake Nahwatzel Resort, 360-426-8323.

Spencer Lake: Spencer Lake Tavern, Shelton, WA 98584. 360-426-2505.

Okanogan County
WDFW Region 2
Washington Department of Fish and Wildlife, 1550 Alder St. NW, Ephrata, WA 98823-9699. Phone 509-754-4624

Sprawling across 5332 square miles-an area larger than the state of Connecticut-Okanogan is the largest county in Washington, pushing north across the top of the state through the vast Pasayten Wilderness Area against British Columbia, west into the rugged North Cascade Mountains and rolling east almost 100 miles through national forest, the state's largest Indian reservation, and open pine forests where there are more mule deer and trout than year-round residents.

Water managers have counted 930 lakes in the county, 534 of them over 2,500 feet elevation, including 215 over 4000 feet. This east-central county offers some of the best lowland and high mountain lake fishing in the state. Some of the lakes are among the most popular opening day attractions in Washington, and several in the Winthrop area are being managed specifically to provide ice fishing.

River and stream fishing, however, has suffered dramatically in recent years. Most of the streams and rivers, especially the larger ones, are either closed to fishing or tightly restricted because of ESA listed steelhead, salmon or bull trout. Because of the fluidity of ESA listings, streams in this guide will include resident fish species, and locations but not current fishing conditions. Unless specifically noted in the current WDFW regulations, it's best to assume that the bubbling stream just a tempting cast away is closed. No streams or rivers are now stocked with hatchery trout, and the county's only major steelhead river—the Methow—and its tributaries, are closed to steelheading. Winter whitefishing is allowed on the entire river, and there's summer catch-and-release trout fishing below Winthrop. Most lakes are fry-planted and some have supplemental stockings of catchables to sweeten the pot just before openings.

The Methow River system drains most of west Okanogan and the Okanogan River, an unsung smallmouth stream, drains the central and north portion. The highest point is North Gardner Mt. at 8956 feet about 15 miles west of Winthrop.

One of the most unusual features is Omak Lake, 3244 acres, over 300 feet deep in places, fills a rock-walled 7.7 mile-long canyon on the Colville Indian Reservation. The lake has no outlet and deprived of flow the high mineral content of the water has accumulated, through evaporation, producing a solid mineral content with high salinity. The cold, deep, salty water is unfit for most trout, but has proved great habitat for Lahontan cutthroat and there are some monsters here.

The climate produces hot, dry summers and cold winters. Midsummer temperatures at Omak are usually in the upper 80s, and lows have been measured at -26 degrees. My mid-Oct. expect freezing nights and snow far down on the peaks in the Pasayten Wilderness. Valley lakes are snow free on the Apr. opener, but most backcountry lakes are iced in until mid May, longer at higher elevaitons. Precipitation is measured in feet along the summit of the Cascade Range, but only about a foot—much of that snow—falls at Omak.

The county is lightly populated with just under 37,000 year-round residents. Biggest city is Omak with a population of 4300.

Most of the county, especially in the north and west, is public land within the 1.5 million acre Okanogan National Forest, including all or part of Pasayten, Lake Chelan-Sawtooth wilderness areas, North Cascade National Park and the WDFW Methow Wildlife Area. DNR manages a large tract in the Chopaka Mountain/Sinlahekin Valley region W. of Loomis. Most of the popular fishing lakes have state park, forest service, DNR or private camping and WDFW boat accesses.

Major fishing areas are centered around Winthrop, Oroville, Tonasket, Omak and Conconully. The Colville Indian Reservation includes a large section north of Grand Coulee Dam and east of the Okanogan River and supports many excellent trout lakes that can be fished by buying tribal permits. Tribal headquarters are at Nespelem.

Main routes into the county are the North Cascade Scenic Highway 20 (closed in winter) which runs east-west between I-5 on the coast and the east county line near Republic. US 97 runs north-south along the Columbia River from Wenatchee to the Canadian border, and Hwy. 155 rolls across the Colville reservation. An updated map of the Okanogan National Forest is critical to unraveling the county's myriad of backroads and fishing holes.

AENEAS LAKE. An excellent fly-only spring and fall rainbow and brown trout planted lake. Carryovers in the 15 to 18 inch class are available in the 27 acre lake. WDFW access. Drive 3.5 miles SW of Tonasket on County Road 9400/Pine Creek Road crossing the Okanogan River to the lake.

ALTA LAKE. Heavy plants of rainbow are made each year in Alta, and the lake comes through despite heavy early pressure. It covers 187 acres and lies 1.5 miles W. of Pateros on Hwy. 153, then S. for 2 miles to lake. State park with boat launch and camping, plus a resort.

ANDREWS CREEK. A rainbow and cutthroat stream which enters Chewuch River at Andrews Creek campground 19 miles N. from Winthrop on Chewuch River Rd. Trail 504 follows the stream upstream 13 miles to headwaters under Remmel Mt. in Pasayten Wilderness.

BARNSLEY LAKE. Private 9 acre lake that tends to winter kill 1.5 miles SW of Winthrop.

BEAVER LAKES. A pair of lakes holding rainbow and brookies. "Big" Beaver is 30 acres and 5 acre "Little" Beaver is 100 ft. E. The lakes are at 2700 and 2675 elev. and offer best fishing in late spring. Hwy. 20 about 18 miles E. of Tonasket, then N. 12 miles past **BONAPARTE LAKE** to Big Beaver where there are two FS campgrounds. County Rd. 9480 from Little Beaver leads 0.5 miles to **BETH LAKE**, 13 acres, which has rainbow and cutthroat. Ramp on Big Beaver. FS campground and launch on Beth.

BIG TWIN LAKES. The largest of two adjoining rainbow-planted lakes, Big Twin covers 77 acres 4 miles SW of Winthrop. Heavily stocked with rainbows and Lahontan cutthroat and is a crowded favorite on opening weekend. Selective gear

rules, electric motors only. From Hwy. 20 at the east edge of Winthrop turn SW onto County Rd. 9120/Twin Lakes Rd. for 2 miles to Big Twin. WDFW access, ramp, private resort. Fishing peaks in May.

BLACK LAKE. 66 acre mountain lake at 4000 feet with rainbow and ESA listed bull trout. Selective gear regs. Outlet, Lake Creek from Black Lake to the confluence of the Chewuch River is closed. Drive N. from Winthrop about 20 miles up Chewuch River to FS 100, then NW for 2.5 rough miles to road end. Lake Creek Trail 500 continues about 3 miles to lake. **HALFMOON LAKE**, 15.5 acres, lies 2700 feet above Black Lake 1.4 miles cross country W. of Black Lake in Pasayten Wilderness. It has cutthroat. **KIDNEY LAKE**, a 12.5 acre cutthroat lake is 1 mile S. from Halfmoon.

BLACK PINE LAKE. An 18 acre lake at 3900 feet, planted with brookies. From Hwy. 20 at Twisp drive 4 miles W. along S. bank of the Twisp River on County Rd. 1071/Poorman Creek Rd., then S. on FS 300 about 6 miles up Poorman Creek to lake, campground.

BLUE LAKE (SINLAHEKIN). An excellent prospect for large rainbow and brown, plus planted brook trout at the head of Sinlahekin Valley on the Sinlahekin WRA at 1686 feet elev. Covers 186 acres and holds trout 12 to 18 inches. 1 fish daily limit, selective gear rules. Gravel launch. Hwy. 97 about 5.5 miles N. of Riverside turn W. onto County Rd. 9410 for 8.5 miles to **FISH LAKE** then N. another 4 miles to Blue Lake.

BLUE LAKE (WANNACUT). Covering 110.6 acres 5 miles SW of Oroville. Annual plants of brookies, rainbow and Lahontan cutthroat.

BONAPARTE LAKE. A pretty, often overlooked 158-acre year-round lake that produces kokanee salmon, brookies, rainbows

Chopaka Lake.

and mackinaw. Fishing holds up well from late spring through summer in this big lake at 3554 feet elev. FS campground with pier at lake's S. end, plus a resort. From Tonasket drive E. on Hwy. 20 for 20 miles, then due N. up County Rd. 4953/FS 32 for 6 miles along Bonaparte Creek. Boat ramp.

BONNER LAKE (Ward). 15.7 acre private lake, no public access. Largemouth bass and black crappie. About 2.4 miles N. of Twisp.

BOULDER CREEK. Large tributary flowing into Chewuch River 7 miles N. of Winthrop from Pelican Pass. The creek, supports brook trout, is paralleled by FS 37 from its mouth. FS 37 connects the Chewuch drainage with Conconully lakes area. From Winthrop drive N. for 7 miles on paved County Road 9137 up E. side of Chewuch River which crosses FS 37 and creek at mouth.

BUCK LAKE. A large FS campground focuses a lot of pressure on this 15 acre lake at 3247 feet 9 miles N. of Winthrop. Planted after ice-out with about 2500 rainbows. Some largemouth bass and brown bullheads. There is a small pond 800 feet S. of Buck. Drive N. from Winthrop up W. side of Chewuch River on Chewuch River Rd/FS 51 for 9 miles to Eight Mile Creek Rd./FS 100 jct. on left, then 0.4 miles W. to Buck Lake Rd. for 2 miles to lake. Small trout, frequent winter kills.

BUCKSKIN LAKE. A 11.6 acre Pasayten Wilderness cutthroat lake at 6000 feet, N.

of Slate Peak on SE side of Buckskin Point. Drains to Middle Fork Pasayten River. From Harts Pass Rd./FS 5400 hike N. on Trail 498.

BUFFALO LAKE (Annum). A 121-foot deep, 542 acre lake on the Colville Indian Reservation offering rainbow, kokanee salmon and warm-water species. Good fishing through summer. Some large rainbow are taken in Buffalo. Resort, a public access on W. shore. Hwy. 155 for 12 miles SE of Nespelem, then E. 5 miles on Buffalo Lake Rd.

BUZZARD LAKE. Private 15 acres at head of Little Loup Loup Creek, 3380 feet elev. Rainbow.

CAMPBELL LAKE. A WDFW Methow WRA lake covering 11 acres, with a split management program. Summer fishery is catch and release, changing to catch-and-keep winter fishery (Sept.-Mar.). Predictably good fishing, especially in fall before ice-over. Winter access can be snow-difficult. Annually gets about 4000 catchable rainbows in late summer. WDFW access, small launch. From S. side of Winthrop head NE on Bear Creek Rd., past golf course and Davis Lake Road, then E. on Lester Rd. about 4 miles to lake.

CASTOR LAKE. Private 17.9 acre lake located 3.7 miles NW of Riverside.

CHEWUCH RIVER (AKA CHEWACK). Once considered a fair light tackle bet for rainbow, cutts and brookies in summer and fall this rumbling, pool pocked tributary to the Methow is now tightly restricted to protect two ESA species. From mouth at Winthrop to Eight Mile Creek it's open June-Sept. for catch-and-release fishing, selective gear. From Eight Mile to Pasayten Wilderness it's closed to all fishing from Apr.-Mar. Winter whitefishing is allowed in both sections. Paved roads from Hwy. 20 at Winthrop follow both sides of the stream and are connected by a bridge. The W. side road/ FS 51 leads upstream to Thirty Mile CG where trails continue upstream into Pasayten Wilderness. 7 FS campgrounds.

CHILIWIST CREEK. Once stocked with brookies. 2 miles SW of Malott on W. side of Okanogan River turn W. on road which follows the creek about 5 miles.

CHOPAKA LAKE. An exceptionally popular trophy rainbow lake set aside for fly-fishing only. Chopaka is well known for swarming callibaetis mayfly hatches and memorable dry fly and chironomid fishing, especially in the shallower S. end. Pack along leech, woolly buggers and Montana nymphs for fish that want a mouthful down deep between mayfly eruptions. Best from float tubes or small boats. There's a lot of 14 to 20 inch rainbows caught here, and although one fish a day is allowed, most anglers release everything, a big part of why the lake produces so many large trout. Rough road especially early in the season. From Loomis heads N. then S. on FS 39, then N. up Chopaka Creek Rd./DNR 1000 about 7 miles to lake WDFW access and DNR campground. Chopaka 1.5 miles long and covers 148.8 acres at 2921 feet elev.

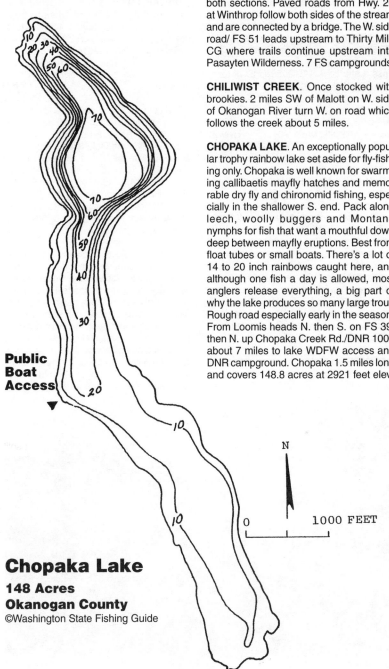

Public Boat Access ▼

N

0   1000 FEET

Chopaka Lake

148 Acres
Okanogan County
©Washington State Fishing Guide

CONCONULLY LAKE, UPPER, (AKA SALMON LAKE). Nearly always one of the top trout lakes in a region of good trout lakes. Annually planted with about 20,000 rainbow fry that measure about 11 inches with a few carryovers in the 14 inch range. Best in May-June. Respectable kokanee salmon trolling in late summer and early fall when the rainbows become active again. Some largemouth and smallmouth bass. Lake covers 313 acres E. of town, strung out behind a dam on Salmon Creek along the sage brush base of Silver Hill. Water fluctuations are common. Road on N. side. Resort, dock, rental boats, WDFW launch, camping on N. side. From Hwy. 20 at Riverside, turn NW on Hwy. 215 to Conconully, past reservoir, and E. to lake.

CONCONULLY RESERVOIR. Planted with about 10,000 rainbow fry 450-acre lake is on the S. side of Conconully, and while typically not as productive as its lanky eastern neighbor, this pan-shaped impoundment still a fair to good May into June prospect for rainbows that average around 10 inches. A few self-sustaining kokanee are available and bite best during mid summer. Large state park with camping, ramp, plus resorts with full facilities. From Hwy. 20 at Riverside, turn NW on Hwy. 215 . Reservoir is at roadside on S. edge of Conconully.

CONNERS LAKE. A small brookies planted lake on Sinlahekin WRA. Gravel ramp.

COPPER LAKE (Silver Nail). A private 5.4 acre bass and bluegill pond 4 miles N. of Oroville adjacent to W. side of US 97.

COUGAR LAKE. A small Winthrop-area winter-fishing lake planted before Sept. opener with about 3500 catchable rainbows. Covers 3 acres on WDFW Methow WRA, 1.5 miles N. of **CAMPBELL LAKE** Rd. Turn left 1 mile after crossing Bear Creek en route to Campbell Lake. WDFW access.

CRATER LAKE. Located at 6900 feet elev. 14 miles SW of Twisp, this 13 acre alpine lake holds 'bows and cutts. Drains to Methow River via Gold Creek. From Hwy. 20 about 6 miles NW of Methow, turn W. onto Road 1034, then 10 miles NW. up Gold Creek on FS 4340, W. up FS 300 along Raven Ridge and Crater Creek to trail 416. It's a 3.5 mile hike to lake. Because of elevation, Crater is a late summer and fall show.

CRAWFISH LAKE. Located at 4475 feet elev. on the boundary dividing Okanogan NF and Colville Indian Reservation, Crawfish covers 80 acres, supports a good population of brookies, rainbows and—crawfish. Along with a trolling rod, bring a trap. Boiled, like shrimp, and dipped in lemon butter or seafood sauce, shucked crawfish tails are fine eating and great trout bait. From Omak go E. on Hwy. 155 about 2 miles than N. along E. side of Okanogan River turning E. on Lyman Lake Rd. up Tunk Valley to Craw-

Conconnully Lake.

fish Lake Road to the lake. FS campground on NE shore plus a ramp.

CRUMBACHER LAKE. Private. No access. Brookies were planted in this 4.6 acre pond adjacent to W. side of US 97 about 7 miles N. of Riverside.

CUB CREEK. No longer stocked. Previously brookies were planted in beaver ponds along this Chewuch River tributary, now under selective tackle rules. From Hwy. 20 at W. side of Winthrop follow W. side of Chewuch River 5 miles N. then NW on Rd. 1251 along the creek for 10 or more miles. Fish marshy areas. Tributaries, First, Second and Third creeks flow seasonally.

DAVIS LAKE. Primarily a winter-fishing lake covering 39.3 acres and planted with about 15,000 catchable rainbows in Aug. Catch and release rules from Apr.-Aug. and catch and keep Sept.-Mar. Often a very good producer for winter fishery, and in spring there is usually a good number of large carryovers to challenge. WDFW access, resort. Davis is 4 miles SE of Winthrop. From Hwy. 20 at the SE bridge, turn sharply E. onto road along E. side of Methow River, then left on Bear Creek Road, past golf course to marked Davis Lake Road on right.

DIBBLE LAKE (Garrett). About 700 catchable rainbow are planted in this 5.3 acre lake, 3.4 miles S. of Winthrop. From Hwy. 20, turn W. on Twin Lakes Rd. then left on first dirt road.

DUCK LAKE (Bide-a-Wee). A surprisingly deep mixed-species lake with rainbow, bass, bluegill and crappie. Covers 29 acres, up to 65 feet deep, 3 miles N. of Omak and 1 mile W. of Omak airport. Road from Omak leads N. to lake. Inlet is a canal from Salmon Creek.

DUFFY LAKE. Lake Chelan-Sawtooth Wilderness lake, of 9 acres at 6500 feet. Some large cutthroat plus brookies reported. From Hwy. 20 at Twisp, go W. on Twisp River Rd./FS 44 to War Creek CG, cross bridge, then left (SE) on FS 4420, then right (S) up FS 080 to Trail 4104 to Oval Lakes. Hike 4.5 miles S., then cross country E. for 1 mile to Duffy. To reach **OVAL LAKES** at head of Oval Creek, continue 7 to 9 miles on trail. Lakes cover 18, 8 and 21 acres and support cutthroat and rainbow at 6200 to 6600 feet.

EARLY WINTERS CREEK. Closed to fishing. A tributary to Methow River 1.5 miles NW of Mazama. FS campground. Hwy. 20 follows creek upstream for 13 miles. The stream carries rainbow and cutthroat. From Hwy. 20 Spur Rd. 400 leads to trail 483 up Cutthroat Creek to **CUTTHROAT LAKE,** a 9 acre lake at 4935 feet which holds small cutthroat.

EIGHT MILE CREEK. Carries both rainbow and brookies plus protected summer steelhead. Selective gear rules. The creek spills into the Chewuch River 8 miles N. of Winthrop at Eight Mile Ranch. Good FS Rd. follows creek NW for over 15 miles upstream ending about 1 mile from Pasayten Wilderness boundary. 4 FS campgrounds are spaced along Eight Mile Creek Rd..

ELL LAKE. Managed as a quality lake with selective gear rules, and a 1 fish limit, Ell delivers rainbow averaging 12 inches with many in the 15-18 inch range. Covers 21 acres in the Aeneas Valley, 17 miles SE of Tonasket adjacent to Hwy. 20. The addition aerator seems to have solved a long-time problem with oxygen-depletion die offs. WDFW launch. **LONG LAKE**, 16 acres, and ;**ROUND LAKE,** 20 acres, are also on the highway near Ell. All 3 have public access, hold rainbow and deliver best for fly fishermen.

FAWN LAKE. Cutthroat have been stocked in this 5.8 acre lake at 5500 feet in the Pasayten Wilderness near headwaters of N. flowing Ashnola River. Drains SE to Lake Creek. From W. Chewuch River Rd. go NW on FS 3801 to Trail 500, hike past Black Lake for about 6 miles to Fawn under the divide.

FISH LAKE. Most of this 102 acre lake is on the Sinlahekin WRA about 4.5 miles NE of Conconully on County Rd. 219. WDFW access at E. end. Stocked with rainbows that offer fair spring fishing for 11 inch trout, and a fair number of 14-inch carryovers. Route is E. of Conconully on Rd. 4015 along N. shore of **CONCONULLY LAKE** past Sugar Loaf campground to lake shore. Also from US 97 about 6 miles N. of Riverside by turning W. on Rd. 9410/Pine Creek/ Fish Lake Rd.

FORDE LAKE. 24 acre reservoir on Sinlahekin WRA 6 miles S. of Loomis. Wild brook trout. WDFW launch.

FRENCH CREEK. Selective gear rules allow fishing in this Methow River tributary entering on N. side of Methow. Beaver ponds offer marginal fishing for brookies. Road from Methow follows creek NE about 5 miles.

FRY LAKE (Loon). 10 acres 200 feet W. of **DUCK LAKE** about 3 miles N. of Omak with trout, largemouth bass, crappies.

GOLD CREEK. A tributary of the Methow River closed to fishing from the mouth 6 miles NW of Methow to North Fork Gold Creek. Small wild rainbow. FS 4340 parallels N. bank about 10 miles to the headwaters. FS campground Foggy Dew Creek 5 miles from Hwy. 20.

GOLD LAKES. A pair of brookie lakes on the Colville Indian Reservation 14 miles N. of Nespelem up the Nespelem River. The upper lake is 19 acres, with Lower Gold covering 11 acres. May is best.

GOOSE LAKE (Big). Colville Indian Reservation lake 17 miles W. of Nespelem. The 181 acre lake has bass and crappie, and usually is best in summer. Road from SW end of **OMAK LAKE** leads 5 miles to Goose. Low water level has hurt fish population.

GOOSE LAKE (Little). An 8 acre lake 6.5 miles SE of Okanogan adjacent to the Okanogan Airport Road. Plants of brookies and rainbow in the past. It is on the Colville Indian Reservation.

GREEN LAKE (Upper). A pair of mixed management lakes developing popular winter ice fishing reputations. Upper is 5 miles N. of Okanogan, covers 44 acres, with WDFW access. Route is up Salmon Creek NW of Okanogan 4.5 miles then N. about 2 miles to lake. Holds rainbow and brookies. **LOWER GREEN** , 9 acres, is 1500 feet S. of Upper Green.
Catch and release, selective gear fishing from Apr.-Nov. then catch and keep, bait, fishing Dec.-Mar. Fishing is good for trout averaging 10 to 14 inches.

HESS LAKE. A narrow, 6 acre lake in Scotch Creek planted with rainbow, 6.2 miles W. of Hwy. 97 at Riverside. Drains to Johnson Creek.

HORSESHOE LAKE. Lahontan cutthroat are in this 28.7 acre lake 5.2 miles NW of Riverside on Cave Mt.. Follow Coulee Creek Road to end, then hike E. Drains to Okanogan River.

INDIAN DAN LAKE. A 13.8 acre lake in Indian Dan Canyon 3.9 miles W. of Brewster with largemouth bass and bluegill.

LEADER LAKE. Sitting in a long, tree-lined bowl this popular 159 acre reservoir is 9 miles W. of Okanogan N. of Hwy. 20 has been planted with catchable rainbows and generally offers fair fishing in spring and fall. DNR campground and launch on SW shore. Roadside shore fishing access.

LITTLE TWIN LAKE. Adjoins 77-acre Big Twin Lake 4 miles SW of Winthrop. From Hwy. 20 turn SW onto County Rd. 9120/ Twin Lakes Rd. Little Twin covers 24 acres and is open for catch-and-release Apr. 1- Nov. 30 and for catch-and-keep (bait OK) ice fishing from Dec. 1-Mar. 31. WDFW access, ramp. Excellent selective gear fishing for 12 to 16 inch rainbows in spring, and becoming a very popular ice-fishing spot.

LOST CREEK. Holds small rainbow and brookies. About 24 miles SE of Tonasket on the Aeneas Valley Road flowing into the San Poil River West Fork. A road 1 mile W. of Aeneas leads S. up the creek over 10 miles. A FS campground 2 miles up creek.

LOST LAKE. 46 acres 6 miles N. of **BONAPARTE LAKE**, about 30 miles NE of Tonasket. Offers brookies and rainbow. FS campground at N. end. Boat launch. Hwy. 20 for 17 miles E. from Tonasket to Road 4953 then N. past Bonaparte Lake to paved FS 33 then W. through Box Canyon to lake.

LOUIS LAKE. Cutthroat and rainbow, some large, are in this 27 acre mountain lake at 5300 feet in Lake Chelan-Sawtooth Wilderness. Drive 22 miles W. of Twisp on Twisp River Road/FS 44 to South Creek CG. Hike 2 miles on Trail 401 along South Creek to Louis Creek Trail 428 then 3 miles to lake.

LYMAN LAKE. Annually stocked with about 2000 catchable rainbows and 1000 brook trout fry. This 3.5 acre lake is 2.5 miles SW from Aeneas, drains to Lyman Creek. FS campground and boat ramp.

MARPLE LAKE (Bench, Rainbow). Frequent winter kill plagues this 3 acre private pond which may contain rainbow. 15 miles SE of Tonasket up the Aeneas Valley.

McGINNIS LAKE. A 115 acre brook trout lake on the Colville Indian Reservation. Drive 7 miles S. of Nespelem on Hwy. 155, then E. and S. past **REBECCA LAKE** 5 miles to W. tip of McGinnis. Public access.

METHOW RIVER. Starts high in the snow fields on E. side of the Cascade Crest under Snowy Lakes Pass and Mount Hardy, elev. 8080 feet and flows SE through the Methow Valley to enter the Columbia River at Pateros on US 97. Between Early Winters on the North Cascade Scenic Highway 20 to the Columbia confluence, the Methow River is paralleled by Hwys. 153 and 20. Five FS campgrounds are along upper stretches above Mazama where the river is more of a large stream filled with shallow, wadeable riffles, pools and tailouts—classic wild trout freestone water. WDFW and roadside access sites are scattered downstream from Winthrop where the Methow, fattened with flows from the Chewuch, Lost, and Twisp rivers, is wide, deep and although rocky and challenging is suitable for rafts and shallow draft river boats. It was once a respectable trout fishery, supplemented with hatchery plants, and an above average summer-steelhead and salmon river. However, in recent years, WDFW has suspended trout stocking, steelhead and the river's native bull trout are on the ESA list and trout fishing is either closed or tightly restricted. Catch and release fishing has been allowed (check current regs) from Gold Creek S. of Carlton to (Hwy. 20) Weeman Bridge about 8 miles upstream from Winthrop, but all summer fishing has been closed from Gold Creek downstream. The slough-water at the mouth, a famous steelhead trolling and jig fishing spot is now, along with the rest of the river, closed to all steelhead fishing. WDFW may open winter whitefish seasons Dec.-Mar. Before you drop a line into this picturesque mountain river, check current regs and ask about emergency regulations.

MOCCASIN LAKE. A private "trophy trout" fee lake covering 33 acres 4 miles S. of Winthrop off Twin Lakes then Patterson Lake roads.

MOLSON LAKE. 20 acres and fair to good early fishing for 4000 annually stocked catchable rainbows. Prone to winter kills. Adjacent to E. side of **SIDLEY LAKE** about

11 miles E. of Oroville. Take Tonasket Creek Road 8 miles E. from Oroville, then N. 5 miles through Molson to Molson Lake.

OKANOGAN RIVER. A large, sluggish Columbia River tributary flowing S. from Osoyoos Lake on the Washington-British Columbia border to enter the Columbia River near Fort Okanogan State Park near Brewster. A respectable smallmouth bass river, especially in the Oroville area and between Riverside and Tonasket. Also holds a few trout (trout fishing closed) whitefish and steelhead however ESA listing of steelhead has closed all steelhead fishing and substantially modified river regulations. Smallmouth averaging 10 to 12 inches, a few to 5 pounds, are the big attraction from June-October. Possibly because of the distance from metro areas, the Okanogan's considerable smallmouth potential is under recognized. Lots of good bank spots, but best from boats. From Oroville to Tonasket the river flows through a vast, marshy area of small ponds, sloughs and backwaters. Lower river walleye action improving in recent years, especially for boaters floating between Malott and the mouth where there is little bank access. Night fishing is sometimes effective for the bass during the heat of summer. Pockets of panfish, including perch, crappie and pumpkinseed. River often roiled by irrigation pumping. US 97 follows the river between Brewster and the British Columbia border providing lots of access.

OMAK CREEK. Flows into Okanogan River at Omak from the E. Hwy. 155 roughly follows the creek's N. side about 20 miles through Disautel on Colville Indian Reservation. Wild rainbow and brookies, few steelhead.

OMAK LAKE. The largest natural lake in the county, this 3242 acre water is 7 miles SE of Omak at 950 feet elev. on Colville Indian Reservation (Tribal fishing permit required.). There are 7 inlets but no outlets to this huge, 300-feet deep lake which has an exceptionally heavy sodium cabonate content, a saline solution that suits the habitat needs of the lake's giant Lahontan cutthroat which were stocked in the 1970s and have evolved into a true trophy fishery. The largest Lahontan ever caught in Washington, slightly over 18-pounds was caught here in 1993, and biologists will be surprised if a 20 pounder isn't taken. The lake is surrounded by dramatic cliffs and plunging shorelines. Open year-round, but tackle is limited to barbless artificials. No bait. Trolling large spoons, spinners, plugs and flies is the technique of choice. Ramp at N. end. Resort, guides, full fishing services.

OSOYOOS LAKE. Split by the US/Canada line, (about 2036 acres are in Washington) Osoyoos is a 10-mile long, multi-species lake open year round 1 mile N. of Oroville adjacent to Hwy. 97. Okanogan River flows through it. Generally poor for cold water fish, including naturally reproducing rainbow to 14 inches and kokanee salmon 10 to 14 inches. Best fishing is for smallmouth and largemouth bass, yellow perch and crappie. Some burbot. Large state park with boat launch and camping.

OVAL LAKES. String of 3 cutthroat planted lakes at head of Opal Creek 16.5 miles SW of Twisp in Lake Chelan-Sawtooth Wilderness. Sizes are 8, 21.3 and 21 acres. Elevations are 6200 to 6500 feet on the crest between Eagle and Fish Creek passes. Drain to Oval and Eagle Creeks to Twisp River. Follow Twisp River Rd./FS 44 W. from Hwy. 20 to War Creek CG, cross bridge, turn left to Rd. 080 to Trail 410. Fork left onto Trail 410A up Oval Creek to lakes.

PALMER LAKE. A large, remote and really good smallmouth bass lake. A natural lake covering 2063 acres at 1145 feet elev. in the distant Sinlahekin Valley. In addition to large numbers of smallmouth the lake offers largemouth bass, kokanee salmon, rainbow trout, catfish and crappie. Burbot (freshwater ling) are caught through the ice in winter but this fishery has been failing. The lake is fed by Sinlahekin Creek and feeds into the Similakeen River. BLM and DNA campgrounds at each end of lake plus a resort, and a picnic site at NE end. Drive N. 4 miles N. from Loomis on Loomis-Oroville Rd. which closely follows E. shore.

PATTERSON LAKE. A slow starter, but dependable May and June for catches of 9-inch planted rainbows and brookies and there's always a fair number of carryovers to 15 inches. 143 acres 7 miles SW of Winthrop in Methow WRA. Resort and WDFW access. From Hwy. 20 turn W. on Twin Lakes Rd. past **TWIN LAKES** to Patterson Lake Rd.

PEARRYGIN LAKE. One of the most popular trout lakes in the Methow, cover-

ing 212 acres and heavily stocked (usually 65,000 fry) with rainbows each year. Spring opener sees a lot of 10-inch trout and some very nice holdovers around 15 inches. Lots of bank fishing access and good stillfishing with bait. Troll small lures, flies. Success typically runs fair to good from opener to Sept. closure except at peak of playboat period. Located on Methow WRA, the lake has resorts, a large popular state park with boat launch and camping, and a primitive WDFW launch. S. side of lake is undeveloped. Disabled access. Lake is 1.5 miles NE of Winthrop on Pearrygin Lake Rd. N. from center of town.

PROCTOR LAKE. 7 acres with rainbow and brookies plants 3.5 miles N. of Omak and about 300 feet N. of Duck Lake.

RAMON LAKES. Three of the most remote mountain lakes in WA. These small cutthroat planted lakes of 2 to 3 acres at about 7000 feet in headwaters of Ramon Creek on N. side of Sheep Mountain in Pasayten Wilderness. Lakes are only 700 feet S. of U.S.-Canada border. Drain to Ashnola River. From Andrews Creek trailhead on Chewuch River Rd. NW up Trail 504, then W. on Trail 533, then N. on Trail 529 around Sheep Mt.

RAT LAKE. Primarily a winter ice fishing lake, this 62.5 irrigation reservoir 5.5 miles N. of Brewster is formed by a dam in Whitestone Creek. Annually planted with

Pearrygin Lake.

about 4000 rainbow and brown trout fry. Trout 12 to 18 inches available for summer catch and release fishery, and winter catch and keep. Drive 3.5 miles N. from Brewster up Swamp Creek on Paradise Hill Rd. to Rat Lake Rd. WDFW access, launch. Road often not snow plowed.

REMMEL LAKE. A mountain cutthroat lake covering 13.2 acres at 6500 feet near the N. boundary of Pasayten Wilderness in the spectacular headwaters of the Chewuch River. It lies 2.2 miles N. from Remmel Mt. and drains to Chewuch River. From 30 Mile CG, hike NW on Trail 510.

ROCK LAKES. Two lakes of 3.5 and 4.5 acres 11 miles NW of Okanogan. Route is via Loup Loup Road, to Rock Lakes Road. DNR campground. Brook trout.

ROUND LAKE. 20.3 acres in Aeneas Valley 16 miles E. of Tonasket. It receives rainbow plants. Drains to W. Fork San Poil River. Public access.

ROWEL LAKE. Brookies and rainbow in 4 acres 10.5 miles N. of Brewster in Rowel Canyon. Drains to Whitestone Creek.

SALMON CREEK. Main stem closed to fishing. North and West Forks are open. Flows into N. end of Conconully Reservoir at Conconully. FS Rd. 38 follows upstream about 8 miles to Salmon Meadows CG. 4 other campgrounds along this stretch. Creek holds wild rainbow and brookies. Lower creek flows from S. end of **CONCONULLY RESERVOIR** SE about 15 miles to join the Okanogan River at Okanogan. The Okanogan-Conconully Road parallels the creek most of its length.

SALMON LAKE (See Upper Conconully Reservoir).

SAN POIL RIVER. West Fork. Heads in the hills N. and S. of Long, Round and Ell Lakes about 17 miles SE of Tonasket. Road up Aeneas Valley follows the San Poil about 10 miles from the river's junction with Aeneas Creek E. and S. through Aeneas and into Ferry County. There is a FS campground 2 miles inside the Okanogan County line. The river offers larger than average brookies, rainbows, whitefish and in its lower section (Ferry County) near Lake Roosevelt there are walleyes. Fishes best in late spring after runoff. Tribal fishing permit required on Colville Indian Res-

ervation. Hwy. 21 follows most of the river and provides excellent access.

SASSE LAKE. A 6 acre reservoir on the Sinlahekin WRA, about 1 mile NE of the outlet of **FISH LAKE.** Subject to summer kill and is not planted.

SCHALLOW POND. Formed by a dam across Fish Lake outlet. 10 acre pond 4.5 miles NE of Conconully on Sinlahekin WRA. Rainbow and brookies.

SCHEELITE LAKE. A small, remote high mountain lake on the NE side of Pasayten Wilderness, planted with golden trout, about 2 miles S. of U.S.-Canada border between Scheelite Pass and Bauerman Ridge. Lake is N. of Trail 533 which comes in from the E. at Iron Gate Trailhead at end of Hodges Horse Pasture Rd.

SIDLEY LAKE. Heavily planted in June with 10,000 catchable rainbows this 108-acre lake, 1 mile S. of the U.S.-Canada border and 1 mile NW of Molson provides quality fishing for rainbows 12 to 18 inches. Open year-round. The lake is at 3675 feet elev. and has been planted in the past with Lahontan cutthroat. WDFW access and resort. Lots of excellent, open shore fishing for non boaters.

SILVER LAKE. 3 acre lake in Lake Chelan-Sawtooth Wilderness, stocked with cutthroat. It lies 16 miles SW from Twisp and 1.9 miles NE from Eagle Pass at 5550 feet. It drains to Eagle Creek. From Twisp River Rd./FS 44 turn S at War Creek CG to Trail 410 up Eagle Creek.

SIMILKAMEEN RIVER. Enters Washington from British Columbia 6 miles N. of **PALMER LAKE,** and flows about 25 miles SE into the Okanogan River at Oroville. Loomis-Oroville Rd. follows the river. The Similkameen supports rainbow, steelhead and whitefish, and delivers best fishing in late spring and early summer. Prime fishing water between Nighthawk and Oroville. Enloe Dam, an old hydroelectric facility near Oroville, blocks anadromous summer steelhead and salmon from potential spawning areas upstream. Partially because of this obstruction, the river is now closed to ESA listed steelhead. Open June-Aug. for trout and Dec.-Mar. for whitefish. River tends to freeze over.

SINLAHEKIN CREEK. Runs N. through

Similkameen River.

the Sinlahekin Valley and WDFW WRA into Palmer Lake. Access can be difficult but good fishing for brookies and rainbows. Selective gear rules, and the season is short—June through Aug —between Palmer Lake and Cecile Creek bridge. Road follows the creek through mostly private land.

SOUTH CREEK. A Twisp River tributary with cutthroat in Lake Chelan-Sawtooth Wilderness entering at South Creek CG 22 miles NW of Twisp at FS 44. Trail 401 follows the stream for about 5 miles into the wilderness and continues across South Pass into NCNP.

SPECTACLE LAKE. Covering 314 acres and opening more than month earlier than most lakes in this area, this heavily stocked and very popular lake is an excellent place to tackle larger than average rainbows from 11 to 16 inches. Stocked near the Mar. 1 opener with 30,000 catchable rainbows and 2000 triploids to sweeten a fishery already swollen with a fry plant of 170,000 rainbows and 22,000 browns. 3 resorts and a WDFW access, ramp. The long, narrow lake closes at the end of July and fishing is usually very good all season for still fishermen, trollers and fly fishermen. From US 97, S. of Tonasket just S. of the Okanogan River bridge, turn N. on Tonasket-Oroville West Side Road, then W. on Loomis-Oroville Rd., past **WHITESTONE LAKE** to Spectacle Lake which is 2.5 miles E. of Loomis.

SPRING LAKE. A 15-acre oblong shaped lake on Methow WRA NW of Twisp. Planted with catchable rainbows and supports carryovers to 16 inches. Fish early. Mosses in early summer. Small boats and lots of open bankfishing. May winter/summer kill.

Nearby Dead Horse Lake may hold a few trout. From Hwy. 20 at Twisp, turn NW onto North Twisp River Road/FS 44 about 3 miles then right (N.) onto dirt road to lake.

STARZMAN LAKES. Lakes of 8 and 5.5 acres which hold brookies and rainbow. Head N. from Brewster on road to Wakefield 1.5 miles, then turn left to follow Starzman Creek 8 miles to S. end of Lower Starzman.

STEVENS LAKE. An 11 acre lake in Horse Springs Coulee with brookies. Stevens is reached by road on W. side of Okanogan River in town of Tonasket which leads 8 miles SW and then N. to mouth of Horse Springs Coulee where a rough road continues N. 3 miles to lake. Sometimes winter kills.

SUGARLOAF LAKE (Pine Tree). Brook trout have been planted in this 6 acre lake 750 feet N. of **UPPER CONCONULLY LAKE.**

SUMMIT LAKE. Rainbow are the attraction in this 9.9 acre Colville Indian Reservation lake located about 11.5 miles NE of Nespelem near head of Coyote Canyon. Drains to Omak Creek.

TORODA CREEK. Heads N. of Wauconda 20 miles E. of Tonasket on Hwy. 20, and flows NE about 20 miles to join the Kettle River in Ferry County. A road follows Toroda Creek for its full length from Wauconda to Toroda, but private property hampers access. Best for brookies and a few rainbows in late spring.

TURNER LAKE. A narrow, 2300 foot long lake of 16.5 acres at 4164 feet. Turner winter-kills and is not planted. It is S. of Wauconda.

TWIN LAKES (See Big and Little Twin Lakes.)

TWISP RIVER. Once a popular trout and camping stream this long river has lost a lot of its luster because of ESA complications and the end of WDFW's river trout stocking program. A major tributary pouring from headwaters in the Lake Chelan-Sawtooth Wilderness into the Methow River at Twisp on Hwy. 20. Paved Twisp River Rd./FS 44 parallels the river for over 25 miles W. and N. of the mouth, passing 5 FS campgrounds. Many trout-bearing tributaries, including Poorman, Newby, Coal, Little Bridge, Buttermilk, Lime, Eagle, War, Williams, Reynolds, South and North Creeks. Below War Creek CG the river is open June-Sept. for catch and release fishing with selective gear, but much of this reach flows through private property. Above War Creek, in the national forest, it is probably closed and in recent years there has been no special winter whitefish season anywhere. Many trailheads from FS 44 lead hikers to high lakes in Lake Chelan-Sawtooth Wilderness and NCNP.

VARDEN LAKE. Cutthroat lake covering 4.5 acres 17.5 miles NW from Silver Star Mt. and S. of Hwy. 20 from Klipchuck CG on Snagtooth Ridge. Drains to Varden Creek, Early Winters Creek and Methow River. Bushwhack access.

WANNACUT LAKE. A pretty and slightly saline lake of 411 acres that holds up for fishing well into June because of its depth, 158 feet at deepest point. Wannacut produces chunky 12-16 inch rainbow, is planted regularly, and has large carry-overs. Nice for fly fishing and light tackle trolling. Resort with camping and rental boats, WDFW access, ramp. Drive S. from Oroville 2.5 miles on W. side of Okanogan River, then W. 3 miles on County Rd. 4510/Blue Lake Rd. past Blue Lake to north tip of Wannacut. Rd. 4491, a rougher route, comes N. from Enterprise between **SPECTACLE LAKE** and **WHITESTONE LAKE**.

WAR CREEK. Selective gear fishing for wild cutthroat and rainbow in this Twisp River tributary entering at War Creek CG about 15 miles W. of Twisp. Road 100 extends 2 miles up War Creek to Trail 408 then up the creek about 10 miles under War Creek Ridge to headwaters at War Creek Pass into Lake Chelan-Sawtooth Wilderness.

WASHBURN LAKE. 2.1 miles NE of Loomis, Washburn covers 12.8 acres and hosts planted brookies along with largemouth bass and bluegill. Drains to Spectacle Lake. Open April-Sept. Both state fishing license and Colville Tribal permits are required.

WHITESTONE LAKE. A long, shallow lake this is one of the most popular warm-water lakes in the county, Whitestone covers 173 acres and offers small perch and pumpkinseeds, plus channel and bullhead catfish and largemouth bass. The lake's well known crappie fishery has declined

dramatically. Most of the lake is less than 10 feet deep, offering lots of structure for bass and panfish. deepest water is a 25 foot hole at midlake, but there's a 20 foot pocket at SE end. Whitestone is 5.5 miles N. of Tonasket near **SPECTACLE LAKE** and is open year-round. Drive N. from Tonasket on W. side of the Okanogan River 4.5 miles, then W. for 3 miles on Loomis-Oroville Rd. to Whitestone. Good WDFW access, ramp, camping.

WOLF CREEK (Little). A spring fed stream near Winthrop. Closed because of ESA complications. Beaver ponds in lower reaches support brookies. In upper reaches there are wild rainbow and cutthroat off Wolf Creek Rd./FS 100 which is reached by driving W. From bridge at S. edge. of Winthrop toward fish hatchery, then bearing right (W.) at Twin Lakes Rd. turn-off.

Okanogan County Resorts

Alta Lake: Alta Lake State Park, 509-923-2473. Whistling Pines, 509-923-2548.

Big Twin Lake: Big Twin Lake Campground Winthrop, 509-996-2650.

Bonaparte Lake: Bonaparte Lake Resort, 509-486-2828.

Buffalo Lake: Reynold's Resort, 509-633-1092.

Conconully Reservoir: Shady Pines Resort, 509-826-2287. Liar's Cove, 509-826-1288.

Conconully Lake: Conconully Lake Resort, 509-826-0813.

Davis Lake: Davis Lake Resort, 509-996-2169.

Palmer Lake: Chopaka Lodge, 509-223-3131.

Patterson Lake: Patterson Lake Resort-Sun Mt. Lodge. 509-996-2226.

Pearrygin Lake: Derry's Resort, 509-996-2322. Pearrygin Lake State Park, 509-996-2370. Silverline Resort, 509-996-2448.

Spectacle Lake: Spectacle Lake Resort,. 509-223-3433. Spectacle Falls Resort, 509-223-4141. Rainbow Resort, 509-223-3700.

Twin Lakes (Winthrop): Big Twin Campground, 509-996-2650.

Wannacut Lake: Sun Cove Resort, 509-476-2223.

Pacific County

WDFW Region 6

Washington Department of Fish and Wildlife, 48 Devonshire Rd. Montesano, WA 98563-9618. Phone 360-249-4628

Miles of good fishing water surround Pacific County. Wedged in the elbow between the Pacific Ocean, Columbia River, Willapa Hills and 35-mile long Willapa Bay, Pacific is the most southwesterly county in the state and offers a mix of anadromous steelhead, salmon, cutthroat and sturgeon, trout, bass and panfish, plus marine access to offshore rockfish, ling cod, halibut, albacore tuna and salmon. Its bays and beaches are well known for razor clams, Dungeness crabs and succulent Pacific oysters. Unfortunately, most of the really good oyster beaches are on private tidelands in Willapa Bay, the mouth of which is a popular spot for shallow-water, small boat fishing for chinook salmon.

The wide, tidal flow at the mouth of the Columbia River delivers the famous Buoy 10 summer chinook and coho salmon small boat fishery, some of the best white and green sturgeon fishing flats in the state, and a charter boat base at Ilwaco that books ocean trips for salmon, bottomfish and tuna. Only half a dozen lakes receive regular trout stocking, but there are 15 lakes with good numbers of bass and panfish. Most are located on Long Beach Peninsula, a tourist and recreation spit between Willapa Bay and the Pacific Ocean. The largest lake in the county is Loomis at only 151 acres.

Several small winter steelhead, salmon and sea-run cutthroat streams wind through the 970 square mile county which ranks 30th in size in the state. The Willapa, Naselle, North and Nemah Rivers, while mere shadows of their production in the late 1980s, still produce anadromous fish from late Sept. into March.

The upland county is a rumple of low, heavily clear-cut stump knobs rising to a high spot of only about 3,000 feet near the Grays River's headwaters. There are a few trace tracts of the once magnificent forests that encased this year, but the hills are mostly a region of vast clear-cuts, dense tree farms and thick brush. Excluding the massive Columbia River, the county's largest flows are the Willapa River which drains the central portion of the county into Willapa Bay, and the Naselle River drains the S. part to Willapa Bay. Both are small enough to cast across, wadeable and can be productive steelhead and salmon fisheries.

Public land is scarce, but most timber company lands are open to the public. Several segments of the Willapa National Wildlife Refuge are in the bay and the north tip of Longbeach Peninsula, which bills itself as the "world's longest beach drive." Ramps in the refuge and at Palix and Smith Creek units of the WDFW Johns' River Wildlife Area provide small boat access to Willapa Bay. A ramp and dock at Toke Point in Tokeland is popular for bay crabbing and with salmon fishermen targeting the September run of chinook at the bar. There is a good public ramp with lots of parking in the Ilwaco boat harbor. Other ramps are near the mouth of the Willapa River at Raymond and at South Bend, the county's largest towns. Raymond, a logging and mill town, is the largest community with about 3000 residents, and full services for traveling fishermen.

The Shoalwater Tribe has a small reservation near Tokeland. Fort Canby State Park is at the base of the North Columbia River jetty. One of the most popular state parks, it covers several hundred acres, provides more than 200 camp sites, beach access and a good boat ramp into a protected bay on the Columbia River.

Main routes are US 101 which crosses N-S from Aberdeen to Astoria. Hwy. 4 follows the Columbia River from Longview E-W to US 101 N. of Ilwaco. Hwy. 6 is a winding two-lane running E-W from I-5 at Chehalis to Raymond along the Upper

Chehalis and Willapa rivers. Hwy. 105 cuts S. from Westport along the N. edge of Willapa Bay to Raymond.

The climate is mild, warm, wet and smells of ocean air. While mid summer is often warm (in the high 70s and low 80s) and dry, the rest of the year gets swamped with Pacific rain squalls. Average rainfall varies from 86 inches at Willapa Harbor to more than 113 inches at the mouth of the Naselle River. For comparison, Seattle gets 35 annual inches of rain. Freezes are rare, and there's always open water fishing available.

ALDER CREEK. A small, brushy cutthroat stream entering the East Fork Naselle River just above the North Fork. Road from Naselle leads E. and N. up the N. Fork with logging roads providing access to about 5 miles of the creek. Best fishing late summer and fall.

BEAR RIVER. Fair for sea-run cutthroat in the fall, with very limited steelheading in lower river Dec. and Jan. US 101 crosses at the mouth into Willapa Bay, and may be fished upstream for a short distance above US 101. Access to the upper river is limited, but a road 1 mile E. of Illwaco leads E. 2 miles, then NE 2.5 miles to the stream.

BLACK LAKE. 30 acres 0.5 miles N. of Ilwaco. Stocked with 4500 rainbow in April that provide a spring fishery. Summer is for largemouth bass, yellow perch and brown bullhead. Drains to Cranberry Marsh and Willapa Bay. Some shore access.

BREAKER LAKE. Largemouth bass and perch are in this 7-foot deep, 20.3 acre lake, 1.5 miles N. of Long Beach. Drains into ocean.

CANYON CREEK. Tributary to South Fork Palix River with fair sea-run cutthroat fishing. The brushy creek may be reached by turning N. at South Bend's W. city limits. At about 5 miles the road meets and follows the creek for 2 miles.

CASES POND. A 2 acre kids-only pond 1 mile E. of Raymond. Planted with 1700 legal rainbow in Apr., May and June for juvenile fishing. Adult coho salmon sometimes planted in Oct.-Nov.

CEDAR RIVER. Empties into Willapa Bay 4 miles E. of North Cove on Hwy. 105. Logging roads follow the river upstream, but may be gated. Sea-run cutthroat are taken in Sept-Oct.

CLAM LAKE. A shallow, weedy 10 acre lake that holds largemouth bass, crappie and perch, 2.4 miles N. of Long Beach . A road runs close to the N. tip of the lake.

COLUMBIA RIVER. The mouth of the Columbia River is one of the most popular fishing spots on the entire river. Most years in Aug., Sept. and Oct. there is an extremely popular small boat fishery inside of Buoy 10 targeting summer and fall chinook and coho salmon bound for upriver spawning areas and hatcheries. Every one of the Columbia River's legendary salmon come through here. Nearest access and ramp is through Ilwaco. Year-round sturgeon fishing is excellent, especially for green and white sturgeon that fit into the catch-and-keep slot limit. The flats near Megler-Astoria/US 101 Bridge are very good for sturgeon. Flounders are caught in the river, and the North Jetty at Fort Canby State Park offers rockfish, ling cod, greenling, surf perch, flounders and occasionally a late summer salmon. Crabbing is popular near the river's mouth. The bar at the mouth of the Columbia is one of the most hazardous crossings in North America and no place for small boats. Stay well inside. That's where most of the fish are, anyway.

The docks at Ilwaco are worth probing for pile and striped perch. Charter offices at Ilwaco book sturgeon and Buoy 10 salmon trips inside the bar, as well as ocean salmon (especially coho), spring and summer rockfish, spring halibut and late summer albacore salmon trips. Shad, steelhead and smelt migrate upstream through here but there is no concentration point and very limited harvest. Boat ramps at Ilwaco boat harbor, Fort Canby State Park, and Chinook.

COURTHOUSE POND. Stocked with about 400 rainbow trout in April and May.

CRANBERRY LAKE. An 18-acre bass and panfish lake. Best for largemouth and perch. Lies 3.5 miles N. of Long Beach drains into Willapa Bay. County road parallels W. shore.

DEER LAKE. Largemouth bass and perch are found in Deer, a 7.6 acre lake located 2 miles N. from Long Beach. It drains to Pacific Ocean.

FALL CREEK. Joins upper North River at

Brooklyn in NE county. Cutthroat, best in fall. The road to Pack Sack Lookout follows the creek S. from Brooklyn for about 2 miles. A maze of logging roads head SE from the lookout to lead to upper reaches of Fall Creek.

FORT CANBY LAKE (O'Neil). A shallow, stumpy 10-acre lake about 2 miles SW of Ilwaco at Fort Canby State Park. Offers largemouth bass and a few rainbow. The road to North Jetty at the Columbia River mouth goes just S. of the lake.

FRESHWATER LAKE. 5.1 acres with perch and largemouth bass 5 miles N. of Long Beach. Drains to Willapa Bay.

GILES LAKE. 18 acre lake on the North Beach Peninsula with largemouth bass, perch and crappie. Located 2.5 miles N. of Long Beach. County roads near N. and E. shore.

GOOSE LAKE (Mallard). The northern lake in a chain N. of Long Beach on the North Beach Peninsula. Covers 5 acres and supports bass, perch and panfish. Other lakes in the chain include Lost, Island, Tape, Cranberry, Clam, Briscoe, Deer, Breaker, Clear and Tinker. From Hwy. 103 follow county roads to the lakes. Many of these lakes are open year round.

ISLAND LAKE. A shallow, 8-foot deep, 55 acre lake with public access that produces largemouth bass and perch through the summer. Lake is 4 miles S. of Ocean Park on North Beach Peninsula. A road leads E. from Hwy. 103 to the lake.

LITSCHKE LAKE. Largemouth bass and yellow perch are in this very shallow, 5.2 acre lake 4 miles N. of Long Beach.

LOOMIS LAKE. The largest lake in the county, Loomis is narrow, 2.5 miles long, 9 feet deep, covering only 151 acres. It's 2.5 miles S. of Ocean Park off Hwy. 103. One of the best trout lakes in the county with fishing fair to good from April into August for 2000 catchable rainbows stocked in Apr. Best trout month is May. Best fishing, though, is for warm-water species. Perch bite well most of the summer, especially toward fall. Also, crappie, bluegill, brown bullheads, pumpkinseeds and largemouth bass. You don't hear much about the bass fishing, but I suspect there are a few good fish around all that brush. WDFW access, shallow launch, dock.

LONG BEACH PENINSULA. There's a potential to surf cast for redtail surf perch on the ocean side of this sandy peninsula, but few anglers ever try it. Miles of public beach. Locate a low spot and stillfish with pyramid sinkers anchoring No. 6 hooks sweetened with bits of clam neck or sand shrimp. Willapa Bay side will provide perch flounders, and sole. Razor clam digging in season from Grayland to North Cove on Twin Harbors Beach.

LOST LAKE. A 1.5 acre pond with perch, 1.7 miles SE of Klipsan Beach. Drains to ocean.

MILL CREEK. Willapa River tributary joining 3 miles SE of Raymond. Creek supports a few fall cutthroat. Road from Raymond heads SE up the creek for 5 miles.

NASELLE RIVER. A small, picturesque riffle and pool river that produces winter steelhead, chinook, coho, chum salmon and sea-run cutthroat but in recent years the biggest news has been the concentration of white sturgeon in the wide, slow lower river and just off the mouth. According to WDFW the Naselle sturgeon catch, in recent years, has rivaled the productive Chehalis River. In the late 1980s this little river produced almost 1000 winter-runs. By 1999 that figure fell to just 57 hatchery winter steelhead most taken in Dec. and Jan. It does get a run of catch-and-release wild fish toward the end of the season. The Naselle delivers pretty fair sea-run cutthroat from July through Dec. and salmon run all fall. In late August the first kings come in, followed by Sept.-Dec. coho and Nov.-Dec. chums. Public launch in Naselle. The river enters Pacific County from Wahkiakum County 3.5 miles E. of Naselle and flows NW about 10 miles to Chetio Harbor in Willapa Bay. US 101 crosses the sturgeon water at the mouth and Hwy. 4 follows the N. bank for about 7 miles. A secondary road follows the river to its headwaters. The tidewater section is best boated, but the upper river is a delight to wade and cast.

NEMAH RIVER. A big stream, really, with 3 lightly-fished forks emptying into Willapa Bay between Bay Center and Johnson's Landing on US 101. Marginal fishing at best. The North Fork gets most fishing attention and is paralleled by road upstream for 5 miles. Logging roads follow the Middle Nemah for 5 miles, while US 101 runs along the pretty South Fork. Plants of several

North Fork Nemah River.

thousand steelhead smolts in the North. Fork produce a catch of about two dozen hatchery steelhead a year most in Dec-Jan. Sea-run cutthroat are found in tidal reaches of all 3 forks from late Aug.-Dec. Best fishing is usually for a late October run of chums in tide water. Also gets chinook and coho runs.

NORTH RIVER. An excellent sea-run cutthroat stream from late July into Sept., with early winter returns of hatchery steelhead. Anglers take about 60 winter-runs a year, most in Jan. The slow-moving river heads in Pacific County, then runs into Grays Harbor County and back to Pacific to flow SW to Willapa Bay 8 miles E. of North Cove on Hwy. 105. Public boat launch site at mouth of **SMITH CREEK** which joins North River in its tidewater area. US 101 crosses the North in Grays Harbor County with a logging road following the stream downstream to near its mouth. Easy method of fishing the river is to launch a boat at mouth of Smith Creek on an incoming tide and drift upstream about 4 miles to the falls. Some coho fishing in Sept.-Nov. Chinook are in the river, but there's no season on them most years.

PALIX RIVER. A small river with small runs of winter steelhead, sea-run cutthroat and salmon. Best bet is the sea-run cutthroat in the lower river Aug.-Dec. If you catch a salmon or a steelhead call the local paper—it'll make headlines. The Palix heads in the hills S. of South Bend and meanders about 7 miles SW to an arm of Willapa Bay 2 miles

SE of Bay Center. US 101 crosses the mouth, where a boat launch provides access to lower river. A network of logging roads runs links the Middle and South Forks.

RADAR PONDS. A pair of small, 3.2 and 4.6 acres, year-round trout ponds 4 miles N. of Naselle near the radar station. Stocked in Apr. with 5700 catchable rainbows. Also cutts and brookies., and some years adult coho are stocked in Oct.-Nov. Head NW of Naselle 1.5 miles on Hwy. 4, then N. up Holm Creek 3 miles.

RUE CREEK. Enters South Fork Willapa River about 1 mile W. of Menlo. Road from Menlo leads S. up the creek for about 4 miles. Holds sea-run cutthroat in late summer and fall.

SALMON CREEK. A sea-run cutthroat stream joins the Naselle River 1 mile E. of Naselle. Followed by Hwy. 4 about 3 miles E. from mouth, then NE in and out of Wahkiakum County and on up to Salmon Creek's headwaters.

SKATING LAKE. A skinny 2.5 mile-long lake covering 66 acres with yellow perch. 1 mile S. of Oysterville.

SMITH CREEK. Produces 30 to 50 winter steelhead most in Jan. in lower stretches, but is best known as a sea-run cutthroat and jack salmon producer. Smith Creek flows into Willapa Bay at mouth of North River where it's crossed by Hwy. 105. Boat ramp at this site Aug. and Sept. are peak cutthroat and jack salmon months. Upper stretch of the creek is crossed by US 101 between Raymond and Aberdeen and a road 1 mile S. of this point continues E. to the creek's headwaters.

SOUTH BEND MILL POND. A popular 1.8 acre kids-only pond where about 1700 catchable rainbow are stocked Apr.-June. Pond is 1.4 miles W. of South Bend and drains to Willapa River.

TAPE LAKE. Only 7 feet deep, this 9.9 acre lake supports largemouth bass, and perch. Early summer best. 4 miles N. of Long Beach, drains to Willapa Bay.

TINKER LAKE. An 11 acre, 6-foot deep lake on NE side of Long Beach. Offers largemouth bass and yellow perch. Drains to Willapa Bay.

TRAP CREEK. A Willapa River tributary joining 10 miles SE of Raymond. Hwy. 6 crosses creek mouth, and logging roads follow upstream about 5 miles to headwaters near Trap Creek Lookout. Fair bet for fall cutthroat

WILLAPA BAY. This huge 35-mile long bay is the second largest bay on Washington's coast (behind Grays Harbor), but its fishing value is seriously compromised by extreme shallow depth, and a bar to the ocean that often is sanded shut. Still, it offers salmon, winter steelhead, sea-run cutthroat, sturgeon, crabbing and an assortment of marine perch and flounders. Sturgeon and chinook salmon are the big attractions. Sturgeon fishing is very good off the mouth of the Naselle River almost year round. From mid-Aug. into Sept. light tackle fishermen launch at Tokeland and head W. to troll herring in 10 to 20 feet of water just inside the bar on the N. side of the bay along Washaway Beach for chinook salmon that ride across the sand on incoming tides. Hit this one right and you'll be into 20 to 30 pounds of line-shredding memories. In Sept-Dec. coho and chums come in, but most anglers let them hit the rivers before fishing. While the bay coho and chum fisheries aren't as popular as that for kings, there are fish to catch. Sea-run cutthroat are in the shallows near shore, just about everywhere, especially around inlet mouths, islands and oyster beds. Dungeness crabbing can be very good in the Tokeland area, where there is an ex-

cellent ramp and dock. Also ramps at South Bend, mouth of North River, Raymond, Johns River Wildlife segments, and Willapa National Wildlife Refuge. The Johns River and WNWR sites are used most often by duck hunters. WNWR dominates much of the S. bay. Lots of oyster farms in the bay, all private, and none friendly to "accidental" picking. There is a public oyster and hardshell clam beach at Nahcotta Tidelines. The bar between the bay and ocean is shallow and easy to run aground on, difficult at best to cross and impossible most of the time. This bar is a dangerous place for small boaters. Stay inside. Hwys. US 101, 105 and 103 follow most of the shoreline.

WILLAPA RIVER. Winter steelhead, chinook, coho, chums and sea-run cutthroat attract fishermen to this pastoral stream from Aug-Mar. The Willapa is the best fishing river in the county, and though it's suffering, it's still one of the best in the region. It heads in SE Pacific County and flows NW about 30 miles before entering the N. tip of Willapa Bay at Raymond. Hwy. 6 between Raymond and Chehalis parallels the Willapa through farm land for many miles. From Nov.-Mar. boat fishing is banned, but may be used for transport. The Willapa season opens in July when sea-run cutthroat and jack salmon begin filtering in. The runs last into Oct. In Sept. and Oct. there's a fishable run of chinook targeted in the tide water of the lower river. Coho come in from Sept. through Dec. and there's a run of chums in Nov. and Dec. Steelheading for legal hatchery fish is best in Nov. and Dec. when anglers now take about 150 to 250 fish, tragically below the 1000 to 1500 winter-runs that hit the bank in the mid 1980s. There's a run of stocky natives for catch-and-release fun just before the winter closure. The South Fork enters the mainstem at Raymond where a road follows the stream S. about 5 miles. The South Fork delivers about 2 dozen hatchery winter steelhead in Dec. and Jan. A rare summer-run is sometimes taken in June-July. Also has wild sea-run cutthroat. Boat launch at Willapa.

WILSON CREEK. A Willapa River tributary which joins at community of Willapa. Boat launch at mouth provides access to Willapa. Wilson is primarily sea-run cutthroat water. Roads follow the creek E. upstream to headwaters.

Pend Oreille County
WDFW Region 1
Washington Department of Fish and Wildlife, 8702 N. Division St., Spokane, WA 99218. Phone, 509-456-4082.

Rolling like a lumpy green blanket across the extreme NE corner of Washington, Pend Oreille County (pronounced Ponderay) holds a lot of promise for fishermen, especially trout fishermen. The county covers 1428 square miles, most of it lightly-populated, wooded, mountainous, and sprinkled with small lakes and cold rivers. The county abuts the borders of Canada and Idaho, is 66 miles long, about 22 miles wide and ranks 25th in size. Pend Oreille County offers anglers lots of public land, and more than 170 lakes, 106 of them above 2500 feet in the Colville and Kaniksu national forests in the Selkirk and Pend Oreille Mountains, foothills of the Rockies. The major river is the Pend Oreille which slides into Washington from Idaho and flows north into the Columbia River in Canada near the U.S.—Canada border. It's one of the state's largest rivers and one of the few to flow north. The PO is a wide, fairly gentle river and one of Washington's most neglected trout and warm water fishing opportunities. The river's wealth of rainbows, browns, bass and panfish are largely unknown outside of closed-mouthed local anglers.

Except for a lowland region in the south-central part of the county near Diamond and Sacheen lakes, and the Pend Oreille River Valley, the county is mountainous. The mile-plus high wall is an topographic obstruction to clouds sweeping eastward off the dry, flat Columbia Basin. Rain and snow clouds bank against the mountains and dump almost 30 inches of annual precipitation, twice what falls just W. in neighboring Ferry County. The moisture feeds lush brush, salal, Oregon grape, snow berries and dense stands of twisted vine maple and dog-hair trees more reminiscent of Puget Sound's forest than the open woodlands of semi-arid central and eastern Washington. The highest point is Gypsy Peak at 7309 feet, in the Salmo-Priest Wilderness Area at the extreme NE corner of the county.

Summer fishermen usually enjoy warm, dry weather with temperatures rarely climbing above the mid 80s. Winter can be brutal. Temperatures frequently hover in the zero range, and rarely climb out of the teens. The lowest temperature on record is -41.

The main access route to fishing opportunities is Hwy. 20 which parallels the Pend Oreille River from Idaho to Tiger. Hwy. 31 continues into Canada.

BEAD LAKE. A 720 acre lake which lies in a beautiful mountain setting at 2850 feet elevation NW of Newport. WDFW does not stock this large lake. Wild Mackinaw, kokanee and burbot are available though. To reach the lake from Newport cross the Pend Oreille River to the E. bank and LeClerc Creek Road, then NW 8 miles on LeClerc to Bead Lake Road. Follow the lake road N. to the S. shore. Bead Lake Trail provides access from FS boundary on S. side of lake. A small USFS fee boat ramp is at the S. end of the lake. Occasionally it's closed. Contact the Newport Ranger District for schedule. Summer fishing pressure is light on this year-round lake, but in the winter lots of ice-anglers target the lake's abundant burbot. Jig near bottom with leadheads sweetened with meat baits or nightcrawlers. Just after ice-out there can be some very good near-surface trolling for Mackinaw. As the weather warms these husky lake trout head for the bottom where anglers troll plugs. Also some fair spring and summer trolling for kokanee salmon.

BOUNDARY LAKE. Not stocked, but rainbow are present in this 9 acre lake which is adjacent to Hwy. 31 about 10 miles N. of

Boundary Reservoir.

Metaline Falls just inside the U.S.-Canada line.

BOUNDARY RESERVOIR. A 1600 acre bass, perch and trout impoundment on the Pend Oreille River about 8.8 miles N. of Metaline Falls. Largemouth and smallmouth bass and yellow perch are the dominant catch. Occasionally planted with catchable trout. Picnic and boat launch areas.

BOX CANYON RESERVOIR. A lanky 6000-acre Pend Oreille PUD reservoir on Pend Oreille River 2.8 miles N. from Ione. Good fishing in sloughs and shoreline shallows for largemouth bass, black crappie, yellow perch and brown bullhead catfish A cooperative net-pen rearing project provides some rainbow trout fishing. Ramps at Ione and Edgewater where there is also a nice campground.

BROWN'S LAKE. One of the state's most popular "fly fishing only" lakes, 88-acre Brown's Lake is dominated by 10 to 12 inch cutthroat, with carryovers in the 14-inch class. This pretty, undeveloped lake is at an elevation of 3450 feet. It's wedged between steep hills, which makes bank fishing tough and the lake slow to shed winter ice. Best fishing is in spring and fall. Access is from Usk. Cross to the E. side of the Pend Oreille River, drive N. on Kings Lake Road 5 miles, then NE about 6 miles to S. shore of the lake where a FS campground and boat launch ramp are located. Near the lake Kings Lake Road becomes

FS 5030. A fish viewing platform, handicap accessible, is located 0.5 miles E. on inlet stream. Best to view cutthroat spawning in May.

CALDWELL LAKE. An brookies planted lake of 14.8 acres located 7.4 miles SE from Ione. Drainage to Scotchman Lake to Pend Orielle River.

CARL LAKE. A 7 acre lake stocked with rainbows. Route is Tiger-Colville road from town of Tiger for 4 miles, then S. on rough road 1.5 miles to lake.

CHAIN LAKE. A 125-foot deep enlargement of Little Spokane River covering 77.6 acres in a 1.2 mile stretch of two connected segments. It has kokanee, yellow perch and largemouth bass. Location is 3.6 miles NE from Elk.

CONGER PONDS. Pair of small ponds of 3.2 and 5.3 acres in headwaters of Trimble Creek 5 miles NW from Cusick. Planted with rainbow fry.

COOKS LAKE. Rainbow stocked lake which lies at 3075 feet. It covers 11 acres. the lake is 4 miles past **BEAD LAKE** about 5.2 miles NE of Usk.

CRESCENT LAKE. A 21.6 acre lake located 9 miles N. of Metaline Falls adjacent to W. side of Hwy. 31. Crescent is stocked with 3000 rainbow fry which are often in the 9-10 inch class by opening day. Fair angling from July to October. Campground, picnic area and small boat launch on S. shore. High water will flood campground.

DAVIS LAKE. This 145.9 acre lake at 2150 feet offers brookies, rainbow, kokanee salmon, largemouth bass and sunfish. It has a public access area on N. end. From Usk drive S. on Hwy. 211 for 5.7 miles. Davis comes on early and then again in fall months.

DIAMOND LAKE. A 754 acre, popular recreation lake at 2360 feet adjacent to US 2 abut 7 miles SW of Newport. A once robust trout fishery has been severely compromised by illegal stockings of warm water species. It's stocked in Mar. with about 25,000 catchable size rainbows and browns which provide some decent trout fishing in the early spring. There's also summer catches of yellow perch and largemouth bass. There is a public access plus resorts on Diamond. Route is 7 miles SW of Newport on Hwy. 2 which parallels the SE shore of the lake. It drains to Sacheen Lake. Public access and resorts.

FAN LAKE This pretty little 72.9 acre lake has a public access and lends itself to fly fishing for rainbow. It is located 8 miles NE of Deer Park, 2.5 miles W. of Hwy. 195

at 1930 feet. Best fishing is in spring and fall.

FRATER LAKE. An 11 acre cutthroat planted lake located 6.5 miles S. of Ione on Hwy. 31, then 6 miles SW on Hwy. 20. Drainage is into **LEO LAKE**, and most productive fishing comes during spring and September and October. Small boats may be launched from shore.

GOOSE CREEK. A remote creek which flows into the upper West Branch inside the Idaho line. Top stretch of the creek carries small cutthroat and brookies and is crossed by the road running NE from Usk 16 miles between North and South Skookum Lakes. A rough trail follows the stream.

GRANITE CREEK. Only the upper reaches of this Priest Lake tributary are in Washington. Closed for bull trout protection.

HALFMOON LAKE (Moon). A 14 acre mountain cutthroat lake located 7.5 miles NE of Usk at head of Halfmoon Creek. A road parallels E. shore of the lake. Spring and fall offer best fishing.

HARVEY CREEK. The creek heads in Bunchgrass Meadow on the E. slope of

Davis Lake.

Molybdenite Mtn. and flows NW into Sullivan Lake. Best fishing for the creek's rainbow and cutthroat comes after July 1. Route is road from Ione about 7 miles NE toward **SULLIVAN LAKE**, then E. and S. up Harvey Creek 8 miles to Bunchgrass Lake at 4950 feet.

HORSESHOE LAKE. Kokanee, Mackinaw and rainbow along with largemouth bass, crappie, perch, sunfish and catfish inhabit this 128 acre lake. It is a steady producer of medium sized kokanee. The lake lies in a deep bowl, and is reached via road from S. end of **ELOIKA LAKE** in Spokane County 8 miles to lake shore. There is a public access on Horseshoe. Elevation is 1975 feet.

IONE MILL POND. This 37 acre lake lies adjacent to W. side of Hwy. 31 at Ione. Marginal fishing.

KINGS LAKE. This 53.2 acre lake at 3250 feet 6.5 miles NE of Usk has been closed since the 1940s and used for WDFW fish production. It is one of Washington's two sources for broodstock westslope cutthroat.

LAKE OF THE WOODS. An 8 acre rainbow lake at 2400 feet about 6 miles E. of Camden on Spring Valley Road. Access problems.

LEADBETTER LAKE (Loon). A brook trout lake covering 22 acres. Leadbetter is 5 miles N. of Metaline Falls. Follow the road running along the W. side of Pend Oreille River. Private. Limited access is available via a primitive boat launch on the E. shore.

LEAD KING LAKES. Rainbow and brookies planted lakes of 4.2 and 2.4 acres at 2550 feet. Location is 5.5 miles N. from Metaline Falls and about 1.9 miles N. from **LEADBETTER LAKE**.

LEO LAKE. A 39-acre cutthroat lake adjacent to the S. side of US 20 at the Pend Oreille-Stevens County line. Leo offers action during spring and fall. FS campground and boat launch at N. end.

LITTLE SPOKANE RIVER (East Fork). A nice little trout river crossed by US 2 near the SW limits of Newport. Turn S. on Scotia Valley Road which parallels the river for several miles. The river runs through Chain Lake and continues into Spokane County.

The Little Spokane offers wading anglers small brookies and pan size rainbows and can be a lot of fun with light tackle, especially fly rods. **WEST FORK LITTLE SPOKANE RIVER** flows SE from Sacheen Lake into Trout Lake, then into Horseshoe and upper Fan Lake before crossing into Spokane County and **ELOIKA LAKE**. The river supports brook and rainbow trout, plus warm water species in the stretch between Horseshoe and Eloika Lakes.

LITTLE LOST LAKE. Brookies and rainbow have been stocked in the 5.7 acre lake at 3150 feet. Location is 5.5 miles N. from Ione at head of Lost Lake Creek. Drains to Pend Orielle River.

LOST CREEK. Rainbow and brook trout in this small stream tributary to Pend Oreille River S. of Tiger. Series of fishable, hike-in beaver ponds are along the creek.

LOST LAKE. A 22.1 acre brook trout lake 9 miles NW of Elk and 1.1 miles W. of **TROUT LAKE**. Drains to W. Branch Little Spokane River.

LUCERNE LAKE (Yorke). Brookies are in this 17 acre lake, 8 miles N. of Metaline Falls on the W. side of Hwy. 31 about 0.4 mile S. of **CRESCENT LAKE**. Private lake.

MARSHALL LAKE. Plants of 30,000 catchable size rainbow and cutthroat fry maintain a good fishery at this scenic 188 acre lake near the Idaho border NE of Newport. It is fed by Marshall and Burnt Creeks. From Newport cross the US 2 bridge to the E. side of the Pend Oreille River, and then N. on Bead Lake Road for 6.5 miles , veer NE. on Marshall Lake Road to S. end of lake. Marshall holds up well throughout the season . Public access, ramp and resorts.

MEADOW LAKE. A 70-acre mountain lake about 20 miles NE from Colville at elevation of 3450 feet. Planted with rainbows.

MILL CREEK. A tributary running into the Pend Oreille River at Babbitz Landing off US 20 about 14 miles N. of Usk. Mill Creek is followed upstream 6 miles by a road on the N. bank. It produces small brookies and cutthroat during late summer.

MUSKEGON LAKE. Cutthroat are the attraction in this 7.5 acre lake. Elevation is 3450 feet. It lies 16 miles SE from Metaline Falls and about 1300 feet W. from

Washington-Idaho border. Drainage is to Priest River.

MYSTIC LAKE. A 17 acre lake stocked with cutthroat. Elevation is 2975 feet, and route is 4 miles beyond **BEAD LAKE** on the Bear Paw road. Good camp site, heavily used.

NILE LAKE. Rainbows, browns, brookies and cutthroat trout and pumpkinseed panfish are in Nile, which lies at 3190 feet elevation and covers 23 acres. The lake is 5 miles SW of Tiger adjacent to E. side of US 20. Nile is a good fly fishing prospect in June and September. Small boats may be launched along shore.

NO NAME LAKE. Planted with fingerling cutthroat, this rich 15 acre lake is located 1 mile past **BEAD LAKE** off Bear Paw road. FS campsites.

PARKER LAKE. A 22.1 acre lake adjacent to 27 acre marsh. Parker has been planted with rainbow and brook trout. Dispersed campsites on FS land. About 6 miles N. of Cusick on US 20, turn onto Cusick Creek Rd./County Rd. 2441 and continue 3.5 miles to lake.

PEND OREILLE RIVER. The largest river in Pend Oreille County and an excellent destination for fishermen who enjoy a mix of trout and warm water fish. Sometimes more than 200 yards wide, the Pend Oreille heads in Idaho's massive Lake Pend Oreille, and crosses into Washington at Newport. It flows N. the length of Pend Oreille County enters B.C. 10 miles N. of Metaline Falls and flows into the Columbia River. It is one of the few north flowing rivers in the state. US 20 and Hwy. 31 follow the river, providing great access, and some roadside fishing. The most productive fishing, however, is from trailerable boats. The fishing holds up well all year, for a sweeping variety that includes, large and small-mouth bass in the sloughs and shorelines, schools of perch, crappies, some nice browns, pen-raised rainbow, lots of whitefish, and a few cutthroat. Fishing holds up throughout the year. Campsites and boat ramps are sprinkled along most of its length.

PETIT LAKE. A cutthroat lake of 10 acres located at 3975 feet on the N. flank of Diamond Peak. From Ruby on Hwy. 31 turn onto LeClerc Creek Rd. and continue to lake. No outboards.

Pend Oreille River largemouth.

POWER LAKE DAM. A 55 acre reservoir at 2,421 feet elev. on Calispell Creek's N. Fork that produces rainbow and brook trout during the summer. From Usk go SW on Hwy. 211 about 7 miles, turn W. on Calispell Rd, continuing past Calispell Lake watershed to Middle Fork Rd., to FS 3520 which goes to N. end of lake. Water levels fluctuate.

PRIEST RIVER (Lower West Branch). A remote, pretty stream that delivers small wild cutthroat and brookies. Best route is through Idaho. Follow Hwy. 57 N. from town of Priest River turn NW up the river at Falls Ranger Station to the mountain headwaters in Kaniksu National Forest north of Bead Lake.

RUBY CREEK. Brookies and rainbow have been planted in beaver ponds on this stream which enters Pend Orielle River at Blueside. From US 20 go SW on Ruby Creek Road to follow creek.

SACHEEN LAKE. Big plants of brookies, browns and rainbows produce good fishing at this popular 319 acre lake. Steep banks are great for trollers, but there several good bank fishing areas exist. Stocked annually with 20,000 brookies and 5000 rainbow. Lake is 70 feet deep, but much of it runs 30 to 40 feet, and trolling is popular.

Spring and early summer are the most productive, although some good fly action for big brookies and browns takes place in the fall. Drive 11 miles SW from Newport on US 2 or 25 miles N. from Spokane to Jct. of Hwy. 211. Turn N. on Hwy. 211 for 4 miles to the lake. Resorts, rental boats, docks, camping plus a public boat launch area on the NE shore. Elevation is 2250 feet.

SALMO RIVER (Upper). Located in NE corner of the county, heading under Little Snow Top Mountain on the Idaho line, and flowing NW about 6 miles to enter B.C. From Metaline Falls take FS road 302 E. up Sullivan Creek for about 11 miles to FS Road 654. Follow this road about 12 miles to trail 506 which leads 3 miles to river.

SKOOKUM LAKES. Plants of rainbow trout boost South Skookum (32 acres) and North Skookum (38 acres).Some brookies. Both lakes lie at slightly over 3500 feet elevation, 6 and 7 miles N. of Usk on Hwy. 31. Follow Skookum Creek Road upstream. Mid-May is best fishing period. There is a FS campground and boat ramp on South Skookum, and a state campground on **NORTH SKOOKUM**, as well as a resort.

SLATE CREEK. A producer of small cutthroat and brook trout, Slate flows into the E side of the Pend Oreille River 6 miles N. of Metaline Falls. Hwy. 31 crosses the creek near its mouth. FS Road 3155 tracks the N. bank for about 6 miles providing excellent access.

SULLIVAN LAKE. This is a lake for lunker chasers, and it still holds the record for producing the biggest brown trout ever caught in the state—a 22 pounder landed in 1965. It has a deserved reputation for producing trout that are weighed by the pound, especially browns, cutthroat and rainbows. Trout to 5 pounds are not rare. There's a bunch of brookies and small kokanee that attract both the big, predatory trout as well as anglers. Burbot, sometimes called freshwater ling, are also in the lake and provide an excellent ice fishery. Most big-fish anglers troll with large blue back plugs that resemble kokanee. This 1290 acre lake is E. of Hwy. 31 and Metaline Falls. From the town go E. on Sullivan Lake Road up Sullivan Creek about 4 miles past

SULLIVAN MILL POND, then 2 miles S. where FS Road 303 parallels the W. shore for 3.5 miles. There are FS boat launches and campgrounds at both ends of the 1290 acre lake. A rough road goes up the E shore along the steep hill.

TACOMA CREEK. Crossed by Hwy. 31 about 3.5 miles N. of Cusick, the small stream yields brook trout, rainbows, browns and cutthroats. Roads follow the creek upstream for several miles.

TROUT LAKE. A private 95 acre lake that holds rainbow, brookies, perch, bass and sunfish. A few large 'bows are taken early each year. From Pend Oreille State Park, follow road NW for 4 miles to lake .

VANES LAKE. Stocked with brookies, a 4 acre lake at 3000 feet. Location is 1 mile N. from **NO NAME LAKE** in a marshy area.

WEST BRANCH PRIEST RIVER (Lower). Fair fishing for brook trout and cutthroat, the stream is reached by driving N. from town of Priest River in Idaho 12 miles on Hwy. 57 to Falls Ranger Station, then NW up the stream into Washington, where the road runs along the river for approximately 10 miles. **UPPER WEST BRANCH** is reached via a road NW from Idaho's Hwy. 57 N. of Priest River. A road follows river for about 7 miles in Washington through Squaw Valley. Primitive campsites along stream.

YOCUM LAKE. Plants of cutthroat produce fair to good fishing in this 41 acre lake which lies at 2875 feet elevation. South of Ione from LeClerc Creek Wildlife Area follow West Branch LeClerc Creek Road 6 miles, turn W. at jct. of Yocum Lake FS Rd. for about 3 miles to lake shore. Access can be difficult early in the season. Primitive campsite at lake.

Pend Oreille County Resorts

Marshall Lake: Shadow Bay Resort, 509-447-3332. Marshall Lake Resort, 509-447-4158.

North Skookum Lake: Marshall Lake Resort, 509-447-4158.

Sullivan Lake: USFS Sullivan Ranger District. 509-446-2681.

Pierce County
WDFW Region 6

Washington Department of Fish and Wildlife, 48 Devonshire Rd. Montesano, WA 98563-9618. Phone 360-249-4628

The most extreme topography in the state is found in Pierce County ranging from sea level to the icy crest of Mount Rainier at 14,411 feet.

Between the two extremes are 1789 square miles of saltwater fishing, a wealth of small lowland lakes and impounded reservoirs stocked with trout, kokanee salmon, bass and panfish, a couple of notable steelhead rivers, and hike-in alpine trout lakes tucked between ragged folds deep in the high Cascade Range.

One of the state's most populous counties, this Puget Sound metro area ranks 19th in size among the 39 counties. About 323 square miles lie within the boundaries of Mt. Rainier National Park. Approximately one-half of the lakes are located above 2500 foot elev. The Puyallup and Nisqually River systems drain all but the NE portion which is drained by the White River. All three have runs of anadromous steelhead and salmon, and run straight off the glaciers at Mount Rainier. Summer melt on these glacial headwaters will fill all three with glacier flour, a silt that transforms them from gin-clear freestone flows into rivers that resemble troughs of liquefied concrete. Glacier flour is a summer phenomena that ends in fall when cold weather freezes the runoff melt and while glacier silt sometimes interferes with early salmon seasons it's usually ended by the start of winter steelheading.

The saltwater includes some fine winter blackmouth and seasonal runs of chinook, coho and to a lesser degree chum salmon. There are a few areas like the Narrows and Tolivia Shoals that still produce ling cod, and some nice rockfish. The Tacoma area was once famous for producing mountains of true cod and walleye pollock, but these fish are now rare and protected by management restrictions. The county wraps around a number of marine islands, including Anderson, McNeil, Fox, Herron, Ketron, Raft, Day, Cutts, Tanglewood, Grave, Eagle and Pitt.

Most of the east county is in the Cascade Range and foothills, including 323 square miles within Mount Rainier National Park (MRNP). This area features steep mountains, deep canyons and forested valleys. Maintained National Forest trail systems link many of the high lakes.

The White River (AKA Stuck) drains the NE part of the county rumbling along the Chinook Pass Hwy. 410 scenic route through Mud Mountain Dam to join the Puyallup at Sumner. The Puyallup and Nisqually rivers drain the rest. The Puyallup River flows into Tacoma's Commencement Bay and is the county's most popular steelhead and salmon river. Both are also tribal treaty rivers with commercial gillnet seasons.

The lowland climate is maritime, mild and fishable year-round. Annual precipitation at Puyallup is 40 inches. At Longmire 2762 feet up the slopes of Mount Rainier it measures more than 81 inches, climbing to 106 inches just 4 miles NE and 2788 feet higher at Paradise.

Pierce County has 361 recorded lakes and reservoirs and nearly half are mountain lakes at elevations above 2500 feet. Many high lakes are in the Mount Baker-Snoqualmie and Gifford Pinchot national forests including Clearwater and Glacier View wilderness areas. Most of the high lake trailheads require FS parking permits. Also, refer to the Mount Rainier National Park section.

Much of the foothill land between Mount Rainier and Alder Lake E. of Hwy. 161 and S. of Hwy. 410 is owned by private timber companies that require annual access permits for vehicles. The major owners are Weyerhaeuser which owns the White River

Tree Farm SE of Enumclaw and Champion which owns much of the land in the Kawposin-Eatonville area. Some companies allow free foot, horse or bicycle access, and some areas are closed. Much of the timber company land includes valleys and undulating lowlands with pockets of trout in beaver ponds, small rarely fished streams and mountain lakes. All permit areas are posted.

The largest lake in Pierce County is Lake Tapps, an impounded multi-species reservoir covering 2,296 acres S. of Auburn and E. of Sumner. Much of the trout fishing is centered on a splattering of valley lakes SE of Puyallup near Kapowsin. WDFW has stopped stocking catchable trout into streams in this region, although most of the creeks support resident cutthroat and some rainbows. These wild trout provide mostly catch-and-release opportunties because of 2 fish daily limits and 12 to 14 inch minimum sizes on many streams. Few wild creek trout top 10 inches.

The massive Fort Lewis Military Reservation and McChord AFB complexes dominate the W. county south of Tacoma. Some lakes on the bases are open to fishing with military permits. The Nisqually National Wildlife Refuge is at the mouth of that river just N. of the Thurston County line. The refuge is a great place to watch birds and hunt ducks, but its value to fishermen is limited to a marginal sea-run cutthroat fishery in the colored lower river and nearby **MCALLISTER CREEK** (See Thurston County) and crabbing in the delta. Much of the lower Nisqually flows through restricted access lands, either on Fort Lewis or within the Nisqually Indian Reservation,

Main routes to Pierce County fishing are I-5 N-S through Tacoma, Hwy. 7 and 161 which run N-S. from Tacoma and Puyallup into the Kapowsin lakes area. Hwy. 410 swings up the White River to the N. edge of MRNP and through spectacular Chinook Pass to Yakima County. Hwy. 706 reaches E. into the mountains from the Kapowsin region to MRNP's S. side at Paradise and Longmire.

Steelhead and salmon fishing has taken a serious hit in this region in the past two decades, but there have been some major strides in developing a year-round lowland trout fishery that includes widespread stocking of Triploid rainbows averaging 1.5 pounds when they hit the water and growing rapidly. Numerous largemouth, smallmouth bass and panfish lakes are within an hour's drive of the population center. Most saltwater fishing efforts originate at boat launches at Tacoma's Point Defiance, Narrows Marine, Gig Harbor, or from one of the small island ramps on the W. side of Narrows Bridge. Public fishing piers extend from Tacoma's N. shore into Commencement Bay and Dalco Pass.

ALDER LAKE. Wedged into a corner of logged foothills shared by Pierce, Lewis and Thurston counties, this 2931-acre (at full pool) reservoir is impounded by a Tacoma power dam on the Nisqually River adjacent to Hwy. 7 S. of Eatonville. It's a true mixed species lake and probably very much under fished considering the variety offered. One of the problems is that the water level is frequently and severely drawn down, a fluctuation that makes it tough to grow large fish. Alder has a reputation for providing trollers towing flasher blades and bait with 7 to 12 inch rainbows and kokanee. Best fishing for these is in the upper end of lake. Kokanee are the top draw, hitting best May-July. Few, however, exceed 10 inches. A few cutthroat will hit rainbow trolls. Perch fishing has been growing in popularity in recent years and some wide-bodied fillets hit the skillet from late spring into early fall. The trick is to find a school. Alder also supports small largemouth bass, crappie, and bullhead catfish. Tacoma City Light has public access, ramp, dock and mooring. DNR campsites and launch ramp. Resort and store in Alder has ramp. Hwy. 7 about 5 miles S. of Eatonville follows Alder's N. shore. Open year-round.

AMERICAN LAKE. Heavily stocked and consistently one of the top lakes in the S. Puget Sound area, American covers 1125 acres, is 90 feet deep in places and offers exceptionally large rainbow, cutthroat, and kokanee salmon plus a mixed bag of smallmouth, largemouth, and rock bass, perch and bullhead catfish. Located 8 miles SW of Tacoma near Fort Lewis, American is 3.5 miles long, includes 4 islands and is fed by a series of creeks and natural springs. Fishing holds up well all year. In May WDFW sweetens the pot with more than 60,000 catchable rainbows, plus a helping of 14-inch and up Triploids. There is an exceptional carry-over fishery and naturally re-producing strain of steelhead rainbows. Anglers have taken rainbows in the 10 to 13 pound range and 5 pounders create big smiles every year. Trolling near shore is a

American Lake
1125 Acres
Pierce County
©Washington State Fishing Guide

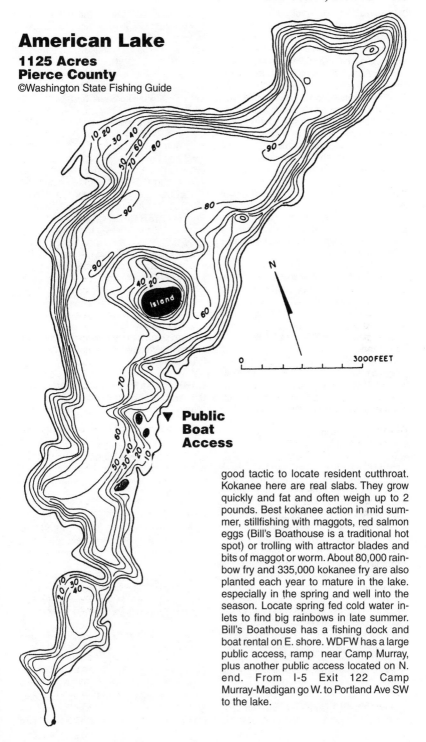

▼ **Public**
Boat
Access

good tactic to locate resident cutthroat. Kokanee here are real slabs. They grow quickly and fat and often weigh up to 2 pounds. Best kokanee action in mid summer, stillfishing with maggots, red salmon eggs (Bill's Boathouse is a traditional hot spot) or trolling with attractor blades and bits of maggot or worm. About 80,000 rainbow fry and 335,000 kokanee fry are also planted each year to mature in the lake. especially in the spring and well into the season. Locate spring fed cold water inlets to find big rainbows in late summer. Bill's Boathouse has a fishing dock and boat rental on E. shore. WDFW has a large public access, ramp near Camp Murray, plus another public access located on N. end. From I-5 Exit 122 Camp Murray-Madigan go W. to Portland Ave SW to the lake.

BAY LAKE. An excellent spring rainbow producer covering 119 shallow acres on the Longbranch Peninsula. The lake is fertile and may deliver holdover 'bows to 16 inches. Stocked with 10,000 catchable rainbows in April, but is heavily fished, warms quickly and is usually done for the year by June. Also gets a fry plant of 10,000 brook trout and 50,000 rainbows. Some largemouth bass and brown bullhead catfish. WDFW access. From Purdy W. and S. on Hwy. 302 to Key Center then S. on Gig Harbor-Longbranch Rd. 7 miles to lake S. of Penrose Point State Park.

BEAVER CREEK Tributary to Big Mashel River 4 miles E. of Eatonville. Supports cutthroat and rainbow. Road from Eatonville leads up the Mashel about 3 miles, then swings SE to parallel Beaver Creek for 2.5 miles.

BENBOW LAKES. Chain of 5 lakes including Whitman, Byron, Upper and Lower Twin plus an unnamed lake. All are private except Whitman, a 29 acre lake which has a public access, rainbow, cutthroat and panfish. Lakes are 2.5 miles W. and S. of Kapowsin.

BONNEY LAKE. A 17-acre lake stocked with 1300 catchable rainbows in Mar., offering largemouth bass, perch and pumpkinseed. WDFW ramp on NW shore. From Sumner go SE on Hwy. 410 for 2.5 miles then N. for 1 mile on Myers Rd. to 77th SE, then E. to circle lake.

BOWMAN LAKE. Rainbow and warm water species. Covers 11 acres 4.5 miles SE of Auburn. Drains is to the Stuck River.

BRADLEY POND. This 13-acre pond east of South Hill Mall in Puyallup is stocked with about 2000 catchable rainbows by early Apr., plus largemouth bass, crappie, perch and bullhead catfish. Adult coho salmon sometimes stocked in Oct.-Nov. Open year-round

CARBON RIVER. A heavily silted glacial stream flowing from Mt. Rainier NW to join Puyallup River about 3 miles N. of Orting. Receives winter steelhead plants. Generally delivers about 50 summer-runs, most in July and Sept. and 50 winter-runs, most in Jan.

CARNEY LAKE. Annually planted with 2500 catchable and 15,000 fry rainbow this

Fishing Lake Kapowsin bass structure.

39 acre lake is on the Kitsap County line 4 miles N. of Vaughn. May and June are best. WDFW access.

CARTER LAKE. A 6.3 acre marshy lake 0.5 mile SW of Ponders on McChord AFB. Planted with rainbow, open year-round.

CHAMBERS CREEK. Heads in Steilacoom Lake and flows W. to Puget Sound near Steilacoom. Good sea-run cutthroat fishing at mouth in fall. Lots of juvenile chinook salmon which must be released.

CHAMBERS LAKE. An 80 acre marshy lake dammed on Muck Creek 1 mile NE of Roy on Ft. Lewis military reservation. Holds rainbow, cutthroat and largemouth bass.

CLARKS CREEK. A tributary to Puyallup River flowing from Maplewood Spring SW of Puyallup to the Puyallup a few miles W. of town. Steelhead hole at mouth of Clark, with some creek sea-run cutthroat in fall. Road follows W. bank upstream. Receives winter steelhead plants.

CLEAR LAKE A popular, 155-acre lake, spring stocked with about 11,000 catchable rainbow, and a few hundred triploids, plus 50,000 kokanee and 35,000 rainbow fry. Some nice carryovers. Rainbow action peaks in May and June, giving way to summer kokanee. WDFW access, ramp and resort facilities. 5.5 miles N. of Eatonville on W. side of Hwy. 7.

CLEARWATER RIVER. Flows from Clearwater Wilderness near MRNP to White River at Hwy. 410 about 10 miles E. of Enumclaw. Logging road runs S. along E. bank of this quick, shallow, freestone rocky river upstream to where it's bridged. Lightly fished for small wild rainbow and cutthroat in late spring and summer. Vehicle access requires Weyerhaeuser permit.

CRESCENT LAKE. A rainbow and cutthroat planted lake of 47 acres 4 miles N. of Gig Harbor. Stocked with 2500 catchable rainbows before opener. Some largemouth. Public access, ramp

ECHO LAKE. A 61.4 acre mountain lake in Norse Peak Wilderness reached via a 5 mile trail from Corral Pass. Drains to upper Greenwater River. Cutthroat in 7-8 inch range. From Hwy. 410 near Silver Springs turn N. on FS 7174 climbing to Corral Pass at 7000 ft. elev. then Trail 1176 to lake at 3819 feet elev.

DALLES LAKES. Pair of small lakes, 2.5 and 0.8 acres, 7 miles SE from Greenwater at N. end of Dalles Ridge. Elevation is 4550 feet. Drain to White River.

DECOURSEY POND. A 1-acre juvenile-only pond. planted with rainbows and adult coho salmon. Pond is a side channel in Clarks Creek Park wet of Western Washington Fairgrounds in Puyallup.

EAST LAKE. Cutthroat lake of 4 acres at 4000 ft. elev. about 15 miles SE from Enumclaw on N. side of Cayada Mountain. Drains to Carbon River.

EATONVILLE POND. 4 acre rainbow pond, 0.5 miles S. of Eatonville. Drains to Mashel River.

FLORENCE LAKE. Located on Anderson Island this 66.5 acre lake is open year-round for brown trout, holdover rainbows, largemouth bass and bluegill. Primitive ramp at county park on N. shore.

FOREST LAKE. A 6.3 acre lake with brown and rainbow trout, rock bass and pumpkinseed. 3.4 miles S. of Orting.

GEORGE POND. 1.6 acre mountain lake with cutthroat N. of Corral Pass, 26 miles SE of Enumclaw on N. side of Noble Knob at 5470 feet. Drains to Greenwater River.

GIG HARBOR. A congested, but picturesque harbor NW of Narrows Bridge. Sheltered ramp off Randle St. on NW shore. Convenient small boat access to salmon and bottomfish areas in the Narrows, Dalco Pass, Point Defiance. WDFW reports fair surf smelt raking on beach near ramp Oct.-Mar. Follow signs N. from Hwy. 16.

GRAVELLY LAKE. Access to this 148 acre lake is difficult since private homes ring entire lake. Has bass and panfish. 0.5 miles NW of Ponders Corners.

GREENWATER LAKES (Meeker). A chain of hike-in lakes on Pierce-King county line on upper Greenwater River. Upper lake covers 6 acres, with the lower lake 4 acres. They hold small brook trout, cutthroat and rainbow. From Hwy. 410 S. of Greenwater, turn E. on paved FS 70 and continue to trailhead parking lot where pavement turns to gravel and road crosses river. Trail 1176 follows the river upstream through a park-like setting of towering old growth for about 2 miles to the lakes at elevs. of 2780 and 2846 feet. Easy, popular hike. FS permit required.

HARTS LAKE. A year-round lake, plumped in the spring with 8500 catchable rainbows that attract a lot of pressure in April and May. A few trout are taken throughout the summer in spring areas, but the best warm weather action is for largemouth bass, crappie, pumpkinseed, perch, channel cats and yellow and brown bullhead. A round lake that covers 109 acres. Resort facilities, rental boats and a WDFW boat launch. Road leads SE from McKenna about 5 miles to the lake. **LITTLE HART LAKE**, 10.6 acres, is 600 feet S. from Harts. Holds brown bullhead.

HELEN'S LAKE. Rainbow in this 5 acre lake at 4000 feet 7.5 miles NE from National. Drains to Puyallup River.

HERRON LAKE. A private 10 acre rainbow lake adjacent to Case Inlet 1 mile S. of Herron.

HILLE LAKE. Fair fishing in a 3 acre pond for rainbow, bass and panfish. Adjacent to the E. side of Lake Tapps' N. end.

HORSESHOE LAKE. Private 12 acre lake with warm water species. 3 miles N. of Eatonville at SW end of **OHOP LAKE** on Northwest Trek property. No fishing access.

JOSEPHINE LAKE. On the E. shore of Anderson Island, Josephine covers 72 acres and hosts bass and panfish.

KAPOWSIN LAKE. A stump bedded, log riddled, brushy pocket of perfect large-mouth bass habitat spread over 512 irregular acres. A year-round lake, planted with 15,000 catchable rainbows in early April, Kapowsin is about as close to a perfect bass lake as it gets in Western Washington. It's 58 feet deep on the S. end, but most of the rest is less than 20 feet and filled with wood debris, islets, stumps, old log rafts, and shorelines thick with over-hanging brush that provides a labyrinth of excellent cover for largemouth bass to 5 pounds and quite a few in the 1 to 3 pound range. It also holds rock bass, black crappie, bluegill, pumpkinseed, yellow perch and brown bullhead. Kapowsin sometimes comes on in early fall for fly fishermen targeting large rainbow. Open year-round. Champion owns a boat launch site and campground on N. end of lake that may be closed. Bank access on W. side, and there is a resort with rental boats. From Puyallup, go S. on Hwy. 161 about 14 miles then E. on Kapowsin Road to lake.

KREGER'S LAKE (Alder). Private 42-acre lake 1 mile SW of **SILVER LAKE** and 5.5 miles W. of Eatonville. Bass.

LILLY LAKE. 10 acres at 4080 feet elev. in Clearwater Wilderness. Has cutthroat and rainbow. Drains into Clearwater River. Accessible with White River tree farm permit.

LOUISE LAKE (Balch). A small plant of 1000 catchable rainbows provides trout fishing into early June in this 39 acre lake. Also holds largemouth bass and brown bullhead. Lies in a bowl 1.5 miles SE of Steilacoom with access via Old Military Road to 99th Ave. SW to Lake Louise Drive which circles lake.

MASHEL RIVER. Small wild cutthroat are in this Nisqually River tributary. Road from bridge in Eatonville leads upstream for about 7 miles. The **LITTLE MASHEL** joins the Big Mashel 1 mile S. of Eatonville with a road following the stream to its headwaters. Waterfall 1 mile above mouth. This stream contains wild rainbow and cutthroat. Hwy. 161 to Eatonville.

MORGE LAKES. Trio of cutthroat lakes at 4400 feet covering 1.5, 3.0 and 2 acres. Located 4.4 miles NE from National at head of Busywild Creek. Drain to Nisqually River.

MUCK CREEK. A seasonal creek that flows through Roy and then W. for 4 miles inside Fort Lewis to Nisqually River. Often goes dry in late summer. Some sea-run cutthroat in fall. The mouth is a good hole for Nisqually winter steelhead.

MUD LAKE. A private 20 acres bass and panfish lake 4 miles NW of Eatonville and 1 mile W. of Clear Lake. .

NATIONAL MILL POND. Cutthroat in this 9 acre pond adjacent to N. side of Nisqually River at National.

NISQUALLY LAKE. Located on the Fort Lewis military reservation 4 miles NW of Roy. Holds rainbow and varies from 40 to 100 acres.

NISQUALLY RIVER. A horrible testimony to greed. In 1989 this huge river delivered more than 2000 winter steelhead to anglers. Today it's closed and there's no indication that a winter-run season will re-open soon. Nisqually winter-runs, famous for pushing 20 pounds, were practically netted out of existence by tribal gillnetters and poachers. Fishing is now limited from June 1-Nov. 30 and targets mostly Sept. chinook and Nov. chum salmon and fall sea-run cutthroat. There's a little upriver trout fishing, but in summer the large, glacial flow pours off melting glaciers on Mt. Rainier and runs W. like a culvert of liquid concrete to empty into Puget Sound at the Nisqually National Wildlife Refuge N. of Olympia. In late summer and fall the lower-river and delta can deliver pretty good sea-run cutthroat mixed in with the salmon. The Nisqually Indian Reservation is on the river SE of I-5 where tribal netters set gill nets.

OHOP LAKE. A narrow, 2.4 mile-long lake covering 235 acres with a mix of 16,000 April planted rainbows, and a fair summer fishery for largemouth bass, crappie, perch and brown bullhead. Sometimes comes on for larger 'bows in fall. WDFW access, ramp. Lake is 1.5 miles N. of Eatonville. From Hwy. 161 turn N. onto Orville Road which hugs the W. shoreline.

ORTING LAKE (Forest). A marshy 4 acre pond with rock bass about 2 miles NE of Orting. Drains to Puyallup River. Foot access only.

POINT DEFIANCE. For most anglers this is the hub of Tacoma-area saltwater fishing where the high cliff of Point Defiance Park meets the riptides swirling between the Tacoma Narrows and Dalco Pass. A large public multi-lane boat ramp with docks is adjacent to the Vashon Island ferry terminal. Point Defiance Boathouse, just W. of the ramp, has a fishing pier, rental boats, full line of tackle, marine fuel and the latest information. It's possible to walk the beach around the cliffs to the Claybanks and fish for salmon and surf perch, but it's also possible to get stranded here if you don't watch the tides. E. of Point Defiance, two public fishing piers reach out from Ruston Way into Commencement Bay. Good night squid jigging in winter. The Point Defiance area is one of the most productive salmon spots in Puget Sound. It's a concentration point for summer and fall migrants and supports immature blackmouth chinook that provide a popular winter fishery.

PUYALLUP RIVER. A popular but seriously declining steelhead and salmon river flowing from the glaciers on Mount Rainier through Puyallup into Commencement Bay on Tacoma's N. side. Once one of the state's best winter steelhead streams, in 1986 it gave anglers more than 2400 winter-runs. In 1999 only 369 winter-runs were caught, most in Jan. Roads parallel both banks of lower river from Sumner to Tacoma offering easy access. The best stretch for steelhead and salmon is from Sumner upstream to the mouth of the Carbon River at Orting. Good drift boat section and lots of bank access. August provides chinook in silt-colored waters, but by late Sept. into Nov. the river has greatly cleared in time for a fair to good run of hatchery coho. Sea-run cutthroat are available in late summer and fall and there is minor rainbow fishing in upper Puyallup. A Nov.-Dec. chum fishery is gaining popularity. Major tributaries include the White at Sumner, Carbon at Orting and South Prairie Creek. Most of the river upstream from Commencement Bay is followed by paved road. Puyallup Indian Reservation borders the diked, channelized section of river between Puyallup and Tacoma and gillnets are set during run peaks.

PITCHER MT. LAKE. A rainbow lake of 7 acres 1.8 miles W. of **SUMMIT LAKE** on NW side of Pitcher Mt. Elev. is 4650 feet. Drains to Carbon River.

RAINIER SCHOOL POND. Stocked with about 1000 catchable rainbows in April for kids fishing.

RAPJOHN LAKE. Brown and rainbow

Point Defiance area salmon fishing.

trout are in this 56 acre lake, plus large-mouth bass, black crappie, pumpkinseed, yellow perch and brown bullhead. Spring planted with 5000 legal 'bow and a few hundred large triploids. WDFW access, ramp and resort. About 5 miles NW of Eatonville between Hwys. 7 and 161.

ROY LAKE (Muck). A private 26-acre lake 0.5 miles NE of Roy. Holds panfish..

SECUALLITCHEW LAKE. Located on Fort Lewis military reservation 1.5 miles NE of Dupont, covers 81 acres planted with kokanee salmon and rainbow trout. Drains through Edmond Marsh to Puget Sound.

SILVER LAKE. A 138 acre lake heavily spring planted with 30,000 rainbow, and 12,000 brown trout, plus perch, bass, brown bullhead, pumpkinseed and black crappie. Silver furnishes good fishing from May into Sept. A resort on NE shore adjacent to Hwy. 7 provides ramp, dock and shore access. Silver is about 5 miles W. of Eatonville.

SNELL LAKE. A 2 acre rainbow lake 1.4 miles SE from Wilkeson. Drains to Wilkeson Creek.

SOUTH PRAIRIE CREEK. A one-time steelhead producer now offering wild rainbow and cutthroat. Heads in the Three Sisters area SE of Mud Mt. Dam and flows W. to join the Carbon River 2 miles N. of Orting. Crossed by Hwy. 165 SW of Buckley then flows between Hwy. 162 and South Prairie-Carbon River Rd. SW to Carbon River confluence.

SPANAWAY LAKE A popular year-round lake 0.5 miles W. of Spanaway on Hwy. 7 about 10 miles S. of Tacoma. Spring stocked with 18,000 catchable rainbows plus several hundred large triploids that really attract a crowd in April and May. A fry plant of 26,000 rainbows provides seed for next year. In summer, anglers target perch, smallmouth and largemouth bass, brown bullhead, pumpkinseed, and crappie. Covers 262 acres. County park at NE end provides shore fishing access, ramp and a boathouse. Drains to Spanaway Creek to Clover Creek into Steilacoom Lake.

STEILACOOM LAKE. A year-around lake with a few large rainbow, largemouth bass, rock bass, cutthroat and brown bullhead.

Usually poor fishing. Steilacoom is 313 acres 3 miles E. of Steilacoom. Interlaken Drive SW bridges the lake in the middle.

STUCK RIVER (See White River).

SUNSET LAKE. An artificial lake of 7.7 acres 1.5 miles E. of Wilkeson. It has received rainbow plants. Drains to Sunset and South Prairie creeks.

SURPRISE LAKE. 1.5 miles E. of Milton adjacent to the S. side of Hwy. 514. 9th St. NW parallels the W. shore. Surprise is 30 acres, planted with rainbow, bass and panfish. Best in May and June.

TANWAX LAKE. A 173 acre lake heavily stocked in May with 28,000 catchable rainbows, including a couple of hundred triploids, plus largemouth bass, perch, pumpkinseed, crappie, brown bullhead. The lake provides a lot of the planted rainbow in May and June, and produces mostly warm water species during mid summer. Rainbows, some surprisingly large, stir the surface in fall. WDFW ramp and access, plus two resorts with dock and boat rentals. Outlet crosses Hwy. 161 about 1 mile N. of Clear Lake.

TAPPS LAKE. At 2296 acres this White River diversion impoundment flooded a group of 7 small lakes to become the largest lake in Pierce County. In the summer it's a good looking, cold water lake with numerous inlets and irregular shoreline that, unfortunately, rarely lives up to the potential of its appearance. Much of the reason goes to the dramatic draw downs that occur each winter leaving acres of lake floor dry. By summer, the lake is at full pool. A few rainbow trout are caught, but most fishermen concentrate on smallmouth and largemouth bass, rock bass, perch, crappie, and bluegill. The lake has also been stocked with sterile tiger muskies which, if they survive, will contribute to the fishery about 2005. Lots of jet ski and play boat activity in the main lake in summer. The reservoir is perched on the ridge 3 miles NE of Sumner and N. of Bonney Lake off Hwy. 410.

TULE LAKE. A 31 acre rainbow lake 1.5 miles SE of **HARTS LAKE**. Largemouth bass, black crappie, yellow perch and brown bullhead. Road from McKenna leads SE about 7 miles to E. shore, passing Harts Lake.

VOIGHT CREEK. Small Carbon River tributary joining at Orting. Fair for wild cutthroat. A road leaves Hwy. 162 at Crocker 2 miles E. of Orting and follows the creek upstream for about 11 miles to junction with McGuire Creek.

WAPATO LAKE. Bring the kids, this 28 acre juvenile-only lake is stocked with about 3500 catchable rainbows in Mar. and Apr. and also holds pumpkinseed and brown bullhead catfish. Open year-round. Located in Tacoma park. Alaska Street runs along W. shore.

WAUGHOP LAKE (Mud). A marshy 21.7 acre lake in Fort Steilacoom Park planted Mar-May with 2800 catchable plus 8000 fry rainbows. Also, largemouth bass, crappie, perch, and brown bullhead catfish. Sometimes stocked in Oct.-Nov. with adult coho. Open year-round, 1.5 miles E. of Steilacoom. Drains to Puget Sound.

WEST LAKE (Hidden Lake). Rainbows in this 6 acre lake 7 miles NE of National at 4600 feet. Drains to South Puyallup River.

WHITE RIVER (Stuck). Flowing from a glacier on Mount Rainier along Hwy. 410 through Mud Mountain Dam, between Enumclaw and Buckley into the Puyallup River at Sumner where most folks call it the Stuck. A horrible fishing bet. The milky glacial color for which the river is named restricts summer fishing in the White which is the only season it's open in the upper reaches. This river once flowed into the Green River, but was rerouted into the Puyallup and dammed. That bit of manipulation pretty well finished off the river's potential for steelhead and salmon. Today, the river serves as the boundary between Pierce and King Counties for much of its length. The lower reaches offer a few winter steelhead and the hole at the mouth of

the Puyallup is a pretty fair salmon and steelhead holding area. The upper river, along Hwy. 410 has whitefish, cutthroat, (protected) Dolly Varden and a few rainbow. Unfortunately for anglers, just as the first good freezes of fall stop the glacial silt melt and allows the river to run clear (which it does all winter) the June-Oct. fishing season ends. About 3 miles SE of Greenwater (see King County, **GREENWATER RIVER**), on Hwy. 410 turn SW onto FS 74, a paved road, which crosses the White and follows the West Fork White River 11 miles ending about 1 mile from MRNP boundary. From either end of FS 74 turn E. on graveled FS 75 and switch back into the mountains to FS 7530 which ends at **MULE LAKE** and **LONESOME LAKE**, a pair of small lakes near 5000 ft. elev. with poor cutthroat and brook trout fishing. Vehicle accessible campground at Lonesome Lake. FS 75 loops into FS 74.

WHITMAN LAKE. 29.6 acres planted with 1200 rainbows in Mar. plus largemouth bass, pumpkinseed, yellow perch and brown bullhead. The largest of the Benbow Lakes group .Small WDFW access, ramp. Open year-round, drains to Tanwax Creek. 6.5 miles N. of Eatonville.

Pierce County Resorts

American Lake: Bill's Boathouse, 360-588-2594.

Puget Sound: Narrows Marina, 253-564-4222. Point Defiance Boathouse, 253-591-5325.

Spanaway Lake: Spanaway Lake Park Boathouse, 253-531-0555.

Silver Lake: Henley's Silver Lake Resort, 360-832-3580.

Tanwax Lake: Rainbow Resort, 360-879-5115.

San Juan County

WDFW Region 4

Washington Department of Fish and Wildlife, 16018 Mill Creek Blvd., Mill Creek, WA 98012. Phone 425-775-1311.

San Juan County is spread across 172 land miles all of it on islands in North Puget Sound which makes it the smallest county in the state, and a tough prospect for freshwater fishermen. The three largest islands are Orcas, San Juan and Lopez, but there are over 400 islands within the county which is one of the most popular recreation and vacation destinations in Washington.

The islands feature rocky, abrupt shorelines, rising to a high point at the 2,409-foot summit of Orcas Island's Mt. Constitution. A number of hills climb 1000 feet above sea level, but most of the land is flat or gently rolling.

Most of the islands have little or no surface water, and streams are intermittent. Largest lake is Mountain Lake on Orcas Island, but several smaller lakes are exceptionally high in nutrients are provide unexpectedly large trout or bass. Little Egg Lake is famous for fat trout. Saltwater fishing is good especially for salmon, ling cod and rockfish. Some of the state's largest feeder chinook (blackmouth) are caught at N. end of San Juan and off Orcas Island. Some of the largest lakes, especially on San Juan and Orcas Island are closed to the public, either through private ownership or water source restrictions.

While summers in the Olympic Mountain rain shadow are fairly dry, winter's can be moderately wet. Annual rainfall on the S. shore of Orcas Island is 28.77 inches, and the average temperature is 50 degrees.

All access from the mainland is by ferry, private boat or small plane. Washington State Ferry service from Anacortes is the popular route.

CASCADE LAKE. Located on Orcas Island 3.5 miles SE of East Sound in popular Moran State Park this 171 acre lake is stocked with cutthroat, rainbow and kokanee. May is prime for rainbow and cutthroat and a kokanee bite develops at mid summer. Some lunker cutthroat caught here each year. Rental boats at park. Public boat launch.

EGG LAKE. A 7 acre lake on NE end of San Juan Island annually stocked with 1000 rainbow, and largemouth bass are present. Park with boat launch adjacent to road on W. shore.

HUMMEL LAKE. A fertile 36 acre lake on N. Lopez Island. Hummel produces some exceptionally nice rainbow. 14 inchers are common. Annually stocked with about 1500 catchable rainbows that enjoy quick growth in the rich water. Lake also offers largemouth bass and bluegill Low water can be

a problem during dry years. Take road from ferry landing about 3 miles to lake shore. Public access on N. shore.

HUNTER BAY. A county park provides beach access on Lopez Island. Surf smelt raking, plus flounder fishing. DNR beach just E. of boat ramp sometimes the best smelt spot.

KILLEBREW LAKE. A 13 acre Orcas Island Lake with a public launch and fishing for largemouth bass and bluegill. A few rainbow trout. From Orcas drive Dolphin Bay Rd. for about 4 miles. Drains to Grindstone Harbor.

MOUNTAIN LAKE. A 198 acre year-round Orcas Island lake that comes on strong in June, July and September. It holds cutthroat, brook trout and kokanee. Located 4.4 miles SE of East Sound on Orcas Island in Moran State Park. Campground and

Black rockfish may be caught on light tackle.

rental boats on lake. Small boats may be launched from SW shore. Mountain Lake serves as water supply for communities of Doe Bay and Olga.

SALTWATER. The best fishing recreation in this freshwater-short county is in salt-water. Resident blackmouth chinook and seasonal runs of ocean chinook, coho, and pinks are available throughout the county, especially off the points on San Juan and Orcas islands. Good shrimp fishing, and year-round non commercial crab zones are rebuilding populations of Dungeness crabs at Mud Bay and Fisherman Bay on Lopez Island, Blind Bay on Shaw Island, Deer Harbor on Orcas and Garrison Bay on San Juan Island. Popular clam beaches are at Spencer Spit State Park and English Camp at Garrison Bay on San Juan. Dock fishing for pile and striped perch near ferry docks and at Friday Harbor marina. Many beaches also offer surf smelt raking.

SPORTSMAN'S LAKE. A shallow 66 acre lake 3.5 miles NW of Friday Harbor on San Juan Island. This spring-fed lake is a top largemouth bass producer. Open year-round, best in fall when water level retreats from brushy shoreline. WDFW launch on N. side.

TWIN LAKES. A pair of 8 and 3 acre lakes 3500 feet by trail N. of Mountain Lake on Orcas Island. Rainbow and cutthroat. Some shore fishing.

San Juan County Resorts

Cascade Lake: Moran State Park, Eastsound, WA. 360-376-2326.

Skagit County
WDFW Region 4
Washington Department of Fish and Wildlife, 16018 Mill Creek Blvd., Mill Creek, WA 98012. Phone 425-775-1311.

Stretching over 1775 square miles between the saltwater in Rosario Strait and the jagged crest of the north Cascade Mountains, the 22nd largest county in Washington runs from flat agricultural sloughs dividing tulip fields through foothill clear-cuts to rugged mountains glistening with remote rarely fished alpine lakes. Through the center runs the Skagit River, one of the largest rivers in Washington and once a nationally lauded steelhead and salmon river. The Sauk River, another storied anadromous fish producer, flows N-S wide and fast along the base of the mountains, pouring into the Skagit at Rockport at a spot appropriately named Howard Miller Steelhead Park. The confluence is one of the best steelhead and salmon fishing holes on the river.

More than 280 lakes offer trout and warm-water fish, a good number of them in the broad delta that covers much of the SW county along I-5. The largest lake is man-made Shannon Reservoir on the Baker River near Concrete.

Nearly three- fourths of Skagit County is mountainous. High point 9200 foot Mount Buckner is on the Cascade crest at the Chelan County border in North Cascades National Park. Many peaks rise to more than 8000 feet. E. of the I-5 corridor there is little residential development. Much of this heavily forested land is within vast Mt. Baker-Snoqualmie National Forest, North Cascades National Park and Glacier Peak Wilderness.

The alpine lakes in the toothy crags of E. Skagit County are among the most scenic anywhere, and most rarely see a fisherman. Compared to the often congested Alpine Lakes Wilderness Area between Stevens and Snoqualmie passes this region is absolutely lonesome.

Part of the reason is the steepness and lack of trails. Typically major trails follow large river and creek valley floors to smaller trails that climb quickly, sometimes with switchbacks, to beautiful top-of-the-world lakes at 6500 to 8000 feet. Many other lakes are reached by bushwhacking cross country from established trails or on unofficial siwash trails. USGS contour maps are critical to enjoying the North Cascade high country. Many of the peaks are mantled with snow year-round, and most lakes are iced over until July. Snow falls every month.

The Skagit River drains most of the county and is fed by major tributaries Sauk and lower Suiattle rivers. The Samish River drains a small NW area . The Cascade River is an almost unheard of trout stream that flows W. from the edge of the Glacier Peak Wilderness, into the Skagit at Marblemount. A good Forest Service road follows it almost to the headwaters. All have seen much better fishing days, but are still notable producers of anadromous trout and salmon. This is also one of the few areas in the state where it is still legal to fish for and keep Dolly Varden char, although it's wise to check annual regs.

The weather is typical of Puget Sound's maritime climate although it tends to rain and snow a lot more in the foothills surrounding the Skagit than in the rain shadow of the Olympic Mountain that protects the coast. Annual precipitation at Anacortes is 26 inches. Eighty-five miles E. at Concrete on the Skagit, it rains and snows 64.40 inches. The average annual temperature is 51 degrees creating mild winters and summers with summer fishing temperatures in the 60s and 70s.

There are two primary routes into the county: I-5 runs N-S and Hwy. 20/North

Cascades Scenic Route parallels the Skagit River. The two highways meet at Burlington N. of Mount Vernon. Hwy. 530 winds N. from Arlington to follow the Sauk River. A favorite trout route for fishermen is Hwy. 9 a N-S link connecting some of the county's best freshwater lakes.

ALDER CREEK. Tributary to the Skagit River crossed by Hwy. 20 about 1.5 miles E. of Hamilton. Marginal cutthroat fishing.

ARROWHEAD LAKE. A seldom-fished 14.9 acre mountain lake at 4500 feet 9.5 miles SE from Marblemount. Has rainbows. Drains to Cascade River.

BACON CREEK. Enters the Skagit 5 miles NE of Marblemount at a popular winter steelhead hole. Bacon is a popular fly fishing stream for native rainbow, Dolly Varden and some brookies in top stretches. FS Rd. 1060 leaves Hwy. 20 and follows the stream N. for 5 miles and into Whatcom County. Picnic area at creek's mouth.

BASIN LAKE. A 2.5 acre rainbow pond 8 miles SE of Marblemount at 4200 feet. Drains to Cascade River. May winter kill.

BEAR CREEK. A small creek that flows into **SHANNON LAKE** from the W. at the Bear Creek power house, about 6 miles N. of Concrete on the Baker Lake Road. Produces small cutthroat and rainbow early in the season.

BEAR LAKE. 2 acre lake at 3900 feet at headwaters of Irene Creek. Plants of cutthroat. Route is E. from Marblemount across the Skagit and E. up Cascade River Rd. about 8 miles to Marble Creek campground. Cross the Cascade look for an old trail to lake.

BEAVER LAKE. A warm-water species lake, with some cutthroat. Covers 73 acres and is fed by **CLEAR LAKE** Best fishing is for largemouth bass, crappie, perch, and brown bullhead. WDFW boat launch and access on W. shore. Take Hwy. 9 1 mile SE of village of Clear Lake and turn E. along S. end of Clear Lake to Beaver Lake

BIG LAKE. Plenty of variety is offered in Big, a 545 acre year-round lake 5 miles SE of Mt. Vernon. Hwy. 9 skirts the lake's E. shore. A public access is located on W. side, and resort facilities are available. Fish include some rainbow, cutthroat, lots of largemouth bass, perch, brown bullhead and crappie. Big lake is best known for large bass. Best in the spring and early summer, but holds up well through the warmer months.

BOULDER LAKE. Rainbow are in this 55 acre mountain lake 13.5 miles NE of Darrington on SW flank of Hurricane Peak at 5000 feet. FS Rd. 2640 goes to the lake, but may be gated. Drains to Suiattle River.

BULLAR LAKE. A 2 acre pond planted with rainbow, at 3500 feet 4.5 miles SE of Marblemount. Drains to Cascade River.

CAMPBELL LAKE. A popular 410-acre, shallow warm-water fishery on Fidalgo Island, 5 miles S. of Anacortes on Hwy. 20. Campbell holds largemouth bass, perch, bullhead catfish, and a few rainbow. Open year-round, slot limit on bass. Some disabled facilities. Resort, WDFW public access, launch on N. side. Campbell is fed by **ERIE LAKE**.

CANNERY LAKE. Perch and bullhead catfish are in this 18 acre lake 3 miles W. of Anacortes adjacent to beach at Shannon Point. Drains to saltwater in Guemes Channel.

CAREYS LAKE. Cutthroat, some rainbow in this 4 acre lake 1 mile NE of Hamilton off Hwy.20. Drains to Hamilton Slough.

CASCADE RIVER. A little known mountain river with steelhead, rainbow, cutthroat, Dolly Varden, and salmon. The Cascade flows into the Skagit at Marblemount. FS campgrounds at Marble Creek and Mineral Park. WDFW hatchery, boat launch at Marblemount. Winter and summer steelhead have been planted in Cascade River providing catches of about a dozen summer-runs in October and 135 winter-runs in Nov.-Jan.   On the E. side of Marblemount, from Hwy. 20 cross the Skagit River bridge and continue E. upstream on river road for about 20 miles to within 2 miles of Cascade Pass on Cascade Crest. Trail 744 continues into North Cascade National Park and the upper Stehekin River in Chelan County.

CASKEY LAKE. A private 5 acre brook trout, rainbow lake and brown bullhead lake 6 miles S. of Rockport on W. side of Sauk River.

CAVANAUGH LAKE. This 844 acre year-round lake is often a slow starter, but delivers fine late summer and fall fishing for rainbow, cutthroat, kokanee salmon, a few brookies and largemouth bass. Good fishing in August, but expect heavy competition from play boaters. The lake has a public access, ramp on SE shore. Cavanaugh is 10 miles NE of Arlington below Frailey Mt. From Hwy. 530 NE of Arlington at Oso turn N. on Lake Cavanaugh Rd. and continue 5 miles to lake. From Hwy. 9 at Pilchuck, turn NE on 44th Ave. NE/Granstrom Rd. and continue N and E. 14 miles up Pilchuck Creek to lake.

CLEAR LAKE. 223 acres 3 miles S. of Sedro Woolley at Clear Lake. Stocked in April with about 5000 rainbow, plus largemouth bass, perch, crappie, pumpkinseed panfish and bullhead catfish. Open year round. WDFW access, ramp on the N. shore. Drains to **BEAVER LAKE**.

CLIFF LAKE. Remote 5 acre rainbow trout lake at 4800 feet about 12 miles from Marblemount. Drains to Big Creek which crosses the Suiattle River Rd.

CRANBERRY LAKE(Little). A shallow, hour-glass shaped 27-acre residential lake on the SW. side of Anacortes. Stocked with largemouth bass.

CUB LAKE. A high mountain 11-acre rainbow lake at 5400 feet elev. about 25 miles E. from Darrington in Glacier Peak Wilderness. Drains to **ITSWOOT LAKE** and Sulphur Creek.

CYCLONE LAKE. Golden and rainbow trout have been stocked in Cyclone's 55.5 acres. Elev. is 5300 feet ll.5 miles SE from Marblemount at head of Found Creek on NE side of spectacular Snowking Mt. Drains to Cascade River.

DAVIS SLOUGH. Cutthroat and rainbow are in this 7 acre slough adjacent to the S. side of Hwy. 20 about 1.8 miles E. of Hamilton. Closed for rearing steelhead smolts.

DAY CREEK. Feeds into the Skagit River E. of Sedro Woolley S. of Lyman. Sea-run cutthroat, a few steelhead. Road from S. side of the Skagit parallels Day Creek high on the ridge on W. side upstream to **DAY LAKE**, about 7 miles, with a rough section about halfway at Rocky Canyon. From Hwy. 9 bridge S. of Sedro Woolley, turn E. on South Skagit Rd. to Day Creek Rd.

DAY LAKE. Best route to this 136 acre lake is from Oso on Hwy. 530 along the Stillaguamish River 4 miles NW to Lake Cavanaugh, then about 8 miles N. to Day Lake. The lake has rainbow and brookies. Beaver ponds at the head of the lake offer brookies.

DEVILS LAKE. A private brook trout lake of 31 acres at 826 feet elev. about 6 miles SE of Mt. Vernon. No access. Outlet, Devils Creek, also contains brookies and a few cutthroat, but it is tough brushy fishing.

ENJAR LAKE. Golden and cutthroat trout share these 12 acres 1.5 miles N. of Snowking Mt. at 4300 feet and 3 miles E. of **SLIDE LAKE** which is 8 miles SE from Marblemount. A faint trail leads about 2 miles up Slide Creek to Enjar.

ERIE LAKE. A heavily stocked shallow, 111-acre trout and largemouth bass lake on Fidalgo Island 2 miles SW of Anacortes. Stocked with 14,000 catchable rainbows plus another 500 large triploid rainbows. Usually a hot spot on opening weekend. SE of Anacortes turn S. on Hwy. 20, go about 1.5 miles then W. on Campbell Lake Rd., continuing past **CAMPBELL LAKE** about 1.5 miles, to lake shore.

EVERETT LAKE. An 8 acre lake 1 mile NE of Concrete, draining into Everett Creek and **SHANNON LAKE**. Everett has rainbow, brookies and cutthroat. Access from Baker Dam Rd.

FALLS LAKE. A pair of mountain lakes 5.4 miles S. of Marblemount. The lower lake covers 60.4 acres at 4200 feet elevation and Upper Falls, at 4500 feet, is 22.4 acres. Both have been stocked with rainbow. Drain to **JORDAN CREEK** and **CASCADE RIVER**. A rough road follows Jordan Creek to Falls Lakes outlet.

FINNEY CREEK. Finney Creek flows into the S. side of the Skagit River about 1 mile upstream from Birdsview. Fair for rainbow in July and August. Carries a few summer steelhead. At Concrete cross Skagit River on Dalles Bridge then drive downstream 8.5 miles cross Finney Creek then SE turn up Finney Creek Road/FS 17 which continues 7 miles. To follow the Upper Finney Creek pickup FS 17 which intersects S.

Granite Lake grayling.

Skagit Rd. S. of Rockport. FS 17 follows the creek and leads to a network of mountain roads.

FLY LAKE. A 2 acre rainbow planted pond at 4000 feet, 7.4 miles SE of Marblemount. Drains to Irene Creek S. of Marble Creek Campground on Cascade River.

FLUME CREEK PONDS. Series of beaver ponds 5 miles S. of Rockport on W. side of the Sauk River. Ponds total 4 acres, produce brook trout in April and May. Route is up Flume Creek 1.5 miles from road on W. side of the Sauk.

FRIDAY CREEK. Joins the Samish River just above Old Hwy. 99 bridge. Creek supports sea-run cutthroat, rainbow and steelhead. Friday Creek drains from **SAMISH LAKE**.

GEE POINT LAKE. A 4 acre rainbow lake at 4100 feet elev. 8.5 miles SE of Concrete. **LITTLE GEE**, 1.5 acres, lies 4750 feet SE. Lakes drain to Skagit River. On S. side of Skagit River follow FS 17 SW from Concrete-Sauk Valley Rd. up Finney Creek then N. on FS 1720 to Little Gee Lake and trailhead to Gee Point Lake.

GRANDY LAKE. A 56 acre roadside cutthroat and largemouth bass lake that does well for fly fishermen in spring and fall. The cutts are in the 9-inch range. From Hwy.

20 E. of Hamilton turn N. up Baker Lake Hwy/FS 11 about 4 miles to lake. County park and small boat launch on N. shore.

GRANITE LAKES. Big Granite is one of the few grayling lakes in Washington state. Catch and release. A deep, 144 acre lake at 5000 feet at head of Boulder Creek about 7 miles SE of Marblemount at N. edge of Glacier Peak Wilderness. Granite Lakes No. 1, 2 and 3 are 4, 7 and 38 acres. All hold cutthroat and rainbow. From WDFW hatchery follow rough road upstream along S. bank of Cascade River to Boulder Creek. Hike up E. side of main creek to Big Granite Lake a steep 0.5 mile root and rock route.

HAWKINS LAKE. A 7 acre rainbow lake at 3500 feet 9.4 miles NE of Hwy. 530 at Oso. Drains to Deer Creek.

HEART LAKE (Hart). A well-stocked rainbow lake of 61 acres about 2 miles S. of Anacortes. An opening day honey hole where anglers target about 12,000 stocked rainbows, some weighing a pound or more. From downtown Anacortes turn S. on Heart Lake Road to access on E. shore.

HILT LAKE. A marshy 3 acres with brookies. Cross Skagit River at Rockport, drive S. on Hwy. 530 for 1.5 miles then E. and S. on FS 16 for about 5 miles to power line road near N. end of lake.

JACKMAN CREEK. Best fishing in this Skagit River tributary is in July and August for cutthroat. Excellent winter steelhead drift at creek's mouth. Upper trout water is reached from Hwy. 20. About 2 miles E. of Concrete turn NE up FS 14 which follows the creek several miles upstream. Wild cutthroat are reported in creek upstream from FS 14 bridge.

JORDAN CREEK. Enters Cascade River about 0.5 miles above Skagit River confluence at Marblemount at WDFW hatchery. Jordan is best in mid-summer and fall for small wild cutthroat and rainbow. A logging road on the creek's E. bank leads upstream for 4 miles to within 0.5 miles of **FALLS LAKE**. The 60 acre lake lies at 4200 feet elevation and drains into Jordan Creek via a cascading outlet. Both the lower lake and the upper (22 acre) lake offer cutthroat.

JORDAN LAKES. The lower lake, 4150 foot elev. is 59 acres. Upper Jordan covers 65 acres at 4550 feet about 2300 feet E. of the lower lake. Both lakes planted with cutthroat. Trail from end of logging road goes 4 miles up Jordan Creek to L. Jordan Lake.

JOSEPHINE LAKES. The upper lake covers 3 acres. Lower Josephine is a 2 acre pond. Upper lake has brookies, lower lake cutthroat. Drive 5 miles NE of Hamilton on Mt. Josephine Rd. to 3000 feet elev. Tough drive and tougher 0.4 mile hike from road end E. to lake.

LA RUSH LAKE. Boggy 3 acres planted with rainbows 7.4 miles SE of Marblemount at 3200 feet. Drains to Cascade River.

LIZARD LAKE. Brookies are in this 2 acre pond 2.8 miles N. of Blanchard.

LILY LAKE, also 2 acres, lies 2200 feet S. from Lizard. The lakes drain into Oyster Creek to Samish Bay.

LOUISE LAKE. (White Lake). A 6 acre rainbow lake at 5000 feet S. of Illabot Peak about 8.7 miles S. of Marblemount. Drains to White Creek then into Sauk River S. of county park campground.

MARTIN LAKE. Rainbow are in this 10 acre lake 5 miles S. of Marblemount at 4650 feet. Drains to Skagit River.

McMURRAY LAKE. Good spring and early summer fishing in this popular 160 acre lake for rainbow and cutthroat, and summer-long largemouth, smallmouth, perch and crappie action. Planted with 17,000 rainbows in April. Lots of trout in the half to three-quarter pound range. Bass up to 8 pounds. WDFW ramp and access on S. shore and resort on N. end. Hwy. 9 hits the E. shore about 9 miles NW of Arlington.

MINKLER LAKE. A narrow, 10-foot deep slough-like 37 acre lake with cutthroat and largemouth bass adjacent to Hwy. 20 about 3.5 miles E. of Sedro Woolley.

MUD LAKE. 8 acre largemouth bass, crappie, perch and bullhead catfish lake in the community of Clear Lake.

NOOKACHAMPS CREEK. Flows N. from Big Lake about 6 miles to the Skagit River near Burlington. The E. Fork of creek enters main creek from the E. near community of Clear Lake. Nookachamps provides small wild rainbow and cutthroat. Roads follow and cross creek most of its length.

NOOKSACK RIVER SOUTH FORK. July and August are good months to tackle this stream's wild rainbow. Route is NW from Hwy. 20 at Hamilton about 6 miles up Jones Creek through Scott logging works, then E. to follow Nooksack 12 miles upstream nearly to Whatcom County line. Trails from this point head E. up Wanlick Creek 3 miles, and N. along S. Fork to its headwaters at **ELBOW LAKE**. Road access often restricted on the logging road. Another route to upper South Fork is via Rocky Creek road which leaves Baker River road just below Baker Dam in Whatcom County.

NEORI LAKE. Rainbows are in this remote 13 acre mountain lake at 4400 feet elev. about 12 miles SE of Marblemount. Drains to Cascade River.

PASS LAKE. Adjacent to Hwy. 20 this 99-acre lake is one of western Washington's premier fly fishing only lakes. Pass is at the N. end of Deception Pass Bridge 6 miles S. of Anacortes. Catch-and-release regulations have developed a solid fishery for exceptionally large rainbows, browns and cutthroat to 28 inches. Most trout are in the 15 inch range. Atlantic salmon have been stocked but success has been marginal. Open year round and offer excellent success in early spring, fall and sometimes during the winter when hatches develop. Boat launch off Hwy. 20, and campsites in Deception State Park. No gasoline outboard motors.

PHEBE LAKE. Located near center of Cypress Island. Phebe, at 15 acres, is the largest of 3 adjoining lakes. Has cutthroat, rainbow and kokanee. From Strawberry Bay on the island's W. flank walk trail 1 mile.

PILCHUCK CREEK. Planted with winter steelhead, some wild cutts and rainbow. It heads N. of **CAVANAUGH LAKE.** From Hwy. 9 at Pilchuck turn NE onto 44th Ave. NE/Grandstrom Rd. and continue along creek. At Lake Cavanaugh Rd. bear E. and continue upstream.

PRAIRIE LAKES. Lower Prairie covers 5 acres and Upper Prairie 3 acres. The lakes lie at 1500 and 1600 feet elev. 8.5 miles NE of Darrington on slopes of Prairie Mt. Stocked with rainbow and brookies. From N. side of Darrington, turn E. on Sauk Prairie Rd. and continue on logging road to lakes. Drain to Suiattle River.

SALTWATER. The W. side of Skagit County has several developed saltwater fishing opportunities. **CAP SANTE MARINA** and **SKYLINE MARINA** W. of Anacortes on Fidalgo Island offer jigging for surf smelt during the winter. **FIDALGO BAY** and **MARCH POINT** have year-round surf smelt raking opportunities east of the Shell Oil pier and N. of the railroad bridge. Best smelt jigging in this area is on the Deception Pass State Park pier at Cornet Bay. Good crabbing in this area. **LACONNER,** at the S. end of **SWINOMISH CHANNEL** offers fair surf smelt jigging in Oct.-March. Smelt runs have fallen dramatically at LaConner. Annual smelt derby in February. Excellent crabbing in **SKAGIT, FIDALGO, SAMISH AND PADILLA BAYS AND MARCH POINT.** E. March Point has decent clam digging, and the E. shore of Padilla Bay has oysters. There's fishing piers at Anacortes and Bowman's Bay at Deception Pass State Park, and LaConner Marina. Boat launches to Puget Sound salmon and bottomfish at Washington Park W. of Anacortes, Cap Sante and Skyline marinas, LaConner and Bayview. Shore fishing at Deception Pass State Park, and Washington Park.

SAMISH RIVER. A good sea-run cutthroat, fair salmon, and poor steelhead river. This small stream produces about 50 winter steelhead in Dec. and Jan., sea-run cutthroat in summer and fall and fall runs of hatchery chinook, chum, and coho salmon. Beginning in August a fishable run of chinook comes in, followed by a fair Octo-

Lower Granite Lake, Upper Granite Lake at right.

ber run of coho and a poor run of November chums. Easily waded except in lower reaches where it enters Samish Bay at Edison. This lower portion is excellent for cutts in late summer and fall. Sea-run cutthroat also in upper reaches. Most popular steelheading area is from old Hwy. 99 downstream for about 3 miles. The Samish is bridged below Hwy. 99 at Allen, Thomas Road, Farm to Market Road and at Edison. One mile N. of Hwy. 99 bridge a road turns E. and N. to follow river to its headwaters in Whatcom County. WDFW salmon hatchery.

SAUK RIVER LOWER. A large powerful glacial tributary flowing into the Skagit River at Rockport at the jct. of Hwy. 530 and Hwy. 20. The Sauk offers winter and summer steelhead, Dolly Varden, sea-run cutthroat, spring and a troubled fall chinook and coho salmon. Salmon fishing is usually closed. Winter steelheading is best in February. A legendary March run of large natives that provided a great catch-and-release fishery, has been protected by seasonal closures. A very poor summer steelhead fishery almost develops in late summer. Dolly Varden fishing can be very good, especially in the fall during the salmon run. There's a 20-inch minimum if you're fishing Dollies for dinner. Can be fished from boat or bank. It's a powerful river, though and requires some drift boating skill. Boat fishing is best below the Hwy. 530 bridge that crosses the Sauk N. of Darrington, just above the mouth of the Suiattle. Hwy. 530 tracks the E. bank 11 miles to the Skagit at Rockport. The Concrete-Sauk Valley Road runs along the W. side. Lots of primitive camping, FS camps at Clear Creek and Bedal. County campground at Flume Creek, and major campground at Steelhead Park in Rockport.

SHANNON LAKE. A lanky kokanee salmon lake, formed by a power generating dam on Baker River just N. of Concrete. The hour-glass shaped reservoir covers 2148 acres and is fed by Rocky, Sulpher, Bear, Thunder, Everett and Three Mile Creeks, plus the Baker. Shannon holds rainbow, Dolly Varden, cutthroat, silver and sockeye salmon, but is most heavily fished by leaded line trollers looking for the lake's big population of small kokanee. Annually planted with 250,000 kokanee fry. Kokanee fishing is predictably good beginning in May and to protect the lake's run of sockeye, there is a 6 inch minimum and 18 inch maximum. Best trout fishing is near the

tributary creeks. Dolly Varden are protected. A difficult boat launch is near mouth of Everett Creek on SE. side of lake. From Hwy. 20 about 0.4 miles E. of Baker River bridge at Concrete turn N. on Baker River Rd. which goes to the boat launch and continues along E. shore for approximately 8 miles, then crosses the narrow neck dividing Shannon and Baker Lake in Whatcom County.

SAUK LAKE. A 10-acre alpine bowl at 4025 feet elev. in an open, rocky basin below the cock's-comb crest of Sauk Mt. Planted with rainbows and cutthroat. The lake is about 3 miles N. of Rockport. From Rockport State Park go N. on FS 1030, a steep, switchback gravel road to Sauk Mt. trailhead. Trail 613 crosses the ridge to the lake. Drains to Bark Creek.

SHELF LAKE. A 3.5 acre mountain lake with rainbow. Elev. is 4050 about 9 miles NE from Oso and 1100 feet SW from **HAWKINS LAKE.** Drains to Deer Creek.

SIXTEEN LAKE. An excellent opening day prospect, and good May fishery for 7000 planted cutthroat and rainbow. This 42 acre lake is known for producing fat fish, many in the .75 pound range. WDFW access, launch on W. From I-5 at Conway, go E. on Hwy. 534 about 2 miles. WDFW sign marks the turnoff N. for 0.4 miles to the lake.

SKAGIT RIVER. Once a world-celebrated steelhead and chinook salmon producer, the powerful Skagit River has not escaped the problems crippling all West Side rivers at the turn of the century. It is still an important anadromous fish producer, but winter steelhead catches have fallen from years of upwards of 35,000 fish caught to the less than 1300 caught in 2000. While comparatively low, those numbers rank the Skagit 4th behind the Cowlitz, Bogachiel and Skykomish. Numbers are even worse for salmon, especially the once plentiful and coveted 50 to 70 pound spring chinook. That season has been closed for years. The Skagit heads in Canada as a trout river and is blocked in Whatcom County by 3 Seattle power dams, all without fish ladders. It enters Skagit County 2 miles downstream from Newhalem alongside Hwy. 20 and flows into Skagit Bay 2 miles S. of LaConner. The South Fork empties into same bay at Milltown on Skagit-Snohomish County line. The river is annually planted with about 400,000 winter-runs and 21,000 summer-run smolts. Salmon plants number in the millions, and include spring, summer and fall runs of chinook, fall coho, chums and odd-numbered year runs of pink (humpy) salmon, and a few sockeye. Fishing for pinks is very popular in late Aug. and Sept. and chums are gaining popularity as a Nov.-Dec. target of opportunity. Sea-run cutthroat and Dolly Varden are common throughout the river below Sedro Woolley, especially in late summer and fall near the mouth. Both of these light-weight game fish still provide very good fishing. The minimum size on Dollies, however, is 20 inches. The lower North Fork is popular, in season, for large chinook, silvers, chums and humpies in late summer. When there's a salmon season Young's bar near Mount Vernon resembles a picket fence of plunking rods. Access is no problem. Good roads roughly parallel both banks from I-5 to Marblemount, and Hwy. 20 continues along the N. bank to the first dams. Because it's such a wide, deep powerful river most anglers prefer fishing from boats, but there's plenty of bank casting room and bank fishing can be very productive, especially in known salmon and steelhead stacking holes. Plunking is most popular in the lower river, especially from I-5 down, and drifting bait or plug fishing dominates the water from Rockport upriver. Professional guides work the Skagit daily. Contact through local sporting goods dealers. Four major tributary rivers feed the Skagit; Baker, Suiattle, Sauk and Cascade, plus dozens of large streams and creeks that are used for wild fish spawning.

SKARO LAKE. 12 acre alpine lake surrounded by cliffs. Rainbow plants. Elev. 4450 feet about 12 miles SE of Marblemount .05 mile SW of Found Lake. Drains to upper Cascade River.

SLIDE LAKE. A short hike leads to the rainbows in this 37 acre mountain lake at 3300 feet. Lake is 8 miles SE of Marblemount and drains to Illabot Cr. From Hwy. 530 just S. of Rockport, turn E. on FS 16 . At end of road, FS Trail 635 continues 1 mile to lake.

SNOW KING LAKE. A picturesque 26.3 acre mountain lake with rainbows at 4600 feet about 13 miles SE of Marblemount and NE of the glaciers on Snowking Mt. Fed by **CYCLONE LAKE.** Drains to Found Creek and Cascade River.

SPRINGSTEEN LAKE. Cutthroat are the attraction in this 19.2 acre lake at 3550 feet, 7.5 miles NW of Concrete and 0.8 miles SW of Washington Monument Mt. Drains to South Fork Nooksack River. Trails up Grandy and Bear creeks to Goat Mt. continue NW to lake.

SUIATTLE RIVER. A long, tumbling lightly-fished wilderness stream flowing from the glacier encrusted flanks of Glacier Peak, elev. 10,541, centerpiece of the Glacier Peak Wilderness Area into the Sauk River 6 miles N of Darrington at the Hwy. 530 bridge. Most of the upper Suiattle is in Snohomish County. Dolly Varden are legal in this river, and there are some large ones (20-inch minimum), along with wild rainbow, cutthroat and a few summer steelhead and chinook salmon. Hot days will create glacial melt that discolors the river, but shouldn't stop a good bait fisherman from poking into deep holes for Dollies. The N. bank of the Suiattle is paralleled by FS Road 16 from Hwy. 530 bridge at Sauk R. confluence continuing upstream 20 miles and ending at the trailhead to Trail 784 just E. of Sulphur Creek campground. Trail 784 follows the river through a deep green valley around Glacier Peak and provides easy access to rarely fished reaches. This trail is an arterial to many secondary trails spiraling from the valley to PCT 2000 and wilderness high lakes. FS 16 is an important access road to trailheads leading hiking anglers N. and S. into Glacier Peak Wilderness lakes. Roadside FS campgrounds are at Buck, Downey and Sulphur creeks in Snohomish County.

SUMNER LAKE. An 8 acre, marshy lake with rainbow and warm-water fish 2.8 miles NE of **MCMURRAY LAKE.** Drains into Big Lake.

TEN LAKE. Brookies, cutthroat, kokanee and rainbow are in this 16 acre lake between Devils and Scott mtns. Drains to Carpenter Creek. From Big Lake, follow Devil Mt.. Lookout Road which passes close to the lake. A trail starts at gate and heads downhill 0.4 miles to the lake.

TEXAS PONDS. 6 miles N. of Darrington on Hwy. 530 almost to Sauk River bridge then NW on FS 29 about 2 miles to these 6 acre ponds at 1500 feet. Brookies, some very large, and a developed picnic area.

THUNDER CREEK. A major tributary flowing from the W. side of Noisy Diobsud Wilderness into the E. side of **SHANNON LAKE.** Fair for wild rainbows and cutthroat in May and June especially in the lower reaches. From Concrete on Hwy. 20, turn N. past Baker Dam up the E. shore 4 miles then E. on rough road about 5 miles along the creek.

TUPSO LAKE. Located 9.5 miles S. of Marblemount, E. of Suiattle Mt. at head of Grade Creek. This 4 acre lake holds rainbow at 4500 feet elev. and drains to Suiattle River. From FS 16/Suiattle River Rd., turn N. on FS 2640 and continue on 2642 then hike a few hundred yards NW along ridge to lake. Several small ponds nearby.

VOGLER LAKE. April plants of 1000 catchable rainbows and some holdover brookies give this 3-acre pond a lift in early spring. WDFW access. Hwy. 20 drive N. on Baker Lake Rd. 3 miles to lake which is on Burpee Hill Rd., just S. of jct.

WHALE LAKE. A 50.1 acre mountain lake with rainbow trout, 9 miles SE of Marblemount at 4600 feet in the headwaters of Found Creek. Whale is just below the ridge between the Granite and Found lakes, and drains to Cascade River.

WHISTLE LAKE. Walk-in access holds down fishing pressure at this 29.7 acre lake 3.5 miles S. of Anacortes on Fidalgo Island. Stocked with cutthroat, largemouth bass and perch and open year-round. Usually offers fair spring and summer fishing. Drains to Skagit Bay.

Skagit County Resorts

Campbell Lake: Lunz's Resort, 360-293-6316.

Skagit River: Blake's RV Park & Marina 360-445-6533. Rockport Steelheader State Park, 360-853-8461.

Lake Shannon: Creekside Camping, 360-826-3566.

Skamania County
WDFW Region 5
Washington Department of Fish and Wildlife, 2108 Grand Blvd. Vancouver, WA 98661-4624 Phone 360-696-6211.

The 1691 square miles of Skamania County are caught between the slow-swirl of the Columbia River and the restless volcanoes of the south Cascade Mountains including most of the Mount St. Helens National Volcanic Monument (NVM), west edge of Mount Adams Wilderness and the rolling Indian Heaven Wilderness. Most of this lightly populated county is within the Gifford Pinchot National Forest and there is little settlement north of Hwy. 14 which cuts through the little river towns of Skamania, Stevenson and Carson at the edge of the Columbia River Gorge National Scenic Area. Stevenson is the biggest of the lot and only 1,165 folks call it home.

If you're driving into the county, you'll arrive in the south end on Hwy. 14 or on a Forest Service Road. Granted, many of FS roads here are paved, including FS 90 and 25 around Mount St. Helens, FS 30 up the Wind and FS 86 up the Little White Salmon, but all are snow-closed during winter.

This is one of those rare spots in the world where a really quick fisherman can battle a 10-foot white sturgeon, land a prized spring chinook, dart a shad, jig up a walleye, plug 3-pound smallmouth, and backpack into a wilderness trout lake all before lunch. If the region has a fishing failing, it's that typical stream steelhead fishing can be tough to find. Few locals, however, complain about trolling or bank casting for summer-runs at the mouth of the Wind and the Columbia backwater known as Drano Lake. The county, however, sits at the heart of some pretty spectacular spring and fall salmon fishing, thanks largely to a massive releases from federal hatcheries at Carson and Willard (on the upper Wind R.) Little White Salmon (Drano Lake) and Spring Creek on the Columbia W. of White Salmon.

Skamania County includes a lot of unusual geologic features that reflect its fire and ice volcanic roots. Hot springs spill into the Wind River, almost within sight of Beacon Rock the largest monolith north of Rock of Gibraltar, the Big Lava Bed, a monstrous 40-square mile welt of hardened lava that literally encases the forest in stone, miles of lonesome Wind River trout fishing, a beautiful and almost unknown stretch of the upper Lewis River and tiny Trapper Creek Wilderness—possibly the least known wilderness area in the state, and an ice cave that suddenly opens in the floor of the forest E. of Indian Heaven.

The ragged, exploded crown of Mt. St. Helen's summit, 8363 feet, is the highest point in the county. The lowest point is 75 feet elev. below Bonneville Dam. Three areas hold most of Skamania's lakes. One rocky area between North Bonneville and Stevenson contains over 60 natural rock-bound lakes. Indian Heaven Wilderness about 25 miles north of Carson and the Columbia River, has more than 175 lakes many with trout. The third lake area has more than 40 lakes, most at elevations between 4000 to 5000 feet in the headwaters of Green and North Fork Toutle rivers. The 300 lakes in Skamania County however, include only one large lake—10-mile long Swift Reservoir.

The county is 24th in size in the state. The topography is mostly rolling terrain above 2000 feet with a few peaks reaching above 5000 feet. The county seems to sit on a ball with streams draining off in all directions. Much of the north county drains into the Cispus, Green and Toutle rivers. The Lewis River collects most of the streams west of Mount Adams. The southern county flows into the Washougal, Wind and Little White Salmon rivers, and a very small area south and west of Mount Adams drains into the Big White Salmon River.

Weather wise, the county is in a transition zone that gets equal doses from the wet west and arid east. Along the Columbia it shows much of the topography of eastern Washington (including poison oak). Summers can reach into 80s and low 90s, and winter's bring heavy snows above 2000 feet that don't leave until April. Weather along the river often has no relationship to the weather you'll find a few miles north into the mountains. There's lots of places to park a camper or pitch a tent and years of intense logging have left a network of forest roads to explore.

ASHES LAKE. This 51 acre, 25-foot deep lake offers largemouth and smallmouth bass, bluegills, and some husky channel catfish. It lies 1.8 miles SW of Stevenson of Hwy. 14. Best fishing is from January through June. Summer moss is a big problem. Limited shore fishing area. Nearby **LITTLE ASHES LAKE** is stocked with rainbows and covers 2 acres, 2 miles SW of Stevenson adjacent to the N. side of Hwy. 14 . Can be fished from shore. Use bobbers to dangle baits above the weeds.

BASS LAKE. Planted in June with 500 rainbow trout. Overflow water from the Columbia River has introduced largemouth bass to the lake's 10 acres. Lake is NW from North Bonneville near Greenleaf Slough.

BEAR CREEK. Flows from St. Helens Lake 1.5 miles S. into Spirit Lake. Another Bear Creek, closed to fishing, flows into the Wind River 2.5 miles N. of Carson.

BEAR LAKE. One of several hike-in trout lakes in a cluster in Indian Heaven Wilderness, this 8 acre rainbow lake at 4750 feet elev. is 2.5 miles SW of Cultus Creek Campground on the NE side of wilderness on FS 24. It is a fairly easy 3 mile hike to the lake. **ELK, CLEAR, LEMEI** and **DEER** Lakes are within a 0.5 mile radius from Bear. The lakes are adjacent to or located on spur trails from PCT 2000.

BIG CREEK. Wild rainbows are in this rollicking creek about 7 miles E. of the E. end of Swift Reservoir. FS 90 along the North Fork Lewis crosses Big Creek at the Big Creek Falls observation area. To reach the upper creek, however, turn SE off FS 90 S. of the viewpoint onto FS 3211 and loop N. on 3220 around Burnt Peak to where the creek cuts through Skookum and Cayuse meadows. The creek's headwaters are near Surprise Lakes at the N. end of Indian Heaven Wilderness. It's crossed by several logging roads. Swampy in sections, but there can be some surprisingly good trout fishing for anglers who don't mind a lot of work.

BLACK CREEK. A brook trout stream with beaver ponds on upper Wind River. Closed to fishing in recent years. Drive upstream on Wind from Carson on Rd. 30 for 9 miles, then NE up FS 60, 7 miles to Black Creek. Spur roads reach the creek in several spots.

BLUE LAKES. Series of three small brook and cutthroat lakes. From Hwy. 14 about 1.5 miles W. of Stevenson turn north on Ash Lake Road to Blue Lakes Road, then to gravel pit parking area where trail begins.

BLUE LAKE. Located in the rolling south center of Indian Heaven Wilderness this 12 acre lake contains brook trout. Located on PCT 2000 at 4640 feet elev.

BLUFF LAKE. 5 acres 3.5 miles N. of Beacon Rock and 5.7 miles W. of North Bonneville. Holds a few rainbow, cutthroat and bass. Drains into Woodward Creek.

BRADER LAKE. 3 acre brook trout lake about 19 miles N. of Carson and 1200 feet SE from **EUNICE LAKE**.

Beacon Rock on the Columbia River.

CHAIN OF LAKES. A string of approximately 10 small lakes that hold brook and brown trout. Largest lakes in the chain are 6 and 9 acres and elevation is 4300 feet. Route is S. on FS 23 from US 12 near Randle to **TAKHLAKH LAKE** campground at N. edge of Mount Adams Wilderness. From Takhlakh Road 022 leads 1 mile N. to Chain lakes, campground.

CLEAR LAKE. A 13 acre lake at 4800 feet elev. in Indian Heaven Wilderness 2 miles SW of Cultus Creek campground (See Bear Lake). A 2.5 mile hike to brookies, rainbow and cutthroat .

COLUMBIA RIVER. The Skamania County section of the Columbia includes Bonneville Dam, the lowest impoundment on the river and is the first barrier hit by migratory fish moving upstream. The dam area is a seasonal hot spot for summer steelhead, spring and fall chinook, shad and sturgeon. The large boulders that line the N. shore downstream from the dam offer good fishing for smallmouth bass and fair fishing for walleye. Summer steelhead, spring and fall chinook and coho salmon are caught above and below the dam. Sturgeon fishing is very productive from bank and boat. One of the best sturgeon bank fishing area on the river is beneath the power lines and along Hamilton Island, just downstream from Bonneville Dam. This is where anglers fish for "oversize" sturgeon, the 7 to 11 foot monsters that run upriver to spawn or feed on shad each June and July. The hottest shad fishing on the Columbia takes place from mid May through June from the dam downstream. Bank fishermen cast into the spillways, off Hamilton Island and into the eddy at the mouth of the Beacon Rock slough. Sturgeon boaters anchor in deep holes from Beacon Rock State Park downstream. Good boat launch with dock at Hamilton Island between N. Bonneville and the dam, and a steep launch with docks at Beacon Rock State Park. The mouth of the Wind River is one of the most popular salmon fishing spots on the entire Columbia, especially for spring chinook. Above the dam, fishing is also good in the Bonneville Pool. Steelhead trolling usually peaks in August in the Wind and at Drano Lake, the backwater at the mouth of Little White Salmon River. Above the dam boaters launch at Wind River mouth, Drano Lake, Home Valley off Hwy. 14.

COMCOMLY LAKE. A 5 acre brook trout lake at 4500 feet on E. edge of Indian Heaven Wilderness off FS 6035 and spur 051 NE of Forlorn Lakes. Drains to (Big) White Salmon River.

COUNCIL LAKE. 48 acre mountain lake with brookies, rainbow, cutthroat and drive-in access. It lies at 4200 feet at NW edge of Mt. Adams Wilderness. Council is 24.5 miles SE from Randle. Drive SE from US 12 on FS 23 along Cispus River, at FS 21 jct. turn S. cross river and follow Canyon Creek up Council Bluff to lake. Drains to Cispus River. Campground.

CULTUS CREEK. A small, brushy stream that heads under Bird Mt. in N. Indian Heaven Wilderness, flowing NE to join Trout Lake Creek. Drive SW from Trout Lake on Hwy. 141 for 7 miles to Peterson guard station, then N. on FS 24 for 9 miles to Cultus Creek Campground at NE edge of wilderness area. The creek supports wild brook trout..

CULTUS LAKE. 500 feet SW of Deep Lake in Indian Heaven Wilderness at jct. Trails 179 & 34 at 5000 feet. Cutthroat. Drains to White Salmon River.

DEADMAN'S LAKE. A short hike to this 34 acre brook trout lake at 4330 feet elev. just inside the NE corner of Mt. St. Helens NVA. Maximum depth 60 feet. Leave US 12 at Randle and drive S. on FS 25 to FS 26, then S. on FS 26 about 10 miles to a spur road leading right to FS 2608. Leave main road and switchback up Red Spring Creek to Trail 218A Goat Mt. trail.

DEE LAKE. Brookies and cutthroat in this 2.5 acre lake at 4500 feet on SW side of Indian Heaven Wilderness. Short hike on trail from leaving FS 65 about 3 miles N. of Falls Creek Horse Camp.

DEEP LAKE. Tiny brook trout lake 1 mile E. of Deadman's at 3963 feet off Red Spring Creek Rd. just outside NVA . See Deadman's directions.

DEEP LAKE. 6 acre rainbow and cutthroat lake in Indian Heaven Wilderness at 4950 feet 1.7 miles SW of Cultus Creek campground (See Bear Lake).

DEER LAKE. Indian Heaven Wilderness 5-acre brook and cutthroat lake at 4800 feet 2.5 miles SW of Cultus Creek Campground (See Bear lake). Drainage to North Fork Lewis River.

DRANO LAKE. A 220-acre backwater of the Columbia River of the mouth of the Little White Salmon River famous statewide for summer steelhead and chinook salmon trolling. Drano is 7 miles W. of White Salmon adjacent to the N. side of Hwy. 14. Fed by Little White Salmon River, Drano offers a cold water layover for summer-run steelhead bound for upriver spawning areas and is home to thousands of chinook salmon released from and returning to Little White Salmon National Fish Hatchery. Salmon fishing is especially productive for spring chinook trolling (herring wrapped Flatfish, Kwikfish, Wigglewarts, large spinners) in May and June, and fall chinook in September, and steelhead in August and September. Best from boats, but bank fishermen take their share, too. Some smallmouth and a few sturgeon are taken. A few trout may trickle down from upper river which is stocked with about 3500 rainbows in May near popular campgrounds. Access area off Hwy. 14, launch. Launch provides access to Bonneville Pool. May be dangerously windy. Extremely crowded during peak seasons. Night fishing for steelhead popular during late summer heat. Check the regs, this one is tightly managed.

ELK LAKE. Popular Indian Heaven Wilderness lake with rainbow and cutthroat. Covers 13 acre at 4700 feet, 2.5 miles SW of Cultus Creek Campground off PCT 2000.

EUNICE LAKE. A 6.5 acre Indian Heaven Wilderness lake at 4500 feet planted with brook and cutthroat. FS 65 along W. side of wilderness 3 miles N. of Falls Creek Horse Camp, then hike E. on Trail 111 past Dee Lake.

FOREST LAKE (Doris). Located on Skamania-Cowlitz County line at 3900 feet elev. just outside Mt. St. Helens NVA. Holds browns and cutthroat. N. of Coldwater Ridge visitors center. Off Weyerhaeuser Rd. 3500.

FRANZ LAKE. Covering 99 acres, Franz is part of a National Wildlife Refuge 7 miles SW of North Bonneville between Hwy. 14 and Columbia River. It contains largemouth bass and brown bullhead. Has been closed to fishing.

EAST CANYON CREEK. Cutthroat and rainbow are taken from this creek which is paralleled by road for all of its 10 miles.

Drive SE from Randle on FS 23 to North Fork Campground at forks of Cispus River, then up main Cispus for about 7 miles on FS 23 to creek. Unimproved camping along creek.

FALLS CREEK. From Carson go N. on Wind River Rd. 4 miles to FS 65, then N. on road 65 for 14 miles to where road crosses stream's upper reaches. Creek supports wild brook and rainbow. May be closed.

FISH LAKE (Little Fish). 4 acre brookie and cutthroat lake at 3800 feet 1.5 miles NE of Steamboat Mt. and about 18 miles NW of **TROUT LAKE**. on FS 88 from to FS 8845 which leads W. 1 mile to lake.

FORLORN LAKES. A cluster of popular, mostly shallow lakes at 3500 feet just outside the SE edge of Indian Heaven Wilderness, about 1 mile N. of Goose Lake. Largest covers 14 acres. Planted with browns, rainbow and brookies. Best soon after snow melts. Lots of primitive camping. From Carson drive N. on Wind River Road then NE on FS 65 up Panther Creek to Jct. with FS 60 & 6050 (40). Turn E., past Goose Lake Campground to lakes on FS 6040. Camping is usually better than the fishing and in September the lakes are a great base for a combination, blue and huckleberry pick, grouse hunt, and trout fry.

FROG LAKE (School House). 4 miles E. of Carson adjacent to road. 4 acres with a few brook trout and a variety of warm water fish.

GHOST LAKE. A 5-acre cutthroat and brookie lake at 3767 feet elev. FS 99 to Bear Mt. viewpoint. Take Boundary trail 1 on N. side of road for 0.5 miles to Ghost Lake spur 1-H. on trail #1 to trail #181, and then 1 more mile to lake. **STRAWBERRY LAKE**, which covers 10 acres at 5374 feet, is 0.5 miles NE of Ghost. It contains brookies.

GILLETTE LAKE. Brookies have been stocked in this 3.5 acre pond 1.5 miles N. of North Bonneville adjacent to power line road.

GOOSE LAKE. A popular brown trout and cutthroat producer covering 58 acres at 3050 feet 13 miles N. Carson between the SE corner of Indian Heaven Wilderness and Big Lava Bed. Road access. Small

Forlorn Lakes.

boats may be launched at FS campground. Very popular for fly fishing. Stocked with 4000 browns after ice-out, widely known for excellent October action. on stocked cutthroat. See Forlorn Lake driving directions.).

GRANT LAKE. 11 acres 5 miles E. of Carson adjacent to N. side of Hwy. 14 below Dog Mt. Holds largemouth bass and bullhead catfish.

GREENLEAF LAKE (Slough). 48 acres, N. of Hwy. 14 at North Bonneville, holds bass and panfish and in spring a few wild rainbow and cutthroat migrate up from Hamilton Creek and down from Greenleaf Creek. A road follows N. shore, or fishermen walk up Hamilton Creek from the park at North Bonneville. Limited access.

HAMILTON CREEK. Previously planted with winter steelhead and cutthroat, now offers wild rainbow and cutthroat (wild cutthroat release) in June. 2 fish, 12-inch limits. Surprisingly deep in spots, nice light tackle and fly pools, and grassy banks upstream to Greenleaf Slough. Tributary to Columbia, entering river on W. side of North Bonneville through park. Flows from W. end of Greenleaf Slough under Hwy. 14 and railroad. From Hwy. 14 turn S. into North Bonneville Park. Creek borders W. side.

HANAFORD LAKE (Frances). One of the **FAWN LAKES** group at 3900 to 4000 feet N. and W. of Elk Prairie at headwaters of Coldwater Creek N. of Coldwater Ridge Visitor Center, and just outside the NVA. Fawn Lake is 1 mile W. of the Skamania-Cowlitz line. Other lakes in group are **FOREST** and **ELK**. Hanaford is 23 acres with cutthroat, brookies and rainbow. Elk covers 30 acres, and Forest, 8. They hold brookies and rainbows. Group is on logging company land Rd. 3500.

HEMLOCK LAKE (Trout Creek Reservoir). A 14-acre artificial impoundment in Trout Creek 7.5 miles N. of Stevenson along the Wind. Brook trout. May be closed.

HIDDEN LAKES. Two adjacent mountain lakes at 4050 and 4100 feet 1 mile E. of Cultus Creek Campground. Covering 5 and 10 acres with brook trout. From FS 24 on NE side of Indian Heaven Wilderness, hike E. on Trail 106.

HORSESHOE LAKE. A 24-acre roadside brookie lake at 4150 feet just NW of Mt. Adams Wilderness. FS campground on E. shore. From US 12 at Randle drive SE up Cispus River on FS 23 past **TAKHLAKH LAKE**, then 7 miles NE along wilderness boundary on FS 2329 to Spur 078 to lake **GREEN MOUNTAIN LAKE** is 2000 feet

NW of Horseshoe, 4 acres planted with brookies.

ICEHOUSE LAKE (Bridge). A heavily and frequently stocked 2.5 acre lake on Hwy. 14 at N. end of Columbia River Bridge of The Gods. Open year-round planted with more than 2000 browns, 7000 rainbows including 20 to 26-inch brood stock and Triploids, surplus winter steelhead and cutthroat. Also largemouth bass and bluegills. Managed for year-round fishing, is frequently restocked and offers best action from late fall through early summer when weeds become a problem. Bring the kids, bobbers and worms.

INDIAN HEAVEN LAKES. More than 50 hike-in lakes and ponds along PCT 2000 in Indian Heaven Wilderness, a mostly gentle plateau region popular for combination hiking-fishing trips. Scenery, huckleberries, lakes, trout, and gently undulating trail network make this a very popular summer and fall area. The wilderness is bordered on all sides by good FS roads. FS 65 follows the W. side, FS 60 runs along the S. end, FS 24 and 6035 go up the E. side and along the N. end through Surprise Lakes. From Trout Lake follow FS 24 and from Carson go N. on FS 60. PCT 2000 runs N-S through the heart of the wilderness and most spur trails to lakes spur off the PCT. Major access at Cultus Creek Campground. Trails lead into the wilderness at several spots from border roads. Major lakes include Blue, Bear, Elk, Clear, Deer, Cultus and Deep (See individual listings). Most lakes on main trails are heavily fished and offer marginal success. Bushwhack to smaller lakes can have bigger rewards. Good area for small rafts and float tubes.

KIDNEY LAKE. Heavily stocked 12 acre cutthroat and rainbow lake 1 mile N. of North Bonneville on power line. Because of its 59-foot depth, the lake holds up well into summer. Seeps to Columbia River. Planted in April, May and Dec. with more than 7000 rainbows including Triploids averaging 1.5 pounds. No ramp, but easy carry-in access. Open April through Feb. 28.

KWADDIS LAKE. Brookies and cutthroat are stocked in this 3.5 acre lake at 4300 feet, nicely off the beaten path on W. side of Indian Heaven Wilderness. Drains across FS 65 to McClellan Meadows.
LARSON LAKES (Nelson). A string of 3

lakes covering 1 to 3 acres 4 miles N. of Home Valley on Hwy. 14. Hold brookies and rainbow. Gravel road from Home Valley leads NE about 6 miles to lakes just NW of Augspurger Mt.

LAVA LAKES. 7 small lakes with surface acres estimated at 4 acres on the power line 1.7 miles NW of Stevenson. Supports brookies, rainbow and cutthroat. **FRENCH LAKE**, 2 acres, **BIG** and **LITTLE MAIN LAKES**, 3 and 2 acres, and **SARDINE LAKE**, 2 acres, are within a short distance of Lava Lakes. These small ponds carry rainbow. Sardine has cutthroat in addition to rainbow.

LEMEI LAKE. Small mountain brook trout lake on W. side of Lemei Rock at 5000 feet. Drains to North Fork Lewis River. More grassy pond than lake.

LEWIS RIVER NORTH FORK. Above Swift Reservoir this famous steelhead and salmon river evolves into a beautiful, long stretch of under-recognized catch-and-release wild trout water. Down river dams at Merwin, Yale and Swift reservoirs block anadromous fish, isolating the upper river for wild rainbow, cutthroat and bull trout although the char are fully protected by ESA regulations. Best fishing is after snow runoff from mid July into October. Large

Bonneville Dam shad fishing.

trout are occasionally caught just above **SWIFT RESERVOIR**, especially in the early summer when lake rainbows are looking for river spawning water. Most of these wild trout are brightly colored and 5 to 12 inches with an occasional surprise around 15 inches. A series of spectacular water falls divides the river into fishing segments. FS 90 follows the river, usually high up the bank above the water, on the S. side, bridges the river downstream from Lower Falls campground at mile 14, and continues along the N. bank. Trail 31 follows the river between Upper Falls and Curley Creek Falls. Except for bridge crossing areas, and a couple of spur road access points, the water requires short, but often steep hikes down from FS 90. Easily waded, perfect for fly or light spinning gear, the North Fork is 30 to 50 feet wide, rocky, with riffles, pools, runs and long glassy glides. Best action rewards anglers willing to hike into the most inaccessible stretches. Campgrounds at Lower and Middle Falls, lots of primitive camping.

LILY LAKE (Hamilton Creek Pond). 8 acre brookie lake 7 miles W. of Stevenson that drains into Hamilton Creek. Best route is via Beacon Rock Hill Road to Three Corner Rock Road, then 3 miles N.

LITTLE WIND RIVER. Flows into Wind River from the E. just above mouth at Carson. The stream is wadeable and carries a few steelhead in lower reaches. Home Valley road leads to power line road which extends to mouth of Little Wind River.

LOST LAKE. An 8 acre brook trout lake 3 miles by trail W. of road end at Government Mineral Springs at Trapper Creek Wilderness. Elevation of the lake is 3760 feet. Tough hike.

MEADOW CREEK. An often marshy creek N. of Indian Heaven Wilderness. Reached from Wind River Road 25 miles N. of Carson, through Old Man Pass. Meadow Creek meanders through Lone Butte Meadows for about 4 miles before emptying into Rush Creek near the road crossing. The creek provides rainbow and brook fishing and access is relatively easy to fish in meadow area. FS Rds. 30 and 32 follow creek through Lone Butte Meadows button-hooks E. and S. again to join FS 24 and pass **SURPRISE LAKES** and Cold Spring campground and crosses upper portion of creek. Top fishing during July.

META LAKE. The 9 acre lake at 3580 feet supports brook trout that survived the St. Helens eruption. It is on FS 26 the main road to NVA's Windy Ridge Viewpoint. An interpretive area and trail provides information about the eruption and how aquatic life survived.

MOSELY LAKES. 5 small lakes 2 miles W. of Stevenson that drain into Rock Creek. The lakes cover about 3 acres and have been planted with brookies and rainbows Early season best. From Hwy. 14 turn onto Ash Lake Road to Blue Lake Road.

MOSQUITO LAKES. Fall fishing can be productive for brook trout in both Big and Little Mosquito lakes. The larger lake covers 24 acres; the smaller, 5 acres. From Peterson Prairie campground W. of Trout Lake, drive 15 miles N. on FS 24 to E. tip of Big Mosquito Lake. Elevation is 3900 feet. Lakes drain to Trout Lake.

MOUSE LAKE. A shallow 9 acre cutthroat lake at 4500 feet 18.5 miles SE of Randle. Drains to Cispus River.

MUDDY RIVER. Once considered a good bet for fall rainbow and cutthroat fly fishing. Flowing off the erupted flanks of Mount St. Helens, the Muddy is glacial-fed and cloudy much of the year, although it clears slightly when cold temperatures freeze snow melt. This fast-dropping stream enters upper end of **SWIFT RESERVOIR**, at FS Road 25 which follow river N. for about 4 miles, offering access after a hike of about 1 mile. Road ends at bridge with dramatic volcano views. Clearwater FS campgrounds. Tributaries may provide cutts and rainbow from mid-summer. Try **CLEAR CREEK, CLEARWATER CREEK**, and **SMITH CREEK.** FS road 93 crosses Clear Creek, the best fishing stream, about 1 mile from mouth and a rough road, 9303, parallels the creek for about 4 miles. Some whitefish are present in these streams. **PINE CREEK** joins the upper end of Swift about 0.5 miles below mouth of Muddy River, roughly paralleled by a road NW for 8 miles. It contains rainbow and cutthroat, but fishing is poor.

NORTHWESTERN LAKE (See Klickitat County).

OBSCURITY LAKE. A 10 acre brook trout lake at 4337 feet in the Mt. Margaret back country area. Access from Norway Pass

Swift Reservoir.

trailhead on Trail 211, a hike of about 6 miles. Permit camping only. Information from National Volcanic Monument headquarters.

OLALLIE LAKE (Sheep). A pretty 15-acre mountain lake NW of Mt. Adams Wilderness on upper Cispus River. Stocked with brookies, browns and cutthroat and lies at 4250 feet. From US 12 at Randle drive SE on FS 23 for 27 miles, bear onto FS 21 to Adams Fork Campground, then S. on FS 5601 to lake-shore campground. Fishes best in late summer.

PANHANDLE LAKE. A 15 acre lake which lies at 4520 feet 10 miles by trail over Norway Pass on Lakes trail 211, approximately 7 miles. Permit camping. Brookies and rainbow.

PANTHER CREEK. A very pretty trout stream with forest road access, lots of camping and a no fishing restriction. This is a major tributary of Wind River, entering at FS 65 jct. with Wind River Road about 4 miles above the Columbia River. FS 65 follows the stream NE from Wind River Road.

PLACID LAKE. A 19-acre cutthroat lake which at 4000 feet 1 mile SE of Lone Butte. From Wind River Road N. of Carson turn NE up Panther Creek on FS 65, then 1 mile E. on FS 420 where the trail begins.

ROCK LAKE. A 2 acre brook trout pond in Indian Heaven Wilderness.

RYAN LAKE. No fish survived Mt. St. Helen's eruption.

SOUTH PRAIRIE LAKE. A marshy 14 acre lake 9.5 miles N. of Willard on NE side of Big Lava Bed. Stocked with brookies. Drains to White Salmon River. From Willard, drive NW on FS 66 along Big Lava Bed to lake near Jct. of FS 6610.

ST. HELEN'S LAKE. A casualty of the Mt. St. Helen's eruption, the lake basin is closed to all public access and is reserved for research purposes

SHOVEL LAKE (African). A 21 acre mountain lake at 4653 feet with brook trout. Reached from Norway Pass trailhead on Lakes Trail 211, approximately 8 miles. Permit camping only.

SNOW LAKE (Burgoyne). 1 mile W. of Shovel Lake at 4700 feet. No fish.

SPIRIT LAKE. Once one of the state's most beautiful lakes, Spirit was devastated by the eruption of Mt. St. Helens on May 18, 1980. Lake information is available at Coldwater Ridge Visitor's Center 7 miles from Mt. St. Helen's crater. Spirit Lake is not open to the public, and fishing is closed, but in 2000 WDFW biologists found a large number of steelhead strain rainbow trout weighing several pounds that apparently survived the epic blast and are re-populating.

STEAMBOAT LAKE. Brown and brook trout are the attraction in this 9 acre lake

13 miles at 4050 feet N. of Indian Heaven Wilderness. Follow FS 24 through Mosquito Lakes to Spur 021, a rough road that leads 2.5 miles E. to N. end of lake.

STRAWBERRY LAKE. A 10-acre brookie lake at 5374 feet. See **GHOST LAKE** for access.

SURPRISE LAKES. A splattering of 15 small lakes and ponds 2.5 miles S. of Mosquito Lake near Jct. of FS 24 and 30 NE of Indian Heaven Wilderness. Some of these shallow lakes support brook trout, and some are barren. Several campgrounds, including Surprise Lake Indian Camp, Cold Spring Indian Camp, Meadow Indian Camp, Saddle and South campgrounds. PCT 2000 goes through lake area. Great huckleberry picking.

SWIFT RESERVOIR. Once an excellent producer of rainbow trout, 4589 acre Swift Reservoir is the upper most impoundment on the North Fork Lewis River. FS 90 rides the steep hillside 100 feet above the N. side of the 10 mile long reservoir. Development is limited to a few campgrounds and summer homes on the E. end. Only boat launch at Swift Forest Campground. Hand carry from Eagle Cliff on E. end. After a series of floods and excessive siltation in the late 1990s, fishing crashed and WDFW has been working to rebuild it by introducing different stocks of rainbow fry. There is an excellent potential of recovering the once-exceptional trout fishery as the water clears which will promote plankton growth and other nutrients. Rainbows are the dominant fish, but there are also a few cutthroat and ESA protected bull trout which must be released. From the April opener into May rainbows concentrate at tributaries and near the dam, scattering throughout the lake by late June. These trout are very depth oriented and where you catch one, keep fishing. A large island at Drift Creek on the SE end makes a good base for boat campers. Water draw downs for power generation can leave ramps high and dry or blocked by log debris. For lake levels call, 1-800-547-1501. East of Cougar, **SWIFT POWER CANAL** a channelized river flow between Swift and Yale reservoirs, is usually stocked with 1000 catchable size rainbows in June. The canal is crossed by a bridge on FS 90, an extension of Hwy. 503 from I-5. **TAKHLAKH LAKE**. A picturesque mountain lake with cutthroat and brook trout covering 35 acres at 4350 feet elev.

Stocked in May with 4000 brookies. The lake is at the NW edge of Mount Adams Wilderness 24.5 miles SE of Randle. Route is on FS 23 upstream along Cispus River to Adams Fork Camp, then S. on FS 5601 for 1.5 miles to lake campground. Small gravel launch. Popular camping destination with several nearby fishing lakes. Spectacular view of Mt. Adams.

THOMAS LAKE. A shallow, 10.5 acre Indian Heaven Wilderness lake at the head of Outlaw Creek 19 miles N. of Carson. Brookies and rainbows. From Wind River Rd., turn NE onto FS 65 up Panther Creek then N. along W. side Indian Heaven Wilderness to Trail 111. Hike 0.5 mile into wilderness to lake's W. shore.

TRADEDOLLAR LAKE. 12 acre cutthroat lake at 3552 elev. N. of Coldwater Visitor Center at Mt. St. Helens NVA. Access by timber company road 3500 to Elk Prairie past **FAWN, HANFORD**, and **ELK LAKES** to within a short distance from Tradedollar. Road may be gated.

TROUT CREEK. An easy to-reach tributary of Wind River, but closed to fishing. Trout Creek is about 7 miles NW of Carson on Wind River Road, then 1 mile W. on Hemlock road to FS road 43 which parallels Trout Creek about 5 miles. **HEMLOCK LAKE**, a shallow 16 acre lake at junction of Hemlock Road and FS 43 with rainbow and brookies. Closed to fishing in recent years.

TROUT LAKE CREEK. Heading under Steamboat Mt., Trout Lake Creek flows SE about 18 miles through Trout Lake in Klickitat County to join the White Salmon River near that town. From Trout Lake go NW on FS 88 and 8810 for much of its length. Creek has wild rainbow, brookies and cutthroat. Best fishing in July-August. Trout Lake Creek Campground on FS 88 at Skamania-Klickitat county line makes a nice fishing base.

TUNNEL LAKE (Stump, Mud). Open year-round, a 13 acre rainbow stocked lake adjacent to Hwy. 14 on the Columbia River about 2 miles E. of Cook. Stocked with about 4,000 catchable rainbows, including a helping of 14-inch and up trout, in April and Dec. Some perch and lunker largemouth bass. No ramp, but carry-in boat access and good bank fishing. Good spot for kids.

VENUS LAKES. Rainbow and cutthroat lakes of 8 and 12 acres at 4600 and 4920 feet on E. side of Mt. Venus in Mt. Margaret area on W. side of NVA. Drain to Green River. No trail, no camping allowed.

WAPIKI LAKE. A very scenic 10 acre rainbow and cutthroat lake, Wapiki and several small adjoining pond are at 4700 feet on E. edge of Indian Heaven Wilderness. From FS 24 about 0.5 mile NW of FS 6020, take Trail 34 about 4 miles to lake.

WHITE SALMON RIVER (See Klickitat County).

WHITE SALMON RIVER UPPER. Beginning on the glaciated W. slope of Mt. Adams, the Upper White Salmon flows W. and S. into Klickitat County 3 miles N. of Trout Lake and then into the Columbia River at Underwood. Planted with both summer and winter steelhead. Paved FS 23 from Trout Lake leads NW about 13 miles along upper river to Swampy Meadows, allowing easy access at many points for trout fishermen targeting the stream's wild rainbows and brook trout. The Skamania County portion of Upper White Salmon offers best fishing in June and July.

WHITE SALMON RIVER LITTLE. One of the best rainbow and brook trout streams in the county for anglers willing to work, and one of the few still stocked by WDFW which adds 3500 catchable rainbows in late May. The Little White Salmon is a rocky, fast river which shows riffles, pools and white water for most of its length. It heads under Monte Cristo lookout station just E. of the Skamania-Klickitat County line and flows about 15 miles S. through Willard National Fish Hatchery to enter the Columbia River at Drano Lake near Cook. FS 86 then FS 230 parallel the Little White Salmon from its mouth to Monte Cristo. Fishermen can find seclusion and good fishing by exploring the river's steep canyon areas. Best fishing from mid-June into fall. Watch for rattlesnakes and poison oak in lower stretches. Oklahoma Campground makes a good base for summer fishermen.

WILMA LAKE (Strawberry). Located 0.5 mile NE of Ghost Lake, covering 10 acres at 5374 feet. Holds brookies (See Ghost Lake for route).

WIND RIVER. In recent years the mouth and the extremely tough, steep canyon sections have become the top spring chinook fishery on the Columbia, usually in April and May. During the peak of the springer run this little area, serviced by a two-lane ramp, and dock can be as close to combat fishing as most anglers want to see. In mid July summer steelhead begin to stack at the mouth and anglers where anglers will score into Sept. In recent years, WDFW has closed the upper river, above Shipherd Falls, including all of Wind River tributaries to trout and steelhead fishing. The falls may be reached, with difficulty, by driving 1 mile E. of Carson, then left on Shipherd Fall's spur and hiking gorge walls to falls. Several hot springs flow into the Wind in the Carson area. N. of Carson, FS Road 30 follows the Wind to connect with FS 90 on North Fork Lewis and FS 24 to Trout Lake.

WOODWARD CREEK. A tumbling tributary pouring into the Columbia 0.4 miles W. of Beacon Rock State Park on Hwy. 14. A road leads along W. bank upstream for approximately 2 miles. The stream supports steelhead but is closed during winter season.

WOODS LAKE. Located in Indian Heaven Wilderness on the N. side of Bird Mt., Woods is a 13-acre brook and cutthroat lake at 5000 feet. From FS 24 at Cultus Creek Campground, take Trail 108, 2 miles W. Drains to North Fork Lewis.

ZIG ZAG LAKE. A 2 acre pond at 3400 feet elev. at head of East Fork Lewis River. Offers brook trout. Short trail from FS 42 which crosses the divide between East Fork Lewis and Wind River near Cougar Rock.

Skamania County Resorts

Columbia River: Skamania Lodge
     Stevenson, 800-221-7117.

Snohomish County

WDFW Region 4

Washington Department of Fish and Wildlife, 16018 Mill Creek Blvd., Mill Creek, WA 98012. Phone 425-775-1311.

Snohomish is a good county for fresh or saltwater fishermen who love variety. More than 460 lakes have been officially recorded, split almost equally between roadside lowland trout/warm-water fish lakes and remote mountain lakes with rainbows, cutthroat, brookies and goldens scooped out of remote, sometimes spectacular basins along a thread of hiking trails. Largest lake in the county is 1021-acre Lake Stevens a residentialy-surrounded multi-species lake E. of Everett.

On the W. are some of central Puget Sound's most productive seasonal salmon, crabbing and clamming areas. The E. border runs along the ragged mile-high crest of the Cascade Mountains. The S. is bordered by King County and the N. by Skagit County. In between are half-a-dozen of the most promising steelhead, sea-run cutthroat and salmon rivers flowing off the W. slopes of the Cascades, plus hundreds of brushy, but fishable, creeks and beaver ponds. Major drainages and anadromous fish rivers are the Stillaguamish River and its Forks which drain two-thirds of the county, plus upper Sauk, Suiattle, Skykomish, Snohomish, Wallace, Beckler and Sultan. All are closely followed by highways and paved or improved gravel roads. The Stillaguamish, Sauk, Skykomish and Snohomish rivers are popular with boat fishermen. The Whitechuck River is a remote, roadless mountain gush that feeds into the Sauk River S. of Darrington.

Rivers that don't support anadromous fish are no longer stocked by WDFW and depend on wild fish reproduction to support sport fishing. Catch and release is required in some areas, and advised anywhere wild fish are targeted. The state has also stopped stocking brook trout in this county, but many of the lakes and ponds have reproducing populations of these colorful char. On the upside trout plants have been increased in many lowland lakes many of which are also getting supplemental plants of triploid rainbows-sterile fish that usually weigh at least 1.5 pounds when stocked and increase in weight rapidly.

About half of the county's 2112 square miles are heavily forested and mountainous, owned either by large timber-cutting corporations or within Mount Baker-Snoqualmie National Forest. All or part of 4 designated wilderness areas lie within the county, including the Alpine Lakes, Henry M. Jackson, Boulder River, and Glacier Peak which includes the county's high point—the permanent snowfields and icy glaciers at the 10,541 foot summit of Glacier Peak. Snohomish is the state's 13th largest county. Lower river valleys are mostly agricultural and the population center, with a couple of small town exceptions, is along the I-5 corridor on the W. side of the county. It's a mild maritime climate averaging about 50 degrees in the lowlands, with lots of rain and snow and moderate temperatures. At Everett the county averages 34.81 inches of precipitation, at Darrington 80.38 inches, 200 inches in the Sultan Basin and near Stevens Pass.

Winter steelheaders rarely fight freezing temperatures in the far W. and S. parts of the county, but freezes are common in the N. county. Most high lakes, between 2500 feet and 4000 feet, some accessible by logging roads, will be ice-free in late April or May, but many of the highest lakes, especially in the heavily-shaded pockets in Glacier Peak Wilderness, don't thaw until July.

On Puget Sound, saltwater salmon seasons vary considerably depending on ESA status and management decisions. Blackmouth (immature chinook) are available from Nov. through April, and in recent years the season has been in late winter. Ocean chinook begin arriving in late July and August, followed by coho in late Aug. and Sept., and chums in Oct. and Nov. During odd numbered years there is a heavy very popular pink salmon run that concentrates off the mouth of the Snohomish River. Several parks and fishing piers offer saltwater shore-fishing opportunities. The major boat launch into the sound is at Everett, with a smattering of smaller launches available.

Salmon fishing is allowed in rivers only during years of good returns. The Snohomish River system, including the Skykomish River is by far the most popular steelhead and salmon river. The Snohomish System is one of the largest in Western Washington and often ranks number one in winter steelhead catches, and in the top five for summer-runs. The Skykomish River delivers almost half of the winter and summer catch recorded for the entire Snohomish System. WDFW salmon and steelhead hatcheries are on the Skykomish E. of Sultan.

Access to the county's fishing areas is from I-5 on the W. which is paralleled at a distance by two-lane Hwy. 9 which touches many of the best lowland lake opportunities. U.S. 2 crosses E-W between I-5 and Stevens Pass, following the Skykomish River for most of its course. One of the most spectacular fishing drives is along the Mountain Loop Highway that cuts a circular route through the mountains E. of Granite Falls along the S. Fork Stillaguamish, turns N. at Barlow Pass at the edge of the Henry M. Jackson Wilderness and follows along the headwaters of the Sauk before returning to Hwy. 530 at Darrington. Hwy. 530 runs NE-SW between Arlington and Darrington following the Stillaguamish and Sauk systems.

ARMSTRONG LAKE. Plants of triploid and catchable size rainbows plus holdover cutthroat deliver a strong, popular opening day and May fishery at this 31 acre lake. To thwart heavy cormorant predation WDFW usually plants larger than average trout in Armstrong, many weighing 0.5 to 0.75 of a pound on opening day. Largemouth bass are also available. From Arlington go N. on Hwy. 9 about 1.5 mile then E. on Armstrong Rd. Drains to Stillaguamish River via Armstrong and Harvey Creeks. WDFW public access, ramp on S. shore.

ASHLAND LAKES. A pair of foothill lakes on state land. Lower Ashland covers 12.9 acres and upper lake 7 acres at 2700 and 2870 feet elev. Both have brookies. Lakes are 5 miles SE of Verlot. From Mountain Loop Hwy. at Wiley Campground go S. on FS Rd. 4021 to trailhead at end of road. Drain to Wilson Cr. and Pilchuck River.

BALLINGER LAKE. A 103-acre residentially encircled lake on Hwy. 104 the Edmonds Ferry Terminal route just W. of I-5. Annually stocked with 6000 catchable rainbows in April. Also offers largemouth bass, perch, crappie, and bullhead catfish. Summer and fall are productive months for bass and perch. Drains into McAleer Creek and Lake Washington. Public access, ramp, pier reached through park on NE shore.

BANDANA LAKE. Rainbow stocked 3 acres in Boulder River Wilderness 6.8 miles N. of Verlot on N. side of Meadow Mt. Outlet to Meadow Creek. From Mountain Loop Hwy. N. on FS 41 to Trailhead 641 on Tupso Pass.

BARCLAY LAKE. A popular family hiking destination on the N. side of Baring Mt. E. of Index. Planted with rainbow fry, and most fish are 6 to 11 inches, a few larger. Barclay covers 11 acres and is brushy and swampy. Best fished with a raft. Open year-round. The lake is located at 2300 feet elev. drains into S. Fork of the Skykomish River, and is reached by turning N. from Hwy. 2 at Baring onto FS road 6024 along Barclay Creek ending at Trail 1055 which continues 1.5 miles to the lake. Campsites.

BATH LAKE. Golden trout have been stocked in this remote, top-of-the-world 14.7 acre lake at 5950 feet elev. in Glacier Peak Wilderness high above the deep Canyon Cr. drainage. It is the largest in a group of four lakes 2.5 miles NE of Sulphur Mtn. Drains to Bath Creek and Suiattle River.

BEAR LAKE. Cutthroat are stocked in this 19.8 acre lake at 2775 feet 2.8 miles SE from Verlot on E. side of Mt. Pilchuck. Drains to S. Fork Stillaguamish River. From Wiley Campground g SW on FS 4021 to lake edge.

BEAVER PLANT LAKE. A 3.2 acre lake planted with rainbow and cutthroat about 6 miles SE of Verlot. Trail from FS Rd. 4021 E. of **BEAR LAKE.**

BECKLER RIVER. Only the upper stretches of the Beckler are in Snohomish County. The Beckler flows into Skykomish River's S. Fork at Skykomish on Hwy. 2 and supports small wild rainbow, cutthroat and a few whitefish. Best fishing June, July and August. A FS campground is just N. of Skykomish on FS Road 65 which runs 14 miles along Beckler's entire length and continues to join FS Rd. 63 on North Fork Skykomish River at Garland Mineral Springs. FS 6530 cuts NE from FS 65 and follows the **RAPID RIVER.**

BEECHER LAKE. A crescent shaped 17 acre old river channel lake 0.5 mile E. of Cathcart on the Connelley Road. Holds largemouth bass, cutthroat, pumpkinseed, crappie and catfish. Drains into Snohomish River 4 miles S. of Snohomish.

BEVIS LAKE (Beaver). A 6 acre bass and brookie lake N. from Monroe up Wood Creek on Wood Creek Road for 7.5 miles, then E. for 1.5 miles to lake which is on Boy Scout of America property.

BITTER LAKES (Tom, Dick and Harry). Trio of small brook trout lakes 4 miles NE of Index on NW end of Jumpoff Ridge. Drain to North Fork Skykomish.

BLACKMANS LAKE. A popular 60-acre year-round, multi-species lake on Hill Road in Snohomish. Access from 13th street. Stocked in May with 7500 catchable cutthroat, some holdover rainbow trout, and 550 large triploids. Also largemouth bass and perch. Disabled access to two fishing docks in park on NE shore and WDFW boat ramp with bankfishing area on S. shore.

BLANCA LAKE. A 179-acre mountain lake with rainbow and cutthroat in the 12 inch class accessible in mid-July. The lake is at 3975 feet elev. on the S. side of glacier encrusted Monte Cristo Peak. Silt flour from Columbia Glacier discolors the water. From Hwy. 2 at Index turn N. on FS 63 up the North Fork Skykomish River past Garland Mineral Springs to FS Trail 1052 which leads 3.5 steep miles to lake in Henry M. Jackson Wilderness.

BLUE LAKES. A pair of 22 and 3 acre lakes

nestled under the Cascade Crest at 5600 and 5700 feet. Cutthroat. From Mountain Loop Hwy. turn E. at Bedal Campground onto N. Fork Sauk River Road/FS 49 to Sloan Creek FS campground. FS Trail 652 leaves the campground along Sloan Creek then switchbacks up ridge and continues 9.5 miles to the lakes. Trail 652 continues 2 miles past lakes to PCT 2000 at Dishpan Gap and trails from Little Wenatchee River.

BOARDMAN LAKE. This 49 acre lake at 2981 feet sheds ice and is fishable for rainbows and brookies early. It's 6 miles SE of Verlot an easy 1 mile hike with only 200 feet elevation gain from the end of FS Rd. 4020 on Trail 704. Follow Mountain Loop Hwy. E. of Verlot 4.6 miles to Wiley Camp, then S. on FS 4020 for 4 miles to **EVAN LAKE** and trailhead. **EVAN** has brookies, cutthroat and rainbow, and covers 12 acres. Trail continues S. about 1 mile to Boardman.

BOSWORTH LAKE. Most anglers target a heavy spring plant of 9500 catchable rainbows and another 1000 triploids. Also some large cutthroat and a growing population of largemouth bass. Bosworth covers 95 acres about 2.5 miles S. of Granite Falls. A WDFW access, launch on NE shore. From Granite Falls go S. on Robe-Menzel Rd. to Utley Rd. then SW 0.5 miles to lake.

BOULDER CREEK. Sometimes called Boulder River, the upper reaches deliver fair to good wild rainbow fishing from July into fall. A few cutthroat and Dolly Varden. Crosses Hwy. 530 and flows into N. Fork Stillaguamish 1 mile E. of Hazel. About 2 miles E. of Hazel FS Rd. 2010 goes S. from Hwy. 530 and 4 miles up French Creek crossing drainge to Boulder Falls at the edge of Boulder River Wilderness. Trail 734 continues upstream into the wilderness 3 miles to Boulder Ford.

BRYANT LAKE. A 20 acre lake with largemouth bass, crappie and cutthroat. Bryant is adjacent to E. side of Hwy. 9, about 3 miles NW of Arlington.

BUCK CREEK. A large, rarely fished mountain drainage flowing S. out of Glacier Peak Wilderenss into Suiattle River below Huckleberry Mountain at Buck Creek Campground on FS 26 about 13 miles above the Sauk River confluence. After snow run-off Buck Creek can delivers fair summer rainbow angling. FS campground at mouth.

Boardman Lake.

CANYON CREEK. A small, fast but exceptionally productive winter and summer steelhead stream that joins South Fork Stillaguamish 1 mile N. of Granite Falls. Siltation and slides from clear-cuts in headwaters have damaged this watershed and diminished summer steelhead fishing. Still, this is the most productive tributary on the Stilly, far outproducing the South Fork. Top summer steelheading is in Sept. and Oct. and winter fishing peaks in Jan. Access is difficult due to summer homes, real estate developments and timber company holdings along lower river. Road from Granite Falls leads N. to cross Stillaguamish, then follows Canyon Creek 2 miles E. FS 41/ Canyon Creek Rd. leads N. from Mountain Loop Hwy. about 6 miles NE of Granite Falls. **CANYON LAKE**. Planted with cutthroat and brook trout fry it lies at 2700 feet elev. on the S. side of Green Mt. and covers 5 acres. Drive E. from Granite Falls on the Mountain Loop Hwy. 7 miles to FS Rd. 41, then 2 miles to FS Rd. 4110, to FS Rd. 4111 to FS Trail 720 which crosses Benson Creek and climbs ridge about 1 mile to lake. Drains into Wiley Creek.

CASSIDY LAKE. A popular 124-acre multi-species lake 3 miles E. of Marysville. Stocked with perch, crappie, pumpkinseed, brown bullhead, and largemouth bass. Marshy shore lines. There is a WDFW disabled access and boat ramp. Drains via Catherine Creek to Pilchuck River. Best fishing July through October. From Hwy.

9, 2 miles N. of Lake Stevens turn E. on Lake Cassidy Rd. to W. side of lake.

CAVANAUGH LAKE (LITTLE). Rainbow swim in Little Cavanaugh which varies from 4 to 8 acres, and lies in a logging area at 1500 feet elev. 5 miles S. of Goldbar. Nearby beaver ponds offer brookies. Drive E. on Hwy. 2 for 6.3 miles E. of Goldbar to **NO NAME CREEK**, then S. on FS 62 for 5.2 miles to small road on right. Follow this road about 0.7 miles and turn left to lake.

CEDAR PONDS. Brookies are in this brushy 9 acre private pond near **TOMTIT** and **DAGGER LAKES**.

CHAIN LAKE. A year-round, 23 acre lake 3 miles N. of Monroe. Stocked with 1500 catchable rainbows in April. Also has largemouth bass, pumpkinseeds and crappie. Drains to Snohomish River via French Creek. Drive N. from Monroe on Lewis Street/195th Ave. SE 3 miles to S. shore.

CHAPLAIN LAKE (Reservoir). Fishing is not allowed in this Everett water supply reservoir. Chaplain is a natural lake raised by dam and fed by Sultan River diversion. Has brookies and cutthroat, covers 443.7 acres 5.8 miles N. of Sultan.

CHAPLAIN POND. A shallow, weedy 11-acres just below the Everett water treatment plant, 4.5 miles N. of Sultan below

Chaplain Lake. Stocked with coastal cutthroat fry. Use a float tube. From Hwy. 2 W. of Sultan turn N. on Reiner Rd.

CHITWOOD LAKE. A lanky, marshy 6 acre lake 4 miles E. of Granite Falls, open year-round. Naturally produced coho and wild cutthroat. Drains to Worthy Creek. A logging road leads to the lake, but is gated two miles short, requiring a road hike, or mountain bike ride.

CICERO POND. Rainbow, catfish and largemouth bass in this 4 acre pond adjacent to Hwy. 530 about 0.5 mile E. of Cicero. Reached by walking abandoned RR grade 0.4 miles E. from Cicero.

CLEAR CREEK. Rainbow, cutthroat, Dolly Varden and a few brookies in Clear Creek, which joins the Sauk River about 2 miles S. of Darrington. From Darrington go S. on Mountain Loop Hwy./FS Rd. 20 along Sauk River to Clear Creek FS campground at mouth, then upstream on FS 2060 for 5.5 miles. Trails from this road into Boulder River Wilderness. A primitive trail siwashes 0.5 miles downhill to **COPPER CREEK.** Both creeks produce best July and August.

COAL LAKE. From Mountain Loop Hwy. just beyond Big Four picnic area, turn N. on FS Rd. 4060 for 4 miles to 6 acre Coal Lake. Very scenic route. Coal Lake has brookies and cutthroat and lies at 3420 feet elevation. Trail 605 continues N. for 0.5 miles to 2.5 acre **PASS LAKE** at 3700 feet, which has cutthroat and rainbow. Campsites at Pass. Continue to end of Rd. 4060 where Trail 712 leads 1.5 mile along ridge to **INDEPENDENCE LAKE** at 3700 feet, which has cutthroat and rainbows.

COCHRAN LAKE. A 33.6 acre rainbow lake NE of Monroe. Public access area on N. shore. From Monroe go N. on Woods Creek Rd. 6 miles. Just N. of jct. with Upper Woods Cr. Rd. a road forks W. to the lake's SE tip. Drains to Woods Creek.

CONEY LAKE. A 5 acre mountain lake at 5000 feet 1.4 miles NE of Curry Gap. Has rainbow. Drains to Sloan Creek and North Fork Sauk River. Coney Lake outlet enters Sloan Creek where FS Rd. 49 crosses.

CONNER LAKE. Largemouth bass and pumpkinseed are in this 8.9 acre lake 1 mile E. of Hartford. Drains to Pilchuck River.

COWBELL LAKE. Rainbow planted lake of 3.4 acres at 3420 feet, 1000 feet NW of **UPPER BOARDMAN LAKE**.

CRABAPPLE LAKE. A deep, 36 acre lake N of Tulalip Indian Reservation. annually planted with 1500 rainbows, usually has a few carry-over 'bows at spring opener. Also, pumpkinseed panfish. WDFW access, launch on N. side. From I-5 about 6 miles N. of Marysville, turn W. on Fire Trail Rd./ 140th St. NE 5.5 miles to Wenberg State Park entrance on E. side of **LAKE GOODWIN** where a road leads E. for 0.5 miles to Crabapple from Lake Goodwin Road. Watch for signs.

CRESCENT LAKE. A 9 acre slough with largemouth bass, crappie, catfish, and perch S. of Monroe. Drains to Snoqualmie River, just above Skykomish River confluence. Drive S. from Monroe on Hwy. 203 to W. on High Rock Rd. to High Bridge Rd. to E. shore.

CUTTHROAT LAKES. Group of 7 small cutthroat lakes at 4300 feet on NE side of Bald Mt. summit. Drain to South Fork Stillaguamish. From Mountain Loop Hwy. at Red Bridge Campground turn S. on FS Rd. 4030, bear W. on 4032 to top of Mallardy Ridge and S to Trail 706.

DAN CREEK. Fair for rainbow and cutthroat in late summer. Enters Sauk River 2 miles NE of Darrington. FS Rd. 24 follows stream for 4 miles.

DEVILS LAKE (Lost). Public access area on SW shore of this 13 acre cutthroat and rainbow lake E. of Maltby. Drains to Ricci Creek and Snoqualmie River. Best fishing early in season. Head E. from Maltby 1.5 miles on Hwy. 202 then S. on Echo Lake Road for 1.5 miles, then E. on Lost Lake Road 0.7 miles to lake.

DIAMOND LAKE. Rainbow are in Diamonds's 9.6 acres, at 5250 feet elev. about 0.8 miles SE from Meadow Mt. Drains to Suiattle River. E. on Whitechuck River Rd./FS 23 then N. on FS Rd. 2700 to FS 2710 and continue to Rd. end where Trail 657 goes E. to lakes.

DOLLAR LAKES. Rainbow planted lakes of 6 and 2 acres at 3950 and 3900 feet 2.8 miles N. of Index and 1 mile SE from E. end of Lake Isabel.

DOWNEY LAKE. Cutthroat are in this 13 acre mountain lake at 5500 feet elev. 20 miles E. of Darrington. Drains to Downey Creek and Suiattle River. From Suiattle River Rd./FS Rd. 26 go N. on Trail 768 which crosses outlet below lakes.

DUFFY CREEK. Fair to poor summer cutthroat fishing in this tributary to Skykomish River. From Hwy. 2 at Sultan, turn S. cross Skykomish River then E. on Mann Rd./164th St. 7 miles to creek.

DUFFY LAKES. Rainbow lakes of 2.5 and 3.5 acres at 3000 and 3180 feet 4 miles S. of Gold Bar in headwaters of Duffy Creek.

EBEY LAKE (Little). Can be hard to find, but good fly fishing at times for large cutthroat, Ebey covers 10 acres and is located on Ebey Hill. Outlet is Hell Creek which drains into North Fork Stillaguamish River. Boat launch on N. side. Hwy. 503 to Trafton, then SE about 5 miles, then W. for 1.5 miles uphill to lake shore.

ECHO LAKE (Eatons). A 17 acre year-round rainbow lake with WDFW access, ramp on E. shore. 1 mile S. of **DEVILS LAKE** and 3 miles SE of Maltby. It is 50 feet deep and sometimes supports carry-over 'bows. Also pumpkinseeds. Drive NE from Maltby on Hwy. 522 then SE on Echo Lake Road which encircles lake.

ECHO LAKE. 9 miles N. of Sultan at 1670 feet, this Echo is 25 acres and contains rainbow and brook trout. Sometimes excellent fishing. Outlet is a 120 foot falls and empties into Pilchuck River. Reached from old Monroe log camp walking or mountain biking from gate up Echo Lake Truck Trail. Brushy, bring a raft.

EMERALD LAKE (Meadow). An 11 acre lake rainbow lake at 5150 feet 17 miles E. of Darrington on E. side of Meadow Mt. Falls tumble 70 feet at outlet. Drains to Lime Creek to Suiattle River. Hike-in access from White Chuck River Rd/FS 23 , N. on FS Rd. 2700 and 2710 to Rd. end where Trail 657 continues E.

EVAN LAKE. A 12.8 acre rainbow lake at 2750 feet elev. at end of FS Rd. 4020 from Wiley Campground on Mountain Loop Hwy. Drains to Boardman Creek.

FLOWING LAKE. A popular, heavily fished

Edmonds fishing pier.

135 acre year-round lake planted lightly in April and again with 14,000 rainbow trout in May. Some largemouth bass. Fed from Storm Lake 800 feet W. WDFW disabled, access, launch on E. shore, park and resort. Drive E. from Snohomish on 68th St. SE then on Three Lakes Road for 4.5 miles to Flowing Lake Road then 1 mile to lake. County park with good wheelchair, bank fishing access.

FONTAL LAKE. One of the best lakes for rainbow and large brook trout in Snoqualmie Valley. Fontal covers 37 acres 4.5 miles SE of Monroe behind a locked Campbell Group gate, 2.5 miles from the lake. Walk or bike ok. Raft best. From Hwy. 203 about 3 miles S. of Monroe turn E. and S. on High Rock Road then NE 7.5 miles to SW side of **HANNAN LAKE** and another 0.5 miles to E. tip of Fontal which is open year-round.

FORTSON MILL POND #2. A kids only 2 acre rainbow planted pond 9.5 miles E. of Oso on Hwy. 530 at Fortson. Drains into North Fork Stillaguamish.

FRENCH CREEK. Fair for summer rainbows. Enters North Fork Stillaguamish River 2 miles E. of Hazel on Hwy. 530. From highway FS Rd. 2010 leads S. 1 mile to French Creek FS campground and upstream.

GISSBERG PONDS (Smokey Point Ponds). Two 5 acre year-round ponds in Gissberg County Park just W. of 1-5 and S. of Smokey Point. A great place for kids to bank fish for 10,000 catchable rainbows planted in spring plus 400 large triploid rainbows, largemouth bass, perch, bluegills, and channel catfish.

GOAT LAKE. A pretty, early ice-out 64 acre mountain lake 4 miles E. of Barlow Pass with brookies and rainbow at 3154 feet. Take Mountain Loop Hwy. FS 20 to about 3 miles N. of Barlow Pass, then SE on FS 4080 about 1 mile to Elliott Creek Trailhead and 4.8 miles to lake.

GOBLIN CREEK. Upper Goblin Creek offers fair summer rainbow and cutthroat fishing. Flows into North Fork Skykomish. Best route is from Index N. on US 2 at Index N. on FS 63/North Fork Rd. past Garland Mineral Hot Springs to where the stream enters the Sky.

GOODWIN LAKE. One of the most popular fishing lakes in Snohomish County, this 547 acre year-round lake is stocked with 15,000 cutthroat and rainbow. Best for trout in May and June then summer for largemouth and smallmouth bass, crappie, perch and pumpkinseed panfish. Access through Wenberg State Park on lake's E. shore which has a boat launch and camping. Drive N. from Everett on 1-5 about 9 miles to Smokey Point Exit 206, then W. on Lake Goodwin Rd. 5 miles to N. end of lake.

GREIDER LAKES. A pair of golden-trout planted lakes. Lower Greider is 8.5 acres at 2900 feet. Upper Greider covers 58.4 acres at 2930 feet just S. of Spada Reservoir. From Hwy. 2 E. of Startup turn N. on Kellogg Lake Rd./FS 61 then E. on Sultan Basin Rd. to S. side of reservoir. At the fork, there's a trailhead and short hike up Greider Creek.

GULCH LAKES. Trio of small rainbow lakes at 3600 feet 9.5 miles N. of Index on E. side of Hard Pass. From US 2 go N. on North Fork Skykomish Rd./FS 63 then W. and N. on FS 6335 to a rough trail up Silver Creek to confluence of Gulch Lake outlet.

HALCYON LAKE. Cutthroat planted 5.3 acre lake in a logging area 3.4 miles S. of Gold Bar. Drains to Skykomish River.

HALL LAKE. A 6.1 acre neighborhood lake between Hwy. 99 and I-5 just S. of Hwy. 104. Poor to fair for largemouth bass, panfish and drains to **LAKE BALLINGER**.

HANNAN LAKE. 48 acres with rainbows and brookies. It often holds husky hold-over 'bows. Church owned and access often limited. See Fontal Lake driving directions.

HANSON LAKE (McAllester). Large cutthroat and brookies attract anglers to this shallow 10 acre lake 5.5 miles SE of Granite Falls on gated Scotty Road. Hike or bike, ok. Produces best early. Year round.

HEATHER LAKE. Cutthroat lake of 17.5 acres at 2450 feet 8.5 miles E. of Granite Falls on NW side of Pilchuck Mt. Just E. of Verlot turn S. on FS Rd. 42 to Trail 701.

HELENA LAKE. Golden trout stocked 27.5 acre lake at 3050 feet 8 miles S. of Darrington, E. of FS Rd. 2060 at head of Helena Creek.

HEMPLE LAKE. A 7 acre rainbow lake at 3150 feet 10 miles E. of Granite Falls. Drains to South Fork Stillaguamish.

HOWARD LAKE. Plants of 4000 rainbows, 14 inches and up, have made this 27 acre lake an excellent opening day bet. Lake is 9 miles NW of Marysville and 1.4 miles W. of N. end of **GOODWIN LAKE**. From I-5 go W. at Exit 202 Smokey Pt. Rd. to 45 Rd. then NW past Lake Ki and Lake Goodwin to Lakewood Rd.

HUGHES LAKE. Cutthroat, brookies and largemouth bass in this 20 acre lake 8 miles N. of Monroe on Woods Creek Road. S. of Lake Roesiger turn NE on spur road 0.5 mile to lake.

INDEPENDENCE LAKE. A 5.5 acre, deep rainbow lake at 3700 feet about 5 miles NE of Silverton. Headwaters of Coal Creek, drains to South Fork Stillaguamish River.

ISABEL LAKE. A large low "high" lake with brookies, rainbow, kokanee, cutthroat and a few large mackinaw. Covering 176 acres at 2842 feet elev. Maximum depth of 201 feet. From Gold Bar on US 2 drive N on FS Rd. 6010 to trail that follows the outlet 0.8 mile N. to lake.

JANUS LAKE. Located along PCT 2000 6 miles NE of Stevens Pass, Janus is 29 acres at 4220 feet elev. Cutthroat. Drive E. of Stevens Pass on Hwy. 2 for 4.5 miles then N. on Smith Brook Road/FS 6700 for 2 miles to Janus Lake Trail to PCT. Hike is 3.7 miles.

JAY LAKE. A 5-acre widening on the inlet of Wallace Lake in Wallace Falls State Park N. of Gold Bar on US 2. Hike or bike access at 1900 feet elev. Brushy. Good fishing after mid May for wild cutthroat and brook trout. Small campground at state park.

JOAN LAKE. A 3.5 acre lake once planted with Atlantic salmon. The lake is at 5100 feet elev. 6 miles NW of Stevens Pass. Drains to Rapid River.

JULIA LAKE. An abused 8 acre pond with small cutthroat and brookie in a logging area 5 miles SE of Granite Falls on Scotty Road. Road gated requiring a 5 mile hike or bike. Bring a raft. Clear-cuts have depreciated fishing.

KELCEMA LAKE. A 23.2 acre cutthroat lake at 3282 feet elev. 2.8 miles N. of Silverton at head of Deer Creek. Drains to South Fork Stillaguamish. From Mountain Loop Hwy. near Coal Creek Bar, turn N. on FS Rd. 4052 up Deer Creek to Trail 718 and short hike to lake in Boulder River Wilderness.

KELLOGG LAKE. Kellogg is 20 acres in two basins connected by a long snaking waterway surrounded by an extensive peat bog. Offers largemouth bass, black crappie, perch, cutthroat and bullfrogs. Drains into Bear Creek to Wallace River. Open year-round, best fished from a raft or tube. From US 2 go 3 miles NE of Sultan on Sultan Basin road, then 1 mile E. on Kellogg Lake Rd. Best fishing is in April and October.

KETCHUM LAKE. 20 acre year-round rainbow stocked lake 3 miles N. of Stanwood. About 1000 catchable rainbow are stocked in April supplementing a self-sustaining population of bluegill, largemouth bass, bullhead catfish and pumpkinseed. From Stanwood N. 2.5 miles on Hwy. 530 then E. on Ketchum Lake Rd. for 0.4 miles to WDFW access, small boat launch on N. end of lake.

KI LAKE. A heavily planted trout and warmwater fish lake and an excellent opening

weekend-early May prospect. Stocked in mid April with 15,000 catchable and 1000 triploid (averaging 1.5 pounds) rainbows. Decent summer largemouth bass and perch fishery. Located 8 miles NW of Marysville. Covers 97 acres. County road access on N. shore. From I-5 Exit 202 at Smokey Point, then W. on Smokey Point Rd. 4 miles then NW on the 45 Rd. to lake.

KING LAKE. A deep, 9 acre brookies and cutthroat lake in a Weyerhaeuser logging area SE of Arlington. Open year-round, best fishing April and May. Drive E. and S. of Arlington on Homestead and Jordan roads for 9 miles (passing Jordan) then hike or bike E. and N. about 1 mile on rough gated road. Difficult, confusing access. Drains to Jordan Creek.

KING LAKE. A 12 acres cutthroat lake 2 miles W. of **HANNAN LAKE**, draining into **MARGARET LAKE**. From Monroe 3 miles S. on Hwy. 203, then E. and S. on High Rock Road for 1 mile, then E. for 2.5 miles, then N. 1 mile to lake.

KLEMENTS MILL POND. Largemouth bass, rainbow and limited numbers of cutthroat in this 3 acre pond. Route is 0.5 miles N. of Granite Falls on Mountain Loop Hwy., then NE for 0.5 miles to lake on NW slope of Iron Mt.

KROOZE LAKE. A 2 acre cutthroat pond 3.5 miles NE of Arlington, drains to North Fork Stillaguamish River. Drive 3 miles out of Arlington on Hwy. 530 Pond borders W. side of road. Poor fishing.

LIME LAKE. A spectacular, remote alpine lake stocked with golden trout on Lime Ridge in Glacier Peak Wilderness. A deep 10.9 acre lake at 5550 feet elev. Drains to Lime Creek, Suiattle River. From Mountain Loop Hwy./FS 20 at White Chuck campground, turn E. on FS Rd. 23 then NE on 2700-2710 to Trail 657. Nearby cutthroat lakes are **BOX LAKE** and **UPPER RIVORD** and **LOWER RIVORD**.

LITTLE CAVANAUGH LAKE. A rainbow fry plant maintains a fair trout fishery in this logging area pond that varies from 4 to 8 acres. From US 2 at Index, turn S. on FS Rd. 62/Proctor Creek Rd. and continue about 5 miles to lake. May be gated requiring hike or bike access.

LOMA LAKE. Plants of 1000 catchable

Upper Rivord Lake, Lime Ridge.

and 500 large triploid rainbow boost success in this 21-acre year-round lake just N. of Tulalip Indian Reservation, 5 miles NW of Marysville. Public access on NE shore. Produces best in April and May. At Stimson Crossing turn W. on 140th St. NW for 3 miles, then 0.5 miles N. to Loma on Lake Drive which circles the lake.

LOST LAKE (DEVIL'S). 13 acre year-round lake with native cutthroat, 1000 spring planted rainbow, and largemouth bass. Public access on W. shore, ramp. 2.5 miles E. of Maltby on Hwy. 522 cross Snoqualmie River then S. on Welch Rd. to lake

LOST LAKE. Year-round 18-acre brown, cutthroat and rainbow lake 1 mile W. of Lake Chaplain in Everett city watershed. Drains to Woods Creek. Considered excellent for fly-fishing from float tube or raft. Brushy shoreline, small public pier. From Monroe drive N. on Woods Creek Road 7 miles to gated spur road. Walk E. on road into watershed to lake.

MARTHA   LAKE   (ALDERWOOD MANOR). Plants of 8000 catchable and 600 triploid rainbows makes this 59 acre lake a spring favorite and good numbers of holdover trout and largemouth bass, perch and bullhead catfish extend the productive season into summer. Martha Lake AM has a depth of 48 feet has a WDFW access and ramp on its SE. shore, and a large county park on the S. end with two fishing piers. From I-5 drive N. 2 miles the E. on 164th St. SW. about 1.5 miles to S. end of lake.

MARTHA LAKE (WARM BEACH). Plants of large rainbow, plus 1000 triploids and a hold-over population of cutthroat, plus largemouth bass and perch make this a good year-round bet, best in April and May. Public access, launch on NW side of the 58 acre lake. I-5 Exit 206 to Smokey Point then W. on Lake Goodwin-Warm Beach Road NW on 45 Road and W. on Lakewood Rd.

MARTHA LAKE (LITTLE). This 13.4 acre Martha is 3.4 miles E. of Marysville near the N. tip of Lake Cassidy and offers largemouth bass, perch and bullhead catfish.

MAY CREEK. Wild rainbows. Flows into Wallace River about 1.5 miles E. of Gold Bar.

MEADOW LAKE. A 9 acre mountain lake at 4500 feet elev. in headwaters of Meadow Creek. Holds rainbow and cutthroat in the 11 inch range, with a few larger fish. Mountain Loop Hwy. to mouth of White Chuck River, then E. on FS 23 for 5.5 miles, N. on FS 2700/Meadow Mt. Rd. to FS 2710 to trail 638. Hike 4 miles to lake, passing. **CRYSTAL LAKE** at the 1 mile mark. Crystal is 21 acres and contains rainbow and cutthroat.

MEADOW LAKE. A private 14 acre lake with rainbow and cutthroat, 3 miles N. of Monroe.

MENZEL LAKES. Private lakes of 13 and 3 acres SE of Granite Falls. Three beaver ponds above the lakes have been planted with cutthroat fry.

METAN LAKE. A 3.5 acre cutthroat lake 12.5 miles SE of Darrington on SW side of Pugh Mt. at 2800 feet elev. Drains to Sauk River. From FS 20 turn NE on FS 2095 to Trail 644 to lake.

MONTE CRISTO LAKE. A 14-acre lake on South Fork Sauk River adjacent to Mountain Loop Hwy. 2 miles N. of Barlow Pass. Holds rainbow, cutthroat and brookies. Best July into fall.

NORTH LAKE. Cutthroat in 10.6 deep acres, 8.8 miles SE of Darrington at head of North Falls Creek. Drains to Sauk River.

OLSON LAKE. Fair summer fishing for crappie and cutthroat in this 3 acre pond 3 miles SE of Arlington on W. side of Service Road where power line crosses the road.

PANTHER LAKE. A 47 acre year-round lake with largemouth bass, crappie, pumpkinseed sunfish and brown bullhead at former community of Three Lakes. WDFW access on W. shore. From Snohomish drive E. on 68th St. SE about 6 miles, then N. on Panther Lake Road 1.5 miles.

PASS LAKE. A 2.4 acre rainbow pond at 3700 feet 3.8 miles NE of Silverton on Mountain Loop Hwy. at head of Coal Creek. From Mountain Loop Hwy. go N. at Big Four Camp to FS 4060 to Coal Lake picnic area. Short walk NE on trail 605.

PEACH LAKE. 17-acre mountain cutthroat lake at 4800 feet about 10 miles N. of Stevens Pass. Access from PCT 2000. Drains to Beckler River.

PEEK-A-BOO LAKE. Rainbow planted lake, 22.4 acres, 10 miles SE of Darrington at head of Peek-A-Boo Creek. Drains to Sauk River. At White Chuck Campground, go W on FS 2080 and continue to end of main road and trail 656 to lake.

PICNIC POINT POND. A 4 acre pond 0.4 miles N. of Picnic Point adjacent to RR. tracks and Puget Sound. Stocked with rainbow. Hike N. up RR. tracks from Picnic Point park.

PILCHUCK CREEK. A small cutthroat and steelhead stream that enters the Stillaguamish River 0.5 mile W. of where the creek crosses I-5. Sea-run cutthroat in lower reaches spring and fall. Few summer-run steelhead in June, and winter-runs in February. Clears and drops rapidly after high water and can produce steelhead when larger streams are out of shape. Upper portions carry small cutthroat and rainbow, 14-inch trout minimum. Norman Road offers access at mouth. The Stanwood-Bryant road crosses the creek 1.5 miles N. of the I-5 bridge. Hwy. 9 bridge is about 4.5 miles N. of Bryant.

PILCHUCK RIVER. The Pilchuck is a quick, narrow, rocky steelhead river that heads N. of Sultan under Bald Mt. and flows W. and S. for 30 miles to the Snohomish River at E. edge of Snohomish. Open only during the winter, and produces about 300 winter-run steelhead a year, most are wild and most are caught January and February. Also has sea-run cutthroat and salmon but no salmon season. Boat fishing is prohibited. The river may be waded at riffles, and is paralleled along lower stretches between Snohomish through Machias by Machias Road. The Robe-Menzel Road leads S. from Granite Falls along the river for 4 miles. Upper reaches are reached by driving SE from Granite Falls on Anderson Road 4 miles, then E. about 6 miles. This road swings S. to Sultan.

PINNACLE LAKE. Cutthroat and brookies planted in 6.5 acre lake at 3820 feet elev. 10 miles E. of Granite Falls on E. side of Pilchuck Mt. in Mount Pilchuck State Park. Drains to S. Fork Stillaguamish River.

POWERLINE POND. A 2 acre pond with small rainbow, cutthroat and brookies 5.4 miles N. of Bothell on power line. Drains to North Creek.

PROCTOR CREEK. Poor rainbow fishing in this tributary of Skykomish River entering 1 mile E. of Gold Bar. At Index, Rd. 62 runs S. to meet and follow creek. Road often gated.

PUGET SOUND. Artificial bottomfish reefs,

public piers and one of the best boat ramp facilities on Puget Sound at Everett, bring saltwater fishing, crabbing and shrimping to the W. edge of Snohomish County. Good pot and hand crabbing for Dungeness and red rock in many near-shore areas, especially in the non-commercial crab zone along the south edge of Port Gardner Bay, and off the Everett jetty. Crab, dock shrimp, chinook, coho, ling cod, rockfish and squid are targeted at the public fishing pier in Edmonds which is bolstered with nearby artificial bottomfish reef. Public piers at Mukilteo (where there is also a horrible, unprotected boat launch) and at Stuart's Dock in Everett offer good fishing platforms for flounder, perch, smelt and herring and a variety of bottomfish. In late summer, the Edmonds pier, adjacent to the ferry terminal, is one of the best salmon fishing piers on the Sound. It produces year-round. Many gravel beaches support good numbers of littleneck, butter, cockles and horse clams, but be alert for access, private property and red tide complications. The Everett multi-lane city ramp just inside the Snohomish River is an excellent facility. In Edmonds a public sling launch is S. of the Ferry terminal. Edwards Point and Point Wells S. of Edmonds, and Possession Point and Possession Sound off Mukilteo are excellent winter and summer salmon spots. In odd-numbered years Port Gardner Bay and Humpy Hollow are hot spots for staging Snohomish River pink salmon.

RAPID RIVER. Even the most dedicated stream fishermen rarely know of this quick mountain trout stream pitching off the Cascade crest from several small lakes along PCT 2000 SW below Johnson Ridge into Beckler River 9 miles N. of Skykomish. Pocket picking water for small wild rainbow and cutthroat. From US 2 at Skykomish turn N. on FS Rd. 65 then E. at the mouth of the Rapid onto FS 6530 which continues E. along the stream to Henry M. Jackson Wilderness. June-October best. Bring light tackle.

RILEY LAKE. Plants of 3000 rainbow in April boost this 30 acre lake's spring prospects. Public access on SE end. From Hwy. 530 about 4 miles NE of Arlington at Trafton turn E. onto Trafton Rd. 6 miles to Riley Lake Road, then N. 2 miles to S. end of lake. Peat bog shore. Best from small boats.

ROESIGER LAKE. A large, reproducing kokanee population, plus WDFW plants of 8000 rainbows, largemouth bass, bluegill, crappie, perch and brown bullhead make this 352-acre lake a fine year-round prospect. Roesiger is hour-glass shaped, 115 feet at deepest point and delivers respectable success all summer. Catchable rainbow are stocked in the south arm in late March. In May the center and northern arms are stocked. Most summer trout and kokanee anglers concentrate on trolling the deep N. arm, while the shallower central and south ends are great summer bets for warm-water species—especially bass. WDFW access/launch on S. shore. Snohomish County park on E. shore offers bank fishing. Drive N. from Monroe up Woods Creek Road for 10 miles to S. tip of lake. Roads up W. and E. shores.

ROUND LAKE. Snow fed 12 acre mountain lake at 5100 feet in Glacier Peak Wilderness. Rainbows. Drains to White Chuck River. From Mountain Loop Hwy. at Bedal turn E. on FS 49 to Trail 646 and a tough, switch-back climb N. through Bingley Gap and E. to lake which lies in a deep cirque.

RUGGS LAKE. 11 acre private lake S. of Everett with rainbow, cutthroat, bullhead and warm-water fish. Fed by Silver Lake 1 mile NW. No public access.

SAUK RIVER UPPER. Scenic upper reaches of this major Skagit River tributary (See Skagit County) are in Snohomish County and provide some winter and summer steelheading but is best for wild cutthroat, whitefish and it's one of the few legal Washington bull trout fisheries. Some very nice bull trout in this river which has a 20 inch minimum size. The White Chuck River flows into the upper Sauk about 9 miles SE of Darrington often dumping in milky glacial-floured water. Above that confluence, the Sauk runs clear and often shallow with trout pools. The North and South Forks merge to form the mainstem at Bedal Campground 15 miles SE of Darrington on the Mountain Loop Hwy. From Bedal, the **NORTH FORK SAUK** is followed by FS Rd. 49 E. around Bedal Peak up the North Fork 7 miles to Sloan Creek campground where FS Trail 649 continues upstream eventually linking to PCT 2000. The road crosses the North Fork at Sloan Creek campground and continues 6 miles up Sloan Creek about 10 miles to Trail 650 which continues to alpine lakes on the glaciated E. flanks of Monte Cristo Peak. The upper river is more of a creek and fishes best July-Sept. **SOUTH FORK SAUK** flows around the W. side of Bedal Peak and is paralleled by Mountain Loop Hwy. to Barlow Pass. At the pass, gated FS Road 4710 continues upstream to form Monte Cristo campground below Poodle Dog Pass and trailheads into Henry M. Jackson Wilderness and alpine lakes in a spectacular setting surrounded by glaciated peaks.

SCRABBLE LAKE. A 3 acre rainbow lake at 5000 feet on W. side of Scrabble Mt. in Henry M. Jackson Wilderness. Drains to Rapid River NE of Skykomish.

SCRIBER LAKE. A 3.4 acre year-round neighborhood lake in Lynnwood's Scriber Lake Park. Stocked with largemouth bass and perch. Small fishing pier.

SERENE LAKE. April and May are top months for this year-round lake's 1500 planted rainbow and cutthroat. Lake is 3 miles N. of Lynnwood adjacent to Hwy. 99. A WDFW access, launch on W. shore. From Hwy 99 take Shelby Road W. to 43rd Ave. W., then N. to access.

SHAW LAKE. The uppermost lake in the chain ending with Wallace Lake in Wallace Falls State Park near Gold Bar. It's an excellent fishery for cutthroat up to 16 inches. Open year-round, elev. 2075 feet. Access is walk-in, difficult and worth the effort. Best in late May, June.

SHOECRAFT LAKE. Shoecraft is one of several lakes just N. of Tulalip Indian Reservation W. of I-5. It's 600 feet SW of **GOODWIN LAKE and** is linked by a narrow canal. Shoecraft covers 137 acres, is planted in May with 5000 large rainbows. Also holds large and smallmouth bass, black crappie, perch, pumpkinseed and bullhead catfish. Open year-round. WDFW access, launch on SW shore off 43rd Ave. W.

SILVER CREEK. Flows into the North Fork Skykomish River 8 miles NE of Index. Offers fair to good summer fishing for small wild rainbow. FS 63 from Index to FS 6335 at Galena which leads up creek approximately 5 miles. A non-maintained trail continues NE about 3 miles to **SILVER LAKE** at 4200 feet elevation in Henry M. Jackson Wilderness which has cutthroat. Silver Lake is best reached from Monte Cristo

by hiking S. through Poodle Dog Pass on Trail 708.

SILVER LAKE. A year-round lowland lake on the Everett-Bothell Hwy. this 102 acre water is heavily stocked in April with 1000 triploid rainbows and in May with 4500 catchable rainbow and kokanee salmon. Also offers largemouth bass and perch. No developed trailerable boat ramp. Portable craft may be launched at SE corner of lake. Lots of shoreline fishing access and public dock along the highway. City park, fishing pier on W. shore.

SKYKOMISH RIVER (MAIN). Fed by two major salmon and steelhead hatchery/rearing pond facilities, dozens of spawning tributaries with a long run from the crest of the Cascades to the dairy farm lowlands in Snoqualmie Valley the main stem Sky is the most productive summer and winter anadromous fish producer in the greater Seattle region. A broad, deep, boulder-bed-pool, riffle-and-rapid freestone river paralleled by access roads along both banks for most of its length, the Sky's productivity is equaled by its popularity. It's easily the top target for the majority of Seattle metro area steelheaders. In recent years the Sky has ranked No. 3 in state winter-run production and No. 4 for summer-runs. Rarely does it rank out of the top 5 in either category.

Still, the Skykomish is suffering the same downward trends of all Puget Sound

Skykomish River steelheaders.

drainages, only at a slower rate. For comparison in 1999 the Sky produced almost 2000 winter steelhead and 3000 summer steelhead. Ten years earlier anglers caught about 5000 winter-runs and 3000 summer runs.

Good numbers of summer-runs are caught May-October peaking in July and August. Winter steelheading starts strong in November, spikes sharply in January when most hatchery fish come in, then drops dramatically in February when it's mostly a wild steelhead show. Some years a popular wild steelhead catch-and-release fishery is allowed in March. When salmon returns are high, the lower Sky is occasionally opened for chinook, and often opened for chums, odd-year pinks and hatchery coho. While steelhead action extends upriver beyond US 2/High Bridge to WDFW's Reiter Ponds and on into the Forks, most salmon fishing is from Gold Bar salmon hatchery downstream, often centering in the first miles either side of Monroe. First salmon run of the year is chinook which arrive in late July and August and the last is chums which are sometimes caught into December. Odd-year pinks are very popular September targets in the lower river. The salmon runs are also shadowed by strong runs of sea-run cutthroat and Dolly Varden which prey on the salmon spawn. Dollies are protected in many rivers, but in recent years have been legal in the entire Snohomish system including the Sky June-February. Dollies to 10 pounds have been caught here, and the catch and keep minimum is 20 inches. From Monroe upstream the Sky supports a large population of 7 to 12 inch mountain whitefish which bite well in late winter, yet are ignored by most anglers.

The mainstem Sky flows approximately 25 miles between the North and South Fork confluence at Index to where it merges with Snoqualmie River 3.5 miles SW of Monroe at Hwy. 202 bridge forming the broad, tidal-influenced Snohomish River. The north bank is followed by US 2 for the river's entire length. The south bank is followed between Monroe and Sultan by Ben Howard Road. WDFW Ben Howard access on the S. side of river 2 miles E. of Monroe bridge is a favorite take-out for drift boats fishing down from Sultan and a launch point for jet boats working the Monroe area. Another WDFW ramp is at Hwy. 203 bridge in Monroe. Other exceptionally popular bank-fishing and boat access points are the mouth of the Sultan River, US 2/High Bridge and WDFW's Reiter Ponds steelhead rearing facility. Bank access is limited between Sultan and High Bridge which is a prime drift boat float. South Fork Sky drops into King County near Baring.

SKYKOMISH RIVER NORTH FORK. The North Fork flows SW from the crest of the Cascades near PCT 2000 at Cady Pass to merge with the South Fork at Index. It's fed by dozens of streams. Anadromous fish, mostly steelhead, go 16 miles upstream as far as Deer Falls just above Goblin Creek which is less than 2 miles from the end of FS Rd. 63 at the boundary of Henry M. Jackson Wilderness. Between 20 and 50 summer and winter steelhead are caught each month June-February, mostly in the lower river. Below and above Deer Falls are a fair number of wild cutthroat and rainbow, mostly 6 to 9 inches. From US 2 at Index turn NW on North Fork Road/FS 63 which parallels the North Fork 18 miles. At Garland Mineral (Hot) Springs, FS Rd. 65 forks SE crosses Jack Pass and loops along the Beckler River to Hwy. 2 at Skykomish. At the E. end of FS 63 several major trailheads continue to alpine lakes in Henry M. Jackson Wilderness and link to PCT 2000.

SKYKOMISH RIVER SOUTH FORK. This branch of the Sky flows about 13 miles between its confluence with the North Fork just downstream of Sunset Falls at Index and its beginning at the confluence of the Beckler and Tye rivers near Skykomish. It's entirely followed by US 2 on the N. bank and much of the S. bank by FS 6030. Only about 4 miles of the South Fork are in Snohomish County (See King County). Most of the river, including the Beckler and Tye, is fair for wild rainbows and a few cutthroat.

SMELLING LAKE. Smelling Lake plunges 107 feet deep, yet covers only 7 acres. Open year-round, it holds small wild cutthroat and brookies, and fishes best in April, May and October. Drains to Worthy Creek. From Granite Falls drive 4.5 miles SE on Scotty Road

SNOHOMISH RIVER. A large, pastoral lowland river formed by the confluence of the Skykomish and Snoqualmie rivers 3 miles SW of Monroe. Rising and falling with tide changes the Snohomish flows NW to enter Port Gardner Bay at Everett. The

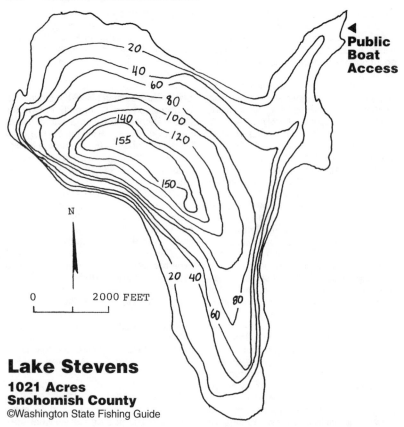

▲ **Public Boat Access**

N

0   2000 FEET

Lake Stevens
1021 Acres
Snohomish County
©Washington State Fishing Guide

sluggish flow splits near I-5 into Union, Ebey and Steamboat Sloughs. These year-round waters provide good sea-run cutthroat and Dolly Varden fishing from August into November. Pilings, log jams and old landings around the mouth attract large numbers of beautiful sea-run cutthroat much of the year with peaks spiking in May-June and Sept.-Oct. There is a little known, but growing white sturgeon fishery in the deepest holes between Snohomish and Everett. Sturgeon are not plentiful, but there are more than enough to target, especially in spring. The Snohomish is a broad, slow often muddy-bottomed conduit for steelhead and salmon headed for its major tributaries. It carries some of the largest steelhead and salmon runs in the state, but except for a few experienced plunkers and trollers, most anglers target the Snohomish's fish in the more angler-friendly Skykomish and Snoqualmie rivers. The Snohomish's claim to fame is chum, hatchery coho, odd-year pink salmon fish-

ing in the sweeping bends and eddies between Snohomish and Monroe. Thomas' Eddy is a famous pink salmon hole with WDFW access. The Snohomish's placid flow is easily fished with outboard prop and jet boats. Launches at Everett, Snohomish and Monroe. Bank side roads provide lots of access.

SNOWSLIDE LAKE (Slahal). Rainbow are in this 10 acre mountain lake at 4300 feet 5 miles N. of Index on Ragged Ridge at head of Excelsior Creek. Drains to North Fork Skykomish River.

SOUTH LAKE. A 13.2 rainbow hike-in lake at 4200 feet elev. 5.8 miles N. of Barlow Pass on N. side of Stillaguamish Peak. Drains to Sauk River.

SPADA LAKE. A 760 acre reservoir impounded by a dam on Sultan River in Sultan Basin for City of Everett water storage. Not stocked but has a reproducing population of rainbow and cutthroat that occasionally hit 18 inches. Well known as a fly-fishing lake. Quality regs in effect, no bait, single hooks, 12-inch minimums, no gas powered motors. Fishing holds up well all summer. Success has been declining in recent years but is still a fair prospect. Drive E. from Sultan .05 miles on US 2, then N. on Sultan Basin Road/FS 61 for 14 miles to lake. FS 61 follows 5.5 miles along S. shore to two FS boat ramps, observation points and trailhead to Greider Lakes.

SQUIRE CREEK. A trouty tributary of North Fork Stillaguamish River 2.5 miles W. of Darrington. County park 0.8 miles upstream from mouth along Hwy. 530. Supports wild rainbow, cutthroat and Dolly Varden. Top fishing in May and June. To reach upper creek drive FS Rd. 2040 W. and S. from center of Darrington about 2 miles to hit Squire at Buckeye Creek and continue 6.5 miles up Squire to FS trail 654 which continues upstream about 5 miles crosses Squire Creek Pass to Eight Mile Creek to Clear Creek.

STEVENS LAKE. The largest natural lake in Snohomish County this 1021-acre year-round residential lake delivers good, but surprisingly overlooked fishing for a variety of cold and warm water gamefish. Anglers hit the water from several public parks and 2 fee boat ramps. The best ramp is Wyatt County Park, on the SW side off Davies Road, has access, swim beach, 3-lane ramp and fishing pier. A city boat ramp and dock is in downtown Lake Stevens. Bank access at Lundeen County Park on N. shore, and Sunset County Park on SE side. Stevens is best known for large (2 pound) kokanee salmon, from plants of 200,000 fry, that go on the bite in mid May and continue through summer. Most anglers troll for the tasty salmon, but chumming is legal which attracts still fishermen. Respectable shoreline/dock casting for largemouth (to 7 pounds) and smallmouth bass (5 pounds), and in late April-May look for schools of black crappie in brushy shorelines. Late August and September produce 8 to 14 inch perch. Year-round anglers may target rainbows and cutthroat in the 160-foot deep lake. Annually planted with 65,000 rainbow fry. Fishing pressure is inexplicably light for the quality of action available. Unfortunately for fishing diehards, this is also a major summer play lake and mid-day anglers compete with whining jet skis, water skiers and similar abomi-

nations. Lake Stevens drains into Pilchuck River. The small town of Lake Stevens is on the NE corner of the lake on Hwy. 9 about 5.5 miles E. of Everett.

STICKNEY LAKE. A 26 acre year-round lake with perch, largemouth bass, black crappie and bullhead catfish 4.5 miles NE of Lynnwood and .05 miles E. of Hwy. 99. Public access, launch on E. shore. Drains to Swamp Creek into Lake Washington. From Hwy. 99 go N. on Manor Way, S. on Admiralty Way, then N. on 20th Place W. to lake.

STILLAGUAMISH RIVER (Main). 16 miles of pretty lightly fished steelhead and salmon water. The main Stilly crosses the northern part of Snohomish County sliding under I-5 W. of Arlington en route to a braided flush into Port Susan south of Stanwood. The main stem produces good fishing for sea-run cutthroat, Dolly Varden (closed to dollies in recent year) in spring and fall, summer and winter steelhead. Beginning in August there are runs of chinook, coho, chums, plus pink salmon in odd-numbered years. The main Stilly is rarely opened for kings or coho fishing but there have been recent openings for chums and pinks. the forks above Arlington are closed to salmon fishing. The lower river offers some of the finest sea-run cutthroat fishing in the region in May-June and August-September, and a developing sturgeon fishery spring through fall. Hwy. 530 provides access.

STILLAGUAMISH RIVER NORTH FORK. Set aside by WDFW for fly-fishing only from mid-April through November, the North Fork is one of the most popular and storied summer steelhead streams in W. Washington. From Dec. 1-Feb. 28 it's open to conventional tackle. In the "good ol days" the Stilly attracted famous fishermen from across the country, including Zane Grey, and Roderick Haig-Brown and continues as a contemporary favorite of fly fishermen. The years have not been kind to this famous river. In the last 10 years catches have fallen from around 1700 winter-runs a season to about 600. Summer-runs have dropped from 550 a year to slightly more than 100. Some of the difference is undoubtedly traced to an increase in catch-and-release fly fishing. Best summer fishing occurs in July, October and November. Winter steelhead peak in December. Lower third of this fork is plagued by muddying clay slides. Good numbers of sea-run cutthroat follow the salmon into the North Fork from mid-summer into fall. Hwy. 530 tracks the stream E. from Arlington to Darrington. FS Rd. 2810 continues N. from Darrington ranger station for 7 miles along the headwaters.

STILLAGUAMISH RIVER SOUTH FORK. The South Fork supports very small runs of summer and winter steelhead (anglers often catch less than dozen of each annually), fair sea-run cutthroat and a few coho, chinook and pink salmon. Usually closed to salmon fishing, however. Above Granite Falls it's a mediocre prospect for wild rainbow and cutthroat from mid-June into fall. Clay slides muddy the lower river but the upper river is usually clear. Stehr Road leads SE from Arlington along the W. bank to Granite Falls. Homestead and Jordan roads parallel E. side. E. of Granite Falls Mountain Loop Hwy. closely follows upstream for approximately 25 miles to headwaters at Barlow Pass. Campers can select from 14 FS campgrounds along the South Fork/Mountain Loop Hwy.

STONE LAKE. Rainbow are reported in this 1.5 acre lake at 3800 feet, 1800 feet S. of Eagle Lake N. of Baring. From Hwy. 2 at Baring go N. on FS 6024 to Trail 1055 to E. side of Merchant Peak. Drains to South Fork Skykomish River.

STORM LAKE. Planted in late April with about 10,000 catchable rainbows, this 78 acre lake is a popular opening day-early May prospect. Also a growing number of largemouth bass. Public access, narrow ramp on W. shore. Go E. from Snohomish on 68th St. SE and Three Lakes Road, past Flowing Lake then S. on Storm Lake Rd.

SULTAN RIVER. A major tributary of the Skykomish River at town of Sultan where there is a boat launch to the Sky. City of Everett has dammed the Sultan about 12 miles from its mouth. Anglers take about 45 winter-run steelhead—most in December—in the lower stretch which flows through a steep canyon. The river gives up a couple of dozen summer-runs annually. Dolly Varden are legal here, and there are a few to catch. Often a good alternative when the nearby Skykomish is high and dirty. Reiner and Pipeline roads follow river's W. side, Sultan Basin Road leads up E. side for approximately 14 miles to mouth of **WILLIAMSON CREEK**, and then continues another 7 miles to road end near

Sheep Gap Mt. Fair to good fishing for wild rainbow and cutthroat in upper river. A rough road heads N. up Williamson Creek for 5 miles.

SUNDAY LAKE. Largemouth bass, black crappie, perch and pumpkinseed plus rainbow provide fishing these 39 acres. Primitive public access on N. shore. Located 5 miles E. of Stanwood. Drains into lower Stillaguamish River. Drive 3 miles E. from Stanwood on Stanwood-Bryant Road, then SE 1 mile on Sunday Lake Road.

SUNSET LAKE. Golden trout are the attraction in this remote 34.4 acre mountain lake at 4100 feet 7 miles E. of Index on N. side of Burley Mt. Drains to North Fork Skykomish.

SWARTZ LAKE (Waite's Mill Pond). Cutthroat and panfish, possibly largemouth bass, are in this small lake 1.5 miles SE of Granite Falls. Swartz covers 17 acres and drains to Milard Lake.

TEMPLE POND. An 8-acre pond (largest of several) in Lord Hill Regional Park SE of Snohomish. Stocked with cutthroat and brown trout fingerlings, and illegal largemouth bass. Open year-round

THIRTYSIX LAKE. A 5 acre pond in the center of a logging area peat bog at the headwaters of Elwell Creek about 5.5 miles S. of Sultan. Open to year-round fishing for good size cutthroat.

THOMAS LAKE. A shallow, boggy 7 acres, Thomas is 7.5 miles N. of Bothell and 2 miles SE of **SILVER LAKE** on York Road. Holds cutthroat, bass and perch.

TOMTIT LAKE. Largemouth bass are the attraction in this 27.9 acre lake in a logging area 3 miles S. of Sultan. Drains to Skykomish River.

TROUT LAKE (Mud). Formerly used for rearing steelhead, this 19 acre lake is a natural producer of cutthroat trout, with best fishing in the summer months. Drive NE from the bridge across the South Fork Stillaguamish near Granite Falls 3 miles to the Scott Paper company road, then N. 2.5 miles across Canyon Creek to the lake. Take left fork in road after crossing Canyon Creek.

TWENTY TWO LAKE. Rainbow plants are

made regularly in this 44 acre lake which drains into South Fork Stillaguamish River via Twenty Two Creek. Drive E. of Granite Falls on Mountain Loop Hwy. for 12 miles (1.5 miles E. of Verlot) then head S. up Twenty Two Creek 2 miles to lake at 2460 feet elev.

TWIN LAKES. Plants of cutthroat and rainbow have been made in Twin Lakes which cover 32 (Lower Twin) and 34 (Upper Twin) acres. Also, brookies and possibly a few steelhead. Lakes drain into Cub Creek, then into Jim Creek, and are located on a U.S.N. reservation. Limited access and may be closed to non-military. Follow Hwy. 530 from Trafton for 7 miles, then S. another 2 miles to check in at Navy radio station. Boat launch on upper lake.

TWIN LAKES. A pair of alpine lakes in a spectacular setting at 4700 and 4800 feet elev. 3 miles S. of Monte Cristo. Lower Twin covers 24 acres; Upper Twin, 69 acres. The lakes offer rainbow, cutthroat and a few brookies. Outlet from upper to lower Twin plunges down a 75 foot falls into Troublesome Creek. From Mountain Loop Hwy. hike old road to Monte Cristo and then Trail 708 over Poodle Dog Pass to lakes.

WAGNER LAKE. Planted in early April with 2500 rainbows to supplement a largemouth bass fishery. Wagner covers 20 acre 2.5 miles NE of Monroe. Take Wood Creek Road NE of Monroe for 1.5 miles, turn N. on Wagner Road for 1 mile passing Wagner community club, then right 100 yards to lake. WDFW access, ramp on SE.

WALLACE LAKE (Walton). Rainbows, mackinaw, cutthroat and brook trout are in the 100 feet depths of this 55 acre lake at 1850 feet elev. It's a 4 mile road hike to this year-round lake which drains into North Fork Wallace River. Best from rafts or tubes. Wallace Lake Road goes N. from Gold Bar on US 2 for about 6 miles to lake shore.

WALLACE RIVER. Poor winter steelheading and good whitefish angling in lower stretches of the Wallace, decent wild trout fishing for native cutthroat in the clear water above Wallace Falls in the undeveloped state park. Overgrown logging roads access much of the trout water. The Wallace flows into the Skykomish 1.5 miles E. of Sultan and flows under US 2 at E. outskirts of Startup. Trails lead upstream along both banks for a short distance. Wallace Lake Road crosses the river just below lake. Road from Gold Bar runs up E. side of the river, touching the stream near Wallace Falls.

WEDEN LAKE. Rainbow are in Weden's 5.5 acres at 4400 feet elev. 3.5 miles S. of Barlow Pass. From Monte Cristo Road hike S. on Trail 724 to Foggy Lake then follow outlet from Weden.

WHITECHUCK RIVER. Limited summer fishing is available in the Whitechuck because of heavy glacial silt from glaciers on surrounding peaks and headwaters in Glacier Peak Wilderness. The tumbling, rifflerich stream usually clears in fall and can be fished for Dolly Varden, and trout until the end of Oct. You may find a stray steelhead or salmon in the lower river just above the Sauk River which collects the Whitechuck 9 miles SE of Darrington on Mountain Loop Hwy. FS Road 23 follows the Whitechuck E. from Whitechuck Campground for 10 miles providing easy access. Trail 643 continues upstream for another 10 miles or so past Kennedy Hot Springs to headwaters under White Chuck Cinder Cone S. of Glacier Peak. Spectacular country.

WINTERS LAKE. A 11.2 acre lake with largemouth bass 3 miles NE of Sultan. Drains to Bear Creek.

WOODS CREEK. Native Dolly Varden, cutthroat, and a few winter steelhead are found in this Skykomish River tributary NE of Monroe. Florence and Lower Woods Creek roads follow the lower portion of stream E. and N. from Monroe. Woods Creek Road parallels middle stretches..

Snohomish County Resorts

Goodwin Lake: Lake Goodwin Resort, 360-652-8169.

Spokane County

WDFW Region 1

Washington Department of Fish and Wildlife, 8702 N. Division St., Spokane, WA 99218. Phone, 509-456-4082.

With nearly 500 lowland lakes, some exceptionally fertile, a beautiful rock and gravel river system, long summers and plenty of public access Spokane County is a remarkably productive fishing region despite being the population center of eastern Washington.

The concentration of lowland lakes and the surprising quality of the Spokane River/tributaries form one of the state's most promising fishing areas on the outskirts of the city of Spokane's population of 188,800—many of them fishermen.

Most fishing takes place on lakes or small ponds and is split between trout and warm water species. In the last decade there has been a major increase in the amount of warm water fishing available and a corresponding rise in popularity of fishing for bass, walleye, crappie and other panfish. Generally speaking, trout and kokanee salmon fishing is best Apr.-May and Sept.-Oct. and warm water species anchor the mid-summer. Most public lakes are stocked by WDFW, have developed public access/boat ramp areas, and the larger lakes also have resorts with dock fishing, rental boats and cabin or camping areas.

Topographically, the county dominates a low divide between the treeless plateaus of the Columbia Basin and the low, wooded foothills into the Rockies. The E. county is mostly rolling prairie, sage, pasture and crops on the edge of the Columbia Basin. A few miles from Spokane thin, open stands of pine and fir trees begin to appear and thick brush crowds the banks of most rivers and creeks. Forests growth is heavier in the NE and E. parts of the county where there are two minor mountain areas with elevations reach above 5000 feet. Mica Peak, 17 miles SE of the city, is 5,205 feet and the highest point is 5,878 feet at the top of Mt. Spokane, 23 miles NE. The W. part of the county is scabland, etched with coulees and lots of small surface-water lakes. Part of the county drains N. into Lake Roosevelt/Columbia R. and part S. into the Palouse. The Little Spokane River drains the NE part of the county, the Spokane River the E. and central portions, while the SW county flows S. into Palouse River system.

Summers are hot and dry with temperatures ranging in the low 80s. Winters are fairly cold averaging about 20 degrees. Total annual precipitation is 17.19 inches, much of it falling as winter snow. Primary access is from I-90, US 2, US 395 and US 195. The county covers 1777 square miles ranking 21st In size among Washington's 39 counties.

AMBER LAKE (Calvert). Tackle restrictions and catch-and-release seasons aimed at improving the quality of fishing, plus plants of 5000 catchable rainbow, plus rainbow and cutthroat fry and some hefty holdovers make Amber an excellent spring prospect. The lake covers 117 acres and is located 11 miles SW of Cheney. From Hwy. 904 go S. on Mullinex Road, turn W. on Pine Spring Road to lake shore community of Amber. Best fishing is in April and May. Selective gear rules.

BADGER LAKE. This 244 acre lake is stocked with rainbow and cutthroat fry. Resorts and a public access are located on Badger. Best fishing period is April, May and September. A locally famous mayfly hatch in mid-May can trigger excellent dry fly fishing. Lake is 12 miles S. of Cheney. From Hwy. 904 go S., SW. on Mullinex Road, turn S. onto Dover Road and follow to lake.

BAILEY LAKE. A 16 acre private lake with

marshy shores, 5 miles NE of Deer Park. It holds rainbow, but is not stocked. Outlet is Bear Creek.

BEAR LAKE (Kuester). Rainbow and warm water species, including largemouth bass, black crappie, and yellow perch. This 33.8 acre lake is 6 miles SE from Deer Park in a county park on US 2. Only juveniles or licensed adults accompanied by a juvenile are allowed to fish. Drains to Little Spokane River.

BLANCHARD CREEK. A pretty little brook trout stream which can provide good fishing all summer. It runs from near the look-out on Mount Spokane on the N. side of Mount Spokane State Park NE into Idaho. From Blanchard Valley near the Idaho border turn SW on Blanchard Creek Road.

BONNIE LAKE. A lanky, heavily silted 4.5 miles long enlargement of Rock Creek, Bonnie covers 366 acres, including about 82 acres in Whitman County. The lake offers poor fishing for largemouth bass, crappie, perch, sunfish and catfish. The S. shoreline is sheer rock cliffs up to 300 feet high. Route is S. and E. from Cheney 15 miles on Cheney-Plaza Road through Trumbull National Wildlife Refuge, then S. about 1.5 miles on private road. Boats may be launched from N. end.

CHAPMAN LAKE. This "S" shaped lake of 146 acres, best known as a kokanee lake, also offers rainbow trout, smallmouth and largemouth bass, perch and crappie. Resort facilities. Drive 9 miles S. of Cheney on Cheney-Plaza road, then turn E. for 1 mile to S. tip of lake. Bass fishing usually is good through summer and fall kokanee can be very good.

CLEAR LAKE. Excellent family fishing lake just S. of Fairchild AFB and N. of I-90. Heavy fall fry plants and spring stockings of 20,250 catchable rainbows, 15,000 brookies and 1500 1$^{1/2}$ pound Triploid rainbows, delivers excellent action at this popular lake. Located 2 miles S. of the community of Medical Lake, Clear Lake produces rainbow, brown and lake trout plus good shoreline fishing for largemouth bass fishing and brown bullheads. Nearly 3 miles long but covers only 375 acres. Good mayfly hatch in N. end in late May. Public access, ramp is at S. end, and there are 2 resorts. Boat, dock and shoreline fishing all produces. Most trout fishermen troll or

stillfish with bait. Mid summer can bring low water problems for the ramp. From I-90 about 14 miles E. of Spokane, exit W. onto Hwy. 902/Salnave Rd. and turn N. onto Clear Lake Rd.

DOWNS LAKE. A fast-warming, shallow lake in the SW corner of Spokane County, Downs is a 423 acre lake with extensive marshy shorelines and a good reputation for warm water fish. The lake receives periodic rainbow and brown trout plants and also contains largemouth bass, yellow perch and brown bullhead. Drive SE from I-90 at Sprague go S. on Hwy. 23, then E. on Williams Lake Rd. Turnoff is just E. of Lincoln Co. line. About 30 acres of Downs Lake are in Lincoln County.

ELOIKA LAKE. Considered one of the state's top warm water species lakes, Eloika offers a variety that includes largemouth bass (6 pounders are not uncommon), large crappie, bullhead catfish, perch and pumpkinseed. Open year around, but peak fishing is spring and summer. Bass and crappie are hot in the spring and early summer and perch do well from late summer into fall. WDFW stocks about 4000 catchable brown trout annually in Mar. or Apr. and brookies are also occasionally taken. The lake is largely undeveloped and covers 659 acres with lots of weed beds, cattails and lily pads. It has a resort with a boat launch plus public ramp. Lake is 7 miles N. of Chaytaroy on US 2, about 22 miles N. of Spoken. Two miles S. of Pend Oreille County line turn W. on Eloika Lake Rd. Public access is S. of Grays Landing.

FISH LAKE. Heavy annual WDFW stockings of catchable, brood stock and fry brook trout have made this one of the best brook trout fisheries in eastern Washington. Excellent prospect for spring and fall action. Bring lots of earthworms. Lake elevation is 2171 feet. It covers 47 acres. Gasoline powered boats are not allowed. Resort with dock, baits. County park boat launch. Drive 2.5 miles NE of Cheney on Cheney-Spokane Rd.

HOG CANYON LAKE (Deep). A winter-only fishing water, Hog Canyon Lake covers 53 shallow acres. Planted with around 14,000 catchable rainbows in the spring and 14,000 fry. A fertile lake where trout grow quickly to 10 to 12 inches by the Dec. 1 opening. The lake is located 13 miles SW of Cheney. Drive SW from Spokane on I-90 to Fishtrap Lake exit. Turn E. on Peterson Rd., cross R.R. tracks and follow dirt road to public access on S. end.

HORSESHOE LAKE. A 68 acre marshy lake with little open water 10 miles W. of Nine Mile Falls. Horseshoe gets 12,000 rainbow plants and contains brown bullhead catfish. Drive S. from Nine Mile Falls to state park, then W. on 7-Mile and Coulee-Hite roads 11 miles and then 1.5 miles N. on McLaughlin Road to lake. Boats may be launched at lake shore.

LIBERTY LAKE. Heavily fished for a mix of trout and warm water species. Liberty gives a good account of itself and can be productive early in the season, and has a reputation for delivering large bass and panfish. Now you can add large trout. The 711 acre lake is stocked with 20,000 catchable and broodstock rainbows, 2500 triploids (1½ lbs. and up) and brown trout, plus walleye, largemouth bass, bluegill, crappie, yellow perch, pumpkinseed and brown bullhead. There is a public, disabled access, state park, and RV park. Liberty Lake is 15 miles E. of Spokane 2 miles S. of I-90 at town of Liberty Lake.

LITTLE SPOKANE RIVER. A fun fly and light tackle stream. Excellent for winter whitefish. Heading in Pend Oreille County, the river enters Spokane County at Camden and meanders 30 miles SW to Spokane River at Old Fort Spokane on Stevens County line. US 2 crosses the river at Chattaroy. County roads follow stream for its entire length, but access can be tough because of posted land. Little Spokane offers brookies, brown trout, rainbow, whitefish and suckers. Lots of 7 to 10 inch trout, and a few that will be measured by the pound.

LONG LAKE. A productive year-round 5020 acre reservoir, (aka Spokane Lake) behind a power dam on Spokane River 23 miles NW of Spokane. The lanky reservoir extends 24 miles upstream from Lake Roosevelt providing miles of shoreline structure, coves and points. The reservoir is half in Spokane County, half in Stevens County. Game fish include perch, crappie, walleye, largemouth, smallmouth bass, bullhead catfish and a few northern pike. Planted with brown trout, lake trout and rainbow. Most productive spring and fall. Several resorts. DNR camp and boat launch sites 3 miles E. of Long Lake Dam.

Road from Nine Mile Falls parallels S. bank.

MEDICAL LAKE. Husky brown trout attract fly fishermen and light tackle (selective gear rules) to this 148.9 acre lake adjacent to W. side of town of Medical Lake. Annual plants of brown trout which grow large under a 2-fish, 14-inch minimum retention limit, and selective gear regs. Some largemouth bass. Public access and boat ramp. Lake closes at the end of Sept.

NEWMAN LAKE. Big, fishy, year-round lake. Planted with rainbow, large triploids, brown trout, tiger muskies (36-inch minimum), bass and a slug of panfish, Newman is a far better than an average fishing prospect especially for large bass. It covers 1190 acres, but is only 30 feet deep at the most which promotes a lot of insect and aquatic food. The lake is 14 miles E. of Spokane not far from the Idaho border. Drive E. on Hwy. 290 to Moab, then N. 3 miles on Newman Lake Rd. to E. shore. Anglers tackle largemouth and smallmouth bass, (some very large;), perch, crappie, bluegill, yellow bullhead catfish and pumpkinseed. There is a resort and a public access site with disabled, wheelchair accessibility on E. shore.

NORTH SILVER. Managed for catch-and-release, fly-fishing only, this is an unusually promising year-round prospect for large trout. It's a fertile, shallow, 87 acre rainbow-stocked lake 1.1 mile E. of Medical Lake. Rich waters grows large trout. Easy access. It is divided from Silver Lake by a road fill.

SILVER LAKE. A 559-acre year-round lake 1 mile E. of Medical Lake that in recent years has been infested with tench and offers, at best, fair angling success for planted rainbow trout and poor fishing for brown trout and largemouth bass. A county road crosses N. end of lake. Resorts, and a public access on N. shore.

SPOKANE LAKE. See Long Lake.

SPOKANE RIVER (Main Stem). This is the largest river in Spokane County flowing W. from Idaho just N. of I-90, through Spokane where it's the centerpiece of Riverfront Park, then swings NW into **SPOKANE LAKE** (Long Lake) near Nine Mile Falls. After spring runoff about 10,000 catchable rainbows are planted in the Riverfront Park

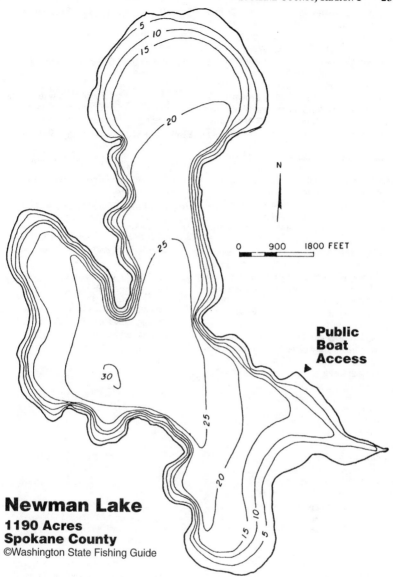

N

0   900   1800 FEET

**Public
Boat
Access**

▶

Newman Lake
**1190 Acres
Spokane County**
©Washington State Fishing Guide

area. Between Idaho state line and Spokane there is fair wade and bank fishing during the summer for rainbows, brookies and brown trout. WDFW has been attempting to establish a quality-type fishery by tightening fishing regulations to a 1 fish, 12-inch minimum limit, and restricting fishermen to selective tackle from the upper dam to Idaho line. This stretch is also only open June through Oct. Below the upriver dam, the river is wider, open year-round

and produces a few trout, landlocked salmon, bass, walleye and panfish. The lower sections are best fished from boats. Walleye are popular targets for trollers near Long Lake. Best fishing is spring and summer.

WEST MEDICAL LAKE. Historically an outstanding rainbow lake that is heavily stocked with 120,000 rainbow and 20,500 brown trout fry, 15,500 catchable rainbows and 700 large triploids. Carry-over trout of 13-17 inches are common. The lake is fertile, produces a lot of fly hatches and trout grow quickly to bragging size. It covers 235 acres. West Medical has a resort plus a handicap-accessible public access site with wheelchair fishing area on W. shore. The lake is located 1 mile W. of town of Medical Lake. From I-90 about 14 miles W. of Spokane, exit onto Salnave Rd. and go N. to a W. turn onto Fancher Rd. and continue .4 mi. to the south end of lake.

WILLIAMS LAKE. Mid May during the mayfly hatch is a great time to be on the water at this excellent rainbow lake. Williams also produces a few cutthroat. The lake covers 319 acres in a long, narrow footprint. The deepest part is a 115-foot hole in the extreme E. end. Just E. of mid-lake the water is 7 to 25 feet deep which makes it a prime feeding area. A 47 foot deep trench along the steep N. shore attracts trollers. Stillfishing with bait and fly casting are also popular. Williams lies about 12 miles SW of Cheney. From the S. side of Cheney drive S.W. on Hwy. 904 for 1 mile to Mullinix Rd. Turn S. on Mullinix and continue to W. shore. The public boat launch is on NE shore, and there are 2 full service resorts. Tent and RV camping, fish docks, boat rentals. Lake opens last week in April, closes Sept. 30.

Spokane County Resorts

Badger Lake: Badger Lake Resort, 509-235-2341.

Chapman Lake: Chapman Lake Resort, 509-523-2221.

Clear Lake: Mallard Bay Resort, 509-299-3830. Rainbow Cove Resort, 509-299-3717.

Eloika Lake: Jerry's Landing, 509-226-3843.

Long Lake: Willow Bay Resort, 509-276-2350. Forshee's Last Resort, 509-276-8568.

Newman Lake: Osborn's Cherokee Landing, 509-226-3843.

Silver Lake: Picnic Pines Resort, 509-299-3223. Ruby's Last Resort, 509-299-7273.

West Medical Lake: West Medical Lake Resort, 509-299-3921.

Williams Lake: Klink's William's Lake Resort, 800-274-1540. Bunker's Resort, 509-235-5212.

Stevens County
WDFW Region 1

Washington Department of Fish and Wildlife, 8702 N. Division St., Spokane, WA 99218. Phone, 509-456-4082.

Speckled with hundreds of small lakes, and a few large ones, Stevens County lies mostly in the Okanogan Highlands, of NE Washington and includes several small north-south running mountain ranges. Valleys are narrow, framed by rolling pine-wooded hills, and less than 10 percent of the 2551 square miles are in crops. If you like woods, water and fish—Stevens County is a good place to be.

It's the 5th largest county in the state, lightly populated (if you count people instead of rainbows, cutthroats, brookies, white-tailed deer and turkeys) and has a lot to offer fishermen. More than 300 lakes are officially listed for the county with more than 100 of these located at or above 2500 feet elevation. Many are small, others are private, and some are difficult to get into. Many, however, are stocked by WDFW and offer good fishing and camping facilities. The county is also stitched with small, quick trout streams, most of them supporting a mix of brookies and rainbow and nearly all of them hemmed in dense brush.

Most of Stevens drains into the Colville River system then into the Columbia River. Canada borders the county on the N., massive Lake Roosevelt separates it from Ferry County on the W. The largest lakes are Loon (long-time holder of the state record trout), Deer and Waitts Lakes. One of the centerpieces of the county is the Little Pend Oreille Wildlife Area (LPOWA) and chain of lakes SE of Colville and N. of Chewelah in the Colville National Forest which encompasses much of the N end of the county.

Summers are generally comfortable, rarely exceeding the mid-80s with cool nights, warm days and low humidity. Winter can be bitterly cold, dropping to zero at the blink of a cold front with highs often in the low 20s. The record low is -29 degrees. Deep snow blankets the mountains until April sometimes early May. Annual precipitation at Colville is 17.36 inches, much of it snow. Rain and snow is light in the foothills but can be heavy in the higher mountains. The highest point is 7,308 feet at Abercrombie Mountain 15 miles from Northport. Elevations at most of the foothill and valley lakes are 2000 to 2700 feet, and some will still be frozen at the late April opener of fishing season.

Main access through the county is US 395 which runs N-S connecting Deer Park, Chewelah and Colville. Hwy. 20 runs E-W through Colville.

BAYLEY LAKE (Cliff). A marshy, 17-acre fly-fishing only lake on the LPOWA NE of Chewelah. It holds large brookies and is lightly planted with rainbow. Route from Chewelah is up N. Fork of Chewelah Creek/Sand Canyon Rd. about 5 miles, then N. up Bayley Creek to lake. **POTTERS POND**, covering about 2.5 acres, just N. of Bayley Lake on W. side of Bayley Creek holds brookies and rainbow.

BENJAMIN LAKE. A 12.7 acre lake on Spokane Indian Reservation 2 miles SW from Wellpinit. Planted with rainbow, and drains to Spokane River.

BIG SHEEP CREEK. Located in the extreme, remote NW corner of the county, Big Sheep Creek offers excellent fishing for rainbow and brook trout to 14 inches in the upper reaches. It enters Stevens County from British Columbia about 1.5 miles NE of Lead Pencil Mt. and flows SE 10 miles to a confluence on the north shore of the Columbia R. about 2 miles N. of Northport. Top portion of creek has deep pools, is brushy and supports brookies, while lower stretches show white water and rainbow. Drive N. from Northport on Hwy. 25, cross the Columbia River, then NW on Sheep Creek Road which follows creek to Canadian border. Sheep Creek FS Campground is 7 miles upstream from Hwy. 25. Road near campground leads W. up American Fork of Big Sheep Creek. Little Sheep Creek, also offers brookies and rainbows, but is followed by Hwy. 25 and is less productive than its more remote Big fork.

BLACK LAKE. A beautiful 70 acre secluded rainbow trout lake at 3700 feet elevation. Receives limited fishing pressure. Rainbows are in the 8-12 inch class. Drive E. from Colville on Hwy. 20 for 15 miles, then N. on Black Lake-Squaw Creek Rd. up Gap Creek 1.5 miles to E. shore of lake where there is a resort. The road continues W. for 1 mile from N. end of Black to **TWIN LAKE** (formerly Spruce and Cedar Lakes, but joined by a FS dam). There are FS campgrounds on lake. It holds cutthroat.

BROWN'S LAKE. A 17 acre private lake located SW of Chewelah, Brown's drains into the Colville River via Huckleberry Creek.

CEDAR LAKE. Plants of 20,000 rainbow fry plus carry-over browns provide a good fishery in this remote 51 acre lake. Browns are no longer stocked, but there are a few large carry-overs. Cedar Lake is reached by driving NE on Hwy. 251 along the E. shore of the Columbia R. About 0.4 miles before the Canada border turn S. up Cedar Creek 4 miles to lake. Best fishing is during May, June and July.

CHAMOKANE CREEK. Rated "fair" for rainbow with some brown trout, Chamokane drains into Spokane River. Top fishing is from May to September. The creek is reached by driving W. from Loon Lake. Just W. of Springdale swing SW on Springdale-Hunters Rd. which follows the creek up Camas Valley.

CHEWELAH CREEK. A large stream that flows into the Colville River at Chewelah. The N. and S. Forks join at outskirts of town near Hwy. 395. Roads follow both branches upstream to headwaters. There are rainbow and brookies in the creek and forks with top fishing just after runoff in May and June. Lots of brush, but good road access. Primitive campsites in Colville NF.

CLARK LAKE (Bissel, Charles). This 24 acre private lake is situated at 1800 feet. Location is 8 miles N. from Hunters.

COFFIN LAKE (aka Devils & Fuhrman). A 10 acre lake 2.7 miles NE of Kettle Falls and 1200 feet NW of Lee Lake. A primitive DNR access is on N. shore. Several species of trout plus kokanee and warm water species. Elevation is 2280 feet. Rough boat launch site.

COLVILLE RIVER. This large, brown trout river heads S. of Waitts Lake along Hwy. 231 and flows NE to enter Lake Roosevelt 2 miles S. of Kettle Falls. US 395 parallels river for approximately 35 miles in the Colville Valley through Chewelah and Colville, but much of the access is across private land and requires permission. Offers mostly browns, but there are some rainbows. Top fishing section is from Chewelah to mouth from June through October. This river holds some large fish especially browns, but you'll work for them. The lower river, just above Lake Roosevelt, sometimes offers walleye, kokanee and panfish.

COTTONWOOD CREEK. Brookies and rainbow. Best fishing in summer months. The creek is reached by driving .5 mile E. from Chewelah toward 49° North Ski Area, then S. on Cottonwood Cr. Rd.

Lake Roosevelt rainbow trout.

DEEP LAKE. Fingerling plants develop good spring and fall catches of cutthroat and brookies. The lake covers 210 acres, at an elevation of 2025 feet. Public access. Drive 9 miles SE from Northport on Colville-Aladdin-Northport Rd. to Spirit, then 2 miles NE on Deep Lake-Boundary Road to lake.

DEER LAKE. A very popular fishing and boating lake just 26 miles N. of Spokane and E. of US 395, Deer Lake is one of the largest lakes in Stevens County. It offers a mix of salmon, trout and warm water species that appeals to family fishing. Covering 1163 acre and up to 75 feet deep Deer Lake is stocked with rainbow, kokanee, brookies, large and smallmouth bass, perch, crappie, pumpkinseed, catfish and lake trout. It's planted in the spring with more than 25,000 catchable rainbows, another 15,000 fry, plus brookies and rainbow releases from net pen rearing projects. The lake is also annually stocked with 158,600 kokanee salmon fry. Fishing holds up well throughout most of the season. Trout action, including lake trout, is best in spring, kokanee from mid summer into September and the warm water species do well from opening day through September. Two resorts offer full facilities plus a public access area with ramp. Drive US 395 to 3 miles N. of Loon Lake then E. on Lake Loop Rd. 1.5 miles E. to lake.

DOUGLAS LAKE. A shallow 4 acre pond N. of Colville, draining into Mill Creek. About .05 mile E. of Colville city limits a road heads N. from Hwy. 20 for 3.5 miles to within a short distance of Douglas. Winter kills. Seldom stocked.

ELBOW LAKE (Crown). Brook trout are in this 14 acre lake at 2775 feet elev. in headwaters of Crown Creek's W. Fork. A marsh divides the lake into nearly equal segments. Lake is 12 miles from Hwy. 25 N. of Northport. From the highway head N. and W. up Big Sheep Creek, turning W. up American Fork of Big Sheep to shore of lake. This road continues W. another 9 miles to **PIERRE LAKE**.

FRANKLIN D. ROOSEVELT LAKE (UPPER). The largest lake in the state at 79,000 acres, 151 miles long, created by Grand Coulee Dam on Columbia River 28 miles NE of Coulee City. The reservoir stretches across the northcentral part of the state, and forms the north border of Lincoln County continuing E. into Ferry and forming much of the W. boundary of Steven County before nudging into British Columbia. It is located in a relatively remote, low mountain region. The lower lake is in the Columbia Basin, a dry region of hot summers framed by rolling, rocky hills, sagebrush, willows, basalt columns and coulees. As the lake moves E. into the low mountains of Stevens County the shoreline increasingly supports conifer forest and enjoys cooler summer temperatures than found in the lower lake.

Lake Roosevelt supports one of the widest varieties of freshwater fish in the state. Species include cutthroat, rainbow, brookies, Dolly Varden, lake whitefish, kokanee, Kamloops, sturgeon, large and smallmouth bass, crappie, perch, sunfish, walleyes, carp, suckers, tench, shiners, chub, and an assortment of other rough fish. Best game fishing is at mouths of countless inlets along both shores of huge reservoir.

Fishing success in the upper reservoir rises and falls dramatically, seasonally and often by species. One time rainbows—some to 6 pounds—will be the hot ticket, next will be kokanee or walleye and when that's not working some anglers enjoy huge success casting to shoreline rocks for bass. Smallmouth are almost ignored in the upper lake. The once great kokanee fishing has fallen in recent years and the daily limit has been trimmed to 2 fish. These are large, beautiful kokes, though. The mouth of Spokane River is one of the state's historic walleye spots. Net pen rearing projects at Seven Bays, Keller Marina, Hunters and Kettle Falls have endowed the lake with some excellent rainbow trout fishing, with fish often going several pounds.

One of the most enjoyable ways to fish this big lake is by boat camping, or renting a houseboat and towing a fishing boat. The 660 miles of lake shore and 35 recreational areas in Coulee Dam RA are administrated by National Park Service. All recreational areas may be reached by boat. Facilities include house boats rentals, 8 full service campgrounds, many primitive lake shore camp sites accessible by boat, multiple concrete boat ramps, docks, picnic areas, swimming spots. Information center for the recreational areas is at the W. end of Coulee Dam at Grand Coulee Dam National Recreation Area headquarters where maps and service directories are available. Call: 509-633-0881. Hwy. 25 parallels much of the S. shore in Stevens County and US 395/Hwy. 20 crosses the lake at a narrows just NW of Kettle Falls. Grand Coulee Dam is accessible from Hwy. 155 N. from Coulee City and Hwy. 174 N.W from Wilbur on US 2. Fishing regulations and bag limits vary and should be read carefully before fishing this massive year-round reservoir. The San Poil R. arm is closed in late winter and early spring, and the Kettle River Arm is closed from April through May.

HATCH LAKE. A 34-acre winter-only fishing lake SE of Colville, delivers rainbow trout to ice fishermen from Dec. 1-Mar. 31. Public access. Elevation is 2141 feet. **LITTLE HATCH LAKE** is a private, 14-acre brook trout lake 500 feet W. of Hatch. Drive E. from Colville for 5 miles on Hwy. 20, turn S. on Artman-Gibson Rd. for 1 mile to lakes.

HUNTERS CREEK. Heading on W. slope of Huckleberry Mt., the creek flows W. for 11 miles to join **Lake Roosevelt** 1.5 miles W. of Hunters. Holds rainbow and is best in summer. From Hunters on Hwy. 25 a road follows upstream for 5 miles, then continues along S. Fork for another 8 miles.

JUMPOFF JOE LAKE. A roundish 105-acre lake with planted and carryover rainbows, browns and brookies. Trout from 8 to 14 inches are typical and there are always a few in the 18-inch range. Small largemouth bass, pumpkinseed and yellow perch are present. The lake is also infested with giant goldfish. Jumpoff Joe lies in a timbered region at 2031 feet. There is a resort with full services, public access and ramp. From Chewelah drive S. on US 395 for 7.5 miles, then W. and S. on E. Jumpoff Joe Rd. for 1.5 miles to the lake's E. shore.

KEOUGH LAKES: Two private marshy lakes of 13.6 and 4.8 acres, separated by a narrow strip of land, with brookies and rainbows. Lakes are 4.5 miles SE from Colville with drainage to Prouty Creek to Little Pend Oreille River. Permission to fish required.

KETTLE RIVER. This rebuilding trout stream is the boundary between Stevens and Ferry Counties. It enters U.S. at Laurier and flows S. approximately 25 miles to join **LAKE ROOSEVELT** 3 miles S. of Boyds in Ferry County. Stevens County roads follow river for about 12 miles, but the best access is from Hwy. 395 in Ferry County. This major highway parallels the entire length along the W. bank. Fish include rainbow, brown trout and whitefish. Walleye sometimes caught near Lake Roosevelt. Special regulations, including catch-and-release and selective fishery regs are in effect to protect native spawners and rebuild what was once a very good trout fishery. Decent trout fishing most of the summer and fall. Whitefish action can be terrific in winter.

LITTLE PEND OREILLE LAKES. A series of small picturesque, mountain trout lakes, most adjacent to Hwy. 20, about 23 miles E. and N. of Colville near WDFW's Little Pend Oreille Wildlife Area. LPO Lakes include **Sherry**, 26 acres the lowest in the chain, **Gillette**, 48 acres; **Thomas** 163 acres; **Heritage**, 71 acres; all in Stevens County. **Leo** and **Frater**, the two top lakes, are in Pend Oreille County. All lakes are annually stocked with 7 to 12 inch cutthroat, and some also deliver a few carry-over rainbow and brook trout. Fishing is always good, but success can be spotty. Fly fishermen favor the fall. A canal links Sherry, Gillette, Thomas and Heritage lakes. **Coffin Lake** (see Coffin Lake) is also part of the LPO lakes and is about 3 miles S. of Sherry. A resort is on Gillette and FS campgrounds at Gillette, Thomas and Leo Lakes. FS boat ramps are on Leo and Gillette Lakes. Elevation of lakes is 3160 feet and some ice is possible on opening day. If you're looking for an exceptional place to camp and fish this is it.

LITTLE PEND OREILLE RIVER. A small 25-mile-long river that drains the Little Pend Oreille Lakes, and flows into Colville River at Arden, 6 miles S. of Colville on Hwy. 395. Brookies and rainbow provide fair to good angling May through September. The upper section is followed by Bear Creek Road. The Lower section holds browns and may be fished by heading E. on Artman-Gibson Rd. upstream from Arden. Spur roads lead to N. bank. Hwy. 20 from Colville E. and N. to Middleport touches and roughly follows upper 10 miles of stream to source.

LONG LAKE. A 14 acre lake located 8 miles SE from Colville. Has received brown trout and smallmouth bass plants. No defined inlet or outlet. From US 395 turn E. on Moran Creek Rd. and continue about 2 miles, turning N. on a dirt road a little more than a mile to lake.

LOON LAKE. This sprawling one-time holder of Washington's trout record (a 30-

Little Pend Oreille Lakes.

pound, 4-ounce Mackinaw) is regularly planted with catchable browns, rainbow, lake trout, brookies, and fry plants of kokanee. It also affords some pretty decent fishing for small and largemouth bass, perch, crappie, pumpkinseed and brown bullhead. This 1119 acre lake is often an excellent fishing hole throughout the season. Kokanee start in May. Kokanee catches have been off in recent years, but still attract a lot of fishermen. Several full service resorts ring the lake and a public access/ramp is on the W. shore. Wheelchair access. The lake lies at 2381 feet elevation, 28 miles N. of Spokane via US 395 which runs along lake's E. shore.

McCOY LAKE. A 36 acre brook trout lake managed by the Spokane tribal agency. It is located at 1644 feet elevation. From Fruitland on Hwy. 25, go S. about 8 miles to lake, passing Newbell and Mudgett Lakes.

-

McDOWELL LAKE. Walk-in access, fly-fishing only, catch-and-release regulations have developed a good fishery for the large rainbow planted in this 33 acre water at 2325 feet, 11.5 miles SE of Colville. Drains to Little Pend Oreille River. From Hwy 20 at Little Pend Oreille Wildlife Area turn S. on Narcisse Creek Rd., cross the river, and park at gate on W. side of Rd. Walk is about .25 mile.

MILL CREEK. A tributary of Colville River, joining that stream 2 miles NW of Colville. Mill provides fair to good fishing for rainbow and brookies. Follow Colville-Aladdin Rd. N. and NE from E. limits of Colville for 2 miles to meet and follow creek. Turn E. on Northport Rd. to follow creek to Three Forks. The S., Middle and N. Forks of Mill Creek come together at Three Forks, approximately 8 miles upstream from Colville. The road up S. Fork continues over ridge to drop into **LITTLE PEND OREILLE LAKES** group on Hwy. 20, a distance of about 10 miles. From Colville-Aladdin Rd., bear NW to follow Douglas Falls Rd. along stream, to Douglas Falls and beyond.

MUDGETT LAKE. A 32 acre lake with a public access. Drive 2 plus miles S. of Fruitland on Hwy. 25, turn SE onto Old Highway 22-McCoy Lake Rd. to lake which offers planted rainbows.

PHELAN LAKE. Closed to fishing in 2000. It has brookies and is 18 acres.

PHILLIPS LAKE. A 1.3 acre brookie stocked pond 2 miles SE of Bailey Lake. It drains to Colville River.

PEPOON LAKE. Brookies and rainbow are stocked in this 11 acre lake. Location is 5.5 miles W. from Northport in headwaters of

Rattlesnake Creek at 2450 feet. Drains to **LAKE ROOSEVELT**.

PIERRE LAKE. Occasionally cutthroat to 5 pounds have been taken in this beautiful 106-acre lake but most trout are 8-14 inches. It has a few sizable holdover brookies, plus kokanee, brown bullhead, black crappie and largemouth bass. Regularly planted with rainbow and cutthroat. It lies at 2012 feet elevation in the headwaters of Toulou Creek. Follow US 395 N. from Kettle Falls to Rock Cut. Turn E. on Sand Creek Road, then S. for 1 mile on Barstow-Pierre Lake Road. **LITTLE PIERRE LAKE** is S. on Barstow-Pierre Rd. There is a Colville National Forest campground and ramp on Big Pierre. Drains to Kettle River.

POTTER LAKE. Stocked with rainbows, a 3.9 acre lake 3.5 miles N. from Colville at 2420 feet. Drainage to Colville River.

ROCKY LAKE. The lake covers 20 acres and holds planted rainbow. DNR camp and launch sites. From SE limits of Colville go S. on Rocky Lake Rd. for 3.5 miles.

SHEEP CREEK. A rainbow trout tributary to Colville River, joining that river about 5 miles S. of Valley. Hwy. 231 and 292 S. from Colville River Junction provide access at various points.

STARVATION LAKE. Rainbow are the attraction in this 28 acre lake. Top fly fishing. The catch-and-keep season only lasts from opening day through May 31. From June 1 to the end of October, catch-and-release, selective gear rules apply. Starvation is 9 miles E. of Colville on Hwy. 20, then S. on Starvation Lake Rd. .05 miles to lake. Public access and campground. Elevation is 2375 feet.

SUMMIT LAKE. A 6.9 acre rainbow trout lake at 2600 feet 7.4 miles NE from Orient and 2.7 miles S. of U.S.—Canada. border. Drains to Kettle River. At Laurier, turn E. on Box Canyon Rd.

TWIN LAKES (Spruce). The Twins cover 26.8 acres and are located 12 miles E. of Colville. They are planted with cutthroat and drain to Little Pend Oreille River.

TURTLE LAKES. Lakes of 8.9 and 1.7 acres on Spokane Indian Reservation 4.5 miles NW of Wellpinit on Wellpinit-Hunters Road. Rainbow planted.

WAITTS LAKE. Waitts is a rich 455 acre lake where trout attain excellent growth, with fish of 3 to 5 pounds not uncommon. The state record rainbow hails from here, a 22-pound, 8 ounce monster. Big trout are still available. Fair perch and largemouth bass fishing. Annually stocked with 40,000 fingerling browns and 22,500 catchable rainbow, several hundred brood stock trout. Several resorts and a public access on lake. From Chewelah drive S. on US 395, turn SW on Hwy. 231 to Valley, turn W. on Waitts Lake Loop Rd. 4 miles to lake.

WILLIAMS LAKE. Rainbow are stocked in Williams, 38 acres at 1980 feet elevation 16.5 miles N. of Colville. From Hwy. 25 S. of China Bend turn E. on Williams Lake Rd. 3 miles to NE shore.

WRIGLEY LAKE. A 6.8 acre marshy lake at 2531 feet 2.5 miles W. from Echo on Echo Mt.. Planted with rainbow, it drains to **LAKE ROOSEVELT.**

Stevens County Resorts

Deep Lake: Wilderness West Resort, Colville, WA 99114. 509-732-4263.

Deer Lake: Sunrise Point Resort, 509-233-2342. West Bay Park, 509-233-3010. Deer Lake Resort, 509-233-2081.

Jump Off Joe Lake: Jump Off Joe Resort, 509-937-2133.

Lake Roosevelt: Colulee Dam National Recreation Area Headquarters, 509-633-0881.

Little Pend Orelile Lakes: Beaver Lodge Gillette Lake, 509-684-4995.

Loon Lake: Granite Point Park, 509-233-2100. Shore Acres Resort, 800-900-2474.

Waitts Lake: Silver Beach Resort, 509-937-2811. Waitts Lake Resort, 509-937-2400. Winona Beach Resort, 509-937-2231.

Thurston County
WDFW Region 6

Washington Department of Fish and Wildlife, 48 Devonshire Rd. Montesano, WA 98563-9618. Phone 360-249-4628

A small county disappearing into the fingers of saltwater at the extreme south end of Puget Sound and state headquarters for WDFW, Thurston has a surprising number of good trout and warm water species lakes which anglers mix with sheltered saltwater salmon, rockfish, and sea-run cutthroat fishing.

The county lacks a good steelhead river, but an hour or two on I-5 and US 101 leads to popular steelheading in N. Puget Sound, Southwest rivers and Olympic Peninsula waters.

More than 100 lakes have been documented in the county and all are classified as lowland lakes below 2500 feet elev. Most of the lakes receive heavy plants of catchable-size trout in spring and many also get a boost of thousands of fry planted to mature in the lakes. The saltwater opportunity is built around four major inlets, Henderson, Budd, Eld and Totten. The city marina is at the foot of Budd Inlet. On Johnson Point, there's a good ramp and marina at Zittles. More saltwater ramps at Boston Harbor, Luhrs Beach at the mouth of the Nisqually, and Puget Harbor.

Thurston covers only 761 square miles, the 32nd largest county in the state. Most of the county is either river bottom valleys, prairie or rolling low hills. The high point is 2984 feet near Alder Lake at the edge of Lewis County. There are two low mountainous regions, the Bald Hills in the SE part of the county and the Black Hills which rise in the W. The county is drained by the Nisqually River (see Pierce County), which forms boundary with Pierce County, and by the Deschutes, upper Skookumchuck and Black Rivers.

The Deschutes River flows through Tumwater and S. Olympia through Capitol Lake entering Puget Sound at a concrete dam where chinook salmon leap in early fall. Olympia has an excellent marina with full facilities a short cast from the old WDFW headquarters building at 600 Capitol Way. The underplayed Black River produces sea-run cutthroat and largemouth bass.

WDFW has stopped stocking catchable trout into streams in this region, although most of the creeks support resident cutthroat and some rainbows. These wild trout provide mostly catch-and-release opportunities because of 2 fish daily limits and 12 to 14 inch minimum sizes on many streams. Few wild creek trout top 10 inches.

The maritime climate is warm and dry in the summer, mild and wet in the winter. Olympia gets about 46 inches of rain a year, more than Seattle, but less than half of what falls on Aberdeen directly W.

Most of the public grounds are DNR lands in the Black Hills, Capitol Forest SW of Olympia, and in the logged foothills E. of Hwy. 507 between Yelm and Tenino. WDFW has public hunting and fishing areas at Scatter Creek and Skookumchuck Reservoir. Gifford Pinchot National Forest touches the SE corner of the county. A big chunk of Fort Lewis Military Reservation is SE of Olympia near Yelm.

Major fishing routes are I-5 which connects with US 101 and Hwy. 8 in S. Olympia. Hwy. 507 threads along the upper Skookumchuck River from Lewis County through Tenino and Yelm.

ALDER LAKE (See Pierce County).

BALD HILLS LAKE. A 45 acre lake only 15 feet deep that weeds badly by mid sum-mer. Best in late spring for largemouth bass, perch and catfish. Open year-round, 11.5 miles SE of Yelm and 1 mile E. of Clear Lake. Head from Yelm through Four Corners and continue 2 miles to fork. Take left fork for about 3 miles, then S. at forks for 3 miles past **CLEAR LAKE**.

BARNES LAKE. 14 acres 3 miles S. of Olympia with largemouth bass and bluegill. Drains to Percival Creek.

BASS LAKE. Yellow perch and largemouth bass are in this 6.6 acre lake in Bald Hills region.

BIGELOW LAKE. Yellow perch and largemouth bass in 13.8 acre lake 2 miles NE of Olympia. Drains to Budd Inlet.

BLACK LAKE. The largest lake in the county, well stocked with 16,000 catchable rainbows in Mar. adding to survivors from a fry plant of 117,000 and cutthroat Black delivers good late spring and summer trout fishing to go with its solid population of smallmouth, largemouth and rock bass, bluegills, black crappie, pumpkinseed, yellow perch and brown bullhead. Brushy banks and a dish shaped bottom combine to offer good fishing conditions for trout trollers and bank casters. Bullheads run large here and the south end is a favorite nighttime fishing spot. Lots of bass there, too. This year-round, 576 acre lake is only 4 miles SW of Olympia, a mixed blessing because it also attracts a pox of jet skies and play boats during the heat of summer. WDFW access, ramp on SE shore. Black drains into Capitol Lake via Black Lake Ditch and Percival Creeks. Route to lake is W. of I-5 on US 101 then S. 1.5 miles to N. end of lake on Black Lake Blvd.

BLACK LAKE DITCH CREEK. A cutthroat stream flowing out of N. end of Black Lake and joining Percival Creek before entering Capitol Lake.

BLACK RIVER. A regionally rare stream because of its slow, meandering flow, the Black runs SW about 20 miles to enter Chehalis River E. of Oakville. The upper 5 miles are swampy (Bring a duck gun in the fall). Hwy. 801 from Little Rock follows river downstream for several miles. Boating is most effective way to fish the brushy, slow-moving river for sea-run cutthroat and largemouth bass. May and June and again in fall are good periods for cutthroat, while bass take during summer. Boats and canoes may be launched downstream from Littlerock and at the Rochester-Oakville Hwy. 12 bridge crossing.

CAPITOL LAKE. A 306 acre lake and park centerpiece in Olympia formed by a dam at mouth of Deschutes River. Has sea-run cutthroat and jack and adult chinook salmon in fall. Some winter steelhead, rainbow and a few panfish. Stocked in early June with about 2000 rainbows. Aug. and Sept. bring chinook to the upper end of the lake at Tumwater Historical Park and below I-5 overpass. When legal these big salmon provide a popular sport fishery for anglers in small boats and bank casters. Lots of access and complex regs. Better check the WDFW booklet before wetting a line in this one.

CHAMBERS LAKE. Open year around, but heavily weeded in summer Chambers offers a few wild cutthroat, fair fishing for largemouth bass, warmouth, perch. crappie bullheads and channel catfish. It's been planted with grass carp to control weeds. The 72 acre lake is only 8 feet deep. It's connected to **LITTLE CHAMBERS LAKE**, 49 acres, on the E. WDFW access, launch on NW shore. Chambers is 3 miles SE of Olympia. From Hwy. 510 take county road 1 mile S. to lake.

CLEAR LAKE (Bald Hills). An exceptionally popular and productive rainbow, brown, cutthroat trout and largemouth bass lake. Covers 173 acres SE of Yelm. Very popular opening day lake because of the number of fish and their size. Stocked just before the April opener with 15,000 catchable rainbows, plus 1000 large triploids. Also gets up to 51,000 fry each year. Browns to 6 pounds are taken. By fall rainbows often reach 12 to 14 inches and with the browns and triploids provide a potentially good big trout fishery all summer. Route is SW from Yelm through Four Corners and Smith Prairie 11 miles to SW tip of lake. Resort and WDFW access, ramp. Limited parking.

COOPERS POTHOLE. 700 feet E. of Lake St. Clair, this 4.9 acre pond has largemouth bass.

DEEP LAKE (Deep Drake). A mixed species state park lake stocked with 6000 catchable rainbows in the spring that furnish fair trout fishing from May into June. Summer and fall fishing is a good bet because of the large numbers of largemouth bass, bluegill, perch, and pumpkinseed panfish. Despite its name, most of this Deep Lake is only about 15 feet deep. It covers 66 acres 9.5 miles S. of Olympia. I-

5 Exit 95 at Maytown then E. Maytown Rd. SW about 2.5 miles to N. turn. Millersylvania State Park offers campsites, and boat launch. Resort.

DESCHUTES RIVER. Beginning in Lewis Country this small river flows 35 miles NW across Thurston County to enter Capitol Lake in S. Olympia at head of Budd Inlet. June best for resident cutthroat in upper stream. A very few winter steelhead. The mouth sometimes provides a good Sept. chinook fishery (**See Black Lake**) Sea-cutthroat plants have been discontinued, but the stream still attracts fair number of sea-runs moving upstream with the chinook. Crossed by roads at numerous points, and a road SE from Olympia's airport roughly parallels river to Hwy. 507 about 2 miles SW of Rainier. County and logging roads continue SE up river into Lewis County.

EATON CREEK. A cutthroat trout stream that gets a "fair" rating in June. A tributary of **ST. CLAIR LAKE** reached by driving E. of Tumwater up Evergreen Valley Rd.

EATONVILLE POND. Usually stocked with 1000 catchable rainbows in late April.

ELBOW LAKE. A 36-acre Bald Hills lake with largemouth bass, crappie, perch, catfish and cutthroat. 3500 feet NE of Clear Lake. State park and boat launch site at NW end. See **CLEAR LAKE** for route.

FIFTEEN LAKE. Largemouth bass are in this 4.2 acre lake 1.5 miles SE of Rainier. Drains to Deschutes River.

FRY COVE. A county park on the W. shore of Eld Inlet that offers Pacific oysters. Sea-run cutthroat fishing in spring and fall.

GEHRKE LAKE. 1.4 miles E. of Rainier an 8 acre pond with largemouth bass. Drains to Deschutes River.

GRASS LAKE. A 120-acre marsh with largemouth bass, perch, crappie and brown bullhead catfish. 2 miles W. of Olympia. Drains to Budd Inlet.

HEWITT LAKE. 26 acres in a deep bowl 2 miles SE of Tumwater. Some cutthroat mostly largemouth bass and perch. Private residences ring lake. Access difficult.

HICKS LAKE. Spring planted with 15,000 catchable rainbows, 1100 large triploid rainbows, plus cutthroat and brown trout (some in the 5-pound range), Hicks is a popular fishing lake covering 171 acres. Summer fishery targets rock and largemouth bass, pumpkinseed, warmouth and yellow perch. WDFW access, ramp. About 2 miles E. of Lacey on Hwy. 510, then S. for 1.5 miles to lake. Drains to **PATTISON LAKE**.

KENNEDY CREEK. Heading on W. slope of Rock Candy Mt., Kennedy flows NW past the W. tip of **SUMMIT LAKE** to enter Mason County at Kennedy Falls. The creek provides fair resident cutthroat and fall sea-runs and a few winter steelhead and salmon. Hwy. 8 crosses the creek W. of Summit Lake. A road follows it for about 2 miles.

LAWRENCE LAKE. A good mixed species lake, Lawrence is stocked with rainbows, browns and cutthroat trout, and also offers largemouth bass, perch and brown bullhead catfish. Shallow water warms quickly and retards trout bite. After June best fishing is for warm water species. Covers 339 acres and drains into Deschutes River. WDFW access, launch. 6 miles S. of Yelm and 6 miles SE of Rainier. Road from Yelm leads E. to Four Corners. Turn right on Vail Loop Rd. and follow signs to lake.

LOIS LAKE. 2.5 acres with rainbow. N. from Lacey on N. side of Hwy. 99. Drains to Henderson Inlet.

LONG LAKE. 2 lakes joined by a narrow, weedy neck, Long covers 2 miles and about 311 acres 5.5 miles E. of Olympia. Brown trout to 6 pounds, and spring plants of 26,000 catchable rainbows, a couple of hundred triploids, plus largemouth bass, rock bass, crappie, warmouth, pumpkinseed and yellow perch. Large WDFW access, ramp. Turn S. from I-5 at Marvin Rd. exit onto Hwy. 510 then E. at Union Mill to Carpenter Road which runs between Long and Hicks lakes.

LONGS POND. Just for the kids, this juvenile-only pond in Lacey is stocked with 3500 catchable rainbows and cutthroat in Mar., Apr. and June. Also largemouth bass, sunfish and perch. Open year-round.

McALLISTER CREEK. Delivers late summer and early fall sea-run cutthroat. Flows into Nisqually River delta. From I-5 Exit 111 E. to road which parallels creek. Hatchery upstream provides fall chinook and chum salmon. Nice spots to fly fish from roadside.

MCINTOSH LAKE. A shallow, narrow, 1.4 mile long lake covering only 116 acres along the N. side of Hwy. 507 about 3 miles E. of Tenino. Spring planted with 10,000 cutthroat and rainbow catchables plus large triploid rainbows. Also gets about 100,000 rainbow and cutthroat fry. This is a fertile lake that promotes fast growth and delivers quality trout. Also offers largemouth bass and lots of yellow perch. WDFW access, ramp on N. shore. May provide best trout fishing, perch and bass kick in in June.

MCLANE'S CREEK. A small 4 mile long creek which heads W. of Black Lake and flows N. into Mud Bay 3 miles W. of Olympia. A road leads S. from Hwy. 8 up creek. McLane produces sea-run cutthroat in spring and fall, and fall salmon.

MUNN LAKE. Planted with 3200 rainbows and cutthroat in the spring. Covers 29.8 acres 4 miles S. of Olympia. Drains to Deschutes River. Bluegill and largemouth bass. WDFW access and ramp.

OFFUT LAKE. This a fisherman's lake. A 5 mph speed limit keeps out the playboat riffraff and one of the last trout lake resorts in the region caters to anglers and campers. Husky trout from Mar. and Apr. plants of 23,000 rainbows and several hundred 14-inch cutthroat, plus 50,000 rainbow fry. Exceptional number of large holdovers that are weighed by the pound. This 192 acre lake is 25 feet deep and trout fishing holds up well into June, recovers nicely in Sept. and Oct. and surprisingly can deliver good action in mid-winter. Mid summer is for perch, brown bullhead and above average largemouth bass action with bucketmouths to 5 pounds. Illegally stocked smallmouth are also gaining a foothold and fish in the 3-pound range are not uncommon. Troll, stillfish, or throw a fly, there's something for everyone to target. Open year-round. Resort with fishing dock and boat rentals and WDFW access, ramp. Drive 3 miles S. of Olympia airport on Tumwater-Tenino Rd., then E. 1 mile E. on Waldrick Rd. to lake.

PATTISON LAKE. Previously spelled, Patterson, this 257-acre Lacey lake provides fair fishing for browns and 20,000 spring planted rainbows early in the season. Summer fishermen target perch, crappie, rock bass, bluegill and largemouth bass. Patterson has a WDFW access, ramp. and is 6 miles SE of Olympia. Fol- low Hwy. 510 to Lacey, then 3 miles SE from center of town to lake.

PERCIVAL CREEK. A tributary to Capitol Lake which supports rainbow and sea-run cutthroat.

PERCIVAL LAKE, 22 acre enlargement at creek mouth into Capitol Lake. Used as a salmon raising pond. Leave US 101 a short distance W. of Olympia on Mottman road and drive S. for .05 miles to creek. Stream may also be fished upstream from mouth.

PRIEST POINT PARK. A large saltwater park N. of Olympia with beach access on Budd Inlet N. of Ellis Cove. Marginal fishing for flounders. WDFW reports surf smelt available to dip in Sept.-Feb. Head N. from downtown Olympia on Boston Harbor Rd.

REICHEL LAKE. Largemouth bass, 9 acres, 3.4 miles E. of Vail. Drains to Deschutes River.

SCOTT LAKE. Cutthroat, perch, largemouth bass and brown bullhead in 67 acres 9 miles S. of Olympia. Turn E. from 1-5 about 6 miles S. of Tumwater and drive approximately 1 mile to lake shore. Access is limited.

SIMMONS LAKE (Ken). Covers 24.6 acres, holds largemouth bass and perch. 2 miles W. of Olympia in marshy area. Drains to Budd Inlet.

SKOOKUMCHUCK RIVER. Heads on W. slope of Porcupine Ridge in SE Thurston County and flows W. and S. for about 20 miles before entering Lewis County near Bucoda. Upper reach above reservoir delivers small resident rainbow and cutthroat in summer. Check WDFW regs for restrictions. Below the reservoir anglers find winter steelhead, especially in March stacked in a congested hole below the dam. Lower stream offers fair fall sea-run cutthroat fishing. Hwy. 507 runs S. from Tenino 2 miles to Prairie where a county road leads E. to follow Skookumchuck upstream. Hwy. 507 continues downstream. The Skook joins the Chehalis Rive at Centralia. No access to reservoir

SMITH LAKE. A shallow, 17.7 acres with perch and largemouth bass 4 miles SE of Olympia. Drains to Deschutes River.

SOUTHWICK LAKE. 37.1 acre lake a few

Upper Skookumchuck River.

cutthroat, mostly largemouth bass and brown bullhead. 5 miles SE of Olympia about 0.5 mile from N. end of Pattison Lake to which it drains.

SOUTH COUNTY PONDS. A collection of small ponds scattered in the Bald Hills of southern Thurston County with good numbers of largemouth bass, perch, brown bullhead catfish and crappies. Some of the ponds have been planted with cutthroat fry.

SPRINGER LAKE. Brown bullhead and largemouth bass in 5.5 acres, 2.5 miles W. from Offutt Lake. Drains to Deschutes River.

ST. CLAIR LAKE. One of the most under publicized lakes in the region, but a fun multi-species spot. More than 110 feet deep, 245 acre St. Clair is a ragged maze of inlets, points and coves. Once reported to hold mackinaw but there hasn't been one sighted in recent memory. Today it's known as a trout and kokanee lake, stocked in Mar. and May with 19,000 catchable rainbows and cutthroat, plus a few hundred in the 1.5 pound range. Also gets about 80,000 rainbow and cutthroat fry, and almost 100,000 kokanee fry that develop into a fine summer fishery for trollers towing blade strings and bait. The kokanee aren't overly large, but they can provide a lot of action and some delicious eating. St. Clair

also offers rock bass, largemouth bass, crappie, pumpkinseed, warmouth and perch. Some large carryover rainbow are taken each year. Open year-round. 2 public access areas, ramps. From I-5 at Marvin Road Exit, turn S. on Hwy. 510 which runs near N. tip of lake.

SUMMIT LAKE. A deep (110 feet) 522 acre lake SW of Olympia with some large rainbow and cutthroat plus kokanee and largemouth bass, yellow perch and brown bullhead. A slow starter but develops well and by mid summer usually provides good fishing especially for the average-size kokanee. It gets a plant of 38,000 catchable rainbows, including a few hundred 14 inchers, in late Mar. supplementing fry plants of 100,000 rainbows and 160,000 kokanee. WDFW access and ramp on SW shore. Turn NW from Hwy. 8 onto Summit Lake Road about 11 miles W. of I-5 and drive 1.5 miles to lake which is circled by a paved road.

SUSAN LAKE. 3.5 acres 700 feet from N. end of **MUNN LAKE**. Holds largemouth bass, bluegill and a few rainbow.

TRAILS END LAKE. Channel catfish have been stocked in this 12.8 acre lake 4 miles S. of Olympia and 600 feet S. of **MUNN LAKE**. Drains to Deschutes River.

TROSPER LAKE. A shallow 17 acre lake with largemouth bass, perch and brown bullhead, 3.5 miles S. of Olympia. Drains to Budd Inlet.

WADDELL CREEK. Wild cutthroat in June. The creek flows into Black River near Little Rock on Hwy. 121. County road from Little Rock follows NW up creek about 5 miles.

WARD LAKE. Usually a good opening day producer. 67-acre lake stocked with about 6000 catchable rainbows in Mar., plus several hundred triploids and cutthroat, supplementing fry plants. Annual stockings of 15,000 kokanee salmon fry provide a marginal summer salmon fishery. Because of the lake's depth, up to 67 feet, the water is cool enough to keep kokanee action in mid summer. Warm months are best for largemouth bass, crappies and bluegills. WDFW access, ramp. Road from Tumwater SE to Rainier passes within .04 miles of lake about 1.5 miles E. of Tumwater. County road skirts W. shore.

Thurston County Resorts

Black Lake: Salmon Shores RV Park, 360-357-8618.

Harts Lake: Harts Lake Resort.

Offut Lake: Offut Lake Resort,360-264-2438.

Puget Sound: Zittle's Johnson Point Marina, 360-459-1950.

Wahkiakum County
WDFW Region 5

Washington Department of Fish and Wildlife, 2108 Grand Blvd. Vancouver, WA 98661-4624 Phone 360-696-6211.

A small, lightly populated county W. of I-5 wedged between the Columbia River and the clear-cut knobs of the Willapa Hills.

With a couple of noticeable exceptions, Wahkiakum County offers a minimum of interest for anglers, and nothing for lake specialists. One tiny lake, unnamed, and covering barely an acre, is the only stillwater listed for this 269 square mile county which ranks 37th in size in the state. Highest point is 2673 feet about 11.5 miles N. of the river town of Cathlamet.

The southwest county is bordered on the S. by some pretty fair sturgeon water in the Columbia River, on the E. by Cowlitz County, the W. by Pacific County and Lewis County on the N. The southern, heavily logged slopes of the Willapa Hills frame most of the county north of its only major arterial, Hwy. 4 which crosses the southern edge of the county en route from I-5 at Longview to Hwy. 101 and the ocean.

Besides the Columbia River, the Elochoman and Grays rivers provide most of the fishing action. The Elochoman drains most of the E. part of the county and N. and W. county is drained by the Grays and Deep rivers.

The county gets about 90 inches of precipitation, mostly rain, a year, but temperatures are mild and the climate maritime. You can comfortably fish 12 months a year. There's an excellent marina and launch at Cathlamet, an interesting river town.

BROOKS SLOUGH. Approximately 2 miles long, Brooks Slough is fed by Alger and Risk creeks and is adjacent to the S. side of Hwy. 4. Mouth of slough is at Skamokawa where Skamokawa Creek joins it from the N. Brooks is bridged at mouth and the county road doubles back to parallel slough's S. bank. The slough offers largemouth bass, perch, crappie and bluegill fishing during summer. May be fished from shore. Boat ramp and fishing areas adjacent to Hwy. 4 about 1 mile E. of Skamokawa.

COLUMBIA RIVER BARS. The most popular fishing bars in the county are located at Sunny Sands on Puget Island, and County Line Bar between Cowlitz and Wahkiakum Counties. June and July are best steelheading months for plunkers, while jack salmon fishing begins in September. Chinook and coho salmon are taken in August and September. A few wild cutthroat provide limited action from July to October, but are no longer stocked. Boats may be launched into Columbia River at Abernathy Creek, Willow Grocery Park, mouth of Brooks Slough, Port of Cathlamet, Deep River. Several pull-over sturgeon fishing spots on the shoulder of Hwy. 4 E. of Cathlamet.

DEEP RIVER. Enters Grays Bay on the Columbia River 16 miles W. of Skamokawa on Hwy. 4. Deep River county road leads upstream from Hwy. 4, for 3.5 miles and then into Pacific County. Fee ramp at Hwy. 4. The river is named for its considerable depth, which allows prop boats to roam 3 or more miles upstream from its mouth. Lots of duck hunting in the marshes. The lower 5 miles is a deep tidal slough that offers anglers largemouth bass, crappie, catfish, occasional cutthroat and perch. Some salmon and steelhead available.

ELOCHOMAN RIVER. The hottest hot spot in the county, especially in winter when anglers turn out for an exceptionally heavy winter steelhead return. Best fishing is in December and January. Anglers in recent years take about 650 winter-runs, thanks

Columbia River.

mostly to a productive Beaver Creek Hatchery upstream. In past years it has produced as many as 6000 winter-runs. This little river heads in Cowlitz County and flows SW about 15 miles in Wahkiakum County before joining Columbia River 2 miles NW of Cathlamet. Two-lane Hwy. 407 parallels the river about 10 miles upstream from the mouth and provides a lot of bank-fishing access. A few wild sea-run cutthroat show during fall months, but like most SW rivers, the Elochoman is no longer stocked with cutts. Wild cutts must be released. Steelhead holding water is well defined and usually marked by parked cars every day of the season.

GRAYS RIVER. Another Columbia River tributary that produces poor to marginal steelhead success, despite fairly heavy smolt plants. Anglers will catch, most years, 100 to 200 winter-runs, most in January. In fall cutthroat and wild chinook and chum salmon swim the lower stretches, all cutthroat must be released and salmon sea-

sons are rare. Hwy. 4 touches the river at community of Grays River. About 3 miles from the mouth, Hwy. 403 leaves Hwy. 4 and goes SW along the east bank to Washington's only covered bridge. Some years smelt enter the Grays in March. There can be decent shallow-water sturgeon fishing in Grays Bay between the mouths of the Grays and Deep rivers. Boat launch near Hwy. 403 bridge at Rosburg Grange.

SKAMOKAWA CREEK. A wide creek crossed at its mouth by Hwy. 4 at Skamokawa 8 miles NW of Cathlamet. East and Middle Valley county road follows creek upstream for 4 miles. Lots of steelhead smolts are planted and disappear. In recent years, diehard local steelheaders take about 60 winter-runs, most in Nov.-Dec. Lower sluggish reaches holds crappie and largemouth bass. Some fall cutthroat fishing. There is a rough boat launch near the mouth.

Walla Walla County
WDFW Region 1
Washington Department of Fish and Wildlife, 8702 N. Division St., Spokane, WA 99218. Phone, 509-456-4082.

This is a tough, dry place for lake fishermen. There are no natural lakes in Walla Walla County. Fishermen head for the big water of the Columbia and Snake River impoundments, the smaller flows in the Touchet and Walla Walla Rivers and a few stocked ponds.

Located in the semi-arid SE part of the state, the county covers 1299 square miles and is the 26th largest. Highest point is Lewis Peak at 4880 feet. Walla Walla County is bordered on the NW and N. by the Snake River and Franklin County. On the E. are the wheat fields of Columbia County and the northwest slope of the Blue Mountains and Umatilla National Forest. The W. border is the Columbia River and Benton County, and the S. portion looks into the Milton-Freewater area of Oregon. Most of the county is agricultural or rangeland and trees are few and far between. Less than 2.5 percent of this county is classed as forest.

When you find a place to fish, don't expect crowds. The county is one of the most lightly populated. Most residents are clustered in the far S. county, along US 12 and the city of Walla Walla. The vast, nearly uninhabited Eureka Flats, Touchet Valley, rolling river breaks and dry canyon lands to the N. are populated by small agricultural communities and scattered farms.

Summers are warm, dry and sunny with temperatures usually in the high 80s and low 90s. Winters average around freezing, but January temperatures have fallen as far as -29. There is little humidity and precipitation is light—mostly falling as rain during November. The annual rain and snow fall is 15.07 inches at Walla Walla.

The main route into the county is US 12 which runs across the bottom of the county connecting the Columbia River, Walla Walla and Waitsburg. The center of the county is crossed E-W by Hwy. 124 which follows the Touchet River to Waitsburg. The far N. is held together by far flung county roads. There's a lot of horizon in this county.

Most of the best fishing is found in the lakes and sloughs of the Snake River along the north end of the county. Several small ponds get regular WDFW plants of rainbow, including Bennington, College Place and Jefferson Park.

BENNINGTON LAKE (MILL CREEK RESERVOIR). An excellent trout fishery, possibly the best in the county. This 52-acre lake is created by a U.S. Army Corps of Engineers dam on Mill Creek 3 miles E. of Walla Walla just S. of WDFW McNary Wildlife Area. It is heavily planted with 24,500 catchable rainbows, plus about 1000 tripolids, some up to 5 pounds. Offers limited warm water species fishing. Good bank access and boat ramp. No internal combustion outboards.

BURBANK SLOUGH. A 700 acre elbow shaped slough, rarely more than 11 feet deep, formed by backwaters of McNary Dam located S. of Burbank. It supports mostly largemouth bass and bluegill. Part of the Slough is on the McNary National Wildlife Refuge. There is a boat launch on the SE. side just W. of US 12 before the bridge.

CASEY POND. A 60 acre lake on McNary W.R.A. 4.5 miles SE of Burbank. It offers both large and smallmouth bass plus crappie, perch, sunfish and bullhead catfish. Can be pretty fair fishing early in the season.

COPPEI CREEK. Wild rainbow provide action early in season. The stream heads in the Blue Mtns. and flows NW about 14 miles to the Touchet River at Waitsburg. US 12 follows Coppei 3 miles S. from Waitsburg, then Coppei Road parallels creek another 9 miles SE along forks to headwaters.

CURLEW POND. Located on McNary game range about 5.4 miles SE from Burbank. Largemouth bass and bluegill. Drains to **WALLULA LAKE**.

DRY CREEK. A fair early season producer of small native rainbow. The creek joins Walla Walla River 4 miles E. of Touchet. A county road leads from Hwy. 12 at the mouth NE upstream for approximately 16 miles to cross Hwy. 12 at Dixie and continues another 5 miles to headwaters in the Blue Mtns.

FISH HOOK POND. Formed by seepage from the Snake River's Ice Harbor Pool, the pond is about 2 acres and holds rainbow. Bank fishing only. It is situated E. of Burbank between Fish Hook Park and Ice Harbor Dam on S. side of RR tracks. It's stocked annually with 6000 catchable rainbows plus a few hundred larger trout.

GARRISON CREEK. Primarily a backyard kids creek that provides rainbow trout, with May usually the best fishing month. The creek flows into Walla Walla River. Access is a problem as the stream, a diversion of Mill Creek, runs through private land.

JEFFERSON PARK-LYONS PARK PONDS. Urban ponds stocked with 10 to 12 inch rainbow trout (a few larger) and restricted to juvenile fishermen. Open year round. Located in parks in Walla Walla and College Place.

McNARY POOL (Lake Wallula). Fluctuations in water levels influence fishing in these waters. Fishing takes place all year, but the warm water species are normally from spring to fall for walleye, large and smallmouth bass, crappie, perch, sunfish and bullhead catfish which are taken in good numbers. the McNary pool can produce some exceptionally good smallmouth action in spring and early summer after water temperatures near 60 degrees. Best fishing areas are pumping plant above Hwy. 12 bridge on Snake River, Casey Pond-Burbank area, and Walla Walla River estuary. Boats may be launched at S. end of US 12 bridge on Snake River, at Casey

Pond, "2 Rivers Area", and at mouth of Walla Walla River. McNary Pool is the name given water backed up by McNary Dam on Columbia River. It extends from dam at Umatilla, Oregon to Richland, Washington. There is a winter-spring sturgeon fishery that slips into a catch-and-release fishery after July 1 and some of these fish are long enough that if they stood on their tails they could look down into a basketball hoop. Steelhead move in during late summer into fall and are targeted by trollers. Walleye diehards will troll and jig the pool for these fine eating fish year-round.

MILL CREEK. Heading high in the Blue Mts. in Columbia County, Mill Creek loops SW into Oregon, then NW again into Walla Walla County. It enters Walla Walla River 3 miles W. of College Place. Roads follow stream for virtually its entire length. Upper stretches are reached by leaving US 12 at Eastgate scale house and driving E. and S. 13 miles into Oregon where the road ends. Upper reaches are in Walla Walla watershed which is closed to public entry except by permit. A trail continues upstream. Mill Creek can offer good fishing throughout season except during spring runoff. The lake used to be planted with rainbow, but future stockings are uncertain. There are also bull trout (protected), native rainbow, whitefish and a run of summer steelhead. Because of the road-side access the creek receives a fair amount of pressure.

MUD CREEK. Rated poor this rainbow stream flows into Walla Walla River. Some angling is available from mouth upstream.

QUARRY LAKE. A 9 acre lake crammed with 22,000 rainbows, plus several hundred 14-inch plus trout. It is on the McNary Wildlife Refuge Area. It has a public access area and gets the nod for good May and June angling. Drive 5 miles SE of Burbank on US 12. Turn right to lake at public access sign. Latest fishing conditions may be obtained from recreation headquarters located in Burbank. .

SNAKE RIVER. This wide, dammed river is the N. and W. boundary of Walla Walla County, and joins the Columbia River S. of Burbank. US 12 crosses the mouth at McNary National Wildlife Refuge. Ice Harbor Dam blocks river 8 miles upstream and forms Lake Sacajawea which extends 32 miles upstream to base of Lower Monumental Dam. Game fish found in this section of the Snake include summer steelhead, spring and fall chinook (usually protected), channel catfish, crappie, perch, sunfish, bullhead catfish, large and smallmouth bass and white sturgeon. Best fishing period for the various species is as follows: Steelhead, August to end of October; chinook (when legal) May through September; channel catfish, March to October; sturgeon, March through September; smallmouth bass, May through September; smallmouth bass, March through October. Top fishing areas on Snake include down stream from Ice Harbor Dam to mouth for all species. Steelheading is best at Ayer, Field's Gulch and Lyon's Ferry, Page, Levey, "25 mile", Walker's Pit, Burr Canyon and most inlets on Ice Harbor Reservoir are best for all species of warm water species. Good smallmouth bass fishing at Burbank Heights, pumping plant, Ayer, Field's Gulch and Lyon's Ferry. Boats may be launched at Burbank, immediately above Ice Harbor Dam, Page, Walker Pit, Ayer and Lyon's Ferry. Best access to the lower river is from the N. bank in Franklin County. The Pasco-Kahlotus Rd. follows the river at a distance, with access roads branching off to the river. On the NE side of Walla Walla County there is S. side access at Lower Monumental Dam, Ayer Road and Lyons Ferry State Park on Hwy. 261.

TOUCHET RIVER. A small river, easily waded in most stretches, with a reputation for good trout fishing—especially brown trout that attract anglers to the Dayton area. The river also holds rainbow, steelhead and protected bull trout, plus a few whitefish.

Top fishing period is June through October. The Touchet flows W. from Dayton in Columbia County, entering Walla Walla County at Waitsburg, then turns S. to join Walla Walla River at town of Touchet. Good roads follow stream in the county, providing access—much of it across private property requiring permission. Steelheading takes place below the Wolf Fork Bridge at Dayton from Dec.- Mar. This small river can be surprisingly productive for steelhead.

WALLA WALLA RIVER. This could be the best prospect in Washington to hook a giant catfish. The Walla Walla is a medium-size stream which heads in Oregon and flows NW into Walla Walla County 3 miles S. of College Place, and then W. to **WALLULA LAK**E adjacent to the Columbia River at Wallula Junction. It has warm water species and steelhead. Bass fishing is good in lower reaches during March. Channel catfish up to 20 pounds are taken during late spring. Lots of night fishing with meat baits. The mouth is a channel cat hot spot. This fishery gets more popular every year. There is good steelheading in the lower river from Sept. into Dec. In some years more than 1000 steelies hit the bank here. Access can be a problem. There are public access areas W. of College Place at Whitman Mission, and two near McDonald Bridge.

YELLOW HAWK CREEK. A diversion of Mill Creek, the creek branches off Mill Creek 2 miles E. of Walla Walla and flows SW 10 miles to the Walla Walla River. Access is difficult in some stretches

Whatcom County
WDFW Region 4

Washington Department of Fish and Wildlife, 16018 Mill Creek Blvd., Mill Creek, WA 98012. Phone 425-775-1311.

Snug beneath the British Columbia border, Whatcom County is one of the largest and, when you travel east of the I-5 corridor, thinly populated counties on the West Side. For fishermen the 2180 square miles are a backwoods trove of lightly fished lowland and alpine lakes, brushy streams, chalky rivers and roughly 30 miles of productive saltwater shoreline, including two exceptional state parks.

Roughly three quarters of the county, Washington's 11th largest, are mountainous and heavily forested, much of it within the Mount Baker-Snoqualmie National Forest and North Cascades National Park. Much of the remote central county is dominated by Mount Baker Wilderness and Mount Baker National Recreation Area. A finger of Noisy-Diobsud Wilderness reaches up from Skagit County E. of Baker Lake. Whatcom County claims the most spectacular and jagged peaks in the Cascade Range. Many elevations soar to above 8000 feet with rocky, lung-searing, dagger-like summits. The skyline of eastern Whatcom County is a ragged, serration white with glaciers and permanent snow fields. More than half of the county's fishing lakes are above 2500 feet and many of those above 5000 feet are rarely ice free until July. Lakes in the 7000 foot range rarely open until late August and smaller ones tend to winter kill. The skyline is dominated by two glacier encrusted volcanoes; Mount Baker at 10,778 feet—the highest point in the county—and Mount Shuksan 9127 feet. Most forest and recreational roads end near Mount Baker and the rugged mountains east of there are some of the most remote and isolated in the contiguous US. Much of it lies within North Cascades National Park (NCNP) and hiking trails are few with miles of mountains in between. If you need to fish unfished—and possibly unstocked—lakes in spectacular surroundings this is your place.

West of the national forest the county dramatically flattens into a lowland of conifer and deciduous forests, folding into a tabletop of Midwest-like agricultural ground that runs W. to saltwater. A few lakes in this area are planted with catchable trout. Many streams are colored by agricultural siltation and ditched in the lower reaches. The gray concrete of I-5 crosses N-S through the farm ground, the arterial that connects nearly every important recreational highway in the county. I-5 is paralleled at a distance by Hwy. 9 an excellent two-lane alternative through small town-Whatcom County. On the N. Hwy. 524/Mount Baker Hwy. connects the recreation and ski areas at Mount Baker with Bellingham and a web of secondary roads at saltwater.

Only three rivers drain this massive county; the Nooksack, Baker and Skagit river systems The Nooksack and its three long forks drain most of it, 737 square miles in the western part of the county emptying into Bellingham Bay. The Skagit and Baker rivers drain the SE and E. parts of the county and streams in the far north run further north into Canada's Fraser River. Three huge reservoirs, Diablo and Ross impounded on the upper Skagit River, and Baker Lake on the Baker River provide summer fishing for cold water game fish particularly in late summer and fall. Whatcom Lake covers more than 5000 acres and Samish Lake another 814.

WDFW has stopped stocking catchable trout into streams in this region, although most of the creeks support resident cutthroat and some rainbows. These wild trout provide mostly catch-and-release opportunities because of 2 fish daily limits and 12 to 14 inch minimum sizes on many streams. Few wild creek trout top 10 inches.

Despite its tremendous drainage area, the Nooksack's once productive steelhead fishery has collapsed. Recent checks show fewer than 100 steelhead caught annually in the entire system, mostly winter-runs hooked in January in the main stem, North and Middle Forks. Compare that dismal total to the mid-1980s when anglers were catching almost 2000 fish a winter. During summer, snow melt from glaciers in the headwaters silt the river with glacial flour and color the water murky gray. The Nook' does collect a lot of coho, chum and pink salmon thanks to heavy lower river hatchery plants intended mostly to subsidize industrial and tribal net fishing. The Nooksack rolls into Bellingham Bay at the E. edge of the Lummi Indian Reservation, which has treaty netting rights.

Summer fishing temperatures are cool, and most freshwater bites are slower to develop than in counties to the south. Upland lakes fish best in May and June and the large reservoirs in fact, don't hit their prime until August and September, especially those with kokanee salmon.

Whatcom County is a wet place. Bellingham gets 33.63 inches of precipitation and just 60 miles E. at Newhalem rain and snow annually average 77.66 inches. Mount Baker holds the national record for snowfall, piling so deep that ski chairlifts ran through snow ditches. The lowlands are cool maritime areas while the high Cascades are largely influenced by the hot, arid Columbia Basin weather blowing W. up the Okanogan and Methow valleys.

ANN LAKE. Brookies, cutthroat and rainbow inhabit this high mountain lake (4700 feet elevation) of 6 acres. Leave Hwy. 542 at Austin Pass (near Mount Baker Ski area) and hike 4 miles SE on FS Trail 600 to lake.

ATHEARNS PONDS. A series of beaver ponds, covering about 5 acres, holding brookies adjacent to South Fork Nooksack River about 4 miles SE of Saxon,.

BACON CREEK. Flows S. into Skagit County and Skagit River from its headwaters in Green and Berdeen Lakes. Bacon enters the Skagit 5 miles NE of Marblemount. FS Rd. 1060 follows upstream for about 5 miles, with a very rough trail continuing upstream into NCNP. A very few summer steelhead are taken along with small wild cutthroat, rainbow and the odd Dolly Varden.

BAGLEY LAKES. A pair of 9 and 11 acre lakes at 4200 feet elev. SW of Mt. Baker Lodge. The lakes hold brookies and cutthroat. Austin Pass picnic area is just above the lakes.

BAKER LAKE. A popular 10-mile long, 3616-acre fishing and boat-camping reservoir impounded behind a pair of power generating dams on the Baker River. Boat fishermen enjoy a spectacular view of Mount Baker which seems to sit squarely in the N. end of the lake. Baker Lake supports a good April-June kokanee salmon fishery especially in the south end, and several thousand catchable rainbow are planted in early July. There's also wild cutthroat, whitefish. There are Dolly Varden/bull trout but it's illegal to fish for them. Best trout fishing is near the mouths of the tributary streams. In a management twist from most lakes there is an 18-inch maximum size limit on all trout and kokanee salmon. West shore boat ramps are at Baker Lake Resort on the lake's NW shore, Shannon Creek Campground, Panorama Point Campground, Horseshoe Cove campground, Kulshan Campground. Several primitive flat spots on the roadless E. shore are used for boat camping. Hiking Trail 610 follows the E. shoreline from a trailhead just E. of the dam. Spur roads access the lake's W. shore from Baker Lake Rd./FS 11. From Hwy. 20 5 miles E. of Hamilton turn N. on Baker Lake Road for 17 miles to the W. shore.

BAKER RIVER UPPER. The river above Baker Lake heads on the W. slope of 8207 foot elev. Mt. Challenger in NCNP, and flows SW about 12 miles to the upper end of **BAKER LAKE.** FS Rd. 11 follows the stream for about 1 mile above the NE end of lake and Trail 606 continues upstream 5 miles into the park. Late summer and early fall fly-fishing for small wild rainbows.

BARRETT CREEK. A short-run creek, less than 1 mile in length, that drains **BARRETT LAKE** into Nooksack River 1 mile SE of Ferndale. Spring and fall cutthroat fishing.

BARRETT LAKE. Cutthroat and largemouth bass are in this long, skinny 40 acre lake 1 mile E. of Ferndale. Axton Road leads to the lake. May is top month.

Baker Lake.

BERTRAND CREEK. May and June are best months for Bertrand's rainbow and cutthroat. From Lynden drive SW for 4 miles along the N. bank of the Nooksack River to the creek confluence.

BLUE LAKE. An easily reached 13 acre mountain lake at 4000 feet elev. 7 miles N. of Concrete. Holds cutthroat, brookies, brown trout and rainbow, and drains via Bear Creek into **SHANNON LAKE**. From Hwy. 20 go N. on FS 11 then W. on FS 12 around Sulphur Butte to FS 1230. From end of 1230 follow Trail 604 less than a mile to lake.

BLUM LAKES. Group of 4 NCNP lakes at elevations from 4950 to 5900 feet beneath the glaciers on Mt. Blum, elev. 7680. The lakes are E. of the N. end of Baker Lake. The lakes range from 1.5 to 145 acres. Stocked with rainbow. Drain to Upper Baker River.

CAIN LAKE. An excellent early season 72-acre fishery about 9.5 SE of Bellingham about 2 miles S. of **WHATCOM LAKE**. Stocked with 7000 rainbows, many almost a pound, plus there are largemouth bass and perch. WDFW access, ramp on SW shore. From I-5 Exit 240 to Alger then N. on Cain Lake Rd.

CALIFORNIA CREEK. Sea-run cutthroat furnish fair fishing during spring and fall in this 6 miles long creek flowing into Drayton Harbor at Blaine. I-5 parallels the E. bank and several county roads cross it. Best fishing near mouth.

CAMP CREEK BEAVER PONDS. These shallow ponds are reported barren. They are located near Skookum Creek which joins South Fork Nooksack near Saxon.

CANYON CREEK. A long tributary to Nooksack River with Dolly Varden/bull trout, brookies and rainbow. Best fishing after snow run-off ends in mid June. Canyon Creek Road/FS 31 leaves Mt. Baker Hwy. just E. of Douglas Fir campground reaches the creek in 4 miles and parallels it upstream 14 miles where a left fork leads to **DAMFINO LAKES** trail. No fish reported. From end of right fork hike cross-country uphill to **BEARPAW MT. LAKES** (Church Lakes) at 4450 and 5150 feet. Cutthroat plants.

CANYON LAKE. Rated good for rainbow in May and June this low mountain lake covers 45 acres at 2250 feet elev. in logging area E. of Mount Baker Hwy. Road from Deming leads NE along Nooksack River's Middle Fork on N. side for 4 miles to Canyon Creek, then E. up creek to within 1 mile of lake. A trail continues to lake.

CEDAR LAKE. A 4-acre cutthroat lake on NE slope of Chuckanut Mt. From S. Bellingham go through Chuckanut Village to a trail to lake. Best in May.

CLEARWATER CREEK. Late summer is best for the wild rainbow and cutthroat in this mountain stream flowing into Middle Fork Nooksack River 7 miles S. of Kulshan. From Middle Fork/FS Rd. 38 E. of Deming, turn N. on gravel rod which continues about 2.5 miles NE up Clearwater.

COPPER LAKE. A very remote 8 acre rainbow lake at 5250 feet elev., in NCNP 11.4 miles E. of Shuksan and 1.8 miles SE of Copper Mt. Adjacent to Trail 692 which is a continuation of Trail 674 from Hannegan Trailhead at the end of FS Rd. 32. Drains NE to Chilliwack River.

DAKOTA CREEK. A slim, 9 mile long stream which begins SE of Blaine and flows NW into Drayton Harbor. I-5 crosses Dakota at its mouth and county roads provide easy access upstream. Spring and fall runs of sea-run cutthroat. A few steelhead are taken in December, January and February.

DIABLO LAKE. The 300-foot deep center link in a three link chain of city of Seattle dams impounding the upper Skagit River, Diablo covers 910 acres and 4.5 miles between Gorge and Ross lakes. Hwy. 20/North Cascade Scenic Highway bridges Thunder Arm S. of the main reservoir. The big reservoir starts yielding native rainbows and cutthroat in April and improves in May and June. Can be a very good fall fishery . Most anglers troll and concentrate on the inlets. Large numbers of ESA protected Dolly Varden/bull trout. Tributaries include Riprap, Sourdough, Happy, Thunder and Colonial creeks. Good boat launch at NCNP campground near mouth of Colonial Creek at the Thunder Arm bridge. Another launch is on the N. shore at Sourdough Cr. and there are more campgrounds at Buster Brown Flats and Hidden Cove. A road between Gorge and Diablo lakes provides access to N. shore. Between April and Nov. Hwy. 20 continues E. on an exceptionally scenic route over the North Cascade Range into Okanogan County at Winthrop. The highway is gated in winter. Resort with store, camping.

DIOBSUD LAKES. Three alpine rainbow lakes of 2, 2.5 and 3.5 acres 9.5 miles NW from Marblemount at the headwater of Diobsud Creek in Noisy-Diobsud Wilderness. Elevations are 4075 to 4490 feet. Drain to Skagit River. Best route is up the E. side of Baker Lake on FS 1107 to road end then SE on Trail 611.

ELBOW LAKE. One of several small trout lakes on Sister Divide. Elbow is a 5 acre lake at 3400 feet elev. 6.5 miles SW of summit of Mt. Baker on Sister Divide. Cutthroat and rainbow. Route is up Baker River Road then W. on FS 12/Rocky Creek Road to its end on South Fork Nooksack River at edge of Mount Baker Wilderness. Logging road comes within .05 miles of lake. **DOREEN LAKE** is 400 feet S. of Elbow. It holds rainbow. **WISEMAN LAKE** lies at 4250 feet 1 mile W. of Elbow, covers 18 acres and offers brookies, rainbow and cutthroat.

FAZON LAKE. A year-round 32 acre lowland lake located in a boggy area 1.5 miles NW of Goshen S. of the Nooksack River. Well stocked with warm water fish including tiger muskies, bluegill, largemouth bass, perch, brown and yellow bullheads and possibly a few channel catfish which are no longer planted. May also support some hold-over rainbows from earlier stockings. WDFW access, ramp on S. shore. From Hwy. 544/Evereson Goshen Road turn E. on Hemmi Rd. to S. shore. Some strange regulations at this lake, including a ban on boat fishing Oct. 4-Jan. 15.

FERGUSON PONDS. About 10 acres of water in this group of ponds near Saxon Bridge on the South Fork Nooksack River. Ponds hold cutthroat and rainbow.

FISHTRAP CREEK. Fair for wild rainbow in May, some cutthroat in fall. The stream flows through Lynden into Nooksack River about 3.5 miles SW. Several roads cross the creek providing easy access.

FOUNTAIN LAKE. A 14 acre largemouth bass and catfish lake 3 miles SE of Lynden. Drains to Nooksack River. Head S. from Lynden on Hannegan Rd. 2 miles, then E. on Hwy. 544 for 1 mile then N. on access road to lake. Best fishing comes in mid-summer.

FRAGRANCE LAKE (Lost, Gates). A 6

acre cutthroat lake in Larrabee State Park on W. side of Chuckanut Mt. Top angling in May. Road up the mountain passes within 0.4 miles of lake. Good trail. **LOST LAKE**, a 12 acre rainbow lake lies 2400 feet E. of Fragrance Lake. Continue past Fragrance Lake on trail to Lost Lake.

GALENA CHAIN LAKES (Galena). Four small lakes clustered 2 miles W. of Mt. Baker Lodge at 4800 feet elev. in Mt. Baker Wilderness. The lakes are Arbuthnot (5 acres), Hayes (13 acres), Mazama (1 acre), and Iceberg (36 acres). Most contain rainbow and brookies. From end of Mt. Baker Hwy. at Artist Point hike trail 682 NW 2 miles to lakes. Best fishing in late summer and fall. Drain to North Fork Nooksack.

GOAT LAKE (Mud). Cutthroat are in this 4 acre pond 1 mile from W. end of Samish Lake. Access from logging road near Luther Wood camp.

GOODELL CREEK. July and August are premium fishing months for this stream's cutthroat, brookies and rainbow. It joins Skagit River at Newhalem. A road, possibly gated, leads upstream 2.5 miles. Goodell Creek campground is at creek's mouth at Hwy. 20.

GORGE LAKE. The lowest of three Seattle City Light impoundments on upper Skagit River, the lake is formed by Gorge Dam at Gorge Creek Falls. A narrow lake, Gorge is about 4 miles long and is paralleled on the N. bank by Hwy. 20 to foot of Diablo Dam. Poor to fair summer fishing for native rainbow. Dolly Varden/bull trout are illegal. Boat launch at head of reservoir near company town of Diablo.

GRANITE CREEK. PCT 2000 follows Granite Creek from its source near Rainy Pass in Skagit County and Hwy. 20 parallels the creek from its mouth nearly to its source. Late summer and fall fishing is best for small wild rainbow and cutthroat.

GREEN LAKE. An 80 acre mountain lake at 4300 feet elev. in NCNP 11.5 miles N. of Marblemount with cutthroat and rainbow. Lake is on N. side of picturesque Bacon Mt. at head of Bacon Creek. Tough hike in.

GREEN LAKE (McLeod). A lowland lake 4 miles SE of Lynden, adjacent to Hwy. 544. Covers 19-acres and offers perch and brown bullhead.

HIGHWOOD LAKE. A 2 acre rainbow pond 1500 feet E. Mt. Baker Lodge at 4100 feet.

HOZOMEEN LAKE. An excellent brook trout lake of 111 acres at 2800 feet elev. about 3 miles E. of head of Ross Lake. Trail 748 from Hozomeen Camp leads approximately 4 miles to lake. Road to Hozomeen camp and boat ramp on Ross Lake enters from Hope, British Columbia (See Ross Lake).

HUTCHINSON CREEK. Poor to fair fishing for small rainbow and brookies in this stream which flows into the South Fork Nooksack 1 mile SE of Acme. To fish, turn E. from Hwy. 9 just N. of Acme onto Mosquito Lake Rd. to follow about 2 miles of the creek. June is most productive.

JERRY LAKE: Lower of four Jerry Lakes, covers 30 acres at 5900 feet 1.5 miles N. from Crater Mt. in Pasayten Wilderness about 7 miles E. of Ross Lake below Jack Mt. glaciers. Planted with rainbow. Drains to Devil's Creek and Ross Lake.

JOHNSON CREEK. Heading in B.C. Johnson flows S. through Clearbrook and enters Nooksack River near Everson. Supports wild rainbows.

JOHNSON CREEK. This Sumas River tributary usually starts producing well at season opener. It offers cutthroat, brookies and rainbow. Best fishing in lower 2 miles.

JORGENSON LAKE. A marshy 12 acre lake 6 miles SE of Deming with brown bullhead. From Hwy. 542 go S. on Mosquito Lake Road which passes the E. shore

JUDSON LAKE (Boundary). A 112 acre largemouth bass and black crappie lake on the U.S.-Canada border 8 miles NE of Lynden. From Lynden drive W. on Halverstick Rd. then N. on Van Burien Rd. to lake.

KENDALL LAKE. Wild cutthroat and brookies are the attraction in this shallow 12 acre lake. It drains via Kendall Creek to North Fork Nooksack, and is 1.4 miles N. of Kendall. Dries up occasionally.

LITTLE CANYON CREEK. Outlet of Canyon Lake flowing 3.5 miles W. into Middle Fork Nooksack at Kulshan. The creek holds Dolly Varden (protected) and native cutthroat. Road parallels Canyon Creek from Kulshan about 2 miles upstream.

MAIDEN LAKE. Remote 17 acre rainbow lake at 3900 feet elev. in Mount Baker Wilderness N. of and draining via Swift Creek into **BAKER LAKE** at Baker Lake Resort.

MARTEN LAKE. Cutthroat have been reported in this 5 acre lake at 3650 feet elev. From W. shore of Baker Lake at Boulder Creek Campground go N. on FS Rd. 1130 for 5 miles. Then it's cross country 1.5 miles NW to the lake at the edge of Mt. Baker Wilderness.

MIRROR LAKE. 14 acre rainbow lake produces best in spring. It is 0.5 mile NW of Wickersham and drains into **WHATCOM LAKE**. Best in April and May.

MOSQUITO LAKE. Channel catfish and brown bullhead are in this 7 acre lake 5.7 miles SE from Deming. From Hwy. 542 at Kulshan turn S. on Mosquito Lake Rd..

MUD LAKE. Small pond with black crappie, perch and brown bullhead .08 miles SE of Deming..

NOISY CREEK. July and August are the months to fish for wild cutthroat and rainbow. It is a tributary to **BAKER LAKE** flowing in on the roadless upper E. shore. Boat to creek mouth in a small bay then hike upstream on Trail 6103 into Noisy-Diobsud Wilderness.

NOOKSACK RIVER. The dominant drainage in N. Whatcom County, but in recent years has deteriorated into a poor fishing opportunity. The North, Middle and South Forks merge and form the mainstem Nooksack about 1 mile SE of Deming. It flows NW 15 miles to Lynden, then SW another 15 miles to enter Bellingham Bay near Marietta. Roads follow within striking range along its 30 mile length. Since the mid 1980s annual steelhead catches have plummeted from about 2000 to less than 100. The Lummi Indian Reservation, with treaty netting rights, sits at the mouth of the Nook'. Most catches are winter-runs taken in December and January, but a few summer-runs filter in during Sept. and Oct. There are heavy runs of hatchery coho, pinks and chums in the lower river, released primarily to subsidize industrial and tribal net fisheries. Some years there are sportfishing seasons for salmon, especially during odd-year pink runs. Early summer through fall can offer fair sea-run cutthroat and some Dolly Varden. Most of the sum-

mer the glacier-fed Nooksack is milky and difficult to fish. Long finned smelt enter the lower river in November and December and can offer a fun dip netting below Ferndale.

NOOKSACK RIVER NORTH FORK. Clouded with glacial silt most of the summer, the North Fork doesn't come on until fall when the ice melt freezes. This fork heads under glaciers on Mt. Shuksan's N. flank, and is closely followed for 25 miles by Hwy. 542 which leads to Mt. Baker N. and E. of Deming. Falls at mouth of Wells Creek, 6.5 miles E. of Glacier, block anadromous fish. Above the falls are wild rainbow, brookies, Dolly Varden and a few cutthroat. Tough fishing.

NOOKSACK RIVER MIDDLE FORK. This tributary flows 20 miles W. and N. from S. side of Mt. Baker to join North Fork 3 miles E. of Deming. From Hwy. 542 at Kulshan turn S. on Mosquito Lake Road which follows the river to FS 38 which continues upstream to the edge of Mt. Baker Wilderness. Light tackle fishing for wild rainbow, cutthroat. ESA protected Dolly Varden, plus a very few salmon and steelhead are in the Middle Fork. Best trout fishing in fall.

NOOKSACK RIVER SOUTH FORK. South Fork enters main river 1 mile SE of Deming. Produces a rare steelhead in winter (reported catch in 1999 was 3 steelhead), and is mostly fished for cutthroat and rainbow in summer and fall. Hwy. 9 follows the stream for 6 miles, offering some access. Lots of private land in valley. Upper South Fork is in Skagit County and is reached by from Hwy. 20 by turning NE at Hamilton and continuing about 16 miles up Jones Creek to old logging camp near Lyman Pass (See Skagit County).

PADDEN LAKE. Bring the kids, this is a great place for family fishing. Heavily stocked with more than 18,000 rainbows, averaging 0.75 of a pound, this 152 acre centerpiece of Bellingham City Park is surrounded by excellent bank-fishing opportunities. A launch is available for boats without gasoline motors. Hwy. 99/Samish Way runs along the lake's E. shore. Padden, located on the S. edge of Bellingham just E. of I-5, also is stocked with kokanee salmon and a few cutthroat which begin biting well in late May and June. This is usually one of the best lakes in Western Washington on opening weekend. Padden Creek drains lake into Bellingham Bay.

PINE LAKE. A 6 acre lake at 1570 feet elev. on the E. side of Chuckanut Mt. 5 miles S. of Bellingham NW of Samish Lake . Brookies, cutthroat and rainbow. April, May and June are best.

RACEHORSE CREEK. Limited cutthroat fishing in this small tributary flowing into North Fork Nooksack River about 6 miles NE of Deming. From Kulshan go N. 3 miles on North Fork Rd. to mouth of Racehorse just below Nooksack Hatchery.

ROCKY CREEK. Baker Lake Hwy./FS 11 crosses Rocky Creek 10 miles N. of Concrete. FS Rds. 12 and 1220 parallel creek about 6 miles W. Late summer best for small wild rainbow and cutthroat.

ROSS LAKE. One of the most visible, beautiful and lightly fished lakes in Washington. Ross Lake is the highest of 3 Seattle City Light impoundments damming the Skagit River. The reservoir stretches nearly 24 miles through a narrow, mountain shouldered valley that winds N. from North Cascades Scenic Hwy. 20 into Canada. Ross covers 11,678 acres and it's the lack of easy access, not fish, and certainly not the spectacular surroundings that holds down fishing pressure. The only way to get a trailerable boat on the lake is through Hope,

British Columbia, coming S. on sometimes rough road to Hozomeen campground and ramp on the NE shore. South of Hozomeen the only access is from hiking trails, carrying in a small craft or by renting a motor boat at Ross Lake Resort near the dam. The SE shore is followed by an excellent trail that begins at Ruby Creek on Hwy. 20 and runs N. to Desolation Peak Lookout. Along the way are several developed, and numerous primitive campsites. A trail also goes up the SW. side from the resort to Big Beaver Campground. Many primitive sites are used by boat campers fishing their way S. from Canada. Fishing is allowed from July 1-Oct. 31 for native rainbows (Lots of Dolly Varden/bull trout that must be released). Recent regulations have set a 3-fish, 13-inch minimum limit. This big cold lake is a notoriously slow starter, usually not developing good catches until late summer running strong into fall. Most anglers troll near tributary mouths, especially Pierce, Big Beaver, Skymo, Noname, Arctic, Little Beaver, Silver, Howlett, Hozomeen, Lightning, Dry, Devils, May Roland and Ruby Creeks. Some tributaries are closed near mouths. The access road is 1.5 miles W. of Hope, B.C., and heads S. along Silver Creek about 40 miles to head of Ross Lake on B.C.-U.S. border at Hozomeen guard station. The road ends

Ross Lake.

about 2 miles inside U.S. line. Washington route is from Hwy. 20 about 7 miles E. of Newhalem to Milepost 134 where a trail leads 0.5 miles to lake and a phone connects with the resort. Resort facilities include small boat portages, rental canoes, kayaks and fishing boats, shuttle service for backpackers, and cabins. The entire lake is within the Lake Ross National Recreation Area, bordered on the W. by NCNP and on the E. by Pasayten Wilderness.

SALTWATER FISHING. The saltwater laps at the W. edge of Whatcom County in a series of large, somewhat protected bays that offer a myriad of saltwater possibilities including shore fishing, shellfishing, clamming and crabbing. At Semiahmoo Spit County Park in Blaine surf smelt spawn on the beaches and south of the base of the spit. Smelt raking is best July-January. Good crabbing can be found adjacent to most marine beaches, and a year-round, no-commercial zone, is in Chuckanut Bay and Birch Bay. Birch Bay State Park offers excellent clam digging and the beach has been salted with Pacific oysters. Surf smelt can be harvested at Little Qualicum Park on Bellingham Bay and fishing is available the 6th St. dock, Boulevard Park pier, Ferry Terminal pier and Blaine Dock. Squalicum Mall Marina is a good place to jig surf smelt in winter. Boat launches at Larrabee State Park, Post Point, Bellingham Marina, and Blaine's Drayton Harbor. A hand-carry access at Birch Bay State Park.

SAMISH LAKE. Best known for its summer kokanee salmon bite, this year-round 814 acre lake S. of Bellingham is also a decent prospect for largemouth bass, perch, crappie, and good-size cutthroat and rainbow. Kokanee bite often begins in June and improves to fall when fishing is often excellent. Most kokanee anglers troll since chumming was banned in 1998. The pothole at the upper end of the lake is 145 feet deep and the main lake drops to 75 feet. Best bass and panfish action takes places on the shallow, weedbeds at the S. end. Resorts and a public access/ramp on the lake 6.5 miles SE of Bellingham. I-5 parallels the E. shore. Lots of summer play boating competition.

SAMISH RIVER (See Skagit county).

SHUKSAN LAKE. A short steep hike from the upper end of Baker Lake leads to this 28 acre brook trout tarn at 3700 feet elev.

From Hwy. 20 follow FS 11 up the W. side of **BAKER LAKE** N. on FS Rd. 1160 to end, then N. 2 miles on Trail 608.

SILVER LAKE (Fish). An excellent 173 acre early season prospect for 18,000 large rainbows stocked in April. Some cutthroat to 18 inches. Silver is N. of the North Fork Nooksack, 3 miles N. of Maple Falls and Hwy. 542 at head of Maple Creek. Public access, ramp and a county park. Best in spring and again in the fall.

SKAGIT RIVER UPPER. Only 10 miles of the Skagit River are in Whatcom County and that includes 4.5 mile long **GORGE LAKE**. Upstream of Gorge Lake the Skagit is imprisoned in a power dam reservoir system that extends into Canada. It enters Whatcom County about 3 miles SW of Marblemount and is a paralleled by Hwy. 20. Campgrounds at Newhalem and Goodell Cr. The Skagit doesn't carry much fishing promise in this area, but there is always a chance of hooking rainbow, Dolly Varden, cutthroat, steelhead, salmon or whitefish. A road crosses the river at Newhalem and forks. The S. fork follows Newhalem Cr. and the W. fork hugs the S. bank of the Skagit almost to the county line.

SKOOKUM CREEK. A small tributary of South Fork Nooksack River with wild cutthroat and brookies. Skookum enters South Fork 3 miles SE of Saxon where a road across South Nooksack leads up Skookum Creek about 2.5 miles.

SQUALICUM LAKE. A walk-in, fly fishing-only lake 6.5 miles NE of Bellingham. Stocked with cutthroat and brown trout, some exceptionally large. From I-5 go E. on Hwy. 542/Mt. Baker Hwy. Just E. of Mission Rd. turn S. on gravel road .04 mile to trail. Drains into Squalicum Creek. Walk-in access from N. side.

SUMAS RIVER. Heading on W. slope of Sumas Mt., the placid river flows N. just E. of Hwy. 9, through mostly farm ground to Sumas and into British Columbia. Wild cutthroat and a few rainbow may be taken. Country roads provide access.

SWIFT CREEK. A mountain stream fair in July and August for wild cutthroat and rainbow. Most productive in lower 2 miles. Swift is a Baker Lake tributary. From Hwy. 20 drive N. up Baker Lake Road to Baker Lake Resort where FS Rd. 1144 goes N. toward

Rainbow Falls and Baker Hot Springs to Trail 607 which follows the creek upstream.

TENNANT LAKE. A marshy 43 acre large-mouth bass lake 1 mile SE of Ferndale. Drains to Bellingham Bay.

TENMILE CREEK. Small, brushy stream born in a swamp between Goshen and Wahl flowing W. about 10 miles passing through **BARRETT LAKE** into Nooksack River 1 mile NE of Ferndale. Spring cutthroat fishing. County roads provide access.

TERRELL LAKE. A productive 440 acre warm-water fish lake on WDFW's Lake Terrell W.R.A. From I-5 Ferndale exit then W. on Mountain View Rd. 3.3 miles to Lake Terrell Road. The deepest spot is about 11 feet and acreage varies over the season. Fishing dock and boat ramp on W. shore. No boat fishing Oct. to mid Jan. Offers largemouth bass, brown bullhead, perch and cutthroat. Open year-round, best fishing April, May, June and September.

THORNTON LAKES. Golden trout have been stocked in (Middle) Thornton Lake which covers 11 acres at 4680 feet 3.8 miles W. of Newhalem. Cutthroat and rainbow in upper and lower lakes. Spectacular views of glaciers on 7231 foot Mt. Triumph and Pickett Range. All three Thornton Lakes drain to Skagit River. From Hwy. 20 at milepost 90 turn N. on gravel FS rd. to closure then continue up old roadbed to trailhead.

THUNDER CREEK. A great hiking trail follows this major tributary to Diablo Lake at Thunder Arm. Offers rainbow, Dolly Varden and cutthroat from June to October. Hwy. 20 bridge crosses Thunder Arm at Colonial Creek campground where Thunder Creek Trail heads upstream 20 miles into Skagit County and Park Creek Pass. Spectacular peaks in upper reaches. Creek drains Fisher Creek and begins as melt from Thunder and Boston glaciers on Forbidden and Boston mtns. May be discolored by glacier flour.

THUNDER LAKE. An 8 acre lake adjacent to the Hwy. 20 about .05 mile NW of the Thunder Arm bridge across Diablo Lake. Holds cutthroat.

TOAD LAKE (Emerald). Stocked in April with about 7000 rainbows in the 0.75 pound

Thorton Lake.

range, this 30 acre lake on N. side of Squalicum Mt. is a hot opening day prospect that usually holds up into July. Decent kokanee action from June on. WDFW access and launch on W. end. From the N. end of Lake Whatcom follow Toad Lake Rd. 1 mile N.

TOMYHOI LAKE. An 82 acre brook trout lake which .05 mile inside U.S.- B.C. border at 3700 feet elev. Drains N. into Canada's Chilliwack River. Best fishing from mid-July into fall. From Hwy. 542/Mt. Baker Hwy. turn N. at Shuksan on FS 3065 up Swamp Creek about 3 miles to switchback trail 686 over Gold Run Pass 4 miles to lake.

WANLICK CREEK. Good fishing for wild cutthroat and rainbow in July and August in this tributary to South Fork Nooksack River. From Hwy. 20 go N. on Baker Lake Rd. to Rocky Creek bridge, then W. on FS 12/Loomis-Nooksack road about 10 miles.

WELLS CREEK. Small glacial stream with brook trout fishing when cool weather slows snow melt. Joins North Fork Nooksack River 6 miles E. of Glacier just below Nooksack River Falls.

WHATCOM CREEK. Outlet of Whatcom Lake flowing from N. end of lake through Bellingham to Bellingham Bay. The creek supports rainbow and cutthroat.

WHATCOM LAKE. A long 500 acre 340 feet deep mixed species lake at the east city limits of Bellingham. The huge cutthroat that once attracted anglers from throughout the state, have declined to where fishing for them is now banned. Anglers, instead, concentrate on large numbers of kokanee salmon (more than 2.5 million fry planted), remnant rainbows,a few largemouth bass, perch and what has become one of the state's best smallmouth bass fisheries. The NW side is best for smallmouth May-Aug. Mackinaw have been reported. Kokanee fishing is best in May-June, September-October. No chumming. A public access area with boat launches and WDFW kokanee hatchery on S. shore. N. end ramp at Bloedel-Donovan City Park. Water source for Bellingham.

WISER LAKE. Hwy. 539 splits this 123 acre year-round, warm-water species lake 8 miles N. of Bellingham and 3 miles SW of Lynden. Largemouth bass, perch and brown bullhead, may hold a few rainbow, cutthroat and crappie. May and June are most productive. Public access, ramp on N. shore.

Whatcom County Resorts

Baker Lake: Baker Lake Resort, 360-853-8325.

Ross Lake: Ross Lake Resort, 360-386-4437.

Diablo Lake: Diablo Lake Resort, 206-386-4429.

Yelloweye rockfish.

Whitman County
WDFW Region 1

Washington Department of Fish and Wildlife, 8702 N. Division St., Spokane, WA 99218. Phone, 509-456-4082.

The rolling wind-washed Palouse hills, horizon-to-horizon wheat, scab lands, dust devils and Washington State University are what put this chunk of Washington on the map. Fishing follows in the distance. This is low, rolling country. Only 10 of Whitman County's 140 lakes lie above 2500 feet. Most of Whitman's 2179 square miles (12th largest in the state) are about 1000 feet elevation. Few of these lakes offer good fishing potential though. Many, however, dry up during the summer. It's a big, dry, nearly treeless county wedged between the Columbia Basin and Idaho.

The NW section is mostly scab land with rocky channels and coulees. The Palouse River flows westerly across the county and enters a deep rocky canyon below Hooper dropping 185 feet over Palouse Falls. The biggest non impounded lake in the county is 7-mile long Rock Lake which is protected by vertical cliffs towering 300 feet high above the water. Highest point in the county is Tekoa Mountain at 4006 feet. The Snake River, which forms the S. border of Whitman, and the Palouse River provide most of the county's fishing.

Summer's are surprisingly mild, although temperatures can level off in the high 80s. The heat is often fanned by a steady prairie wind that either soothes or scorches you. The record low in this county is -26 degrees. Annual precipitation is about 21 inches at Colfax, often in the form of thunderstorms. More than 90 percent of the county is agricultural ground.

The main routes through the county are, State Hwys. 26, 127 and US 195 which comes south from Spokane to Pullman.

ALKALI FLAT CREEK. A small rainbow stream which offers limited angling in early spring. It enters the Snake River at Riparia. Roads follow the creek NE upstream for about 35 miles.

COTTONWOOD CREEK. Heads S. of Steptoe Butte and flows W. to join Rock Creek SW of Ewan. Few rainbows.

GILCHRIST POND: A small pond due S. of Colfax near Union Flat Creek. Stocked with several though catchable size rainbows. Open year-round.

LOWER GRANITE DAM RESERVOIR. A 9000 acre reservoir formed by Lower Granite Dam on Snake River. The pool is 39 miles long. Large variety of fish including large and smallmouth bass, black crappie, white crappie, bluegill, yellow perch and channel catfish. Can be very good for summer steelhead trolling. Salmon are also in the river but have been fully protected in recent years. There is an excellent boat ramp at the dam and upstream on the E. shore at Wawawa River Rd. Contact the corps for a map of access points.

MILLER LAKE. This 25 acre lake is 3.5 miles N. of Ewan at the N. end of Rock Lake. Road from Ewan leads to the lake shore. No plants.

PALOUSE RIVER. Incredibly this pretty river is 125 mile long, making it one of the longest in the state, yet it offers little to serious fishermen. It forms the boundary between SW Whitman County and Franklin and Adams Counties, then swings E. and S. to Colfax where the N. and S. Forks come together. Best period is during summer months for channel catfish and smallmouth bass below Palouse Falls.

PAMPA POND (LaCrosse). A 3 acre pond

Rock Lake.

annually planted with more than 5000 rainbows, some 14 inchers. It is 4 miles W. of LaCrosse between the RR. track and highway.

PENAWAWA CREEK. Rated "fair" for rainbow in May. The creek is a tributary of Snake River converging at Penawawa, 10 miles W. of Almota. It is reached and fished by driving up Penawawa Canyon where the road follows the creek. Limited fishing.

RIPARIAN POND: A small pond just blow Little goose Dam on north side of the Snake Rive. Stocked with about 2000 pan-size rainbows every year. Good place for kids.

ROCK LAKE. Primarily a warm water species lake—largemouth bass and black crappie—with 8000 annually planted rainbow and 4000 browns. This long skinny lake covers 2147 acres and is located 1 mile N. of Ewan. There is public access area at S. end. Rock Lake is an enlargement of Rock Creek and stretches more

than 7 miles. Basalt cliffs more than 300 feet high hem the lake. Best fishing May and June, and again in September and October. Water conditions vary due to run-off from farms in area. Lake is subject to muddy conditions. Bring a boat, you'll need it.

SILVER CREEK. A limited producer of rainbow, Silver flows into Palouse River's N. Fork at Elberton. It heads in Idaho 10 miles NE of Elberton, and roads from that community provide easy access.

UNION FLAT CREEK. A tributary of Palouse River entering 5 miles W. of LaCrosse. May and June are the best months for Union Creek's small rainbow. Roads parallel stream for most of its length.

WILLOW CREEK. Heading approximately 8 miles E. of LaCrosse, Willow flows W. 17 miles to the Palouse River on Whitman-Adams County line. It hosts a few rainbow.

Yakima County

WDFW Region 3

Washington Department of Fish and Wildlife, 1701 S. 24th Ave., Yakima, WA 98902. Phone 509-575-2740.

The second largest county in the state, Yakima County is a picturesque composite of mountain lakes and streams and heavily stocked lowland lakes flowing eastward into a nearly arid scabland. The county offers a lot of trout, and limited warm-water fishing opportunities. Fishing success has been bolstered by recent stockings of large triploid rainbows and an increase in the number of year-round waters.

Yakima County is bordered on the W. by the Cascade Mountain Crest, on the N. by Chinook Pass Hwy. 410 and Wenas Valley, on the E. by the Columbia R. and arid Rattlesnake Hills and on the S. by Klickitat County. The sprawling Yakama Indian Reservation includes nearly all of the land between the Yakima River and Mount Adams Wilderness Area, S. of Union Gap and N. of Satus Pass. Tribal permits are required to fish.

The county covers 4286 square miles and contains more than 300 lakes, about 180 of them mountain lakes over 2500 feet elevation. Highest point is Mt. Adams, second highest mountain in Washington at 12,307 feet, tapering to less than 600 feet near the Columbia River. Much of the mountain area is within the Wenatchee and Gifford Pinchot national forests.

This huge county is drained by an extensive braid of rivers including the lower Yakima, Bumping, American, Tieton, Naches, Little Naches, Cowiche, and upper Klickitat, plus several major native trout creeks including Wenas, Selah, Oak, Rattlesnake, Nile, Crow, Milk, and Ahtanum; all, except Selah and lower Wenas, are small picturesque mountain streams with marginal fishing opportunities for wild trout. Selah and Lower Wenas Creek are major drainages with little value to fishermen, and flow through sagebrush, private property, livestock pastures and cow pies.

WDFW no longer stocks these rivers and streams with supplemental hatchery trout. Most flowing water in Yakima County supports native populations of rainbow and cutthroat trout, a few brookies and also bull trout (formerly Dolly Varden), which are federally protected under Endangered Species Act conservation closures. Bull trout may not be fished for. Many of the mountain lakes, especially hike-ins in the Norse Peak, William O. Douglas and Goat Rocks wilderness areas, are excellent for brookies, rainbow and cutthroat trout from mid-summer into early fall. Irrigation reservoirs support kokanee salmon, burbot and trout, but are subject to periodic drawdowns. The major reservoirs are popular camping, boating and fishing destinations. Good numbers of whitefish are in most rivers and streams and some reservoirs.

The slopes along the Cascades in the W. part of the county are mostly timbered and heavy precipitation near the crest produces thick brush. Timber thins and the forest opens up at about Cliffdell on the Chinook Pass Hwy., and from Yakima east trees are rare. The lower Yakima River valley is flat, agricultural ground that runs 40 miles SE toward the Columbia River.

The climate in the mountains is warm and dry during the summer, moderate to brutally cold in the winter, with deep, deep snow above 3500 feet. There is a big temperature swing between Yakima where 90-95 degree days are common, and the slopes of the Cascade where few days push into the 80s. Annual precipitation at Yakima is only 7.21 inches. The county gets most of its moisture from April and May snow-runoff from the mountains, and by late summer water levels in streams and lakes can be extremely low.

The city of Yakima is the heart of the county and all routes to top fishing areas lead there. From the N., I-82, Hwy. 821 (Ellensburg/Yakima Canyon Road), and Umtanum/Wenas Road drop S. from I-90 at Ellensburg. From the E. are Hwys. 24 and 241 across the Rattlesnake Hills, and from the S. are US 97 and Hwy. 22 crossing the Yakama Nation Reservation to the Columbia River Gorge corridor and Tri-Cities regions.

The two most scenic routes into the county are on the W. from the I-5 corridor. US 12 and Hwy. 410 both skirt Mount Rainier National Park and plunge into the county at the mile-high crest of the Cascade Mountains. Hwy. 410 crosses spectacular 5430-foot elev. Chinook Pass and follows the American and Naches rivers downstream through Wenatchee National Forest campgrounds, elk meadows and aspen bottoms to Yakima. This highway is closed in winter between Morse Creek and Crystal Mountain. US 12 enters through White Pass on a two-lane line between William O. Douglas and Goat Rocks Wilderness areas, past Rimrock Lake along the foam-flecked edge of Tieton River. The two mountain routes merge under the watchful gaze of bighorn sheep at WDFW's Oak Creek Game Range and continue E. along the base of Clemans Mt. into Naches and Yakima.

AHTANUM CREEK. Fair fishing for 8-9 inch rainbow June-Aug. Small cutthroat in top sections. 1.7 miles of the North Fork is closed from Grey Rock Trailhead Bridge to Shellneck Creek to protect bull trout. Selective gear rules. Turn W. at Union Gap from US 97 onto Lower Ahtanum Rd. which follows creek W just above N. boundary of Yakama Indian Reservation. Campground, cabins at Soda Springs about 35 miles upstream from Union Gap. **FOUNDATION CREEK** joins Ahtanum near Soda Springs and offers small cutthroat.

AMERICAN RIVER. A cold, nutrient poor, but beautiful small river that offers poor to fair fishing during mid-summer for wild cutthroat, brook trout and whitefish. Selective tackle restrictions, no bait. The American River, gin-clear, shallow and spilling in stair steps is followed by Hwy. 410 for its entire length downstream from Mount Rainier National Park at Chinook Pass. The Rainier Fork is the upper few miles in a deep, steep canyon far below the highway which joins the American Fork just SW of Morse Creek gate. Has small cutthroat. From Morse Creek downstream the river and highway share the same elevation. Numerous stream-side FS campgrounds and trailheads. The American joins the Bumping River at Bumping Lake Rd. on Highway 410 about 32 miles NW of Naches. A few miles downstream the Bumping is joined by the Little Naches fork and becomes the Naches River. Rental cabins, RV park, gas, store, restaurant at Whistling Jack's Resort in Cliffdell, and Squaw Rock, and in the Bumping River drainage at Goose Prairie and Bumping Lake Resort. American River Fork is the outlet of **DEWEY LAKES** on American Ridge

reached from Chinook Pass by hiking PCT 2000, 2 miles S. This pair of small mountain lakes is easily reached and heavily fished for brook trout. In mid-August the lower American River is a good place to see spring chinook spawning. Don't harass or fish for these protected ocean migrants, though. Major elk and black-tailed deer summering area. Mountain goats sometimes visible on the surrounding peaks.

ASPEN LAKE. An urban artificial pond on Naches River near 16th Ave. in Yakima. Pumpkinseed, largemouth bass and channel catfish. No public access, permission required.

BACHELOR CREEK. Rainbow stream S. of Yakima city limits along lower Antanum Rd. near airport.

BARTON CREEK BEAVER PONDS. Series of small ponds near E. end of Bumping Lake. Late summer fishing for rainbow and brook trout when there's water in the ponds.

BASIN LAKE. Cutthroat are in this 4.6 acre lake, elev. 5820 feet, at head of N. Fork Union Creek. 6.7 miles NE of Chinook Pass. Drains to American River.

BEAR LAKE. A 5-acre, rainbow-stocked pond on Oak Creek Wildlife Area at head of Oak Creek. Accessible by rough road in late May. Produces rainbow of 8-10 inches, possibly wild brook trout. Early summer best. Lynne Lake adjoins Bear.

BENCH LAKE. Yakama Indian Reservation lake of 18.4 acres with rainbow and brook trout lake at 4850 feet 11.2 miles NW of Glenwood and 5.2 miles SE from Mt. Adams summit. Drains to Klickitat River.

BERGLUND LAKE. A14 acre lake planted with largemouth bass, black crappie and pumpkinseed, and a few rainbow. Located within Yakima at confluence of Yakima and Naches Rivers. No access.

BIRD LAKE. Six acre Yakama Indian Reservation lake. Rainbow and brook trout. Lake is at 5575 feet 11 miles NW from Glenwood Drains to Klickitat River.

BLANKENSHIP LAKES. Group of 3 hike-in lakes in lush meadows between 5230 and 5820 feet in Mosquito Valley. Drive almost to the end of the Bumping Lake/Deep Creek Road, to Trail 1105 and hike about 2 miles S on Trail 1105. Lakes are 1 mile NE of Tumac Mt. Cutthroat lakes ranging from 4.1 to 9.6 acres. Big and South Blankenship Lakes drain to Tieton River and N. Blankenship drains into Deep Creek and Bumping River.

BLUE LAKE. Rainbow are in this 3.5 acre lake at 6200 feet, 7.8 miles SW of Rimrock Lake's Tieton Dam and 2000 feet SW from Blue Slide Lookout. Drains to S. Fork Tieton River. Best access from Ahtanum Creek.

BYRON PONDS. Two weedy, year-round ponds totaling 50 acres on Sunnyside Game Range. Largemouth bass and pumpkinseed panfish.

BUMPING LAKE. A 1310 acre kokanee and trout reservoir impounded by an irrigation dam on Bumping River, about 2 miles SW of Goose Prairie. In late summer this lake can be drawn down to about 600 acres. From Hwy. 410 turn SW on Bumping River Road at American River confluence NW of Cliffdell. The lake is 12 miles up the Bumping River on mostly paved road. To reach the resort on north side of the lake turn right and drive across dam. Lake is at 3426 foot elevation and snow may block access until mid-May, which is when small kokanee salmon in 7-9 inch range start hitting trollers using flasher blades and maggot baits. Rainbows 8-11 inches are taken from mid-June through fall. Occasional cutthroat and whitefish, and large numbers of protected bull trout. Public access and 2 developed FS campsites along E. end and S. shore of the lake. Bumping Lake Resort on NE shore has cabins, campsites, hookups, store, supplies, some tackle and rental boats.

BUMPING RIVER. Paralleled by paved road from Hwy. 410, and littered with scenic FS campsites, this tumbling stream is heavily fished below Bumping Lake for 8-9-inch wild rainbows, cutthroat and a few brookies. Above Bumping Lake, hiking anglers follow Trails 970-971 upstream into

Bumping Lake.

the William O. Douglas Wilderness enjoying fair trout action. Generally flush with snow runoff until mid June. No bait except during winter whitefish season. Developed FS campgrounds at American Forks, Cedar Springs, Soda Springs and Cougar Flat. Groceries, supplies, some tackle, restaurant, cabins at Goose Prairie, and Bumping Lake Resort. Many trailheads to mountain lakes begin at the river road.

CLEAR CREEK. The spectacular waterfall outlet of Dog and Leech lakes just E. of White Pass. Flows far below road into Clear Lake. Best access is from W. end of Rimrock Lake turning S. from White Pass/Hwy. 12 and continuing to N. end of Clear Lake. Turn right (NW) onto Rd. 840 which follows the creek for 2 miles. Brook trout in adjoining beaver ponds, a few small rainbows and cutthroats in creek. Four FS campgrounds at Clear Lake.

CLEAR LAKE. Heavily stocked with 30,000 catchable rainbow trout and another 20,000 fry, this 265-acre lake is one of the best fishing bets in this area. Two FS campgrounds with a total of 78 sites, FS boat (fee) launch on E. shore, and picnic area. This popular lake 1 mile W. of Rimrock Lake, 5.7 miles east of White Pass. Most trout are in the 8-12 inch bracket. Clear is a irrigation reservoir formed by dam on the N. Fork of Tieton River, at an elevation of 3615 feet. In recent years the lake has been stabilized, although its vulnerable to extreme draw downs for irrigation.

CONRAD LAKES: (Long Creek Lakes). One tiny 1.2 acre cutthroat pond and a fishless 1-acre wetland at 5290 feet, 8.5 miles S. of Clear Lake dam. Drain to S. Fork Tieton River.

COUGAR LAKES. A trio of alpine lakes at the head of Cougar Creek in the headwaters of Bumping Lake. Trailhead at road end W. of Bumping Lake Marina. Trail 970 goes 3 miles to **SWAMP LAKE** 51 acres, and continues another 2 miles to Big Cougar, 82 acres and **LITTLE COUGAR,** 13 acres. All have rainbow and brookies

COWICHE CREEK. Fair to good producer of wild rainbow and cutthroat, especially in upper forks, best in late spring. Road from Cowiche follows creek for 15 miles. No bait.

CRAMER LAKE. One of several dozen potholes, marshes and small lakes along PCT 2000 on high plateau N. of US 12/White Pass. Cramer is a 19-acre rainbow lake on FS trail 1106 which leads from SW shore of Dog Lake campground 2 miles E. of White Pass. Hike 3.2 miles to lake at 5025 feet elevation. One-half mile NW is **DUMBBELL LAKE** in Lewis County. A large number of small lakes are in this area, most hold rainbow, cutthroat or brookies.

DEVILS WASHBASIN LAKE. A cutthroat lake of 1.9 acres located at 6268 feet 8.2 miles S. from White Pass. It drains to N. Fork Tieton River.

DOG LAKE. One of 2 popular lakes at the summit of US 12/White Pass. Dog Lake covers 61 acres below impressive Spiral Butte, 2 miles E. of summit, at 4207 feet elevation adjacent to N. side of highway. By early June it offers fair fishing for 7-11 inch rainbow and brookies. FS campground, boat launch. About 1000 feet downstream from lake outlet on S. side of US 12 is a FS viewpoint of Clear Creek's 100-foot waterfall. Several trailheads lead N. from Dog Lake to hike-in lakes in the William O. Douglas Wilderness Area.

ELTON LAKE North. A 14 acre winter-season lake E. of 1-82, 6 miles N. of Yakima. Stocked with catchable rainbows, bullhead catfish, perch, whitefish and largemouth bass. Public access. No public access to South Elton Lake.

FENNER LAKE. Once planted with cutthroat, now barren, this 3.1 acre mountain lake is at 5460 feet in Norse Peak Wilderness about 3 miles SW from Raven's Roost Lookout.

FISH LAKE. 10 acre brook trout lake near PCT 2000 just E. of Carlton Pass about half way between the W. end of Bumping Lake and Hwy. 123 at 4114 feet. A 7-mile hike on Trial 971 from Bumping Lake around Crag Mountain or 2.5 miles from end of Carlton Creek Road reached from Hwy. 123. **CRAG LAKES** lie about 1 mile N. of Fish.

FREEWAY LAKE (AKA **Rotary Lake**). A heavily-stocked 23 acre rainbow and brown trout lake best in spring and fall for 8 to 12 inchers. Also largemouth bass to 7 pounds and pumpkinseed panfish. Follow paved Greenway Trail in Yakima .04 miles from public parking area at Boise-Cascade or .03 mile from Harlan Landing.

FLATIRON LAKE. 7 acre rainbow lake at 5700 feet 1.6 miles SW of Little Bald Mt. Lookout near FS 1600/Clover Springs Rd. Drains to Bumping River at Soda Springs Campground. From the campground hike Trail 975 up the outlet.

GIFFIN LAKE: A shallow 104.8 acre lake on Sunnyside Game Range 2.8 miles NW of Mabton. Stocked with rainbow trout, largemouth bass, black crappie, pumpkinseed and brown bullhead.

GREEN LAKE. 4.5 acre rainbow lake at 5900 feet, 7.4 miles S. of Tieton Dam-Rimrock Lake, 1.4 miles E. of Blue Slide Lookout and Lake. Accessible by dirt road.

GRAHAM-MORRIS POND. Gravel pits near Toppenish with largemouth bass, bluegill, perch, pumpkinseed and crappie. No public access.

GRANGER LAKE. Small pond in Granger stocked with rainbow, largemouth bass, bluegill and channel catfish.

HELL LAKE. A cutthroat planted 3.4 acre lake at 5414 feet, 1.4 miles SE of US 12/ White Pass on PCT 2000. Drains to N. Fork Tieton River.

HILL LAKE (AKA Tumac Lake). A 5.8 acre hike-in rainbow lake at 5110 feet elev. 4.6 miles NE of White Pass in Cowlitz Pass area, 1 mile S. of Tumac Mt.

HORSESHOE POND. Year-round, 59 acre lake about 4 miles NW of Mabton adjacent to N. side of Yakima River. Has largemouth bass, crappie and perch.

I-82 PONDS. Seven popular, small former gravel pit ponds open year-round along I-82 between Union Gap and Zillah. **Pond 1** (15 acres) between Wellis and Donald Rds. has largemouth bass, walleye, perch and pumpkinseed. **Pond 2** (25.5 acres) no longer stocked with trout but has largemouth, bluegill and bullhead. **Pond 3** (19 acres) E. of Donald Rd. has bluegill, largemouth bass, perch and pumpkinseed. **Pond 4** (29.5 acres) stocked with rainbow and brown trout and has walleye, largemouth bass, black crappie, bluegill and bullhead. **Pond 5** (27 acres) has largemouth bass, crappie, bluegill, pumpkinseed and bullhead. **Pond 6,** on Buena Loop Rd., has been planted with rainbow trout, largemouth bass and bullhead. **Pond 7** (8 acres)

E. of Buena has largemouth bass, crappie and pumpkinseed. Walk-in access to all ponds except Pond 7. Gasoline motors not allowed.

KLICKITAT RIVER (Upper). Remote upper section between hatchery and Mount Adams can produce rainbow and cutthroat in summer. Discolored by glacial melt on warm days. This part of the Klickitat is on the Yakama Nation Reservation N. of Glenwood. Reached by driving W. past Ahtanum Ranger Station to Klickitat Meadows Rd. Yakama tribal permit required. S. of reservation the river flows into Klickitat County through WDFW Klickitat Wildlife Area to Columbia River at Lyle.

KRAMER PONDS. Small private ponds S. of Zillah and N. of Yakima River with warm water species. No public access.

LEECH LAKE. One of 2 popular roadside lakes adjacent to US 12 at White Pass. Leech is a 40 acre lake at 4412 feet elev. restricted to fly-fishing only for brook trout 8-12 inches, some larger. Open year-round, generally ice free by June. FS campground, small-boat launch, no gas motors. Mosquitoes can be nasty. PCT 2000 heads N. from lake into high lakes in William O. Douglas Wilderness Area.

LILY LAKE. 5.3 acre cutthroat lake near SW shore of Bumping Lake N. of FS Rd. 1800.

LITTLE NACHES RIVER. A pretty, heavily fished mountain stream that flows through a long valley peppered with FS campgrounds and heavily used by fishermen, campers, hikers, RVers, ORVers, and hunters. Turn N. from Highway 410 at the confluence of the Naches River, about 29 miles NW of Naches. Little Naches River is paralleled by paved FS Rd. 19 upstream 14 miles where the pavement merges into gravel surfaced FS 1914 and climbs into Western Washington through Windy Gap/ Naches Pass/Government Meadows connecting with paved FS 70/Greenwater River Road. River supports wild rainbow in 8-9 inch range taken after mid-June, small cutthroat in forks. WDFW no longer stocks this stream and fishing can be very tough. In early fall spring Chinook spawn here, but may not be fished for. Selective gear rules, no bait.

The **SOUTH FORK LITTLE NACHES** joins the river at Lost Meadows and is paralleled by FS 1906. **MIDDLE and NORTH FORKS** join above Timothy Meadows. All have small cutthroat. Numerous FS campgrounds, some with water and pit toilets, are along FS 19. About 2 miles N. of Kaner Flat Campground FS 1902 bridges river to Crow Creek FS Campground and eventually Raven's Roost Lookout at Cougar Valley access to Norse Peak Wilderness. A 3.5 mile hike from end of Rd. descends into Cougar Valley to cutthroat in **CROW CREEK LAKE**. Lake is shallow, heavily silted, but may produce fish to 14 inches. Several small cutthroat lakes in this vicinity include Sheepherder, Janet, Rae and Anna. **CROW CREEK** is a romping tributary that flows from Crow Creek Lake through a steep mostly roadless canyon in Norse Peak Wilderness to join the Little Naches River at Crow Creek Campground. Deep pools and runs in creek support native cutthroat and a few rainbow, ESA protected bull trout and a few chinook salmon. Anglers must be willing to bushwhack. Hike upstream from Crow Creek Campground/bridge, or continue on FS 1920 (Fife's Ridge Road), turn W on FS Rd.1922 to end and hike downhill.

LONG JOHN LAKE: A narrow, 1200-foot long, 4.8 acre cutthroat lake in Cowlitz Pass area 4.2 miles N. of US 12/White Pass summit. Use FS Trail 1142.

LOST LAKE. 9 acre lake with rainbow to 12 inches. From US 12 east of Rimrock Lake just W. of Hause Creek campground turn S. on paved FS Rd. 1201 and follow to lake at 3675 feet elev. Small boats may be launched. Road continues S. 3 miles to Pickle Prairie Trail 1125 which turns E. .04 miles to LONG LAKE, an 8 acre brook trout lake at 4350 feet elev.

MAL LAKE. A 4 acre mountain lake at 5100 feet with brook trout near Timberwolf Mt. LO and headwaters of Three Creek. From Hwy. 410 turn S. at Eagle Rock cross Naches River, then S. on FS Rd. 1500 up Rattlesnake Creek.

McDANIEL LAKE. A popular, marshy 10 acre rainbow lake at 3550 feet 8 miles SW of US 12 near Meeks Table Natural Area in headwaters of Rattlesnake Creek. Road access. From Hwy. 410 turn S. at Eagle Rock cross Naches River, then S. on FS Rd. 1500 up Rattlesnake Creek to Rattlesnake Springs then NW on FS 1502 to lake. Best early in season for WDFW planted 8-

12 inch trout. May dry up during drought years.

MILK CREEK, POND and LAKE. See Kittitas County.

MORGAN LAKE. A shallow, 24.6 acre pond on Sunnyside W.R.A. 2.5 miles N. of Mabton on McGee Road. Open year-round for largemouth bass and pumpkinseed. Continue .05 mile W. to 105-acre **GIFFIN LAKE**.

MUD LAKE. Large Triploid and catchable rainbows to several pounds are stocked in Mud Lake's cattail-encircled 4 acres at 2500 feet elev. on the sunbaked S. side of Clemans Mt. Open year-round, selective gear rules, 1-fish limit, no bait. Best fished from float tubes, small car-top boats. About 7.4 miles NW of Naches turn N. on rough, unpaved road at Horseshoe Bend from Hwy. 410/Chinook Pass Hwy. Lake is about 1.5 miles from highway, and drains to Naches River which is visible below the access road. Popular in early spring before general opener.

MYRON LAKE. Aggressive WDFW stocking programs have created an excellent and popular fishery in this small man-made lake W. of Yakima between Fruitvale Blvd. and US 12. Public access. Stocked with rainbow and brown trout, including broodstock to 12 pounds, and Triploid rainbows averaging a half-pound each. Selective gear rules, no bait, 1 fish limit. Open year-round.

NACHES RIVER. A broad, shallow river with pools, deep runs, riffles and eddies, this bouncy mountain river looks great but fishes tough. No longer stocked by WDFW, the river has a thin population of wild rainbow, cutthroat and lots of whitefish. It is intensely fished mostly because of the campgrounds, summer homes and convenient access from US12/Hwy. 410 which rides the shoulder of the river for 40 miles from its headwater tributaries below Chinook Pass to its confluence with the Yakima River 3 miles W. of Yakima. Rainbow best in the low water of August and September and largest trout between Naches and Yakima R. confluence. Whitefish in winter. Best trout fishing above Rattlesnake Creek. Special whitefish only winter season. No fishing allowed for bull trout, steelhead or spring chinook which spawn in the river. Selective gear rules, no bait, 2 trout daily limit, 12-inch minimum, 20-inch maximum. The Naches is formed above Cliffdell from the confluences of the Little Naches, Bumping and American rivers. The Tieton River is a major tributary entering at the US 12 jct. with Hwy. 410.

NILE CREEK. Brushy tributary to Naches River about 32 miles NW of Yakima. Supports wild rainbow in lower reaches and cutthroat higher up. June and July best. From Hwy. 410/Chinook Pass Hwy. turn S. at Eagle Rock onto paved Nile Road continue on S. side of creek for 3 miles through private property, then S. on FS 1600 along N. Fork of Nile into national forest for about 15 miles past Little Bald Mt. LO. and Clover Springs. Rarely fished in upper canyon reaches.

NORTH ELTON POND. A 15-acre winter-fishing lake near Selah along I-82. Usually stocked by WDFW prior to Dec. opener with half-pound rainbows.

OAK CREEK. A small creek running through WDFW Oak Creek Wildlife Area on E. side of Bethel Ridge. Enters Tieton River just S. of headquarters. Wild rainbow, cutthroat and brook trout, most 6 to 10 inches.

OTTER LAKE. Cutthroat are in this 7.2 acre lake 4 miles NE of White Pass at 5030 feet. Follow FS Trail 1106 N. from Dog Lake.

PEAR AND APPLE LAKES. Mountain lake headwaters of Indian Creek which flows into the W. end of Rimrock Lake. Both offer brook trout. Shortest access is from Bumping River Road/FS 18 to FS Trail 1105 near Deep Creek Campground. Take Trail 1105 past Blankenship Lakes to Indian Creek Meadows, then N. 1 mile on Trail 1148. Also reached from US 12 by turning N. on Indian Creek Rd. at W. end of Rimrock Lake for approximately 3 miles, then hiking FS Trail 1105 about 5 miles to Trail 1148. The lakes lie side-by-side. Pear is 20 acres, Apple is 9 acres. Elevation is 5060 feet.

PLACER LAKE. An old mining dig filled with 4.7-acres of water and cutthroat trout, 5380 feet elev. at head of Morse Creek, 2.7 miles NE of Hwy. 410/Chinook Pass. Easy 1-mile trail hike from end of unpaved Morse Creek Road.

RATTLESNAKE CREEK. Catch-and-release, selective gear management is showing big results in this major tributary to the Naches River 30 miles W. of Yakima. Wild cutthroat and rainbow 6 to 12 inches are plentiful, especially in hike-in reaches. The creek is paralleled by paved FS 1500 Rd. on S. side for about 10 miles where side roads lead to headwater tributaries and trails. This is a canyon creek and the road, while excellent, is often high above it. Most creek access is a steep, rock scramble. In the headwaters, Little Rattlesnake Creek is very good for 8-10 inch rainbow in June and July. Upper walk-in forks have wild cutthroat. From US 12 turn SW at Eagle Rock, cross Naches River, then S. onto FS 1500.

RIMROCK LAKE. The largest lake in the Yakima area, popular camping, boating, water play destination and the best kokanee salmon producer in the region. This 2530 acre reservoir, open year-round, is 12.5 miles E. of White Pass/US 12, impounded behind Tieton River dam at 2918 feet elev. US 12 follows N. shore. Numerous public and private camping sites. FS fee boat launch at E. end, plus resort ramps. Delivers 8-11-inch kokanee best trolling from mid-May through Aug. Some rainbow to 16 inches and whitefish. ESA listed bull trout are common but fishing is prohibited. High afternoon winds are common in summer. Rimrock is an irrigation reservoir and fishing quality and quantity depends on drawdown levels. In the past it has been drained to little more than the old river bed requiring fishery to be completely rebuilt. Several resorts, boat rentals, RV camps, bait, tackle, restaurants, groceries.

ROOT LAKE. A pretty 5.1 acre hike-in rainbow lake at 5300 feet on N. side of Miners Ridge 2 miles S of Bumping Lake. Follow FS 18/Bumping Lake Rd. SW then W. on FS 1800, then S on FS 1809 past Granite Lake to road end trailhead.

ROTARY LAKE. Urban Yakima lake heavily stocked with rainbow and brown trout plants, catchables 8-12 inches and Triploids to several pounds. Also largemouth bass to 7 pounds and pumpkinseed panfish. Great place for kids. 23 acres, open year-round. The lake is near Greenway Trail, about .33 mile from Harland Landing or the Boise-Cascade parking lot. Disabled access.

SATUS CREEK. Trout stream on Yakama Nation reservation S. of Toppenish. Hwy. 97 follows creek between Toppenish and Satus Pass. Closed to non-Indian fishing.

SANDSTONE LAKE. 3 acre cutthroat lake at 3800 feet, 2.2 miles S. from mouth of Bumping River.

SARGE HUBBARD PARK POND. A 3.5 acre juvenile and licensed disabled angler pond in Yakima. Regularly stocked with catchable rainbows trout and fingerling channel catfish. Pond is on Greenway Trail in Sarge Hubbard Park.

SELAH CREEK: A long, shallow drainage E. of I-82 in the treeless sagebrush canyon between Umtanum and Yakima ridges much of it on the Yakima Firing Center military reservation. No angling value.

SHEEPHERDER LAKE. A 3.3 acre cutthroat lake at 4931 feet S. of Crow Creek Lake. From Chinook Pass follow PCT 2000 N. to Big Crow Basin, then E. on Trail 953.

SNOWPLOW LAKE. 6 acre rainbow lake at 4500 feet elev. 8 miles SE of Mt. Adams and 1.2 miles SE from Snowplow Mt.. on Yakama Nation Reservation. Drains to Klickitat River.

SURPRISE LAKE. A remote, hike-in 14-acre cutthroat lake at base of Goat Rocks. Fish are 8-10 inches. FS Rd. 1000 follows S. Fork of Tieton from E. end of Rimrock Lake about 12 miles past Grey Creek campground through Conrad Meadows to end of Rd. Trail 1120 continues about 5 miles to lake at 5300 feet elev.

SWAMP LAKE. 51-acre mountain lake in the headwaters of Bumping River. Follow Cougar Lake trail 971 from N. shore of Bumping Lake, to a right hand fork near Cougar Creek onto FS Trail 970 then climb 2.5 miles to Swamp Lake at 4797 feet. Excellent fly fishing for rainbow from open NW shoreline. Some brook trout. Bush-whack trail N. to cutthroat in **CEDAR LAKES**.

TIETON RIVER. Mainstem Tieton River is one of the few rivers still stocked with trout. The North and South Forks collect behind Rimrock Lake Dam and form the mainstem Tieton River which flows SE along US 12 from the dam to join the Naches River. To fish the upper **South Fork** follow FS Rd. 1000 from E. end of Rimrock Lake about 12 miles past Grey Creek campground through Conrad Meadows, then follow trail upstream to source at Surprise Lake. A 10 mile section of the South Fork is closed between Rimrock Lake and falls. Above the falls The South Fork supports small 'bows and cutthroat. **North Fork** is reached from W. end of Clear Lake, above Rimrock Lake. Follow FS Rd. 1207 SW. Pleasant fly fishing for wild brookies, small cutthroat and rainbow. The mainstem **Tieton River** is stocked after snow runoff in June and July with catchable-size rainbow. Whitefish plentiful, special winter season. In 1961 this small, fast river produced the state record bull trout, 22-lb.-8-oz., but these char are now officially protected as endangered species and fishing for them here is closed. Several pleasant riverside campsites accessible from US 12. River is a conduit for agricultural water and fluctuates with irrigation demands. High water common in late summer.

TWIN SISTERS LAKES. Two of the largest hike-in lakes on a high plateau in the William O. Douglas Wilderness Area littered with trout lakes, ponds and marshy swales N. of White Pass. Best route to Twin Sisters is from Hwy. 410, turn SW on Bumping Lake Rd./FS 18. Continue to road end at Deep Creek camp. Follow FS Trail 980 about 2 miles to Little Twin Lake at 5150 feet elev, and continue a few hundred feet to Big Twin. Trail 980 continues 2 miles to PCT 2000. Big Twin Sister Lake covers 104 acres and Little Twin Sister 31 acres. Both support brook trout, and attract heavy fishing pressure. A cluster of several dozen small lakes are within 4 miles of Twin Sisters. Major lakes include **PILLAR, LONG JOHN, DANCING, OTTER, SHELLROCK** and **DUMBELL, BLANKENSHIP, APPLE, PEAR, FRYING PAN, JUG, and SNOW**. These lakes hold brookies, rainbow or cutthroat. Sometimes winter-kill. Plateau is very pretty, gently rolling, heavily forested with large meadows, bisected by PCT 2000, easy hiking, and there is lots of wildlife, especially elk and mosquitoes. This is a spectacular hike-fish area in late September when blueberries are ripe, elk are bugling, trout are biting and mosquitoes have been frosted. July through early Aug. mosquitos can suck a small backpacker dry.

WENAS CREEK: A long, narrow, brushy creek that heads on N. side of Bald Mountain and flows E. between Manastash

Ridge and Clemans Mt. through Wenas Lake, emptying into Yakima River N. of Selah. Above Wenas Lake creek runs through WDFW game range or FS land and can be fished for small rainbow and cutthroat. Below Wenas Lake impoundment dam, Wenas Creek is a badly altered agricultural stream. Irrigation diversions reduce summer flow to a trickle between eroded banks where cattle stand in knee deep muck. Some fishing in the .25 mile above the Yakima. Rainbow and brown trout escapees lurk just below Wenas Lake but access is difficult.

WENAS LAKE. A very fishy, fertile and popular 61 acre reservoir impounded on Wenas Creek 12 miles W. of Selah. Well known for producing large trout. Heavily stocked with catchable and triploid rainbows, browns, and channel catfish. A very good rainbow producer and one of the best brown trout lakes in the state. 13 pounders caught. Lots of 8 to 12 inch rainbows and quite a few that are measured by the pound. Channel catfish were planted in the late '90s and should grow quickly in this fertile, sun seared lake. Bait fishing takes the biggest browns. Trolling and stillfishing popular. Wenas is open year-round, produces best early in season, again in fall and lately a winter ice fishery has been developing. WDFW public access, disabled access, boat ramp and a fishing resort with full services. Scenic route is S. from I-90 at Ellensburg, Exit 106 bear E. to Umtanum/Wenas Road, and S. on graded gravel road across Manastash and Umtanum ridges through Ellensburg Pass and L. T. Murray State Wildlife Area. Winter elk feeding area just W. of lake where Wenas Road swings N. Also reached from I-82 via Exit 26 to Selah then NW on Wenas Road.

WIDE HOLLOW CREEK. Small creek in Yakima stocked with rainbow trout. The creek skirts SW border of Yakima where it

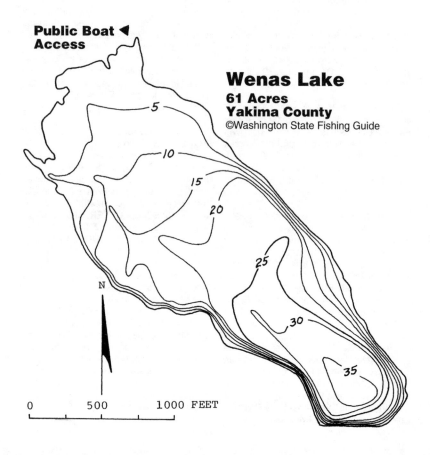

Public Boat ◀ Access

Wenas Lake
61 Acres
Yakima County
©Washington State Fishing Guide

5

10

15

20

25

30

35

N

0   500   1000 FEET

Yakima River, Ellensburg Canyon.

is polluted and developed. Cottonwood Canyon Rd. follows creek W. of Yakima.

WILDCAT CREEK. Fair creek fishing for wild, small rainbow and cutthroat. Joins lower Tieton River NE of Rimrock Lake. From US 12 turn N. on FS Rd. 1306 to fol- low creek upstream. At road end Trailhead 1113 leads to Russell Ridge and eventually Bumping River Rd./FS 18.

YAKIMA RIVER (See Kittitas County.) Above Roza Dam this is the best river in the state for large trout, especially in canyon stretches between Selah and Ellensburg. Below the dam the river is heavily exploited by irrigators In the semi-arid farm and orchard area near Yakima and suffers agricultural and industrial run-off pollutants. Summer water warms substantially, supports few trout. Smallmouth, largemouth bass, panfish and channel catfish are caught in lower reaches, especially just above the mouth near Tri-Cities. Occassional spring chinook, coho season openings. Below Wapato diversion the river is subject to extreme low water and a stew of nasty pollutants that include DDT.

Yakima County Resorts

Wenatchee National Forest, Naches RD, 509-653-2205

Bumping Lake: Bumping Lake Resort:

Naches River: Whistlin' Jack Lodge Cliffdell, 800–827–2299. Squaw Rock Resort Naches, 509-658-2926.

Rimrock Lake: Silver Beach Resort, 509-672-2500.

Wenas Lake: Wenas Lake Resort, 509-697-7670.

Mount Rainier National Park

This is not a park for fishermen.

Fishing in Mount Rainier National Park requires leg work, good lungs, imagination, and a willingness to measure success in terms of fantastic scenery not by the number of fish available to pull your string.

Virtually all productive waters are far removed from roads, most fish are small, and the park not only has a no re-stocking policy, but at times has worked to eliminate non native fish by gillnetting and seining.

While not actively discouraging fishermen, the present park administrators make no effort to encourage it. No response was made by park personnel to repeated efforts to obtain specific lake and stream information to guide anglers. Fishermen find open discouragement on the park's internet web site which states:

"Mount Rainier National Park isn't known for its fishing, so don't be disappointed if you fail to catch fish, or if the fish are small. Only experienced anglers do well and then only during limited times of the season. Experience tells us that anglers' success is often less than anticipated. Park waters are not stocked, but dependent on natural reproduction to replenish the fish population. We encourage you to use barbless hooks and artificial lures and to release uninjured fish."

Persistent anglers have more than 260 miles of trails to wander within the 235,625 acres of park, which lead to at least 384 permanent lakes and 470 rivers and streams. Consider, however, that only 27 lakes still have reproducing populations of fish including brook trout, rainbow and cutthroat. Because of the elevation most lakes do not shed ice until late-June at the earliest, icing up again in October. Many access roads close after the first deep snowfall. Most streams fall rapidly, stair stepping steeply downhill through small pools and plunging falls.

Official seasons mirror WDFW general seasons. Lakes and ponds are open from the last weekend in April through October. Rivers, streams and beaver ponds, open in June through October. Check WDFW regulations for exact dates Daily catch and season limits follow WDFW regulations.

No license or permit is required to fish in the park, but back country permits are required for overnight trips..

Most of the trout available are self-sustaining brookies, often small. A cousin of these colorful char, bull trout, are a federally listed threatened species and fishing for bull trout in the park is prohibited.

Other closed park waters include: Klickitat Creek above the White River entrance water supply intake. Ipsut Creek above the Ipsut Creek campground water supply intake. Laughing Water Creek above the Ohanapecosh water supply intake, Frozen Lake, Reflection Lakes, Shadow Lake and Tipsoo Lake.

The picturesque Ohanapecosh River and its tributaries, flowing along Hwy. 123 near the Steven County entrance, are open to fly fishing only. Fly-only tributaries include, Ollallie, Panther, Boulder, Deer, Kotsuck and Chinook creeks.

It's also illegal to: Possess or use of live or dead bait fish, amphibians, non-preserved fish eggs, or roe; chum with fish eggs, food, drugs, etc.)to attract fish; fishing with nets, seines, traps, drugs or explosives, or any means other than hook and line.

Non-motorized boats, float tubes and rafts are allowed on all waters except: Frozen, Reflection, Ghost and Tipsoo lakes.

The major rivers, with one exception, are fed by glaciers on the ice-encrusted slopes of 14,411 foot high Mount Rainier and in summer glacial melt fills them with particles called "glacier flour" that turns the naturally clear water into the color of concrete sludge. During the peak of the fishing season glacial streams are too cloudy to fish. In narrow windows that appear in-season during spring and fall when glaciers are frozen, these glacial streams provide marginal angling: Nisqually, Tahoma, Puyallup (both N. and S. Forks), Carbon, N. and S. Forks of Mowich, W. Fork of White, Stevens and Frying Pan.

Ohanapecosh River, which is restricted to fly fishing, is a clear running stream and may be fished most of the season. Actually there are more than 200 miles of clear water streams in the park but most of these are tumbling, brush-choked and offer little fishing opportunity.

Fees are charged to enter the park, $5 per individual and /or$10 per vehicle, good for 7 days. Camping fees at road accessible sites range from $8 to $12 for sites with water, tables, grills, restrooms. Reservations are accepted at some sites by calling 1-800-365-2267.

A back country permit (no charge) is required for all overnight use and is available at the various ranger stations and access gates. Since 1988 approximately 97 percent of the park has been designated wilderness.

The park surrounds Mount Rainier between Seattle and Yakima and is bordered by Snoqualmie-Mount Baker, Wenatchee and Gifford-Pinchot national forests. Several wilderness areas meet the edge of the park.

Routes into the park from the W. are Hwy. 410 from Enumclaw following the White River to the White River entrance which leads to trailheads at Sunrise Visitor Center. A few miles beyond the Sunrise entrance, at Cayuse Pass (elev. 4675), Hwy. 410 meets Hwy. 123. From this jct., Hwy. 410 turns N. to Tipsoo Lake and Chinook Pass (elev. 5430). Hwy. 123 turns S. along the E. edge of the park through Ohanapecosh River valley past the Stevens Canyon/Paradise entrance and connects with US 12, the White Pass Hwy. to Yakima.

Coming from the S. and I-5, US 12 runs through Packwood to Hwy. 123. From the Puyallup area, Hwy 7/706 from Elbe passes through Ashford to the Nisqually Entrance and climbs to the lodge, information centers and trailheads at Paradise. Beyond the lodge complex, the road loops down Stevens Canyon to connect with Hwy. 123 the only through route in the park.

Both Hwy. 410 and US 12 link the park with Yakima. Probably the least known entrance is an extension of Hwy. 165 from Buckley up the Carbon River to Mowich.

Entrance fees are charged except where Hwys. 410, 123 and US 12 pass through the park. Highways 410 and 123 are normally snow closed mid-Nov. through May.

Contact: Mount Rainier National Park Tahoma Woods, Star Route Ashford, Washington 98304 Phone: 360-569-2211

ADELAIDE LAKE. An 8 acre lake at 4584 feet elevation lying N. of James and Ethel Lakes. Contains chunky rainbow. One of a group of 4 lakes (See Marjorie and Oliver Lakes).

ALLEN LAKE. A 5 acre cutthroat and brook trout lake at 4596 feet. Fishing is often good, because the lake is difficult to reach. Route is via a very steep 2.5 mile climb along an informal trail.

BEAR PARK LAKE. Cutthroat lake of 1.9 acres at 5400 feet. Difficult access across a divide E. of Palisades Lakes in White River drainage.

BENCH LAKE. An open lake of 7 acres at 4600 feet in burned-off country 0.7 miles by trail from Stevens Canyon Road. Sup- ports brook trout, rainbow and cutthroat.

SNOW LAKE is a short distance above Bench at 4678 feet. It offers cutthroat, large brook trout and possibly a few rainbow.

CARBON RIVER. Paralleled by Hwy. 165/ Carbon River-Mowich Road, from Buckley, this glacial stream is surprisingly lightly fished, and when it's running clear it can provide respectable catches of pansize rainbows, cutthroat and whitefish. There's also a good chance of hooking a ESA protected bull trout which must be released. Fishes best after the first September freeze stops glacial bleed that fills the river with gray silt all summer. From the end of the Carbon River road, good trails continue upstream to pocket-picking water.

Bench Lake.

CHENUIS LAKE. No trail into this 3 acre cutthroat lake at 5090 feet. Check route with ranger at Carbon River entrance.

CHINOOK CREEK. A pretty stream that begins below Tipsoo Lake on Chinook Pass Highway 410, and flows S. along E. side of the park to join the Ohanapecosh River. Followed by Hwy. 123 for 2 miles S. from Cayuse Pass. Also accessible by road from Ohanapecosh. Holds small brook trout, cutthroat and rainbow. Fly fishing only.

CLOVER LAKE. An open lake of 7 acres reached by trail from Sunrise Point. No fish reported.

CRYSTAL LAKES. Two small cutthroat and rainbow lakes in a pretty, open basin at 5830 feet. The larger lake is 8 acres. Best route is a 3-mile hike on PCT 2000 from Chinook Pass N. through Sourdough Gap. Also reached from Hwy. 410 by a steep 2.5 mile switchback hike from Silver Springs.

DEADWOOD LAKES. A pair of small lakes at 5300 feet. The clear, shallow lakes contain cutthroat. May winter kill. Hike N. from Chinook Pass through low saddle for 0.5 mile to the lakes.

DEWEY LAKES. Actually just outside the park, the Deweys are heavily fished lakes at 5200 feet. They are on PCT 2000 just S. of Naches Peak on Chinook Pass. It's about 2.5 mile hike on PCT 2000 from the parking lot at the pass. Lower Dewey is 51 acres, Upper is 8. Both are brook trout lakes.

ELEANOR LAKE. A 20 acre rainbow lake at 4960 feet in open, alpine country. Follow the Wonderland Trail from Sunrise Lodge past Frozen Lake and Berkeley Park to Grand Park, then N. and E. through Grand Park to the lake. Total distance is 9.3 miles through beautiful, open parks. Campsites.

GEORGE LAKE. A shelter and campsites on this beautiful 26 acre lake at 4232 feet. Drive to summit of Round Pass on the W. side road from Nisqually entrance. Marked trail takes off from Round Pass parking lot 0.8 miles to the lake. George is heavily populated with sculpin.

GOLDEN LAKES. A group of small lakes at 4556 feet S. of Mowich Lake near the headwaters of Rushing Water Creek. Only two of the lakes support fish. The largest lake, which lies about 0.5 miles NW of the shelter cabin, and the smaller lake into which it drains, both have brook trout. The lakes are reached from the Nisqually entrance to the W. side road which is closed to vehicles beyond Fish Creek. Trail starts at the N. Puyallup bridge and continues 4.5 miles to the lakes, which lie at head of **RUSHING WATER CREEK**. Access also from Mowich trailhead near Mowich Lake.

GREEN LAKE. A 10-acre cutthroat lake at 3000 feet reached by trail up Ranger Creek from the Carbon River Road.

GREEN PARK LAKES. Cutthroat in the largest lake which covers 11 acres. Elevation is 5400 feet. From Sunrise Point hike on the Hidden Lake trail, then NW cross-country.

HIDDEN LAKE. Brook and rainbow trout are in this 5 acre lake at 5926 feet. Clover Lake trail N. Hidden is hidden in a depression about 4 miles N. of Sunrise Point.

HUCKLEBERRY CREEK. This large, fishable stream heads a short distance N. of Sourdough Ridge and the upper stretches are reached by trail from Sunrise Lodge. Lower portions of Huckleberry are brushy but may be fished by leaving the Chinook Pass Highway 410 about 6 miles E. of Greenwater N. of The Dalles CG where FS 73 follows the creek upstream toward the park. A trail continues from the road terminus into the park. The creek supports cutthroat with best fishing between mouth of Josephine Creek and park boundary.

KENWORTHY LAKE. 8 acre rainbow lake N. and below Gobbler's Knob Lookout at 4700 feet.

KOTSUCK CREEK. A cutthroat tributary to Chinook Creek. Take Deer Creek trail from Hwy. 123 about 4 miles S. of Cayuse Pass, then follow Owyhigh Lake Trail along the creek. Fly fishing only.

JAMES LAKE. Route to this 10 acre rainbow lake is through the Carbon River entrance to Ipsut Creek CG, then across the Carbon River on a foot bridge 1.3 miles above the campground. Trail takes off here, switch-backing steeply to Windy Gap, climbing 3000 feet. At the gap the trail drops 2500 feet to James at 4370 feet elevation. Total distance is 5.8 miles. No camping permitted. **ETHEL LAKE** is about 0.4 miles NW of James and is connected by a rough trail. Ethel covers 21 acres and contains rainbow. Steep and brushy shore lines make fishing difficult. Elevation of Ethel is 4287 feet.

LOST LAKE. Brookies are in this tiny (2 acre) lake which drains into Huckleberry Creek. Check with rangers as the lake is really "lost" and very difficult to locate.

LOUISE LAKE. Brookies are in this 11 acre lake and provide fair to good fishing. Elevation is 4592 feet. Reached from Stevens Canyon Road about 1.5 miles E. of junction with Longmire-Paradise road. Visible from the road.

MARJORIE LAKE lies at 4,555 feet between Adelaide and Oliver Lakes. An informal fishermen's trail starts slightly W. of the outlet of Ethel and leads about 0.8 miles to Marjorie. The lake is 11 acres and holds rainbow. **OLIVER LAKE** is 20 acres. Elevation is 4458 feet. There are rainbow in Oliver. The lake is located about 100 yards W. of Marjorie. **ADELAIDE LAKE** is situated over a small ridge about 0.7 of a mile NE of Oliver. It contains rainbow.

MARSH LAKE. A beautifully situated cutthroat lake of 4 acres at 3900 feet. An informal trail takes off from across the road from Box Canyon picnic area to climb to Marsh. A 2 acre pond adjoins Marsh. It's about 1 mile hike.

MOWICH LAKE. The largest lake in the park and it's reached by road in late July after snow has melted. This 100 acre, 190 feet deep lake supports kokanee and brook trout, and may have a few rainbow and cutthroat. Limited camping. Use the Car-

Mowich Lake.

bon River (Hwy. 165) entrance to ranger station at SW tip of the lake.

MOWICH RIVER. A Puyallup River tributary accessible via the Paul Peak trail from Mowich Road/Hwy. 165 about 1 mile inside the park. Upper stretches are reached by hiking 2 miles downhill from Mowich Lake. When clear and low this large glacial river offers cutthroat and rainbow fishing. Clouded most of the summer.

MYSTIC LAKE. An 8 acre cutthroat lake at 5700 feet with some rainbow and brook trout reached by a trail of 7.6 miles from Ipsut Creek CG. Trail crosses Carbon River at foot of Carbon Glacier. The lake may also be reached by a 10 mile trail crossing the foot of Winthrop Glacier out of Yakima Park. Shelter on Mystic. Infamous for summer mosquitoes.

NISQUALLY RIVER. This large glacial stream is usually too clouded with glacial flour to fish, but does contain brookies, cutthroat and rainbow. Hwy. 706 to Paradise-Longmire Road which parallels the river from Nisqually Park entrance upstream to Nisqually Glacier bridge.

OHANAPECOSH RIVER. A beautiful, gin clear, and exceptionally challenging small river that streams through a wonderland of fine colored gravel, rustling vine maple and giant old growth along the E. side of the park paralleling Hwy. 123 for several miles.

Ohanapecosh River.

It could be the perfect trout stream—if it had more trout. The ultra clear water is very cold, and nearly infertile, factors that severely limit the number and size of fish. A trail follows the W. bank. This strikingly beautiful stream supports small cutthroat, brook trout and rainbow. Fly fishing only. Large campground at Ohanapecosh off Hwy. 123. You may share the river with black-tailed deer, elk, ruffed grouse or black bear. This is one of those chosen rivers that's a pleasure to fish, even when you know you'll go fishless—especially in the fall when vine maple and mountain ash paint the green woods with streaks of brilliant red.

PARADISE RIVER. Aptly named, this small river runs into the Nisqually River near Cougar Flats CG. Brushy and difficult to fish, but has a few rainbows, cutthroat and brookies.

PALISADES LAKES. Two rainbow and brook trout lakes of 3 and 5 acres at 5500 and 5800 feet. Reached via a 1 mile trail beyond Hidden Lake (See Hidden for route).

REFLECTION LAKE. Filled with the mirrored image of Mount Rainier, this beautiful lake along the Stevens Canyon entrance below Paradise is one of the most photographed lakes in the park. It has good numbers of brook trout, despite park eradication programs, but is closed to fishing to prevent shoreline damage.

STEVENS CREEK. Rainbow, cutthroat and brook trout available when it is clear enough to fish. The creek plunges through Stevens Canyon well below the road between Paradise and Ohanapecosh. Best access is from Wonderland Trail which follows about 1.5 miles of the pool and pocket stream.

SUNRISE LAKE. A 4 acre lake located at 5800 feet elevation. No fish reported.

TAHOMA CREEK. Snow melt discolors this creek during warm weather, but rainbow, brook trout and cutthroat fishing is available and sometimes possible before and after runoff. Tahoma is crossed by the Longmire Road 1 mile inside the park entrance, and is paralleled upstream to its junction with Fish Creek.

TATOOSH CREEK. Outlet of Reflection

Lake, Tatoosh is a clear stream which holds brook trout and can offer surprisingly decent fishing. Empties into Paradise River about 1.5 miles below Narada Falls.

TIPSOO LAKE. A beautiful but barren snow-melt lake lying near the summit of Chinook Pass at 5314 feet, adjacent to Hwy. 410. No fishing permitted because of the fragility of the lake shore ecosystem. Spectacular view and photograph point of Mt. Rainier and jagged Tatoosh Range.

WHITE RIVER (West Fork). FS 74/West Fork Road leaves Chinook Pass Hwy. 410 about 3 miles E. of Greenwater and follows the West Fork upstream for several miles to within 2 miles of the park boundary. Cutthroat and rainbow in this swift, rocky river. The main river continues along the highway to the park's White River entrance. Above the White River CG it falls steeply from Emmons Glacier and is heavily clouded with glacial silt all summer, sometime clearing by mid October. Generally poor fishing.

Mount Rainier NP high lake.

North Cascades National Park

High jagged peaks, heather ridges, plunging slopes, avalanche chutes, cascading waterfalls, the 684,000 acres encompassed by the park complex are easily some of the most spectacular in America. Few roads reach into the backcountry, but a network of hiking trails leads to alpine lakes, valley streams and lonesome rivers. Many of the rivers pour from the 300 glaciers in the park, more than any other national park in the contiguous US.

The park is bordered on the north by British Columbia and on the south by Lake Chelan National Recreation Area. On the east it's bordered by the remote Pasayten Wilderness Area. The park spans the Cascade Crest and offers both the rain forest lushness of the West Slope and the semi-arid dry of the East. The complex is divided into four management units covering 1,053 square miles of magnificent but physicaly challenging mountains. The units include north and south units of North Cascade National Park which are divided by scenic SR 20 and the Ross Lake and Lake Chelan National Recreation Areas.

The park and recreation areas include the greatest concentration of ragged 8,000-plus feet peaks in Washington and were created in 1968. These summit and basins hold hundreds of pristine lakes, most of which have been stocked with rainbow, cutthroat or brook trout. Winter comes early and stays late in the high country and many NCNP lakes are ice-free only from late June to mid-September. Lakes at elevations in excess of 7,000 feet are generally frozen until July. Expect snow at any month when fishing the high lakes.

Most streams and rivers depend on natural propagation and catch and release where not required is advised. Nearly all of the streams and rivers are free-stone streams light on nutrients with pansize and small trout. The larger drainage streams and rivers are all worth exploring with a light rod and tiny lures or flies.

Washington fishing licenses are required in the park and recreation areas. Hunting is permitted in season in the recreation areas only and state licenses are required.

While roads are scarce there are approximately 360 miles of hiking and horse trails in the four units all of which lead to wilderness-type fishing. Free permits required for back-county camping may be obtained at any park service office or ranger station. Headquarters for the North Cascades group is in Sedro Woolley.

The North Cascades National Scenic Highway/SR 20 cuts E-W through the heart of the park and the Ross Lake Recreation Area. Crossing the Pacific Crest Trail (PCT 2000) at 4680 foot Rainy Pass. The highway links I-5 on the west side of the Cascades Mountains with Winthrop on the east slope. Because of extreme snowfall and frequent avalanches the highway is closed during winter—usually mid-November to mid-April. The following lakes and streams are wholly or partially within NCNP, Ross Lake National Recreation Area or Lake Chelan National Recreation Area.

A WDFW fishing license is required and state regulations apply.

The park and recreation areas are always open, but access is limited by snow in winter. State Route 20 (North Cascades Scenic Highway), is closed from approximately mid-November to mid-April. Seasonal opening and closing dates depend on weather, snow depths, and avalanche hazards.

Generally, the best weather for fishing occurs between mid-June and late-September. Most years snow is off all but the highest trails by July. Summer rain and snow storms can be common especially in high areas.

No admission fees but a Northwest Forest Pass is required for parking in NCNP along the Cascade River Road and at some trailheads along Hwy. 20 in Ross Lake National Recreation Area. Day pass $5, annual $30.

Between May 1 and Oct. 31 boaters must have a Dock Fee Permit to use the docks in Lake Chelan National Recreation Area. Cost is $8 day, $40 annual.

Developed campgrounds in the North Cascades are accessible by road. NCNP does not accept camping reservations. Free campgrounds are primitive. For RVers: Goodell Creek Campgound has mainly back-in sites and a few pull-throughs. Newhalem Creek Campgound has some (paved) pull-throughs in each of its 3 loops. This is generally the easiest of the campgrounds in which to park an RV. Colonial Creek Campground has mostly unpaved, back-in sites. Maneuvering space is limited.

Access to NCNP and Ross Lake is from I-5 at Burlington, west of the mountains, and Winthrop on the east, following Hwy. 20. Well marked branch routes to Baker Lake, the Cascade River, and Pasayten Wilderness Area.

The only road access to the shore of Ross Lake is through Canada, via the Silver-Skagit Road (gravel) near Hope, British Columbia. Boats may be trailered to Ross Lake through Canada but the going can be gravel-road rough and slow. A free permit is required for overnight use of lakeshore camps.

The main access to Stehekin, in the Lake Chelan NRA, is by float plane from Chelan on Hwy. 97, by boat or air. There is no road access into Stehekin, or Lake Chelan National Recreation Area. During summer, anglers can reach Stehekin by hiking from Hwy. 20 trailheads..

Two roads, both gravel, enter North Cascades National Park: the Cascade River Road from Marblemount and the Stehekin Valley Road, which does not connect to any roads outside the Stehekin Valley.

For neighboring lakaes and streams see county listings. For additional NCNP information:

North Cascades Complex, 2105 State Route 20, Sedro-Woolley, WA 98284. Phone: 360-856-5700

North Unit

BACON CREEK. Upper stretches in the park are rather inaccessible. It is reached by heading N. from Hwy. 20 on a gravel road 5.5 miles NE of Marblemount. Fish species include cutthroat, rainbow, Dolly Varden/bull trout and steelhead. Cutthroat are below Berdeen Lake.

BAKER RIVER. Lower portions above Baker Lake accessible by trail from the north end of lake. Rainbow, cutthroat and Dolly Varden/bull trout. The lower river is closed from its mouth to fish barrier dam from June 1-Aug. 31.

BERDEEN LAKE. A remote 127-acre lake at 5000 feet elevation, draining into Bacon Creek. It lies 12.5 air miles N. of Marblemount and holds small numbers of Montana blackspot cutthroat. A smaller, unnamed cutthroat lake lies below. It.

CHILLIWACK RIVER (Lower). Reached by trail from head of Chilliwack Lake in B.C., or from Hannegan Pass. Fish species include whitefish, Dolly Varden/bull trout, cutthroat, sockeye and kokanee, which spawn in August. **LITTLE CHILLIWACK**

RIVER enters the main river from the west near the park border. It holds cutthroat and dollies. No trails.

COPPER LAKE. Cutthroat and rainbow inhabit Copper's 8 acres. The lake is at 5250 feet and is reached by trail over Hannegan Pass from FS Hannegan Campground. Drains to Chilliwack River. Campsite at lake.

GOODELL CREEK. Lower reaches in Ross Lake NRA reached by rough road heading NW for 1 mile at S. outskirts of Newhalem. Upper portion of stream is in N.C.N.P. Fish include rainbow, steelhead and Dolly Varden/bull trout.

GREEN LAKE. An 80 acre lake at 4300 feet 11.5 miles N. of Marblemount. No trail to the rainbow and cutthroat lake which drains into Bacon Creek.

NOOKSACK RIVER (North Fork). Source is several glaciers in the Nooksack Cirque. Sparse numbers of rainbow and cutthroat. Glacial flour discolors water during summer melt.

North Fork of the Nooksack River.

THORNTON LAKE. Three alpine lakes on the west side of Trapper Peak. Lower Thornton, 56 acres, has cutthroat trout and is at 4450-feet elevation. Nearby Middle Thornton, elev. 4,680 feet, and 11 acres, is stocked with golden trout and rainbow. Periodic stocking. Upper Thornton, elev. 5040, and 31 acres is believed barren. Route is SW from Hwy. 20 on a dirt road which takes off about 3 miles SW of Newhalem for 4 miles where a trail leads 5 miles to lake.

South Unit

CASCADE RIVER (North Fork). Paralleled by gravel road to Cascade Pass. Produces small rainbow and some dollies. Dolly Varden/bull trout may be retained from June 1-Feb. 28.

DAGGER LAKE. A 10.5 acre high mountain lake draining into the Stehekin River, reached by trail over Twisp Pass from the Stehekin road or the Bridge Creek trail from Rainy Pass. It holds cutthroat.

HIDDEN LAKE. Rainbow and small golden trout are in this 55 acre lake at 6000 feet 12 miles E. of Marblemount. A rough trail follows Sibley Creek from Cascade River Road.

MONOGRAM LAKE. Trail to this 28 acre lake leaves Cascade River road about 7 miles from Marblemount. There are cutthroat and rainbow in the lake which is at 4850 feet. Camp at outlet which drains into Cascade River.

TRAPPER LAKE. A remote 147-acre lake at 4165 feet located in upper Stehekin River drainage. Holds cutthroat. Can be reached via way trails from W. side of Cascade Pass and from Stehekin road near Cottonwood.

Ross Lake N.R.A.

DIABLO LAKE. SR. 20 passes above the shore of this 910 acre impoundment of the Skagit River at Colonial Creek. Boat launch site at Colonial Creek. Rainbow, Dolly Varden/bull trout and cutthroat are available. The lake is more than 300 feet deep and most of the good fishing is found by trolling near shore especially cove areas. Campgrounds, resort, boat ramp, RV/tent sites, public access.

GORGE LAKE. Covering 210 acres, Gorge holds rainbow, cutthroat and Dolly Varden/bull trout. Access from SR. 20, with a boat launch at town of Diablo. Campground at north end of lake.

HOZOMEEN LAKE. A 3.5 mile trail from Hozomeen area at head of Ross Lake leads to this 111 acre lake at 2800 feet elevation. It contains eastern brook. **ROSS LAKE.** Naturally spawning rainbow, cutthroat, Dolly Varden/bull trout and eastern brook offer good fishing in this spectacular Skagit River impoundment of 11,678 acres. Boat access, campground and boat launch is at Canadian end of lake only. Follow Hwy 401, then south on Silver Creek Road about two miles west of Hope, B.C. No car, just trail and resort access to S. end of lake. There is no accessible boat launch on the S. end of lake, although Ross Lake Resort has rental boats, gas, food, cabins, and water shuttle to campsites (Phone 360-386-4437). Trail follows the shoreline into Pasayten Wilderness Area. There are several FS campgrounds on the lake. Best fishing is trolling near shore, especially at inlet coves and points.

SKAGIT RIVER. The 10 mile stretch of free-flowing river in the recreation area contains steelhead, salmon, rainbow, cutthroat, Dolly Varden/bull trout and whitefish. SR 20 parallels this section.

WILLOW LAKE. A 27 acre lake at 2900 feet located 1.4 miles SE of Hozomeen Lake. Contains rainbow and cutthroat.

Lake Chelan N.R.A.

BOULDER CREEK. A plunging stream reached by a short trail upstream from Stehekin road. Cutthroat and rainbow are present. Fishing is tough.

BRIDGE CREEK. A rumbling mountain stream paralleled by Bridge Creek/PCT trail from Stehekin road at Boullion to US 20. Creek crosses US 20 east of Rainy Pass. Headwaters are north of Liberty Bell Mountain Primarily a cutthroat stream with some rainbow and brook trout.

CHELAN LAKE. Road access to south end of lake via US 97 at Chelan, Manson, 25 Mile Creek and a few other areas. From the north, the lake is accessible only by hiking trials to Stehekin and the north end of the lake. The most popular hike from US 20 is Bridge Creek Trail/PCT trailhead at Rainy Pass. Trail connects to the Stehekin shuttle road at Boullion and is an arterial to Rainbow Lake and Rainbow Creek trails both of which end in Stehekin. Anglers will find rainbow, cutthroat, lake trout, kokanee salmon, ling (burbot) and smallmouth bass. In 1974 chinook salmon were stocked and annual plants have developed a decent troll fishery for 10 to 20 pounders. Spacious state parks south of NCNP 9 mi. west of

Image Lake and Mt. Shuksan.

Chelan and at 25 Mile Creek, (509-687-3710). Fishing guides are available. Fishing is allowed year-round in the south end, but closed during April-June in extreme upper end. Late winter fishery is mostly a 5-hook setline or jig fishery for burbot. Kokanee April-June, catchable rainbows stocked in south end in April. Fair to good trout fishing all summer. State record Mackinaw, 31-lb. 2.75 oz., caught here in 1999.

COMPANY CREEK. A lower Stehekin River tributary reached from the Company Creek road off Stehekin/Boullion road. A trail parallels lower reaches. Most of stream is in Glacier Peak Wilderness. Cutthroat, rainbow, brook trout and kokanee salmon.

COON LAKE. Reached by short hike on trail from High Bridge on Stehekin road, the 9 acre lake is situated at 2172 feet elevation. Holds cutthroat with some brooks in outlet stream. No camping on lake.

McALESTER LAKE. This 15 acre lake may be reached by trail from Rainy Pass, Twisp River road over South Creek Pass, or from Stehekin road up Rainbow Creek. It lies at 5500 feet and hosts an abundant number of small cutthroat. Campsites at lake.

RAINBOW CREEK. Access to lower sections from Stehekin road and trail. Rainbow and cutthroat plus kokanee in fall at confluence with Stehekin River.

STEHEKIN RIVER. Flows quickly from NCNP into Lake Chelan at Stehekin. Excellent road access between Stehekin and Cottonwood Campground below Cascade Pass from the paralleling Stehekin/Boullion road. The road, however, can only be accessed from Stehekin (shuttles and rentals available) and the river is closed above Agnes Creek at the PCT jct. This fast-flowing river is lightly fished for native rainbow up to 5 pounds, and cutthroat, with cutthroat only above High Bridge. Good for fly and spin-fishing. Catch and release only from Mar. 1-June 30. From July 1-Oct. 31 anglers are allowed to use selective gear, two fish limit, 15-inch minimum. Read the regs carefully.

TRIPLET LAKES. Two tiny lakes of 3 and 4 acres at 6100 feet elev. S. of War Creek Pass in Four Mile Creek drainage. It's a 1 mile cross-country hike from the Summit trail. They hold cutthroat. Drainage is to Lake Chelan.

Olympic National Park

The heart of the Olympic Peninsula beats in the nearly 1400 square miles on the skirts, valleys and peaks of the hacksawed, snow-capped summits that define Olympic National Park (ONP).

At most points, the park begins where the land turns vertical. In some areas that's within a few miles of the beach, in other it's actually on the beach. Much of the east and south border is buffered by Olympic National Forest. Few roads reach deeply into the park, with the exception of the lofty Hurricane Ridge Road from Port Angeles which climbs to a spectacular dead-end below 6,450 ft. Obstruction Peak.

For fishermen, the park is a mixed blessing. On the plus side are remote alpine trout lakes, and rarely fished streams with difficult access. On the down side, fish management is geared to protecting ESA threatened species and little effort is made to encourage recreational fishing opportunities.

Because fishing is not high on the park administration's totem pole of desirable recreation, most lakes are either fishless or abandoned to become self-sustaining. In most instances, to fish the park successfully, requires above average pre-fishing investigation.

ONP is rare in the range of species and topography that it offers anglers. Theoretically, park fishermen may start a day challenging trout in mile-high alpine mountain basins where the water is chilled by dripping glaciers, drop tiny flies into pockets of cascading creeks plunging through tunnels of lush vegetation, run plugs for river steelhead, salmon, and sturgeon and finish by fishing in salt water.

The park is surrounded on all sides by salt water drainages and many of the streams support anadromous trout and salmon plus ESA protected bull trout. The streams may have special closures and protective lure, season restrictions. The park is open 365 days a year. Most roads are open year round, although some may be closed during winter because of snow. Some campgrounds are open year round.

The peninsula has a moderate marine climate Summers are generally fair and warm, with high temperatures between 65 and 75 degrees. Late summer is driest, with heavy precipitation the rest of the year. Winters are mild, with temperatures at lower elevations in the 30's and 40's. At higher elevations, snowfall is generally heavy, with accumulations of up to 10 feet common. Near sea level, much of the precipitation is rain and infrequent snow..

All fishing destinations in the park can be reached from U.S. Highway 101, which circumnavigates the Olympic Peninsula. From the Seattle area, anglers may reach U.S. 101 by crossing Puget Sound on a state ferry, Hwy. 16 across the Tacoma Narrows Bridge or driving south around Puget Sound.

Entrance permits and passes are sold spring through fall at park entrances. $10 per vehicle for seven consecutive days at any park entrance. Camping fees range from $8 to $12. ONP charges fees for all overnight trips into the park's wilderness back country. The wilderness fee program has two components. The Individual Nightly Fee is $2 per person per night in the back country.

Summers are sometimes crowded at road accessible campgrounds, and fees are charged. Some campgrounds close in winter. No campsite reservations. Most campgrounds provide water, toilets, and garbage, picnic table and fire pit or grill. No hook-ups, showers, or laundry facilities. Sites accommodate trailers 21 feet or less. Major campgrounds have a few sites for larger RV's.

Often referred to as "three parks in one", ONP encompasses three distinct ecosystems—rugged glacier capped mountains, over 60 miles of wild Pacific coast, and stands of old-growth and temperate rain forest. In sharp contrast to the clear-cut scalpings on national forests and private timbers lands around the park, these diverse ecosystems are still largely pristine in character and about 95 percent of the park is designated wilderness

Isolated for eons by glacial ice, the waters of Puget Sound and the Strait of Juan de Fuca, the Olympic Peninsula has developed its own distinct array of plants and animals. Eight kinds of plants and five kinds of animals are found on the peninsula that live nowhere else in the world.

Best hiking and fishing time is from mid-summer into fall since most of the park's prime fishing lakes are above 3500 feet elevation. Portions of the Queets, Hoh, Quinault, Duckabush and Dosewallips rivers, all supporting steelhead, salmon, sea-run cutthroat and bull trout, are within the park. The upper Elwha River cut-off from saltwater by two ladderless dams, provides good to excellent fly-fishing for wild stream trout.

The park service no longer stocks fish in ONP.

A fishing licenses is not required in ONP but WDFW limits and seasons apply and catch report cards are necessary when fishing for anadromous steelhead and salmon. Angling regulations are available from park headquarters.

Because of fluid regulations, ESA listings and impacts on park areas it is important that fishermen read these regulations before making trips. Park shelters are being phased out, and there are areas with fire and lake-side restrictions.

Contact: Superintendent , Olympic National Park, 600 East Park Avenue, Port Angeles, WA 98362. Phone 360-452-4501

ANGELES LAKE. Easily reached by good trail 3.5 miles above Heart 'O The Hills CG 6 miles S. of Pt. Angeles at 4196 feet. The 19 acre lake is one of the largest alpine lakes in ONP. Steep cliffs on three sides make shore fishing difficult. Lots of brook trout. Usually ice free in June.

BARNES CREEK. Major inlet of Lake Crescent, and principal spawning stream for the lake's cutthroat. Trail to Marymere Falls and/or to Mt. Storm King parallels Barnes, then trail continues upstream to vicinity of Happy Lake. Brook trout in higher regions, good cutthroat in the canyon stretch below Mt. Storm King.

BIG CREEK. Enters N. side of Quinault River about 4.5 miles above Lake Quinault. Holds brook trout, protected bull trout, cutthroat, steelhead and some sockeye and coho salmon in lower reaches. Middle stretch flows underground except in rainy weather.

BLACKWOOD LAKE. A small, beautiful lake at 3000 feet at base of the ridge separating the Sol Duc and Bogachiel drainages. Take Mink Lake trail from Sol Duc Hot Springs to divide, go W. for 0.5 miles on trail then drop .08 miles down steep terrain to lake. Large numbers of brook trout.

BOGACHIEL LAKE. A 2 acre, shallow lake 1 mile SW of Deer Lake at head of S. Fork Bogachiel River. Accessible from the Deer Lake-Mink Lake trail on poorly defined trail. Sharp drop of 0.4 miles to lake. Holds some

brook trout in 7 to 9 inch range. E. and S. shores best.

BOGACHIEL RIVER. Heads in forks S. and W. of Seven Lakes Basin. Trail follows main river and N. Fork. Holds both summer and winter steelhead, rainbow, cutthroat, whitefish, protected bull trout and a few brook trout. Adult and jack coho salmon run high in the river. A rough trail from Bogachiel RS over Indian Pass leads to upper Calawah River. Bogachiel flows W. of Forks, and then into Quilayute River.

BOULDER CREEK. Flows into Lake Mills on the Elwha River from the W. May be reached by trail along W. side of Lake Mills, 2 miles from boat launch site. Has rainbow and brook trout. Upper sections of Boulder Creek reached by Olympic Hot Springs Road. Public campground at end of road.

BOULDER LAKE. A 3.5 mile hike from Boulder Creek campground on excellent trail. Many good campsites. Elevation of lake is 4450. Contains brook trout in 8-10 inch range with some larger. W. shore inlet area best fishing. Beautiful lake and setting.

BUCKING HORSE CREEK. Enters Elwha River about 23 miles upstream from Whiskey Bend. Elwha trail crosses creek. Holds rainbow, Dolly Varden, brook trout and some cutthroat.

BUNCH LAKE. A 10 acre lake at 3,000 feet at head of Bunch Creek. Reached from E.

Fork of Quinault Road by rough, cross-country travel. Reported to contain rainbow.

CALAWAH RIVER. South Fork. Tough going on the Indian Pass Trail north from Bogachiel RS over Indian Pass. Some excellent fishing, but rough country. Rainbow, cutthroat and protected bull trout.

CAMERON CREEK. A Gray Wolf River tributary. Trail leads from Deer Park 4.5 miles to Three Forks. Also reached by trail from Slab Camp. Contains rainbow, Dolly Varden and cutthroat.

CAT CREEK. Feeds into S. end of Lake Mills. A good sized stream has rainbow and supports protected bull trout. Access by boat.

CEDAR LAKE. 21 acres at 5,500 feet. Fine fishing for rainbow in the 10-15 inch bracket. Leave Gray Wolf trail at Falls Shelter and head S. for 3 miles over meadows and through forest on indistinct trail. Excellent campsites along open shoreline.

CONSTANCE LAKE. Reached by 2 miles of steep, difficult trail from Dosewallips River Rd. Elevation is 4750 feet, and lake is surrounded by rock cliffs on three sides. Campsites on S. shore. Holds rainbow and brook trout. Mountain goats sometimes seen from the lake.

LAKE CRESCENT. The second largest lake in ONP, Crescent covers 4700 acres and is about 9 miles long by 1 mile wide on the N. side of the park. Crescent is most famous for its huge but rare strain of Beardslee (rainbow) and Crescenti (cutthroat) trout, although it is questionable whether pure strains of these fish remain. Over the years Crescent has received brook trout, cutthroat, steelhead, kokanee and many strains of rainbow. Trout to 10 pounds are still sometimes taken and the record is a 16-pound, 5 ounce Beardslee rainbow. The big trout have a sweet spot for trolled plugs (sometimes more than 100 feet deep) that imitate the lake's huge population of small kokanee salmon. The kokanee are caught all summer by anglers trolling blade strings with bits of bait or small spoons. Both trout and salmon are often stratified very deep in the ultra clear water. Use a depth sounder to locate kokanee schools and you'll probably also locate the feeding depth of large cutthroat and rain-

Crescent Lake Beardslee trout.

bows. Public campgrounds, ramps, resorts offer current fishing information and accommodations including trailer space. Hwy. 101 twists and turns along the S. shore of this huge lake and provides road-side access.

DEER LAKES. A pair of 8 and 1 acre lakes at 3525 feet reached by good trail 4 miles from Sol Duc Falls parking area. Brook trout and rainbow in good numbers. Wooded shorelines.

DOSEWALLIPS RIVER. A good trail follows the Dosewallips from the end of FS 2610 to the headwaters at Dose Meadows below Hayden Pass. The trail branches 1.5 miles upstream from the trailhead. One branch follows West Fork 9 miles to Anderson Pass. The other trail climbs through virgin timber about 9 miles before entering alpine meadows above Camp Marion. West Fork holds rainbow, while the main branch of the Dosewallips has rainbow and brook trout plus a few Yellowstone cutthroat trout in the steep-walled canyon stretches near Camp Marion. Steelhead and salmon are found in lower reaches, and some mountain whitefish are taken. The Dosewallips flows into Hood Canal at Dabob Bay.

DUCKABUSH RIVER. Approximately 13 miles of fishable water inside the park along the Duckabush. Heads at O'Neil Pass and is fed by Hart, Marmot and LaCrosse

Lakes. Road up N. side of Duckabush from Hood Canal ends about 5 miles from park boundary. Rainbow are primary fish in this brushy stream, although salmon and steelhead are in lower portions. Trail follows river all the way to headwaters.

EAGLE LAKES. Three small lakes on N. slope of Aurora Ridge above Lake Crescent at about 3000 feet. Largest is 1.5 acres. Populated with brook trout to 13 inches. Aurora Ridge Trail passes within 0.5 miles of Eagle. Good way trail. Shoreline is brushy. Camp on high ground above lake to avoid mosquitoes. **ELK LAKE**. A 6 acre lake at 2550 feet on Glacier Creek which feeds into the Hoh River. About 14.5 miles from end of Hoh River road on excellent trail that touches E. side of Elk on way to Mt. Olympus. Campsites. Elk Lake holds brook trout of 7-11 inches some larger.

ELWHA RIVER. One of finest fly fishing trout streams in the state and the best in the park. A well-used trail follows the river for 28 miles into the heart of ONP from a parking area at Lake Mills at Whiskey Bend 9 miles S. of U.S. 101 and W. of Pt. Angeles. The river grade is moderate with lots of long pools, riffles and tailouts, except for a quick drop in and out of Lillian River Canyon. Campsites are at mile points 8.8, 11.5, 11.7, and 20.9. Major tributaries include Lillian, Long, Goldie and Hayes rivers. Fishermen's trails upstream and furnish good fishing for rainbow to 20 inches. Lots of ESA protected bull trout to several pounds. Release 'em all. As a rule, the further you hike, the better the fishing gets. Most anglers don't wet a line until they hit Mary's Falls at 9.7 miles from the trailhead, then they fish seriously for the next 9 miles upstream. Some of the tributaries are very much worth exploring and fishing (See Clallam County). Check current WDFW and park regs carefully.

FLAPJACK LAKES. Two lakes of 7 and 6 acres at head of Madeline Creek draining into North Fork Skokomish River. Trail from the upper end of Lake Cushman at Staircase continues 7 miles N. to lakes. Good camping spots. A stream connects the lakes, which hold rainbow and brook trout. Lower lake produces largest fish. Brookies 7-14 inches; rainbows 7 to 18 inches. Elevation 3900 feet.

GLADYS LAKE. The highest of three lake in a series in Grand Valley. It covers about

6 acres and lies at 5,400 feet. Gladys hosts rainbow and brook trout, with the 'bows to 14 inches. The brookies are 7-8 inches. Good campsites.

GODKIN CREEK. Enters Elwha River about 10 miles above Elkhorn RS. Holds rainbow, brook trout, Dolly Varden and a few cutthroat.

GRAND CREEK. Drains Grand, Gladys and Moose lakes and joins Gray Wolf River at old Three Forks shelter, 4.5 miles from end of road at Deer Park under Green Mt. Grand Lake-Badger Valley Trail follow upper Grand Creek for several miles. No trail access from Badger Valley to Three Forks area. Rainbow plus protected bull trout in lower reaches.

GRAVES CREEK. A good sized tributary to Quinault River. Trail leaves road at mouth of stream and follows creek about 5 miles to Graves Creek Basin. Trail continues about 1.5 miles to and past Sundown Lake. Contains rainbow and protected bull trout. Campground at mouth.

GRAND LAKE (ETTA). 13 acres at 4740 feet elev. Trail leads 3.5 miles from end of Hurricane Ridge/Obstruction Peak Road. Brookies and small rainbows. S. and SE shorelines best. Outlet stream sometimes produces.

GRAY WOLF RIVER. Major tributary of Dungeness River. Popular fishing spot where Grand and Cameron Creeks pour into the Gray Wolf below Green Mt. Popular trail from Slab Camp at end of FS Rd. 2926 up Gray Wolf offers access to river at many places before climbing to Gray Wolf Pass and dropping into Dosewallips drainage. Rainbow, protected bull trout, steelhead, salmon and some brook trout are in the river. Leave Hwy. 101 at Sequim State Park and drive to Dungeness Forks, bearing W. on about 2 miles to end of road and start of trail or via Slab Camp Road/FS 2926

HAPPY LAKE. A shallow, grassy lake at 4,875 feet at head of Barnes Creek in basin between Crescent and Boulder lakes drainages. Trail from Olympic Hot Springs Road—about 5.5 miles. Hit Happy Ridge Trail above Lookout Point. Campsites along E. shore. No recent reports. Had brookies to 14 inches but may have winter killed.

HAYES RIVER. Enters Elwha River 16.8

miles upstream from Whiskey Bend trailhead at Lake Mills. Trail follows the Hayes for a mile or so. Rainbow fishing.

HART LAKE. A long hike to a beautiful alpine lake at head of Duckabush River at 4900 feet in a glacial cirque basin. Hart covers 16 acres. Excellent campsites along the open shores. Trail up Duckabush River for 21 miles or 16 miles from end of Skokomish N. Fork Road. Rainbow and brook trout. May not be ice-free until July.

HOH LAKE. A beautiful lake that produces rainbow and brook trout. Hoh Lake lies at 4600 feet in the headwaters of the Hoh River. Covers 10 acres. 9.5 hike on Sol Duc River-Deer Lake route past the High Divide Trail which ties into Hoh River trail. N. shore one of top fishing spots for larger trout.

HOH RIVER. Largest Olympic Peninsula river, the Hoh begins as glacier melt on Mt. Olympus and Mt. Tom. It carries glacial silt during summer and is difficult to fish, but many varieties of fish are present despite the gray colored water. Winter and summer steelhead, chinook and coho salmon, sea-run cutthroat, protected bull trout and whitefish all are found in the river. Inside the park the river is fast and tumbling and pocket picking is mostly for small wild trout and chars. Road leads 19 miles E. from Hwy. 101 to the Hoh RS and campground, where the trail starts and follows the river to Glacier Creek, which it parallels to Elk Lake and Glacier Meadow. A branch takes off 9.5 miles from end of the road to Hoh Lake, Bogachiel Park and Sol Duc Hot Springs.

IRELY LAKE. A log-filled, 10 acre lowland lake at 550 feet adjacent to Big Creek, a tributary to the Quinault River. Trail takes off 1 mile short of end of N. Fork of Quinault Road for 1 mile to lake. Carries rainbow, cutthroat and brook trout. Catch and release rules.

LA CROSSE LAKE. An alpine lake at head of the Duckabush River at 4800 feet. La Crosse covers 15 acres 1 mile N. of Hart Lake. No fish reported.

LILLIAN RIVER. Tributary to Elwha River. Elwha trail crosses Lillian River 4.6 miles upstream from Whiskey Bend Lake Mills trailhead. Fishermen's trail follows bank of stream for several miles. May offer good fishing for rainbow and brook trout.

LITTLE RIVER. Enters Elwha River at Hwy. 101 bridge above Lake Aldwell. Only upper stretch is in park. Fishing is poor.

LOST RIVER. Another Elwha River tributary which joins the Elwha about 1.5 miles above Elkhorn approximately 13 miles by trail from Whiskey Bend. Lost River is good sized and supports rainbows and bull trout.

MARGARET AND MARY LAKES. At 3600 and 3550 feet respectively, the lakes are 6 and 3 acres in the Low Divide separating Mt. Seattle and Mt. Christie. Drains to Elwha River. Mary Lake, the smaller, furnishes brook trout. Margaret winter kills and has no fish. The lakes lie about 16 miles by trail from end of Quinault's N. Fork Road.

MARMOT LAKE. Just below Hart Lake at 4300 feet at head of Duckabush River. Trail 21 miles up Duckabush. Few if any trout.

MILLS LAKE. Formed by the uppermost dam on lower Elwha River, Mills is about 2.4 miles long by 0.4 miles wide and covers 451 acres. Offers tough fishing for rainbow, brook trout, Dolly Varden and a few cutthroat. Boat launch at lower W. end. Road to Whiskey Bend trailhead up the Elwha parallels E. side. May be good fishing where Elwha flows from sharp-walled canyon at upper end of lake, particularly in fall months (See Clallam County)

MINK LAKE. A marshy 10.5 acre lake 2.5 miles by trail from Sol Duc Hot Springs. Elevation is 3080 feet. Brook trout. Bring lots of mosquito repellent.

MOOSE LAKE. 7 acres in Grand Valley at head of Grand Creek. Lake is at 5,100 feet and holds brook trout. Rough trail of 4.4 miles from end of Hurricane Ridge/Obstruction Peak Rd. leads to Moose. Best fishing in deep water at inlet streams for 9-10 inch trout.

PELTON CREEK. Upper Queets River tributary. Campsite at confluence. Contains rainbows and protected bull trout.

P.J. LAKE. At N. base of Eagle Point about .05 mile by rough trail from Waterhole picnic site on the Hurricane Ridge/Obstruction Peak Road. Brookies of 7-10 inches in a 2 acre lake at 4700 feet. Top fishing spot is between the two inlets along SE shore.

QUEETS RIVER. Road from Hwy. 101 follows river 14 miles to campground at road end. Accessible at a number of spots along this road. At the end of road, wade the Queets to the N. side, hit trail up the river. Summer and winter steelhead plus spring and fall chinook, cutthroat, bull trout, whitefish and fall coho salmon. Because of glacial silt and clay bank bleed the river is often off color.

QUINAULT RIVER. Road up S. side of main Quinault River above lake continues upstream past Graves Creek CG about 22 miles from Hwy. 101. Summer steelhead in late June into fall. Check the regs for closures. The canyons above Graves Creek best. Dolly Varden, whitefish and rainbow are also present. The Quinault flows from Enchanted Valley, and an easy, graded trail offers access and campsites at many places..

QUINAULT RIVER NORTH FORK. Road up S. side of main Quinault River crosses bridge at forks and continues N. up the N. Fork. Total distance from Hwy. 101 is about 16 miles. Trail leads from this point 16 miles to Low Divide. The North Fork holds rainbow, steelhead, salmon, protected bull trout and whitefish.

REFLECTION LAKE. At head of Big Creek, a branch of the Quinault's North Fork. The lake is at 3500 feet and covers about 1 acre. Trail leaves North Fork Quinault Road about 2.5 miles upstream from forks, passes N. shore of Irely Lake and continues about 5 miles to Reflection and Three lakes where there is a campsite. Reflection lies 0.4 miles below the Skyline Trail and is not visible from trail. Brook trout are plentiful and measure 7-10 inches. Campsites on W. shore.

ROYAL CREEK. This Dungeness River tributary enters the river about 10 miles upstream from Dungeness Forks. Drains from Royal Basin and Royal Lake.

ROYAL LAKE. At head of Royal Creek, Royal Lake lies at an elev. of 5,100 feet and covers 2 acres. Holds brook trout. Trail up Dungeness River and then up Royal Creek.

RUSTLER CREEK. A major tributary to the North Fork Quinault River that enters the river 4 miles upstream from end of the North Fork Road. Fishermen's trail follows creek about 2 miles. Holds rainbow, protected bull trout and a few cutthroat.

SALMON RIVER. Heads in Jefferson County and flows through the Quinault Indian Reservation, Salmon enters ONP at the Queets River about 1.5 miles NE of Hwy. 101 on the Queets River Road. Winter steelhead.

SCOUT LAKE. NE of Mt. Stone drains in Duckabush River. Elevation is 4250 feet,

Morganroth and No Name lakes in Seven Lakes Basin.

and the lake covers 15 acres. Rough, poorly marked trail leads 2 miles from Upper Lena Lake, dropping over 600 feet in last 0.5 miles to lake. Rainbow to 18 inches. Campsite near inlet which forms One Too Many Creek.

SEVEN LAKES BASIN. Group of lakes in upper Sol Duc River drainage at elevations ranging from 3,500 to about 5,000 feet. Lakes are located N. of Bogachiel Peak and hold brook trout and rainbow. They include Soleduck, Morganroth, No Name, Long, Clear, Lake #8, Lunch and Round lakes. Lunch and Round reached by trail from end of Sol Duc Hot Springs Road. Rest of lakes accessible by way trails or cross country in open, sub-alpine region. Trail distance 8 miles.

SKOKOMISH RIVER NORTH FORK. A popular, especially with fly fishermen, catch-and-release river above Lake Cushman in ONP. The lower river attracts fish from the lake, including large Dolly Varden, kokanee, landlocked chinook, cutthroat and rainbows. Expect fall closures in this area to protect spawning chars and salmon. Upstream from Staircase Rapids, the river holds mostly wild rainbows, a few cutthroat and bull trout. Some to 15 inches. The trail follows river upstream to the headwaters on a divide between Mts. Steel and Hopper. A very pretty small river, with clear water (no glacial melt) that's usually fishable from June into Oct. Pocket picking for wild rainbows and cutts in many of the tributaries. From the divide, the trail drops into Duckabush River drainage. FS 24 leads from US 101 to SW campground and trailhead at Staircase.

SMITH LAKE. 7 acres at 4000 feet in a steep basin at head of Hammer Creek on North Fork Skokomish River. Contains brook trout. About a 6 mile hike from end of North Fork Skokomish River Rd. Final 0.5 mile is a steep way trail to lake.

SOL DUC RIVER. Upper stretches of this white water river are in the park reached by leaving Hwy. 101 about 1.5 miles from W. end of Lake Crescent. Road continues approximately 14 miles to Sol Duc Hot Springs CG. The Sol Duc carries both summer and winter steelhead, plus native rainbow, salmon, bull trout and a few brook trout and cutthroat. Heavily used trails from

end of road branch out to many sections of the park.

SUNDOWN LAKE. At 3900 feet at head of Graves Creek tributary to the Quinault River. 8 acres with rainbow. Hike 8.5 miles up Graves Creek Trail from Quinault River Road.

TOM CREEK. A quick stream that enters North Fork Hoh River 3 miles from end of road at Hoh RS. A trail heads S. about 1 mile along the creek which holds rainbow, cutthroat and protected bull trout.

TSHLETSHY CREEK. A major tributary of the Queets River about 7 miles upstream from end of road at Queets campground. Summer steelhead gather at mouth of the creek and in the Queets just below. Trail follows Tshletshy Creek to high ridge and then drops into the Quinault drainage. The creek holds rainbow, protected bull trout, steelhead and a few cutthroat.

UPPER LENA LAKE. A 10 acre lake at 4500 feet 2.5 miles W. of **LOWER LENA** (55 acres at 1800 feet). Drain into Hamma Hamma River. Follow Hamma Hamma River to Lena Creek CG then by trail N. 3.5 miles to **LOWER LENA** where a rough trail takes off for **UPPER LENA**. The **LENA** lakes contain rainbow. **MILK LAKE**, a small lake, is located 1.5 miles S. of **UPPER LENA**. Brook trout.

WILDCAT LAKE. A brook trout lake at head of Tumbling Creek which enters Dosewallips River from the S. about 1 mile from end of Dosewallips Road. Elevation is 4150 feet. Rough trail via Muscott Way Trail. When the trail enters meadows in Muscott Basin, head NE to the ridge and cross into Wildcat Lake Basin.

Olympic National Park Resorts

Lake Crescent: Fairholm Resort, Star Rt., Box 15, Port Angeles, WA 98362. 360-828-3020. Lake Crescent Lodge, Star Rt., Box 11, Port Angeles, WA 98362. 360-928-3211. Log Cabin Resort, Rt. 1, Box 416, Port Angeles, WA 98362. 360-928-3325.

Sol Duc River: Sol Duc Hot Springs Resort. 360-327-3583.

Major Saltwater Salmon Fishing Areas

Washington's coastal and inland saltwater fisheries are regulated on an emergency basis, with regulations changing to meet changing conditions and management goals. Seasons and regulations listed in the Washington Department of Fish and Wildlife annual regulations booklet, are often modified by change orders, conservation closures, and imposed federal regulations.

The prime fishing periods recommended for the major saltwater areas listed may not coincide with current legal fishing periods.

The publishers' recommend that you always review current regulations for area-specific emergency closings, openings, and tackle restrictions before all saltwater fishing trips. WDFW Olympia office provides a hot line recorded message of current rules, seasons and emergency regulations. WDFW Regulation Hotline: 360-902-2500

JOHNSON POINT. Winter blackmouth Nov. into early spring, a few spring chinook show in April-June, and fall chinook in Aug.-Sept. Resident coho and sea-run cutthroat provide a light-tackle fishery in spring and summer. Best bite on tide change. For salmon, mooching is productive in winter but dogfish can make bait-fishing a terror, and the only option is to troll with flasher and squid. Boat ramp, fuel, bait, tackle at Zittle's Marina.

ANDERSON ISLAND. Winter blackmouth and spring chinook. Possibly the best year-round salmon bet in the south Sound. Concentrate on the south side, especially Devil's Head and Lyle Point. Mooch or troll. Flood tide best in summer, ebb in winter.

TOLIVIA SHOAL. Coho, chinook, blackmouth and pinks in odd years. Best salmon fishing takes place in April-June on the flood tide. Troll the rip lines. Decent bottom fishing for rockfish and ling cod in rocks.

SQUAXIN ISLAND. Winter blackmouth, chinook salmon, sea-run cutthroat. Net pen rearing projects generate some fall returns of chinook. Troll spinner-cut herring. Winter and fall action best.

MINTER CREEK. A public access/ramp at the head of Carr Inlet. Best in late summer for chinook, coho and sea-run cutthroat.

This is mostly an early-morning fishery, although a flood tide bite is worth fishing. Small lures, spinner cut herring work well here.

FOX ISLAND. A good spring, April-July, fishery for small blackmouth, resident coho, and winter blackmouth in Dec.-Jan. Hale Pass and Point Gibson are top prospects. Public ramps on the island and at Narrow's Marine in Tacoma. Mooch winter and run troll gear in summer.

POINT DEFIANCE. Top salmon spot in the Tacoma area, offering year-round salmon; winter blackmouth, summer and fall coho, late summer chinook and occasionally a wayward pink or chum. Best fishing areas are the clay banks on the Point, rips south and north of the Point, breakwater east of Tacoma Yacht Club, and the south end of Vashon Island at Point Dalco, drop-off at the mouth of Quartermaster Harbor, Piner Point and Point Robinson. Salmon anywhere in Dalco Pass between Point Defiance Park and Vashon Island.

Shore fishing is available from a railing in the boathouse, and at Les Davis Public Fishing Pier on Ruston Way. Squid fishermen use the piers on winter nights. During low summer low tides some foolhardy fishermen will walk the beach around the Point to the rocks below the cliff and cast jigs and spoons into deep water. Be aware. the shoreline south of the Point is underwater during average tides. Don't get trapped between the cliffs and an incoming tide.

There is a public three-lane fee boat ramp with docks at the Vashon Ferry dock. Point Defiance Marine has elevator launches, rental boats, bait, tackle, fuel, snacks and daily fishing information.

COMMENCEMENT BAY. Popular fishing spots are off the mouth of the Puyallup River and in the rip lines that parallel the north bank. Troll or motor mooch for chinook, and odd-year pinks in Aug. and Sept.. Early morning and tide change bites. Nearby Browns Point is a good spot for everything that collects in the Bay, plus Sept.-Oct. coho and winter blackmouth. Troll or motor mooch the 90-110 foot line between Browns Point and Redondo boat ramp.

VASHON ISLAND. Located between Tacoma and Seattle, Vashon Island provides some of the finest salmon fishing still available in Central Puget Sound. The northern tip of the island marks the WDFW regulatory division between Marine Areas 10 and 11, and Area 11 is one of the few places left in the sound with a realistic chinook salmon season. The island offers good habitat for herring and other baitfish that supports salmon year-round. Blackmouth and resident coho are taken winter and spring and incoming ocean chinook and coho arrive in late July and stay until November.

Popular fishing areas beginning at the north end and running clockwise around the island are Allen Bank off Blake Island (exceptional blackmouth), Dolphin Point, Point Beales, Point Robinson (actually on Maury Island) Point Piner, mouth of Horseshoe Bay, Point Dalco, in Colvos Passage at Point Richmond, Olalla and Southworth. There is a bottomfish refuge/preserve in Colvos Pass north of Gig Harbor. Trolling for salmon is allowed in the preserve, not mooching or drifting.

Chinook arrive first at Blake Island, generally in late July and most move south along the east side of Vashon toward Tacoma. The first coho show up about Labor Day although the main run often doesn't arrive until the end of September. Winter fishing for blackmouth, when allowed, can be excellent especially at Point Dalco, Dolphin and Point Robinson. Pile perch are found near the ferry docks and piers. Point Dalco once was a premier area for large

Pacific True Cod, and a few are still found here, but the stocks were so severely over harvested that they have not recovered.

Chinook in summer and blackmouth in the winter. Best bet is to troll or motor mooch along the 90 foot drop-off usually marked by a ripline on the tide change. Troll for a small run of Sept.-Oct. coho. For both chinook and coho work the ripline north to Three Tree Point and south to Dash Point. Public ramp, dock and fishing pier in Poverty Bay on Redondo Beach Drive. Squid fishermen favor the pier on winter nights. A 4-ton sling is available at Des Moines Marina.

ALLEN BANK. In recent years the Allen Bank, on the north end of Vashon Island, has become a favorite winter and spring chinook spot. There's a ramp at Harper and hoist at Southworth, and the bank is an easy run from ramps at Bremerton or West Seattle. Bait, especially herring, sometimes collects in this area. Motor mooching is very productive, followed by trolling flasher-squid or thin-blade spoons. An artificial reef attracts bottomfish, including ling cod.

DUWAMISH HEAD-ELLIOTT BAY. Chinook available year-round. Green River kings and coho, plus salmon headed further south, will stage here in Aug.-Nov. Best bite is at daylight. Good spots are the Duwamish Head buoy, and mouth of the Duwamish River. Flounders in the bay, some rockfish off Duwamish. Excellent multiple lane launch at Armenie Ramp on Harbor Avenue in West Seattle.

SHILSHOLE BAY. Chinook are present year-round and coho in Aug. and Sept.. Early morning and slack tide bite. Dogfish sharks can be a problem. Excellent multiple lane ramp at Golden Gardens Park.

POINT JEFFERSON. One of the most reliable salmon spots in central Puget Sound. Jeff Head has chinook year-round, coho during the summer into early fall. Some bottomfish in deeper areas, including sablefish (aka: black cod). Mooch or troll, tide changes, early morning bite. Ramps at Suquamish.

POSSESSION POINT/BAR. A submerged ridge extending off the southern tip of Whidbey Island, the bar is one of the most consistently productive year-round salmon areas in Puget Sound. Chinook are found year-round, with major ocean migrants arriving in May and again in July, Aug. and Sept. Resident coho peak in April ocean coho best in Aug.-Sept. Good for pinks on odd numbered years. Good water for both mooch and troll tactics. Generally fishes best on ebb tide. Some rockfish, flounder and occasional halibut. Launch ramps in Kingston, Hansville, Mukilteo and Everett. Sling at Edmonds Marina.

POINT NO POINT. Good chinook year-round, best in July-Aug.; coho in Sept. and Oct. Mooch herring on ebb tide. Sling, trolley launch, fuel, bait at Point No Point Resort, ramp at Eglon public access.

HAT ISLAND. Sometimes called Gedney, this is a favorite summer destination run due west from the Everett ramp for chinook, coho and pinks. Best bite is early morning and tide changes. North side best for coho on mooch or troll. Decent bottom fishing at artificial reef.

MISSION BAR. Best fished July-Oct. from mouth of Snohomish River to Tulalip. Chinook, coho present. This is a favorite trolling area for Snohomish River pinks on odd-numbered years.

EDMONDS-POINT WELLS. Chinook year-round, coho in late summer. Best fishing July-Sept. Troll flashers/squid or motor mooch herring in 90 feet of water at the drop-off. Public pier and artificial reef north side of Edmonds Marina for salmon jigging, some flounder, pile perch, and popcorn shrimp. Fresh herring available at south end of marina. Sling launch.

BUSH POINT. Good late summer fishing for migrating chinook, coho and pinks that collect in the rips off the point to feed on herring balls and candlefish in the protected bay. This is a hot spot for odd-year pinks in Aug. In winter, there is a productive steelhead beach fishery casting Spin-n-Glos with hoochies. Rail launch or beach carry. Ramps at Keystone Ferry Dock at Fort Casey SP and Mutiny Bay.

PORT TOWNSEND. Good winter blackmouth chinook jigging on Midchannel Bank's candlefish spawning flats southeast of town. Summer troll/mooch in the rips and eddies at Point Wilson Lighthouse for migrating chinook, coho, and odd-year pinks. On some tides these fish can be reached by casting from beach. Best ramp is fee launch at Fort Worden SP. More ramps in town at Boat Haven Boatyard and Point Hudson.

OAK BAY/LIPLIP POINT. Winter blackmouth, and summer chinook in July-Aug.. Good daylight bite. Ramp at Hood Canal Bridge, Marrowstone Island. Decent ling cod fishery at offshore rocks.

DOUBLE BLUFF. Winter blackmouth and summer chinook and coho. Try ebb tide troll with spinner-cut herring. Launch at Mutiny Bay.

TSKUTSKO POINT. Located just north of Seabeck in Hood Canal, can offer decent winter blackmouth, and in late summer chums and coho are in offshore rips. Cross the mouth of Dabob Bay and troll north along the west shoreline for chinook and sea-run cutthroat. Launch at Seabeck.

MISERY POINT. Late spring spot for blackmouth. From late summer into fall tide rips between Misery Point and Oak Head sometimes provide good fishing for feeding coho, some chums. Ramp at Misery Point and sling at Seabeck Marina.

LILLIWAUP/HOODSPORT. Best known for Nov. chum salmon fishery near Hoodsport Hatchery. Beach casting or from small boats with green yarn flies or lures. From Aug.-Oct. there is sometimes a daylight bite for resident blackmouth and ocean chinook, and excellent July-August fishing for odd-year pink salmon. Sea-run cutthroat in shoreline shallows. Ramps at Hoodsport, Potlatch SP and Union.

UNION/TAHUYA. The elbow and sock of Hood Canal, these areas have seen their best days, but can still produce blackmouth and kings for trollers on ebb tide near the Skokomish Delta. A few coho show in late Oct. and Nov..

DECEPTION PASS. Skagit River-bound chinook in July-Aug. in extreme shallows at West Beach. Go out to deeper water for coho and odd-year pinks. There is also decent king fishing in late summer in the ebb tide eddy just west of bridge. Rockfish and lings in rocky areas, some perch along shoreline structures. Ramps at Deception Pass SP and Coronet Bay.

HOPE ISLAND. Once a tremendous fishery for 40-pound plus Skagit River kings.

Success mirrors the Skagit return which in recent years has been dismal. Diehard Hope Island traditionalists still pin their hopes on slow trolling large spoons and plugs May to early Aug. The east end of the island fishes best on the flood and the west side on the ebb.

GUEMES CHANNEL. Decent winter blackmouth fishery, mostly trolling with hoochies and flashers or flashers and herring. Also late summr coho and odd-year pinks. Ramp at Washington Park.

POINT LAWRENCE. A large peninsula on the east side of Orcas Island, Lawrence is good in late spring through early fall for blackmouth and coho. Lummi Rocks, east of Lawrence, produces chinook and coho during the summer, and offers fair bottom fishing including ling cod. Good odd year pinks. Ramps at Bellingham and Lummi Island.

EAST SOUND. Troll or mooch the entrance to this big Orcas Island bay in winter for blackmouth. Ramp at East Sound.

MOSQUITO PASS. Northwest end of San Juan Island. Large feeding chinook are in the shallows of the pass in late winter and early spring. In Sept., ocean coho arrive in the deep waters off the south end of the pass. Good bottomfish, ling cod area. Best access is from ramp at Snug Harbor Marina.

NORTH ORCAS ISLAND. Troll for summer chinook along north shore, then turn out to rips for passing coho in Aug. and Sept. Some pink fishing. Good bottom fishing in this area.

DALLAS and PARTRIDGE BANKS. Found north of Port Townsend and west of Whidbey Island these open water banks are favorites with spring halibut fishermen, and in July-Sept. there are chinook, coho and odd-year pinks. Mostly trolling for salmon, spreader bars and bait for halibut. Ramps at Point Wilson and west shore of Whidbey Island.

SEQUIM BAY. A lightly fished local spot for blackmouth in the winter. Herring trolled or mooched. Excellent ramp at John Wayne Marina.

DUNGENESS SPIT. Summer fishery for chinook tight to the north side of spit. Pinks in late July and coho from late Aug. to Oct.

Spring chinook appear in the Bay in late April and May. Blackmouth and kings from July through Sept. and pinks in Aug., and halibut off Green Point between Dungeness Spit and Ediz Hook. Ramp on Dungeness Bay.

EDIZ HOOK. Summer fishery for mature kings, and winter for feeder blackmouth. Most fish are taken June through Sept. Almost always a morning bite. In late summer head offshore to rips for coho and pinks. Ramp on the hook.

PILLAR POINT. One of the best Strait of Juan de Fuca summer spots for kings and coho. Early morning and tide change bites. Coho are in the rips offshore, sometimes several miles, and kings tend to hug the steep shoreline. There's also pinks in July-Aug. Ramp at Pillar Point but often unusable at low tide. Bring an anchor.

SEKIU. Numerous favorite spots are reached from this one-time great Strait salmon port. Most popular in mid-summer to fall, but locals enjoy a decent winter blackmouth fishery for unusually large fish that move in to gorge on spawning candlefish. Top summer spots will be The Coal Mine in early morning for chinooks, Mussolini Rock, for kelp bed kings early mornings in Aug., The Caves, just west of Sekiu Point is the most popular spot for kings in July-Aug. Coho and odd-year pinks tend to run further offshore in the east-west rip lines. Ramps in Sekiu and Clallam Bay from July-Sept. Excellent coho and pink trolling.

NEAH BAY. Located at the spectacular and lonely northwest corner of the Olympic Peninsula on the Makah Reservation, Neah is a solid summer bet for kings and coho. Steep mountains dive into the Strait of Juan de Fuca on the north and the Pacific Ocean on the west and provides excellent mooching structure for kings. Coho school along rip lines anywhere from a few hundred yards offshore at Waadah Island to a mile or so at The Whistle Buoy. Odd year pinks swarm the rip lines off the mouth of the Strait. Excellent near-shore, kelp bed fishing for black rockfish, ling cod and halibut. April, May and June are excellent months for light-tackle rockfish action at breakwater, Waadah, Sail, Seal and Tatoosh islands. Ramp, moorage, gas, bait, cleaning tables, and tackle at the marina. Motels, groceries, restaurant in town.

GRAYS HARBOR/WESTPORT. Best known for its offshore charter boat fishing out of Westport, but the harbor and boat basin are good bets in Sept. and Oct. Pen-reared coho and chinook, raised for sport-fishing, return to the Westport Boat Basin and provide a popular bank fishery in Oct. and Nov. Ocean charter boats are available for salmon, albacore tuna and bottomfish. Inside the harbor between the South Jetty to the Boat Basin is good for coho and kings when open in Sept. and Oct. Troll plug cut herring and rig for shallow water. Good bottom fishing around the Westport revetments and south jetty and from charter boats headed outside to rock pinnacles for rockfish and lings and to the flats for halibut. Late winter and spring rock fishing is exceptionally productive here. Launch ramp in Westport at the Coast Guard station.

WILLAPA BAY. Ocean salmon, winter steelhead and sea-run cutthroat surge into the bay from late Aug. well into early winter, most headed for the Willapa and Naselle rivers. Chinook arrive first, generally late Aug. through Sept. Mooch with 2-oz weights and herring on the incoming tide along the north side of the bay just inside the treacherous bar at the mouth. Water is often less than 12 feet deep. Washaway Beach is another good mooching bet. Salmon will ride the flood tide over the shallow bar. Coho arrive from late Sept. through Dec. The late run of coho is not widely publicized or heavily fished and it can produce exceptionally large ocean hooknose. A few anglers will brave the holiday season winds and rains to fish the incoming and flood tide at the bar. Most, (Don't confuse most with many. There are never many anglers in this fishery.) however, will troll the more protected area off the river mouths. Sea-run cutthroat prowl the pilings, river mouths and island shorelines year-round, and winter steelhead are in the bay in late fall and early winter, especially near the Willapa and Naselle river mouths. There is also a pretty fair shallow-water winter/spring sturgeon fishery near the river mouths. The best access to the bar is from the ramp at Tokeland where you can also get bait, dock space and enjoy a restaurant or motel. Ramps are also available in Raymond, South Bend, Smith Creek, the mouth of the Willapa River and at the Palix River on Hwy. 101 at Bay Center.

ILWACO. At the mouth of the Columbia River, Ilwaco is a launching point for charter boats that fish the ocean for salmon, albacore tuna and some bottomfishing. This is also the launching point for a fleet of small boats that hit river salmon in the popular Columbia River Buoy 10 fishery in Aug. and Sept. Charters that run offshore as a rule, catch far more coho than kings, and in recent years the blue-water trips for albacore fishing have been productive. The Columbia River inside the mouth can be fished with most trailerable boats, but never be tempted to cross the bar into the ocean in a small boat. When ebb tides and onshore wind waves collide this can be one of the nastiest and deadliest bar crossings in the world. The U. S. Coast Guard comes here to practice rolling boats. Excellent summer sturgeon fishing in the river between Ilwaco and Astoria and on the flats a mile or so downstream from the Astoria Bridge. Not too much bottomfish action here, except for red-tail surf perch which feed in depressions along the sandy surf line of Long Beach Peninsula. Black rockfish and sometimes ling are taken from the rocks of the north jetty. Good launch ramps, docks in Ilwaco harbor and Fort Canby State Park.

Public Saltwater Fishing Piers

In recent years there has been a concerted effort to build piers that can be enjoyed year-round by saltwater fishermen. While still far short of ideal, there are now more than 60 public piers and docks available to boatless saltwater fishermen in the Straits of Juan de Fuca, Hood Canal, Puget Sound and Grays Harbor.

Just about any fish that swims Washington's saltwater may be caught at the piers, and often pier fishermen are allowed to continue salmon fishing when seasons are closed for boaters. Check WDFW regs every year for pier fishing exceptions to salmon closures. Most salmon fishermen cast jigs (Buzz Bombs, Darts, etc) but in some areas feeder blackmouth and migrating chinook and coho are caught by dangling live or plug cut herring several feet below a sliding bobber.

Most pier anglers stillfish on the bottom with bait. Popular baits are clam necks, shrimp, pile worms, herring chunks, and squid. Common catches are flounders, sole, greenling, pile and striped perch, ratfish, skates, dogfish sharks and occasionally—

Edmonds fishing pier and artificial reel offers sports angling oasis off limits to commercial fleet net fishing at boundary.

especially at night—black rockfish and ling cod. Piers are also productive spots to dangle traps for Dungeness and red rock crabs, dock and popcorn shrimp, and to jig winter nights for squid. Some piers are popular with smelt jiggers in the spring, especially in the North Sound. Some of the largest piers also have artificial reefs built nearby to attract feeding fish. Best fishing is almost always on an incoming or high slack tide.

Most of the developed piers are wheelchair accessible, have railing rod holders, fish cleaning tables and running water. Piers attract everybody and all levels of expertise from gear-enhanced old pros to kids with soda can reels and handlines. You'll see it all on a public fishing pier and enjoy great camaraderie and wonderful fish tales.

Try These Public Fishing Piers:

Port Angeles City Pier
Blaine Dock Port of Bellingham
Gooseberry Point Ferry Dock
Boulevard Park Pier (S. of Bellingham)
6th St. Dock, Bellingham

Anacortes Municipal Pier
Friday Harbor Marina (San Juan Is.)
LaConner Marina Dock
Bowman's Bay Pier,(Deception Pass)
Cornet Bay Docks

Whidbey Naval Seaplane Base Pier
Oak Harbor Pier, Flintstone Park
Coupeville Pier,
Kayak Point Snohomish County Park
Langley City Pier

John Wayne Marina (Sequim)
Fort Worden (Port Townsend)
Port Hudson (Port townsend)
Fort Flagler (Marrowstone Is.)
Port of Everett Pier

Mukilteo Ferry Dock Pier
Meadowdale Pier (N. of Edmonds)
Edmonds Pier
Indianola Pier
Suquamish Pier

Keyport Pier
Brownsville Pier
Silverdale Pier
Illahee City Pier (Bainbridge Is.)
Point White/Gibson Pier

Illahee State Park Pier
Coal Dock Lion's Community Park (Brem.)
Park Avenue Pier, Bremerton
Bremerton Pier/First Street Dock
Waterman Point Pier (Sinclair Inlet)

Annapolis Dock (Retsil Pier)
Port Orchard Pier
Shilshole Marina (A-Dock, Seattle)
Elliott Bay (Seattle, N. of Myrtle Edwards Pk., and on Elliott Ave.)
Duwamish Head, West Seattle

Spokane Street Bridge
Blake Island Pier
Harper Pier
Des Moines Marina Pier
Redondo Marina Pier

Dash Point County Park Pier
Tramp Harbor Pier
Port Defiance Park Pier
Les Davis Pier, Ruston Way
Old Town Dock (Tacoma)

Clyde Davidson Memorial Pier
(Steilacoom)
Luhr's Beach Pier (Nisqually Delta)
Twanoh Park Pier
Hoodsport Pier
Point Whitney Pier

Hood Canal Bridge Pier
Port Townsend City Dock
Westport Boat Basin Pier
Ilwaco Marina Docks

Where To Find Artificial Marine Reefs

Artificial reefs have been built on the bottom of Puget Sound and Hood Canal by WDFW to attract and provide habitat for a variety of bottomfish, including rockfish, ling cod, greenlings, cabezon, perch and flounders.

Reefs are made mostly of scrap concrete and rock, and are about 200 feet long around 50 feet wide in 45 to 100 feet of water. They may provide excellent bottomfishing fishing opportunities, mostly for boaters, but a few are within reach of public fishing piers. Because they support herring and other baitfish, the reefs also attract salmon.

The reefs are marked with two buoys, one at each end. Major artificial reef locations are:

Possession Point, 600 feet W. of buoy, 55-100 feet deep.

Gedney (Hat) Island, 3000 feet S. of the S. tip 45-70 feet deep.

Edmonds, 200 feet W. of public pier, 30-80 feet deep (no boat fishing).

Onamac Point, 1000 feet N. of navigation light, 45-100 feet deep

The Trees, 2.1 miles S. of Point Wells 45-100 feet deep.

Misery Point, 600 feet N. of navigation light, 45-100 feet deep.

Blake Island, 800 feet S. of S. tip, 60-90 feet deep.

Point Heyer, Vashon Is., 1000 feet SE of radio tower, 45-100 feet deep.

Toliva Shoal, 1300 feet NW of navigation buoy, 60-90 feet deep.

Itsami Ledge, Johnson Pt., 1100 feet NW of South Bay nav. light., 50-70 feet deep.

Saltwater Fishing Rigs

Bottomfish Pier Rigs

Standard Bottom Rig

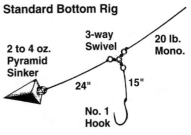

2 to 4 oz.
Pyramid
Sinker

3-way
Swivel

20 lb.
Mono.

24"

15"

No. 1
Hook

Sliding Bottom Rig   **Sliding Split Ring**

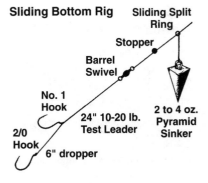

Stopper

Barrel
Swivel

No. 1
Hook

2/0
Hook

24" 10-20 lb.
Test Leader

6" dropper

2 to 4 oz.
Pyramid
Sinker

Bottomfish Pier Rigs

Pile Perch Rigs

Double Dropper Flounder Rig

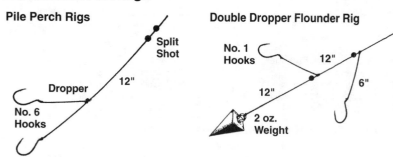

Split Shot

Dropper 12"

No. 6 Hooks

No. 1 Hooks

12"

12"

6"

2 oz. Weight

Salmon Trolling Rigs

Flasher/Squid

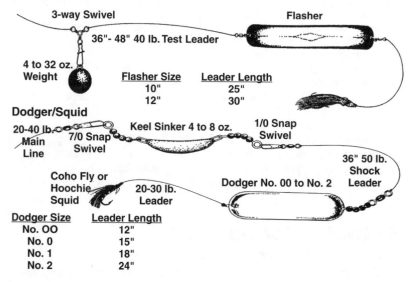

3-way Swivel

36"- 48" 40 lb. Test Leader

Flasher

4 to 32 oz. Weight

Flasher Size	Leader Length
10"	25"
12"	30"

Dodger/Squid

20-40 lb. Main Line

7/0 Snap Swivel

Keel Sinker 4 to 8 oz.

1/0 Snap Swivel

36" 50 lb. Shock Leader

Coho Fly or Hoochie Squid

20-30 lb. Leader

Dodger No. 00 to No. 2

Dodger Size	Leader Length
No. OO	12"
No. 0	15"
No. 1	18"
No. 2	24"

Salmon Mooching

Mooching Herring

Insert lowest hook in cavity and out spine. Pull both hooks through top hole.

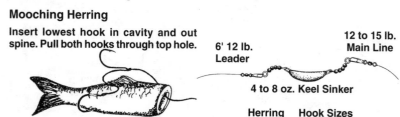

6' 12 lb. Leader

12 to 15 lb. Main Line

4 to 8 oz. Keel Sinker

Insert lowest hook, turn, and insert top hook on opposite side.

Top View

Herring Length	Hook Sizes Bottom	Top
4"	1/0	1
5"	2/0	1/0
6"	3/0	2/0
8"	4/0	3/0

Designed by Northwest Anglers for Northwest Fish!

Worden's Rooster Tail, Lil' Corky, Spin-N-Glo, Hawg Boss Super Toad, Timber Tiger, FlatFish, Triple Teazer and others are some of the most productive lures around ...catching trout, walleye, salmon, steelhead, bass, perch and just about everything else that swims in the lakes and streams of the Northwest. Worden's makes lures right here in Washington for fish of the Northwest. That's how we got started over 60 years ago and why we're still here today!

Catching Made Easier

Worden's®

Yakima Bait Co.
PO Box 310, Granger, WA 98932, (509)854-1311
www.yakimabait.com

Fishing With Kids

Leave Your Rod Home And Take That Youngster Fishing

This page is directed to fathers, mothers, uncles, aunts, brothers, sisters or neighbors who know of a youngster who wants to go fishing. Take 'em, and if you don't fish, all the better.

I suspect that many kids don't get to fish because their dad or mom doesn't know what equipment is necessary, how to rig the gear, or where to go. It isn't that tough. You'll make yourself a hero by getting your offspring out on lake or stream and into some fish. Kids don't care about size, they want to watch a bobber bounce and zip under the water, and they want numbers—a dozen 6-inch perch or sunfish will do just fine.

Even if you don't like fishing yourself, neither you nor your youngster will ever forget those beginning fishing experiences together. In fact, I recommend that adults, like good professional guides, don't fish. That way you're relaxed, not worried about *your* bite, have the patience to untangle tangles, and to direct your entire effort at helping the kid. Kids don't want to watch you catch a fish, they want to catch a fish. Forget the fancy equipment. You can buy a small, open-face spinning reel loaded with six pound test monofilament line, plus a 6 or 7 foot light spinning rod for under $20. For the $20 you'll probably be able to include a dozen snelled (hooks with leaders tied to them) number 8 hooks, a dozen small snap swivels, some split sinkers and four or five pencil-shaped floats. That's it. You may want to buy a jar of salmon eggs, but common garden worms are as good or better bait.

Case's Pond, Pacific County.

Practice a bit

Before making the trip, string the line through the rod guides and tie a rubber eraser or small weight to the end. Then go outside set up bunch of tin can targets, and let the youngster try casting. Spinning reels are simple. A 6-year-old can learn to cast reasonably well in 15 minutes. Now, where to go? Look in your county listings for lakes that contain warm-water fish, or the story that list many of the waters in the state that support panfish. It is not necessary to get up early for perch, crappie, sunfish or catfish, the type fish your boy or girl is going to catch. Late afternoon into evening hours on a sunny day in mid-summer is a good fishing time.

Fish from shore

You may fish from a boat, but with a little guy along I prefer to fish from shore. They get wiggly sometimes. If there is a resort on the lake, ask the resort operator where the best panfishing areas are. Or walk around the lake until you find a place where there are logs, lily pads or brush in the water. String line through the rod guides and tie a swivel to the end. Snap the swivel to one hole in the bobber. Attach another snap swivel to the other hole in the bobber and tie the leader to the swivel. Let your youngster select his worm and hook it in several places, permitting the ends to squirm. Then direct him to cast as close to the logs or other cover as he can (If you need help on proper fishing knots, see illustrations elsewhere in this book).

Keep moving

If the bobber doesn't start dancing in 10 minutes, try another spot. When you locate fish and they start attacking the worm, try to keep the youngster from setting the hook until the bobber goes completely under the water. Your youngster will want to keep those first few fish, but after several trips suggest releasing fish. Take a pail along, fill it with lake water and place fish in it. When you are ready to go home, the youngster can select a few "choice" fish and enjoy releasing the rest. Kids love to release fish, to watch them wiggle then dart away to be caught another day. Started out this way kids are not likely to turn into game hogs when they get older. It really IS that simple.

Fishing Waters For Kids Only

Small ponds scattered throughout the state have been set aside exclusively for kids 14 and under to fish without adult competition. Adults are encouraged to help though.

All of the ponds are stocked by WDFW, usually in the spring, and some several times a year. Check locally for specifics, and additions or deletions to the following list of juvenile waters.

Lakes and streams set aside for juveniles (14 years old and younger), and in a few cases disability license holders, seniors and families are listed alphabetically by county, followed by the open fishing season.

Adams County: Para-Juvenile Lake (shared with Grant County); Mar. 1 through July 31.

Asotin County: Headgate Pond (also open to seniors and disability license holders); last Saturday in Apr. through Oct.

Benton County: Columbia Park Lagoon (near south end of U.S. Hwy 395 bridge. Also open to junior and adult anglers when accompanied by a juvenile); year-round.

Chelan County: Cashmere Pond; year-round. Enchantment Park ponds; year-round. Nason Creek Fish Pond also open to disability license holders); year-round.

Clallam County: Lincoln Pond; year-round. Peabody Creek; last Saturday in Apr. through Oct. 31. Valley Creek; last Saturday in Apr. through Oct.

Columbia County: Dayton Pond; year-round.

Garfield County: Pataha Creek (within Pomeroy city limits); June 1 through Oct.

Grant County: Para-Juvenile Lake (shared

with Adams County); Mar. 1 through July. Columbia Basin Hatchery Creek (from the hatchery outflow to confluence with the mainstem Hatchery Creek. Also opened to disability license holders); year-round. Columbia Basin Hatchery Creek (excluding the section previously described for juveniles and disability license holders — Family Fishing rules: also open to junior and adult anglers when accompanied by a juvenile); year-round.

Grays Harbor County: Mill Creek Pond; year-round. Vance Creek Pond # 1 (also open to seniors and disability license holders); last Saturday in Apr. through Nov.

King County: Coal Creek (near Snoqualmie — from mouth to I-90); last Saturday in Apr. through Oct.; Kimball Creek (near Snoqualmie); last Saturday in Apr. through Oct. Mill Pond (Auburn); last Saturday in Apr. through Oct. Old Fishing Hole Pond (Kent); last Saturday in Apr. through Oct. Soos Creek (from mouth to bridge near hatchery residence juveniles-only for salmon Sept. 30 through Oct. 15.

Kittitas County: Mercer Creek (within Ellensburg city limits); June 1 through Oct.. Naneum Pond; year-round. Wilson Creek (two branches within Ellensburg city limits); year-round.

Klickitat County: Jewitt Creek; June 1 through Oct. Little Klickitat River (within Goldendale city limits); last Saturday in Apr. through Oct. 31.

Lewis County: Fort Borst Park Lake (Family Fishing rules: also open to junior and adult anglers accompanied by a juvenile); last Saturday in Apr. through Feb.

Lincoln County: Goose Creek (within Wilbur city limits — also open to disability license holders); year-round.

Okanogan County: Jasmine Creek; year-round.

Pacific County: Cases Pond; last Saturday in Apr. through Nov. South Bend Mill Pond; year-round.

Pierce County: DeCoursey Pond; last Saturday in Apr. through Nov. Wapato Lake; year-round.

Skagit County: Northern State Hospital Pond; last Saturday in Apr. through Oct.

Snohomish County: Fortson Mill Pond #2; last Saturday in Apr. through Oct. Jennings Park Pond; last Saturday in Apr. through Oct.

Spokane County: Bear Lake (Family Fishing rules: also open to junior and adult anglers accompanied by a juvenile — also open to disability license holders); year-round.

Thurston County: Long's Pond (Lacey); year-round.

Walla Walla County: Jefferson Park Pond; year-round. Lyons Park Pond (College Place); year-round.

Whatcom County: Fishtrap Creek (from Koh Road to Bender Road); June 1 through Oct. Johnson Creek (from Northern Pacific railroad tracks to Lawson Street footbridge in Sumas); June 1 through Oct. Whatcom Creek (from stone bridge at Whatcom Falls Park to Lake Whatcom); last Saturday in Apr. through Oct.

Whitman County: Garfield Juvenile Pond; year-round.

Yakima County: Sarge Hubbard Park Pond (also open to disability license holders); year-round. Yakima Sportsmen's Park ponds; year-round.

Steelhead Secrets

**Winter, Summer, Baits, Jigs, Plugs, Rods, Rains,
Barometer, and more**

Winter Steelhead

Winter steelheading in Washington is a four month show, with first appreciable number of hatchery fish appearing in December and generally peaking in January. Wild steelhead arrive from February to early April. Most steelhead will ride a wave of high water into the lower river then filter upstream, individually and in small schools. They move substantially on any freshet. When the water is low and clear, these big fish will hold in deep runs and surge forward under low light conditions, dawn, dusk, overcast days.

It's a sure bet that every flush of water brings new fish into major steelhead streams.

Wait for water drop

Steelhead don't do much traveling when rivers are at flood stage. Rather than fight the forceful flows they hunker behind logs, rocks and sometimes even the willows at shoreline. When the water turns a thick green and starts to drop steelhead will be on the move. During this period fish will be located throughout lower stretches of the river, and not always in drifts. Using the rule of thumb that "the higher the water, the lower in the pool steelhead will hold," tail-outs or fans of pools should be systematically fished. Fish in front of, in back of, and on both sides of every rock or stump that elbows the current. Fish at your feet. Steelhead won't fight high velocity currents when there are easier routes. Wait two to four days after rivers first start dropping. By then steelhead will have found holding riffles and pools, and rather than hitting the odd fish you can work on clusters. This is the time they gang.

Fish need cover

Cover is the only defense river steelhead have against predators that often arrive from above in an explosion of feathers and talons. If you can see bottom in the fishy portion of the drift, forget it. Almost with exception, good holding water must have rocks, logs, over-hanging branches or depth. Besides protection, rocks and logs provide "soft" water where steelhead may hold against the current with little or no effort. Current boils and threads indicate rugged bottom that means cover—and fish.

Set alarm early

Productive drifts are those located either just above or below rough stretches of rapids. Watch for first good slicks upstream or downstream from long, flat sections or river where cover is at minimum. These particular spots are excellent prospects for early morning trips since steelhead wait for cover for darkness to pass water in which they are vulnerable. They'll often take the first bait or lure offered. Steelhead also school in first holding water below falls or rough rapids. Upstream movement is done primarily at night and is governed by amount of water coming over falls or other barrier. Fish below the falls during low water periods, and in first few good drifts above this point following a raise in water. Mouths of feeder streams should not be over looked. When the main river is dirty the clear-dark line caused by clean water spilled by the creek should be worked. Sometimes it is the feeder stream dumping mud which offers cover for steelhead in the main river.

Rains rule

Besides bringing new steelhead in from saltwater, a flush of rain raises water temperatures and oxygenation which improve fishing, since fish tend to be sluggish when river water registers in the chilly 30's. Save the rising barometer theory for other fish. That's not the way it works for winter steelhead which live in snow-fed rivers. They react to the warmth brought by rain water by hitting more freely.

Although fishermen may locate the lay holes for steelhead by busting brush, it is much easier to drift the river in a boat. Boating should be done with great caution. Every steelhead season fishermen are drowned in boating mishaps. It is wise to locate five or six top holding drifts in a ten mile section of river. First location would probably be near tide water. Since steelhead must undergo biological changes in moving from salt to fresh water, they follow several high tides into lower holes before committing themselves to the river. Find the last good riffle that is touched by tidal waters and work the drift thoroughly.

Don't dally

Each of the pre-located drifts should be fished in order. An hour of hard fishing at each location should be maximum time spent unless fish are hit. Most novice steelhead fishermen expend far too much time on one drift before moving on. The time to carefully comb every possible section of the drift is after steelhead have been located. Characteristically, steelhead that haven't been spooked will bite the first time lure or bait is properly presented if they want to hit. Once a fisherman is satisfied that he has worked the key water at correct depth and speed, it's time to move on.

Not much time

Rivers will not remain in top condition for more than a week at most. Four days is more realistic. Steelheading will be good when water levels and color are right and beginners and semi-skilled fishermen will score along with the pros during this period. The situation gets a bit tough when rivers drop and clear. Even though steelhead are there, they aren't too cooperative. Water temperatures drop as rain water runs off, and it is necessary to place bait or lure close to steelhead as they become less active. Clear water means spooky fish.

The rule that steelhead will be found where there is cover always applies. The long, deep drifts that held fish when water levels were up become clear. Now the situation is reversed, and it's "the lower the water the higher in the pool" rule to follow. It is helpful to use longer, lighter leaders, smaller lead and lures, or bobber and jig combos and to cover all riffle or white water thoroughly.

Lay it there

Precision casting is imperative. Up-stream casts are particularly effective during low water periods. This technique will exact a heavy toll of terminal tackle but steelheaders who hook fish in this manner don't complain. Just reel quickly, hold the rod high and set on every hesitation.

Work back side

An effective method of connecting with steelhead when rivers are low is to fish the back side of the creek. This appears obvious, but it is surprising how fisherman after fisherman will approach a drift, plant his boots in the tracks of the man who just left a drift and cast repeatedly to the same spot that has been pounded all day. First angler through may hook a fish, but after the drift has been beat for hours the fish will lay tight against the far bank in snags or rocks, or in undercuts of the bank.

All but the largest steelhead streams may be waded during low water. A steelheader wearing chest-high waders can usually make it at tail of pools. Crossing to the back side of the heavily worked drift will put you right on top of fish.

Fishing equipment

A standard winter steelhead rod is 8 to 8 1/2 feet long. It's stout in the butt section so that heavy hooks may be set in a steelhead's tough mouth, but the last 12 to 18 inches of the tip section is sensitive. This aids anglers in detecting the light pickup of steelhead. Handle of the rod back of the reel seat extends approximately the length of the angler's forearm to provide needed support. Heavy-duty spin reels or level wind reels are standard, with minimum of 150 yards of 12 to 15 pound test mono line usually required. Use lower test line than your main line for leaders so that hang-ups will not result in excessive main line loss.

Mix'em up

Choice of lures or bait is governed by water conditions, lateness of season and by individual preference. Experienced steelheaders may stick with a favored style spoon, Corkie bobber, jig, fly or bait through high water and low, but their success in hooking fish is because they are getting it in front of fish consistently. Less skilled steelheaders would do well to mix their offerings. Sand shrimp, prawns, nightcrawlers or clusters of salmon eggs are popular natural baits. After systematically sweeping every bit of good looking water with bait, re-rig and take it from the top again using a spoon or spinner. No action? Rig a float and jig and try it again. Floats and jigs have gained a large following in recent years, and are very effective for covering long slow pools, and near-side troughs. I've sometimes had success by using a black or purple yarn and Corkie setup when everybody else is using orange, green or cerise. Don't be afraid to throw something different, especially when you know there are fish in heavily hammered water.

Toward end of the winter steelhead season as fish approach spawning they more aggressively hit spoons, spinners, plugs and brightly painted bobbers. Buck steelhead, particularly, chase spoons, flashy spinners and diving plugs during late season. When steelheading, especially when plug fishing the rule is, the longer you keep the lure in front of the fish, the more likely it is that you will provoke that fish into striking. Heavier leads may snag more frequently, but they slow a lure's drift and will produce more fish. Plugs should be worked slowly downstream. The idea is drive a steelhead backward with the plug and when it hits the tailout, hold-on!

Mark the hot spots

Year after year fish will come to the same holding drift. A rock ledge, stump, root or brush that hangs into the river to provide cover for steelhead will harbor them repeatedly. When fish are caught in such a spot, others will move in. As fishermen take time to examine and understand why the big sea-run rainbows act as they do under varying water conditions, they will hook steelhead consistently.

Hot Spots

While winter steelheading is but a shadow of what it was less than 20 years ago, it's still an exciting and challenging sport. Washington steelheaders catch about 25,000 winter-runs a year, less than the 25,000 summer-fish reported. Here's some of the most productive winter steelhead rivers to target.
More than 100 rivers support winter steelhead. The list below includes the top 10 rivers in the state (in this order) in 1999 and while this order may shuffle somewhat year-to-year, they are all dependable fisheries from Dec.-Feb.

Top Winter Rivers

Cowlitz, Quillayute, Bogachiel, Skykomish, Skagit, Quinault, Calawah, Snoqualmie, Sol Duc, Hoh below Hwy. 101 and Green-Duwamish.

Summer Steelhead

For the last few years Washington anglers have been catching more summer-run steelhead than winter-runs, reversing the traditional concept of Northwest ironheading. More Washington streams carry summer-run steelhead than most anglers realize, and steelheaders with the pioneering spirit can help themselves to some top sport if they want to explore. Approximately 100 of the state's rivers and creeks host this fish, which is the finest of all game fish in the opinion of many experts.

Summer run steelhead move in from the ocean during June, July, August and September, but may enter home rivers as early as February. Even though the fish come in early, they spawn about the same time as winter steelhead in March and April. Summer steelhead live in deep pools while waiting for eggs and sperm to mature. They feed a little bit after leaving the ocean, but rely mostly on fats stored in their bodies for nutrients. An early summer or "springer" steelhead taken in March or April, particularly, is loaded with energy and is a rough fish to control. Summer-runs, as a rule, are more acrobatic than winter fish, often leaping clear of the water several times.

The Columbia River and tributaries, produce many of the state's summer steelhead, although approximately 20 major river systems in W. Washington now carry them. Average yearly summer-run catch has been dropping each year and is now around 35,000 fish, which is about 10,000 more than the total number of winter steelhead caught.

Use Light Gear

Because summers offer low, clear water in most rivers, lighter terminal tackle is used, and leaders are lengthened to 20 to 30 inches. Summer steelhead are often in fast, white water during the day or when fished hard, because even in deep pools the clear water may not provide enough cover. Summer fishermen prefer 6 to 8 pound test line and "invisible" fluorocarbon leaders. A few split shot rigged on a dropper to slide off if snagged, is often all the weight that's needed for a good presentation. Summer-runs are usually more active than winter fish and will sometimes chase baits. At other times, especially during the heat of the day, you have to hit a fish on the nose to provoke a strike. Sight fishing is common during the summer. Single eggs work well, along with small egg clusters, spinners and spoons. Sand shrimp and nightcrawlers are also effective summer baits. Keep your shadow off the water and cast delicately, summer fish spook easily. Night fishing with glow bobber/bait rigs is sometimes the best way.

Some of the top summer-run rivers are the Columbia and Snake system, Cowlitz, Little White Salmon (Drano Lake), Kalama and Skykomish. Because of ESA listings some of these rivers may not be open or may be seasonally closed. Consult current regulations.

Following are among Washington best summer steelhead streams listed by months in order of their productivity: **SNOHOMISH RIVER SYSTEM**, July-Sept.;**BOGACHIEL**, June, July. **CANYON CREEK**, June. **COLUMBIA**, July, Aug., Sept., Oct. **CASCADE**, May, June. **CLEARWATER**, July. **COWLITZ**, July, June. **DUNGENESS**, June, July. **ELWHA**, July, June, Oct. **GREEN** (King Co.), Sept., June, July, Oct. **HOH**, Sept., Oct., July. **KALAMA**, June, July, May. **KLICKITAT**, Sept., Oct., July, Aug. **LEWIS**, June, July, May. **NORTH FORK LEWIS**, Sept. **EAST FORK LEWIS**, June, July, May. **NOOKSACK**, July. **QUEETS**, Aug., July, Sept. **SAUK**, July, Sept. **SKAGIT**, June, May. **SKYKOMISH**, June, July. **NORTH FORK SKYKOMISH**, Aug. July. **SOUTH FORK SKYKOMISH**, June. **SNAKE**, Oct. **SNOQUALMIE**, June, July. **SOL DUC**, June. **STILLAGUAMISH**, Oct., June. **NORTH FORK STILLAGUAMISH**, June. **WASHOUGAL**, June, May, July. **BIG WHITE SALMON**, Aug., Sept., July. **LITTLE WHITE SALMON/DRANO LAKE** Sept., July, Aug. **WIND**, June, July, Sept., Aug. **WYNOOCHEE**, Aug., July. Often only a few fish will separate a "best" month from a preceding or following month and summer steelhead are in most rivers other months.

Steelhead Drift Fishing Techniques

One of the tough features of winter steelhead fishing is that the big, ocean run rainbows lie in snag country, close to the bottoms of rivers. Tough, because fishermen have to get bait or lures down where the fish live and where the rocks and branches are. This bottom fishing in the steelhead zone takes a heavy toll of terminal gear. At least some of the frustration, loss of gear and time might be avoided by paying more attention to sinker hookups.

Break-away hookup

Many steelheaders use break-away lead hookups exclusively, figuring to give up some lead to save a bobber or spoon. Standard hookup involves a small barrel swivel tied with a jam knot to the end of the line. The leader goes on the other end of the swivel, then a lighter piece of leader material, about three or four inches long, is tied to one of the swivel's (Incidentally—small swivels should be used since large swivels are a source of hang-ups as they jam between rocks.)

A common practice is to allow three or four inches of leader material to extend after tying a jam knot. Hollow core pencil lead, large "cannonball" buck shot or grooved or slotted pencil lead are clamped on the dropper line in both cases. The advantage of the lighter dropper line is that even though the lead won't slip off in some cases when hung up, the light line will break leaving the terminal gear with the fishermen. A disadvantage is that it takes more time.

The trick to clamp on type sinkers is to put them on tight enough so that they won't sail out across the river and into the alders on a cast, but loose enough to slide off when they jam under a grabby rock.

Three-way swivels with surgical tubing tied with dental floss to the hanging arm of the swivel is another method. Pencil lead is inserted in the tubing. This method probably results in more hang ups than the others.

A simplified and the most popular technique of sinkering consists of cutting surgical tubing into one inch pieces, then bending the tubing near one end and cutting a notch with scissors. The main line, just above the swivel, is doubled, pushed down through the notch in the tubing, then brought outside the tubing. This provides a snubber effect. Pencil lead is inserted. A better way is to use a snap swivel on the end of the line, attach the drift tackle leader and mainline to the round eye of the swivel. Open the clasp and run it through one side of the tubing and shut it. This rig will cast long and well, but if it hangs up, a few solid jerks will force the wire clasp to cut through the tubing and save the gear.

Another simple sinker system involves slipping a two inch piece of surgical tubing on the main line above the swivel, then jamming pencil lead into the tubing so that it is parallel to the line. A disadvantage of this system is that your line is more subject to abrasion from the bottom.

Drift Hookups For Steelhead

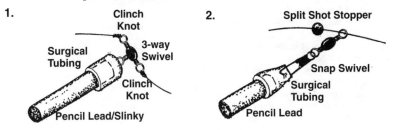

1. Surgical Tubing — Clinch Knot — 3-way Swivel — Clinch Knot — Pencil Lead/Slinky

2. Split Shot Stopper — Snap Swivel — Surgical Tubing — Pencil Lead

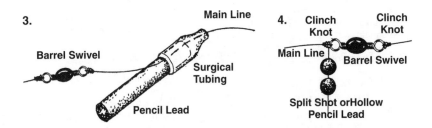

3. Barrel Swivel — Main Line — Surgical Tubing — Pencil Lead

4. Clinch Knot — Clinch Knot — Main Line — Barrel Swivel — Split Shot or Hollow Pencil Lead

5.

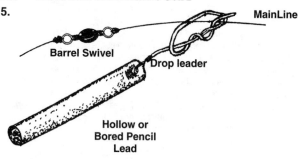

Float Fishing

Canadian steelheaders first developed an effective system of float fishing that is now the rage among their stateside counterparts. The technique involves using a large, color-topped cork or styro-foam float to suspend bait or artificial jigs just off river bottoms.

Advantages of float fishing for steelhead, in addition to the obvious off-the bottom factor, include the ability to extend a drift. By spilling line, anglers are able to keep their float, and the bait under it, working downstream along a fishy looking current thread. When the float reaches a particularly good looking pocket, the float may be "stalled" by lifting the rod tip, thus keeping the bait in the hot spot for those important few more seconds.

Float fishing comes into its own in slow, "soft" water and for bank fishing troughs at your feet. Even though the water is ruffled by wind or current, the brightly colored float may be easily seen and provides an instant signal to a steelhead strike. With conven-

tional steelhead gear, the bait or lure might hang up on bottom in this type of water.

Another plus is that slower water may be thoroughly worked without the hang ups that happen with even the lightest lead when using the bottom-banging technique. The float allows fishermen to keep close track of their bait, since there is little line belly in the short piece of leader between the float and hooks. It also is a visual aid to strikes. When a steelhead takes the bait, the float will go under the surface of the water either partially or all the way. This should tend to make a steelhead fisherman a bit suspicious . Anglers use floats with clusters of salmon eggs (especially for chinook salmon and winter-run steelhead), nightcrawlers, sand shrimp, weighted jigs dressed with scented yarn and marabou, or several inches of bright pink plastic worms.

Long Rods and Level Wind Reels

Experienced float anglers prefer long rods and capable of casting longer distances than is possible with more conventional steelhead gear, enable

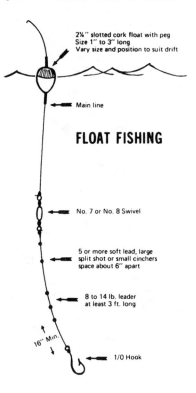

fishermen to keep more line out of the water, reducing slack-line drag. Long rods also make it easier on strikes to sweep out line slack, which is a problem with float fishing, and ram the hooks past the barbs.

Long rods, from 10 1/2 to 13 feet, are used because the floats are fixed on the line and sufficient leader must be tied below them to reach close to the bottom. Thus, when fishing water that is around ten feet in depth, about nine feet of leader, lead and bait dangles under the float which is reeled in close to the rod's tip.

Level wind reels loaded with 15 pound test line are standard for float fishing although some use spinning reels that will hold around 200 yards of 15 pound test line.

How To Rig Floats

Floats are made of cork, plastic or Styrofoam and are three to six inches long. Bright red paint is applied to the top of the float to increase visibility. Floats can be made from wine corks, by drilling a hole through the center. Plastic cocktail straws are slathered with glue and pushed through the hole. Run the fishing line through the straw. Beads slightly larger than the hole in the straw, may be added below the float as stoppers. Leader length can also be adjusted by wedging a toothpick into the straw and pinning the line. Floats should be constantly readjusted to hold the jig or bait just off the bottom.

The line extends from the bottom of the float about two feet, depending upon the depth of water being fished, where a barrel swivel is tied in with a jam knot. A leader sized to depth is tied to the swivel, and jigs, or bait hooks are tied on. Cannon ball split shot is spaced at intervals down the leader to sink the bait. It's also acceptable to use a piece of pencil lead and surgical tubing.

Shrimp, Eggs & Worms

Ghost (sand) shrimp, fished live, are a popular bait. The two hook terminal set-up is particularly suited when using live ghost shrimp. The shrimp is lightly hooked with the top hook near the head, then no-knot line is wrapped around the body securing it to the bottom hook. Single salmon eggs, or soft plastic replicas, threaded onto small, No. 6 baitholder hooks also work well during low water. Few anglers do it, but I have used hooks as small as No. 14 effectively when single egging. Single eggs fit well on these small short-shank hooks which bite deeply and doesn't give the fish any leverage to throw it. Single egging is especially productive when steelhead are spooked or attempting to hide from a high hot sun. Small clusters of fresh eggs, about the size of a fingernail, rolled along the bottom are very hard for aggressive fish to pass up. Attach with an egg loop knot to small hooks ranging from No. 4 to 1. Also try nightcrawlers, hooked once through the head, or bright pink plastic worms hooked once in the midsection so that both ends wiggle.

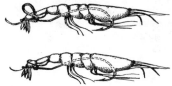

Insert shrimp hook through tail and position point near head. Secure tail to hook shank with a loop knot

River Salmon Fishing

River fishing for salmon is getting tougher in Washington because of dwindling salmon numbers, threatened runs and ESA protections that have stopped or greatly restricted fishing on salmon in their smaller spawning rivers. A solid troll, hogline and plunk fishery continues in the Columbia River downstream from Vernita for spring, summer and fall chinook, and fall coho.

But while river fishing for salmon may have slowed, it is a long way from eliminated, and whenever a season is opened you can expect a lot of enthusiastic anglers. Many southwest counties have spring and fall chinook and coho seasons (especially the Columbia River and its tributaries), Olympic Peninsula rivers generally are open, and seasons are infrequently opened on Puget Sound rivers. In recent years the state has liberalized river fishing for chum salmon attempting to encourage a recreational fishery on what has been a traditional commercial salmon. WDFW also hopes that encouraging chum fishing will in some respect make up for the loss of fishing opportunity on highly prized coho and chinook. Chums are strong, acrobatic fish and definitely worth a shot in the lower rivers. They darken rapidly, however.

Approximately 50 Washington rivers carry significant numbers of salmon and may be open to sport fishing. All 5 Pacific salmon run Washington rivers; including fall and spring chinook (king), coho (silvers), chums (dog) and humpies (pinks), and sockeye. The humpies run only in odd numbered years in state rivers, (except for even year runs in the Hoh, Dosewallips and Duckabush Rivers) while chinook, silvers, and chums make annual runs. There is rarely a river fishery opened for sockeye. Some of the fastest action involves small, aggressive jack chinook and coho. Jacks are 2-year-old salmon always males, which mature early and return to native streams. They are capable of spawning, often are present in large numbers and are much more aggressive than mature 3 to 6 year old salmon.

River Salmon Species

COHO (SILVER) SALMON. Mature in 3 years. Young silvers live in parent rivers about 18 months before migrating to the saltchuck. They spend 18 months in the ocean before making spawning runs at 3 to 30 pounds. Silvers of 14 to 20 pounds are not uncommon. Puget Sound resident silvers are smaller, with adults in the 3 to 6 pound bracket. Silvers enter rivers from July to January and spawn mainly during November and December.

SILVER JACK SALMON. Mature in 2 years. They spend same amount of time in home rivers as do other silvers, but live in the ocean only 4 to 5 months. Weights vary from .05 to 3.5 pounds. Silver jacks enter rivers from September to November.

FALL CHINOOK SALMON. Mature in 3 to 5 years. They spend about 90 days in freshwater before going to sea where they stay until they approach maturity. There is great variance in spawning weights, but most fish are 10 to 35 pounds. In large river systems chinook in the 30 and 40 pound class are not uncommon. Fall chinook enter rivers in August and September and spawn principally during October and November.

CHINOOK JACK SALMON. Mature in 2 years. They live in native river for 90 days, then go to sea until nearly mature. They weigh from 2 to 8 pounds when entering rivers during August and September. Some are heavier.

SPRING CHINOOK. Mature in 4 to 5 years. The springs live in home rivers for about 18 months before migrating to sea where they stay until the spring of their final year. Most weigh from 12 to 30 pounds at spawning. Spring chinook enter rivers from February through May and spawn principally during September.

PINK (Humpy). Mature in 2 years. Fry head for saltwater immediately after wriggling out of the gravel. They spend about 18 months in the ocean. Adults commonly weigh 4 to 8 pounds with some heavier. They spawn in odd-numbered years in Washington, except for even year runs in the Hoh, Duckabush and Dosewallips rivers, entering rivers from July through September. Most pinks spawn during October.

CHUM. Mature in 3 to 5 years. They stay in home rivers for about the same period as pinks and live in saltwater for most of their remaining life. Average spawning weight is about 10 pounds, and spawning occurs from September to December.

SOCKEYE. Mature in 3 to 5 years. Sockeyes leave native streams after hatching, dropping into lakes in the river system where they live for about a year. They live in saltwater until nearly mature. Average spawning weight is 4 to 7 pounds. Sockeyes enter rivers from May to September and spawn in October and November. All Pacific coast salmon, including jacks, die after spawning.

Locating Salmon

Salmon are found in a bit different type water than steelhead. They usually favor slower and deeper runs. Coho and especially pink salmon are often active and can be spotted rolling and jumping in rivers. Chinook may jump, but more commonly roll through the surface leaving bathtub size holes, and chums tend to keep their bellies glued to the bottom. Many fishermen locate rolling fish before settling down to seriously, and patiently pounding the water. Rolling fish tend to be more aggressive than stratified or stacked fish, but there are some big time exceptions to that rule. Generally, the more fish that are stacked in front you, the better the odds are that one of them is a biter. All river salmon seem to go through bite phases. Fishing may be dead for hours and then suddenly for no apparent reason fish are rolling, and rods start going down one after the other. It's not uncommon for this burst of action to start at the top of a pool and progress to the tailout. These spontaneous bites usually shut down as fast they start up, and occur several times a day. The trick is to be there when it happens.

Techniques & Tactics

COHO (Adult). Fish deep, slack water with logs, rocks, over-hanging brush or undercut banks. This is also the type water that holds sea-run cutthroat. Watch for rolling fish and pitch single-hook spinners, winged bobbers or small, thin colorful wobbling spoons. Hot pink, red and fluorescent green are top colors. In slow, pea gravel bottomed water it sometimes pays to rig a Colorado blade, above a single unbaited hook, and jig the light rig along the bottom in front of stacked fish. Silvers will also sometimes pick up egg and yarn offerings. Medium weight steelhead tackle is ideal.

CHINOOK (Adult). Prefer to stack along the breakline dividing heavy current and deep pools. Long sweeping bends are favorite lies. Fish deep and slow. The slower the better. It sometimes takes a lot of aggravation to provoke a chinook strike. Spring chinook are typically more aggressive than fall fish, and may be found a bit higher in the pool. Boaters slowly backtroll plugs, or backbounce large clusters of salmon eggs, sand shrimp, or herring, slowly edging downstream through holding water. Keep the offering within a foot of the bottom. If there's a lot of fish stacked, run back to the top and drift the pool again. From shore, anglers use float-fishing rigs (see how-to story) with silver-dollar size clusters of salmon eggs, winged Spin-n-Glo type bobbers sweetened with eggs or shrimp, and to a lesser degree large spinners, wobbling spoons and egg and yarn setups. In SW Washington rivers fresh prawns are used effectively. Rig to handle 15 to 30 pound s of powerful fish.

PINK These salmon commonly gang in deep pools and are often very active. Tiny wobblers fished deep and slow, will entice them, as will small spinners.

JACKS (Chinook and Coho). The jacks are found with adult salmon, and also frequent riffles. Cluster eggs are probably the most effective bait, but spinners and spoons will take them. Light spinning gear will handle jacks. The salmon provide great sport when taken with tackle geared to their size. Here's where and when to catch them when seasons are opened. Always check current regulations and emergency regulations before fishing for river salmon.

River Salmon Locations & Seasons

BOGACHIEL RIVER. Fall chinook, jack chinook, silvers, jack silvers. October best, September good.

CALAWAH RIVER. Fall chinook, jack chinook, silvers, jack silvers. October best, September good.

CAPITOL LAKE (Olympia). Fall chinook, jack chinook, silvers, jack silvers. September best, October good.

CHEHALIS RIVER. Spring and fall chinook, jack sockeye, chinook, silvers, jack silvers. August best for springs. Fall chinook best in October, with silvers and jacks taken in September, October, November and December. Good late silver fishing. Best fishing below mouth of Satsop River.

CLEARWATER RIVER (Queets tributary). Silver and chinook jacks. Best in September. August and October good.

COLUMBIA RIVER. Fall and spring chinook, silvers. Chinook and silver jacks. Best spring chinook fishing in April. September best for fall chinook. October best for silvers. Salmon are taken from March into November.

COPALIS RIVER. Silvers and silver jacks. October best, September good.

COWLITZ RIVER. Fall and spring chinook and jacks, silvers and silver jacks. Salmon available from April to October. April best for springs. October best for fall salmon.

DESCHUTES RIVER. Chinook jacks. Best in October.

DEWATTO CREEK. Silver jacks. October best.

DOSEWALLIPS RIVER. Silvers and jack silvers. Best in October. Good in September. A few spring chinook in mid summer. Humpies in lower river during both odd and even years.

DRANO LAKE (Mouth of Little White Salmon River). Fall Chinook and jacks. September best, October good.

DUCKABUSH RIVER. Silvers and jack silvers. Best in October, September good. Humpies in lower river odd and even years.

DUNGENESS RIVER. Chinook, silvers, and chums. October best. September and November good. Some spring chinook.

DUWAMISH RIVER. Chinook and silver jacks. October best, September and November good.

GREEN RIVER. Chinook, silvers and chums. October best, September and November good .

HAMMA HAMMA RIVER. Silvers and silver jacks. October best, September good. Humpies in lower river.

HOH RIVER. Fall and spring chinook, chinook jacks, silvers and silver jacks. August best, May and November good.

HOQUIAM RIVER. Chinook jacks, silvers, silver jacks. October best, September and December good.

HUMPTULIPS RIVER. Fall chinook and jacks, silvers and silver jacks. October best, August and December good.

ICICLE CREEK. Spring chinook.

JOHN'S RIVER. Silvers, silver jacks, and summer chinook. October best, September good.

KALAMA RIVER. Fall chinook and jacks, silvers and jack silvers. September best, August and October good.

LAKE SAMMAMISH. Fall Chinook and jacks, silvers and silver jacks. October best, September and November good.

LAKE WASHINGTON. Fall chinook and jacks, silvers and silver jacks. October best, September and November good. Sockeye from June through September.

LEWIS RIVER, N. FORK. Fall chinook and jacks, silvers and silver jacks. Best in September, good in August and October.

NASELLE RIVER. Fall chinook and jacks, silvers and silver jacks. Best in September, good in August and December.

NEMAH RIVER. Chinook and silver jacks. September best, August and November good.

NISQUALLY RIVER. Closed. Jack, chinook, chums, and silvers. September best, August and November good.

NOOKSACK RIVER. Fall and spring chinook, chinook jacks, silvers and silver jacks, humpies. October best, May and November good.

NORTH RIVER. Fall chinook and jacks, silvers and silver jacks. October best, December good.

PUYALLUP RIVER. Chinook, chums, and silver jacks. October best, November good.

QUEETS RIVER. Fall and spring chinook, chinook jacks, silvers and silver jacks. August best, May and October good.

QUILCENE RIVER. Jack chinook and silvers. October best. September, November good.

QUILLAYUTE RIVER. Fall and spring chinook and jacks, silvers and silver jacks. October best, August good.

QUINAULT RIVER. Spring and fall chinook, chinook jacks, silvers and silver jacks, sockeye. October best, June and November good.

SAMISH RIVER. Chinook and silver jacks. October best, September and November good.

SAMMAMISH RIVER. Chums, chinook, sockeye, and silvers. October best, November good.

SATSOP RIVER. Chinook, chums, silvers and silver jacks. December best, August good.

SKAGIT RIVER. Spring and fall chinook, chinook jacks, silvers, silver jacks, humpies. September best on odd-numbered years (big humpy runs). August best on even-numbered years. April and October good.

SKOKOMISH RIVER. Spring and fall chinook. Chinook jacks, silvers, silver jacks, chum. September best for jacks, October good.

SKYKOMISH RIVER. Jacks, chinook, chums, pinks, and silvers. Best in October, good in September.

SNAKE RIVER. Fall and spring chinook, jack chinook. July best, good in May and September.

SNOHOMISH RIVER. Fall chinook and chinook jacks, silvers, silver jacks, pinks, and chums. October best, August and November good.

SNOQUALMIE RIVER. Chinook, chums, and silver jacks. Best in October, good in September and November.

SOL DUC RIVER. Fall and spring chinook, chinook jacks, silvers, silver jacks. October best, September, November and May, June good.

STILLAGUAMISH RIVER. Spring and fall chinook, chinook jacks, silvers and silver jacks, humpies. September best on odd-numbered years due to heavy humpy run. Best in October in even numbered years. July good.

TAHUYA RIVER. Silver jacks. Best in October, poor fishing.

TOLT RIVER. Silver jacks. Best in October.

TOUTLE RIVER. Fall chinook and jacks, silvers, silver jacks. September best, August and October fair.

TUCANNON RIVER. Spring chinook. Best above Marengo in June. May good.

UNION RIVER. Silver jacks. October best

WALLA WALLA RIVER. Chinook, August and September.

WASHOUGAL RIVER. Silvers and silver jacks, fall chinook, chinook jacks. September best, October good.

WILLAPA RIVER. Fall chinook and jacks. Silvers and silver jacks. October best. August and November good.

WISHKAH RIVER. Chinook and silver jacks. October best, September and December good.

WYNOOCHEE RIVER. Chinook jacks, silvers, silver jacks. December best, September good.

YAKIMA RIVER. Spring chinook, fall coho.

Fishing With Eggs

Rigging and Fishing Single Eggs

A single salmon egg bouncing along the bottom of a stream or wavering above a lake floor sometimes seems almost irresistible to trout and summer-run steelhead. How irresistible depends on how well that egg is rigged and fished. Single egging is almost an art form when practiced well, and an abomination when it's not.

Techniques from the pros

Expert trout fishermen using eggs will choose a 7 to 8'1/2 foot fly or spinning rod with a very sensitive tip. They'll hang a single action fly reel or light spinning reel on the rod and load both with 4 to 6 pound test monofilament. Lighter lines, particularly when using a fly rod, may wrap the guides on casts.

Clarity of water will somewhat determine the weight of leaders, which may be as light as one pound test. Generally, the lighter the better. The smaller the diameter the more freedom the bait has for a natural presentation. Leaders of 1 to 3 pound test will handle most situations. If used at all, swivels should be very small-No. 14s. When stillfishing, before tying the line to the swivel, add a small egg shaped slip sinker on the line so that it will slide freely on the mainline, but will stop at the swivel.

Hooks and hookups

Hook sizes range from No. 6 for steelhead to No. 14 for trout. Let the size of the egg, determine the size of the hook. Eggs should cover the point and most of the shank. Use short-shank "egg" hooks, and sharpen with a fine stone.

Salmon eggs are placed on the hook by inserting the point just under the skin of the egg, taking care to make as small an opening as possible. The egg is then worked up the shank and over the eye of the hook, rotated and then pushed back down over the point of the hook. The softest eggs will stay on since the bend of hook cradles the bottom of the egg, during gentle, lob casting.

Strip line from the reel and lay in loose coils on the boat seat or bank. Gently lob casts. When the egg and sinker settle firmly to the bottom, secure the rod in a holder (or forked stick), and reel up all slack so there' a taut line running to the bait. Position the rod so that the tip is high. By watching the point where the line enters the water, and also the rod tip, anglers can tell when trout pick up the egg. The slip sinker allows the trout to pick up the egg and head south without drag. Set the hook.

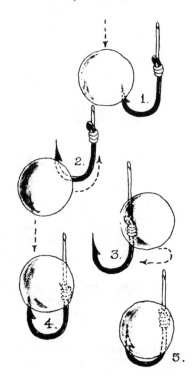

Tactics

Don't fish too long in unproductive lake water. If trout are around they usually find an egg rig within a few minutes. Soak the bait for several minutes while the attractant oils seep into the surrounding water, then retrieve a few inches at a time just enough to activate the egg and catch the attention of fish working up the scent line. Hook disgorgers are in order as trout are often hooked deep with this system. Because of the light leader a soft net is recommended. In streams, use just enough weight to touch bottom and slightly slow the drift. A long leader allows the egg to swing freely, covering a lot of stream bottom. Instead of using the slip sinker recommended for lakes, in streams use a dropper-shot rig. Attach a 4-inch piece of stout monofilament to the swivel and lightly clamp split shot on the line. When the shot hangs up, a smooth, steady pull will usually slide snagged weight off the dropper line, saving the terminal rig.

Putting Up Bait Eggs

Fresh salmon or steelhead eggs are a top bait in the Northwest, whether prepared as clusters for steelhead or salmon, or single eggs for trout, kokanee salmon or summer-run steelhead. Experienced egg-fishing anglers try to avoid baitless days by preserving every skein of eggs they acquire. And, while there are many methods of preserving eggs, the simple way is as effective as any.

Preserving

Separate layers of eggs in the skeins and rub thoroughly with powdered borax. Sprinkle and rub more borax over the outside of the skeins. Wrap each skein separately in absorbent paper towels, then in several layers of newspaper and place in refrigerator to cure. Well wrapped eggs won't smell. How long you refrigerate, depends on how mature the eggs are. Tight skeins require only one day, while juicy eggs from may need three to four days.

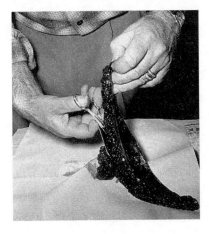

Cluster cuts

After excess moisture has been absorbed by the paper towels and the eggs toughened by the borax, remove the skeins from the refrigerator. Large skeins are cut horizontally into equal sections with scissors, effectively creating four narrow skeins from 2 thick ones. Now, cut the skeins vertically into bait-sized clusters, and be sure that a at least a small strip of membrane is attached to hold the cluster together. Clusters should be about thumbnail size for steelhead baits, twice that for chinook salmon baits. Drop the clusters into powdered borax, roll and shake until completely covered. Be generous with the borax used.

Sprinkle a little borax into a glass jar, fill it to the brim with baits, top with more borax and tightly screw the lid on. Eggs may be stored in a refrigerator for two weeks or frozen. Frozen eggs fish well after a year of freezer life, but once thawed should be used within a week or so.

Sodium Sulfite

Rather than using powdered borax, some anglers prefer the tacky texture of a sodium sulfite cure. Several manufacturers have started marketing sodium sulfite in sporting goods stores, or you can buy it at the pharmacy. Ask for sodium sulfite Merck No. 5201. This is a salt preservative and too much will dry eggs excessively. Sodium sulfite cured eggs will milk well in the water. The clusters are tacky and hold shape better than borax cures. Spread the clusters on a newspaper or stack of paper towels, sprinkle lightly with sodium sulfite, turn over and sprinkle the underside. Allow to air cure (some prefer to cure in the refrigerator) overnight in a cool room. When the eggs reach desirable consistency, bag and either refrigerate or freeze. Sodium sulfite cured eggs may be refrigerated for several weeks between fishing trips, much longer than borax cures. For long term storage I like to enclose a one-day supply of eggs in a small plastic baggy, squeeze out the air, then place that bag into a second bag and vacuum pack. Vacuum packed eggs maintain freshness for a loooong time.

Single eggs

Skeins of large mature, loose eggs—mostly from chinook salmon—can be divided into individual single eggs by lightly forcing through the mesh of a screen or colander. Make sure the mesh size is large enough to accommodate an egg. Six cups of eggs are placed in six cups of cold water to which is added two table spoons of table salt, two tablespoons of borax, two tablespoons of benzoate of soda (pharmacies sell it) and your favorite color of dye. Bring to a slow, rolling boil. Stir constantly and test eggs with a pin every 30 seconds for firmness. When the outer skin becomes tough, but the interior is still soft, remove eggs from the boil and plunge into a container of cold water. When thoroughly chained, drain and pack into eight oz. jars containing one ounce of glycerin. Tightly seal and rotate to coat all eggs with glycerin.

A traditional, on-the-river technique is to strip loose eggs from a ripe female (don't waste the fish) into a can with a bit of water, set the can in the coals of a small fire. When the eggs turn opaque white , they'll stay on a hook and are ready to fish. Don't over cook.

Rigging cluster eggs with steelhead loop knot and yarn.

Specialty Fisheries

Alpine Lakes

High lake fishermen start getting a bit itchy around the first part of June, eye balling the snow, still hanging on the slopes of the Cascades and Olympics Most lakes under 4500 feet will be ice-free and fishable in June higher lakes, especially in the steep cirques of the North Cascades and Olympics may not open until July. Lakes with W. or S. exposures will shed the ice lid first. Sizable streams running in and out of lakes hasten the ice-out time, also. Most high lakes provide good fishing all summer, but snow comes early, often in September. It can snow every month of the year in the mountains.

Early openers

By counties here are some of the high lakes which generally are open, or are partially so, earliest in the season: **KING COUNTY**: Calligan, Dorothy, Hancock. Big Pratt, Granite, Trout, Eagle and Little Eagle. **SNOHOMISH COUNTY**: Airplane, Goat, Isabel, Boardman, Upper Boardman, Ashlands and Island. **WHATCOM COUNTY**: Canyon. **LEWIS COUNTY**: Packwood, Newaukum, Glacier and Backbone. **COWLITZ COUNTY**: Merrill. **SKAMANIA COUNTY**: Goose. **KITTITAS COUNTY**: Manastash, Milk and Lost. **CHELAN COUNTY**: Eight-Mile, Colchuck, Domke, Stuart. **YAKIMA COUNTY**: Lost, Long, Dog and Leech.

Alpine lakes in Mt. Rainier, Olympic and North Cascades national parks usually do not offer open-water fishing until July. September is the best month to fish mountain lakes, but keep an eye on the weather.

Species of fish in Washington's mountain lakes include rainbow, cutthroat, brookies, golden, mackinaw (lake trout) a few Atlantic salmon and grayling.

WDFW has prohibited fishing for grayling which are found in Upper (Big) Granite lake in Skagit county. Grayling plants have been made in King's and Marshall Lakes in Pend Oreille County. Joan Lake in Snohomish County has received Atlantic salmon plants.

Goldens

Golden trout have been stocked in: KING COUNTY. Crawford, Cougar, Edds, Little Hester, Ptarmigan, T'ahl. KITTITAS COUNTY. Glacier, Lemah, Ridge, Summit Chief, Three Queens. CHELAN COUNTY. Choral, Edna, Elsey, Enchanted, King, Rock. OKANOGAN COUNTY. Scheelite. SKAGIT COUNTY. Cyclone, Enjar. SNOHOMISH COUNTY. Bath, Helena, Lime, Sunset. WHATCOM COUNTY. Thornton. NORTH CASCADE NATIONAL PARK. Hidden, Thornton.

Mackinaw

High lakes holding mackinaw include Isabel (Snohomish) and Eight Mile (Chelan). There are also "macks," or lake trout, in such lowland lakes as Deer and Loon in Stevens county; Cle Elum in Kittitas county; and Bonaparte in Okanogan.

There may be a few survivors from largely unsuccessful stockings in Deep (King), Clear (Pierce), Sammamish, Hewitt, St. Clair, Offut, Wallace, Whatcom, Quinault, Pine (King), Keechelus, Kachess, Crescent, Steilacoom, Badger, Chapman, Bear (King), and Black Diamond. Some of these lakes have since been rehabilitated with no signs of lake trout, although there are periodic reports and rumors.

Tiger Muskies

One of Washington's newest and nastiest trophy fish is expanding across the state. Tiger muskies, a sterile hybrid produced from a male northern pike and female muskellunge grow to more than 30 pounds. The hybrid is very much like the true muskellunge in size and appearance and may fight harder. About the only physical difference is that the side stripes on a tiger musky waver. The flesh is white and flaky.

Tigers were first introduced to **Mayfield Lake** on Cowlitz River in 1988 with eggs from Minnesota. The fast-growing fish have already exceeded 30 pounds in Mayfield The fish grew 12 to 18.5 pounds in four years. Tiger musky plants were made into Spokane County's **Newman Lake** in 1992 where some should be over 36 inches, the minimum legal length.

Other lakes with tiger musky plants include a 1995 stocking in **Merwin Reservoir** on Cowlitz County's Lewis River, **Lake Tapps** near Sumner in Pierce County, **Green Lake** in Seattle, **Curlew Lake** in Ferry County, **Redrock Lake** and **Evergreen Reservoir** both in Grant County, and **South Lewis County Park Pond** in Lewis County.

The fish were introduced to state waters through the efforts of WDFW Region 5 biologist Jack Tipping who saw them as a means of controlling Mayfield's huge squawfish and sucker population as well as providing a new trophy fishery. Subsequent testing revealed a substantial reduction in these scrap fish. Because of this welcomed development, rainbow trout are once again being planted in Mayfield from Mossyrock hatchery.

Jack Tipping with 37-inch Tiger Muskie.

While tiger muskies are sterile and cannot reproduce they are voracious predators feeding heavily on squawfish and sucker populations which eat trout and juvenile salmon. Because tigers live and hunt in shallow water there seems to be little if any impact on coldwater species. Although anglers may keep 1-tiger a day (see WDFW regulations) longer than 36 inches most sportsmen release all fish so that they can continue reducing scrap fish numbers and leaving large teeth marks in big, cigar-shaped plugs.

Best fishing periods appear to be afternoons and evenings on hot summer days, fishing near weed beds, sunken logs and grassy reefs. Steel leaders are recommend for these fish because of their sharp teeth. Big lures such as 3/8 oz. bucktail spinners, and noisy 6-inch or longer surface plugs rigged with propellers. These large, noisy lures are cast and retrieved over likely ambush points. The more noise they create, the better. These fish are very aggressive and tough to boat. They can be even tougher to entice, however. Success is generally low for tiger hunters, but the reward—when it comes—will make you smile the rest of the year, maybe longer.

Long term tiger musky action depends on catch-and-release fishing and continued hatchery releases. West side fingerlings are being raised in the Cowlitz and Mossyrock hatcheries and are stocked as 5-inch juveniles. Columbia Basin Hatchery at Moses Lake is raising tiger muskies for release in eastern Washington.

Kokanee Come On in May

Trout fishermen are treated to a second season opener in late May when kokanee (AKA silver trout) a landlocked sockeye salmon, change their preference in food from plankton to more easily imitated insects and other more meaty foods. Until kokanee are about 6 inches long they strain microscopic feed through gill rakers and are difficult to lure to a bait.

Kokanee are 3 or 4 years old and 8 to 14 inches long when their diet switches and they start entering the sport catch. they are most aggressive in May and June which generally offers the best fishing, however in deep, cold lakes the kokanee action will continue right into fall when brightly colored red and green spawners head for natal streams.

Some coho salmon

Most of the "silver trout" planted are kokanee salmon, but a few lakes have been planted with coho salmon. Unlike kokanee, coho salmon go on solid foods early in life, rather than depending upon plankton, and are 2 and 3 year fish when they start nailing baited hooks. Coho range from 6 to 16 inches, with 9 to 12 inches average. Silver salmon do not peak in terms of best fishing period, but provide action from the spring opener into summer. They take worms and eggs and other bait similar to rainbow. The following "how-to" refers to kokanee.

Use soft rods

Soft action rods such as long fly rods with sensitive tips are ideal. Reels should be loaded with 6 to 8 pound test monofilament line. It is important to add about 3 feet of 2 pound test leader and size 10 or 12 single egg hooks. A BB split shot is clamped about a foot above the hook. Add single salmon eggs, maggots, uncased caddis larvae (periwinkles), and worms are used for bait.

Lacking a depth sounder/locator to spot schools begin by lowering the bait to within 6 inches of the bottom, then slowly inch it up until about 15 feet from bottom. When there's a bite, mark the depth, there's a good chance the entire school of salmon is stratified exactly at that depth. Some fishermen actually handline in that first fish so they can mark the depth and return precisely there. Kokanee may be found in up to 70 feet of water.

They are nearly always schooled just below the thermocline which in most lakes is deep in the spring and gradually rises toward the surface as the season progresses. They bite light

Kokanee are very light biters, so the rod tip must be watched very carefully. Most bait fishermen will double anchor their boat to stabilize it against sway, and prop the rod so that it's free of hand movement. Then concentrate on the tip, and set the hook on the first nibble. When in deep water set very hard to offset line stretch. This is where the sweep of a very long rod helps.

In some lakes, like American near Tacoma, Whatcom south of Bellingham, Bumping and Rimrock lakes in Yakima County still fishermen tip a fluorescent whitefish fly with either goldenrod grubs or maggots. Small red salmon eggs (Pautzke Balls O' Fire) are also used with a maggot on a No. 12 egg hook. Often morning hours are most productive for kokanee.

Trolling works, too

Trolling is also effective, and in many lakes the preferred technique. Small gang trolls followed by a leader of about 12 inches with 2 single hooks in No. 8, baited with worms, maggots or single eggs. Downriggers work well, but some anglers prefer the traditional tactic of using leaded line and small, inch-long wobbling spoons. To the leaded line attach 25 feet of 6-pound test monofilament which is tied directly to the end of the leader with a loop knot to maximize lure swing. Leaded line is color-coded so that fishermen may determine exactly how much line is out. The color changes every 25 or 50 feet. A less practiced technique is to troll with salmon weights (banana-shaped) followed by 4-6 feet of leader and a small (4 1/2" long) dodger. Behind the dodger add a 30 inch leader tied to a very small kokanee wobbler spoon. Bright red is a popular lure color.

Vary speed and depth

When trolling blind start shallow and gradually go deeper until you locate the magic stratification zone. Frequent lazy "S" turns and changes in trolling speed often coax kokanee to hit.

Try these landlocked salmon lakes

Landlocked kokanee, and non migratory coho and chinook, by counties, are as follows:

KING COUNTY. Sawyer, Deep, Morton and Wilderness. Lakes Washington and Sammamish kokanee are protected. Bengston Lake has coho (June through July best).

SNOHOMISH COUNTY. Roesiger, Stevens, and Silver. (May through Aug.).

KITSAP COUNTY. Wildcat has coho, (May through July best).

PIERCE COUNTY. American, Alder, Clear, Tapps (May through July best, fall often excellent).

THURSTON COUNTY. Summit, St. Clair, Alder, Ward (May through July best, fall sometimes good).

MASON COUNTY. Cushman, Kokanee, Mason, Devereaux, (best in midsummer).

SKAGIT COUNTY. Cavanaugh, Baker, Shannon. Pass Lake has Atlantic salmon (May through July. Shannon best in October).

WHATCOM COUNTY. Samish, Whatcom, Padden and Toad (May through July best).

ISLAND COUNTY. Cascade, Mountain (May through July best).

CLARK and **COWLITZ COUNTIES.** Yale, Merwin reservoirs, (Mid-summer and fall best).

LEWIS. Mayfield, Riffe has coho and kokanee,

CLALLAM COUNTY. Pleasant, Sutherland, Ozette and Crescent (Mid-summer best).

GRAYS HARBOR COUNTY. Quinault (June-Sept.)

KITTITAS COUNTY. Kachess, Keechelus, Cle Elum and Cooper (June, July best).

CHELAN COUNTY. Lake Chelan kokanee and landlocked chinook; Wenatchee.

OKANOGAN COUNTY: Osoyoss, Bonaparte, Conconully, Upper Conconully, Buffalo

GRANT COUNTY. Long Lake, Billy Clapp (Late spring, summer best). Banks Lake has a remnant kokanee population.

SPOKANE COUNTY. Chapman, (April, May and June).

STEVENS COUNTY. Loon, Deer, Pierre, (June, July best).

PEND OREILLE COUNTY. Bead, Davis, Horseshoe, Sullivan (April and May best).

LINCOLN, STEVENS, FERRY COUNTIES. Lake Roosevelt (Late summer)

YAKIMA COUNTY. Bumping, Rimrock.

Cutthroat Trout

Washington is blessed with an odd assortment of cutthroat trout, providing challenging opportunities from the saltwater to alpine lakes and lowland lakes to desert alkali pits.

Sea-run cutthroat, imperiled by over-fishing, are making a comeback in many areas thanks to several years of restrictive tackle regulations and catch and release quotas. Several traditional sea-run areas, like the Stilliguamish, Forks and Southwest streams and South Puget Sound beaches are enjoing a real surge in catch-and-release sea-run action. Inland, cutthroat are not as heavily stocked as rainbows and browns, but have a devoted following. They are the darling of high-lake fishermen and the Lahontan strain is being expanded into additional Columbia Basin alkali lakes.

A sea-run cutthroat trout's early life is similar to steelhead. They hatch in freshwater, remain in the home stream for two summers, at about 20 months they migrate to sea on a spring freshet. Unlike steelhead, cutts don't roam far, and can generally be caught in the estuary or along the beach not far from their natal stream. In saltwater they feed along gravel beaches, eel grass and near stream mouths Most sea-run cutthroat return to home streams in the fall, usually following the first salmon runs upstream. Their first return to freshwater is usually a feeding run, targeting salmon spawn. Only about 10 percent of the females spawn on their first return to freshwater.

Peak in fall

Cutthroat may enter rivers from the saltchuck every month of the year, but usually do not appear in large numbers until late July or August. The peak is in late September and October. Most spawn by early April, but ripe fish have been caught from January into June.

Landlocked cutthroat vary in appearance from coastal cutts, being chunkier and more colorful. They have fewer black spots, a more prominent red throat slash and are usually darker. Some sea-runs are almost silver and the namesake throat slash is faint.

Fish shallow

Sea-run cutthroat are targeted in fresh and salt water by trolling or casting from or to the beach over a rocky bottom near mouths of streams. In a boat, fishermen are in range as long as they can see the bottom. Typical lures are small spoons, spinners, flies that imitate small candlefish or shrimp, and small herring fished either plug or spinner cut. Since cutthroat often dine on small fish such as bullheads, sand lance, smelt, herring and occasionally salmon fry, sparsely dressed streamer flies are highly effective. In streams the fish prefer slow, snaggy stretches or pools over-hung with brush. Spinner and worm fishing is a standby for both sea run and native cutthroat. Crawfish tails, sucker meat or prawns work great for late evening or night fishing. Stream cutts will also nail large dry flies during grasshopper season. Locate beaver ponds

Some of the finest wild trout fishing in W. Washington is for cutthroat in beaver ponds. Even the smallest stream may have beaver ponds along its length. Fishermen should look for fresh beaver signs, then explore. Patches of dead trees may signal a permanent type pond, since water kills trees after a period. If a beaver pond holds water in late September, the driest month of the year, it is a good prospect. Most major beaver pond systems in W. Washington have at some time been planted with cutthroat (or brookies).

Good fishing areas

Among the better salt water shoreline areas for cutthroat are Hood Canal, Port Gardner, Priest Point, Port Susan, Mukilteo shoreline, beaches along Camano, Whidbey, Bainbridge and Vashon islands. Fox Island, Nisqually Delta, Squaxin Island, Hammersley Inelt, Eld Inlet, and Harstene Island. Many of the inlets and passes in the South Sound with gravel beaches attract sea-runs most of the year.

Promising sea-run rivers include Cowlitz, North, Satsop, Bogachiel, Hoh, Queets, McAllister Creek, Skokomish, Stillaguamish, Skykomish, Samish, and Skagit.

These are some of the best areas, but you can expect to find sea-runs at just about every river or fair sized stream draining directly into saltwater.

Fly fishermen watch for the first hatches of flying ants, then reach for their tackle and head for the river. Spin fishermen should be there with them.

Trout & Kokanee Salmon Rigs

Trolling

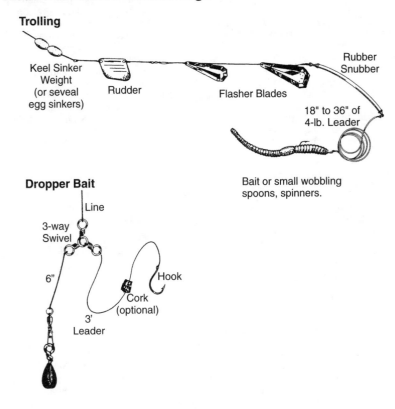

Keel Sinker Weight (or seveal egg sinkers)

Rudder

Flasher Blades

Rubber Snubber

18" to 36" of 4-lb. Leader

Bait or small wobbling spoons, spinners.

Dropper Bait

Line

3-way Swivel

6"

Hook

Cork (optional)

3' Leader

Casting Rigs

Trout & Panfish

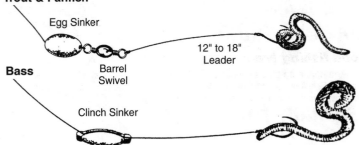

Egg Sinker

12" to 18"
Leader

Barrel
Swivel

Bass

Clinch Sinker

Bobber & Floats

Cinch line to bobber top and bottom.

Bead or knot stopper.

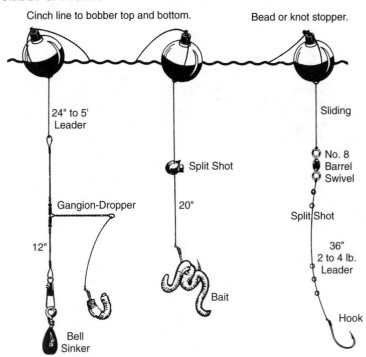

24" to 5'
Leader

Sliding

No. 8
Barrel
Swivel

Gangion-Dropper

Split Shot

Split Shot

20"

12"

36"
2 to 4 lb.
Leader

Bait

Hook

Bell
Sinker

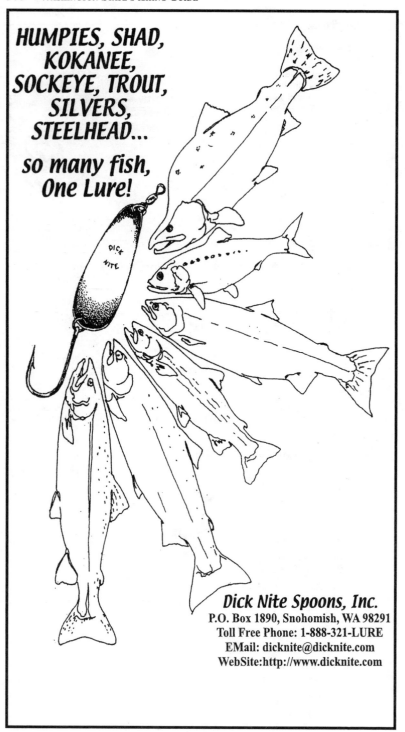

Warm Water Species

Nasty bass, huge walleye, strong catfish, fang-faced tiger muskies and tasty panfish are rapidly expanding through Washington's historically traditional trout country. Both eastern and western Washington now offers tremendous warm water fishing opportunities.

One of the pluses for warm water species is that they start delivering good fishing just about the same time that trout action is tapering off in many lakes. Early summer through early fall are most productive for largemouth, smallmouth, rock and warmouth bass, perch, white and black crappie, bluegill, pumpkinseed, channel and yellow and brown catfish, tiger muskies and walleye. Some lakes also offer ice fishing (See ice fishing story, page 348). Walleye are gaining a huge following by delivering 5 to 15 pounders with amazing regularity, especially in the Columbia River from Vancouver upriver, and in Roosevelt, Moses, O'Sullivan, Banks and Soda lakes.

Largemouth bass.

While largemouth are always a favorite, smallmouth bass have been rapidly expanding in lakes and rivers on both sides of the Cascades. Our chilly waters are proving an ideal habitat for smallmouths 1 to 5 pounds. May and June are top smallie months. Lots of lakes, plus the Yakima, Snake, Columbia and Okanogan rivers. Panfish, especially tasty and aggressive yellow perch are gaining great popularity with fishing families, and in recent years WDFW has been stocking channel catfish—a tough fighter that's great on the table—in many new waters both east and west. The range of tiger muskies has also been expanded on both sides of the mountains. Many of the state's warm water species are generated at the WDFW Columbia Basin Hatchery in Moses Lake.

Warm water lakes and streams

Some of the state's better warm water lakes and streams by counties, include: (See individual county listings for fish species and locations).

ADAMS COUNTY: Black (upper), Butte, Cow, Deadman, Finnel, Green, Hallin, Linda, Royal, Sprague.

BENTON COUNTY: Mitchell Pond, Mound Pond, Palmer Pond, Switch Pond, Yellepit Pond, below Prosser Dam, Umatilla, Wallula.

CHELAN COUNTY: Antilon, Dry (Grass), Entiat, Fish, Meadow, Pateros, Rock Island Pool, Three Lakes Reservoir, Wapato.

CLALLAM COUNTY: Beaver.

CLARK COUNTY: Columbia River sloughs, Lacamas, Lancaster, Long, Mud, Post Office, Round, Vancouver, Widgeon.

COLUMBIA COUNTY: Bryan (Little Goose).

COWLITZ COUNTY: Horseshoe, Kress, Mayfield, Riffe, Sacajawea, Silver.

DOUGLAS COUNTY: Rufus Woods.

FERRY COUNTY: Curlew, Roberta.

FRANKLIN COUNTY: Clark Pond, Dalton, Emma, Herbert G. West, Kahlotus, Mesa, Scootney, Worth.

GRANT COUNTY: Alkali, Ancient, Banks, Billy Chinook, Stratford, Crater,

Crescent, Crescent Bay, Evergreen, Flat, Frenchman Hills, Goose, Long, Mallard, Moses, Potholes (O'Sullivan), Priest Rapids, Roosevelt, Sand, Soda, Stan Coffin, Thompson, Trail, Wanapum, Williams, Willow, Winchester.

GRAYS HARBOR COUNTY: Duck.

ISLAND COUNTY: Cranberry, Deer, Pondilla.

JEFFERSON COUNTY: Crocker, Gibbs, Leland, Ludlow, Sandy Shore, Upper Twin.

KING COUNTY: Angle, Beaver, Bitter, Boren, Desire, Doloff, Fenwick, Green, Haller, Horseshoe Slough, Janicke Slough, Killarney, Larsen, Leota, Meadowbrook, Meridian, Phantom, Pine, Reid Slough, Round, Rutherford Slough, Sammamish, Sawyer, Shadow, Sikes, Spring, Star, Steel, Stickney Slough, Tradition, Twelve, Union, Walker, Washington, Wittenmeyer.

KITSAP COUNTY: Fairview, Flora, Horseshoe, Island, Kitsap, Koeneman, Long, Ludvick, Mission, Panther, Square, Tahuya, Wildcat, Wye.

KITTITAS COUNTY: Fio Rito, McCabe Pond, Sorensen Pond, Woodhouse Ponds.

KLICKITAT COUNTY: Chamberlain, Locke, Rowland.

LEWIS COUNTY: Airport, Carlisle, Davis, Mayfield, Riffe, Swofford.

LINCOLN COUNTY: Coffee Pot, H, Icehouse, Tanwax, Wall, Wederspahn.

MASON COUNTY: Blacksmith, Camp Pond, Collins, Cushman, Forbes, Hanks, Isabella, Island, Jiggs, Limerick, Lost, Mason, Nahwatzel, Simpson, Spencer, Stump, Tee, Trails End, West.

OKANOGAN COUNTY: Bonner, Buck, Duck, Indian Dan, Osoyoos, Palmer, Whitestone, Washburn.

PACIFIC COUNTY: Black, Breaker, Clam, Cranberry, Deer, Freshwater, Gile, Island, Litschke, Loomis, Lost, Skating, Tape, Tinker.

PEND OREILLE COUNTY: Boundary Reservoir, Box Canyon Reservoir, Davis, Chain.

PIERCE COUNTY: American, Bonney, Chambers, Florence, Forest, Harts, Little Harts, Kapowsin, Louise, Ohop, Rapjohn, Silver, Spanaway, Steilacoom, Tanwax, Tule, Wapato, Whitman.

SAN JUAN COUNTY: Egg, Hummel, Killebrew, Sportsman.

SKAGIT COUNTY: Beaver, Big, Campbell, Cannery, Caskey, Clear, Cranberry, McMurray, Minkler, Mud, Whistle.

SKAMANIA COUNTY: Ashes, Bass, Franz, Grant.

SNOHOMISH COUNTY: Ballinger, Beecher, Bosworth, Bryant, Cassisy, Chain, Connor, Crabapple, Crescent, Flowing, Gissberg Ponds, Goodwin, Hall, Kellogg, Ketchum, Ki, Loma, Little Martha, Roesiger, Ruggs, Scriber, Shoecraft, Stevens, Stickney, Sunday, Thomas, Tomtit, Winters.

SPOKANE COUNTY: Bear, Chapman, Clear, Downs, Eloika, Horseshoe, Liberty, Long, Medical, Newman, Queen Lucas.

STEVENS COUNTY: Deer, Jump-Off-Joe, Loon, Pierre, Waitts.

THURSTON COUNTY: Alder, Bald Hill, Barnes, Bass, Bigelow, Black, Chambers, Coopers Potholes, Deep, Elbow, Fifteen, Gehrke, Grass, Hewitt, Hicks, Long, Munn, Offut, Patterson, Pitman, Reichel, Scott, Simmons, Smith, St. Clair, Summit, Susan, Trosper, Ward.

WALLA WALLA COUNTY: Burbank Slough, Casey Pond, Curlew Pond, Sacajawea.

WHATCOM COUNTY: Barrett, Cain, Fazon, Green, Jorgenson, Judson, Mosquito, Mud, Samish, Tennant, Terrell, Weiser, Whatcom.

WHITMAN COUNTY: Lower Granite, Rock.

YAKIMA COUNTY: Berglund, Bridgeman Pond, Byron Pond, Giffin, Granger Pond, Horseshoe Pond, I-82 Ponds, Morgan Pond, Rotary, Yakima River.

Dennis Clay (left) is happy with his "small" sturgeon.

Tackling Dinosaurs: Sturgeon

One of the hottest evolving fisheries in the state is concentrated on the Columbia River's white and green sturgeon. While the lower Columbia and to a lesser degree the Snake rivers attract most of the fishing pressure, there's also respectable sturgeon fishing in the lower Chehalis, Naselle and Willapa rivers. White sturgeon are found in the Columbia, Snake, Chehalis, Naselle and Willapa rivers, with the greens, which prefer a saltier environment, taken in the mouth of the Columbia and in the Grays and Willapa rivers.

Both are caught from anchored boats or plunking from the bank in known sturgeon holes with fresh meat baits tethered to sliding sinkers. Popular baits are smelt, shad, sand shrimp, lampreys, nightcrawlers and large clumps of salmon eggs. Whites are big

The whites are largest of the two—historically reaching up to 20 feet and 1800 pounds. Today, there are still a lot of 8 to 12 foot whites hooked, especially in the June and July catch-and-release oversize fishery between Washougal and Bonneville Dam. Whites are considered better eating than the greens, which commonly reach 7 feet and 350 pounds. Whites migrate freely between fresh and salt water and ascend rivers to spawn in spring. Land-locked whites are in the upper Columbia and Snake Rivers.

Sturgeon are bottom feeders in fresh water, eating mollusks and crustaceans, along with smelt, shad, lampreys, trout and salmon smolts. The fish, which are representatives of an ancient group of fish, has a boneless skeleton made up of cartilage. They grow very slowly, and do not reach spawning age until about 6 feet long, in the case of whites. Washington has had a slot limit for catch-and-keep fishing

STURGEON GEAR

HOOK SIZE 6/0

BARREL SWIVEL

PYRAMID SLIP SINKER

SMELT BAIT

of between 42 and 60 inches to protect immature fish and adult spawners. The most productive catch-and-keep water is near Astoria-Ilwaco at the mouth. The Bonneville Dam area offers fewer fish within the slot limit, but the best opportunity for hooking a monster possibly 12 feet long. Best monster fishing is during the shad run.

The Chehalis and Naselle fisheries are largely overlooked, but can be extremely productive. Both offer shallow-water fishing, less than 10 feet deep in some instances, and light gear opportunities. In the Columbia, powerful water flows may require a pound or two of lead to hold bottom, especially when using large baits like a slab of shad. In the Chehalis and Naselle you can hold bottom with just a few ounces. Rig all weights to slide so there's no resistance when a sturgeon picks up the bait.
Taken all year

Sturgeon may be caught on a year around basis, but usually the best period is from late fall through spring. Tackle is stout—60 pound test line is common with 10 to 32 ounces of lead. Most fishing is done in deep holes, with the bait left to "soak" until a sturgeon picks it off the bottom. Ghost shrimp, in addition to smelt or herring, are used in tidal areas. Surprisingly, to many first-timers sturgeon are great jumpers. It's not at all rare, even for the monsters, to have fish come completely out of the water several times during the fight. They also free jump, soaring above the river like suspended logs.

Sturgeon guides are available year-round on the Columbia Rive, and can be contacted through sporting goods dealers or charter offices in the Vancouver, Portland and Ilwaco areas.

Ice Fishing

Ice fishing in Washington can be divided into two techniques—fishing through ice and fishing around the ice.

Because of our largely mild climate Ice fishing can, but doesn't necessarily mean going out on the ice, spudding out a ragged hole and fishing with bait or jigs.

Many popular winter fishing spots barely freeze over, or leave big areas of open water. This gives the angler with a car topper the chance to break through thin shore ice, or cast from the bank. But some winters bring 6 inches of ice early in-November and it lasts until late March.

In recent years WDFW has made a concerted effort to improve ice fishing opportunities and rewards in the Columbia Basin and Okanogan lakes, especially in the Winthrop/Twisp area where several very good trout lakes are now limited to catch-and-release in the summer then opened to catch-and-keep in the winter when the fish have had a summer to fatten.

Also, several lakes in the basin, especially the Medicare Beach area of O'Sullivan Reservoir and the south end of Banks Lake, are evolving into excellent big trout, open water winter fisheries for the hardy.

One thing for sure, winter trout fishing is gaining speed in central and eastern Washington. The Winthrop area, a long-time spring trout honey hole, is now emerging as an ice fishing hot spot because of WDFW's efforts to expand winter sport fishing opportunities. See current regs. for winter seasons.

Lures and methods

In a few frozen waters, panfish, especially perch, are targeted, but in most lakes it's rainbow trout. Techniques have broadened in the past couple of years. Once most ice anglers still fished bait, sometimes off a bobber. This still works, of course.

Jigging is gaining ground, though.

Ice fishing is gaining popularity.

Most any small (1/8 ounce) jig will work, especially if touched up with a piece of worm or fish eye.

Some jig with small, bright spoons such as the Swedish Pimple, Triple Teazer or midget spinners. Some jig wet flies, tied with an under-body or lead wire to make then sink quickly. Deep purple is a favorite winter color.

Maggots and earth worms are always good ice fishing bets. Other proven natural baits are single red salmon eggs and natural grubs. One of my favorites is a grub that over winters in the center of bulb-shaped galls on goldenrod stalks. It seems to be irresistible to every species targeted by ice fishermen.

Lots of anglers are convinced that Power Bait is impossible to beat. The scented concoction is packed into the tines of a No. 12 treble hook tied 12 to 20 inches below a sliding egg sinker. The floating bait bobs at eye level with every feeding trout that cruises along the nearby bottom hunting for nymphs and other natural goodies.

Winter baits and lures nearly always produce best when fished just off the bottom. Summer trout sometimes stratify and orient to temperature and oxygen bands, but winter trout are bottom oriented.

Impale a piece of bait on the hook of an a 1/32 to 1/8 oz. ice fishing lure, such as a small panfish jig, Swedish Pimple, Kastmaster spoon, crappie spoon or Colorado spinner and slowly bounce it up and down just above the bottom. The movement attracts feeding trout, and the bait triggers the strike. The trick to jigging for ice trout is to bounce the lure slowly pausing for a second or two at the end of each drop. Quick jigging motions are rarely as productive as a slow, deliberate bounce. Cold water trout nearly always take when the bait hangs stationary during the pause at the bottom of the drop. Rarely do you feel any pressure until the rod tip flips upwards setting the hook.

Both trout and panfish are caught on unbaited jigs and tiny thin blade spoons, but the catch count seems to go up when the lure is sweetened with a bit of protein.

You should have, but don't need, a special, short rod for fishing through the ice. Anything from a 9 foot fly rod to a 5 foot bass casting rod will work. However, short spinning rods are the most convenient, easy to use and in ultra-light weights are just plain fun. A few stores are marketing ice fishing rods. Also, a good rod can be made from a broken spinning rod. Cut off the rod just in front of the grip, insert the thin tip end of the rod and glue. You'll windup with a 3-foot, ultra light with a reel seat.

If using a bobber, there's not much need for a rod with a sensitive tip. A broom stick will do. But without a bobber, a rod with a very sensitive tip is a great help, which means one of graphite.

Bobbers come in all sizes, shapes and weights. Most ice anglers like quill or vertical type bobbers — those in which the "stick" is suspended vertically. these give a tip-off to the bite better than round bobbers. My winter tackle box is filled with round bobbers, and they work, too, so go ahead and use a round bobber if that is all you have at hand.

Bait for winter fish is usually worms, salmon eggs, corn or maggots. Perch eyes work beautifully, as do strips of perch meat, cut into angle-worm configuration. Don't forget the maggots and meal grubs.

Easiest way to get a perch eye is not to dig it out with the point of a knife but "pop" it out with the bent end of a large paper clip.

Ice drilling

Axes are commonly used, but are the most inefficient way to chop ice holes. Augers are best. Popular blade sizes are 4, 6 and 8 inch. Six inch holes are perfect, large enough to skate a fish out, and too small to fall through. A heavy iron spud bar can also be used to open a hole, and in a popular area, it's often just as easy to re-open a frozen hole. You'll need an ice skimmer to fish out ice chips.

Packing equipment

Snow sleds are perfect for getting equipment out on the ice. Pack most of the gear in 5 gallon plastic buckets, and use the bucket for a seat or rod prop. Folding camp stools and propane heaters are handy.

Reels and line important

Closed face spinning reels are not a good choice for winter fishing because they trap water inside and may freeze. Open-face spinning reels work best, but fly reels lined with monofilament and small level wind casting reels work. Berkley markets an "Ice" or "Cold Weather" line, which tends to remain flexible when cold.

Fish finders help

A portable depth/fish finder is helpful to locate fish without drilling lots of prospector holes. Most locators can "shoot through" a foot of clear ice. A school of perch can stay in an area for several hours, or move off after a few minutes. There's no sense in waiting at a hole after the school has left. Circle until the school is re-located, drill new holes and fish.

Other considerations

Safe ice should be 4 inches thick, hard and clear. Carry a boat seat cushion tied to at least 50 feet of rope so if someone goes through the ice it's possible to heave a line. If not, you've got a cushion to sit on.

Something warm to drink (coffee, tea, hot chocolate) helps to ward off the chills, and hot soup warms the bones for hours.

Waterproof footwear is a must. This usually means insulated boot-pacs. Rubber boots get cold, and soles on leather hunting boots can be slippery on ice. The nicest days to fish through the ice are sunny and without wind. On some lakes, such as Waitts in Stevens county and Bead in Pend Oreille County, a lot of ice fishing takes place at night. Take a fuel lantern that provides both light and heat.

Snow cover on the ice seems to help the bite.

Top Ice Fishing Lakes

These are some of the top ice-fishing lakes in Washington. Some of the most productive lakes have two seasons, a summer season when catch-and-release fishing (*c&r) is allowed and a more liberal winter season for ice fishing.

During the special winter seasons, on most lakes, general state rules apply including a five-fish daily limit and the use of barbed hooks and bait. These regulations change annually and it's a good idea to review current regulations before heading out. Many year-round lakes also offer excellent winter fishing.

OKANOGAN COUNTY:

Little Twin Lake, Dec. 1-Mar. 31, summer c&r Apr. 1-Nov. 30

Campbell Lake, Sept. 1-Mar. 31; summer c&r Apr. 1-Aug. 31

Cougar Lake Sept. 1- Mar. 31

Davis Lake, Sept. 1- Mar. 31; summer c&r Apr. 1-Aug. 31.

Green Lake, Dec. 1- Mar. 31; summer c&r Apr. 1-Nov. 30

Lower Green Lake, Dec. 1 - Mar. 31, summer c&r Apr. 1- Nov. 30

Rat Lake, Dec. 1 - Mar. 31, summer c&r Apr. 1- Nov. 3

ADAMS COUNTY:

Fourth of July Lake, Dec. 1- Mar. 31,

STEVENS COUNTY:

Hatch Lake, Dec. 1- Mar. 31,

Williams Lake, Dec. 1- Mar. 31

SPOKANE COUNTY:

Hog Canyon Lake, Dec. 1- Mar. 31

YAKIMA COUNTY:

North Elton Pond, Dec.1 - Mar. 31

(* c&r denotes catch-and-release restrictions)

Secret Sauce Fish Barbecue

So you've caught a hatchery steelhead or salmon and you want a real special way to put it on the table. Try this.

Prepare the fish

Sharpen the knife and make a cut along the gill cover as deep as the backbone, then using a limber fillet blade carefully work the blade of along the backbone. Turn the fish over and repeat. You should come up with two nearly boneless slabs.

If the barbecue event is a week or more away, break out a cake pan, add the fillets and fill the pan with water, covering all the fish and freeze. After the fish and water freezes give the pan a sharp rap and pull it free of the block. Stack the block of fish in the freezer.

Remove the fish from the freezer the night before B-Day and lay in a supply of heavy duty aluminum foil and charcoal briquettes. Fire up the barbecue well in advance, making sure that hot coals cover the bottom. Now comes the secret part.

Secret sauce

The barbecue sauce made in advance like this:

One and one-half pound of margarine, 1 cup water, 1 1/2 cup tomato juice, 1/3 T. dry mustard, 3/4 T. salt, 3/4 T. sugar, 3/4 T. chili powder, 1/2 T. Worcestershire sauce, 1.2 T. Tabasco, 3/4 T. black pepper, 1 T. paprika, 1/4 cup vinegar, 1 grated onion, 1 clove garlic. Combine all ingredients and simmer for 30 minutes. Make a double or triple batch if desired and freeze the excess. The sauce freezes well.

This is a Cowboy Sauce concocted by Mrs. Herb Angle of Shelton, Wash.

Cooking method

Make an aluminum foil dish the same size as the top of your barbecue unit, forming a lip of an inch or more all around so that all juices will be retained. Then cut the fish into serving pieces. Grease the grill then place the fish fillets flesh side down on the grill close to the coals. The idea is to achieve a quick sear job.

When those chunks of fish have browned nicely, use a flapjack turner and place them, flesh side up, in the foil pan you've fashioned. Then raise the grill away from the coals and place the pan back over the fire. The fillets should have cracks from the fast searing. Baste the Cowboy Sauce over the fish and into the cracks. Keep spooning. You can't get enough of this sauce over and into the fish. With the cracks in the fillets it is easy to determine when the fish is done. Don't overcook it.

Serve with garlic bread, corn on the cob, fruit or tossed salad. Enjoy!

Where The Hatcheries Are

Since the first Washington salmon hatchery was built in 1895 along the Kalama River, and the first trout hatchery in 1903 at Lake Chelan, Washington Department of Fish and Wildlife has developed the largest network of fish hatcheries in the world, producing salmon, steelhead, trout and a limited number of bass, perch, catfish and walleye.

Washington hatcheries produce 75 percent of all coho and chinook and 88 percent of all steelhead. The state operates 24 complexes with more than 90 rearing facilities.

Most of the hatcheries are open to self guided tours and salmon hatcheries provide a great opportunity in the fall to take the kids where they can see the spawning process, and watch mature coho, chinook, sockeye, chums and pinks. Often the hatcheries have a retaining dam that the salmon will repeatedly try to jump. It's a good show in September and October.

Rivers with direct hatchery releases also tend to be the most productive for salmon and steelhead sports fishing.

WDFW Hatchery Locations

Baker Lake at Baker Lake

Beaver Creek, Cathlamet, steelhead

Bigham Creek, Elma

Bogachiel River, Forks, steelhead

Cedar River, Auburn

Columbia Basin Moses Lake, Warm-Water Species

Columbia River Eastbank Lincoln Rock, Wenatchee

Columbia River Priest Rapids Dam, Beverly, salmon

Columbia River Ringold Springs, Mesa, steelhead

Columbia River, Rocky Reach, salmon

Columbia River Wells Dam, Pateros, trout, steelhead

Colville River, Colville, trout

Coulter Creek, Belfair

Cowlitz River, Winlock, trout

Cowlitz River, Salkum, salmon,

Cowlitz River, Mossyrock, steelhead

Deschutes River Tumwater Falls, Olympia

Dungeness River, Sequim, salmon

Eells Springs, Shelton, trout

Elochoman River, Cathlamet, steelhead

Elwha River, Port Angeles, salmon

Goldendale at Goldendale, trout

Grays River, Grays River, salmon

Green River Palmer Ponds, steelhead

Green River Soos Creek Auburn, salmon

Hoodsport, Hood Canal, salmon

Humptulips River, Humptulip, salmon

Hurd Creek, Sequim, salmon

Issaquah Creek, Issaquah, salmon

Kalama River Falls, Kalama, salmon

Kalama River, Fallert Creek, steelhead

Kendall Creek, Deming,

Klickitat River, Glenwood,

Lake Aberdeen, Aberdeen,

Lake Chelan, Chelan, trout

Lake Samish, Burlington, kokanee

Lake Whatcom, Bellingham, kokanee

Lake Whatcom, Sedro Woolley, salmon

Lewis River N. Fork, Woodland, salmon

McAllister Creek, Olympia, trout

McKernan, Shelton

Merwin Reservoir, Ariel,

Merwin Reservoir, Speelyai Bay, kokanee

Methow River, Winthrop, salmon

Naches River, Naches, steelhead

Naselle River, Naselle, salmon

Nemah River, South Bend, salmon

Okanogan River, Omak, trout

Puget Sound Fox Island, Fox Island, salmon

Puget Sound Peale Pass Net Pens, salmon

Puget Sound, Hupp Springs, Gig Harbor, salmon

Puget Sound, Minter Creek, Gig Harbor, salmon

Puyallup River, Puyallup, salmon

Sauk River, Darrington, salmon

Sherman Creek, Kettle Falls, trout

Similkameen River, Oroville, trout

Skagit River Barnaby Slough, Rockport, steelhead

Skagit River Marblemount, salmon

Skagit River, Arlington, steelhead

Skokomish River George Adams, Shelton, salmon

Skookumchuck River, Tenino, steelhead

Skykomish River Reiter Ponds, Goldbar, steelhead

Skykomish River, Goldbar, salmon

Snake River Lyons Ferry, Starbuck, steelhead

Snoqualmie River Tokul Creek, Fall City, steelhead

Sol Duc River Bear Springs, Beaver, steelhead

Sol Duc River Shale Creek, Beaver, salmon

Spokane River West, Spokane, trout

Spokane River-Long Lake, Ford, trout

Toutle River, North Fork, Toutle, steelhead

Tucannon River, Pomeroy, trout

Turtle Rock, Wenatchee

Vancouver at Vancouver, trout

Voights Creek, Orting, salmon

Wallace River, Sultan, salmon

Washougal River (N. Fork) Washougal, steelhead

Washougal River aboveWashougal, salmon

Willapa River Forks Creek, Raymond, salmon

National Fish Hatcheries

Big Quilcene River at Quilcene, salmon

Entitat River at Entiat, salmon

Icicle Creek at Leavenworth, salmon

Little White Salmon River at Willard and mouth at Columbia R., salmon

Makah Waatch River at Neah Bay, salmon

Methow River at Winthrop, salmon

Quinault River, near Amanda Park, salmon

Spring Creek, Columbia River near White Salmon, salmon.

Wind River at Carson, salmon

Stripping eggs from a salmon at the Willapa River Forks Creek hatchery.

Appendix

Lakes Of Washington

A

LAKE	COUNTY	ACRES	DRAINAGE	ELEVATION	LOCATION
ABERDEEN	Grays Hbr	64	Chehalis R	22	6.5 mi W Montesano
ABERNATHY	Okanogan	4	Methow R	6300	1.5 mi SE Lamont Lk
ABIEL	King	1.5	Nf Cedar R	430	.05 mi SE Annette Lk
ACKER	Skamania	1.5	Nf Lewis R	4650	.03 mi S Bear Lk
ADELAIDE	Pierce	6.8	Wf White R	4584	9 mi N Mt Rainier
ADS	Okanogan	5	Kettle R	3650	1 mi SE Fields Lk
AENEAS	Okanogan	61	Okanogan R	1350	4 mi SW Tonasket
AFRICAN	Skamania	21	Green R	4653	5 mi N Spirit Lk outlet
AGNES	Chelan	7	Stehekin R	6364	8.5 mi SW High Bridge G.S.
AIRPLANE	Chelan	10	White R	5350	32 mi NW Leavenworth
AIRPLANE	Snohomish	2	Skykomish R	3050	3.5 mi SW Gold Bar
AIRPLANE	Snohomish	2.5	Suiattle R	3600	7.5 mi E Darrington
AIRPORT	Lewis	4	Chehalis R	175	2.5 mi S Centralia
AIRPORT PD	Whatcom	2	Bellingham Bay	145	Bellingham Airport
AIRVIEW	Okanogan	5	Chewack R	6200	31.5 mi N Winthrop
ALASKA	Kittitas	35	Yakima R	4230	4 mi NE Snoqualmie Pass
ALBERT	King	1.5	Green R	3100	1.7 mi E Goat Mtn
ALDEN	Okanogan	12	Kettle R	3900	5 mi NW Chesaw
ALDER RES	Pierce	3931	Nisqually R	1207	5 mi S Eatonville
ALDERMAN	Spokane	11	Crab Cr	2360	9 mi W Cheney
ALDRICH	Mason	9	Hood Canal	520	1.5 mi S DeWatto
ALDWELL RES	Clallam	204	Elwha R	321	6 mi W Port Angeles
ALEXANDER	Kitsap	19.5	Sinclair Inlet	238	4 mi SW Bremerton
ALICE	Chelan	4	Wenatchee R	6500	12 mi NW Leavenworth
ALICE	King	33	Raging R	875	2.5 mi S Fall City
ALKALI	Grant	308	Lenore Lk	1085	9 mi N Soap Lake
ALKALI	Spokane	96	Palouse R	2270	9.5 mi SW Cheney
ALLEN	Pierce	5	Nisqually R	4596	4 mi W Longmire
AL'S	King	4.5	Ef Foss R	4600	W Necklace Valley
ALSOP SLOUGH	Chelan	10	White R	1975	6.5 mi NW Lk Wenatchee
ALTA	Okanogan	187	Columbia R	1163	2 mi SW Pateros
AMERICAN	Pierce	235	Puget Sound	1125	8 mi SW Tacoma
AMERICAN	Yakima	3.5	Sf American R	5260	2700' NW Little Cougar Lk
AMES	King	80	Snoqualmie R	240	2 mi W Carnation
AMES POTHOLE	King	1	Snoqualmie R	306	2100' NW Ames Lk
AMES	Lincoln	29	Palouse R	2190	7 mi NE Sprague
AMY	Okanogan	3.5	Okanogan R	1900	3 mi NW Riverside
ANDERSON	Jefferson	59	Pt Townsend Bay	250	.5 mi W Chimacum
ANDERSON	King	2	Taylor R	4500	1.4 mi NE Marten Lk
ANDERSON	Lewis	8	Nisqually R	3900	4.5 mi S Ashford
ANDERSON	Pend Oreille	15	Pend Oreille R	2550	7 mi SE Ione
ANDERSON	Whatcom	2.5	Fraser R	500	5 mi NW Kendall
ANDERSON LKS (4)	Whatcom	1-4	Baker R	5000	1 mi NW Mt Watson
ANDREW	Okanogan	10	Okanogan R	2292	2.5 mi S Conconally
ANGELES	Clallam	20	Juan De Fuca	4196	8 mi S Port Angeles
ANGELINE	King	198	Wf Foss R	5100	9.5 mi S Skykomish
ANGELINE	Snohomish	4	Sauk R	3270	3 mi E Darrington
ANGLE	King	102	Green R	370	12 mi S Seattle
ANN	Kittitas	3	Cle Elum R	6156	19 mi N Cle Elum
ANN	Whatcom	6	Baker R	4700	2 mi W Mt Shuksan
ANNA	Yakima	3	Naches R	4800	1900' N Crow Cr Lk
ANNETTE	King	18	Sf Snoq R	3620	5.5 mi SW Snoq Pass
ANSALDO	Stevens	15	Columbia R	3050	6.25 mi W Northport
ANTILON	Chelan	96	Lk Chelan	2327	10.5 mi NW Chelan
APEX	Ferry	3	FDR Lk	2020	4 mi S Inchelium
APPLE	Yakima	9	Tieton R	5060	7.5 mi NE White Pass
ARBUTHNOT	Whatcom	5	Nk Nooksack R	4800	2 mi W Mt Baker Lodge
ARMSTRONG	Columbia	1	Tucannon R	2400	4 mi S Tac Game Range
ARMSTRONG	Mason	4	Hood Canal	650	3 mi NE Eldon
ARMSTRONG	Snohomish	31	Stilly R	135	2.5 mi N Arlington
ARROW	King	5	Puget Sound	265	2.5 mi S Burien
ARROWHEAD	Skagit	15	Cascade R	4500	9.5 mi SE Marblemount

LAKE	COUNTY	ACRES	DRAINAGE	ELEVATION	LOCATION
ASHLAND LKS (2)	Snohomish	7-13	Pilchuck R	2870	5 mi SE Verlot R.S.
ATHEARNS PD	Whatcom	5 Sf	Nooksack R	450	4 mi SE Saxon
ART	Yakima	2	Tieton R	5230	1400' W Hill Lk
ARTESIAN	Grant	32	Crab Cr	1236	4.5 mi E Gloyd
ASOTIN DAM RES	Asotin	3900	Snake R	842	Town of Asotin
ATKINS	Douglas	140	Jameson Lk	2370	5.5 mi SW St Andrews
AGUSTA	Chelan	26	Wenatchee R	6750	9 ml NW Leavenworth
AUSTIN PASS	Whatcom	1	Nf Nooksack R	4950	1300' N Austin Pass
AUVIL PD	Island	1	Puget Sound	200	S portion Whidbey 191
AVALANCHE	King	3	Mf Snoq R	3780	2600 SW Burnt Boot Lk
AZURE	Whatcom	89	Skagit R	4200	6.5 mi N Newhalem
AZURITE	King	44	Wf Foss R	5100	9.4 mi S Skykomish

B

LAKE	COUNTY	ACRES	DRAINAGE	ELEVATION	LOCATION
B & W	Skamania	1.5	Columbia R	950	RB 5 mi W No Bonneville
BABCOCK RIDGE	Grant	20	Columbia R	1258	3.5 mi W Quincey
BACKBONE	Lewis	3.5	Cowlitz R	2050	6 mi NE Packwood
BADGER	Spokane	244	Palouse R	2180	8.5 mi S Cheney
BADGER	Skamania	2.5	Muddy R	5000	10.5 mi E Spirit Lk inlet
BAGLEY LKS (2)	Whatcom	9-11	Nf Nooksack R	4200	1000' SW Mt Baker Lodge
BAILEY	Spokane	15	L Spokane R	1900	5 mi NE Deer Park
BAILIE PD	Franklin	23	Columbia R	900	1 mi N Mesa
BAKER	Pend Oreille	3.6	Pend Oreille R	2350	11 mi W Newport
BALCH	Klickitat	3	Columbia	600	2 mi NW Lyle
BALD	Skagit	2.5	Skagit R	3750	8.5 mi E Concrete
BALD	Whatcom	2.5	Nf Nooksack R	4400	6 mi N Glacier
BALD EAGLE	King	4	Wf Foss	4500	8 mi SE Skykomish
BALD HILL	Thurston	45	Nisqually R	633	11.5 mi SE Yelm
BALD MTN PD	Skagit	1.5	Stilly R	1050	2 mi NW Cavanaugh Lk
BALLINGER	Snohomish	103	Lk Washington	278	3 mi SE Edmonds
BALLINGER	Spokane	64	Palouse R	2300	5.5 mi SW Cheney
BANDANA	Snohomish	3	Sf Stilly R	3235	7 mi N Verlot
BANDYS	Lincoln	6	Crab Cr	2150	1.5 mi NW Wilbur
BANKS (RES)	Grant	24900	Main Canal	1560	1.6 mi SW Grand Coulee Dan
BANNOCK LKS (3)	Chelan	7-11	Stehekin R	5900	10.5 mi SW High Bridge G.S
BARLCAY	Snohomish	11	Sf Skykom R	2300	3 mi NE Baring
BARING BV PDS	Snohomish	2	Sf Skykom R	850	1 mi NW Baring
BARRINGS	Lincoln	5	Crab Cr	2250	7 mi S Creston
BARKER CANYON	Douglas	12	Banks Lk	1800	4.5 mi S 4 Corners
BARLOW GRAVEL PIT	Pierce	3	Puget Sound	250	2700' E Clover Pk H.S.
BARNES	Thurston	14	Budd Inlet	150	3 mi S Olympia
BARNETT	Pierce	1	White R	2900	2 mi S Silver Cr R.S.
BARNSLEY	Okanogan	9.5	Methow R	1950	1 mi SW Winthrop
BARRETT	Whatcom	40	Nooksack R	20	1 mi E Ferndale
BASALT	Adams	5	Potholes Canal	970	5 mi N Othello
BASIN	King	7	Tye R	5500	8 mi S Scenic
BASIN	Skagit	2.5	Cascade R	4200	8 mi S Marblemount
BASS	King	24	Green R	665	3.5 mi N Enumclaw
BASS	Thurston	7	Nisqually R	500	1900' E Elbow Lk
BATEMAN PD	Yakima	3	Yakima R	990	.05 mi NW Birchfield
BATH	Snohomish	15	Suiattle R	5950	25 mi N Darrington
BATHTUB LKS (8)	Snohomish	10	Pilchuck R	4800	Pilchuck Mtn
BATHTUB	Mason	2	Oakland Bay	350	6 mi N Shelton
BATTALION	Chelan	6.4	Stehekin R	5234	3.5 mi SE High Bridge G.S.
BATTLEGROUND	Clark	28	Columbia R	504	12 mi NE Vancouver
BATT SLOUGHS (2)	Snohomish	3-5	Snohomish R	15	1.5 mi S Snohomish
BAY	Pierce	130	Carr Inlet	27	2 mi S Home
BAYLEY BV PDS (3)	Stevens	3	Colville R	2400	2 mi S Baley Lk
BEACH	Clallam	7	Juan de Fuca	10	Angeles Point
BEALL PDS (3)	Clark	1	Columbia R	280	6 mi N Camas
BEAD	Pend Oreille	720	Pend Oreille R	2850	8 mi NW Newport
BEAR	Chelan	1	Entiat R	6800	21 mi NW Entiat
BEAR	King	49	Taylor R	3670	19 mi NE North Bend
BEAR LKS (3)	King	5	Nf Snoq R	4850	7 mi S Skykomish
BEAR	Kitsap	12	Case Inlet	400	4 mi E Belfair
BEAR	Skagit	2.5	Cascade R	3900	8.5 mi SE Marblemount
BEAR	Skagit	4	Sf Nooksack R	3550	1 mi SW Three Lakes
BEAR	Skamania	11	Muddy R	1700	6 mi E Mt St Helens
BEAR	Whatcom	23	Chilliwack R	5800	1 mi SW Mt Redoubt
BEAR CREEK RES	Skagit	0.2	Baker R	912	5.5 mi N Concrete
BEAR PARK	Pierce	4	White R	5405	11 mi NE Mt Rainier
BEAUSITE	Jefferson	17	Ft Townsend Bay	430	3 mi SW Chimacum
BEAUTY	Jefferson	3	Oueets R	4700	Hwtrs Heehaw Cr
BEAVER	Clallam	36	Sol Duc R	550	3 mi NE Sappho
BEAVER	Columbia	2	Tucannon R	2375	4 mi S G.D. Hdq
BEAVER LKS (3)	King	62	Sammamish R	406	4 mi N Issaquah
BEAVER	Kittitas	1	Yakima R	3450	1 mi SW Snoq Pass
BEAVER	Lewis	7	Cowlitz R	4500	7 mi E Packwood
BEAVER	Skagit	74	Skagit R	30	1 mi SE Clear Lk
BEAVER	Skamania	3	Columbia R	550	4 mi E Carson

LAKE	COUNTY	ACRES	DRAINAGE	ELEVATION	LOCATION
BEAVER PUSS LKS (4)	Kittitas	2	Kachess R	5300	E side Rampart Ridge
BEBE PDS (2)	Cowlitz	2-3	Cowlitz R	560	6 mi NW Castle Rock
BEDAL	Snohomish	3	Nf Sauk R	3500	5.5 mi NE Barlow Pass
BEDARD	Okanogan	13	Columbia R	2460	11 mi NE Bridgeport
BEE	Skagit	10	Suiattle R	4600	10 mi S Marblemount
BEEHIVE RES	Chelan	12	Columbia R	4150	8 mi S Wenatchee
BEECHER	Snohomish	16	Snohomish R	13	.05 mi E Cathcart
BEN LKS (3)	Jefferson	2	Quinault R	4600	1 mi SW Mt Steel
BENCH	King	2.5	Nf Snoq R	4180	17 mi NE North Bend
BENCH	Lewis	3	Ohanapecosh R	5200	6 mi N White Pass
BENCH	Lewis	6	Cowlitz R	4600	5.5 mi E Longmire
BENCH	Skagit	49	Suiattle R	5200	22 mi NE Darrington
BENGSTON	King	4	Nf Tolt R	2600	7 mi S Startup
BENNETTSEN	Mason	25	Tahuya R	381	6 mi W Belfair
BENSON	Stevens	12	Colville R	2750	7 mi E Valley
BERDEEN	Whatcom	127	Skagit R	5000	12 mi N Marblemount
BERGEAU	Lincoln	31	Crab Cr	2100	11 mi SE Wilbur
BERGSTROM	Adams	36	Crab Cr	750	2700' S Royal Lk
BERRY LKS (2)	Kitsap	3	Sinclair Inlet	200	2 mi SW Pt Orchard
BERTHA	King	2	Beckler R	4400	W side Mt Fernow
BERTHA MAY LKS (2)	Lewis	6-30	Nisqually R	3700	7 mi SE National
BESTS	Skagit	15	Skagit Bay	390	Fidalgo Island
BEVIS	Snohomish	6	Skykomish R	540	8.4 mi NE Monroe
BIDDLE	Clark	1	Columbia R	45	6.5 mi E Vancouver
BIG	Kittitas	4	Teanaway R	2380	2.5 mi E Teanaway Jct
BIG	Skagit	545	Skagit R	81	5 mi SE Mt Vernon
BIG BEEF PDS	Kitsap	5	Hood Canal	500	.05 mi E Hintzville
BIG FOUR	Columbia	5	Tucannon R	2525	Mouth Big 4 Canyon
BIGELOW	Thurston	14	Budd Inlet	151	2 mi NE Olympia
BIG GRANITE	Skagit	144	Cascade R	5000	7 mi SE Marblemount
BIG HANKS	Mason	27	Oakland Bay	400	8 mi NW Shelton
BIG HEART	King	191	Wf Foss R	5100	9 mi S Skykomish
BIG HIDDEN	Okanogan	71	Ef Pasayten R	4300	34 mi NW Winthrop
BIG JIM MTN LKS (2)	Chelan	4-5	Wenatchee R	6850	9 mi NW Leavenworth
BIG JOES	Clallam	15	Wf Dickey R	152	10 mi NW Forks
BIG MACK	Okanogan	9	Okanogan R	4000	7.5 mi SE Oroville
BIG SNOW	King	15	Mf Snoq R	5000	8.5 mi N Snoq Pass
BIG SWAMP	Spokane	11	Palouse R	2340	1.1 E Medical Lake
BIG TWIN SISTER	Yakima	104.5	Bumping R	5152	7 mi N White Pass
BILL	Lewis	4	Ohanapecosh R	5000	5.5 mi N White Pass
BINFORD RES	Clark	3	Ef Lewis R	600	2.5 mi NE La Center
BIRD	Yakima	4	Klickitat R	5575	11 mi NW Glenwood
BITTER	King	19	Puget Sound	440	In Seattle
BITTER LKS (3)	Snohomish	3	Nf Skykomish R	3500	4 mi NE Index
BIVIN	Lewis	3	Cowlitz R	980	4.5 mi SW Packwood
BLACK LKS (2)	Adams	14-25	Columbia R	790	8 mi NW Othello
BLACK	King	26	Snoqualmie R	1213	9.5 mi NE Snoqualmie
BLACK	Stevens	70	L Pend Oreille	3701	12 mi E Colville
BLACK	Okanogan	66	Chewack R	4000	24 mi N Winthrop
BLACK LKS (10)	Okanogan	26	Columbia R	2450	9 mi NE Bridgeport
BLACK	Thurston	576	Chehalis R	127	4 mi SW Olympia
BLACK DIAMOND	King	9	Green R	540	1 mi SW Blk Diamond
BLACK DIAMOND	Okanogan	2.5	Okanogan R	2400	2 mi SE Oroville
BLACK & WHITE LKS (3)	Mason	3	Skykomish R	4500	5 mi N Hd Lk Cushman
BLACKMAN'S	Snohomish	60	Snohomish R	140	1 mi N Snohomish
BLACK PINE	Okanogan	19	Twisp R	3900	8 mi SW Twisp
BLACKSMITH	Mason	18	Tahuya R	422	5.5 mi NW Belfair
BLACKWOOD	Clallam	16	Sol Duc R	3000	3 mi SW Sol Duc Hot S
BLAIR RES	Benton	7	Columbia R	445	3 mi S Kennewick
BLAKES PD	Clallam	1	Juan de Fuca	120	1 mi E Sequim
BLALOCK	Walla Walla	6	Walla Walla R	750	4 mi W Walla Walla
BLANCA	Snohomish	179	Nf Skykomish R	4064	7 mi SE Barlow Pass
BLANKENSHIP PTHLS	Yakima	7	Tieton R	5250	6.5 mi NE White Pass
BLANKENSHIP LKS (3)	Yakima	12	Tieton R	5230	6.5 mi NE White Pass
BLAZER	King	6	Pratt R	4060	12 mi SE North Bend
BLETHEN LKS (2)	King	3-8	Taylor R	3198	10 mi NE North Bend
BLUE	Columbia	3	Tucannon R	2150	Tucannon
BLUE	Cowlitz	8	Sf Toutle R	3294	29.5 mi NE Woodland
BLUE	Grant	536	Lenore Lk	1093	11 mi N Soap Lk
BLUE	Lewis	128	Cispus R	4050	15.5 mi SE Randle
BLUE	Lewis	6	Cowlitz R	4550	5.2 mi W Ohanap H.S.
BLUE	Okanogan	186	Similkameen R	1686	9 mi S Loomis
BLUE	Pend Oreille	6.5	L Spokane R	2000	8.5 mi NW Elk
BLUE	Skamania	12	Salmon R	4640	18 mi N Carson
BLUE	Skamania	16	Nf Lewis R	4300	21 mi S Randle
BLUE	Snohomish	22	Nf Sauk R	5600	9 mi S Glacier Peak
BLUE	Whatcom	13	Baker R	4000	7 mi N Concrete
BLUE	Yakima	3.5	Sf Tieton R	6200	8 mi SW Tieton
BLUE GULCH RES	Stevens	1.5	Columbia R	1400	Blue Gulch
BLUFF	Grant	11	Grand Coulee	1445	Lower Grand Coulee
BLUFF	Lewis	8	Cowlitz R	3900	7 mi NE Packwood
BLUFF	Skagit	21	Suiattle R	4000	11 mi S Marblemount

LAKE	COUNTY	ACRES	DRAINAGE	ELEVATION	LOCATION
BLUFF	Skamania	5	Columbia R	2250	6 mi W No Bonneville
BLUFF	Yakima	3	Klickitat R	5800	10.5 mi NW Glenwood
BLUM LKS (4)	Whatcom	2-14	Baker R	5800	18 mi NE Concrete
BLYTHE	Grant	30	Crab Cr	915	10.5 mi NW Othello
BOARDMAN LKS (3)	Snohomish	10-49	Pilchuck R	3420	8 mi SE Verlot Res
BOGACHIEL	Clallam	1.5	Bogachiel R	3525	3 mi SE Sol Duc H.S.
BOILING	Chelan	8	Lk Chelan	6900	30 mi NW Chelan
BOISE-CASCADE MILL P	Yakima	1	Naches R	1450	3500' S Naches
BONAPARTE	Okanogan	159	Okanogan R	3554	18 mi NE Tonasket
BONE	King	1	Green R	4300	6 mi SW Lester
BONER	King	3	Skykomish R	4500	3 mi SW Grotto
BONNEY	Pierce	17	Puyallup R	605	2.5 mi SE Sumner
BONNIE	Whit/Spo	366	Rock Cr	1790	9 mi NW Rosalia
BOOHER	Okanogan	25	Okanogan R	967	4 mi NW Riverside
BOOMERANG	King	1	Nf Snoq R	3215	10.5 NE North Bend
BOOT	Skamania	16	Green R	4550	4.5 mi N Spirit Lk
BOREN	King	15	Lk Washington	300	4 mi N Renton
BORGEAU	Ferry	22	Columbia R	1900	4.5 mi S Inchelium
BORST	Lewis	5	Skookumchuck R	175	Ft Borst Park
BOSWORTH	Snohomish	96	Pilchuck R	563	2 mi S Granite Falls
BOTTOMLESS	Skagit	4	Samish R	200	2 mi N Sedro Woolley
BOUCK	Whatcom	14	Skagit R	4000	3 mi E Newhalem
BOULDER	Skagit	55	Suiattle R	5000	13 mi NE Darrington
BOULDER	Snohomish	22	Sultan R	3750	8 mi N Index
BOUNDARY	King	8	Skykomish R	2310	11 mi NE Carnation
BOUNDARY LKS (2)	Mason	3-4	Sf Skok R	500	12 mi NW Shelton
BOUNDARY RES	Pend Oreille	1600	Pend Oreille R	1990	9 mi N Metaline Falls
BOUNDARY	Yakima	10	Naches R	3300	9 mi S Naches R.S.
BOW	King	13	Puget Sound	340	Opp Sea Tac
BOWERS PD	Snohomish	6	Sf Stilly	940	5 mi NE Granite Falls
BOWMAN	Pierce	2.5	Nisqually	300	Ft. Lewis Res
BOWMAN	Pierce	11	Stuck R	470	4.5 mi SE Auburn
BOWSER	Snohomish	3	Nf Sauk R	4300	9 mi S Barlow Pass
BOX CANYON	Kittitas	2	Kachess R	4500	4 mi E Snoq Pass
BOX MTN LKS (3)	Snohomish	2-24	Suiattle R	5000	19 mi E Darrington
BOYD	Snohomish	13	Pilchuck R	500	2 mi SE Granite Falls
BOYLE	King	24	Snoqualmie R	1040	6 mi NE Snoqualmie
BOYLES	Pierce	3	Puget Sound	230	2 mi SE Steilacoom
BRADER	Skamania	3	Wind R	4600	20 mi N Carson
BRANDENBURG MARSH	Pierce	35	Nisqually R	300	.04 mi NW Roy
BRANDMEIRS BOG	Snohomish	1	Snoqualmie R	1500	9.7 mi NE Carnation
BREAKER	Pacific	20	Pacific	20	1.5 mi N Long Beach
BREWSTER	King	3	Sf Snoq R	1030	3 mi S North Bend
BRIDGEMAN PD	Yakima	6	Yakima R	655	2.5 mi N Mabton
BRIDGES	King	34	Snoqualmie R	1045	6 mi NE Snoqualmie
BRIGGS PD	San Juan	29	Westcott Bay	231	1 mi SE Roche Hbr
BRIGHAM	Chelan	4	Wenatchee R	6500	13 mi NW Leavenworth
BRISCOE	Pacific	11	Pacific Ocean	20	2 mi N Long Beach
BRITT SLOUGH	Skagit	21	Skagit R	15	1 mi SW Mt Vernon
BROKEN ROCK LKS(2)	Grant	20-40	Crab Cr	1251	7.5 mi SW Wilson Cr
BRONSON PD	Snohomish	5.5	Sultan R	710	3 mi NE Sultan
BROWNIE	Pend Oreille	11	P. Oreille R	2350	7 mi N Cusick
BROWNS	Lincoln	42	Crab Cr	167	57 mi N Odessa
BROWNS	Pend Oreille	88	P. Oreille R	3450	8.5 mi NE Cusick
BROWNS	Stevens	17	Colville R	2025	5 mi SW Chewalah
BRYANT	Lewis	2	Cowlitz R	1720	5 mi E Winston
BRYANT	Snohomish	20	Stilly R	146	3 mi NW Arlington
BUCK	Douglas	12	Columbia R	2300	5 mi SW Del Rio
BUCK	King	13	Mf Snoq R	3150	9 mi E North Bend
BUCK	Kitsap	20	Puget Sound	140	1 mi SW Hansville
BUCK	Okanogan	15	Chewack R	3247	9 mi N Winthrop
BUCK	Yakima	2	Bumping R	4660	9 mi S Chinook Pass
BUCK	Yakima	1.5	Naches R	4800	1.5 mi SE Nelson Butte
BUCK & DOE LKS (2)	Stevens	1-1	Colville R	2950	9 mi W Chewelah
BUCKHORN	Jefferson	1	Dungeness R	5150	11 mi W Quilcene
BUCKHORN	King	1	Nf Tolt R	1450	4 mi N Carnation
BUESCH	Lewis	10	Ohanapecosh R	5175	4 mi N White Pass
BUFFALO	Okanogan	542	Columbia R	2042	7 mi SE Nespelem
BUGGER	Okanogan	3	Twisp R	5200	22 mi W Twisp
BULLER	Skagit	2	Cascade R	3500	5 mi E Marblemount
BULLFROG PD	King	3	Skykomish R	800	2 mi SE Baring
BUMPING	Yakima	1310	Bumping R	3426	10 mi Chinook Pass
BUNCH	Grays Hbr	16	Quinault R	3000	7 mi E Quinault Lk
BUNCHGRASS	Pend Oreille	18	P.Oreille R	4950	11 mi SE Ione
BURBANK SLOUGH	Walla Walla	700	Columbia R	341	At Burbank
BURDEN	Okanogan	2.5	Okanogan R	1820	6 mi SW Tonasket
BURKE	Grant	73	Columbia R	1193	7.5 mi S Quincey
BUSHMAN	Thurston	40	Deschutes R	255	1 mi NE Offut Lk
BUSCH PD	Whitman	1	Palouse R	2720	1 mi SE Colton
BUTCH EVANS SLOUGH	King	4	Mf Snoq R	860	1.5 mi SW Pratt R Mouth
BUTLERS PD	Skamania	1.5	Columbia R	150	1 mi N No Bonneville
BUTTE LKS (3)	Adams	30	Crab Cr	B00	7 mi NW Othello

LAKE	COUNTY	ACRES	DRAINAGE	ELEVATION	LOCATION
BUZZARD	Okanogan	16	Okanogan R	3380	7 mi NW Okanogan
BYERS PD	Clallam	1	Sequim Bay	680	9 mi SW Port Angeles
BYRNE	Snohomish	51	Whitechuck R	5550	20 mi SE Darrington
BYRON PDS (2)	Yakima	50	Yakima R	700	4.5 mi S Grandview
BONNEVILLE POOL	Skamania	20200	Columbia R	72	36 mi E Vancouver

C

LAKE	COUNTY	ACRES	DRAINAGE	ELEVATION	LOCATION
CABIN	Grant	4	Columbia R	1250	5 mi SW George
CABIN	Kittitas	5	Teenaway R	2400	2.5 mi E Teenaway Jct
CAD	King	1	Pratt R	4320	2 mi NW Snoq Pass
CADET	Snohomish	2	Nfk Sauk R	5500	5 mi E Barlow Pass
CADY	Mason	15	Hood Canal	450	2 mi SE DeWatto
CAIN	Whatcom	72	Samish R	391	9.5 mi SE Bellingham
CALDWELL	Pend Oreille	15	Pend Oreille R	2560	7.5 mi SE Ione
CALICHE LKS (2)	Grant	10-17	Columbia R	1300	5.5 mi SW George
CALISPELL	Pend Orellle	1031	Callspell R	2028	2 mi SW Usk
CALLIGAN	King	361	Nf Snoq R	2222	9 mi E North Bend
CAMILLE	Ferry	19	Columbia R	1958	2.5 mi W Inchelium
CAMP	Franklin	19	Columbia R	870	5.5 mi N Mesa
CAMP	Skagit	3	Bellingham Bay	1150	Cypress Island
CAMP PD	Mason	6	Tahuya R	350	4 mi NW Belfair
CAMP 1 POND	Pierce	1	Puyallup R	600	E side Kapowsin Lk
CAMP 3 POND	Skagit	2	Skagit R	500	2.5 mi NW Hamilton
CAMP 7 POND	Pacific	4	Willapa R	275	10 mi SE Raymond
CAMPBELL	Adams	115	Pothole Canal	975	5 mi N Othello
CAMPBELL	Clark	247	Columbia R	10	2.5 mi S Ridgefield
CAMPBELL	Pierce	3.5	White R	5500	3 mi NE Chin Pass
CAMPBELL	Skagit	410	Skagit Bay	43	5 mi S Anacortes
CAMPBELL	Spokane	33	Palouse R	2300	4.5 mi SW Cheney
CAMP ROBBER	King	4-5	Ef Miller R	4200	8 mi SE Skykomish
CANAAN	Chelan	2.5	Wenatchee R	5500	8.5 mi NE Stevens Pass
CANAL	Grant	76	Crab Cr	986	6.5 mi N Othello
CANNERY	Skagit	18	Guemes Ch	6	Shannon Pt
CANVASBACK	Clark	167	Columbia R	10	Bachelor Island
CANYON	Snohomish	21	Suiattle R	21	11 mi NE Glacier Pk
CANYON	Whatcom	2	Nf Nooksack R	4775	5 mi NW Shuksan
CAPITOL	Thurston	306	Budd Inlet	0	Olympia
CAREYS	Skagit	4	Skagit R	100	1 mi NE Hamilton
CARLISLE LKS(5)	Grays Hbr	1-4	Copalis R	85	2 mi N Copalis Cross
CARLISLE	Lewis	20	Sf Newaukum R	500	Onalaska
CARLSON PD	Mason	1	Hood Canal	200	1 mi S Union
CARNEY	Pierce/Kit	39	Case Inlet	350	4 mi N Vaughn
CAROLE	King	11	Taylor R	3700	.07 mi W Nordrum Lk
CAROLINE LKS (2)	Chelan	4-8	Wenatchee	5400	10 mi SW Leavenworth
CAROLINE	King	60	Mf Snoq R	4740	6 mi NW Snoq Pass
CARP	Island	7	Saratoga Pass	410	Camano Island
CARP	Klickitat	22	Lk Klickitat	2450	7 mi W Goldendale
CARP	Lincoln	5	Spokane	1900	11 mi N Davenport
CARP	Pierce	11	Puget Sound	240	2 mi SE Steilacoom
CARPENTER	Kitsap	3-5	Puget Sound	30	1 mi W Kingston
CARPENTERS	Skamania	4	Columbia R	630	2 mi NW No Bonneville
CARRIE	Chelan	15	Wenatchee R	5100	11.7 mi N Salmon la Sac
CARTER	Chelan	2	Wenatchee R	6400	1 mi SW Lk Agusta
CARTER	Kitsap	1	Dyes Inlet	230	3.4 mi NW Bremerton
CARTER	Pierce	6	Puget Sound	280	McChord AFB
CARTY	Clark	42	Columbia R	10	Ridgefield
CASCADE	Grant	3	Columbia R	1090	500' N Crystal Lk
CASCADE	San Juan	172	East Sound	346	Morton State Park
CASCADE MILL PD	Yakima	33	Yakima R	1060	NE Yakima
CASEY PD	Walla Walla	60	Lk Wallula	340	4.5 mi SE Burbank
CASTOR	Okanogan	18	Okanogan R	1950	4 mi NW Riverside
CASSIDY	Snohomish	125	Pilchuck R	319	3.5 mi E Marysville
CAT	Clallam	7	Pt Discovery	329	3 mi N Blyn
CAT	Thurston	3	Nisqually R	450	4 mi NW Yelm
CATFISH	Mason	7	Ef Satsop R	460	1000' SE Nahwatzel Lk
CATFISH	Mason	7	North Bay	70	1.5 mi S Allyn
CATHERINE CECILLE	Okanogan	10	San Poil R	2580	SE end Aeneas Valley
CATTAIL	Grant	18	Crab Cr	945	8.5 mi N Othello
CATTAIL	Skamania	5	Columbia R	100	1 mi NW No Bonneville
CAVANAUGH	Skagit	844	Stilly R	1008	10 mi NE Arlington
CAYUSE	Okanogan	11	Okanogan R	1840	5 mi NW Tonasket
CECILIA	Snohomish	1.5	Wallace R	3450	5 mi N Gold Bar
CECIL'S	King	8	Ef Miller R	4400	8.5 mi SE Skykomish
CEDAR	Pierce	36	White R	4200	11 mi SE Enumclaw
CEDAR PD	Snohomish	9	Skykomish R	700	4 mi S Sultan
CEDAR	Stevens	51	P Oreille R	2135	2 mi N Leadpoint
CEDAR	Whatcom	4	Chuckanut Bay	1530	5 mi S Bellingham
CEDAR—LOWER	Yakima	3	Bumping Lk	4750	5 mi SE Chin Pass
CEDAR—UPPER	Yakima	8	Bumping Lk	4750	5 mi SE Chin Pass
CELERY MEADOW	Pierce	1	White R	4700	1800' S Cedar Lk

LAKE	COUNTY	ACRES	DRAINAGE	ELEVATION	LOCATION
CELILORES	Klickitat	11200	Columbia R	160	20 mi SW Goldendale
CEMENT	King	2.5	Sf Skykomish R	4000	3 mi SW Grotto
CHAIN LKS (3)	Chelan	5-8	Wenatchee R	5700	5 mi SE Stevens Pass
CHAIN LKS (6)	King	3.5	Mf Snoq R	5700	W side LaBohn Gap
CHAIN LKS(4)	Lewis	1-4	Ohanapecosh R	5000	7 mi N White Pass
CHAIN	Pend Oreille	78	Spokane R	1950	3.5 mi NE Elk
CHAINOFLAKES(10)	Skamania	30	Cispus R	4300	24 mi SE Randle
CHAIN	Snohomish	23	Snohomish R	390	3 mi N Monroe
CHAIN LKS (4)	Snohomish	2	Nf Stilly R	900	7 mi N Granite Falls
CHAMBERLAIN	Klickitat	81	Columbia R	72	.05 mi W Lyle
CHAMBERS	Lewis	14.5	Cispus R	4525	11 mi SE Packwood
CHAMBERS	Pierce	80	Nisqually R	315	1 mi NE Roy
CHAMBERS LKS (2)	Thurston	49-73	Dechutes R	194	3 mi SE Olympia
CHAPLAIN	Snohomish	444	Sultan R	640	6 mi N Sultan
CHAPMAN	Spokane	146	Palouse R	2154	8 mi S Cheney
CHARLES	Chelan	.11.5	Wenatchee R	6900	13.5 mi NW Leavenworth
CHARLEY—UPPER	Asotin	5	Snake R	2600	16 mi W Asotin
CHARLEY—LOWER	Asotin	6	Snake R	2300	16 mi W Asotin
CHARLEY POND	Yakima	8.5	Yakima R	800	2 mi SE Harrah
CHARLOTTE	Franklin	20	Snake R	440	2 mi NE Ice Hbr Dam
CHARLIA LKS (2)	Jefferson	3-9	Big Quilcene R	5500	12 mi W Quilcene
CHARLIE LKS (4)	King	2-4	Ef Miller R	4000	9 mi Skykomish
CHARLIE BROWN	King	2	Taylor R	4700	16 mi E North Bend
CHASE	Island	5	Holmes Hbr	200	Whidbey Isl
CHASE	Snohomish	1	Lk Ballinger	400	1 mi NW Lk Ballinger
CHAVAL	Skagit	11	Suiattle R	4900	14 mi SE Marblemount
CHENAMUS	Skamania	4	Nf Lewis R	4150	22 mi N Carson
CHENUIS LKS (3)	Pierce	2-4	Carbon R	5000	Chenuis Mtn
CHERRY	King	3	Snoqualmie R	970	6 mi NW Lk Joy
CHESTER MORSE RES	King	1682	Cedar R	1555	7 mi SE North Bend
CHETWOOT	King	111	Wf Foss R	5200	11 mi S Skykomish
CHINA GARDENS DAM R	Asotln	1300	Snake R	910	26 mi S Clarkson
CHITWOOD LKS (2)	Snohomish	1-5	Sf Stilly R	700	4 mi E Granite Falls
CHIWAUKUM	Chelan	67	Wenatchee R	4950	14 mi NW Leavenworth
CHIWAUKUM BV PDS	Chelan	10	Wenatchee R	3500	Below Chiwaukum Lk
CHOPAKA	Okanogan	149	Simlihekum R	2921	6 mi N Loomis
CHORAL	Chelan	1.5	Entiat R	7200	35 mi NW Entiat
CHRISTINE	Pierce	4.5	Nisqually R	4700	6 mi E National
CHRISTMAS	King	8	Sf Snoq R	960	1 mi NE Cedar Falls
CHUCKANUT	Whatcom	2.5	Chuckanut Bay	130	.05 mi NW Chuckanut Vill
CHUKAR	Grant	30	Crab Cr	908	11 mi NW Othello
CHURCH	Whatcom	4	Nf Nooksack R	5150	6 mi NE Glacier
CICERO PD	Snohomish	4	Nf Stilly R	100	.05 mi E Cicero
CINDER	King	7	Lk Sawyer	680	1.5 mi N Blk Diamond
CIRCLE	Kittitas	49	Waptus R	6100	11 mi N Salmon La Sac
CIRQUE	Yakima	7	Tieton R	5650	13 mi SE White Pass
CITY	Jefferson	16	Big Quilcene R	600	1 mi E Discovery Jct
CLARA	Chelan	2	Columbia R	5500	1.5 mi NE Mission Pk
CLARK PD	Franklin	49	Columbia R	758	5 mi SW Mesa
CLARK	Stevens	24	Columbia R	1900	8 mi N Hunters
CLARKSTONE RES	Asotin	4	Snake R	1025	Clarkston Heights
CLAM	Pacific	10	Willapa Bay	20	3 mi N Long Beach
CLARICE	King	41	Tye R	4500	6 mi S Scenic
CLARK RES	Clark	1.5	Columbia R	380	3 mi N Camas
CLAYWOOD	Jefferson	10	Dosewallips R	6100	22 mi S Pt Angeles
CLEAR	Chelan	5	Columbia R	3000	9 mi S Wenatchee
CLEAR	Clallam	6	Sol Duc R	4225	5 mi SE Sol Duc H Spr
CLEAR	Mason	11	Oakland Bay	350	5 mi NW Shelton
CLEAR	Pacific	11	Pacific Ocean	25	1.5 mi N Long Beach
CLEAR	Pierce	155	Nisqually R	772	4 mi N Eatonville
CLEAR	Skagit	223	Skagit R	30	at Clear Lk Vill
CLEAR	Skagit	19	Baker R	4075	8 mi NE Concrete
CLEAR	Skamania	13	Nf Lewis R	4800	2 mi SW Cultus G.S.
CLEAR	Snohomish	2	Sauk R	2240	4 mi NW Silverton
CLEAR	Spokane	7	Palouse R	2190	9 mi NE Sprague
CLEAR	Spokane	375	Crab Cr	2342	2 mi S Medical Lk
CLEAR	Thurston	173	Nisqually R	518	10 mi SE Yelm
CLEAR	Whitman	4	Palouse R	1301	2 mi S Hooper
CLEAR	Yakima	265	Nf Tieton R	3615	6 mi E White Pass
CLE ELUM PDS (2)	Kittitas	5-15	Yakima R	1950	1 mi SW Cle Elum
CLE ELUM RES	Kittitas	4810	Yakima R	2223	7 mi NW Cle Elum
CLEMENTS	Okanogan	3	Okanogan R	1250	3 mi N Omak
CLEVELAND	King	2.5	Miller R	4300	3.4 mi SW Skykomish
CLIFF	Grant	2	Dusty Lk	1060	6.5 mi SW Quincy
CLIFF	Skagit	5	Suiattle R	4800	12 mi S Marblemount
CLOUDY	King	6	Ef Foss R	4800	10 mi SE Skykomish
CLOVER CR PDS	Pierce	1	Puget Sound	300	McChord AFB
CLOVER	Pierce	9	White R	5728	White R Park
COAL	Snohomish	6	Sf Stilly R	3420	3.5 mi SE Silverton
COCHRAN	Snohomish	34	Skykomish R	425	5.5 mi NE Monroe
CODY	Ferry	6	San Poil R	3500	22 mi S Republic
COFFEE POT	Lincoln	317	Crab Cr	1850	12 mi NE Odessa

LAKE	COUNTY	ACRES	DRAINAGE	ELEVATION	LOCATION
COFFIN	Stevens	20	L Pend Ore R	3150	16 mi E Colville
COLCHUCK	Chelan	88	Wenatchee R	5570	10.5 mi S Leavenworth
COLLINS	Mason	4	Tahuya R	410	8 mi W Belfair
COMCOMLY	Skamania	5	W Salmon R	4500	10 mi W Mt Adams G.S.
CONCONULLY RES	Okanogan	450	Okanogan R	2287	at Conconully
CONEY	Chelan	18	Wenatchee R	7400	9 mi SW Leavenworth
CONEY	King	21	Wf Miller R	5300	on Lennox Mtn
CONEY PTHLS (3)	King	1	Wf Miller R	5250	SE side Coney Lk
CONEY	Snohomish	5	Nf Sauk R	5000	1.5 mi E Curry Gap
CONGER PDS (2)	Pend Orelile	3-5	Pend Oreille R	2800	5 mi NW Cusick
CONKLIN	Pend Oreille	8	Pend Oreille R	2100	5 mi SE Usk
CONNIE	Jefferson	7	Sf Quinault R	4200	12 mi E Lk Quinault
CONNOR	Snohomish	9	Pilchuck R	190	1 mi E Hartford
CONRAD LKS (2)	Yakima	1-1	Sf Tieton R	5293	8.5 mi S Clear Lk Dam
CONRADI PD	Cowlitz	12	Cowlitz R	275	5 mi SE Toledo
CONSTANCE	Jefferson	11	Dosewallips R	4750	13.5 mi SW Quilcene
COOK CR PDS	Grays Hbr	5	Ef Satsop R	100	5 mi N Elma
COOKS	Pend Oreille	11	Pend Oreille R	3075	5 mi NE Usk
COON	Chelan	9	Stehekin R	2172	1 mi N High Bridge G.S.
COONEY	Okanogan	8	Methow R	7300	16 mi W Methow
COOPERS PTHL	Thurston	5	Nisqually R	79	700' E Lk St Clair
COOPER	Kittitas	120	CleElum R	2788	3.5 mi NW Salmon la Sac
COOT	Grant	4	Crab Cr	940	6.5 mi N Othello
COPLAY	Pierce	20	Carbon R	4100	13 mi SE Enumclaw
COPPER LKS (2)	Ferry	1-4	San Poil R	3040	3.5 mi SW Republic
COPPER	King	148	Wf Foss R	4000	7 mi S Skykomish
COPPER	Snohomish	2	Sauk R	3300	6 mi NE Verlot R.S.
COPPER	Whatcom	8	Chilliwack R	5250	11.5 mi E Shuksan
COPPER GLANCE	Okanogan	4	Chewack R	6100	20 mi NW Winthrop
CORA	Lewis	28	Nisqually R	3900	9 mi SE National
CORNWALL	Stevens	4	Columbia R	2930	7 mi NE Hunters
CORRAL	Grant	80	Crab Cr	921	11 mi NW Othello
CORRAL	Okanogan	21	Ashnola R	7200	33 mi N Winthrop
CORRAL	Yakima	6	Klickitat R	5800	12 mi S White Pass
COSSALMAN	Spokane	41	Palouse R	2300	3.5 mi S Cheney
COTTAGE	King	63	Sammamish R	231	4 mi E Woodinville
COTTONWOOD	Kittitas	8	Yakima R	3900	5.5 mi S Snoq Pass
COTTONWOOD—UPPER	Kittitas	1.5	Yakima R	4040	6 mi S Snoq Pass
COUGAR—LITTLE	King	9.5	Nf Snoq R	4117	15 mi NE North Bend
COUGAR—BIG	King	20	Nf Snoq R	4123	14 mi NE North Bend
COUGAR	Okanogan	9	Methow R	3400	4 mi E Winthrop
COUGAR	Okanogan	21	Lost R	4200	31 mi NW Winthrop
COUGAR	Snohomish	4	Nf Sauk R	5000	17.5 mi SE Darrington
COUGAR—BIG	Yakima	82	Bumping R	5015	5 mi SE Chinook Pass
COUGAR—LITTLE	Yakima	13	Bumping R	5020	adj Big Cougar Lk
COULEE	Grant	10	Crab Cr	1500	adj Coulee City
COUNCIL	Skamania	48	Cispus R	4200	25 mi SE Randle
COUNDLY	Pierce	16	Carbon R	4150	14 mi SE Enumclaw
COUNTRY LINE PD	Skagit	4	Nf Stilly R	2000	3.5 mi NW Oso
COW	Adams	226	Palouse R	1749	10 mi E Ritzville
COWBELL	Snohomish	3.5	Pilchuck R	3420	7 mi SE Verlot
COWEMAN	Cowlitz	7	Coweman R	2750	22 mi E Kelso
COX	Okanogan	11	Nespelem R	2590	5 mi NE Nespelem
COX PD	Whatcom	1.5	Whatcom Cr	480	.05 mi NW Silver Beach
COYOTE	Adams	10	Crab Cr	815	5.5 mi NW Othello
COYOTE	Lewis	4	Cowlitz R	5100	5 mi SW White Pass
CRABAPPLE	Snohomish	36	Lk Goodwin	415	7.5 mi NW Marysville
CRADLE	Chelan	9	Wenatchee R	6050	16 mi W Leavenworth
CRAG—UPPER	Yakima	5	Bumping R	5020	8 mi S Chinook Pass
GRAIG LKS (3)	Snohomish	6-11	Nf Stilly R	4400	6 mi SW Darrington
CRAMER	Yakima	19	Tieton R	5025	3 mi NE White Pass
CRANBERRY	Island	2	Saratoga Pass	245	Camono Island
CRANBERRY	Island	128	Rosario St	20	Deception Pass Prk
CRANBERRY SL	King	1	Lk Sawyer	550	2 mi N Blk Diamond
CRANBERRY	Pacific	18	Willapa Bay	20	3.5 mi N Long Beach
CRANBERRY	Pierce	26	Nisqually R	644	5 mi NW Eatonville
CRANBERRY	Skagit	8	Samish R	300	4 mi N Sedro Woolley
CRANE	Skamania	1	Lewis R	1750	6 mi E Mt St Helens
CRATER	Grant	25	Columbia R	1230	4 mi W Quincey
CRATER	Skagit	63	Suiattle R	4800	13.5 mi E Marblemount
CRAWFISH	Okanogan	80	Sf San Poil R	4475	15 mi NE Omak
CRAWFORD	King	20	Mf Snoq R	5350	11 mi S Skykomish
CREAM	Jefferson	3	Hoh R	4250	2 mi NW Mt Ferry
CRESCENT	Chelan	2.5	Wenatchee R	5500	8 mi NE Stevens Pass
CRESCENT	Grant	40	Columbla R	994	8 mi N Othello
CRESCENT	Pend Oreille	22	Pend Oreille R	2500	9 mi N Metaline Falls
CRESCENT	Pierce	47	Gig Harbor	166	3.5 mi N Gig Harbor
CRESCENT	Skamania	1.5	Columbia R	780	3 mi SW Stevenson
CRESCENT	Snohomish	9	Snoqualmie R	25	3.5 mi S Monroe
CRESCENT BAY	Grant	70	Columbia R	1290	Grand Coulee
CROCKER	Jefferson	65	Discovery Bay	190	3.5 mi S Pt Discovery Bay
CROSBY	King	1.5	Sf Skykomish R	4500	3.5 mi SW Grotto

LAKE	COUNTY	ACRES	DRAINAGE	ELEVATION	LOCATION
CROW	Okanogan	5	Ashnola R	6800	33 mi N Winthrop
CROWFOOT	Okanogan	7	Okanogan R	2420	11 mi SE Malott
CRYSTAL	Chelan	6	Wenatchee R	7020	11 mi SW Leavenworth
CRYSTAL	Grant	1.5	Columbia R	1160	8 mi SW Quincey
CRYSTAL	King	6.5	Pratt R	4740	3 mi W Snoq Pass
CRYSTAL LKS (2)	King	1-3	Sf Skykomish R	3100	5.5 mi S Skykomish
CRYSTAL	Okanogan	3	Chewack R	6850	25 mi N Winthrop
CRYSTAL	Pierce	9	White R	5830	2.5 mi W Chinook Pass
CRYSTAL	Snohomish	21	White Chuck R	4800	14 mi SE Darrington
CUB	Chelan	28	Lk Chelan	5300	17.5 mi SW Twisp
CUB	Skagit	11	Suiattle R	5400	24.5 mi NE Darrington
CUITIN	Chelan	6	Wenatchee R	5850	8 mi S Stevens Pass
CUMMINGS	Snohomish	2	Pt Susan	375	8 mi NW Marysville
CUP	Chelan	8	Wenatchee R	6400	9 mi E Stevens Pass
CUP	Snohomish	11	Rapid R	4600	6 mi N Stevens Pass
CURL	Columbia	3	Tucannon R	2550	10 mi S Pomeroy
CURLEW	Ferry	870	Columbia R	2333	5 mi NE Republic
CURLEW PD	Walla Walla	35	L Wallula R	340	5 mi SE Burbank
CURTIS	Skamania	2.5	Muddy R	3610	3 mi fm Spirit Lk Inlet
CUSHMAN	Mason	4003	Hood Canal	735	4 mi NW Hoodsport
CUSHMAN PDS	Mason	5	Lk Cushman	800	NE side Lk Cushman
CUTTHROAT	Okanogan	9	Methow R	4935	23 mi W Winthrop
CYCLONE	Skagit	56	Cascade R	5300	11 mi SE Marblemount

D

LAKE	COUNTY	ACRES	DRAINAGE	ELEVATION	LOCATION
D" (DEE)	Chelan	10	Chiwawa R	6400	1 mi N fm W end Schaefer Lk
DAGGER	Chelan	11	Stehekin R	5500	.05 mi W Twisp Pass
DAGGER	Snohomish	28	Skykomish R	662	4.5 mi SE Sultan
DAHLBERG PDS	Snohomish	1-3	Stilly R	1560	3.8 mi N Granite Falls
DAILEY	Stevens	5	Pend Oreille R	2300	3.4 mi E Arden
DALLES LKS (2)	Pierce	1-2.5	White R	4550	7 mi SE Greenwater
DALTON	Franklin	30	Snake R	440	6.2 mi N Ringold
DAMFINO (2)	Whatcom	1.5	Chilliwack R	4500	8 mi NE Glacier
DAMON	Grays Hbr	16	Humptulips R	40	2 mi NE Copalis Crossing
DANCING LADY	Yakima	7	Tieton R	4980	.07 mi NE White Pass
DARLENE	Skamania	2	Wind R	4250	.08 mi SW Gifford Peak
DAVIS	Ferry	17	Kettle R	4550	4 mi SW Barstow
DAVIS	Lewis	18	Tilton R	940	1.4 mi SE Morton
DAVIS	Okanogan	39	Methow R	2350	4 mi SE Winthrop
DAVIS	Okanogan	5	Okanogan R	3450	10 mi SE Tonasket
DAVIS	Pend Oreille	146	Pend Oreille R	2150	6 mi S Usk
DAVIS SL	Skagit	7	Skagit R	120	1.4 mi E Hamilton
DAWN	Clallam	8	Pt Angeles Bay	1800	5.4 mi S Port Angeles
DEAD	Clark	16	Washougal R	180	1 mi N Camas
DEADHEAD	Kittitas	11	Waptus R	5300	9 mi N Salmon La Sac
DEADMANS	Skamania	34	Green R	4330	8.8 mi S Kosmos
DEADWOOD—LOWER	Pierce	7	White R	5250	1.4 mi N Chinook Pass
DEADWOOD—UPPER	Pierce	6	White R	5255	1 mi N Chinook Pass
DECEPTION LKS (3)	King	3-12.5	Tye R	5100	5.5 mi S Scenic
DECEPTION LKS (2)	Pend Oreille	3-4	Pend Oreille R	3100	4 mi E Ione
DEEP	Franklin	10	Palouse R	980	5 mi SE Washtucna
DEEP	Grant	140	Grand Coulee	1231	5 mi SW Coulee City
DEEP	King	39	Green R	770	.08 mi SW Cumberland
DEEP	Kitsap	3	Sinclair Inlet	190	3.5 mi S Pt Orchard
DEEP	Kittitas	53	Waptus R	4450	9.7 mi N Salmon La Sac
DEEP	Okanogan	5	Okanogan R	2150	2 mi SE L Soap Lk
DEEP	Skamania	6	White Salmon R	4950	1.4 mi SW Cultus Cr G.S.
DEEP	Skamania	3	Cispus R	3963	9 mi SE Kosmos
DEEP	Stevens	198	Columbia R	2025	9 mi NE Northport
DEEP	Thurston	66	Black R	198	9.5 mi S Olympia
DEEPWATER	Mason	11	Oakland Bay	240	7.3 mi NE Shelton
DEER LKS (2)	Clallam	1-8	Soleduck R	3525	3.4 mi SE Sol Duc H.S.
DEER	Columbia	2	Tucannon R	2250	10 mi S Pomeroy G.D.R. Hq
DEER	Island	82	Posession Snd	352	1 mi W Clinton
DEER	King	46	Taylor R	3630	18.5 mi NE North Bend
DEER	Kittitas	53	Waptus R	4450	9.7 mi N Salmon la Sac
DEEP	Okanogan	5	Okanogan R	2150	2.2 mi SE Soap Lk
DEER	Mason	12	Pickering Pass	190	10.8 mi NE Shelton
DEER	Pacific	8	Pacific Ocean	25	2 mi N Long Beach
DEER	Skamania	5.5	Nf Lewis R	4800	2.4 mi SW Cultus Cr G.S.
DEER	Skamania	2.5	Green R	2880	6.5 mi N Spirit Lk Outlet
DEER	Stevens	1163	Colville R	2482	32 mi N Spokane
DEER	Yakima	12	Tieton R	5206	1.3 NW White Pass
DEER MEADOW	Mason	3	Nf Skokomish R	720	.08 mi SW Cushman Lk Dam
DEER SPRINGS	Lincoln	60	Crab Cr	1800	11 mi NE Odessa
DEER SPRINGS	Pend Oreille	2	Pend Oreille R	3000	10 mi N Cusick
DE HART	Stevens	2	L Pend Ore R	1650	4.8 mi E Colville
DELANTY	Jefferson	13	Pt Townsend Bay	505	1.4 mi SE head Discovery Bay
DELTA	King	47	Wf Foss R	3500	8.4 mi S Skykomlsh
DEMPSEY MTN PDS	Skagit	4	Grandy Cr	450	5 mi E Hamllton

LAKE	COUNTY	ACRES	DRAINAGE	ELEVATION	LOCATION
DENNY	King	14	Sf Stilly R	43i30	2.5 mi W Snoq Pass
DERPICK	King	37	Mf Snoq R	3686	6.4 mi NW Snoq Pass
DERRY	King	6	Sf Snoq R	744	4.5 mi SE North Bend
DESIRE	King	72	Cedar R	500	5 mi SE Renton
DEVEREAUX	Mason	100	Hood Canal	215	1.5 mi NW Allyn
DEVIL	Chelan	1	Entiat R	6000	24 mi N Leavenworth
DEVILS	Jefferson	12	Quilcene Bay	844	2 mi S Quilcene
DEVILS	Skagit	31	Skagit R	826	5.8 mi SE Mt Vernon
DEVILS	Snohomish	2.5	Sf Stilly R	3820	2 mi W Pass Lk
DEVILS SLIDE	Kittitas	1.5	Naches R	4700	4 mi SW Cliffdell
DEVILSWASH BASIN	Yakima	2	Nf Tieton R	6268	8.2 mi W White Pass
DEWEY—LOWER	Yakima	51	American R	5112	1.7 mi SE Chinook Pass
DEWEY—UPPER	Yakima	8	American R	5140	1.5 mi SE Chinook Pass
DIABLO RES	Whatcom	910	Skagit R	1205	6 mi NE Newhalem
DIAMOND	Kittitas	5	Waptus R	4950	4 mi NW Salmon La Sac
DIAMOND	Pend Orellle	745.5	Wbr L Spokane R	2360	7 mi SW Newport
DIAMOND	Snohomish	10	Suiattle R	5250	.08 mi SE Meadow Mtn
DIAMOND	Yakima	18	Klickitat R	5750	13.5 mi SE White Pass
DIAMOND MTN	Jefferson	10	Dosewallips R	5575	E Side Diamond Mtn
DIBBLE	Okanogan	5	Methow R	1900	3.4 mi S Winthrop
DICKEY	Clallam	527	Wf Dickey R	193	12 mi NW Forks
DIKE 1	Grant	6	Columbia R	997	9 mi N Othello
DILLY	Jefferson	10	Queets R	2350	3 mi SE Spruce B Shelter
DIOSBUD LKS (3)	Whatcom	2-3.5	Skagit R	4075-4490	9.5 mi NW Marblemount
DIVIDE	Klttitas	2	Keechelus Lk	3870	2 mi S Snoq Pass
DIXIE	Skagit	4	Skagit R	3500	9 mi SE Sedro Woolley
DIXONS PD	Lincoln	4	Palouse R	1900	5.5 mi E Sprague
DOC MENIGS PD	Kittitas	9	Yakima R	1455	3.3 mi SE Ellensburg
DOELLE LKS (2)	Chelan	4-8	Wenatchee R	6200	5.4 mi E Stevens Pass
DOG	Yakima	61	Nf Tieton R	4207	2 mi NE White Pass
DOLE LKS (3)	Chelan	3-7	Lk Chelan	6150-6550	6.7 mi W Lucerne
DOLLAR LKS (2)	Snohomish	2-6	Wallace R	3900-3950	2.8 mi N Index
DOLLOFF	King	21	Green R	400	3 mi NW Auburn
DOMKE	Chelan	272	Lk Chelan	2192	35 mi NW Chelan
DON	Mason	17	Hood Canal	520	1.5 mi S Dewatto
DONALD	Chelan	12	Wenatchee R	5800	14.4 mi NW Leavenworth
DOREEN	Whatcom	1	Sf Nooksack R	3380	6.5 mi SW Mt Baker summlt
DOROTHY	King	290	Ef Miller R	3052	7.8 mi S Skykomish
DOSSER	Spokane	9.5	Spokane R	2075	4 mi SE Greenacres
DOUBTFUL	Chelan	30	Lk Chelan	5385	66 mi NW Chelan
DOUGLAS	Stevens	3	Colville R	2500	4.4 mi N Colville
DOW	Snohomish	3.5	Rapid R	4800	4 mi N Stevens Pass
DOWNEY	Snohomish	13	Suiattle R	5500	20 mi E Darrington
DOWNS	Spokane	423	Palouse R	1958	7 mi E Sprague
DRAGON	Jefferson	9	Hoh R	3350	7 mi W Mt Olympus
DRAGOON	Spokane	22	L Spokane R	2080	.04 mi NW Deer Park
DRANO	Skamania	220	Columbia R	72	7 mi W White Salmon
DRAPERS	Lincoln	34	Crab Cr	1900	11 mi S Wilbur
DREAM	King	35	TaylorR	3800	17.5 mi NE North Bend
DREDGE PDS	Cowlitz	4	Sf Toutle R	500	.05 mi E Toutle
DRUNKEN CHARLIE	King	3	Mf Tolt R	1380	4 mi NE Carnation
DRY	Chelan	1.5	Lk Chelan	7000	15 mi SW Twisp
DRY BED—UPPER	Mason	4.5	Satsop R	1250	900' NE Lower Dry Bed Lk
DRYBED—LOWER	Mason	7	Satsop R	1150	15 mi NW Shelton
DRY POND	Mason	2	Tahuya R	400	2.5 mi NE Tahuya
DUCK	Lewis	14	L Nisqually R	3715	7.5 mi N Morton
DUCK	Okanogan	29	Okanogan R	1241	3 mi N Omak
DUFFEY LKS (2)	Snohomish	2.5-3.5	Skykomish R	3000-3180	4 mi S Gold Bar
DUFFY	Okanogan	9	Twisp R	6500	1 mi N Oval Peak
DUFFYS	Lincoln	2.5	Crab Cr	0	8 mi S Almira
DULEY	Douqlas	9	Columbia R	2240	12 mi E Bridgeport
DULEY	Okanogan	53	Columbia R	2430	14 mi S Okanogan
DUMBBELL	Lewis	42	Ohanapecosh R	5200	3.8 mi N White Pass
DUNBAR	Spokane	2.5	L Spokane R	2100	3.7 mi NE Elk
DUNLAP PD	Thurston	2	Chehalis R	220	4.8 mi N Bucoda
DUSTY	Grant	30	Columbia R	888	7 mi SW Quincey

E

EAGLE LKS (3)	Clallam	0.5-1.5	Lyre R	2625-3075	1.5 mi W end Lk Crescent
EAGLE	King	53	Nf Green R	2230	8 mi E Kanasket
EAGLE	Snohomish	20	Beckler R	3750	3.5 mi NE Baring
EAGLE LKS (2)	Okanogan	9-15.5	Methow R	6400-7100	18 mi NW Methow
EAGLE SPRINGS	Lincoln	4	Crab Creek	1740	11.5 mi N Odessa
EARLE	Chelan	16.5	Wenatchee R	6600	8 mi SW Leavenworth
EAST	Pierce	4	Carbon R	4000	15 mi SE Enumclaw
EAST LKS (2)	Whatcom	2-7.5	Skagit R	5600-6100	1.8 mi NE Whatcom Pass
EAST BOARDMAN	Snohomish	25	Sf Stilly R	3370	7.5 mi SE Verlot
EASTER SUNDAY	Stevens	1	Kettle R	3275	10 mi SE Orient
ECHO	King	19	Raging R	910	2.4 mi SW Snoqualmie
ECHO	King	12	Lk Washington	393	6 mi N Seattle

LAKE	COUNTY	ACRES	DRAINAGE	ELEVATION	LOCATION
ECHO	Pierce	61	White R	3819	29 mi SE Enumclaw
ECHO	Snohomish	17	Sammamish R	477	3 mi SE Maltby
ECHO	Snohomish	25	Pilchuck R	1670	9 mi N Sultan
ECHO LKS (5)	Stevens	0.6-3.8	Colville R	1870	8 mi N Colville
EDDS	King	26	Mf Snoq R	4300	4.5 mi NE Snoq Pass
EDGAR	Skagit	4	Shannon Lk	3250	9 mi E Concrete
EDNA	Chelan	3.5	Wenatchee R	6500	13 mi NW Leavenworth
EGG	San Juan	7	San Juan Ch	155	3.5 mi NW Friday Hbr
ELBOW	Douglas	25	Columbia R	2320	1800' S Del Rio G.H.
ELBOW	Ferry	51	Columbia R	2150	13.5 mi N Inchelium
ELBOW	King	6	Mf Snoq R	3900	6.5 mi NW Snoq Pass
ELBOW	Stevens	13.5	Columbia R	2775	9.5 mi W Northport
ELBOW	Thurston	36	Nisqually R	479	9.5 mi SE Yelm
ELBOW	Whatcom	5	Nooksack R	3400	6.5 mi SW Mt Baker summit
ELEANOR	Pierce	20	White R	4960	11 mi NE Mt Rainier summit
ELECTRON RES	Pierce	13	Puget Snd	1540	1 mi SE Electron
ELIZABETH	King	7	Sf Skykomish R	2865	8 mi NW Skykomish
ELIZABETH	Pierce	4	White R	5900	3.5 mi N Chinook Pass
ELK	Clallam	59	Ozette Lk	380	11 mi S Neah Bay
ELK	Grays Hbr	11	Quinault R	3000	6 mi E Quinault Lk
ELK	Jefferson	6	Upper Hoh R	2550	4 mi N Mt Olympus
ELK—LOWER	Mason	6	Hamma Hamma R	1050	1.5 mi S Hamma Hamma G.S.
ELK—UPPER	Mason	3	Hamma Hamma R	1200	1200' S Elk Lk
ELK	Skamania	13	Nf Lewis R	4700	2.5 mi SW Cultus Cr G.S.
ELK	Skamania	30,5	Green R	3978	6 mi NW Spirit Lk outlet
ELL	Okanogan	21	Wf San Poil R	2592	16 mi SE Tonasket
ELLEN	Ferry	78	Columbia R	2300	8.5 mi SE Sherman Cr Pass
ELTON LKS	Yakima	14	Yakima R	—	6 mi N Yakima
ELMER RES	Clark	4	Ef Lewis R	800	6.5 mi N La Center
ELOCHOMAN	Cowlitz	4 5	Ef Elochoman R	1650	12.5 mi NE Cathlamet
ELOIKA	Spokane	659	WB L Spokane	1920	4 mi W Elk SE, end
ELSEY	Chelan	16	Napeegua R	6200	18.5 mi NE Stevens Pass
EMBRO	King	9.5	Tye R	4200	2 mi N Scenic
EMERALD	King	4	Jade Lk	4725	10 mi SE Skykomish
EMERALD	Snohomish	11	Suiattle R	5150	17 mi E Darrington
EMERSON	Pierce	5	American Lk	260	1 mi SW Ponders Corner
EMMA	Franklin	20	Snake R	440	7 mi NE Ice Hbr Dam
EMPIRE LKS (3)	Ferry	0.6-4	Kettle R	3600	11 mi N Republic
ENCHANTMENT LKS(10)	Chelan	1-23	Wenatchee R	6875	10 mi SW Leavenworth
ENJAR	Skagit	12	Skagit R	4300	1.5 mi NW Snowking Mtn
ENTIAT (RES)	Chelan	9860	Columbia R	707	7.5 mi N Wenatchee
ERICKSON RES	Kitsap	2	Manzanita Bay	60	4.5 mi NW Winslow
ERICKSON	Mason	15	Dewatto R	475	4.8 mi NW Belfair
ERICKSON	Stevens	5.5	Colville R	2175	9.5 mi SE Colville
ERIE	Skagit	111	Skagit Bay	140	4 mi S Anacortes
ESCONDIDO	Kittitas	4	Cooper R	4630	10 mi NE Snoq Pass
ETHEL	Chelan	16	Wenatchee R	5400	9.8 mi E Stevens Pass
ETHEL	Pierce	31	Wf White R	4287	8.5 mi NW Mt Rainier summit
ETTA	Clallam	13	Greywolf R	477	16 mi S Port Angeles
EUNICE	Skamania	6.5	Wind R	4500	19.5 mi N Carson
EVANS	King	11	Foss R	3600	4 mi S Skykomish
EVANS	Okanogan	27	Okanogan R	1712	3 mi W Riverside
EVAN	Snohomish	13	Stilly R	2751	6 mi SE Verlot R.S.
EVELYN	King	2	Tye R	5200	7.5 mi S Scenic
EVERETT	Skagit	8	Sherman Lk	650	1 mi E Concrete
EVERGREEN RES	Grant	235	Columbia R	1185	7.5 mi SW Quincey

F

LAKE	COUNTY	ACRES	DRAINAGE	ELEVATION	LOCATION
FAILOR (RES)	Grays Hbr	60	Humptulips R	117	9.4 mi N Hoquiam
FAIRVIEW	Kitsap	7	Case Inlet	380	6.7 mi SW Pt Orchard
FALLS	Skagit	60	Cascade R	4200	4.8 mi SE Marblemount
FAN	Pend Oreille	73	WBr L Spokane	1930	8.4 mi NE Deer Park
FANCHERS DAM RES	Okanogan	20	Okanogan R	3150	11.5 mi NE Tonasket
FARGHER PD	Clark	3	Ef Lewis R	700	3.5 mi W Amboy
FARLEY	Okanogan	14	Okanogan R	2350	6.5 mi SE Malott
FAWN	Cowlitz	24	Green R	3700	6 mi NW Spirit Lk outlet
FAWN	Okanogan	6	Chewack R	5500	29.5 mi N Winthrop
FAZON	Whatcom	32	Nooksack R	128	1.5 mi NW Goshen
FEEKS MARSH	Island	10	Puget Sound	100	3.4 mi W Clinton
FENNER	Yakima	3	Naches R	5460	1.5 mi NW Crow Lk
FENWICK	King	18	Green R	120	1 mi NE Star Lk
FERGUSON	Okanogan	9	Mf Pasayten R	6900	29 mi NW Winthrop
FERGUSON PDS	Whatcom	10	Sf Nooksack R		nr Saxon Bridge
FERN	Chelan	17	Nf Entiat R	6875	34 mi NW Entiat
FERRY	Ferry	19	San Poil R	3329	9.4 mi SW Republic
FIANDER	Thurston	15	Deschutes R	450	4 mi W Yelm
FIDDLE	Mason	1.5	Hood Canal	800	3 mi NE Lilliwaup
FIFTEEN	Thurston	4	Deschutes R	500	1.5 mi SE Rainier
FIGURE EIGHT	Okanogan	31	Okanogan R	2750	11 mi SE Okanogan
FINDLEY LKS (3)	King	1.7-22	Cedar R	3580-3710	14.5 mi E Kanasket

LAKE	COUNTY	ACRES	DRAINAGE	ELEVATION	LOCATION
FINDLEY	Spokane	15	Palouse R	2290	2.4 mi S Cheney
FIO RITO	Kittitas	54	Yakima R	—	5 mi S Ellensburg
FIREWEED PDS (2)	Kittitas	0.9-1.5	Keechelus L	4055	7 mi S Snoq Pass
FIRST	King	2.5	White R	1100	3.4 mi E Enumclaw
FIRST HIDDEN	Okanogan	19	Lost R	4250	32.5 mi NW Winthrop
FIRST THOUGHT	Stevens	2	Kettle R	3500	3 mi NE Orient
FISH	Chelan	513	Wenatchee R	1850	16.4 mi N Leavenworth
FISH	King	16.5	Green R	720	1.5 mi SW Cumberland
FISH	Okanogan	102	Okanogan R	1798	4.5 mi NE Conconully
FISH	Spokane	47	Spokane R	2171	3 mi NE Cheney
FISH	Yakima	10	Tieton R	3400	2.5 mi S Tieton Dam
FISH	Yakima	11	Bumping R	4114	8.5 mi S Chinook Pass
FISHTRAP (RES)	Lincoln	196	Palouse R	1980	6.5 mi E Sprague
FISHER	King	65	Tye R	4850	7.8 mi SE Skykomish
FITCHENER SL	King	3	Nf Snoq R	1470	12.8 mi NE Snoq
FIVEMILE	King	38	Stuck R	400	4 mi SW Auburn
FLANDERS PD	Clallam	2	Pt Discovery Bay	200	2.5 mi NE Blyn
FLAPJACK LKS (2)	Mason	6-10	Nf Skok R	3900	4.3 mi N hd Lk Cushman
FLAT	Lincoln	20	Crab Creek	2150	11.5 mi SE Wilbur
FLAT	Lincoln	11	Crab Creek	2100	2.5 mi SW Govan
FLAT	Mason	2	Sf Skok R	1250	18 mi NW Shelton
FLAT IRON	Yakima	7	Bumping R	57W	1.5 mi SW Bald Mtn L.O.
FLORA	Chelan	11	Wenatchee R	5900	12.8 mi NW Leavenworth
FLORENCE	Lincoln	34	Crab Cr	2300	11 mi S Creston
FLOWING	Snohomish	135	Pilchuck R	526	6 mi N Monroe
FLUME CR BV PDS	Skagit	4	Sauk R	1000	4.7 mi S Rockport
FLY	Skagit	2	Cascade R	4000	7.4 mi SE Marblemount
FOGGY	Snohomish	19	Sf Sauk R	5000	3 mi S Barlow Pass
FOHN	King	1	Wf Foss R	5500	3000' SW Opal Lk
FONTAL	Snohomish	37	Skykomish R	1081	4.5 mi SE Monroe
FORBES	King	7	Lk Washington	250	1.5 mi E Kirkland
FORDE	Okanogan	24	Similkameen R	1560	6 mi S Loomis
FOREST	Pierce	6	Puyallup R	520	3.3 mi S Orting
FOREST	Pierce	2-5	Greenwater R	3900	8 mi SE Greenwater
FOREST	Skamania	8	Green R	3900	5.8 mi NW Spirit Lk outlet
FORLORN LKS (12)	Skamania	1-20	White Salmon R	3700	19 mi N Stevenson
FORTSON MILL PD	Snohomish	2	Nf Stilly R	400	9.5 mi E Oso
FORTUNE PDS (2)	Snohomish	8-1	Nf Skyk R	4600-4700	10.5 mi NW StevensPass
FOUND	Skagit	71	Cascade R	4150	10.8 mi SE Marblemount
FOUNTAIN	Whatcom	14	Nooksack R	70	3 mi SE Lynden
FOUR POINT	Okanogan	16	Chewack R	7100	31 mi N Winthrop
FOURTH OF JULY	Adams	110	Palouse R	1900	2.2 mi S Sprague
FOURTH OF JULY	Snohomish	1	Beckler R	4350	7.5 mi E Index
FOX LKS (2)	Okanogan	4-8	Chewack R	6700	27.5 mi N Winthrop
FRAGRANCE	Whatcom	6.5	Chuckanut Bay	1025	6.5 mi S Bellingham
FRAILEY PDS	Skagit	1	Stilly R	1100	1.4 mi W Cavanaugh Lk
FRANCIS	King	19.5	Cedar R	470	2 mi N Maple Valley
FRANCIS	King	40	Wf Miller R	4200	6 mi SW Skykomish
FRANKLIN ROOSEVELT	Stevens	79000	Columbia R	1288	28 mi NE Coulee City
FRATER	Pend Orellle	11	L Pend Ore R	3200	6.5 mi S Ione
FRAZIER MARSH	King	98	Snoqualmie R	500	7.5 mi S Snoqualmie
FREDS	Okanogan	6	Mf Passayten R	6500	30.4 mi NW Winthrop
FREEWAY	Yakima	23	Yakima R	1070	N side Yakima
FREEZEOUT	Whatcom	9	Skagit R	5800	15 mi NE Ross Dam
FRENCH	Skamania	1.5	Columbia R	440	1.7 mi SW Stevenson
FRENCH CREEK PD	Snohomish	6	Nf Stilly R	900	1.5 mi S Hazel
FRENCH PTHLS/LOWER	Chelan	5	Wenatchee R	5375	11.5 mi N Salmon La Sac
FRENCH PTHLS/UPPER	Chelan	6	Wenatchee R	5875	1500' NW Lower Potholes
FRENCH JOHNS	Ferry	14	FDR Lk	1320	5 mi S Keller
FRESHWATER	Pacific	5	Willapa Bay	20	5 mi N Long Beach
FROG	Kittitas	1	Yakima R	3550	3 mi S Snoq Pass
FROG	Skamania	4	Columbia R	375	4 mi E Carson
FROG	Snohomish	1.5	Sauk R	950	3.4 mi S Darrington
FROSTY	Okanogan	3.5	Similkameen R	5400	22 mi NE Ross Dam
FRY	Okanogan	10	Okanogan R	1242	3.3 mi NW Omak
FRYE	Okanogan	4	Okanogan R	—	.05 mi NW Riverside
FRYING PAN	Lewis	23	Ohanapecosh R	4850	6.5 mi N White Pass
FURY	King	1	Snoqualmie R	1005	6.7 mi N North Bend

G

LAKE	COUNTY	ACRES	DRAINAGE	ELEVATION	LOCATION
GADWELL	Grant	5	Crab Cr	950	8.5 mi N Othello
GALLAGHER HEAD	Kittitas	1.5	Nf Teanaway R	5595	17.5 mi N Cle Elum
GARBER	Stevens	1.5	Colville R	3000	8 mi W Valley
GARFIELD MTN/LOW	King	8	Taylor R	4000	15 mi E North Bend
GARFIELD MTN/UPPER	King	7	Taylor R	4500	1300' SE lower lk
GEE POINT	Skagit	4	Skagit R	4100	8.5 mi SW Concrete
GEHRKE	Thurston	8	Deschutes R	450	1 mi E Rainier
GENEVA	King	29	Commencement B	385	2.5 mi SW Auburn
GEORGE	Grant	5	Crab Cr	1200	0.8 mi NE George
GEORGE	Pierce	33	Nisqually R	4232	5 mi NW Longmire

LAKE	COUNTY	ACRES	DRAINAGE	ELEVATION	LOCATION
GEORGE	Pierce	2	Greenwater R	5470	26 mi SE Enumclaw
GERTRUDE	Lewis	14	Cispus R	5750	20 mi SE Packwood
GHOST	Skamania	5	Muddy R	3767-	.04 mi SW Strawberry Lk
GIBBS	Jefferson	37	Pt Townsend Bay	340	7 mi NW Port Ludlow
GILBERT	Stevens	4	Kettle R	2200	5 mi NE Orient
GILE	Pacific	19	Willapa Bay	20	2.5 mi N Long Beach
GILLETTE	Skamania	3.5	Columbia R	300	1.5 mi N No Bonneville
GILLETTE	Stevens	48	L Pend Ore R	3160	17 mi NE Colville
GISSBERG PDS	Snohomish	5	Snohomish R	—	8 mi N Everett
GLACIER	Lewis	20	Cowlitz R	3000	5.5 mi SE Packwood
GLACIER	King	60	Tye R	4900	3.5 mi S Scenic
GLACIER	Kittitas	21	Cooper R	4750	6.4 mi NE Snoq Pass
GLADYS	Clallam	1	Greywolf R	5500	Hwtrs Grand Cr
GLASSES	Chelan	25	L Wenatchee R	4750	7 mi N Stevens Pass
GLORY	Okanogan	3.5	Ashnola R	6600	31 mi N Winthrop
GLUD PDS	Kitsap	1	Burke Bay	45	3.8 mi S Keyport
GOAT	King	19.5	Mf Snoq R	3600	17.4 mi NE North Bend
GOAT	Lewis	10	Cispus R	6900	9.4 mi SW White Pass
GOAT	Pierce	10	Nisqually R	4300	6.7 mi NE National
GOAT	Pierce	3	White R	5500	7.4 mi N Chinook Pass
GOAT	Snohomish	64	Sf Sauk R	3154	4 mi E Barlow Pass
GOAT MARSH #1	Cowlitz	13	Sf Toutle R	2910	4.4 mi N Merrill Lk
GOAT MARSH #2	Cowlitz	5	Sf Toutle R	2911	750' SE Lk #1
GOLD	King	56	Ef Miller R	5000	9 mi NE Snoq Pass
GOLD—UPPER	Okanogan	19	Wf San Poil R	2950	14 mi N Nespelem
GOLD—LOWER	Okanogan	11	Wf San Poil R	2945	1000' mi NE upper lk
GOLD BASIN PD	Snohomish	1	Sf Stilly R	1100	at Gold Basin
GOLDEN	King	8	Wf Foss R	5200	9.8 SW Skykomish
GOLDEN LKS (3)	Pierce	4-18	Mowich R	4450-4950	7 mi W Mt Rainier summi
GOLDENEYE	Grant	30	Crab Cr	930	10.8 mi N Othello
GOLNICK	Island	2.5	Skagit Bay	325	on Whidbey Island
GOODWIN	Snohomish	547	Tulalip Bay	324	7.5 mi NW Marysville
GOODWIN	Thurston	3	Nisqually R	415	3.4 mi S Yelm
GOOSE LKS (2)	Grant	50-112	Crab Cr	860	9.2 mi NW Othello
GOOSE	Lewis	8	L Nisqually R	2850	8 mi N Morton
GOOSE	Okanogan	181	Columbia R	1225	17 mi W Nespelem
GOOSE	Skamania	58	White Salmon R	3050	15 mi N Carson
GOOSE PD	Thurston	2	Henderson Inlet	170	5 mi E Olympia
GORDON	Skagit	2	Stilly R	3000	on N side Table Mtn
GOSS	Island	55	Holmes Hbr	130	3 mi W Langley
GOUGING	King	11	Wf Miller R	3400	7.4 mi SW Skykomish
GRACE LKS (3)	Chelan	1-7	Wenatchee R	64 6800	7.8 mi SE Stevens Pass
GRANDY	Skagit	56	Skagit R	809	3 mi NW Concrete
GRANITE LKS (2)	King	9-15	Mf Snoq R	2950-3060	8.8 mi SE North Bend
GRANITE	Lewis	29	Nisqually R	4163	7.5 mi SE National
GRANITE	Skagit	16.5	Nf Stilly R	3521	7 mi NE Oso
GRANITE LKS (4)	Skagit	5-144	Cascade R	4500	7 mi SE Marblemount
GRANITE PTHLS (20)	Skagit	1-8	Nf Stilly R	3400	7 mi NE Oso
GRANITE	Yakima	7	Bumping R	5035	1 mi E Miners Ridge L.O.
GRANITE FALLS RES	Snohomish	2	Pilchuck R	680	1 mi E Granite Falls
GRANITE MTN PTHLS (3)	Chelan	2-6	Wenatchee R	6100	SE side Trico Mtn
GRANT	Okanogan	22	Lost Cr	2598	7 mi NW Nespelem
GRANT	Pierce	1.5	Puget Sound	220	1 mi W Du Pont
GRASS	Chelan	3	Wenatchee R	3550	4.2 mi S Stevens Pass
GRASS	King	12	Green R	470	1.7 mi SE Covington
GRASS	Snohomish	2	Nf Rapid R	4700	10 mi N Stevens Pass
GRAVEL	King	9	Mf Snoq R	5100	3.5 mi NE Snoq Pass
GRAVEL PIT	King	1	Green R	655	3.5 mi NW Enumclaw
GREAT WESTERN	Okanogan	5	Nespelem R	2340	4.8 mi NW Nespelem
GREEN	Clark	127	Columbia R	10	8 mi NW Vancouver
GREEN	King	255	Puget Sound	170	In Seattle
GREEN LKS (2)	Okanogan	9-45	Okanogan R	1560	5.4 mi NW Omak
GREEN	Pierce	12	Carbon R	2950	10 mi NW Mt Rainier summit
GREEN	Whatcom	80	Skagit R	4300	11.5 mi N Marblemount
GREEN	Whatcom	19.5	Nooksack R	74	4 mi SE Lynden
GREEN	Yakima	4.5	Yakima R	5900	7.5 mi S Tieton Dam
GREENLEAF SL	Skamania	48	Columbia R	65	.05 mi W No Bonneville
GREEN MOUNTAIN	Skamania	4	Cispus R	4000	24 mi SE Randle
GREEN PARK	Pierce	12	White R	5400	4.5 mi NE Mt Rainier summit
GREEN RIDGE	King	15.5	Mf Snoq R	4200	2000' SW Rock Lk
GREEN VIEW	Chelan	40	Stehekin R	5455	SE side Goode Mtn
GREENWOOD	Lewis	7.5	Nisqually R	4450	9.8 mi SE National
GREIDER LKS (2)	Snohomish	8-58	Sultan R	2935	8.5 mi NE Gold Bar
GRIMES	Douglas	150	Columbia R	1800	8 mi SE Mansfield
GRISDALE PD	Grays Hbr	13	Wynooche R	450	5.4 mi S Camp Grisdale
GRIZZLY	Snohomish	1	Nf Rapid R	4800	9 mi E Granite Falls
GROTTO	King	4	Sf Sky R	3900	NE side Grotto Mtn
GULCH LKS (3)	Snohomish	2-4	Silver Cr	3600	10 mi NE Index
GUNN	Snohomish	6	Lewis Cr	4500	4 mi E Index
GUS'S	King	16	Ef Miller R	4600	10 mi NE Snoq Pass

H

LAKE	COUNTY	ACRES	DRAINAGE	ELEVATION	LOCATION
"H"	Grant	7	Columbia R	1165	7 mi SW Quincey
"H"	Lincoln	26	Crab Cr	2200	6 mi S Wilbur
"H" RES NO 1	Chelan		Squilchuck Cr	4250	7.5 mi S Wenatchee
HAGER	Lewis	2	Cowlitz R	3000	2.5 mi SE Packwood
HAIGS	Clallam	5	Sol Duc R	4675	Hwtrs Sol Duc R
HALCYON	Snohomish	5	Skykomish R	3250	3 mi S Gold Bar
HALE LKS (3)	Spokane	10-24	Badger Lk	2300	6 mi S Cheney
HALFMOON	Adams	27	Crab Cr	820	6 mi SW Othello
HALFMOON	Okanogan	16	Lake Cr	6700	24 mi N Winthrop
HALFMOON	Pend Oreille	14	Pend Ore R	3250	6 mi NE Cusick
HALL	Snohomish	6	Lk Ballinger	340	1 mi S Lynnwood
HALLER	King	15	Thornton Cr	370	In Seattle
HALLIN	Adams	33	Palouse R	1760	11 mi E Ritzville
HAM	King	2	Green R	500	5 mi E Kent
HAMAR	Skagit	2	Skagit R	4310	2 mi SW Snowking Mtn
HAMILTON SL	Skagit	g	Skagit R	90	At Hamilton
HAMPTON—LOWER	Grant	19	Crab Cr	895	7 mi N Othello
HAMPTON—UPPER	Grant	53	Crab Cr	901	7 mi N Othello
HAMPTON SLGHS	Grant	12	Para Lk	875	7 mi N Othello
HANAFORD	Skamania	24	Green Lk	4090	6 mi NW Spirit Lk outlet
HANCOCK	Island	38	Admiralty Inlet	6	1 mi NW Greenbank
HANCOCK	King	236	Nf Snoq R	2172	7 mi NE North Bend
HANGING	Whatcom	74	Chilliwack R	4550	23 mi NE Mt Baker
HANKS LKS (2)	Mason	6-27	Goldsborough Cr	400	8 mi NW Shelton
HANNA	Snohomish	48	Snoqualmie R	1094	5.4 mi SE Monroe
HANS	King	24	Snoqualmie R	490	4.4 mi NE Fall City
HANSON	Snohomish	10	Pilchuck R	1430	5.5 mi SE Granite Falls
HAPPY	Clallam	2.5	Lk Crescent	4875	4.5 mi S Sutherland Lk
HARBOR	Okanogan	3	Okanogan R	3430	8.7 mi NE Tonasket
HARDSCRABBLE (2)	King	8-10	Mf Snoq R	4800	8 mi NE Snoq Pass
HARRY	Skagit	3	Nf Stilly R	3600	10.5 mi NW Darrington
HART	Chelan	11	Wenatchee R	5500	7.5 mi SW Leavenworth
HART	Chelan	33	Lk Chelan	3965	3.5 mi W Holden
HARTS SWAMP	King	7	Snoqualmie R	780	.07 mi NE Duvall
HARTS	Pierce	109	Nisqually R	349	7.4 mi SE Yelm
HASKEL SL	Snohomish	19	Skykomish R	40	.05 mi S Monroe
HATCH	Stevens	34	L Pend Ore R	2141	5.4 mi SE Colville
HATHAWAY	Clark	154	Columbia R	10	1.4 mi S Ridgefield
HATTEN	Lincoln	11	Crab Cr	2150	12.4 mi S Creston
HAUGENS PD	Snohomish	2	Skykomish R	600	4 mi SW Sultan
HAVEN	Mason	15	Sf Skok R	1016	10.8 mi NW Shelton
HAVEN	Mason	70.5	Tahuya R	366	7.4 mi SW Belfair
HAWKINS	Skagit	7	Nf Stilly R	3500	9.4 mi NE Oso
HAYES	Whatcom	13	Nf Nooksack R	4800	400' N Iceberg Lk
HAYES CR PDS	Adams	5	Crab Cr	750	6.5 mi NW Othello
HAZEL MILL PD	Snohomish	2 5	N Stilly R	320	In Hazel
HEART	Grant	26	Crab Cr	978	7.5 mi SW Warden
HEART	Lewis	4	Cowlitz R	5700	9 mi SE Packwood
HEART	Skagit	61	Fidalgo Bay	340	2.5 mi S Anacortes
HEART	Skagit	15	Sf Nooksack R	4050	9 mi N Hamilton
HEART	Skamania	5	Nf Toutle R	4645	4 mi N Spirit Lk
HEATER PD	Pend Oreille	6	Pend Ore R	2050	7 mi N Cusick
HEATHER	Chelan	90	L Wenatchee R	3890	8 mi N Stevens Pass
HEATHER	Okanogan	19	Similkameen R	5700	43 mi NW Winthrop
HEATHER	Skamania	4	Skykomish R	3600	6 mi E Gold Bar
HEATHER	Snohomish	17	Sf Stilly R	2450	8 mi E Granite Falls
HEIDE	Whatcom	1.5	Terrell Cr	20	2 mi S Birch Bay
HELEN	Pierce	5	Puyallup R	4000	7.5 mi NE National
HELENA	Kitsap	6	Case Inlet	390	5 mi E Belfair
HELENA	Snohomish	28	Sauk R	3050	8 mi S Darrington
HELL	Yakima	3.5	Nf Tieton R	5414	1.3 mi SE White Pass
HELLROARING	Yakima	2	Klickitat R	5300	12 mi NW Glenwood
HELMICKS PD	Lewis	1 5	Chehalis R	360	.05 mi NE Pe Ell
HEMPLE	Snohomish	7	Sf Stilly R	3820	10 mi E Granite Falls
HENRY	Lewis	1 5	Ohanapecosh R	5150	5 mi N White Pass
HENSKIN LKS (2)	Pierce	2-3.5	White R	5500-5600	3.5 mi NE Chinook Pass
HERITAGE	Stevens	71	L Pend Ore R	3163	25 mi N Chewelah
HERMAN	Adams	35	Crab Cr	924	6 mi N Othello
HERON	Grant	7	Crab Cr	954	Adj O'Sullivan Dam
HERRON	Pierce	10	Case Inlet	182	1 mi S Herron
HESS	Okanogan	6	Okanogan R	1400	6 mi W Riverside
HESTER LKS (2)	King	67-9.5	Mf Snoq R	4050	5.8 mi N Snoq Pass
HEWITT	Thurston	27	Deschutes R	125	2.5 mi S Olympia
HIBOX	Kittitas	3	Kachess R	4620	6 mi E Snoq Pass
HICKS	Thurston	171	Patterson Cr	158	5 mi E Olympia
HIDDEN	Chelan	10	Wenatchee R	2400	15 mi N Leavenworth
HIDDEN	Chelan	1.5	Columbia R	2000	7 mi NE Chelan
HIDDEN	Clallam	5	Sol Duc R	2625	2 mi SE Sol Duc H.S.
HIDDEN	Pierce	7	Sunrise Cr	5926	1 mi N Clover Lk
HIDDEN	Pierce	2.5	White R	4187	1 mi E Corral Pass

LAKE	COUNTY	ACRES	DRAINAGE	ELEVATION	LOCATION
HIDDEN	Skagit	55	Nf Cascade R	6000	12 mi E Marblemount
HIDDEN LKS (3)	Skamania	3-10	White Salmon R	4100	1 mi E Cultus Cr G.S.
HIDDEN	Snohomish	2	Pilchuck R	1400	4.5 mi SE Granite Falls
HIGHWOOD	Whatcom	2	Nf Nooksack R	4100	1000 NE Mt Baker Ldg
HIIM RES	Clark	6	Ef Lewis R	180	1.5 mi S La Center
HILL	Yakima	6	Tieton R	5110	5 mi NE White Pass
HILLE	Pierce	3	Stuck R	475	4.5 mi NE Sumner
HILLMAN FISH PD	Mason	4	Ef Satsop R	380	9 mi W Shelton
HILLTOP	Grant	6	Columbia R	1300	5.5 mi SW George
HI-LOW	King	4	Mf Snoq R	4300	17 mi NE North Bend
HILT	Skagit	3	Sauk R	1300	4.8 mi SE Rockport
HILTON	Snohomish	3	Snohomish R	375	4.5 mi SE Everett
HINTER	King	5	Ef Miller R	4950	6.7 mi S Skykomish
HINTZVILLE PDS	Kitsap	3	Hood Canal	540	.04 mi S Hintzville
HIRSCH PD	Stevens	7.5	Colville R	2175	3.5 mi E Valley
HOBUCK	Clallam	7	Makah Bay	150	2.5 mi SW Neah Bay
HOG	Spokane	53	Palouse R	2000	9.5 mi NE Sprague
HOFSTADS PTHL	Thurston	3	Nisqually R	21	6.8 mi NW Yelm
HOH	Clallam	19	Hoh R	4500	2700' SW Bogachiel Pk
HOLDEN	Chelan	19	Railroad Cr	5275	3 mi NW Holden
HOLM	King	19	Green R	400	5 mi E Auburn
HOLMSTEDT	Skamania	5	Panhandle Lk	5100	NE side Mt Whittier
HOLOMAN	King	6	Nf Tolt R	3650	5 mi SW Index
HOME	Jefferson	1.5	Dungeness R	5350	14 mi SW Quilcene
HONEY	King	9	Nf Snoq R	3233	13 mi NE North Bend
HONEY	Kitsap	1	Sinclair Inlet	240	2.5 mi SW Pt Orchard
HONOUR	Chelan	6.5	Wenatchee R	5100	14 mi NW Leavenworth
HOO HOO	Skamania	5	Nf Lewis R	1600	6 mi E Mt St Helens
HOOKNOSE	Stevens	2	Pend Ore R	5950	6.5 mi NW Metaline Falls
HOPE	Chelan	2 5	Icicle Cr	4400	3 mi S Stevens Pass
HOPKINS	Okanogan	9	Similkameen R	6400	42 mi SW Winthrop
HORSE	Douglas	12	Columbia R	2200	4 mi NE Sims Corner
HORSE	Skagit	10	Suiattle R	5000	19 mi NE Darrington
HORSESHOE	Adams	13	Palouse R	1670	1 mi NW McCall
HORSESHOE	Chelan	8	Wenatchee R	6275	13 mi SW Leavenworth
HORSESHOE	Jefferson	13	Pt Ludlow	320	4 mi SW Pt Ludlow
HORSESHOE	King	8	Green R	500	2 mi SW Blk Diamond
HORSESHOE	King	8.5	Mf Snoq R	4250	6 mi NW Snoq Pass
HORSESHOE	King	25	Dingford Cr	3500	17 mi E North Bend
HORSESHOE	King	19	Snoq R	50	1 mi N Carnation
HORSESHOE	Kitsap	40	Henderson Bay	270	9 mi S Pt Orchard
HORSESHOE	Lewis	4	Chehalis R	160	2 mi SW Centralia
HORSESHOE	Okanogan	59	Okanogan R	910	5 mi S Oroville
HORSESHOE	Pend Orelile	22	L Spokane R	2125	9 mi NW Elk
HORSESHOE	Pend Orelile	8	Pend Ore R	2150	5.3 mi SE Usk
HORSESHOE	Pierce	9	Ohop Cr	750	3 mi N Eatonville
HORSESHOE	Skamania	24	Cispus R	4150	24 mi SE Randle
HORSESHOE	Spokane	68	Spokane R	2449	9.5 mi W Nine Mi~e Falls
HORSESHOE	Stevens	23.5	Colville R	3050	4 mi NW Othello
HORSESHOE	Yakima	59	Yakima R	650	1.5 mi NW Mabton
HORSESHOE PD	Yakima	59	Yakima	650	4 mi NW Mabton
HORSETHIEF	Klickitat	92	Columbia R	160	2.5 mi NE The Dalles Dam
HOURGLASS	Grant	2	Crab Cr	940	8.8 mi N Othello
HOWARD HANSON RES	King		Green R	1206	6 mi SE Kanasket
HOWARD	Snohomish	3.5	Nf Skykomish R	4000	7 mi NE Index
HOWARD	Snohomish	27	Martha Lk	238	9 mi NW Marysville
HOWARD	Yakima	49	Wf Klickitat R	4887	17 mi S White Pass
HOWELL	Mason	10	Tahuya R	450	2600' S Collins Lk
HOZOMEEN	Whatcom	111	Ross Lk	2800	16 mi N Ross Dam
HUBBARD	Snohomish	6	Sf Stilly R	500	2 mi E Granite Falls
HUBBARD	Thurston	3	Nisqually R	300	6 mi W Yelm
HUFF	Pend Oreille	1	Priest Lk	3150	18.5 mi NE Ruby
HUGHES	Snohomish	20	Woods Cr	540	8 mi NE Monroe
HUGO	Lewis	1.5	Cowlitz R	4100	12 mi SE Packwood
HULL	King	6	Snoqualmie R	822	9 mi N Snoqualmie
HUMMMEL	San Juan	36	Lopez Sound	97	Lopez Island
HUNSINGER	Okanogan	2	Okanogan R	2540	4 mi NW Omak
HUNTER	Okanogan	5	Okanogan R	4050	8.5 mi W Tonasket
HUTCHINSON	Adams	50	Crab Cr	700	4 mi E Chewelah
HUTTULA	Grays Hbr	11	Chehalis R	20	3 mi SW Elma
HYAK	Kittitas	2	Yakima R	3500	2.4 mi S Snoq Pass
HYAS	Kittitas	124	Cle Elum R	3550	11 mi N Salmon La Sac
HYAS	Skagit	4	Suiattle R	4000	11 mi S Marblemount
HYDE	King	5.5	Green R	800	.05 mi W Cumberland

I

I-82	Yakima	8-25	Yakima R		S Union Gap on I-82
ICE LKS (2)	Chelan	21-54	Entiat R	68OU	37.5 mi N Leavenworth
ICE	King	2	Pratt R	4450	4.5 mi NW Snoq Pass
ICE	Lincoln	2	Crab Cr	2400	2 mi SE Creston

LAKE	COUNTY	ACRES	DRAINAGE	ELEVATION	LOCATION
ICEBERG LKS (2)	Jefferson	1-2	Dosewallips R	6100	Hwtr Dosewallips R
ICEBERG	King	21	Mf Snoq R	4850	7.5 mi NE Snoq Pass
ICEBERG	Whatcom	37	Nf Nooksack R	4800	2 mi S Mt Baker Ldg
ICEHOUSE	Skamania	2.5	Columbia R	150	2.5 mi SW Stevenson
IDA	Chelan	16	Wenatchee R	7200	9.5 mi W Leavenworth
IDA	Snohomish	3	Sultan R	830	5 mi N Sultan
ILLABOT	Skagit	4	Skagit R	2550	8 mi SE Marblemount
ILSWOOT	King	48	Ef Ross R	4700	10 mi SE Skykomish
IMAGE	Snohomish	4	Suiattle R	6050	27 mi E Darrington
IMAN	Skamania	2.5	Columbia R	300	1 mi W Stevenson
IMBERT	Grant	15	East Low Canal	1190	2.5 mi SW Warden
INDEPENDENCE	Snohomish	5.5	Stilly R	3700	1 mi W Pass Lk
INDIAN DAN	Okanogan	14	Columbia R	1500	4 mi W Brewster
INDIGO	Snohomish	22	Suiattle R	4500	13 mi E Darrington
INGALLS	Chelan	17	Wenatchee R	6463	15 mi NW Blewett Pass
INKSTER LKS (2)	Lincoln	1-1	Spokane R	2430	12 mi N Davenport
INMAN	Thurston	25	Deschutes R	450	1 mi E Rainier
IONE MILL PD	Pend Orellle	37	Pend Orellle R	2050	At Ione
IPSOOT	Whatcom	9	Baker R	4500	13 mi N Marblemount
IRELY	Jefferson	4	Quinault R	550	9 mi NE Lk Quinault
ISABEL	Snohomish	176	Wallace R	2842	4 mi E Gold Bar
ISABELLA	King	12.5	Nf Snoq R	3510	11 mi NE North Bend
ISABELLA	Mason	208	Mill Cr	150	2.5 mi S Shelton
ISLAND	King	17	Sf Snoq R	4260	13 mi SE North Bend
ISLAND	Kitsap	43	Dyes Inlet	217	2 mi SW Keyport
ISLAND	Mason	109	Oakland Bay	230	2.5 mi S Shelton
ISLAND	Okanogan	9	Okanogan R	2350	11.5 mi S Okanogan
ISLAND	Pacific	59	Pacific Ocean	20	4 mi S Ocean Park
ISLAND	Snohomish	2.5	Pilchuck R	3500	10.5 mi SE Granite Falls
ISLAND	Yakima	1.5	Nf Tieton R	5240	.04 mi E S end Long John Lk
ITSWOOT	Skagit	33	Suiattle R	5100	24.5 mi E Darrington
IVANHOE	Kittitas	21	Waptus R	4700	1 mi NW Salmon La Sac

J

JACK	Chelan	1	Wenatchee R	6300	13.3 mi SW Leavenworth
JACKPOT	Lewis	5.5	Nf Cispus R	4450	9.8 mi S Packwood
JACKSON	Grant	13	Columbia R	450	.04 mi blw Priest Rapids Dam
JACKSON	Pierce	16	Carr Inlet	196	4 mi S Vaughn
JADE	King	28	Ef Foss R	5400	7 mi S Scenic
JADE	King	7	Ef Foss R	4650	10 mi SE Skykomish
JAKES	King	7	Tye R	5000	6.8 mi W Stevens Pass
JAMES	Pierce	19	Wf White R	4370	8 mi N Mt Rainier summit
JAMESON	Douglas	332	Columbia R	1800	Head Moses Coulee
JAMESON PTHL	Douglas	21	Columbia R	1800	Adj S end Jameson Lk
JANELLE	Lewis	7	Wf Tieton R	3300	7.4 mi N Morton
JANET	Yakima	4	Naches R	5032	2.5 mi SW Ravens Roost L.O.
JANICKE SL	King	10	Snoqualmie R	75	2 mi N Fall City
JANUS	Snohomish	29	Sf Snoq R	4220	5.8 mi N Stevens Pass
JAP	Snohomish	1.5	Sultan R	740	4.8 mi N Sunan
JACKSON LKS (3)	Chelan	1.5-7	Wenatchee R	5500	13.4 mi NW Leavenworth
JAY	Snohomish	5	Wallace Lk	1900	3.5 mi NW Gold Bar
JEFFERSON LKS (2)	Mason	3-10	Hamma Hamma R	1800	7 mi W Eldon
JERRY LKS (4)	Whatcom	2-35	Skagit R	5900	7 mi E Ross Dam
JESS	Lewis	8.5	Ohanapecosh R	5175	4.4 mi N White Pass
JEWEL	King	8.5	Ef Foss R	4400	9.3 mi SE Skykomish
JEWEL LKS (2)	King	1.5-2	Ef Foss R	4500	6.5 mi SE Skykomish
JIGGS	Mason	9	Tahuya R	380	1.5 mi NE Tahuya
JOAN	Snohomish	3.5	Rapid R	5100	6 mi NW Stevens Pass
JOE	Kittitas	30	Keechelus Lk	4624	4.8 mi NE Snoq Pass
JOHN SAM	Snohomish	15	Tulalip Bay	506	5 mi NW Marysville
JOHNS	Mason	8	Oakland Bay	240	3.5 mi NW Shelton
JOHNSON	Okanogan	58	Nespelem R	2180	7.3 mi NE Nespelem
JOHNSON	Spokane	'5	Palouse R	2260	12.4 mi S Cheney
JOHNSONS SWAMP	Snohomish	7	Snoqualmie R	1050	4 mi SE Monroe
JONES	King	22.5	Lk Sawyer	530	.05 mi S Blk Diamond
JORDAN LKS (2)	Skagit	59-65	Cascade R	4150	6.5 mi SE Marblemount
JORDAN PDS (3)	Snohomish	3	Sf Stilly R	1600	4.7 mi N Granite Falls
JOSEPHINE	Chelan	22	Wenatchee R	4550	2.3 mi SE Stevens Pass
JOSEPHINE	Pierce	72.5	Puget Sound	196	E side Anderson Island
JOSEPHINE LKS (2)	Skagit	2.5-3.5	Skagit R	2850	5 mi NE Hamilton
JOSEPHINE MTN PDS	Skagit	1	Skagit R	1100	3 mi NE Hamilton
JOY	King	105	Snoqualmie R	527	3.8 mi N Carnation
JUDITH POOL	Grant	1.5	Columbia R	1110	6.4 mi SW Quincey
JUDSON	Douglas	10	Columbia R	2240	9 mi NE Bridgeport
JUDY	King	10	Taylor R	3700	1500' W Nordrum Lk
JUG	Lewis	28	Ohanapecosh R	4550	6.4 mi N White Pass
JUG LKS (2)	Skagit	1-20	Skagit R	3800	10 mi S Marblemount
JULIA	Snohomish	7.5	Pilchuck R	950	4.3 mi SE Granite Falls
JULIUS	Chelan	13	Wenatchee R	4950	10 mi E Stevens Pass
JUMPOFF	Stevens	105	Colville R	2031	10 mi S Chewelah

LAKE	COUNTY	ACRES	DRAINAGE	ELEVATION	LOCATION
JUNCTION	Skamania	8	Nf Lewis R	4750	3 mi SW Cultus Cr G.S.
JUNE	King	3.5	Ef Foss R	4800	7 mi SE Skykomish
JUNE	Skamania	2	Nf Lewis R	3118	3.5 mi S Mt St Helens
JUNGFRAU	Chelan	4 5	Wenatchee R	5450	20.5 mi W Leavenworth
JUPITER LKS (4)	Jefferson	0.5-6	Dosewallips R	3550	11 mi SW Quilcene

K

LAKE	COUNTY	ACRES	DRAINAGE	ELEVATION	LOCATION
KACHESS	Kittitas	4540	Yakima R	2254	2.3 mi NW Easton
KAHLOTUS	Franklin	321	Columbia R	880	40 mi NE Pasco
KALEETAN	King	43	Pratt R	3850	4.5 mi NW Snoq Pass
KANIM	King	18	Nf Snoq R	4300	6.5 mi SW Skykomish
KAPOWSIN	Pierce	512	Puyallup R	600	Adj Kapowsin
KARNES	Jefferson	1	Bg Quilcene R	4600	9.8 mi SW Quilcene
KATHLEEN	King	38.5	Lk Washington	520	5.4 mi NW Maple Valley
KATRINE LKS (2)	King	24-51	Nf Snoq R	2885-4250	12.5 mi NE North Bend
KATY	Grant	8	Crab Cr	1030	7.8 mi W Warden
KEECHELUS	Kittitas	2560	Yakima R	2517	8 mi SE Snoq Pass
KEEFE	Whatcom	4	Nooksack R	25	3.8 mi NE Ferndale
KEENE	Mason	8	Skokomish R	380	2 mi S Union
KEEVIES	King	3.5	Green R	500	2 mi W Blk Diamond
KELCEMA	Snohomish	23	Sf Stilly R	3182	2.8 mi NW Silverton
KELLOGG	Snohomish	20	Wallace R	650	3.8 mi NE Sultan
KENDALL	Whatcom	12	Nf Nooksack R	490	1.3 mi N Kendall
KENDALL PEAK LKS 2	Kittitas	4-7	Keechelus R	4740	W side Kendall Peak
KENDALL PEAK—LOWER	Kittitas	2	Keechelus Lk	4380	1.8 mi E Snoq Pass
KENT	Mason	19	Oakland Bay	350	5 mi NW Shelton
KEPPLER	Spokane	9o	Palouse R	2290	3.5 mi SE Cheney
KETCHUM	Snohomish	20	Skagit Bay	190	3 mi N Stanwood
KETTLE	Yakima	1	American R	5645	8.4 mi E Chinook Pass
KETTLING	Chelan	10	Stehekin R	5500	9.5 mi N Lk Chelan
KI	Snohomish	97	Stilly R	414	7.8 mi NW Marysville
KIDNEY	Okanogan	13	Chewack R	7400	24 mi N Winthrop
KIDNEY	Skamania	12	Columbia R	140	1 mi N North Bonneville
KILLARNEY	King	31	Commencement B	385	3.5 mi SW Auburn
KINGS	King	3	Snoqualmie R	950	1 mi W Boyle Lk
KING	Snohomish	12	Snoqualmie R	1359	3.8 mi SE Monroe
KING	Snohomish	g	Sf Stilly R	460	6 mi SE Arlington
KIRK	Snohomish	1.5	Sauk R	630	.08 mi SW Darrington
KITSAP	Kitsap	238	Dyes Inlet	156	3 mi W Bremerton
KITTITAS GRAVEL PTS	Kittitas	4	Yakima R	1445	3.8 mi SE Ellensburg
KITTITAS PD	Kittitas	2	Yakima R	1660	5.5 mi E Ellensburg
KLAUS	King	62	Snoqualmie R	980	4.8 mi NE Snoqualmie
KLEMENTS MILL PD	Snohomish	3	Sf Stilly R	460	1.4 mi NE Granite Falls
KLONAQUA LKS (2)	Chelan	66-67	Wenatchee R	5450	19 mi W Leavenworth
KLONE LKS (3)	Grays Hbr	2-9	Wynooche R	3175	8.8 mi NE Grisdale
KNOX	Chelan	7	Wenatchee R	6300	10 mi SE Stevens Pass
KNUPPENBURG	Lewis	45	Cowlitz R	4200	1.5 mi SW White Pass
KOUCHEL PD	King	3	Cedar R	640	2.7 mi NE Ravensdale
KREGER	Pierce	42	Nisqually R	532	6 mi W Eatonville
KROEZE	Snohomish	1.5	Nf Stilly R	65	3.5 mi NE Arlington
KULLA KULLA	King	60	Pratt R	3765	11.5 mi SE North Bend
KWAD-DIS	Skamania	3.5	Wind R	4300	18.5 mi N Carson

L

LAKE	COUNTY	ACRES	DRAINAGE	ELEVATION	LOCATION
"L"	Okanogan	7	Omak Lk	2550	6.8 mi SE Okanogan
"L"	Okanogan	21	Wf San Poil R	2592	16.2 mi SE Tonasket
LA BARGE	Snohomish	3	Nf Stilly R	900	7 mi N Granite Falls
LACKAMAS	Clark	315	Washougal R	179	1 mi N Camas
LA CROSSE	Jefferson	3	Duckabush R	5050	2 mi SW Mt La Crosse
LAKE ANDREWS	Okanogan	4.5	Okanogan R	960	6.7 mi S Oroville
LAKE CITY LKS (4)	Stevens	2-7 5	Colville R	1879	2 mi N Echo
LAKE NO 8	Clallam	7	Morganroth Lk	4175	6 mi S Sol Duc H.S.
LAKE OF THE PINES	Okanogan	21	Pasayten R	5750	37.5 mi NW Winthrop
LAKE OF WOODS	Okanogan	2.5	Lost R	6200	25.5 mi NW Winthrop
LAKE OF THE WOODS	Pend Oreille	6.5	LSpokane R	2400	4 mi NE Camden
LAKE SAWYER SWAMP	King	9	Green R	500	1000' SE S end Lk Sawyer
LAKEVIEW PEAK	Cowlitz	3	Kalama R	2950	10.5 mi E Pigeon Springs
LAMONT	Okanogan	5	Methow R	7200	16 mi W Winthrop
LANGENDORFER	King	5.4	Tolt R	580	6 mi NE Stillwater
LANGLOIS	King	40	Tolt R	122	1.4 mi SE Carnation
LANHAM	Chelan	6	Wenatchee R	3900	3.3 mi E Stevens Pass
LARCH	Chelan	31	Wenatchee R	6150	8.5 mi E Stevens Pass
LARCH LKS (2)	Chelan	5-10	Entiat R	5650	32 mi N Leavenworth
LARCH	Skagit	9.5	Nf Stilly R	2300	5.4 mi N Oso
LARSEN	King	7	Lk Washington	260	3 mi E Bellevue
LARSON	Mason	2	Union R	280	1.4 mi W Belfair
LARSON	Mason	9	Hood Canal	400	3 mi E Dewatto
LARSON LKS (3)	Skamania	1-3	Columbia R	1950	5 mi SW Willard

LAKE	COUNTY	ACRES	DRAINAGE	ELEVATION	LOCATION
LA RUSH	Skagit	3	Cascade R	3200	7.4 mi SE Marblemount
LAURA	Kittitas	4	Yakima R	4410	3.5 mi SE Snoq Pass
LAVA LKS (7)	Skamania	3.5	Columbia R	440	1.8 mi SW Stevenson
LAWRENCE	Thurston	339	Deschutes R	421	6 mi S Yelm
LEADER	Okanogan	159	Okanogan R	2273	4.5 mi W Okanogan
LEDBETTER	Pend Oreille	22.7	Pend Oreille R	2575	3.5 mi N Metaline Falls
LEE	Stevens	5	Colville R	2250	6.5 mi NW Colville
LEECH	Yakima	41	Tieton R	4412	In White Pass
LE FAY	King	7	Mf Snoq R	4300	7.5 mi NW Snoqualmie Pass
LEHRMANS PD	Okanogan	3	Okanogan R	950	.05 mi N Oroville
LELAND	Chelan	36	Wenatchee R	4600	19.8 mi W Leavenworth
LELAND	Jefferson	99	L Quilcene R	190	4.5 mi N Quilcene
LEIMI	Skamania	7	Nf Lewis R	5000	2.4 mi SW Cultus Cr G.S.
LEMNA	Grant	3	Crab Cr	950	8.5 mi N Othello
LENA	Grant	25	Grand Coulee	1500	S sd Dry Falls Dam
LENA—LOWER	Jefferson	55.5	Hamma Hamma R	1800	15 mi N Hoodsport
LENA—UPPER	Jefferson	26	Hamma Hamma R	4500	1800 S Upper Lena Lk
LENICE	Grant	100	Crab Cr	—	Crab Cr WRA
LENORE	Grant	1400	Crab Cr		4 mi N Soap Lake
LENNOX	King	~.9	Nf Snoq R	5000	17 mi NE North Bend
LENZ	Stevens	7	Colville R	2175	9 mi S Colville
LEO	Pend Oreille	39	L Pend Ore R	3190	7 mi SW Ione
LEOTA	King	10	Sammamish R	10	2 mi E Woodinville
LEWIS	Pierce	54	Nisqually R	350	3.5 mi NE Yelm
LIBBY	Okanogan	10	Methow R	7600	13 mi SW Twisp
LIBERTY	Spokane	714	Spokane R	2053	15 mi E Spokane
LICHTENWASSER	Chelan	23	Wenatchee R	4754	3.3 mi N Stevens Pass
LIDER	Kitsap	3	Union R	310	2.5 mi NE Belfair
LILA	Kittitas	3	Kachess R	5180	4.4 mi E Snoq Pass
LILLIAN	Jefferson	8	Elwha R	5800	17.5 mi S Port Angeles
LILLIAN	Kittitas	17	Yakima R	4800	3.8 mi SE Snoq Pass
LILLIWAUP SWAMP	Mason	225	Hood Canal	800	6 mi N Hoodsport
LILY	Chelan	15	Columbia R	3100	9 mi S Wenatchee
LILY	Jefferson	2.5	Queets R	3'50	.04 mi N Finley Park L.O.
LILY	Lewis	25	Cowlitz R	3750	3.8 mi W White Pass
LILY PD	Mason	9	Case Inlet	350	6.4 mi N Shelton
LILY	Skagit	2	Samish Bay	2000	2.4 mi N Blanchard
LILY	Skamania	8	Columbia R	1700	6.8 mi W Stevenson
LILY	Yakima	5	Bumping Lk	3860	3.4 mi SW Bumping Lk Dam
LINDBERG	Okanogan	3	Kettle R	4060	2.4 mi NE Molson
LITSCHKE	Pacific	5	Willapa Bay	25	4 mi N Long Beach
LITTLE	Snohomish	23	Nf Stilly R	1509	6.5 mi NE Arlington
LITTLE ASHES	Skamania	5	Columbia R	75	2 mi SW Stevenson
LITTLE BEAVER	Okanogan	6	Kettle R	2675	18.4 mi NW Republic
LITTLE BLUE	Skamania	1	Columbia R	390	2.8 mi SW Stevenson
LITTLE CALLIGAN	King	2	Nf Snoq R	2700	8 mi NE North Bend
LITTLE CAROLINE	Chelan	35	Wenatchee R	5900	10 mi SW Leavenworth
LITTLE CAVANAUGH	Snohomish	8	Skykomish R	1500	5 mi S Gold Bar
LITTLE CHETWOOT	King	1	Angeline Lk	5150	300' N Chetwoot Lk
LITTLE DEEP	Skamania	1.5	Columbia R	150	2.4 mi SW Stevenson
LITTLE DERRICK	King	2	Mf Snoq R	3650	500' NE Derrick Lk
LITTLE EAGLE	King	7	Nf Green R	2150	3900' NW Eagle Lk
LITTLE FISH	Chelan	3	L Wenatchee R	4850	12.4 mi N Stevens Pass
LITTLE FISH	Skamania	4.5	Nf Lewis R	3800	13.4 mi NW Mt Adams R.S.
LITTLE GEE	Skagit	1.5	Skagit R	4240	4750' SE Gee Pt
LITTLE GOOSE	Okanogan	9	Okanogan R	2740	6.7 mi SE Okanogan
LITTLE HART	Pierce	11	Nisqually R	350	3000' SE Harts Lk
LITTLE HEART	King	29	Wf Foss R	4250	7.5 mi S Skykomish
LITTLE HICKS	Thurston	2	Patterson Lk	158	800' S Hicks Lk
LITTLE HORSESHOE	Spokane	68	Spokane R	2440	9.6 mi W Nine Mile Falls
LITTLE ISLAND	Mason	3.5	Case Inlet	330	6.5 mi NE Shelton
LITTLE JOE	Kittitas	5	Cle Elum R	4690	3 mi SW Salmon La Sac
LITTLE KLONAQUA	Chelan	7	Wenatchee R	5450	1300' SE L Klonaqua Lk
LITTLE MASON	King	4	Sf Snoq R	4260	11.4 mi SE North Bend
LITTLE MYRTLE	King	4	Mf Snoq R	4400	9 mi N Snoq Pass
LITTLE PLUG	King	1	Tye R	5500	900' NE Spark Plug Lk
LITTLE PRATT	King	4	Pratt R	4080	2400' E Pratt Lk
LITTLE SI	King	2	Mf Snoq R	1080	1.4 mi NE North Bend
LITTLE SNOW	Lewis	2	Ohanapecosh R	4800	500' W Frying Pan Lk
LITTLE SPEARFISH	Klickitat	6	Columbia R	160	.05 mi NE The Dalles Dam
LITTLE TIFFANY	Okanogan	4	Chewack R	7400	4200' S Tiffany Lk
LIZARD	King	5	Green R	3540	On Cascade Crest
LIZARD	Skagit	2	Samish Bay	1862	2.4 mi N Blanchard
LOCH EILEEN	Chelan	25	Wenatchee R	5200	9.4 mi E Stevens Pass
LOCKE	Klickitat	20	Columbia R	80	3 mi E Bingen
LOCKET	King	56	Ef Foss R	4600	9.5 mi SE Skykomish
LODGE	King	9	Sf Snoq R	3125	1.4 mi SW Snoq Pass
LOIS	Thurston	2.5	Henderson Inlet	150	Adj N fm Lacey
LOMA	Snohomish	21	Tulalip Bay	465	6.5 mi NW Marysville
LONE	Island	17			2.5 mi SW Langley
LONE DUCK	Mason	3.5	Hood Canal	550	1.8 mi S Dewatto
LONELYVILLE	Spokane	23	Crab Cr	2420	3.5 mi SW twn Medical Lake

LAKE	COUNTY	ACRES	DRAINAGE	ELEVATION	LOCATION
LONE PINE	Douglas	10	Columbia R	2200	9.5 mi NE Bridgeport
LONESOME	Pierce	11.5	Wf White R	4860	10.5 mi S Greenwater
LONG	Clallam	15	Soleduck R	3850	5 mi SE Sol Duc Hot Spr.
LONG	Clark	12		10	.05 mi NW Ridgefield
LONG	Ferry	14	Wf San Poil R	3250	11 mi S Republic
LONG	Franklin	2.5	Palouse R	1043	5.4 mi SE Washtucna
LONG (Billie Clapp)	Grant	25	Columbia R	2300	23.8 mi S town Grand Coulee
LONG	Kitsap	314	Yukon Hbr	118	3.5 mi SE Port Orchard
LONG	Lewis	6	Cowlitz R	4000	6.5 mi W Packwood
LONG	Okanogan	20	Columbia R	2650	12.5 mi SE Okanogan
LONG	Okanogan	17	Wf San Poil R	2600	15 mi SE Tonasket
LONG	Thurston	311	Henderson Inlet	153	5.5 mi E Olympia
LONG	Yakima	8	Tieton R	4350	3.5 mi SE Tleton Dam
LONG JOHN	Yakima	5	Tieton R	5140	4.4 mi N White Pass
LONGS	Thurston	10	Henderson Inlet	150	.05 mi E Lacey
LONG-BELL LOG PD	Cowlltz	132.5	Columbia R	10	SE portion Longview
LONG-BELL MILL PD	Lewis	10	Cowlitz R	700	2 mi E Winston
LOOKING GLASS	Skamania	1 5	Whlte Salmon R	5600	12 mi N Mt Adams R.S.
LOOKOUT	Snohomish	1 5	Suiattle R	5575	2300' N Sulphur Mtn summit
LOOMIS	Pacific	151	Paclfic Ocean	17	2.5 mi S Ocean Park
LOON	Stevens	1118.5	Colville R	2381	28 mi N Spokane
LOOP	King	36	Tolt R	550	2.8 mi E Carnatlon
LORRAINE	Chelan	4.5	Wenatchee R	5050	5.8 mi S Stevens Pass
LOST	Chelan	31	L Wenatchee R	4900	9 mi NE Stevens Pass
LOST	Chelan	4	Chiwawa R	5500	20 mi N Leavenworth
LOST	Clark	2	Nf Lewis R	1500	7.5 mi NE Yacolt
LOST	Jefferson	7	Hood Canal	350	2 mi SW Squamish Hbr
LOST	Kittitas	10	Yakima R	4820	20 mi W Ellensburg
LOST	Klttltas	145	Keechelus Lk	3089	6.5 mi S Snoq Pass
LOST	Lewis	21	Cowlltz R	5100	7.5 mi E Packwood
LOST	Mason	122	Oakland Bay	480	7.8 mi SW Shelton
LOST	Okanogan	47	Kettle R	3817	20 mi NE Tonasket
LOST	Pacific	14	Pacific Ocean	20	1.8 mi SE Klipsan Beach
LOST	Pend Oreille	22	W Br L Spokane	2125	9 mi NW Elk
LOST	Pend Orellle	6	Pend Oreille R	3150	5.5 mi N Ione
LOST	Pierce	1	White R	6050	1.5 mi NE Skyscraper Mtn
LOST	Pierce	26	Greenwater R	3985	27 mi SE Enumclaw
LOST	Skamania	8	Wind R	3760	2.5 mi W Gov Mineral Sp G.S.
LOST	Snohomish	9	Skykomlsh R	617	2.5 mi SE Sultan
LOST	Snohomish	18	Skykomish R	980	6 mi N Sultan
LOST	Snohomish	3	Sf Sauk R	2000	2 mi N Barlow Pass
LOST	Snohomish	3	Sf Stilly R	1650	4.4 mi N Granite Falls
LOST	Whatcom	3	Bellngham Bay	140	.04 mi NW Bellingham Airport
LOST	Whatcom	4	Sumas R	2850	3 mi W Kendall
LOST	Yakima	9	Tieton R	3675	3 mi SE Tieton Dam
LOST HAT	Lewis	3	Cowlitz R	4500	3.7 mi NE Packwood Lk outlet
LOST HORSE	Snohomish	3.5	Rapid R	4800	4 mi N Stevens Pass
LOUIS	Chelan	4	L Wenatchee R	4500	8 mi N Stevens Pass
LOUIS	Okanogan	27	Twisp R	5300	21 mi W Twisp
LOUISE	Lewis	17	Cowlitz R	4592	4.8 mi NE Longmire
LOUISE	Skagit	6	Sauk R	5000	8.8 mi S Marblemount
LOWER BEAR PAW MTN	Whatcom	6.5	Nf Nooksack R	4450	6.5 mi NE Glacier
LOWER CATHEDRAL	Okanogan	6	Similkameen R	6000	36 mi N Wlnthrop
LOWER CRYSTAL	Pierce	1.5	White R	5550	8.5 mi SW Quincey
LOWER FISHER	King	3.5	Tye R	4500	8 mi SE Skykomish
LOWER FLORENCE	Chelan	5	Wenatchee R	6000	13.3 mi NW Leavenworth
LUCERNE	King	16	Cedar R	530	4.5 mi NW Blk Diamond
LUDLOW	Jefferson	16	Port Ludlow Hbr	450	4.5 mi W Port Ludlow
LUDVICK	Kitsap	2	Dewatto R	440	2 mi S Holly
LUNA	Whatcom	17	Skagit R	4900	2 mi SE Mt Challenger
LUNCH	Clallam	7	Soleduck R	4475	3200' S Soleduck Lk
LUNKER	King	3.5	Taylor R	4300	800' SE Rock Lk
LYLE	Adams	22	Crab Cr	925	
LYLE	Pierce	9	Clearwater R	4150	4000' E Cedar Lk
LYMAN	Chelan	76	Lk Chelan	5887	48 mi NW Chelan
LYNN	King	6	Green R	3500	10 mi E Enumclaw
LYNNE	Yakima	1.5	Tieton R	4310	Just blw Bear Lk

M

LAKE	COUNTY	ACRES	DRAINAGE	ELEVATION	LOCATION
MAD	Chelan	5	Entiat R	5950	23 mi N Leavenworth
MAIDEN	Whatcom	17	Baker R	3900	18.8 mi N Concrete
MAL	Yakima	4	Naches R	5100	11.3 mi SW Naches R.S.
MALACHITE	King	80	Wf Foss R	4200	7.4 mi S Skykomish
MALLARD	Grant	8	Crab Cr	980	10 mi N Othello
MALLARD	Pacific	5	Pacific Ocean	20	1.5 mi SE Klipsan Beach
MALO	Ferry	2	Kettle R	2300	10.5 mi NE Republic
MALONEY LKS (3)	King	1-1.5	Sf Skykomish R	4000	2.4 mi S Skykomish
MALONEY MEADOW	King	5.5	Sf Skykomish R	4150	3.4 mi S Skykomish
MALONEY	Pierce	5	Hale Passage	248	2 mi W Gig Harbor
MANASTASH	Kittitas	23.5	Yakima R	5000	19 mi W Ellensburg

LAKE	COUNTY	ACRES	DRAINAGE	ELEVATION	LOCATION
MARCO POLO	Grant	10	Crab Cr	1025	8.3 mi N Othello
MARCUS	King	1		610	1.4 mi NE Ravensdale
MARGARET	Chelan	15	Wenatchee R	5500	8.2 mi SE Stevens Pass
MARGARET	King	44	Snoqualmie R	798	4.4 mi NE Duvall
MARGARET	Kittitas	4	Kachess R	4790	4.8 mi SE Snoq Pass
MARIE	King	10	Snoqualmie R	953	2 mi E Fall City
MARION	Chelan	1	Columbia R	5500	1.2 mi NE Mission Pk
MARJORIE	King	10	Wf White R	4555	Adj E end Oliver Lk
MARLENE	King	3	Ef Miller R	4500	8.4 mi S Skykomish
MARLOW	King	3	Green R	420	1.4 mi S Covington
MARMOT	King	135	Tye R	4900	6.7 mi S Scenic
MARPLE	Okanogan	3	Okanogan R	2550	14.8 mi SE Tonasket
MARSH LKS (2)	Lewis	2-4	Cowlitz R	3950	9.8 mi SW Chinook Pass
MARSHALL	Pend Oreille	189	Pend Oreille R	2750	5.5 mi N Newport
MARTEN	King	40	Taylor R	2959	14 mi NE North Bend
MARTEN	Skagit	10	Skagit R	4650	5 mi S Marblemount
MARTEN	Whatcom	5	Baker R	3650	16 mi N Concrete
MARTHA	Grant	12	Crab Cr	1200	.07 mi NE George
MARTHA	Snohomish	59	Sammamish R	450	2.5 mi NE Alderwood Manor
MARTHA	Snohomish	13	Pilchuck R	324	3.4 mi E Marysville
MARTHA	Snohomish	58	Port Susan	186	10.5 mi NW Marysville
MARTIN LKS (2)	Okanogan	5-9	Methow R	6800	16 mi W Methow
MARTINS	San Juan	21.5	East Sound	500	5.4 mi S East Sound
MARY	Chelan	3.5	Wenatchee R	5850	8.5 mi SE Stevens Pass
MARY	Jefferson	3	Elwha R	3550	.04 mi NE Low Divide shelter
MARY	King	3.5	Ef Foss R	s200	2500' W Upper Ptarmfgan Lk
MARY LEE	Pierce	1.5	Mashel R	4350	5.5 mi N Ashford
MARY SHELTON	Snohomish	12	Tulalip Bay	368	5.7 mi NW Marysville
MASON	King	33	Sf Snoq R	4180	12 mi SE North Bend
MASON	Mason	996	Case Inlet	194	8 mi SW Belfair
MASON	Spokane	2	Palouse R	2110	2.4 mi W Amber
MASSIE	Chelan	15	Chiwawa R	5950	39 mi N Leavenworth
MATHEWS	Kitsap	3	Sinclair Inlet	410	4300' S Square Lk
MATSUDA RES	King	1	Quartermaster H	300	1.5 mi S Vashon
33358	Stevens	4	Colville R	2450	2.5 mi N Colville
MAZAMA	Whatcom	1	Nf Nooksack R	4750	2 mi SW Mt Baker Ldg
McALESTER	Chelan	15	Stehekin R	5500	7.5 mi N Lk Chelan
McALLISTER SPRINGS	Thurston	3	Nisqually Reach	15	8.5 mi E Olympia
McBRIDE	Cowlitz	9	Kalama R	2700	28 mi NE Woodland
McCOY	Stevens	38	Spokane R	1644	7.3 mi S Fruitland
McDANIEL	Yakima	10	Naches R	3550	8 mi SW Naches R.S.
McDONALD	King	18	Sammamish Lk	560	6 mi E Renton
McDOWELL	Spokane	81	Palouse R	2300	4.7 mi S Cheney
McGINNIS	Okanogan	115	Columbia R	2375	9.5 mi SE Nespelem
McGOWAN PD	Pacific	2	Columbia R	25	7.4 mi SE Ilwaco
McINTOSH	Thurston	116	Deschutes R	336	4 mi E Tenino
McKINLEY	Lewis	3	Ef Tilton R	3200	7 mi NE Morton
McLEOD	King	13	Nf Snoq R	1006	5 mi N North Bend
McMANNAMAN	Adams	7	Crab Cr	830	6.2 mi NW Othello
McMURRAY	Skagit	161	Skagit R	225	9 mi NW Arlington
MEADOW	Chelan	36	Columbia R	875	1 mi SW Malaga
MEADOW	Grant	5	Grand Coulee	1160	Sun Lks State Park
MEADOW	Okanogan	24	Okanogan R	3550	1.5 mi S Bonaparte Lk
MEADOW	Okanogan	6.5	Chewack R	6400	26.5 mi N Winthrop
MEADOW	Skamania	2.5	Nf Lewis R	3900	2 mi W Mosquito Lk G.S.
MEADOW	Snohomish	20	Skykomish R	500	4 mi N Monroe
MEADOW	Snohomish	9	Suiattle R	4500	14.4 mi SE Darrington
MEADOW	Spokane	32	Spokane R	2371	.05 mi S twn Four Lakes
MEADOWBROOK SL	King	14	Snoqualmie R	400	1 mi E Snoqualmie
MEEKER LKS (2)	Pierce	4-6	White R	2780	26.5 mi E Enumclaw
MELAKWA LKS (2)	King	2-8	Pratt R	4490	3 mi NW Snoq Pass
MENZEL	Snohomish	13	Pilchuck R	470	3.8 mi SE Granite Falls
MERIDIAN	King	150	Green R	370	4 mi E Kent
MERLIN	King	6	Mf Snoq R	4200	2200' W Myrtle Lk
MERRILL	Cowlitz	344	Kalama R	1541	24 mi NE Woodland
MERRITT	Chelan	7	Wenatchee R	5000	2900' SE Lost Lk
MERRITT SL	Chelan	6	Wenatchee R	2100	12.3 mi E Stevens Pass
MERRY	Grant	—	Crab Cr		Crab Cr W.R.A.
MERWIN RES	Clark	4090	Nf Lewis R	239	9.8 mi NE Woodland
MESA	Chelan	4.5	Wenatchee R	6500	500' NE Earle Lk
MESA	Franklin	50	Columbia R	748	1 mi SW Mesa
META	Skamania	9	Muddy R	3580	1.7 mi E Spirit Lk Inlet
METAN	Snohomish	3.5	Sauk R	2800	12.5 mi SE Darrington
METCALF	King	6	Snoqualmie R	1010	6.8 mi N North Bend
METCALF SL	King	5	Snoqualmie R	1040	7.5 mi N North Bend
MICA	Snohomish	13	Suiattle R	5450	4.8 mi NW Glacier Pk
MICHAEL	Kittitas	18	Waptus R	5100	5 mi W Salmon la Sac
MIDDLE HIDDEN	Okanogan	19	Lost R	4300	33 mi NW Winthrop
MILDRED LKS (3)	Mason	6.5-38	Hamma Hamma R	3900	3.8 N Hd Lk Cushman
MILE LONG	Grant	75	Columbia R	996	6.9 mi N Othello
MILK	Jefferson	6	Hamma Hamma R	4800	1800' S Upper Lena Lk
MILK	Kittitas	3	Naches R	4700	4.4 mi NE Cliffdell

LAKE	COUNTY	ACRES	DRAINAGE	ELEVATION	LOCATION
MILL PD	Mason	6	Case Inlet	15	1.5 mi S Allyn
MILL CREEK RES	Walla Walla	52		1205	3 mi E Walla Walla
MILLER MARSH	Mason	15	Hood Canal	650	6.8 mi NE Hoodsport
MILLER	Whitman	25	Palouse R	1865	3.3 mi N Ewan
MILLES	Okanogan	9	Twisp R	2150	3.5 mi NW Twisp
MILLS	Clallam	451	Elwha R	600	11 mi SW Port Angeles
MINERAL	Lewis	277	Nisqually R	1430	At Mineral
MINK	Clallam	11	Soleduck R	3080	1.5 mi S Sol Duc Hot Spr
MINKLER	Skagit	37	Skagit R	60	1.7 mi W Lyman
MINOTAUR	Chelan	24	L Wenatchee R	5575	7.5 mi NE Stevens Pass
MINT MARSH	Mason	10	Hood Canal	800	6 mi N Hoodsport
MIRROR	Chelan	27	Lk Chelan	5490	4 mi SW Lucerne
MIRROR	Grant	4.5	Park Lk	1097	Sun Lks State Park
MIRROR	King	19	Puget Sound	320	2 mi W Steel Lk
MIRROR	Kittitas	29	Keechelus Lk	4195	5.8 mi S Snoq Pass
MIRROR	Okanogan	7	Okanogan R	2840	8.4 mi SE Okanogan
MIRROR	Whatcom	14	Whatcom Lk	350	3200' NW Wickersham
MIRROR	Yakima	1.5	Klickitat R	5250	10.5 mi NW Glenwood
MISSION	Kitsap	88	Hood Canal	516	9 mi W Bremerton
MISSION PD	Kitsap	4	Union R	580	2000' SE Mission Lk
MITCHELL PD	Benton	4	Lk Wallula	340	13.5 mi SE Kennewick
MOCCASIN	Okanogan	33	Methow R	2193	3.9 mi S Winthrop
MOCCASIN	Okanogan	6.5	Kettle R	3600	2 mi NW Wauconda summit
MOIRA	King	5	Dorothy Lk	4600	8.5 mi S Skykomish
MOLSON	Okanogan	20	Kettle R	3675	1800' N Molson
MONEYSMITH	King	22	Green R	415	4.8 mi E Auburn
MONOGRAM	Skagit	28	Cascade R	4850	8 mi SE Marblemount
MONTE CRISTO	Snohomish	14	Sf Sauk R	1970	16 mi SE Darrington
MOOLOCK	King	45	Nf Snoq R	3903	7.3 mi NE North Bend
MOOSE	Clallam	9	Greywolf R	5100	16.5 mi S Port Angeles
MOOSE	Pacific	3	Willpa R	80	7 mi SE Raymond
MORAINE	Skagit	52	Diablo Lk	4500	2.4 mi SE Eldorado Peak
MORGAN	Adams	35	Crab Cr	821	5.8 mi NW Othello
MORGAN MARSH	Kitsap	95	Hood Canal	510	7 mi N Belfair
MORGAN PD	Yakima	25	Yakima R	650	2 mi N Mabton
MORGANROTH	Clallam	10	Soleduck R	4125	5.8 mi SE Sol Duc Hot Sprs
MORGE LKS (3)	Pierce	1.5-3	Mashel R	4400	4.4 mi NE National
MORROW	Mason	5	Ef Satsop R	400	1.5 mi SE Nahwatzel Lk
MORTON	King	66	Green R	500	4 mi W Blk Diamond
MOSES	Grant	6815	Crab Cr	1046	Adj City Moses Lk
MOSES MEADOWS PDS	Okanogan	1-2	Wf San Poil R	3500	19.5 mi E Omak
MOSLEY LKS (5)	Skamania	3.5	Columbia R	700	2 mi W Stevenson
MOSQUITO	King	2	Tye R	5300	3 mi NW Stevens Pass
MOSQUITO	Okanogan	6	Twisp R	5300	6.5 mi N Lk Chelan
MOSQUITO LKS (2)	Skamania	5-25	White Salmon R	3900	14 mi NW Trout Lk
MOSS	Lewis	3.5	Sf Newaukum R	3024	1000' SW Newaukum Lk
MOUND PD	Benton	35	Lk Wallula	340	14.5 mi SE Kennewick
MOUSE	Okanogan	4.5	Columbia R	1680	5.5 mi N Brewster
MOUSE	Skamania	9	Cispus R	4500	18.5 mi SE Randle
MOUNTAIN	San Juan	198	East Sound	914	4.4 mi SE East Sound
MOWICH	Pierce	123	No Mowich R	4929	7.5 mi NW Mt Rainier summit
MOWITCH	King	16	Nf Snoq R	3196	13 mi NE North Bend
MOXEE PD	Yakima	5	Yakima R	990	S side Moxee Hwy
MT ADAMS	Yakima	69	Wf Klickitat R	4500	16 mi N Glenwood
MT FERNOW PTHLS (5)	King	1-3	Beckler R	3900-4500	1 mi N Fernow Mtn
MT ROOSEVELT	King	4	Pratt R	4460	6.4 mi NW Snoq Pass
MUD	Clark	92	Lewis R	15	2.5 mi W La Center
MUD	King	24	Green R	750	1 mi NE Blk Diamond
MUD	King	16	Snoqualmie R	1270	10 mi NE Snoqualmie
MUD	King	12	Sf Skykomish R	2000	3.8 mi S Index
MUD	Lewis	7.5	Nf Cispus R	4850	3.8 mi E Blue Lk
MUD LKS (15)	Mason	20	Chehalis R	400	8 mi SW Shelton
MUD	Pierce	22	Puget Sound	230	1.5 mi E Stellacoom
MUD	Thurston	10	Black R	250	2.4 mi N Tenino
MUD	Whatcom	4.5	Samish R	940	1 mi W Samish Lk
MUD	Yakima	4	Naches R	2500	7.4 mi NW Naches
MUDGETT	Stevens	32	Columbia R	1900	2.3 mi S Fruitland
MULE	Pierce	2.5	Wf White R	4600	10 mi S Greenwater
MULHOLLAND MARSH	Kitsap	6.5	Tahuya R	550	2 mi SW Hintzville
MUNN	Thurston	30	Deschutes R	139	4 mi S Olympia
MURPHY	Douglas	9	Columbia R	2160	9.8 mi E Bridgeport
MURPHY LKS(2)	King	3.5-7	Tye R	4300-4500	1.8 mi S Scenic
MUSKEGON	Pend Orellle	7.5	Priest R	3450	16 mi SE Metaline Falls
MUTUAL	Thurston	2	Chehalls R	325	1.4 mi E Tenino
MY	King	1	Pratt R	3930	3.4 mi NW Snoq Pass
MYRON	Yakima	—	Yakima R	—	W of Yakima
MYRTLE	Chelan	19	Entiat R	3750	35 mi NW Entiat
MYRTLE	King	18	Mf Snoq R	3950	8.5 mi N Snoq Pass
MYRTLE	Skagit	B	Nf Stilly R	3550	6 mi NE Oso
MYRTLE	Snohomish	2	Sf Sauk R	2000	2.4 mi N Barlow Pass
MYSTIC	Pend Orellle	17	Pend Oreille R.	2975	6.3 mi E Usk
MYSTIC	Pierce	7	Wf White R	5700	4.4 mi N Mt Rainier summit

LAKE	COUNTY	ACRES	DRAINAGE	ELEVATION	LOCATION
N					
NADA	Chelan	9	Wenatchee R	5500	7.5 mi SW Leavenworth
NADEAU	King	19	Nf Snoq R	3722	7 mi NE North Bend
NAHWATZEL	Mason	269	Ef Satsop R	440	11 mi W Shelton
NANEUM	Kittitas	1.5	Yakima R	1655	4 mi E Ellensburg
NASELLE PD	Pacific	1	Naselle R	60	2.5 mi E Naselle
NASON	Thurston	6	Budd Inlet	155	2200' NW Bigelow Lk
NATIONAL MILL PD	Pierce	9	Nisqually R	1550	At National
NAZANNE	King	9.5	Wf Foss R	5000	8.5 mi SE Skykomish
NEELYS	Thurston	'0	Nisqually R	400	1.5 mi S Yelm
NEORI	Skagit	'3	Cascade R	4400	1300' W Found Lk
NETTLETON	Stevens	'	Columbia R	1950	3.5 mi N Rice
NEVES	Lincoln	25	Crab Cr	1665	6.3 mi N Odessa
NEWAUKUM	Lewis	'7	Sf Newaukum R	3000	13 mi NE Onalaska
NEWMAN	Spokane	1190	Spokane R	2124	16 mi NE Spokane
NIGGER	Adams	24	Palouse R	1438	3.6 mi S Benge
NIGGER SL	Mason	16	Hood Canal	400	2.4 mi N Tahuya
NIGGERHEAD PD	Lewis	6	Cispus R	2000	11.5 mi SE Randle
NIMUE	King	5	Mf Snoq R	4100	1000' SW Merlin Lk
NINE HOUR	King	6	Mf Snoq R	3931	4800' NE Rainy Lk
NISQUALLY	Pierce	98.5	Nisqually R	229	4.5 mi NW Roy
NO NAME	Pend Oreille	18	Pend Oreille R	2850	9 mi NW Newport
NO NAME	Whatcom	10	Ross Lk	3900	8.5 mi N Ross Dam
NORDRUM	King	60	S Br Taylor R	3800	16.5 mi NE North Bend
NORTH	King	55	Commencement B	390	3 mi W Auburn
NORTH	Okanogan	8	Twisp R	5800	19.5 mi W Winthrop
NORTH	Snohomish	11	Sauk R	4100	8.8 mi SE Darrington
NORTHRUP	Grant	3	Banks Lk	2100	2.9 mi S Electric City
NORTH SILVER	Spokane	—	Crab Creek	559	1.1 mi E turn Medical Lk
NORTH SKOOKUM	Pend Oreille	38.5	Pend Oreille R	3550	7.2 mi NE Cusick
NORTHSTAR	Okanogan	8.5	Nespelem R	4420	13.8 mi N Nespelem
NORTH TEAL	Grant	22	Crab Cr	954	6.4 mi N Othello
NORTH TWIN	Ferry	744	FDR Lk	2572	8 mi W Inchelium
NORTHWESTERN	Skamania	97	White Salmon R	301	2.7 mi N White Salmon
NORTH WINDMILL (2)	Grant	5-22	Crab Cr	1000	6.6 mi SW Warden
NUNNALLY	Grant	—	Crab Cr	—	Crab Cr W.R.A.
O					
OAK	Mason	15	Hood Canal	190	3.8 mi NE Dwatto
OBSCURITY	Skamania	7	Green R	4337	5.4 mi NE Spirit Lk Inlet
ODENRIDER	Lincoln	9	Crab Cr	2050	1.4 mi SW Govan
OFFUTT	Thurston	192	Deschutes R	236	9 mi S Olympia
OHOP CREEK PDS	Pierce	2-2.5	Puyallup R	1900	7.5 mi SE Kapowsin
OHOP	Pierce	236	Nisqually R	524	1.5 mi N Eatonville
OLALLIE	King	13	Sf Snoq R	3780	4.5 mi W Snoq Pass
OLALLIE	Skamania	16	Cispus R	4250	23.5 mi SE Randle
OLD CLE ELUM H PD	Kittitas	2	Yakima R	2080	4.2 mi SE Easton
OLD COLUMBIA MILL PD	Clark	2	Lk Merwin	1450	3.5 mi N Amboy
OLD MILL PD	Pacific	2	Willapa R	20	1.4 mi W South Bend
OLIVER	Pierce	20	Wf White R	4558	8.8 mi N Mt Rainier summit
OLNEY	Yakima	9	Yakima R	1810	7 mi S White Swan
OLSON	Skagit	4	Skagit R	4050	3 mi NW Marblemount R.S.
OMAK	Okanogan	3244		950	7 mi SE Omak
OMALLEY	Pierce	1	White R	2900	0.5 mi W Norse Peak
ONE	Yakima	2	U Bumping R	5050	7 mi SE Chinook Pass
ONE ACRE	Snohomish	1.5	Wallace R	4150	.08 mi SE Stickney Lk
ONEIL	Pacific	~0	Columbia R	25	1.8 mi SW Ilwaco
OPAL	King	3	Ef Foss R	4750	11 mi SE Skykomish
ORR'S PD	Island	1	Possession Snd	200	On Whidbey Island
ORTING	Pierce	4	Carbon R	738	1.8 mi NE Orting
OSBORNE LKS (2)	Mason	2-4	Hood Canal	750	6 mi N Hoodsport
OSOYOOS	Okanogan	2038	Columbia R	9"	1 mi N Oroville
OTTER	King	183	Wf Foss R	4400	9.3 mi S Skykomish
OTTER	Yakima	7	Tieton R	5030	3.5 mi NE White Pass
OVAL LKS (3)	Okanogan	8-21	Twisp R	6200	16.5 mi SW Twisp
OVERCOAT	King	14	Mf Snoq R	5900	8.4 mi NE Snoq Pass
OWENS PDS (3)	Pacific	6	Willapa R	60	5 mi E Raymond
OWL	Adams	21	Crab Cr	825	2.5 mi NW Othello
OZETTE	Clallam	7787	Ozette R	29	15 mi S Neah Bay
P					
P.J.	Clallam	2.5	Juan de Fuca	4700	10.5 mi S Port Angeles
PACIFIC	Lincoln	130	Crab Cr	1650	5.4 mi N Odessa
PACKWOOD	Lewis	452	Cowlitz R	2858	5 mi E Packwood
PALISADES LKS (2)	Pierce	4-4	White R	5500	3200' N Hidden Lk

LAKE	COUNTY	ACRES	DRAINAGE	ELEVATION	LOCATION
PALM	Adams	88	Palouse R	1852	7.5 mi SW Spraque
PALMER PD	Benton	5	Lk Wallula	340	15.5 mi SE Kennewick
PALMER	Okanogan	2083	Similkameen R	1145	4 mi N Loomis
PALMER LKS (2)	Pierce	4-8.5	Case Inlet	50-~70	1.8 mi W Bay Lk
PALMER	Skagit	9	Samish R	525	2600' SW Cain Lk
PAMPA PD	Whitman	3	Palouse R	1370	3.8 mi SW La Crosse
PANHANDLE	Mason	14	Oakland Bay	400	8 mi SW Shelton
PANHANDLE	Pend Orellle	10	L Spokane R	2550	8.5 mi W Newport
PANHANDLE	Skamania	15	Green R	4520	5 mi NE Spirit Lk Outlet
PANTHER	King	33	Green R	440	3.5 mi NE Kent
PANTHER	Snohomish	47	Pilchuck R	455	4.52 mi NE Snohomish
PARA	Grant	12	Crab Cr	832	8.3 mi NW Othello
PARADISE	King	18	Sammamish R	256	4.5 mi NE Woodinville
PARADISE LKS (2)	King	5-23	Nf Snoq R	4050	17 mi NE North Bend
PARK	Grant	341.5	Grand Coulee	1096	14 mi N Soap Lake City
PARKS LKS (2)	Kittitas	9-11	Kachess R	45'0	8 mi E Snoq Pass
PARKER	Pend Oreille	22	Pend Oreille R	2450	10 mi N Cusick
PASS	Skagit	99	Rosario Strait	~30	Fidalgo Island
PASS	Snohomish	2	Sf Stilly R	3700	3.8 mi NE Silverton
PATTERSON	Okanogan	143	Methow R	2380	3 mi SW Winthrop
PATISON (RES)	Thurston	257	Henderson Inlet	'54	8 mi SE Olympia
PAWN LKS (2)	Chelan	2.5-9	Entiat R	4625	23 mi NW Chelan
PAYNES MEADOWS	Okanogan	6	Columbia R	3120	10.2 mi NW Brewster
PEACH	Snohomish	17	Beckler R	4800	1000' S Pear Lk
PEAR	Skagit	10	Suiattle R	5200	13.4 mi NE Darrington
PEAR	Snohomish	33	Nf Rapid R	4800	10.4 mi N Stevens Pass
PEAR	Yakima	21	Rimrock Lk	5060	7.8 mi NE White Pass
PEARRYGIN (RES)	Okanogan	192	Chewack R	'975	1.4 mi NE Winthrop
PEEK-A-BOO	Snohomish	22	Sauk R	4000	10 mi SE Darrington
PEEPSIGHT	Okanogan	6	Ashnola R	7100	30 mi N Winthrop
PEGGYS PD	Kittitas	5	Waptus R	5800	11 mi N Salmon la Sac
PEMMICAN	Snohomish	1	Sauk R	400	5 mi N Barlow Pass
PENOYER	Lewis	6	Ohanapecosh R	5000	5.4 mi N White Pass
PEPOON	Stevens	11	Columbia R	2450	5.5 mi W Northport
PERCH	Grant	15	Grand Coulee	1201	Sun Lks State Park
PERCIVAL	Thurston	22	Capitol Lk		Olympia, W Capitol Lk
PERKINS	Stevens	26	Columbia R	2250	4.5 mi E Barstow
PETE	Kittitas	37	Cle Elum R	2980	23.5 mi NW Cle Elum
PETE LKS (2)	Snohomish	2-3	Rapid R	4900	6 mi N Stevens Pass
PETERSON	King	10	Cedar R	—	6 mi SE Renton
PETERSON	Jefferson	23	Pt Townsend Bay	500	8 mi W Port Ludlow
PETERSON PD	Stevens	9	Kettle R	2050	3.4 mi N Barstow
PETIT	Pend Orellle	11	Priest Lk	3975	12.5 mi NE Ruby
PFEIFFER PD	Snohomish	1	Skykomish R	230	2.8 mi E Monroe
PHANTOM	King	63	Sammamish Lk	250	3.5 mi SE Bellevue
PHANTOM	Yakima	1	Sf Tieton R	4300	7 mi S Clear Lk Dam
PHEASANT	Jefferson	4,5	Hood Canal	390	5.5 mi SW Port Ludlow
PHEBE	Skagit	15	Strawberry Bay	1000	Ctr Cypress Island
PHELAN	Stevens	1B	Colville R	2375	16 mi N Colville
PHILIPPA	King	121	Nf Snoq R	3346	11 mi NE North Bend
PHILLIPS	Lincoln	31	Crab Cr	2200	12 mi S Creston
PHILLIPS	Mason	111	Oakland Bay	188	7 mi NE Shelton
PHILLIPS	Stevens	1	Colville R	3000	9.5 mi N Chewelah
PHOEBE LKS (2)	Chelan	3_13	Wenatchee R	5450	20.5 mi W Leavenworth
PICNIC POINT	Snohomish	4	Possession Snd	10	5.8 mi N Edmonds
PICTURE	Whatcom	3	Nf Nooksack R	4100	1000' NE Mt Baker Ldg
PIERRE	Stevens	106	Kettle R	2012	4 mi NE Orient
PILLAR	Grant	9	Crab Cr	968	8.8 mi N Othello
PILLAR	Yakima	4	Tieton R	5273	1050' NE Long John Lk
PILOT	Snohomish	6	Suiattle R	5500	2200' NE Downey LkAdams
PINES	Adams		Palouse R	1870	3.5 mi S Spraque
PINE	King	88	Sammamish Lk	390	4 mi N Issaquah
PINE	Mason	8	Sf Skok R	2250	23.5 mi NW Shelton
PINE	Whatcom	7	Chuckanut Bay	1570	5 mi S BellIngham
PINE TREE	Okanogan	6		2320	750' N No end Salmon Lk
PINNACLE	Snohomish	6.5	Sf Stllly R	3820	10 mi E Granite Falls
PINUS	Whatcom	1.5	Nf Nooksack R	2450	7 mi E Glacier
PIONEER PD	Snohomish	2	Stilly R	110	1 mi SW Arlington
PIPE	King	52	Cedar R	530	4.5 mi NW Blk Diamond
PIT	Grant	40	Crab Cr	985	6 mi N Othello
PITCHER MTN	Pierce	7	Carbon R	4650	1.8 mi W Summit Lk
PITMAN	Thurston	27	Black R	198	8.8 mi S Olympia
PLACID	Skamania	19	Nf Lewis R	4000	22 mi N Carson
PLATT PD	King	14	Tolt R	560	3 mi SE Carnation
PLEASANT	Clallam	486	Soleduck R	390	12 mi S Sekiu
PLEASANT LKS (2)	Yakima	1-1	American R	3940	11 mi NE Chinook Pass
PLUMMER	Lewis	12	Chehalis R	180	W portion Centralia
POACHER	Grant	1	Crab Cr	945	8.5 mi N Othello
POCKET	Whatcom	2	Baker R	4540	12.5 mi N Concrete
PONDILLA	Island	4	Juan de Fuca	20	W side Whidbey Island
PORTAGE BAY	King	148	Puget Sound	12	In Seattle
POST OFFICE	Clark	77	Columbia R	10	9 mi NW Vancouver

LAKE	COUNTY	ACRES	DRAINAGE	ELEVATION	LOCATION
POTHOLES RES	Grant	28200	Crab Cr	1046	10 mi S city Moses Lake
POTHOLE	King	3	Taylor R	3900	1800' S Dream Lk
POTHOLE	Klickitat	8.5	L Klickitat R	2300	6 mi N Goldendale
POWER	Chelan	3	Wenatchee R	6050	4 mi SW Leavenworth
POWER	Pend Oreille	55	Pend Oreille R	2421	6.4 mi SW Usk
PRAIRIE LKS (2)	Skagit	3-5,5	Suiattle R	1500	8.5 mi NE Darrington
PRATT LKS (2)	King	4 43 5	Pratt R	3385	13.5 mi SE North Bend
PRESTON MILL PDS	King	2-2	Raging R	400	At Preston
PRICE	King	2	Mf Snoq R	4500	6 mi N Snoq Pass
PRICE	Mason	62	Hood Canal	780	4.8 mi N Hoodsport
PRICE	Okanogan	6	Okanogan R	2360	700' SE Medicine Lk
PRICE	Whatcom	40	Nf Nooksack R	3895	N side Mt Shuksan
PRICKETT	Mason	68	Puget Sound	301	5.5 mi SW Belfair
PRIEST RAPIDS DAM R	Grant	7700	Columbia R	488	29 mi E Yakima
PROCTOR	Okanogan	7	Okanogan R	1240	3.5 mi N Omak
PROFITTS PD	King	3	Tye R	1000	4 mi E Skykomish
PTARMIGAN LKS (2)	King	,3-2a	Tye R	4950-5000	I.4 mi SE Skykomish
PTARMIGAN	Okanogan	4	Lost R	6800	32 mi NW Winthrop
PUGSLEY	King	19	Ef Miller R	3650	8.8 mi S Skykomish
PURDY CR PDS	Snohomish	20	Pilchuck R	500	1 mi NE Lk Roesiger
PURDY	Lincoln	16	Crab Cr	2300	6 mi S Creston
PURVIS	King	9 5	Ef Miller R	5100	5.8 mi S Skykomish
PYRAMID	Whatcom	1	Skagit R	2400	1.4 mi S Diablo Dam

Q

LAKE	COUNTY	ACRES	DRAINAGE	ELEVATION	LOCATION
QUAIL	Adams	12	Crab Cr	935	Adj NE Herman Lk
QUARRY	Walla Walla	9	Lk Wallula	340	4.8 mi SE Burbank
QUARTZ	King	1	Mf Snoq R	4800	3000' S Hi-Low Lk
QUARTZ	Okanogan	6	Pasayten R	6900	35.5 mi N Winthrop
QUEEN LUCAS	Spokane	37	Spokane R	2129	5 mi NE Cheney
QUIGLEY	Clark	38	Columbia R	10	.05 mi SW Ridpefield
QUINAULT	Grays Hbr	3729	Pacific Ocean	182	37 mi N Aberdeen
OUINCY	Grant	43	Columbia R	1196	7 mi S Quincy
QUINN	Pierce	1	Greenwater R	38~30	2000' N Lost Lk

R

LAKE	COUNTY	ACRES	DRAINAGE	ELEVATION	LOCATION
RACHEL	Kittitas	27	Kachess R	4600	4 mi E Snoq Pass
RACHOR	King	5	Nf Snoq R	3500	4 mi NE North Bend
RADAR PDS (2)	Pacific	3-5	Naselle R	1000	4 mi N Naselle
RAE	Yakima	1	Naches R	5020	350' E N end Janet Lk
RAINBOW LKS (2)	Chelan	2-4	Stehekin R	5500	6.3 mi N Lk Chelan
RAINBOW	Columbia	10	Tucannon R	2207	2 mi S Game Range H.Q.
RAINBOW	Grant	9	Park Lk	1150	Sun Lks State Park
RAINBOW	King	6	Pratt R	4270	13 mi SE North Bend
RAINY	Chelan	54	Stehekin R	4790	12.5 mi N N end Lk Chelan
RAINY	King	5	Mf Snoq R	3764	12 mi E North Bend
RAMON LKS (3)	Okanogan	2-2.5	Ashnola R	7050	N side Sheep Mtn
RAMPART LKS (5)	Kittitas	0.5-7	Keechelus R	5100	3.8 mi E Snoq Pass
RAMPART	Okanogan	11	Lost R	6600	27 mi NW Winthrop
RAND	Skamania	5	Columbia R	280	2.7 mi SW Stevenson
RAPJOHN	Pierce	56	Nisqually R	632	4.5 mi NW Eatonville
RAT	Okanogan	63	Columbia R	1676	5.5 mi N Brewster
RATTLESNAKE	Douglas	3.5	Columbia R	2430	10 mi NW city Grand Coulee
RATTLESNAKE	King	112	Sf Snoq R	911	.05 mi NE Cedar Falls
RAVENSDALE	King	18	Green R	560	1.4 mi W Ravensdale
RAVENSDALE PDS	King	4	Cedar R	690	.03 mi S Ravensdale
R. B.	Skagit	3	Skagit R	3225	9 mi SE Sedro-Woolley
REBECCA	Kittitas	13	Waptus R	4750	11.7 mi NW Salmon la Sac
REFLECTION LKS (3)	Lewis	1-13	Nisqually R	4861	4 mi E Longmire
REID SLOUGH	King	3	Snoqualmie R	420	1.4 mi N North Bend
REILYS	Okanogan	4.5	Similkameen R	3650	7.4 mi W Oroville
REMMEL	Okanogan	13	Chewack R	6500	33.5 mi N Winthrop
RETREAT	King	53	Green R	731	1.8 mi E Ravensdale
REVEILLE LKS (2)	Whatcom	3-4	Chilliwack R	5000	16.5 mi N Newhalem
R. B.	Mason	13	Oakland Bay	240	3.4 mi NE Shelton
RICE	Jefferson	6	L Quilcene R	140	1.5 mi N Quilcene
RICHMOND	Yakima	1.5	Naches R	5900	E side Nelson Ridge
RIDGE	Kittitas	2	Yakima R	5220	3.5 mi NE Snoq Pass
REBECCA	Okanogan	53	Columbia R	1900	7.8 mi S Nespelem
RED	Stevens	9	Spokane R	1800	5 mi SE Ford
REED	Lincoln	20	Crab Cr	2300	8 mi S Creston
REED	Whatcom	15	Samish R	394	9 mi SE Bellingham
REFFETT PD	Grant	2	Crab Cr	1090	4.8 mi N city Moses Lake
REFLECTION	Jefferson	1	Quinault R	3500	10 mi NE Lk Quinault
RIDGE	Pend Oreille	2.5	Pend Oreille R	3100	9.1 mi SE Ione
RIDLEY	Whatcom	14	Ross Lk	3000	15 mi N Ross Dam
RIFFE	Lewis	—	Cowlitz R	—	Mossyrock
RIGLEY	Stevens	7	Columbia R	2531	2.5 mi W Echo

LAKE	COUNTY	ACRES	DRAINAGE	ELEVATION	LOCATION
RILEY	Snohomish	30	Nf Stilly R	517	2 mi S Oso
RIMROCK (RES)	Yakima	2530	Tieton R	2918	12.5 mi E White Pass
RING	Clallam	2	Nf Boqachiel R	2875	2400' NW Misery Pk
RING	Spokane	23	Crab Cr	2400	1 mi SE twn Medical Lake
ROARING CREEK SL	Pacific	10	Naselle R	20	4.5 mi NW Naselle
ROBE MILL PD	Snohomish	1.5	Sf Stilly R	850	5 mi E Granite Falls
ROBIN LKS (2)	Kittitas	11-34	Cle Elum R	6150	12.6 mi N Salmon La Sac
ROCK	Chelan	3.5	Wenatchee R	5600	7 mi NE Stevens Pass
ROCK	Douglas	16	Columbia R	2400	11 mi NW city Grand Coulee
ROCK	King	23	Wf Foss R	4500	5 mi S Skykomish
ROCK LKS (2)	Okanogan	3.5-4.5	Okanoqan R	3550	11.3 mi NW Okanoqan
ROCK	Whitman	2147	Palouse R	1719	32 mi S Spokane
ROCK CREEK	Skamania	3	Columbia R	1680	8 mi NW Stevenson
ROCK CREEK PD	Skamania	2	Columbia R	1200	7.5 mi NW Stevenson
ROCKDALE	King	2	Sf Snoq R	3540	2.8 mi S Snoq Pass
ROCK ISLAND POOL	Chelan	3470	Columbia R	605	12 mi SE Wenatchee
ROCK QUARRY	King	1	White R	1000	3.5 mi SE Enumclaw
ROCK SLIDE	Snohomish	o.5	Snoqualmie R	1320	5.4 mi S Sultan
ROCKY	Stevens	20	Colville R	2275	3.5 mi S Colville
ROCKY SADDLE PDS 2	Kittitas	1	Naches R	5100	2.3 mi NW Bald Mtn
ROESIGER	Snohomish	352	Skykomish R	570	6.5 mi N Monroe
ROOT	Yakima	5	Bumpinq R	5300	8.3 mi SE Chinook Pass
ROSE	Snohomish	1	Wallace R	4300	5 mi NE Gold Bar
ROSS (RES)	Whatcom	11878	Skagit R	1599	9.4 mi NE Newhalem
ROUND	Chelan	10	Lk Chelan	3250	38 mi NW Chelan
ROUND	Clallam	3	Soleduck Lk	4250	3400' S Soleduck Lk
ROUND	Clark	16	Lake R	10	8 mi NW Vancouver
ROUND	Ferry	52	FDR Lk	2275	5.8 mi W Inchelium
ROUND	King	3	Sammamish Lk	470	1300' SW Tradltion Lk
ROUND	Okanogan	20	Wf San Poil R	2583	16 mi E Tonasket
ROUND	Snohomish	12	White Chuck R	5100	16.5 mi SE Darrinqton
ROUND	Yakima	7	Yakima R	650	1 mi N Mabton
ROWEL	Okanogan	4	Columbia R	2075	10.5 mi N Brewster
ROWLAND	Klickitat	85	Columbia R	72CF	4 mi E Bingen
ROYAL	Adams	102	Crab Cr	780	Near Royal Slope
ROYAL	Jefferson	2	Dunqeness R	5100	15.5 mi W Quilcene
RUBY	Snohomish	4	Nf Sauk R	5200	20 mi SE Darrinqton
RUFUS WOOD (RES)	Douglas	7800	Columbia R	946	1.5 mi SE Bridgeport
RUTH	Chelan	2.5	Wenatchee R	6000	9 mi W Leavenworth
RUTHERFORD SLOUGH	King	18	Snoqualmie R	80	.05 mi N Fall City
RYAN	Skamania	4	Green R	3307	7.5 mi NE Spirit Lk outlet

S

LAKE	COUNTY	ACRES	DRAINAGE	ELEVATION	LOCATION
SACAJAWEA	Cowlitz	48	Columbia R	10	In Longview
SACAJAWEA	Franklin	8370	Snake R	440	10 mi E Pasco
SACHEEN	Pend Orellle	282	L SpokaneR	2250	34 mi N Spokane
SADDLE	Snohomish	4	Nf Stilly R	3780	6.7 mi N Verlot
SAGE LKS (2)	Grant	6	Crab Cr	972	7.4 mi N Othello
SAGO	Grant	1.5	Crab Cr	940	Adj E Hourglass Lk
SAHALEE-TYEE	Skamania	7	White Salmon R	4700	18.4 mi N Carson
SALMON	Okanogan	313	Okanogan R	2324	Adj E Conconully
SAMISH	Whatcom	814	Samish R	273	6.5 mi SE Bellingham
SAMMAMISH	King	4897	Lk Washington	28	10 mi E Seattle
SAND	Grant	28	Crab Cr	1120	Adj N Frenchman Hills
SANDSTONE	Yakima	3	Bumpinq R	3800	2.2 mi S mouth Bumpinq R
SANDY SHORE	Jefferson	38	Hood Canal	470	4.8 mi SW Port Ludlow
SARDINE	Skamania	2	Columbia R	280	1.4 mi SW Stevenson
SARVINSKI LKS (4)	Grays Hbr	9	Chehalls R	30	2 mi S Elma
SASSE RES	Okanogan	7	Okanoqan R	2360	5.6 mi NE Conconully
SATSOP LK NO 1	Grays Hbr	4	Wf Satsop R	2195	6.8 mi NE Grisdale
SATSOP LK NO 2	Grays Hbr	3	Wf Satsop R	220	7 mi NE Grisdale
SATSOP LKS 3, 4 & 5	Grays Hbr	1.5-3	Wt Satsop R	1550	4700' SW Satsop No 1
SAUCER	Snohomish	14	Rapid R	4500	1000' NW Cup Lk
SAUK	Skagit	10	Skagit R	4025	7 mi E Concrete
SAWYER	King	279	Green R	512	2 mi NW Blk Diamond
SAWYER LK SWAMP	King	9	Green R	500	1000' SE S end Lk Sawyer
SCANLON	Okanogan	12	Okanogan R	2380	4.5 mi NW Riverside
SCATTER	Okanogan	7	Twisp R	6900	15.5 mi W Winthrop
SCHAEFER	Chelan	83	Chiwawa R	5050	20 mi NE Stevens Pass
SCHALLOW	Okanogan	10	Okanogan R	1675	4.4 mi NE Conconully
SCHWEDA PD	Lincoln	4	Crab Cr	2100	5.4 mi SW Wilbur
SCOOTENEY	Franklin	217	Columbia R	825	7.5 mi S Othello
SCOTCHMAN	Pend Oreille	34	Pend Oreille R	2500	8 mi SE Ione
SCOTT	Thurston	67	Black R	189	9 mi S Olympia
SCOUT	King	6	Sf Snoq R	3850	5.7 mi SW Snoq Pass
SCOUT	Kitsap	3	Tahuya R	875	2 mi SW Wildcat Lk
SCRABBLE	Snohomish	3	Rapid R	5000	3700' SW Saucer Lk
SEABURY PD	Skagit	2	Stilly R	1325	5 mi NE McMurray Lk
SEAFIELD	Clallam	22	Pacitic Ocean	150	12.4 mi S Neah Bay
SEARS	Pierce	4	American Lk	230	On Ft Lewis Mil Res

LAKE	COUNTY	ACRES	DRAINAGE	ELEVATION	LOCATION
SECOND	King	2.5	White R	1100	3 mi E Enumclaw
SEGELSON	Skagit	3	Nt Stilly R	3500	8 mi NW Darrington
SEQUALLITCHEW	Pierce	81	Puget Sound	206	On Ft Lewis Mil Res
SERENE	Snohomish	53	Sf Skykomish R	2509	2.5 mi S Index
SERENE	Snohomish	42	Puget Sound	540	3.5 mi N Lynnwood
SHADOW	King	50	Green R	540	2.5 mi W Maple Valley
SHADOW	Snohomish	6	Snohomish R	8	1 mi NE Cathcart
SHADOW	Yakima	3	Klickitat R	5500	10.6 mi NW Glenwood
SHADY	King	21	Cedar R	520	3.5 mi NW Maple Valley
SHAMROCK	King	7.5	Mf Snoq R	4014	6.5 mi NW Snoq Pass
SHANNON (RES)	Skagit	2148	Skagit R	438	3500' N Concrete
SHAW	Snohomish	6	Nf Wallace R	2075	5.4 mi N Gold Bar
SHEEHAN	Thurston	4.5	Deschutes R	200	1 mi SW East Olympia
SHEEP	Okanogan	7	Ashnola R	6900	36 mi N Winthrop
SHEEP	Yakima	3	Yakima R	5700	1.7 mi N Chinook Pass
SHEEPHERDER	Yakima	3	Naches R	4931	10.6 mi NE Chinook Pass
SHELF	Skagit	3.5	Nf Stilly R	4050	9 mi NE Oso
SHELLEY	Spokane	36	Spokane R	2025	2.5 mi E Opportunity
SHELL ROCK	Yakima	11	Tieton R	4926	3.8 mi NE White Pass
SHELOKUM	Okanogan	2	Methow R	6347	16 mi W Winthrop
SHERMAN	Ferry	3	San Poil R	5900	12 mi E Republic
SHERRY	Stevens	26	L Pend Ore R	3159	250' S Gillette Lk
SHIELD	Chelan	38	Wenatchee R	6695	9 mi SW Leavenworth
SHINER	Adams	33.5	Crab Cr	701	6.2 mi NW Othello
SHINER	Skagit	5	Skagit R	250	.07 mi NE Montborne
SHOE	Mason	6	Hood Canal	380	8.5 mi W Belfair
SHOE	Yakima	18	Nf Tieton R	6112	3.4 mi S White Pass
SHOECRAFT	Snohomish	137	Tulalip Bay	324	600' SW Lk Goodwin
SHOVEL	Kittitas	27	Waptus R	4000	10.5 mi NW Salmon La Sac
SHOVEL	Skamania	21	Green R	4653	4.8 mi N Spirit Lk outlet
SHOVELER	Grant	6	Crab Cr	940	8.4 mi N Othello
SHUKSAN	Whatcom	28	Baker R	3700	18 mi NE Concrete
SIDLEY	Okanogan	109	Osoyoos Lk	3675	0.7 mi NW Molson
SIKES	King	14	Snoqualmie R	41	At Carnation Farm
SILENT LKS (2)	Chelan	3	Stehekin R	6700	SE side Mt Arriva
SILER MILL PD	Lewis	1	Cowlitz R	1280	4 mi W Morton
SILLS PDS (2)	Snohomish	2	Sf Stilly R	75	.08 mi NE Arlington
SILVER	Cowlitz	2996	Toutle R	484	4 mi E Castle Rock
SILVER	Island	15	Saratoga Pass	325	5.4 mi E Oak Harbor
SILVER LKS (2)	Jefferson	1-2	Dungeness R	5450	9 mi W Quilcene
SILVER	Okanogan	3	Twisp R	5550	16 mi SW Twisp
SILVER	Pierce	138	Nisqually R	605	4.5 mi W Eatonville
SILVER	Snohomish	102	Sammamish R	426	5.5 mi S Everett
SILVER	Spokane	559	Crab Cr	2341	1.1 mi E twn Medical Lake
SILVER	Whatcom	173	Nf Nooksack R	4400	3 mi N Maple Falls
SILVER	Whatcom	164	Ross Lk	6700	19 mi N Ross Dam
SILVER CR PDS	Lewis	7	Cowlitz R	600	3 mi NE Salkum
SILVER NAIL	Okanogan	5	Okanogan R	1000	4 mi N Oroville
SIMMONS	Thurston	25	Capitol Lk	140	2 mi W Olympia
SIMONSON PD	Whatcom	14	Birch Bay	240	3.4 mi SW Custer
SINK HOLE	King	3	Green R	650	1000' NW Beaver Lk
SINLAHEKIN IMP NO 2	Okanogan	3	Similkameen R	1557	700' W Forde Lk
LWR SINLAHEKIN IMP	Okanogan	58	Similkameen R	1500	5 mi S Loomis
SIOUXON	Skamania	2	Nt Lewis R	1480	4 mi NE Yale Dam
SIXTEEN	Skagit	42	Skagit R	427	2.5 mi E Conway
SKARO	Skagit	12	Cascade R	4450	1800' SW Found Lk
SKATING	Pacific	66	Pacific Ocean	20	1 mi SW Oysterville
SKOOKUMCHUCK	Lewis	8	Skookumchuck R	175	At Centralia
SKYLINE	King	2	Tye R	4950	1 mi N Stevens Pass
SKYMO	Whatcom	22.5	Ross Lk	4500	7.4 mi N Ross Dam
SLATE	Okanogan	6	Twisp R	6400	13.4 mi W Winthrop
SLAUGHTERHOUSE	Yakima	15	Yakima R	650	1.7 mi NW Mabton
SLIDE	Skagit	37	Skagit R	3300	8 mi SE Marblemount
SLIM	Skagit	7	Suiattle R	4700	.08 mi E Woods Lk
S.M.C.	King	41	Nf Snoq R	3702	.07 mi NE North Bend
SMELLING	Snohomish	7	Pilchuck R	860	4.3 mi SE Granite Falls
SMITH	Clallam	5	Sequim Bay	625	2.5 mi S Sequim
SMITH	Clallam	3	Freshwater Bay	140	9.5 mi W Port Angeles
SMITH	King	2	Ef Miller R	4500	2200' N Dream Lk
SMITH	Mason	11	Nf Skok R	4000	5.5 mi N hd Lk Cushman
SMITH	Okanogan	3	Similkameen R	7000	17 mi NW Loomis
SMITH	Okanogan	8	Okanogan R	2150	3.5 mi NW Malott
SMITH	Thurston	18	Deschutes R	200	4 mi SE Olympia
SMOKEY POINT PD	Snohomish	5	Possession Snd	110	6 mi N Marysville
SNAKE	Pierce	8	Puget Sound	300	At Tacoma
SNELL	Pierce	2	Carbon R	1150	1.4 mi SE Wilkeson
SNIP	Grant	4	Crab Cr	954	8.5 mi N 0thello
SNOQUALMIE	King	126	N Br Taylor R	3225	9.4 mi N Snoq Pass
SNOQUALMIE PTHLS	King	5	Taylor R	4100	2000' E S end Snoq Lk
SNOQUALMIE MILL PD	King	66	Snoqualmie R	408	At Snoqualmie

LAKE	COUNTY	ACRES	DRAINAGE	ELEVATION	LOCATION
SNOW LKS (2)	Chelan	66-123	Wenatchee R	5420	8 mi SW Leavenworth
SNOW	King	159.5	Mf Snoq R	4016	3 mi NW Snoq Pass
SNOW	Lewis	8	Ohanapecosh R	4975	6 mi N White Pass
SNOW	Lewis	9	Cowlitz R	4678	5.5 mi E Longmire
SNOW	Skamania	5	Nf Toutle R	4700	4.5 mi N Spirit Lk outlet
SNOW KING	Skagit	36	Cascade R	4600	1800' SW Found Lk
SNOW PLOW	Yakima	6	Klickitat R	4500	8 mi SE Mt Adams
SNOW SLIDE	Snohomish	10	Nf Skykomish R	4300	5 mi N Index
SNOWY LKS (2)	Skagit	1-3	Ross Lk	6400	19 mi SE Ross Dam
SNYDER SLOUGH	Lincoln/Whit	60	Palouse R	1937	2.9 mi SE Sprague
SODA	Grant	155	Potholes Canal	998	9.5 mi N Othello
SOLEDUCK	Clallam	31	Soleduck R	3700	4.7 mi SE Sol Duc Hot Spr.
SONNY BOY LKS	Skagit	2.5-4	Cascade R	4400	15 mi SE Marblemount
SOURDOUGH	Whatcom	33	Ross Lk	4400	3.4 mi NW Ross Dam
SOUTH	Okanogan	3	Twisp R	6000	Hwtrs South Cr
SOUTH	Snohomish	13	Sauk R	4200	5.3 mi N Barlow Pass
SOUTH PRAIRIE	Skamania	14	White Salmon R	3140	9.5 mi N Willard
SOUTH SKOOKUM	Pend Orelle	32	Pend Oreille R	3525	6.6 mi NE Cusick
SOUTH TWIN	Ferry	973	FDR Lk	2572	8.5 mi W Inchelium
SOUTHWICK	Thurston	37	Henderson Inlet	173	5 mi SE Olympia
SPADE	Kittitas	122	Waptus R	5050	10.3 mi NW Salmon la Sac
SPANAWAY	Pierce	262	Steilacoom Lk	320	10 mi S Tacoma
SPARKPLUG	King	15	Tye R	5600	3 mi S Scenic
SPAULDING LKS (2)	Okanogan	2.5-5.5	Okanogan R	2300	4 mi W Okanosan
SPEARFISH	Klickitat	22	Lk Celilo	160	1 mi N The Dalles Dam
SPECTACLE	Kittitas	81	Cooper R	4239	6.7 mi NE Snoq Pass
SPECTACLE	Okanogan	315	Okanogan R	1363	2.5 mi E Loomis
SPIDER	King	15	Pratt R	2746	10.5 mi SE North Bend
SPIDER	King	4	Stuck R	420	1 mi NE Fivemile Lk
SPIDER	Mason	23	Sf Skok R	1290	21 mi NW Shelton
SPIRIT	Chelan	2	Wenatchee R	5603	16.7 mi NW Blewett Pass
SPIRIT	Skamania	1262	Nf Toutle R	3198	36 mi E Castle Rock
SPOOK	King	19.5	Tolt R	530	1.4 mi E Langlois Lk
SPRAGUE	Adams	1841	Palouse R	1879	2.2 mi SW Sprague
SPRING	Columbia	5	Tucannon R	2060	0.5 mi S Game Range H.Q.
SPRING LKS (2)	Grant	1	Columbia R	1150	500' W Crystal Lk
SPRING	King	68	Cedar R	500	3 mi NW Maple Valley
SPRING	Okanogan	3.5	Okanogan R	1900	800' W Wannacut Lk
SPRING	Skamania	6	Columbia R	300	1.4 mi NE No Bonneville
SPRINGER	Thurston	5.5	Deschutes R	300	2.5 mi W Oftutt Lk
SPRINGSTEEN	Skagit	19	St Nooksack R	3550	7.5 mi NW Concrete
SPRITE	Chelan	5	Wenatchee R	6050	10 mi N Salmon la Sac
SPRUCE	Stevens	27	L Pend Ore R	3728	12 mi E Colville
SPUD	Lewis	3	St Newaukum R	3025	400' W Newaukum Lk
SPUR 3 PD	Kitsap	1	Tahuya R	500	3 mi S Hintzville
SQUALICUM	Whatcom	33	Bellinham Bay	477	6.5 mi NE Bellingham
SQUARE	Chelan	80	Wenatchee R	4950	4.7 mi S Scenic
SQUARE	Kitsap	8	Sinclair Inlet	400	4.5 mi SW Port Orchard
SQUAW	Chelan	2	Lk Wenatchee	1870	W end Lk Wenatchee
SQUAW	Kittitas	12	Cle Elum R	4850	9 mi N Salmon la Sac
SQUITCH	Kittitas	3	Cle Elum R	,17nn	8.8 mi N Salmon la Sac
ST CLAIR	Thurston	245	Nisqually R	73	6.5 mi NW Yelm
ST HELENS	Skamania	79	Spirit Lk	4567	2 mi N Spirit Lk outlet
ST MICHAEL	Lewis	9	Nf Cispus R	4750	10 mi S Packwood
STACY	Lewis	1	Nisqually R	4500	1.8 mi SE Longmire
STAN COFFIN	Grant	41	Columbia Basin	1170	6.5 mi SW Quincey
STANDSTILL	Mason	6	Hood Canal	735	S end L. Cushman
STANSBERRY	Pierce	19	Carr Inlet	238	3.5 mi NE Vaughn
STAR	Chelan	10	Lk Chelan	7400	33 mi NW Chelan
STAR	King	34	Green R	320	3 mi SW Kent
STARVATION	Stevens	28	L Pend Ore R	2375	9.8 mi SE Colville
STARZMAN LKS (2)	Okanogan	5.5-8	Columbia R	1645	9 mi N Brewster
STATE SOLDIERS HOME	Pierce	2	Puyallup R	220	700' S State Soldiers Home
STEAMBOAT	Skamania	9	White Salmon R	4050	13 mi NW Trout Lk
STEEL	King	46	Commencement B	430	4 mi NW Auburn
STEIGERWALD LKS (2)	Clark	57-258	Columbia R	19	.08 mi SE Washougal
STEILACOOM	Pierce	313	Puget Sound	210	3 mi E Steilacoom
STETSON	Mason	8.5	Hood Canal	500	7.5 mi NE Hoodsport
STEVENS	Mason	8.5	Nf Skok R	600	3.4 mi NW Potlatch
STEVENS	Okanogan	11	Okanogan R	1500	5 mi SE Loomis
STEVENS	Snohomish	1021	Pilchuck R	210	5.5 mi E Everett
STEWART	Okanogan	17	Okanogan R	2700	7.8 mi SE Okanogan
STICKNEY	Snohomish	14.5	Wallace R	3500	2 mi NE Wallace Lk
STIDHAM	Pierce	8	Nisqually R	850	6 mi N Eatonville
STILETTO	Chelan	9	Stehekin R	6800	1.5 mi NW Twisp Pass
STILWELL	Skagit	3	Lk Shannon	4150	8 mi NE Concrete
STINK LKS (3)	King	3	White R	2500	8.8 mi E Enumclaw
STIRRUP	Kittitas	9	Keechelus Lk	3550	3.5 mi W Stampede Pass
STITCH	Snohomish	10	Pilchuck R	215	5 mi E Everett

LAKE	COUNTY	ACRES	DRAINAGE	ELEVATION	LOCATION
STONE	Snohomish	1.5	Sf Skyk R	3800	1800' S Eagle Lk
STONES THROW	Kittitas	2	Kachess Lk	4410	1800' NW Swan Lk
STONY	Pierce	7	Steilacoom Lk	380	3 mi SE S end Spanaway Lk
STORM	Snohomish	78	Pilchuck R	528	5.5 mi N Monroe
STORMO PD	Snohomish	4	Sf Skyk R	800	3.4 mi SE Index
STOUT	Skagit	24	Skagit R	5200	6 mi S Newhalem
STRANGERS	Jefferson	11	Juan de Fuca	150	1 mi SW Port Townsend
STRAWBERRY	Skamania	10	Green R	5374	3.8 mi NE Spirit Lk inlet
STRICKLAND	Pierce	5	Nisqually R	220	.08 mi W Dupont
STUART	Chelan	40	Wenatchee R	5064	12 mi SW Leavenworth
STUMP	Mason	23	Chehalis R	300	7.5 mi NE Elma
STURTEVANT	King	10	Lk Washington	140	1.4 mi NE Bellevue
SULLIVAN	Pend Oreille	1291	Pend Oreille R	2583	4.3 mi SE Metaline Falls
SULPHUR MTN	Snohomish	5	Suiattle R	5200	5000' N Sulphur Mtn summit
SUMMER	Skagit	8	Skagit R	522	2.8 mi NE McMurray Lk
SUMMIT	King	6	Tye R	4600	1.4 mi W Stevens Pass
SUMMIT	Okanogan	10	Okanogan R	3270	6.5 mi SE Disautel
SUMMIT	Pierce	25	Carbon R	5440	13.5 mi SE Enumclaw
SUMMIT	San Juan	10	East Sound	2200	In Moran State Park
SUMMIT	Snohomish	9.5	Pilchuck R	3880	9.4 mi SE Granite Falls
SUMMIT	Stevens	7	Kettle R	2600	7.4 mi NE Orient
SUMMIT	Thurston	523	Totten Inlet	500	9 mi W Olympia
SUMMMIT CHIEF	Kittitas	6.5	Waptus R	6500	10.5 mi NW Salmon la Sac
SUNDAY LKS (2)	King	2-21	Nf Snoq R	1865	13 mi NE North Bend
SUNDAY	Snohomish	39	Stilly R	211	5 mi E Stanwood
SUNDOWN	Jefferson	3	Quinault R	3900	15.5 mi E Lk Quinault
SUNRISE	Okanogan	11	Methow R	7300	16.5 mi W Methow
SUNRISE	Pierce	4	White R	5800	1 mi E Dege Peak
SUNSET	Snohomish	38	Nt Skyk R	4100	7 mi E Index
SURPRISE	Chelan	48	Lk Chelan	6100	33 mi NW Chelan
SURPRISE	King	28	Tye R	4600	2.7 mi S Scenic
SURPRISE	Pierce	10	Carbon R	4450	14 mi S Enumclaw
SURPRISE	Pierce	30	Commencement B	320	3.4 mi NE Puyallup
SURPRISE LKS (15)	Pierce	17	White Salmon R	4200	12.5 mi NW Trout Lk
SURPRISE	Yakima	14	Sf Tieton R	5300	12 mi S White Pass
SURVEYORS	King	5	Sf Snoq R	3980	2 mi S Snoq Pass
SUSAN	Grant	20	Crab Cr	1033	9 mi N Othello
SUSAN	Thurston	3.5	Deschutes R	140	700' W N end Munn Lk
SUSAN JANE	Chelan	3	Wenatchee R	4650	2 mi SE Stevens Pass
SUTHERLAND	Clallam	361	Elwha R	501	12 mi W Port Angeles
SWALLOW LKS (4)	Chelan	5-20	Wenatchee R	5100	20.5 mi W Leavenworth
SWAMP	Kittitas	45	Yakima R	2420	2 mi SE Keechelus Lk dam
SWAMP	Yakima	51	Bumping R	4797	4.5 mi SE Chinook Pass
SWAN	Ferry	52	San Poil R	3641	10.2 mi SW Republic
SWAN	Kittitas	7	Kachess Lk	4040	5.8 mi SE Snoq Pass
SWARTZ	Snohomish	17	Pilchuck R	525	1.5 mi S Granite Falls
SWEDE	Stevens	5	Colville R	2450	4.5 mi SW Valley
SWIFT RES	Skamania	4589	Nf Lewis R	1008	28.5 mi NE Woodland
SWIMMING DEER	Chelan	3	Wenatchee R	4850	E side Cascade Crest
SWITCH PD	Benton	7	Lake Wallula	340	15.7 mi SE Kennewick
SYLVAN	Lincoln	550	Crab Cr	1650	4 mi E Odesso
SYLVESTER	Chelan	20	Wenatchee R	7000	12.4 mi W Leavenworth
SYLVIA (RES)	Grays Hbr	31	Wynooche R	80	1 mi N Montesano

T

T'AHL	King	6.5	Foss R	5200	2750' S Locket Lk
TABLE	Grant	20	Grand Coulee	1500	1.5 mi W Coulee City
TACOMA SPORTSMENS	Pend Oreille	4	Pend Oreille R	2400	7.1 mi N Cusick
TAG EAR	Douglas	9	Columbia R	2230	14 mi E Bridgeport
TAKHLAK	Skamania	35.5	Cispus R	4350	24.5 mi SE Randle
TALARUS	King	18	Sf Snoq R	3270	4.7 mi W Snoq Pass
TANEUM	Kittitas	3	Yakima R	5266	10.5 mi SW Cle Elum
TANK LKS (2)	King	3-4	Wf Foss R	5800	2000' SE Bonnie Lk
TANWAX	Pierce	173	Nisqually R	600	5.5 mi N Eatonville
TAPE	Pacific	10	Willapa Bay	20	4 mi N Long Beach
TAPPS	Pierce	2296	Stuck R	540	3 mi NE Sumner
TAPTO LKS (4)	Whatcom	0.5-10	Chilliwack R	5750	N Whatcom Pass
TARBOO	Jefferson	22	Hood Canal	640	8 mi W Port Ludlow
TATOOSH LKS (2)	Lewis	2.5-10	Cowlitz R	5000	7.5 mi N Packwood
TAYLOR MILL PD	King	3	Sammamish Lk	483	.05 mi N Hobart
TAYLOR	Stevens	1	Kettle R	2200	4.5 mi NE Orient
TEAL LKS (2)	Grant	22-28	Crab Cr	954	6.4 mi N Othello
TEANAWAY	Kittitas	5	Nf Teanaway R	2730	8.5 mi N Cle Elum
TEANAWAY JUNCTION	Kittitas	5	Teanaway R	1820	5 mi SE Cle Elum
TEMPLE PDS (2)	Snohomish	8	Snohomish R	420	3.5 mi W Monroe
TEN	Skagit	16	Sf Skagit R	1210	3.5 mi NE Conway
TENAS	Mason	11	Hood Canal	850	3.5 mi NW Lilliwaup
TENNANT	Whatcom	43	Bellingham Bay	15	1 mi SE Ferndale
TERENCE	Kittitas	14	Waptus R	5550	4 mi N Salmon la Sac
TERRACE LKS (2)	King	2	Tye R	5200	7 mi S Scenic

LAKE	COUNTY	ACRES	DRAINAGE	ELEVATION	LOCATION
TEXAS PDS (2)	Skagit	6	Sauk R	1500	8 mi N Darrinston
TEXAS	Whitman	24	Palouse R	1702	6.4 mi NW Winona
THESEUS	Chelan	31	L Wenatchee R	5150	7.8 mi NE Stevens Pass
THETIS	Kittitas	5	Kachess R	4420	2.5 mi NE Keechelus Lk dam
THIRD	King	2	Green R	1100	3.3 mi E Enumclaw
THOMAS CREEK PDS	Skagit	2	Samish R	300	3.5 mi N Sedro-Woolley
THOMAS	Skamania	10.5	Wind R	4450	19 mi N Carson
THOMAS	Snohomish	7	Sammamish R	387	7.5 mi N Bothell
THOMAS	Stevens	163	L Pend Ore R	3162	17 mi NE Colville
THOMPSON	Grant	14	Banks Lk	1550	7 mi SW Electric City
THOMPSON	King	47	Pratt R	3650	10 mi SE North Bend
THOMPSON	Stevens	7	Colville R	2430	4 mi SE Colville
THORNDYKE	Jefferson	4	Hood Canal	250	2 mi SW South Pt, Hood Canal
THORNTON	Snohomish	3	Suiattle R	5000	E side White Chuck Mtn
THORTON—LOWER	Whatcom	56	Skagit R	4450	3.4 mi NW Newhalem
THORNTON—MIDDLE	Whatcom	11	Skagit R	4680	3.7 mi W Newhalem
THORNTON—UPPER	Whatcom	31	Skagit R	5040	4 mi W Newhalem
THORP	Kittitas	10	Cle Elum R	4670	9.4 mi N Easton
THREAD	Adams	29	Crab Cr	915	3.3 mi N Othello
THREE LAKES RES	Chelan	33	Columbia R	871	5.7 mi SE Wenatchee
THREE LKS (3)	Lewis	1-4	Ohanapecosh R	4850	2.5 mi SE Sheep Lk
THREE LKS (3)	Skagit	1-4	Sf Nooksack R	4000	9 mi N Hamilton
THREE HORSE	Clallam	4	Lk Mills	4140	2.4 mi W Olympic Hot Spr
THREE QUEEN	Kittitas	1.5	Kachess R	5390	1 mi SE Three Queens Mtn
THUN FIELD PD	Pierce	10	Puyallup R	446	2.4 mi SW Orting
THUNDER	Whatcom	8	Diablo Lk	1500	6.5 mi E Newhalem
THUNDER	Yakima	2	Tieton R	3300	1.6 mi NW Tieton Dam
THUNDER MTN LKS (2)	Chelan	4-5	Wenatchee R	6250	4 mi SE Scenic
TIFFANY	Okanogan	20	Chewack R	6550	12.5 mi NW Conconully
TINKER	Pacific	11	Willapa Bay	20	NE side Long Beach
TOAD	Whatcom	30	Bellingham Bay	714	5 mi NE Bellingham
TOKETIE	Chelan	5	Wenatchee R	6500	7 mi SW Leavenworth
TOKETIE	Skagit	17	Suiattle R	5200	14.5 mi NE Darrington
TOKE-TIE	Skamania	3 5	White Salmon R	4700	2200' NE Sahalee-Tyee Lk
TOMBSTONE	Skamania	2.5	White Salmon R	4600	1 mi SE Gifford Peak
TOM, DICK & HARRY	Snohomish	3	Nf Skyk R	3500	4 mi NE Index
TOMTIT	Snohomish	30	Skykomish R	608	3 mi S Sultan
TOMYHOI	Whatcom	82	Chilliwack R	3700	4.5 mi N Shuksan
TONSETH	Okanogan	0.5	Andrews Cr	3100	21.5 mi N Winthrop
TOP	Chelan	7	L Wenatchee R	4700	10 mi N Stevens Pass
TOP	King	5	Foss R	4500	3.7 mi S Skykomish
TOUGAW OLSON	King	1	White R	860	2 mi E Enumclaw
TOWER ROCK BV PDS	Lewis	3	Cispus R	1300	.04 mi SE Twr Rk Forest Camp
TRADEDOLLAR	Skamania	12	Green R	3552	7 mi NW Spirit Lk outlet
TRADITION	King	19	Sammamish Lk	490	1.4 mi E Issaquah
TRAP	Chelan	12	Wenatchee R	5150	3 mi SE Scenic
TRAP	Mason	18	Oakland Bay	230	6.4 mi W Shelton
TRAPPER	Chelan	147	Stehekin R	4165	3 mi SE Cascade Pass
TRAVERS	Lincoln	20	Crab Cr	1740	8 mi N Odessa
TRESTLE SWAMP	Snohomish	5	Snoqualmie R	9OO	4.4 mi NE Duvall
TRIPLETT LKS (3)	Chelan	3-4	Lk Chelan	6100	4.7 mi SE Stehekin
TRIUMPH	Whatcom	4	Skagit R	3650	6 mi W Newhalem
TROSPER	Thurston	17	Budd Inlet	150	3.5 mi S Olympia
TROUT	Chelan	17	Wenatchee R	4850	11.7 mi W Leavenworth
TROUT	Ferry	8	FDR Lk	3000	8.5 mi W Kettle Falls
TROUT	King	18	White R	350	4 mi SW Auburn
TROUT	King	17	Wf Foss R	2012	6.7 mi S Skykomish
TROUT	Pend Orellle	95	Horseshoe Lk	2250	8 mi NW Elk
TROUT	Pierce	5,5	Nisqually R	700	2 mi W Tanwax Lk
TROUT	Skamania	100	White Salmon R	1950	19.5 mi N White Salmon
TROUT	Snohomish	19	Sfk Stillaguamish R		4.7 mi N Granite Falls
TROUT CREEK RES	Skamania	16	Wind R	1100	7.5 mi N Stevenson
TUCK	Kittitas	16	Cle Elum R	5250	8.6 mi S Scenic
TUCKWAY	Whatcom	1.5	Sf Nooksack R	3850	8.5 mi N Concrete
TUCQUALA	Kittitas	63	Cle Elum R	3325	7.5 mi N Salmon la Sac
TULE	Lincoln	127	Lake Cr	1475	4 mi NW Odessa
TULE	Pierce	31	Nisqually R	456	9 mi SE Yelm
TULE	Pierce	8	Puset Sound	290	1.5 mi N Spanaway Lk
TUMWATER	King	2.5	Ef Miller R	4500	5.7 mi SW Skykomish
TUNGSTEN	Okanogan	17	Chewack R	7100	NE side Apex Mtn
TUNNEL	Skamania	13	Columbia R	75	6.4 mi W White Salmon
TUPSO	Snohomish	3	Sf Stilly R	4000	11 mi NE Granite Falls
TURNBULL SL—EAST	Spokane	331	Palouse R	2290	4 mi S Cheney
TURNBULL SL—WEST	Spokane	361	Palouse R	2290	4.5 mi S Cheney
TURQUOISE	Chelan	22	Wenatchee R	5550	18 mi W Leavenworth
TURTLE	Okanogan	8	Okanogan R	2200	7.9 mi SW Tonasket
TURTLE LKS (2)	Stevens	2-9	Spokane R	2475	4.4 mi NW Wellpinit
TUSCOHATCHIE LKS (2)	King	32-58	Pratt R	3420	3.4 mi W Snoq Pass
TWELVE	King	43	Green R	718	1.5 mi NE Blk Diamond
TWENTY SEVEN	Pierce	21	Nisqually R	776	4 mi N Eatonville
TWENTY-TWO	Snohomish	44	Sf Stilly R	2460	9.5 mi E Granite Falls
TWILIGHT	Kittitas	2	Nf Cedar R	3575	6.5 mi S Snoq Pass

LAKE	COUNTY	ACRES	DRAINAGE	ELEVATION	LOCATION
TWIN LKS (2)	Jefferson	2-5	Pt Ludlow Hbr	390	4.5 mi SW Port Ludlow
TWIN LKS (2)	Kittitas	2-4	Keechelus Lk	3090	4.7 mi S Snoq Pass
TWIN LKS—LOWER	Lincoln	45	Crab Cr	1950	13 mi W Harrington
TWIN LKS—UPPER	Lincoln	35	Crab Cr	1957	500' NE Lower Twin Lk
TWIN LKS (2)	Mason	5.5-15	Tahuya R	395	1.5 mi NE Wooten Lk
TWIN LKS (2)	Okanogan	24-77	Methow R	1950	2 mi S Winthrop
TWIN LKS (2)	Okanogan	13	Okanogan R	1975	3 mi W Riverside
TWIN LKS (2)	Pierce	2	Carbon R	4800	14 mi SE Enumclaw
TWIN LKS (2)	San Juan	3-8	Str of Georgia	1100	On Orcas Island
TWIN LKS—LOWER	Snohomish	24.5	Nf Skykomish R	4700	6 mi SE Barlow Pass
TWIN LKS—UPPER	Snohomish	89	Nf Skykomish R	4800	5.7 mi SE Barlow Pass
TWIN LKS—LOWER	Snohomish	32	Nf Stilly R		6.8 mi N Granite Falls
TWIN LKS—UPPER	Snohomish	34	Nf Stilly R	7;	1200' S Lower Twin Lk
TWIN LKS (2)	Snohomish	18-19	Suiattle R	5200	7.5 mi NW Glacier Peak
TWIN LKS (2)	Whatcom	17-20	Nf Nooksack R	5180	3.7 mi NE Shuksan
TWIN FALLS	Snohomish	1.5	Pilchuck R	2030	11.4 mi SE Granite Falls
TWIN SISTERS	Yakima	31-104.5	Bumping R	5152	6.7 mi N White Pass
TWISP	Okanogan	4.5	Sf Twisp R	6300	1.6 mi SW Twisp Pass
TWO LKS	King	1.5	White R	3500	9 mi E Enumclaw
TWO LKS	Yakima	97-118	Wf Klickitat R	4259	11 mi N Mt Adams summit
TWO LITTLE LKS	Chelan	3-10	Entiat R	5750	23 mi N Leavenworth
TY	Yakima	1	Tieton R	4000	.04 mi blw Lynne Lk
TYE	King	3	Tye R	4800	.07 mi NW Stevens Pass

U

UMATILLA	Klickitat	52000	Columbia R	265	9.5 mi SE Goldendale
UNDI	Clallam	15	Bogachiel R	220	I mi SE Forks
UNION	King	598	Puget Sound	14	In Seattle
UPPER CATHEDRAL	Okanogan	9	Ashnola R	6400	36 mi N Winthrop
UPPER CRATER	Okanogan	13	Methow R	6900	14 mi SW Twisp
UPPER FLORENCE	Chelan	4	Wenatchee R	6800	13 mi NW Leavenworth
UPPER RIVORD	Snohomish	13	Suiattle R	5675	1500' E Lime Mtn summit
UPPER WHEELER RES	Chelan	36	Columbia R	4290	10 mi S Wenatchee

V

VALHALLA	Chelan	29	Wenatchee R	5050	3 mi N Stevens Pass
VAN	Snohomish	2	Nf Sauk R	5500	5 mi SW Glacier Peak
VANCE CREEK	Grays Hbr	9	Chehalis R	20	1.5 mi SW Elma
VANCOUVER	Clark	2858	Columbia R	9	3 mi NW Vancouver
VANES	Pend Oreille	4	Pend Oreille R	3000	1 mi W No Name Lk
VANSON	Lewis	10	Green R	4150	6.7 mi S Kosmos
VAN VALKENBERG PD	Whatcom	1	Sumas R	50	1 mi W Sumas
VARDEN	Okanogan	4.5	Methow R	6194	17.5 mi NW Winthrop
VENUS LKS (2)	Skamania	8-21	Green R	4600	5.4 mi N Spirit Lk outlet
VICENTE	Kittitas	11.5	Waptus R	5700	9.9 mi NW Salmon la Sac
VICTORIA	Chelan	27	Wenatchee R	5500	8.6 mi W Leavenworth
VIEW	King	3.5	Wt Foss R	5370	1200' W Jewel Lk
VIRGIN	Grant	20	Crab Cr	1015	8.1 mi N Othello
VOGLER	Skagit	3.5	Skagit R	1060	2.4 mi N Concrete

W

WADDELL	Chelan	10	Stehekin R	4932	4 mi N High Bridge G.S.
WAGNER	Skagit	2.5	Stilly R	3000	10 mi SE Sedro-Woolley
WAGNER	Snohomish	19.5	Skykomish R	300	2.5 mi NE Monroe
WAGON WHEEL	Mason	3	Nf Skok R	4150	2 mi N Lk Cushman
WAITTS (RES)	Stevens	455	Colville R	1959	7 mi S Chewelah
WALKER	King	12	Green R	1140	1.5 mi SE Cumberland
WALL	Adams	15	Palouse R	1600	19 mi SE Ritzville
WALL PD	Benton	4	Lk Wallula	340	15 2 mi E McNary Dam
WALL	Lincoln	32	Crab Cr	2050	10.5 mi NW Harrington
WALL	Lincoln	4	Crab Cr	2200	10 mi SE Wilbur
WALLACE SL	Cowlltz	12	Columbia R	10	2.7 mi S Woodland
WALLULA	Benton	38800	Columbia R	340	20 mi SW Kennewick
WALTER	Lincoln	18	Crab Cr	1650	5.5 mi N Odessa
WALUPT	Lewis	384	Cispus R	3927	15.5 mi SE Packwood
WANAPUM DAM RES	Grant	14680	Columbia R	571	28 mi E Ellensburg
WANNACUT	Okanogan	412		1850	4.6 mi SW Oroville
WAPATO	Chelan	186	Lk Chelan	1229	8.2 mi NW Chelan
WAPATO LKS (2)	Pierce	22-28	Puget Sound	315	At Wapato Park, Tacoma
WAPIKI	Skamania	10	White Salmon	4700	10 mi W Mt Adams R.S.
WAPTUS	Kittitas	246	Cle Elum R	2980	23 mi NW Cle Elum
WARD	Thurston	87	Deschutes R	123	2.5 mi S Olympia
WARDEN LKS (2)	Grant	24-186	Crab Cr	1076	5.7 mi W Warden
WASHBURN	Okanogan	13	Okanogan R	3100	2.1 mi NE Loomis
WASHINGTON	King	22138	Puget Sound	14	E side Seattle
WASHOUGAL	Clark	o,5	L Washousal R	460	5 mi N Washousal
WATSON	Columbia	4	Tucannon R	2350	4 mi S Game Range H.Q.

LAKE	COUNTY	ACRES	DRAINAGE	ELEVATION	LOCATION
WATSON LKS (2)	Whatcom	18-46	Baker R	4375	11.5 mi NE Concrete
WAYHUT	Snohomish	6	Beckler R	4000	9 mi N Skykomish
WEBSTER	King	10	Cedar R	540	2.5 mi N Maple Valley
WEDEN	Snohomish	5.5	Sf Sauk R	4400	3.4 mi SE Barlow Pass
WEDERSPAHN	Lincoln	14	Crab Cr	1655	5.4 mi N Odessa
WELLSIAN	Benton	10		350	S part Richland
WENAS (RES)	Yakima	61	Yakima R	1861	6 mi N Naches
WENATCHEE	Chelan	2445	Wenatchee R	1875	15 mi N Leavenworth
WENTWORTH	Clallam	54	Wf Dickey R	147	7.7 mi NW Forks
WENZEL SL	Grays Hbr	6	Chehalis R	20	2 mi SW Elma
WEST	Pierce	6	Puyallup R	4600	7 mi NE National
WEST MEDICAL	Spokane	235	Crab Cr	2423	1 mi W twn Medical Lake
WEST TRITT	Spokane	107	Palouse R	2290	3 mi S Cheney
WHALE	Skagit	50	Cascade R	4600	9 mi SE Marblemount
WHATCOM (RES)	Whatcom	5003	Bellingham Bay	307	3 mi E Bellingham
WHEELER	Mason	8	Hood Canal	350	1 mi E Tahuya
WHITE MUD	Stevens	59	L Pend Ore R	2168	4.4 mi SE Colville
WHITE RIVER MILL PD	King	23	White R	1040	3 mi E Enumclaw
WHITE ROCK LKS (3)	Chelan	1-20	Stehekin R	6175	8.7 mi S Cascade Pass
WHITESTONE (RES)	Okanogan	170	Okanogan R	1250	5.7 mi N Tonasket
WHITMAN	Pierce	30	Nisqually R	601	6.5 mi N Eatonville
WICKS	Kitsap	9	Carr Inlet	430	5.5 mi E Belfair
WIDGEON	Clark	38	Columbia R	10	1.5 mi W Ridgefield
WIDGEON	Grant	11	Crab Cr	937	8 mi N Othello
WIDOW	King	4	Mf Snoq R	3120	9 mi E North Bend
WILDBERRY	Mason	8	Hood Canal	500	1.5 mi NW Tahuya
WILDCAT	Jefferson	5	Dosewallips R	4150	12.5 mi W Brinnon
WILDCAT LKS (2)	King	19-54	Mf Snoq R	4218	5.4 mi NW Snoq Pass
WILDCAT	Kitsap	112	Dyes Inlet	377	6 mi NW Bremerton
WILDCAT	Yakima	2	Bumping R	5200	1900' N Cousar Lk outlet
WILDERNESS	King	67	Green R	470	2.5 mi S Maple Valley
WILDWOOD	Kitsap	7	Sinclair Inlet	420	.07 mi SE Wildwood
WILEY	Whatcom	6	Ross Lk	6650	12.5 mi NW Diablo Dam
WILLIAMS	Grant	12	Crab Cr	1250	8 mi SW Coulee City
WILLIAMS	King	15	Mf Snoq R	4500	11.5 mi NE Snoq Pass
WILLIAMS	Okanogan	7	Twisp R	6500	18.5 mi W Twisp
WILLIAMS	Spokane	319	Palouse R	2052	11.5 mi SW Cheney
WILLIAMS	Stevens	38	Colville R	1980	14.5 mi N Colville
WILLIAMS	Whatcom	3.5	Sf Nooksack R	350	2.5 mi SE Deming
WILLOUGHBY	Clallam	5.5	Pacific Ocean	200	5.5 mi Ozette
WILLOW LKS (2)	Grant	23-39	Crab Cr	1160	6.5 mi SE city Soap Lake
WILLOW	Lincoln	12	Crab Cr	2100	12.5 mi S Creston
WILLOW	Whatcom	27	Ross Lk	2900	15 mi N Ross Dam
WILSON PD	Kittitas	2	Yakima R	1450	3.5 mi SE Ellensburg
WINCHESTER WSTWY R	Grant	660	Crab Cr	1147	11 mi SE Quincey
WINDMILL	Grant	34	Crab Cr	986	7.1 mi N Othello
WINDMILL PD	Spokane	11	Palouse R	2245	1.4 mi SW Ea Cheney
WINDOM	Snohomish	4	Sauk R	3800	8.7 mi S Darrington
WINDY	King	6	Pratt R	4186	2000' SW Kaleetan Lk
WINDY	Okanogan	2	Similkameen R	7050	17 mi NW Loomis
WING	Skagit	15	Ross Lk	6400	2.7 mi SE Mt Arriva
WINNIE	Lewis	2	Nf Tilton R	2680	12.5 mi NE Onalaska
WINTERS PD	Clallam	4.5	Juan de Fuca	350	1.5 mi SE Mt Pleasant
WINTERS	Snohomish	11	Wallace R	663	3 mi NE Sultan
WISEMAN	Whatcom	18.5	Mf Nooksack R	4250	7.5 mi SW Mt Baker summit
WISER	Whatcom	123	Nooksack R	50	3 mi SW Lynden
WISHRAM	Klickitat	6	Lk Gelilo	160	1 mi E Wishram
WITTENMEYER	King	3	Lk Washington	125	2 mi NE Juanita
WOBBLY	Lewis	8	Nf Cispus R	3400	13 mi S Packwood
WOELFEL	Mason	6	Oakland Bay	350	14.7 mi NW Shelton
WOLVERINE	Chelan	8.5	Wenatchee R	5075	500' NE Square Lk
WOOD	Mason	10	Hood Canal	500	1.8 mi N Tahuya
WOOD	Skamania	12.5	Nt Lewis R	5000	1.5 mi W Cultus Cr G.S.
WOODS	Skagit	35	Suiattle R	5100	23 mi NE Darrington
WOODS	Spokane	32	Spokane R	2419	9.2 mi W Nine Mile Falls
WOOTEN	Mason	70	Tahuya R	407	7 mi W Belfair
WORTH	Franklin	10	Columbia R	770	4 mi NW Mesa
WRIGHT	Lewis	3.5	Cowlitz R	3100	9 mi SE Packwood
WYE	Kitsap	38	Case Inlet	300	3.5 mi SE Belfair
WYNOOCHE	Grays Hbr	1120	Wynooche R		39 mi N Montesano

Y

"Y"	Clallam	5	Lunch Lk	4600	E from Lunch Lk
YAHOO	Jefferson	8	Clearwater R	2350	3.5 mi N mouth Sams R
YAKIMA SPORTSMENS	Yakima	9	Yakima R	1010	2.5 mi E Yakima
YALE RES	Clark	3302	Nf Lewis R	490	20.5 mi E Woodland
YELLEPIT PD	Benton	38	Lk Wallula	340	15 mi SE Kennewick
YELLOW	King	10.5	Sammamish Lk	400	3 mi N Issaquah
YELLOW JACKET	Lewis	2	Cispus R		10.1 mi S Randle
YOCUM	Pend Oreille	42	Pend Oreille R	2875	6.4 mi N Ruby

LAKE	COUNTY	ACRES	DRAINAGE	ELEVATION	LOCATION
Z					
ZIG ZAG	Skamania	2.5	Nf Lewis R	3400	14.5 mi NW Stevenson
ZIMMERMAN PD	Chelan	4	Columbia R	2350	6 mi S Wenatchee
ZOSELS MILL PD	Okanogan	100	Okanogan R	910	At Oroville

Streams Of Washington

STREAM	TRIBUTARY TO	COUNTY	STREAM	TRIBUTARY TO	COUNTY
A			**B**		
ABE CR	Columbia R	Wahkiakum	BCR CR	Quillayute R	Clallam
ABERNATHY CR	Columbia R	Cowlitz	BACHELOR CR	Yakima R	Yakima
ABSHER CR	Chehalis R	Lewis	BACKMAN CR	Skagit R	Skagit
ADA CR	White R	Pierce	BACKMAN CR	Sauk R	Snohomish
ADAMS CR	Cispus R	Skamania	BACON CR	Skagit R	Skagit
ADDY CR	Colville R	Stevens	BACON CR	Klickitat R	Yakima
AENEAS CR	Curlew Cr	Ferry	BACON CR	Kettle R	Ferry
AENEAS CR	Wf San Poil R	Okanogan	BAGLEY CR	Str.Juan de Fuca	Clallam
AENEAS CR	Okanogan R	Okanogan	BAGLEY CR	Nooksack R	Whatcom
AGENCY CR	Yakima R	Yakima	BAEKOS CR	Whitechuck R	Snohomish
AGNES CR	Stehekin R	Chelan	BAKER CR	Satsop R	Mason
AGNEW CR	L Chelan	Chelan	BAKER CR	Black R	Thurston
AHTUNUM CR	Nf Yakima R	Yakima	BAILEY CR	Wf San Poil R	Okanogan
AHTANUM CR	Sf Yakima R	Yakima	BAILEYS(CRYSTAL) CR	Dyes Inlet	Kitsap
AINSLIE CR	Cowlitz R	Lewis	BAIRD CR	Nf Coweman R	Cowlitz
ALCKEE CR	Sol Duc R	Clallam	BAKER CR	Swauk Cr	Kittitas
ALDER CR	Chiwawa R	Chelan	BAKER CR	Willapa Bay	Pacific
ALDER CR	Toutle R	Cowlitz	BAKER R	Skagit R	Whatcom
ALDER CR	Millers Bay	Kitsap	BALDASSIN CR	Beaver Cr	Thurston
ALDER CR	Columbia R	Klickitat	BALLOON CR	Johns R	Grays Harbor
ALDER CR	Nisqually R	Pierce	BANGOR CR	Hood Canal	Kitsap
ALDER CR	Tilton R	Lewis	BARCLAY CR	Skykomish R	King
ALDER CR	Skagit R	Skagit	BAR KER (CASTLE) CR	Dyes Inlet	Kitsap
ALDER CR	Columbia R	Stevens	BARLOW CR	Elk R	Grays Harbor
ALDERBROOK CR	Hood Canal	Mason	BARNABY CR	Columbia R	Ferry
ALGER CR	Columbia R	Wahkiakum	BARNES CR	Lake Crescent	Clallam
ALICE CR	San Poil R	Ferry	BARNUM CR	Hoquiam R	Grays Harbor
ALKALI CR	Snake R	Whitman	BARR CR	Skykomish R	Snohomish
ALLEN CR	Peshastin Cr	Chelan	BARRETT CR	Curlew Lake	Ferry
ALLEN CR	Pend Oreille R	Pend Oreille	BARRETTOUTLET	Nooksack R	Whatcom
ALLEN CR	Lewis R	Skamania	BARRON CR	Tilton R	Lewis
ALLEN CR	Ebey Slough	Snohomish	BASIN CR	Stehekin R	Chelan
ALMOTA CR	Snake R	Whitman	BASIN CR	Sol Duc R	Clallam
ALPINE CR	Snake R	Asotin	BASKET CR	Ef Lewis R	Clark
ALPOWA CR	Snake R	Asotin/Garfield	BATES CR	Wenatchee R	Chelan
ALTA CR	Duwamish R	King	BATTLE CR	L Goodwin	Snohomish
AMAZON CR	Little Pend Ore.	Stevens	BATTLEGROUND CR	Salmon C	Clark
AMBER CR	Toutle R	Lewis	BAYARD CR	Wenatchee R	Chelan
ANACONDA CR	Lewis R	Clark	BEACH CR	Waits Lake	Stevens
AMERICAN R	Bumping R	Yakima	BEACON CR	Woodward Cr	Skamania
AMES CR	Snoqualmie R	King	BEAL CR	Nooksack R	Whatcom
ANDERSON CR	Puget Sound	Kins	BEAN CR	Black R	Thurston
ANDERSON CR	Sinclair Inlet	Kitsap	BEAR CR	Soleduck R	Clallam
ANDERSON CR	Carpenter Cr	Whatcom	BEAR CR	Wishkah R	Grays Harbor
ANDERSON CR	Nooksack R	Whatcom	BEAR CR	Sammamish R	King
ANDERSON CR	Ef Anderson Cr	Whatcom	BEAR CR	Burley Cr	Kitsap
ANDREWS CR	Crocker Lake	Jefferson	BEAR CR	Cle Elum Lake	Kittitas
ANDREWS CR	Elk R	Grays Harbor	BEAR CR	Tilton R	Lewis
ANDY CR	Nf Tieton R	Yakima	BEAR CR	Union R	Mason
ANTOINE CR	ColumbiaR	Chelan/Okan.	BEAR CR	Methow R	Okanogan
ANTON'S CR	Sol Duc R	Clallam	BEAR CR	Wallace R	Snohomish
ANTWYNE CR	Okanogan R	Okanogan	BEAR CR	L Spokane R	Spokane
ARCHER CR	North R	Grays Harbor	BEAR CR	L Pend Oreille R	Stevens
ARIEL CR	Lewis R	Cowlitz	BEAR CR	Nf Bear Cr	Stevens
ARKANSAS CR	Cowlitz R	Cowlitz	BEAR CR	Sf Bear Cr	Stevens
ARMENTROUT CR	Elk In	Thurston	BEAR CANYON CR	Tieton R	Yakima
ARMSTRONG CR	Willapa R	Pacific	BEATTY SPRINGS	Woodland Cr	Thurston
ARMSTRONG CR L	Spokane R	Spokane	BEARDSLEY CR	Lilliwaup R	Mason
ARNOLD SPRINGS	Mud Bay	Thurston	BEASTROM CR	Colville R	Stevens
ARNOLD CR	Kalama R	Cowlitz	BEATY CR	Dempsey Cr	Thurston
ASH CR	Columbia R	Skamania	BEAVER CR	Wenatchee R	Chelan
ARVID CR	Clearwater R	Jefferson	BEAVER CR	Soleduck R	Clallam
ASHNOLA CR	Similkameen R	Okanogan	BEAVER CR	Ef Beaver Cr	Clallam
ASMUS CR	Oakland Bay	Mason	BEAVER CR	Joe Cr	Grays Harbor
ASOTIN CR	Snake R	Asotin	BEAVER CR	Puget Sound	Kitsap
AURORA CR	Lake Crescent	Clallam	BEAVER CR	Cave Cr	Klickitat
AYERS CR	Deschutes R	Thurston	BEAVER CR	Methow R	Okanogan
AXFORD CR	Big Cr	Grays Harbor			

STREAM	TRIBUTARY TO	COUNTY	STREAM	TRIBUTARY TO	COUNTY
BEAVER CR	Toroda Cr	Okanogan	BLIND CR	Cowlitz	Lewis
BEAVER CR	Dragoon Cr	Stevens	BLOCKHOUSE CR	Klickitat R	Klickitat
BEAVER CR	Black R	Thurston	BLOODGOOD CR	L Klickitat R	Klickitat
BEAVER CR	Skagit R	Whatcom	BLOODY RUN CR	Skookumchuck R	Thurston
BEAVER DAM CR	San Poil R	Ferry	BLUE CR	Columbia R	Skamania
BECK CR	Cowlitz	Cowlitz	BLUE CR	Colville R	Stevens
BECKER'S CR	L Washington	King	BLUE CR	Mill Cr	Walla Walla
BECKLER R	Sf Skykomish R	Snohomish	BLYN CR	Sequim Bay	Clallam
BEDDLE CR	L Washington	King	BOARDMAN CR	Stillaguamlsh R	Snohomish
BEECHERS CR	Snohomish R	Snohomish	BODIE CR	Toroda Cr	Okanogan
BEKLER CR	Snohomish R	Snohomish	BOE CR	Big R	Clallam
BELL CR	Sequim Bay	Clallam	BOGACHIEL R	Quillayute R	Clallam
BELL'S CR	Nooksack R	Whatcom	BOISE CR	White R	King
BEN DAY CR	Snake R	Garfield	BOLAN CR	Lewis R	Clark
BENN CR	PacificOcean	GraysHarbor	BONAPARTE CR	Okanogan R	Okanogan
BENSON CR	Methow R	Okanoqan	BOONE CR	Cowlitz R	Lewis
BENSON CR	Stillaquamish R	Snohomish	BONHAM CR	Wf Hoquiam R	Grays Harbor
BERRINGON SPRGS	Columbia R	Klickitat	BOSLEY CR	Quinault R	Grays Harbor
BERGE CR	Wind R	Skamania	BOULDER CR	Quinault R	Grays Harbor
BERNARD CR	Hoquiam R	Grays Harbor	BOULDER CR	Cle Elum R	Kittitas
BERNARD CR	Wenatchee R	Chelan	BOULDER CR	Stehekin R	Chelan
BERRY CR	Wishkah R	Grays Harbor	BOULDER CR	Lake Keechelus	Kittitas
BERRY CR	Pend Oreille R	Pend Orellle	BOULDER CR	Chewack Cr	Okanogan
BERRY CR	Nisqually R	Pierce	BOULDER(ROCK) CR	Wf Methow R	Okanogan
BERRY (SqUAW) CR	Rock Cr	Skamania	BOULDER CR	Nf Stillaguam. R	Snohomish
BERRYMAN CR	Hoquiam R	Grays Harbor	BOULEVARO CR	Bogachiel R	Jefferson
BERT CR	Cedar Cr	Clark	BOU N DARY C R	L Sheep Cr	Stevens
BERTRAND CR	Nooksack R	Whatcom	BOUNDARY CR	Kettle R	Ferry
BIG CR	Humptulips R	Grays Harbor	BOWERS CR	Chambers Cr	Pierce
BIG CR	Yakima R	Kittitas	BOWMAN CR	L Klickitat R	Klickitat
BIG CR	Nf Skokomish R.	Mason	BOXCANYON CR	Kachess Lake	Kittitas
BIG CR	Suiattle R	Skagit	BOXLEY CR	Snoqualmie R	King
BIG CR	L Chelan	Chelan	BOYCE CR	White R	Pierce
BIG CR	Wynoochee R	Grays Harbor	BOYD CR	Nooksack R	Whatcom
BIG CR	Quinault R	Grays Harbor	BOYL CR	Washougal R	Skamania
BIG CR	Wishkah R	Grays Harbor	BRADEN CR	Hoh R	Jefferson
BIG CR	Nisqually R	Lewis	BRACKETT CR	Pend Oreille R	Pend Oreille
BIG CR	Lilliwaup R	Mason	BRAIL CR	Nisqually R	Thurston
BIG CR	Skaqit R	Skaqit	BRAZEE CR	Lewis R	Clark
BIG CR	Lewis R	Skamania	BRECKENRIDGE CR	Sumas R	Whatcom
BIG ALKALI CR	Palouse R		BREMER CR	Tilton R	Lewis
BIG BEEF CR	Hood Canal	Kitsap	BRENNEGAN CR	Entiat R	Chelan
BIG BEAVER CR	Skaqit R	Whatcom	BRICKEY CR	Ef Lewis R	Clark
BIG BOULDER CR	Kettle R	Ferry	BRICKYARD GUL.CR	Latah Cr	Spokane
BIG GRADE CR	Lake Chelan	Chelan	BRIDAL VEIL CR	Skykomish R	Snohomish
BIG MEADOW CR	Chiwawa R	Chelan	BRIDGE CR	Stehekin R	Chelan
BIG MISSION CR	Hood Canal	Mason	BRIDGE CR	San Poil R	Ferry
BIG MUDDY CR	Clark Fork	Pend Oreille	BRIDGE CR	Twisp R	Okanogan
BIG MUDDY CR	Klickitat	Yakima	BRIDGE CR	Sol Duc R	Clallam
BIG QUILCENE R	Quilcene Bay	Jefferson	BRIGHT CR	Cowlitz R	Lewis
BIG R CR	Ozette Lake	Clallam	BRIM CR	Cowlitz R	Lewis
BIG SHEEP CR		Stevens	BRIM CR	Kalispel Lake	Pend Oreille
BIG SOOS CR	Green R	King	BRIM CR	S Br Brim Cr	Pend Oreille
BIG SPRING CR	White Salmon R	Klickitat	BRITTAIN CR	Humptulips R	Grays Harbor
BIG SPRING CR	Clark Fork	Pend Oreille	BROOKS CR	Spoilei R	Cowlitz
BIG SPRING CR	Walla Walla R	Walla Walla	BROOKS CR	Stillaguamish R	Snohomish
BIGTREE CR	Ef Lewis R	Clark	BROWN CR	Pend Oreille R	Pend Oreille
BIRD CR	Outlet Cr	Klickitat	BROWN CR	Colville R	Stevens
BITTER (BLACK) CR	Wynoochee R	Grays Harbor	BROWN CR	Hood Canal	Mason
BITTER CR	North R	Pacific	BROWN CR	Skokomish R	Mason
BJORK CR	Eagle Cr	Chelan	BROWN CR	Sauk R	Snohomish
BLACK (BITTER) CR	Wynoochee R	Grays Harbor	BROWNELL CR	Toutle R	
BLACK CR	Wishkaw R	Grays Harbor	BROWNS CR	HokoR	Clallam
BLACK CR	Satsop R	Grays Harbor	BROWNS CR	Willapa R	Pacific
BLACK CR	Chehalis R	Grays Harbor	BROWNS CR	Lewis R	Cowlitz
BLACK CR	North R	Grays Harbor	BRUCE CR	Nf Bruce Cr	Stevens
BLACK CR	Snoqualmie	King	BRUNDER SPRINGS	Columbia R	Klickitat
BLACK CR	Suiattle R	Snohomish	BRUNNER CR	Miii Cr	Klickitat
BLACK CANYON CR	Methow R	Okanogan	BRUSH(NICKIAM) CR	Cedar Cr	Klickitat
BLACKHORSE CR	Klickitat R	Klickitat	BRUSH CR	Kiickitat R	Klickitat
BLACKJACK CR	Sinclair Inlet	Kitsap	BRUSH CR	Lewis R	Clark
BLACKJACK CR	Stillaguamish R	Snohomish	BRUSH CR	Palouse R	Whitman
BLACK R	Chehalis R	Thurston	BUCHANAN CR	Chehaiis R	Lewis
BLACKMAN CR	Snohomish R	Snohomish	BUCK CR	ChiwawaR	Chelan
BLACKMAN'S CR	Sauk R	Snohomish	BUCK CR	Yakima R	Kittitas
BLACK OAK CR	Whitechuck R	Snohomish	BUCK CR	White R	Pierce
BLACK ROCK CR	Sauk R	Snohomish	BUCK CR	Suiattle R	Snohomish
BLACK SANDS CR	Lewis R	Skamania	BUCK CR	WhiteSalmon R	Klickitat
BLACKWOOD CR	Sol Duc R	Clallam	BUIL DOG CR	Colvllie R	Stevens
BLAIR CR	Nisqually R	Pierce	BUCKEYE CR	Stillaguamish R	Snohomish
BLANCHARD CR	Pend Oreille	Pend Oreille	BUMPING R	Naches R	Yakima
BLANEY CR	Grays R	Pacific	BUNCH CR	Quinauit R	Grays Harbor

STREAM	TRIBUTARY TO	COUNTY
BUNGE CR	L Spokane R	Pend Oreille
BUNKER CR	L White Salmon R	Skamania
BUNKER CR	Puyallup R	Pierce
BURKE CR	San Poil R	Ferry
BURLEY CR	Henderson Bay	Kitsap
BURNHAM CR	Pacific	Pacific
BURKES CR	SilverLake	Cowlitz
BURNS CR	Entiat R	Chelan
BURNS CR	Green R	King
BURNT BRIDGE CR	Vancouver Lake	Clark
BURRIS CR	Columbia R	Cowiitz
BUSH CR	Cloquallum R	Grays Harbor
BURTON (FALL) CR	Cowlitz R	Lewis
BUTCHER CR	Mason Cr	Chelan
BUTCHER CR	Walla Walla R	WallaWalla
BUTLER CR	Klickitat R	Kiickitat
BUTTE CR	Grande Ronde R	Asotin
BUTTE CR	Cowlitz R	Lewis
BUTTER CR	Cowlitz R	Lewis
BUTTERMILK CR	Twisp R	Okanogan
BYRON CR	Lake Whatcom	Whatcom
BYRON CR	Clearwater R	Pierce

C

STREAM	TRIBUTARY TO	COUNTY
C CR	Sol Duc R	Clallam
C CR	Wishkah R	Grays Harbor
CCA CR	Pend Oreille R	Pend Oreille
CCC CR	Chehalis R	Grays Harbor
CABBAGE CR	Palouse R	Whitman
CABBAGE CR	W. Salmon R	Skamania
CABIN CR	Yakima R	Kittitas
CABIN CR	Tieton R	Yakima
CABIN CR	Stehekin R	Chelan
CABIN CR	Wenatchee R	Chelan
CABIN CR	Hamma Ham. R	Jefferson
CABIN CR	Grays R	Pacific
CABLE CR	Spokane R	Spokane
CACHE CR	Palouse R	Whitman
CACHE CR	Toroda Cr	Okanogan
CADWELL CR	Skykomish R	Snohomish
CADY CR	Nf Skykomish R	Snohomish
CALAWAH R	Bogachiel R	Clallam
CALDERVIN CR	Hood Canal	Mason
CALDWELL CR	Walla Walla R	Walla Walla
CALIFORNIA CR	Latah R	Spokane
CALISPEL CR	Washougal R	Clark
CALISPEL CR	Pend OreilleR	PendOreille
CALVIN CR	Lewis R	Colwitz
CALLIGAN CR	SnoqualmieR	King
CAMANO CR	Puget Sound	Island
CAMAS CR	Peshastin Cr	Chelan
CAMAS CR	Wenatchee R	Chelan
CAMP CR	Chehalis R	Grays Harbor
CAMERON CR	Greywolf R	Clallam
CAMERON CR	Columbia R	Cowlitz
CAMP CR	Chehalis R	Grays Harbor
CAMP CR	Cle Elum R	Kittitas
CAMP CR	LPend OreilleR	Stevens
CAMP CR	Sol Duc R	Clallam
CAMP CR	QuinaultR	GraysHarbor
CAMP CR	Queets R	Jefferson
CAMP CR	Twisp R	Okanogan
CAMP CR	Cowlitz R	Skawania
CAMP CR	Whitechuck R	Snohomish
CAMP CR	Colville R	Stevens
CAMPBELL CR	Skagit R	Skagit
CAMPBELL CR	Cowlitz R	Lewis
CAMPEN CR	Washougal R	Clark
CAMP JOY CR	Pend Oreille R	Stevens
CANADA CR	Carbon R	Pierce
CANNONBALL CR	Chehalis R	Lewis
CANOE CR	Lake Quinault	Grays Harbor
CANON R	Palix R	Pacific
CANYON CR	Dungeness R	Clallam
CANYON CR	Lewis R	Clark
CANYON CR	Methow R	Okanogan
CANYON CR	Twisp R	Okanogan
CANYON CR	Washougal R	Skamania
CANYON CR	Sf Stillaguamish R	Snohomish
CANYON CR	Dragoon Cr	Stevens

STREAM	TRIBUTARY TO	COUNTY
CANYON CR	Mf Nooksack R	Whatcom
CANYON R	Satsop R	Grays Harbor
CAPE LaBELLE CR	Wf San Poil R	Okanogan
CAPPS CR	Chehalis R	Lewis
CARACO CR	Dungeness R	Clallam
CARBON R	Puyallup R	Pierce
CAREY CR	L Sammamish	King
CARIBOU CR	Cherry Cr	Kittitas
CARLTON CR	Cowlitz R	Lewis
CARPENTER CR	Skagit R	Skagit
CARPENTER CR	Lake Whatcom	Whatcom
CARPENTER CR	Pilchuck R	Snohomish
CARPENTE R	Sekiu R	Clallam
CARSON CR	Columbia R	Skamania
CARSTEN CR	White Salmon R	Klickitat
CARTER CR	Wynoochee R	Grays Harbor
CARTER CR	Pend Oreille R	Pend Oreille
CASCADE R Nf	CascadeR	Skagit
CASCADE CR	Quinault L	Grays Harbor
CASCADE CR	White R	Pierce
CASCADE CR	Stiilaguamish R	Skagit
CASCADE CR	Nooksack R	Whatcom
CASH CR	Quinault L	Grays Harbor
CASSEL CR	Hoh R	Jefferson
CASTLE CR	Toutle R	Clark
CASTLE CR	Green R	King
CASTLE(BARKER) CR	Dyes Inlet	Kitsap
CATHERINE CR	Kettle R	Ferry
CAT CR	Greywolf R	Clallam
CAT CR	Cispus R	Skamania
CATARACT CR	Carbon R	Pierce
CATHERINE CR	Kettle R	Ferry
CATHERINE CR	Snohomish R	Snohomish
CATHLAMET R	Columbia R	Wahkiakum
CATHY CR	W. Salmon R	Klickitat
CATT CR	Nisqually R	Lewis
CAYADA CR	Carbon R	Pierce
CAVANAUGH CR	Nooksack R	Whatcom
CECIL CR	Sinlahekln Cr	Okanogan
CEDAR CR	Lewis R	Clark
CEDAR CR	Chehalis R	Grays Harbor
CEDAR CR	Yakima R	Kittitas
CEDAR CR	Salmon Cr	Lewis
CEDAR CR	Early Winters Cr	Okanogan
CEDAR CR	Sacheen Lake	Pend Oreille
CEDAR CR	Hamilton R	Skamania
CEDAR CR	Panther Cr	Skamania
CEDAR R	Lake Washington	King
CHAMBERS CR	Puget Sound	Pierce
CHAMOKANE CR	Spokane R	Stevens
CHAPARRAL CR	Klickitat R	Yakima
CHAMPION CR	Green R	King
CHANGE CR	Snoqualmie R	King
CHAPLAIN CR	Sulton R	Snohomish
CHAPMAN CR	Columbia R	Klickitat
CHARLIES CR	Grays Harbor	Grays Harbor
CHEADLE CR	Willapa R	Pacific
CHEADLE CR	Chehalis R	Thurston
CHEHALIS CR	Chehalis R	Grays Harbor
CHEHALIS R	Grays Harbor	Grays Harbor
CHELATCHIE CR	Tum Tum Cr	Clark
CHENOIS CR	Grays Harbor	Grays Harbor
CHENUIS CR	Carbon R	Pierce
CHERRY CR	SnoqualmieR	King
CHERRY CR	Wilson Cr	Kittitas
CHESTER CR	Humptulips R	Grays Harbor
CHEWACK CR	Methow R	Okanogan
CHEWEKA CR	Columbia R	Stevens
CHEWEKA CR	NfCheweka Cr	Stevens
CHEWEKA CR	Colville R	Stevens
CHEWILIKON CR	Okanogan R	Okanogan
CHICKIMAN CR	Chiwawa R	Chelan
CHICKEN CR	L Vancouver	Clark
CHICO CR	Dyes Inlet	Kitsap
CHILATCH CR	Lewis R	Clark
CHILDS CR	Skagit R	Skagit
CHILLIWACK CR	Chilliwack L	Whatcom
CHILLIWISTCR	Okanogan R	Okanogan
CHIMACUM CR	Port Townsend B	Jefferson

STREAM	TRIBUTARY TO	COUNTY	STREAM	TRIBUTARY TO	COUNTY
CHIMACUM CR	Wf Chimacum Cr	Jefferson	COON CR	Columbia R	Paclflc
CHINA CR	Chehalis R	Lewis	COON CR	Pilchuck R	Snohomlsh
CHIWAUKUM CR	Wenatchee R	Chelan	COON LAKE CR	Stehekin R	Chelan
CHIWAWA R	Wenatchee R	Chelan	COONEY CR	Lewis R	Cowlltz
CHOPAKA CR	Sinlahekin Cr	Okanogan	COOPER R	Cle Elum R	Kittitas
CHOW CHOW CR	Quinault R	Grays Harbor	COPALIS R	Pacific Ocean	Grays Harbor
CHRISTMAS CR	Queets R	Jefferson	COPPEI CR	Touchet R	Walla Walla
CHRISTMAS CR	Snoqualmie R	King	COPPER CR	Wf Granite Cr	Ferry
CHUCKALOON CR	Chehalis R	Grays Harbor	COPPER CR	Wf Granite Cr	Ferry
CHUCKANUT CR	Chuckanut Bay	Whatcom	COPPER CR	Nisqually	Pierce
CHUMSTICK CR	Wenatchee R	Chelan	COPPER CR	San Poil R	Ferry
CHURCH CR	Skokomish R	Mason	COPPER CR	Methow R	Okanogan
CINABAR CR	Tilton R	Lewis	COPPER CR	Lewis R	Lewis
CINDY CR	Hoh R	Jefferson	CORNSTALK CR	Stranger Cr	Ferry
CIRCLE CR	Suiattle R	Snohomish	CORRAL CR	Klickltat R	Yakima
CISPUS R	Cowlltz R	Lewis/Skam.	CORRAL CR	Tieton R	Yakima
CLALLAM R	Clallam Bay	Clallam	CORTRIGHT CR	Cowlitz R	Lewis
CLANCY CR	Toutle R	Cowlitz	CORUS (WAUGH) CR	Columbia R	Stevens
CLARK CR	Chumstlck Cr	Chelan	COSNER (DUNN) CR	Colville R	Stevens
CLARK CR	Hood Canal	Mason	COTTONWOOD CR	Kettle R	Ferry
CLARK CR	Puyallup R	Pierce	COTTONWOOD CR	L Deer Cr	Spokane
CLEAR CR	Chiwawa R	Chelan	COTTONWOOD CR	Columbia R	Stevens
CLEAR CR	Dyes Inlet	Kitsap	COTTONWOOD CR	Colville R	Stevens
CLEAR CR	Carbon R	Pierce	COTTONWOOD CR	Yellowhawk Cr	Walla Walla
CLEAR CR	Puyallup R	Pierce	COUGAR CR	Hoh R	Jefferson
CLEAR CR	Muddy R	Skamania	COUGAR CR	Clearwater R	Jefferson
CLEARBROOK CR	Johnson Cr	Whatcom	COUGAR CR	Cowlitz R	Lewis
CLEAR FORK	Cowlitz R	Lewis	COUGAR CR	Stillaquamish R	Snohomish
CLEARWATER CR	Muddy R	Skamania	COUGAR CR	Klickitat R	Yakima
CLEARWATER CR	L Muddy Cr	Yakima	COUGAR CR	Washougal R	Clark
CLEARWATER R	Queets R	Jefferson	COUGAR CR	Lewis R	Cowlitz
CLE ELUM R	Yakima R	Kittitas	COUGAR CR	Big Muddy R	Yakima
CLIFF CR	Duckabush R	Jefferson	COULEE CR	Deep Cr	Spokane
CLOQUALLUM CR	Chehalis R	Grays /Mason	COULTER CR	Nason Cr	Chelan
CLOUGH CR	Snoqualmie R	King	COULTER CR	Case Inlet	Mason
CLOVER CR	Lake Steilacoom	Pierce	COUNTY LINE CR	Totten Inlet	Mason
CLOVER CR	Puyallup R	Pierce	COURTNEY CR	Union R	Mason
CLUGSTON CR	Mill Cr	Stevens	COURTRIGHT CR	Cowlitz R	Lewis
COAL (DRAYS) CR	Columbia R	Cowlitz	COUSE CR	Snake R	Asotin
COAL CR	Lake Washlngton	King	COVIL CR	Juan de Fuca Str	Clallam
COAL (HYAK) CR	Lake Keechelus	Kittitas	COVINGTON CR	Big Soos Cr	King
COAL CR	Crab Cr	Lincoln	COW CR	Palouse R	Adams
COBEY CR	Wf San Poil R	Okanogan	COW CR	Methow R	Okanogan
COE CR	Toutle R	Skamania	COW CR	Snake R	Whitman
COFFEE CR	Sf Goldsbor. Cr	Mason	COWEMAN R	Cowlitz R	Cowlitz
COFFEE CR	Chehalis R	Lewis	COWICHE CR	Naches R	Yakima
COGAN CR	Lake Quinault	Grays Harbor	COWLITZ R	Columbia R	Lewis
COLBURN CR	W. Salmon R	Klickitat	CRAB CR	Columbia R	Grant/Lincoln
COLBY CR	San Poil R	Okanogan	CRAB CR	Lewis R	Skamania
COLBY CR	Dickey R	Clallam	CRANBERRY CR	Oakland Bay	Mason
COLD CR	Columbia R	Benton	CRATER CR	Methow R	Okanogan
COLD CR	Denver Cr	Clallam	CRATER CR	Puyallup R	Pierce
COLD CR	Burnt Bridge Cr	Clark	CRAWFORD CR	Rainey Cr	Lewis
COLD CR	Skykomish R	Snohomish	CRAWFORD CR	Snoqualmie R	King
COLD SPRING	Kalama R	Cowlitz	CRAWFORD CR	L Muddy Cr	Yakima
COLDWATER CR	Toutle R	Cowlitz	CRESCENT CR	Cispus R	Skamanla
COLE CR	Nf Heller Cr	Stevens	CROSS CR	Lake Crescent	Clallam
COLE CR	Lake R	Clark	CROWN CR	Columbia R	Stevens
COLE CR	Icicle R	Chelan	CRUM CANYON CR	Entiat R	Chelan
COLEMAN CR	Yakima R	Kittitas	CRUISER CR	Nemah R	Paciflc
COLLINS CR	Columbia R	Skamania	CRYSTAL CR	Dyes Inlet	Kltsap
COLMAN CR	Nanum Cr	Kittitas	CRYSTAL CR	White R	King
COLOCKUM CR	Columbia R	Chelan	CRYSTAL CR	Sammamlsh R	King
COLONIAL CR	Thunder Cr	Whatcom	CUB CR	Hoko R	Clallam
COLONY CR	Samish Bay	Skagit	CUB CR	Methow R	Okanogan
COLTER CR	Union R	Mason	CUCK CR	Elochoman R	Wahklakum
COLTON CR	Skykomish R	Snohomish	CUITIN CR	Icicle R	Chelan
COLUMBIA R	Pacific Ocean		CULTUS CR	Bogachiel R	Clallam
COLVILLE R	Columbia R	Stevens	CULVERT CR	Okanogan R	Okanogan
COLVIN CR	Lewis R	Cowlitz	CUMBERLAND CR	Toroda Cr	Okanogan
COMMONWEALTH CR	Snoqualmie R	Klng	CUNNINGHAM CR	Ef Lewis R	Clark
COMPANY CR	Stehekin R	Chelan	CUNNINGHAM CR	Kllckltat R	Yakima
CONNAWAC CR	Crab Cr	Grant	CUPPLES CR	Skagit R	Skaglt
CONNELLY CR	Tilton R	Lewis	CURLEW CR	Kettle R	Ferry
CONSTANCE CR	Dosewalllps R	Jefferson	CURLEY CR	Puget Sound	Kltsap
COOK CR	Ef Satsop R	Grays Harbor	CURRANT CR	Deep Cr	Stevens
COOK CR	Quinault R	Grays Harbor	CUSHMAN LK SPILLWAY	Nf Skokomlsh R	Mason
COOK CR	Cherry Cr	Kittltas	CUSICK CR	Clark Fork	Pend Orellle
COOK CR	Cook's Lake	Spokane	CUSSED HOLLOW CR	Lewis R	Skamanla
COOL CR	Bogachiel R	Jefferson	CUTTHROAT CR	Juan de Fuca Str.	Clallam
COOL CR	Yukon Harbor	Kitsap	CYCLONE CR	White R	Klng

STREAM	TRIBUTARY TO	COUNTY
D		
DAIRY CR	Klickitat R	Yakima
DAKOTA CR		Whatcom
DALBY CR	Hood Canal	Mason
DALE CR	Sumas R	Whatcom
DALE CR	Sumas R	Whatcom
DALLES CR	White R	Pierce
DALTON CR	Cowlitz R	Lewis
DAM CR	Cowlitz R	Lewis
DAMON CR	Humptulips R	Grays Harbor
DAN CR	Sauk R	Skagit
DANDY CR	Yakima R	Yakima
DARK CANYON CR	Snake R	Asotin
DARNS CR	Methow R	Okanogan
DARTFORD(SHEEP)CR	L Spokane R	Spokane
DAVIS CR	Cle Elum Lake	Kittitas
DAVIS CR	Cowlitz R	Lewis
DAVIS CR	Methow R	Okanogan
DAVIS CR	Pend Oreille R	Pend Oreille
DAVIS CR	Chehalis R	Grays Harbor
DAVIS CR	Hoquiam R	Grays Harbor
DAVIS CR	Willapa R	Pacific
DAVIS CR	Naselle R	Pacific
DAVIS CR	Green R	King
DAY CR	Kettle R	Ferry
DAY CR	Bogachiel R	Clallam
DAY CR	Skagit R	Skagit
DAWDY CR	Lake Quinault	Grays Harbor
DEAD CANYON CR	Klickitat R	Klickitat
DEADMAN(SHERWD) CR	Kettle R	Ferry
DEADMAN CR	Snake R	Garfield
DEADMAN CR L	Spokane R	Spokane
DECEPTION CR	Tye R	King
DECEPTION CR	Clearwater R	Jefferson
DECKER CR	Satsop R	Grays Harbor
DEEGANS CR	Sf Goldsborough Cr	Mason
DEEP CR	Chiwawa R	Chelan
DEEP CR	Juan de Fuca Str	Clallam
DEEP CR	Spokane R	Spokane
DEEP CR	Columbia R	Stevens
DEEP CR	Kettle R	Stevens
DEEP CR	Humptulips R	Grays Harbor
DEEP CR	Raging R	King
DEEP CR	Chehalis R	Lewis
DEEP CR	White R	Pierce
DEEP R	Columbia R	Wahkiakum
DEER (CARRETT) CR	Curlew Lake	Ferry
DEER CR	Oakland Bay	Mason
DEER CR	Davis Lake	Pend Oreille
DEER CR	Nf Stillaguamish R	Snohomish
DEER CR	Spokane R	Spokane
DEER CR	Colville R	Stevens
DEER TRAIL FORK	Alder Cr	Stevens
DEER CR	Kettle R	Ferry
DEER CR	Cowlitz R	Lewis
DEER CR	Chehalis R	Lewis
DEER CR	Nisqually R	Lewis
DEER CR	Cowlitz R	Pierce
DEER CR	Puyallup R	Pierce
DEER CR	Washougal R	Skamania
DEER CR	Lewis R	Skamania
DEER CR	Skykomish R	Snohomish
DEER CR	Nooksack R	Whatcom
DEER CR	Klickitat R	Yakima
DELABARE CR	Eluha R	Clallam
DELAMETER CR	Cowlitz R	Cowlitz
DELEZENE CR	Chehalis R	Grays Harbor
DELL CR	Chehalis R	Lewis
DELL CR	Naselle R	Pacific
DEMPSEY CR	Black R	Thurston
DENNY CR	Snoqualmie R	King
DERBY CR	Wenatchee R	Chelan
DESCHUTES R	Puget Sound	Thurston
DES MOINES CR	Green R	King
DEVIL'S CANYON CR	Klickitat R	Klickitat
DEVIL'S CANYON CR	Naches R	Yakima
DEVIL'S DREAM CR	Nisqually R	Pierce
DEVORE CR	Stehekin R	Chelan
DEVILS CR	Naches R	Yakima
DEVILS CR	Skagit R	Whatcom

STREAM	TRIBUTARY TO	COUNTY
DEWATTO R	Hood Canal	Mason
DEWEY CR	Chinook R	Pierce
DIAMOND CR	Pend Oreille R	Pend Oreille
DIAMOND CR	Sol Duc R	Clallam
DIAMOND FORK	Klickitat R	Yakima
DIAMOND OUTLET	Lake Sacheen	Pend Oreille
DICK CR	Carbon R	Pierce
DICK CR	Pilchuck R	Snohomish
DICKERSON CR	Chico Cr	Kitsap
DICKEY R	Pacific Ocean	Clallam
DILLENBAUGH CR	Chehalis R	Lewis
DINGFORD CR	Snoqualmie R	King
DIOBSUD CR	Skagit R	Skagit
DISAPPOINTMENT CR	Toutle R	Cowlitz
DISMAL CR	Hoh R	Jefferson
DIXON CR	Cowlitz R	Lewis
DOAKS CR	Nooksack R	Whatcom
DOAN CR	Mill Cr	Walla Walla
DOBSONS CR	Nf Arkansas Cr	Cowlitz
DODGE CR	Chehalis R	Thurston
DOG CR	Columbia R	Skamania
DO-KA-DISHT CR	Skokomish R	Mason
DOMKECR	Lake Chelan	Chelan
DONOVAN CR	Colville R	Stevens
DONOVAN CR	Quilcene R	Jefferson
DOSEWALLIPS R	Hood Canal	Jefferson
DOUBLE DITCH CR	Fishtrap Cr	Whatcom
DOUGAN CR	Washougal R	Skamania
DOUGLAS CR	Columbia R	Douglas
DOWCR	Nf Skokomish R	Mason
DOWANS CR	Bogachiel R	Jefferson
DOWNOY CR	Dungeness R	Clallam
DOWNS CR	Cedar R	King
DOYLE CR	Union R	Mason
DRAGOON CR	L Spokane R	Spokane
DRAYS (COAL) CR	Columbia R	Cowlitz
DRIFT CR	Lewis R	Skamania
DROP CR	Skookumchuck	Lewis
DRUMHELLER SPRGS	Crab Cr	Grant
DRY CR	Chumstick Cr	Chelan
DRYCR	Juan de Fuca Str	Clallam
DRY CR	San Poil R	Ferry
DRY CR	CleElum R	Kittitas
DRY CR	L Spokane R	Spokane
DRY CR	Chamokano Cr	Stevens
DRY CR	Walla Walla R	Walla Walla
DRY CR	Naches R	Yakima
DRY CR	Satus Cr	Yakima
DRY CR	Sol Duc R	Clallam
DRY CR	Soap L	Grant
DRY CR	Hoh R	Jefferson
DRY CR	Snoqualmie R	King
DRY CANYON CR	Klickitat R	Klickitat
DRYWASH CR	Nisqually R	Pierce
DUBUQUE CR	Pilchuck R	Snohomish
DUCK CR	Crab C	Lincoln
DUCKABUSH R	Hood Canal	Jefferson
DUFFEY CR	Skykomish R	Snohomish
DUNCAN CR	Columbia R	Skamania
DUNGENESS R	Juan de Fuca Str	Clallam
DUNN (COSNER) CR	Colville R	Stevens
DURDLE CR	Big Quilcene R	Jefferson
DURHAM CR	Big R	Clallam
DURHAM CR	Duwamish R	King
DUWAMISH R	Elliott Bay	king
DYER CR	Lewis R	Clark
E		
EAGLE CR	Skykomish R	Snohomish
EAGLE CR	Twisp R	Chelan
EAGLE CR	Chumstick Cr	Chelan
EAGLE CR	Lake Crescent	Clallam
EAGLE CR	Hood Canal	Mason
EARLY WINTERS CR	Wf Methow R	Okanogan
EAST CR	Nisqually R	Lewis
EAST BRIDGE CR	Colville R	Stevens
EAST CEDAR CR	Cedar Cr	Stevens
EAST CHEWELAH CR	Colville R	Stevens
EAST DARTFORD CR	L Spokane R	Spokane
EAST DEER CR	Kettle R	Ferry

STREAM	TRIBUTARY TO	COUNTY
EAST DEER CR	Deer Cr	Pend Oreille
EAST MUD CR	Mud Cr	WallaWalla
EAST TORBEL CR	Colville R	Stevens
EAST TWIN R	Juan de Fuca Str	Clallam
EATON CR	St Clair Lake	Thurston
EATON CR	Chehalis R	Grays Harbor
EATON CR	Bogachiel R	Clallam
EDFRO CR	Nooksack R	Whatcom
EDMONDS CR	Puget Sound	Snohomish
EDWARDS CR	Covill Cr	Clallam
EDWARDS CR	San Poil R	Okanogan
EIGHT MILE CR	Columbia R	Klickitat
EIGHT MILE CR	WhiteSalmon R	Klickitat
EIGHT MILE CR	Methow R	Okanogan
EIGHT MILE CR	LQuilcene R	Clallam
EIPPER CR	Deadman Cr	Ferry
ELBOW CR	Quilcene R	Jefferson
ELDER CR	Riddle Cr	Stevens
ELHI CR	Puyallup R	Pierce
ELK (GOLDBAR) CR	Kalama R	Cowlitz
ELK CR	Chehalis R	Lewis
ELK CR	Calawah R	Clallam
ELK CR	Hoh R	Jefferson
ELK CR	Clearwater	Jefferson
ELK CR	Skokomish R	Mason
ELK CR	Willapa R	Pacific
ELK CR	Sultan R	Snohomish
ELKINS CR	Breckenridge Cr	Whatcom
ELLON CR	Nason Cr	Chelan
ELOCHOMAN R	Columbia R	Wahkiakum
ELWELL CR	Skykomish R	Snohomish
ELWHA R	Juan de Fuca Str	Clallam
EMANUEL CR	Kettle R	Ferry
EMPIRE CR	Curlew Cr	Ferry
EMPIRE CR	San Poil R	Ferry
ENIS CR	Port Angeles Harbor	
Clallam		
ENNIS CR	Samish R	Whatcom
ENTIAT R	Columbia R	Chelan
ENTIAT R, Nf	Entiat R	Chelan
ENTIAT R Sf	Entiat R	Chelan
EPPERSON CR	Dungeness R	Clallam
ESSENCY CR	Snoqualmie R	King
ETHOL CR	Myers Cr	Okanogan
EUREKA CR	Sol Duc R	Clallam
EUREKA CR	Okanogan R	Okanogan
EVANS CR	Sammamish R	King
EVANS CR	Carbon R	Pierce
EVARTS CR	Pend Oreille R	Pend Oreille
EVERETT CR	Baker R	Skagit

F

STREAM	TRIBUTARY TO	COUNTY
FAIRCHILD CR	Big Cr	Grays Harbor
FAIRCHILD CR	Willapa R	Pacific
FAIRHOLM CR	Lake Crescent	Clallam
FALES CR	Snohomish R	Snohomish
FALL (BURTON) CR	Cowlitz R	Lewis
FALLERT CR	Kalama R	Cowlitz
FALLS CR	Lake Chelan	Chelan
FALLS CR	Lake Quinault	GraysHarbor
FALLS CR	Rainey Cr	Lewis
FALLS CR	Chewack Cr	Okanogan
FALLS CR	Armstrong Cr	Pacific
FALLS CR	Wind R	Skamania
FALLS CR	Columbia R	Stevens
FALLS CR	Cloquallum C	Grays Harbor
FALLS CR	Hoh R	Jefferson
CALLS CR	Methow R	Okanogan
FALLS CR	Willapa R	Pacific
FALLS CR	Carbon R	Pierce
FALLS CR	Sauk R	Snohomish
FALLS CR	Grays R	Wahkiakum
FALLS CR	Lewis R	Skamania
FAN LAKE OUTLET	West Branch Cr	PendOreille
FARRIER CR	Cowlitz R	Lewis
FENCE CR	Pend Oreille R	Pend Oreille
FENNEL CR	Puyallup R	Pierce
FERN CR	Hood Canal	Kitsap
FIELD CR	Juan de Fuca Str	Clallam
FIFES CR	Bumping R	Yakima

STREAM	TRIBUTARY TO	COUNTY
FIFTEEN MILE CR	Columbia R	Stevens
FIN CR	Lewis R	Skamania
FINCH CR	Hood Canal	Mason
FINLAND CR	Puget Sound	Kitsap
FIR BROOK CR	Wynoochee R	Grays Harbor
FIRST CR	Lake Chelan	Chelan
FIRST CR	Chumstick Cr	Chelan
FIRST CR	Swauk Cr	Kittitas
FIRST (MASON) CR	Nf Teanaway R	Kittitas
FISH CR	Lake Chelan	Chelan
FISH CR	Cedar R	King
FISH LAKE OUTLET	Wenatchee R	Chelan
FISH LAKE STREAM	Wf Klickitat R	Yakima
FISHTRAP CR	Nooksack R	Whatcom
FISK CR	Puyallup R	Pierce
FIVE MILE CR	L Klickitat R	Klickitat
FIVE MILE CR	L Sheep Cr	Stevens
FLAT CR	Columbia R	Stevens
FLAT CR	Stehekin R	Chelan
FLETT CR	Chambers Cr	Pierce
FLIESS CR	Willapa Bay	Pacific
FLUME CR	Lake R	Clark
FLY CR	Lewis R	Clark
FOGGY DEW CR	Gold Cr	Okanogan
FORBES CR	Lake Washington	King
FORD CR	Calawha R	Clallam
FOREST CR	Kettle R	Ferry
FOREST CR	Chehalis R	Grays Harbor
FORKS CR	Willapa R	Pacific
FORKS CR	White R	Pierce
FORKS PRAIRIE CR	Willapa R	Pacific
FORTSON CR	Stillaguamish R	Snohomish
FORTUNE CR	Cle Elum R	Kittitas
FORTY MILE CR	San Poil R	Ferry
FOSS R	Tye R	King
FOSS R. Ef	Ross R	King
FOSS R, Wf	Foss R	King
FOSSIL CR	Grays R	Wahkiakum
FOSSIL CR	Hoh R	Jefferson
FOUNTAIN LAKE OUT.	Nooksack R	Whatcom
FOURTH OF JULY CR	Kettle R	Ferry
FOURTH PLAIN CR	LaCamas Cr	Clark
FOX CR	Entiat R	Chelan
FOX CR	Hoh R	Clallam
FRASIER CR	Outlet Cr	Klickitat
FRAZER CR	Beaver Cr	Okanogan
FRAZIER(TUMWTR.) CR	Port Angeles Har.	Clallam
FRAZIER CR	Klickitat R	Klickitat
FREDRICKSONS CR	Willapa Bay	Pacific
FRENCH CR	Methow R	Okanogan
FRENCH CR	Snohomish R	Snohomish
FRENCH CR	Stillaguamish R	Snohomish
FRENCH CABIN CR	Cle Elum R	Kittitas
FREUND CR	Chumstick Cr	Chelan
FRIDAY CR	Samish R	Skagit
FROSTY CR	Wf San Poil R	Okanogan
FRY CR	Grays H arbor	Grays H arbor
FULLER CR	Chehalis R	Grays Harbor
FURLOUGH CR	Humptulips R	Grays Harbor
FULTON CR	Hood Canal	Jefferson

G

STREAM	TRIBUTARY TO	COUNTY
GABOR CR	Kalama R	Cowlitz
GADDIS CR	Chehalis R	Grays Harbor
GALE CR	Green R	King
GALE CR	Yakima R	Kittitas
GALE(WILKESON) CR	S Prairie Cr	Pierce
GALENA CR	Nooksack R	Whatcom
GALLOP CR	Nooksack R	Whatcom
GALLUP CR	Tilton R	Lewis
GALTON CR	Quinault R	Grays Harbor
GAMAGE CR	Willapa R	Pacific
GAP CR	L Pend Oreille R	Stevens
GARDENA CR	Walla Walla R	Walla Walla
GARNETTS CR	Pend Oreille R	Pend Oreille
GARRARD CR	ChehalisR	Grays Harbor
GARRISON CR	Walla Walla R	Walla Walla
GARRISON CR	Green R	King
GATE CR	Chiwawa R	Chelan
GATTON CR	Lake Quinault	Grays Harbor

STREAM	TRIBUTARY TO	COUNTY
GEE CR	ColumbiaR	Clark
GEE CR	Skagit R	Skagit
GEISLER CR	Wynoochee R	Grays Harbor
GEORGE CR	Greenwater R	Pierce
GEORGE CR	Chehalis R	Lewis
GEORGE CR	Asotin Cr	Asotin
GERMANY CR	Columbia R	Cowlitz
GORMOND SPRINGS	Cowlitz R	Cowlitz
GIBBONS CR	Columbia R	Skamania
GIBSON CR	Chehalis R	Grays Harbor
GIDDINGS CR	Skykomish R	Snohomish
GILBERT CR	Sultan R	Snohomish
GILLAM CR	Duamish R	King
GILLAN CR	Green R	King
GILLETTE CR	Mill Cr	Stevens
GILLIGAN CR	Skagit R	Skagit
GILMER CR	White Salmon R	Klickitat
GIVEOUT CR	Toroda Cr	Okanogan
GLACIER CR	Nooksack R	Whatcom
GLACIER CR	Skagit R	Whatcom
GLADE CR	Columbia R	Yakima
GOAT CR	Wf Methow R	Okanogan
GOAT CR	Toutle R	Cowlitz
GOBLE CR	Coweman R	Cowlitz
GODDARD SPRINGS	White Salmon R	Skamania
GODKIN CR	Elwha R	Clallam
GODS CR	Columbia R	Stevens
GOLD CR	Lake Chelan	Chelan
GOLD (SCATTER) CR	San Poil R	Ferry
GOLD CR	Wf San Poil R	Ferry
GOLD CR	Lake Keechelus	Kittitas
GOLD CR	Methow R	Okanogan
GOLD CR	Myers Cr	Okanogan
GOLD CR	ColvilleR	Stevens
GOLD CR	Naches R	Yakima
GOLDBAR CR	Kalama R	Cowlitz
GOLDEN HARVEST CR	San Poil R	Ferry
GOLDSBOROUGH CR	Oakland Bay	Mason
GOODELL CR	Skagit R	Whatcom
GOODMAN CR	Pacific Ocean	Jefferson
GOODMAN CR	Sauk R	Snohomish
GOOSE CR	Chiwawa R	Chelan
GOOSE CR	Wilson Cr	Lincoln
GORST CR	SinclairInlet	Kitsap
GOSNOLLS CR	Lake Isabella	Mason
GOTCHEN CR	White Salmon R	Klickitat
GRAHAM CR	Chehalis R	Grays Harbor
GRANDE RONDE R	Snake R	Asotin
GRANDY CR	Skagit R	Skagit
GRANITE CR	San Poil R	Ferry/ Okanogan
GRANITE FALLS CR	Lake Chelan	Chelan
GRAPHITE CR	Toroda Cr	Ferry
GRANITE CR	Snoqualmie R	King
GRANITE CR	Yakima R	Kittitas
GRAVES CR	Hood Canal	Mason
GRAYS R	ColumbiaR	Wahkiakum
GRAYS R, Wf	Grays R	Wahkiakum
GRAYWOLF R	Dungeness R	Clallam
GREEN CANYON CR	Reeser Cr	Kittitas
GREEN LAKE OUT.	Ten Mile Cr	Whatcom
GREEN R	Toutle R	Cowlitz
GREEN R	Duwamish R	King
GREENHORN CR	Cispus R	Lewis
GREENLEAF CR	Columbia R	Skamania
GREENWATER R	White R	King
GRIFF CR	Elwha R	Clallam
GRIFFIN CR	Snoqualmie R	King
GROUSE CR	Chiwawa R	Chelan
GROUSE CR	Jump Off Joe Lake	Stevens
GULCH CR	George Cr	Asotin
GUNDERSON CR	Sol Duc R	Clallam
GUNNAR CR	Lewis R	Skamania

H

STREAM	TRIBUTARY TO	COUNTY
HACKETT CR	Coal Cr	Cowlitz
HABER CR	Cowlitz R	Lewis
HAGUS CR	Skokomish R	Mason
HALFMOON CR	Willapa R	Pacific
HALFWAY CR	Chehalis R	Lewis

STREAM	TRIBUTARY TO	COUNTY
HALL CR	Snoqualmie R	King
HALL CR	Cowlitz R	Lewis
HALL CR	Pend Oreille R	Pend Oreille
HALL CR	Cedar Cr	Clark
HALL CR	Columbia R	Ferry
HALTERMAN CR	Stillaguamish R	Snohomish
HAMILTON CR	Columbia R	Skamania
HAMILTON GULCH CR	Wishkah R	Grays Harbor
HAMMA HAMMA R	Hood Canal	Mason
HANAFORD CR	Skookumchuck R	Lewis
HANCOCK CR	Snoqualmie R	King
HANGMAN(LATAH) CR	Spokane R	Spokane/Whit.
HANSEL CR	Peshastin Cr	Chelan
HANSEN CR	Skagit R	Skagit
HANSON CR	Humptulips R	Grays Harbor
HANSON CR	Okanogan R	Okanogan
HANSON CR	Snoqualmie R	Snohomish
HAPPY HOLLOW CR	Hood Canal	Mason
HARDING SPRINGS	American R	Yakima
HARDISON CR	Colville R	Stevens
HARDY CR	Columbia R	Skamania
HARRIS CR	Snoqualmie R	King
HART CR	Nf Tieton R	Yakima
HART LAKE INLET	Hart Lake	Pierce
HART LAKE OUTLET	Nisqually R	Pierce
HARTZOIL CR	Queets R	Jefferson
HARVEY CR	Stillaguamish R	Snohomish
HARVEY CR	Columbia R	Stevens
HATCHERY CR	Kalama R	Cowlitz
HATCHERY CR	Duckabush R	Jefferson
HATCHERY CR	Humptulips R	Grays Harbor
HATHAWAY CR	McCalla Cr	GraysHarbor
HAWK CR	Columbia R	Lincoln
HAYDEN CR	Puyallup R	Pierce
HAYS CR	Lewis R	Clark
HAYS R	Elwha R	Jefferson
HAZARD CR	L Chelan	Chelan
HAZEL CR	Union R	Mason
HAZEL DELL CR	Cowlitz R	Cowlitz
HAZARD CR	White R	Pierce
HEE HEE CR	Queets R	Jefferson
HEITMAN CR	Ef Lewis R	Clark
HELLER (RIDDLE) CR	Colville R	Stevens
HELLROARING CR	Big Muddy R	Yakima
HENDERSON CR	Bonaparte Cr	Okanogan
HENRY CR	Kettle R	Ferry
HERRON CR	Curlew Lake	Ferry
HIERSCH CR	West Passage	King
HIGGENS CR	NaselleR	Pacific
HIGHLAND CR	Tilton R	Lewis
HIGLEY CR	Lake Quinault	Grays Harbor
HILL CR	Hood Canal	Mason
HILL CR	Green R	King
HILLEYS SPRINGS	Puyallup R	Pierce
HIMOS(WOODLAND) CR	South Bay	Thurston
HINTON CR	Johnson Cr	Whatcom
HODGSON (LIME) CR	Kettle R	Ferry
HOFFSTADT CR	Toutle R	Cowlitz
HOGARTY CR	Skykomish R	Snohomish
HOH R	Pacific Ocean	Jefferson
HOH R, Sf	Hoh R	Jefferson
HOKO R	Juan de Fuca Str	Clallam
HOLMES CR	Outlet Cr	Klickitat
HOLYOKE CR	Hood Canal	Mason
HOPKINS(PURCELL) CR	Cowlitz R	Lewis
HOQUIAM R	Grays Harbor	Grays Harbor
HOQUIAM R, Wf	Hoquiam R	Grays Harbor
HORN CR	Nisqually R	Pierce
HORSE CR	Sammamish R	King
HOUSE CR	Tieton R	Yakima
HOWARD CR	Puget Sound	Mason
HOWSON CR	CleElum R	Kittitas
HOZOMEEN CR	Ross L	Whatcom
HUCKLEBERRY CR	Colville R	Stevens
HUDSON CR	Yakima R	Kittitas
HUMPTULIPS R	Grays Harbor	Grays Harbor
HUMPTULIPS R, Ef	Humptulips R	Grays Harbor
HUMPTULIPS R, Wf	Humptulips R	Grays Harbor
HUNTERS CR	Columbia R	Stevens
HURDS (MILL) CR	Cowlitz R	Lewis
HURST CR	Clearwater R	Jefferson
HUTCHINSON CR	Sf Nooksack R	Whatcom

STREAM	TRIBUTARY TO	COUNTY
HYAK CR	Bogachiel R	Clallam
HYAK (COAL) CR	Lake Keechelus	Kittitas
HYLEBOS CR	Puget Sound	King/Pierce

I

STREAM	TRIBUTARY TO	COUNTY
ICE CR	Sekiu R	Clallam
ICICLE CR	Wenatchee R	Chelan
ICY CR	Green R	King
IGNAR CR	Quinault R	Jefferson
ILLABOT CR	Skagit R	Skagit
IMBODEN CR	Cowlitz R	Cowlitz
INDEPENDENCE CR	Chehalis R	Lewis
I I . CR	Willapa Bay	Pacific
INDIAN CR	Grays Harbor	Grays Harbor
INDIAN CR	Nf Teanaway R	Kittitas
INDIAN (Nasika) CR	Cowlitz R	Lewis
INDIAN CR	Hawk Cr	Lincoln
INDIAN CR	Pend Oreille R	Pend Oreille
INDIAN CR	Nf Tieton R	Yakima
I N DIAN CR	Kalama R	Cowl itz
INDIAN CR	Elwha R	Clallam
INDIAN DAN CANY. CR	Columbia R	Okanogan
INGALLS CR	Peshastin Cr	Chelan
INNIS CR	Samish R	Whatcom
IOLA CR	Stillaguamish R	Snohomish
IONE CR	Pend Oreille R	Pend Oreille
IPSUT CR	Carbon R	Pierce
IRELY CR	Quinault R	Jefferson
IRISH CR	Carbon R	Pierce
IRON CR	Chehalis R	Grays Harbor
IRON CR	Cispus R	Lewis
IRON CR	San Poil R	Ferry
ISSAQUAH CR	Lake Sammam.	King
ISSAQUAH CR. Ef	Issaquah Cr	King
ITALIAN CR	Kalama R	Cowlitz
ITWEAT CR	Queets R	Jefferson

J

STREAM	TRIBUTARY TO	COUNTY
JACK CR	Icicle R	Chelan
JACK CR	San Poil R	Ferry
JACK CR	If Teanaway	Kittitas
JACKEL CR	Colville R	Stevens
JACKMAN CR	Skagit R	Skagit
JACKSON CR	Dabop Bay	Jefferson
JACKSON CR	Toutle R	Cowlitz
JASTAD CR	Newaukum R	Lewis
JEFFERSON CR	Hamma Ham. R	Mason
JENKINS CR	Big Soos Cr	King
JENNIE CR	L Boulder Cr	Ferry
JENNINGS CR	Columbia R	Stevens
JENNY CR	Ef Lewis R	Clank
JEWETT CR	Columbia R	Klickitat
JIM CR	Juan de Fuca Str	Clallam
JIM CR	Cedar Cr	Pend Oreille
JIM CR	Sf Stillaguam.	Snohomish
JIMMY COME LATE. CR	Sequim Bay	Clallam
JOE CR	Pacific Ocean	GraysHarbor
JOHN CR	Cedar Cr	Clark
JOHNS CR	Oakland Bay	Mason
JOHNS R	Grays Harbor	Grays Harbor
JOHNSON CR	Navarre Coulee	Chelan
JOHNSON CR	Sequim Bay	Clallam
JOHNSON CR	Lewis R	Cowlitz
JOHNSON CR	Hood Canal	Kitsap
JOHNSON CR	Cowlitz R	Lewis
JOHNSON CR	Okanogan R	Okanogan
JOHNSON CR	Naselle R	Pacific
JOHNSON CR	Sumas R	Whatcom
JOHN TOM CR	San Poil R	Ferry
JONES CR	L Washougal R	Clark
JONES CR	Cowlitz R	Lewis
JONES CR	L Washington	King
JONES CR	Chehalis R	Lewis
JONES CR	Cedar R	King
JONES CR	Nooksack R	Whatcom
JONES CR	Skagit R	Skagit
JORDAN CR	Skagit R	Skagit
JORDAN CR	Toutle R	Cowlitz

STREAM	TRIBUTARY TO	COUNTY
JORDAN CR	Stillaguamish R	Snohomish
JORSTED CR	Hood Canal	Mason
JUDD CR	Puget Sound	King
JULY CR	Lake Quinault	Grays Harbor
JUMP OFF JOE CR	Colville R	Stevens

K

STREAM	TRIBUTARY TO	COUNTY
"K" CR	Skykomish R	Snohomish
KACHESS R	Yakima R	Kittitas
KAHKWA CR	Bogachiel R	Clallam
KALALOCH CR	Pacific Ocean	Jefferson
KALAMA R	Columbia R	Cowlitz
KALISPEL CR	Priest Lake	Pend Oreille
KAMILCHE CR	Skookum Cr	Mason
KAMMERAD CR	Carbon R	Pierce
KANAKA CR	Columbia R	Skamania
KAPOWSIN CR	Puyallup R	Pierce
KARJALA CR	Chehalis R	Grays Harbor
KASTBERG CR	Colville R	Stevens
KATHRYN CR	Coweeman R	Cowlitz
KATULA CR	Chehalis R	Lewis
KEARNEY CR	Black R	Thurston
KENDALL CR	Nooksack R	Whatcom
KENNEDY CR	Totten Inlet	Mason/ Thurston
KENT CR	Pend Oreille R	Pend Oreille
KERRY CR	Kettle R	Ferry
KETTLE R	Columbia R	Ferry
KINICK (DRY) CR	White R	Pierce
KIONA (MASE) CR	Cowlitz R	Lewis
KITSAP LAKE OUT.	Chico Cr	Kitsap
KLAUS CR	Snoqualmie R	King
KLICKITAT CR	Cowlitz R	Lewis
KLICKITAT R	Columbia R	Klickitat/ Yakima
KLICKITAT R, Wf	Klickitat R	Yakima
KLOOCHMAN CR	Clearwater R	Jefferson
KLOSHE CR	Bogachiel R	Clallam
KNOCKEY CR	Mf Hoquiam R	Grays Harbor
KNOWLTON CR	Kalama R	Cowlitz
KOCH CR	Dyes Inlet	Kitsap

L

STREAM	TRIBUTARY TO	COUNTY
LABOR GULCH CR	Okanogan R	Okanogan
LaCAMAS CR	Cowlitz R	Lewis
LaCAMAS CR	Muck Cr	Pierce
LaCAMAS CR	Columbia R	Clark
LaCENTER CR	Ef Lewis R	Clark
LACKEY CR	Carrlnlet	Pierce
LaCLORE CR	Pend Oreille R	Pend Oreille
LADDER CR	Skagit R	Whatcom
LaFLEUR CR	ColumbiaR	Ferry
LAKE CR	Entiat R	Chelan
LAKE CR	Wenatchee R	Chelan
LAKE CR	Soleduck R	Clallam
LAKE CR	Kettle R	Ferry
LAKE CR	Cowlitz R	Lewis
LAKE CR	Pilchuck R	Skagit
LAKE(MARSHALL) CR	Latah Cr	Spokane
LAKE CR	Columbia R	Stevens
LAKE ARMSTRONG OUT.	Hood Canal	Mason
LAKESIDE CR	Lake Quinault	Grays Harbor
LAKEWOOD CR	Columbia R	Skamania
LAMB CR	Hoko R	Clallam
LAMBERT CR	Curlew Cr	Ferry
LANDERS CR	Cowlitz R	Lewis
LANDON CR	Kalama R	Cowlitz
LANE CR	Tahuya R	Mason
LANE CR	Naselle R	Pacific
LANG CR	Willapa R	Grays Harbor
LANGLOIS CR	Tolt R	King
LANKNER CR	Chehalis R	Grays Harbor
LAPAEL CR	Lake Crescent	Clallam
LAPHAM CR	L White Salmon R	Skamania
LARSON CR	Wynoochee R	Grays Harbor
LATAH(HANGMAN) CR	Spokane R	Spoke/Whit
LATAH CR	Nf Latah Cr	Whitman
LATTIN CR	Colville R	Stevens

STREAM	TRIBUTARY TO	COUNTY
LAVA CR	Clear F/Cowlitz R	Lewis
LAVA CR	L White Salmon R	Skamania
LAVIS (LOUIE) CR	San Poil R	Ferry
LAW CR	Kalama R	Cowlitz
LAWRENCE CR	Puyallup R	Pierce
LAWTON CR	Columbia R	Skamania
LEACH(BOWERS) CR	Chambers Cr	Pierce
LEAF CR	Cedar R	King
LEARY CR	Grays Harbor	Grays Harbor
LE CLERC CR	Pend Oreille R	Pend Oreille
LEES CR	Juan de Fuca Str	Clallam
LELAND CR	L Quilcene R	Jefferson
LELAND LAKE INLET	Leland Lake	Jefferson
LENA CR	Hamma Hamma R	Jefferson
LENNOX CR	Snoqualmie R	King
LEONARD CR	Snoqualmie R	King
LESTER CR	Chehalis R	Lewis
LEWIS R	Columbia R	Skamania
LEWIS R Ef	Lewis R	Clark
LEXI NGTON CR	Cowlitz R	Cowl itz
LIBBY CR	Methow R	Okanogan
LIBERTY BAY INLET	Liberty Bay	Kitsap
LIGHTNING CR	Bonaparte Cr	Okanogan
LIGHTNING CR	Skagit R	Whatcom
LILLIWAUP CR	Hood Canal	Mason
LIME (HODGSON) CR	Kettle R	Ferry
LIME CR	San Poil R	Ferry
LIME CR	Wf San Poil R	Ferry
LIME CR	Pend Oreille R	Pend Oreille
LIME CR	Deep Cr	Stevens
LINCOLN CR	Chehalis R	Lewis
LINCOLN CR	Deschutes R	Thurston
LINDCOULEE	Crab Cr	Grant
LINTON(METALINE) CR	Pend Oreille R	Pend Oreille
LION (WILLIAMS) CR	Swauk Cr	Kittitas
LITTLE CR	Yakima R	Kittitas
LITTLE (BEACON) CR	Woodward Cr	Skamania
LITTLE BOULDER CR	Kettle R	Ferry
LITTLEBUCK CR	White Salmon R	Skamania
LITTLE CALISPEL CR	Calispel R	Pend Oreille
LIT. CHUMSTICK CR	Chumstick Cr	Chelan
LITTLE COLLINS CR	Collins Cr	Skamania
LITTLE DEER CR	Deer Cr	Spokane
LIT. DRAGOON CR	Dragoon Cr	Spok/Stevens
LITTLE ELK CR	Smith Cr	Pacific
LITTLE GRADE CR	Lake Chelan	Chelan
LITTLE HOQUIAM R	Mf Hoquiam R	Grays Harbor
LIT. HUCKLEBERRY CR	White Salmon R	Skamania
LITTLE KLICKITAT R	Klickitat R	Klickitat
LITTLE LILLIWAUP CR	Hood Canal	Mason
LITTLE LOUP LOUP CR	Loup Loup Cr	Okanogan
LITTLE MASHELL R	Mashell R	Pierce
LITTLE MISSION CR	Hood Canal	Mason
LITTLE MUD CR	Pine Cr	Walla Walla
LITTLE MUDDY CR	Big Muddy Cr	Pend Oreille
LITTLE MUDDY CR	Wf Klickitat R	Klickitat
LITTLE NESPELEM R	Nespelem R	Okanogan
LITTLE NISQUALLY R	Nisqually R	Thurston
LITTLE NORTH R	North R	Grays Harbor
LITTLE OHOP CR	Ohop Cr	Pierce
LITTLE PEND OREILLE	Colville R	Stevens
LITTLE QUILCENE R	Hood Canal	Jefferson
LITTLE R	Elwha R	Clallam
LITTLE SALMON LA SAC	Cle Elum R	Kittitas
LITTLE SHEEP CR	Sheep Cr	Stevens
LITTLE SOOS CR	Big Soos Cr	King
LITTLE SPANGLE CR	Latah Cr	Spokane
LITTLE SPOKANE R	Spokane R	P Oreille/Spok.
LITTLE TACOMA CR	Tacoma Cr	Pend Oreille
LITTLE TAHUYA CR	Tahuya Cr	Mason
LIT. WALLA WALLA R	Walla Walla R	Walla Walla
LIT. WASHOUGAL R	Washougal R	Clark
LIT. WHITE SALMON R	Columbia R	Skamania
LITTLE WIND CR	Wind R	Skamania
LITTLETON CR	Soleduck R	Clallam
LOCKWOOD CR	Ef Lewis R	Clark
LODGE CR	Columbia R	Stevens
LOHR CR	Hoquiam R	Grays Harbor
LONE RANCH CR	Kettle R	Ferry
LONG ALEX CR	Kettle R	Ferry
LORDS CR	Willapa R	Pacific
LOST CR	Wildcat Cr	Kitsap

STREAM	TRIBUTARY TO	COUNTY
LOST CR	Newaukum R	Lewis
LOST CR	Myers Cr	Okanogan
LOST CR	Wf San Poil R	Okanogan
LOST CR	Pend Oreille R	Pend Oreille
LOST CR	L Pend Oreille R	Stevens
LOST CR	Naches R	Yakima
LOST R	Methow R	Okanogan
LOWRY (MORAN) CR	Colville R	Stevens
LOUIE (LAVIS) CR	San Poil R	Ferry
LOUP LOUP CR	Okanogan R	Okanogan
LUNCH CR	Raft R	Grays Harbor
LYNCH CR	Little Skookum Cr	Mason
LYNCH CR	Ohop Cr	Pierce
LYNX CR	Hall Cr	Ferry
LYON CR	Lake Washington	King
LYRE R	Juan de Fuca Str	Clallam
LYTLE CR	Hoquiam R	Grays Harbor

M

MACKEY CR	Sammamish R	King
MAD R	Entiat R	Chelan
MADISON CR	Elwha R	Clallam
MADSON CR	Cedar R	King
MAHAR CR	Wenatchee R	Chelan
MAIDEN HAIR CR	Wind R	Skamania
MAJORS CR	Columbia R	Klickitat
MALLORY CR	Washougal R	Clark
MALONE CR	Grays R	Wahkiakum
MANASTASH CR	Yakima R	Kittitas
MANILLA CR	San Poil R	Ferry
MANSOR CR	Skagit R	Skagit
MAPLE CR	Cowlitz R	Lewis
MAPLE CR	Wf Granite Cr	Okanogan
MAPLE CR	Nooksack R	Whatcom
MAPLEWOOD SPRGS	Clark Cr	Pierce
MARATTA CR	Toutle R	Cowlitz
MARBLE CR	Cascade R	Skagit
MARCUS CR	Columbia R	Stevens
MARCY CR	Porter Cr	Grays Harbor
M ARGA R ET FALLS CR	Lake Crescent	Clallam
MARIAS CR	Toroda Cr	Okanogan
MARIETTA CR	Kalama R	Cowlitz
MARIETTA CR	Skagit R	Skagit
MARSHALL (LAKE CR	Latah Cr	Spokane
MARTIN CR	Columbia R	Ferry
MARTIN CR	Kettle R	Ferry
MARY ANN CR	Myers Cr	Okanogan
MASE (KIONA) CR	Cowlitz R	Lewis
MASHEL R	Nisqually R	Pierce
MASON CR	Ef Lewis R	Clark
MASON CR	Snoqualmie R	King
MASON (FIRST) CR	Nf Teanaway R	Kittitas
MATHENY CR	Queets R	Jefferson
MATTSON CR	Kettle R	Ferry
MAY CR	Lake Washington	King
MAY CR	Wallace R	Snohomish
MAYFIELD CR	Cowlitz R	Lewis
MAYNARD CR	Port Discov. Bay	Jefferson
McALCOR CR	Lake Washington	King
McALLISTER CR	Nisqually R	Thurston
McALLISTER SPRGS	Puget Sound	Thurston
McCALLA CR	Boulder Cr	Grays Harbor
McCARTY CR	Sf Nooksack R	Whatcom
McCLOSKEY CR	Washougal R	Skamania
McCOY CR	Skykomish R	Snohomish
McCOY CR	Cowlitz R	Skamania
McCREA BRANCH CR	Entiat R	Chelan
McCREEDY CR	Klickitat R	Yakima
McCUMBAR SPRGS	Bird Cr	Yakima
McDONALD CR	Juan de Fuca Str	Clallam
McDONALD CR	Colquallam Cr	Grays Harbor
McDONALD CR	Hood Canal	Jefferson
McEVOY SPRGS BR	WallaWalla R	Walla Walla
McFARLAND CR	Methow R	Okanogan
McKENZIE(REYNOLDS)	Pend Oreille R	Pend Oreille
McLANES CR	Mud Bay	Thurston
McLEOD(WOLFRED) CF	Pend Oreille R	Pend Oreille
McMILLAN CR	Lake Kapowsin Out.	Pierce
McMURRAY LAKE IN.	McMurray Lake	Skagit
McMURRAY LAKE OUT.	Big Lake	Skagit

STREAM	TRIBUTARY TO	COUNTY
MEADOW CR	Lake Keechelus	Kittitas
MEADOW CR	Toroda Cr	Okanogan
MEADOW CR	Sf Deep Cr	Stevens
MORRISON CR	Quinault R	Grays Harbor
METHOW R	Columbia R	Okanogan
MICA CR	Spokane R	Spokane
MIDDLE CR	Nf Teanaway R	Kittitas
MIDDLE NEMA R	Willapa Bay	Pacific
MILOS CR	Lewis R	Cowlitz
MILL CR	Bogachiel R	Clallam
MILL CR	Columbia R	Clark
MILL CR	Salmon Cr	Clark
MILL CR	Columbia R	Cowlitz
MILL CR	Chehalis R	Grays Harbor
MILL CR	Duwamish R	King
MILL CR	L Klickitat R	Klickitat
MILL (HURDS) CR	Cowlitz R	Lewis
MILL (RANDLE) CR	Cowlitz R	Lewis
MILL (GOSNELL) CR	Hammersley In.	Mason
MILL CR	Willapa R	Pacific
MILL CR	Pend Oreille R	Pend Ore.R
MILL CR	White Salmon R	Skamania
MILL CR	Colville R	Stevens
MILL (BEAN) CR	Black R	Thurston
MILL CR	Walla Walla R	Walla Walla R
MILLER CR	Puget Sound	King
MILLER CR	Hood Canal	Mason
MILLS CANYON CR	Entiat R	Chelan
MIMA CR	Black R	Thurston
MINERS CR	Yakima R	Kittitas
MINNOW CR	Davis Lake	Lewis
MIROS CR	Curlew Lake	Ferry
MISSION CR	Wenatchee R	Chelan
MISSION CR	Hood Canal	Mason
MITCHELL CR	Lake Chelan	Chelan
MOCLIPS R	Pacific Ocean	Grays Harbor
MONEY CR	Skykomish R	Snohomish
MOON CR	Black R	Grays Harbor
MOORE CR	Hood Canal	Mason
MORAN CR	Colville R	Stevens
MOROY CR	Spanaway Cr	Pierce
MORGAN CR	Cle Elum R	Kittitas
MORRIS CR	Mill Cr	Pacific
MORSE CR	Juan de Fuca Str	Clallam
MOSER CR	Dyes Inlet	Kitsap
MOSQUITO CR	Drays Cr	Cowlitz
MOSQUITO CR	Pacific Ocean	Jefferson
MOSQUITO CR	Yakima R	Kittitas
MOSS CR	L White Salmon R	Skamania
MOUNT TOM CR	Hoh R	Jefferson
MOX CHEHALIS CR	Chehalis R	Grays Harbor
MUCK CR	Nisqually R	Pierce
MUD CR	Entiat R	Chelan
MUD CR	Dry Cr	WallaWalla
MUD CR	Walla Walla R	Walla Walla
MUDDY FORK	Cowlitz R	Lewis
MUDDY FORK	Cispus R	Skamania
MUDDY R	Lewis R	Skamania
MUIR CR	Palouse R	Whitman
MULHOLLAND CR	Coweman R	Cowlitz
MURDOCK CR	Juan de Fuca Str	Clallam
MURRAY CR	American Lake	Pierce
MYERS CR	Kettle R	Okanogan
MYRTLE CR	Carbon R	Pierce

N

STREAM	TRIBUTARY TO	COUNTY
NABIN CR	Dosewallips R	Jefferson
NACHES R	Yakima R	Yakima
NADLER CR	Columbia R	Skamania
NANCY CR	Columbia R	Ferry
NANEUM CR	Yakima R	Kittitas
NANUM CR	Wilson Cr	Kittitas
NARCISSE CR	L Pend Oreille R	Stevens
NASELLE R	Willapa Bay	Pacific
NASON CR	Wenatchee R	Chelan
NASTY CR	Ahtanum Cr	Yakima
NAVARRE COULEE CR	Columbia R	Chelan
NEFF CR	Colville R	Stevens
NEGRO CR	Peshastin Cr	Chelan
NEGRO CR	Rock Cr	Whitman

STREAM	TRIBUTARY TO	COUNTY
NELLITA CR	Hood Canal	Kitsap
NELSON CR	Lyre R	Clallam
NELSON CR	Columbia R	Skamania
NEMAHR	Willapa Bay	Pacific
NESIKA (INDIAN) CR	Cowlitz R	Lewis
NESPELEM R	Columbia R	Okanogan
NEWSWARTZ CR	Willapa Bay	Pacific
NEUSKAHL CR	Grays Harbor	Grays Harbor
NEWAUKUM CR	Green R	King
NEWAUKUM R	Chehalis R	Lewis
NEWBY CR	Twisp R	Okanogan
NEWHALEM CR	Skagit R	Whatcom
NEWMAN CR	Chehalis R	Grays Harbor
NEWMAN CR	Newman Lake	Spokane
NEWPORT CR	Cle Elum Lake	Kittitas
NEZ PERCE CR	Columbia R	Ferry
NICHLAM(BRUSH) CR	Cedar Cr	Clark
NICHOLSON CR	Toroda Cr	Ferry
NILE CR	Naches R	Yakima
NINE MILE (RABBIT)	San Poil R	Ferry
NINE MILE CR	Osoyoos Lake	Okanosan
NINE MILE CR	Kettle R	Stevens
NINETEEN CR	Tilton R	Lewis
NINETEEN MILE CR	San Poil R	Ferry
NISQUALLY R	Puget Sound	Pierce/ThursT.
NOBLE CR	Yakima R	Kittitas
NOISY CR	Sullivan Lake	Pend Oreille
NOISY CR	Tolt R	King
NOLAN CR	Hoh R	Jefferson
NO NAME CR	Lewis R	Skamania
NOOKACHAMPS CR	Skagit R	Skaqit
NOOKSACK R	Bellingham Bay	Whatcom
NORTH ADDY CR	Colville R	Stevens
NORTH CR	Twisp R	Okanoqan
NORTH FERRIER CR	Oloqua Cr	Lewis
NORTH GRANITE CR	Okanogan R	Okanogan
NORTH LaFLEUR CR	Kettle R	Ferry
NORTH NOMA R	Willapa Bay	Pacific
NORTH PINE CR	Pine Cr	Spokane
NORTH R	Willapa Bay	Grays Harbor
NORTH STREAM	Millers Bay	Kitsap

O

STREAM	TRIBUTARY TO	COUNTY
OAK CR	Columbia R	Klickitat
OAK CR	Tieton R	Yakima
O BRIEN CR	San Poil R	Ferry
O BRIEN CR	Skagit R	Skagit
OHANAPECOSH R	Cowlitz R	Lewis
OHOP CR	Nisqually R	Pierce
OKANOGAN R	Columbia R	Okanogan
OLALLA CR	Puget Sound	Kitsap
OLD LAY CANYON CR	Columbia R	Klickitat
OLEQUA CR	Cowlitz R	Lewis
OLIVER CR	Kiona Cr	Lewis
OLNEY CR	Wallace R	Snohomish
OLSEN CR	Lake Whatcom	Whatcom
OLSON CR	L Pend Oreille R	Stevens
OMAK CR	Okanogan R	Okanogan
ONALASKA CR	Newaukum R	Lewis
ONION CR	Columbia R	Stevens
ORLO CR	Lake Quinault	Grays Harbor
OROPAHAN CR	Columbia R	Stevens
OSOYOOS CR	Okanogan R	Okanogan
OSTRANDER CR	CowlitzR	Cowlitz
OTTER(ARMSTRONG) CR	Spokane R	Spokane
OUTLET CR	Klickitat R	Klickitat
OUTLET CR	E Br Satsop R	Mason
OVINGTON CR	Lake Crescent	Clallam
OYSTER CR	Samish Bay	Skaqit
OXBOW CR	Willapa R	Pacific

P

STREAM	TRIBUTARY TO	COUNTY
PACKARD CR	White R	King
PACKWOOD CR	Cowlitz R	Lewis
PADDEN LAKE OUT.	Bellingham Bay	Whatcom
PAGE CR	Alpowa Cr	Asotin
PAIWAKI CR	Alpowa Cr	Asotin
PALIX R	Willapa Bay	Pacific

STREAM	TRIBUTARY TO	COUNTY
PALMER CR	Similkameen R	Okanogan
PALOUSE R	Snake R	Whitman
PANTHER CR	Wind R	Skamania
PARADISE R	Nisqually R	Pierce
PARIS CR	Cle Elum R	Kittitas
PARK CR	Stehekin R	Chelan
PARK CR	Cherry Cr	Kittitas
PASAYTEN R	Similkameen R	Okanogan
PASS LAKE OUTLET	Deception Pass	Skagit
PATAHA CR	Tucannon Cr	Garfield
PATIT CR	Touchet R	Columbia
PATTERSON CR	Snoqualmie R	King
PAYATO CR	Yakima R	Yakima
PEABODY CR	Port Angeles Hrbr	Clallam
PEARL CR	Klickitat R	Yakima
PEARYGIN CR	Chewack Cr	Okanogan
PEAY CR	Chewelah Cr	Stevens
PECK CR	White Salmon R	Klickitat
PELTON CR	Queets R	Jefferson
PENAWAWA CR	Snake R	Whitman
PEND ORIELLE R	Columbia R	Pend Orielle
PENNINGTON CR	Brooks Cr	Cowlitz
PENNY CR	Big Quilcene R	Jefferson
PESHASTIN CR	Wenatchee R	Chelan
PEENE CR	Deadman Cr	Spokane
PEENY CR	Bonaparte Cr	Okanogan
PERCIVAL CR	Puget Sound	Thurston
PERRY CR	Mud Bay	Thurston
PETERS CR	Cowlitz R	Lewis
PETTIJOHN CR	Bonaparte Cr	Okanogan
PHELPS CR	ChiwawaR	Chelan
PIEDMONT CR	Lake Crescent	Clallam
PILCHUCK CR	Stillaguamish R	Snohomish
PILCHUCK R	Snohomish R	Snohomish
PINE CR	Columbia R	Klickitat
PINE CR	Wagonrd. Coulee	Okanogan
PINE CR	Lewis R	Skamania
PINE CR	Rock Cr	Spok./Whit.
PINE CR	Walla Walla R	WallaWalla
PINE CR	Tieton R	Yakima
PINE CANYON CR	Columbia R	Douglas
PINGSTON CR	Columbia R	Stevens
PISCOE CR	Klickitat R	Yakima
PLUMMER CR	Puyallup R	Pierce
POLSON CR	Wf Hoquiam R	Grays Harbor
POORMAN CR	Twisp R	Okanogan
POPE CR	Entiat R	Chelan
PORTER CR	Chehalis R	Grays Harbor
POTATO CR	Entiat R	Chelan
POWELL CR	Skagit R	Skagit
PRAIRIE CR	Chehalis R	Thurston
PRAIRIE R	Quinault R	Grays Harbor
PRATT R	Snoqualmie R	King
PRESTON CR	Entiat R	Chelan
PRICE CR	Yakima R	Kittitas
PRINCE CR	L Chelan	Chelan
PROCTOR CR	Skykomish R	Snohomish
PROSPECT CR	L Pend Oreille R	Stevens
PURCELL(HOPKINS) CR	Cowlitz R	Lewis
PURDY CR	Skokomish R	Mason
PURDY CR	Carrs Inlet	Pierce
PUYALLUP R	Puget Sound	Pierce
PYRAMID CR	Skagit R	Whatcom
PYSHT R	Juan de Fuca Str	Clallam

Q

QUARTZ CR	Cispus R	Lewis
QUARTZ CR	Lewis R	Skamania
QUARTZCR	Skykomish R	Snohomish
QUARTZ CR	Naches R	Yakima
QUEETS R	Pacific Ocean	Jefferson
QUICK CR	Hamma Hamma R	Mason
QUILASASCUT CR	Columbia R	Stevens
QUILCENE R	Hood Canal	Jefferson
QUILCODA CR	Ebey Slough	Snohomish
QUILLAYUTE R	Pacific Ocean	Clallam
QUINAULT R	Pacific Ocean	Grays Harbor
QUINN R	Ozette R	Clallam

R

STREAM	TRIBUTARY TO	COUNTY
RABBIT (NINEMILE)	San Poi l R	Ferry
RACEHORSE CR	Nisqually R	Pierce
RACEHORSE CR	Nooksack R	Whatcom
RAFT R	Queets R	Grays Harbor
RAGING R	Snoqualmie	King
RAIL CR	Chamokane Cr	Stevens
RAILROAD CR	LakeChelan	Chelan
RAINBOW CR	Stehekin R	Chelan
RAINEY CR	Cowlitz R	Lewis
RAINY CR	Wenatchee R	Chelan
RAMONA CR	Coweman R	Cowlitz
RAMSAY CR	Chewack Cr	Okanogan
RANDLE (MILL) CR	Cowlitz R	Lewis
RAPID R	Beckler R	Snohomish
RATTLESNAKE CR	Columbia R	Ferry
RATTLESNAKE CR	San Poil R	Ferry
RATTLESNAKE CR	White Salmon R	Klickitat
RATTLESNAKE CR	Columbia R	Stevens
RATTLESNAKE R	Naches R	Yakima
REBEL FLAT CR	Palouse R	Whitman
RED CR	Moxlee Cr	Thurston
REESER CR	Wilson Cr	Kittitas
RENO CR	Lewis R	Cowlitz
REPUBLICAN CR	Nf Deep Cr	Stevens
RESER CR	Russell Cr	Walla Walla
RESORT CR	Lake Keechelus	Kittitas
REYNOLDS CR	Twisp R	Okanogan
RICHTER CR	Hood Canal	Mason
RICKEY CR	Columbia R	Stevens
RIDDER(HELLER) CR	Colville R	Stevens
RIFFLE(SULPHUR) CR	Cowlitz R	Lewis
RITTER CR	L White Salmon R	Skamania
RITZ(STONE) CR	Walla Walla R	Walla Walla
RIVERSIDE CR	Yakima R	Kittitas
ROARING CR	Entiat R	Chelan
ROARING CR	Lake Keechelus	Kittitas
ROCK CR	Chiwawa R	Chelan
ROCK CR	Ef Lewis R	Clark
ROCK CR	Kalama R	Cowlitz
ROCK CR	Lewis R	Cowlitz
ROCK CR	Chehalis R	Grays Harbor
ROCK CR	Cedar R	King
ROCK CR	Lake Sawyer	King
ROCK CR	Columbia R	Klickltat
ROCK(BOULDER) CR	Wf Methow R	Okanogan
ROCK CR	Columbia R	Skamania
ROCK CR	L White Salmon R	Skamania
ROCK CR	Latah Cr	Spokane
ROCK CR	Palouse R	Whitman
ROCK CR	Naches R	Yakima
ROCKY CR	Sf Deep Cr	Stevens
ROCKY BROOK CR	Dosewallips R	Jefferson
ROCKY FORD CR	Moses L	Grant
ROCKY RUN CR	Lake Keechelus	Kittitas
ROPER CR	Columbia R	Ferry
ROSLYN CR	Yakima R	Kittitas
RUBY CR	Peshastin Cr	Chelan
RUBY CR	Pend Oreille R	Pend Oreille
RUBY CR	Ross Lake	Whatcom
RUSH CR	Lewis R	Skamania
RUSSELL CR	Yellowhawk Cr	WallaWalla
RUSSELL CR	Nf Tieton R	Yakima
RYAN CR	Columbia R	Stevens

S

SACHEEN LAKE OUTLET	Trout Lake	Pend Orei l le
SADIE CR	E Twin R	Clallam
SAFETY HARBOR CR	Lake Chelan	Chelan
SALMON CR	Black R	Thurston
SALMON CR	Columbia R	Clark
SALMON CR	North R	Grays Harbor
SALMON CR	Pt Discovery Bay	Jefferson
SALMON CR	Cowlitz R	Lewis
SALMON CR	Hood Canal	Mason
SALMON CR	Okanogan R	Okanogan
SALMON LA SAC CR	Cle Elum R	Kittitas
SALMON R	Queets R	Jefferson
SALT CR	Juan de Fuca Str	Clallam

STREAM	TRIBUTARY TO	COUNTY	STREAM	TRIBUTARY TO	COUNTY
SAMISH R	Samish Bay	Skagit	SMITH CR	Lake Crescent	Clallam
SAMMAMISH R	Lake Washington	King	SMITH CR	Cowlitz R	Lewis
SAMS CR	Queets R	Jefferson	SMITH CR	Willapa Harbor	Pacific
SAND CR	Mission Cr	Chelan	SMITH CR	Dunn Cr	Stevens
SAND CR	Cowlitz R	Lewis	SMITH CR	Nooksack R	Whatcom
SAND CR	Kettle R	Stevens	SNIDER CR	Soleduck R	Clallam
SAN POIL R	Columbia R	Ferry	SNOQUALMIE R	Snohomish R	King
SARSAPKIN CR	Sinlahekin Cr	Okanogan	SNOQUALMIE R, Nf	Snoqualmie R	King
SARVIS CR	Huckleberry Cr	Stevens	SNOQUALMIE R, Mf	Snoqualmie R	King
SATSOP R, Ef	Satsop R	Grays Harbor	SNOQUALMIE R, Sf	Snoqualmie R	King
SATSOP R MIDDLE BR	Ef, Satsop R	Mason	SNOW CR	Discovery Bay	Jefferson
SATSOP R Wf	Satsop R	Grays Harbor	SNOW CR	Crocker Lake	Jefferson
SATSOP R	Chehalis R	Grays Harbor	SNYDER CR	Cowlitz R	Lewis
SATUS CR	Yakima R	Yakima	SODA SPRINGS CR	Klickitat R	Yakima
SAUK R	Skagit R	Snohomish	SOLEDUCK R	Quillayute R	Clallam
SCANDIA CR	Liberty Bay	Kitsap	SOLEDUCK R, Nf	Soleduck R	Clallam
SCATTER (GOLD) Ch	San Poil R	Ferry	SOOES R	Pacific Ocean	Clallam
SCATTER CR	Twisp R	Okanogan	SOOS CR	Green R	King
SCATTER CR	Chehalis R	Thurston	SOUTH PRAIRIE CR	Carbon R	Pierce
SCHMIDT CR	Smith Cr	Stevens	SOUTH SLOUGH	Stillaguamish R	Snohomish
SCHNEIDERS CR	Oysfer Bay	Thurston	SPANAWAY CR	Clover Cr	Pierce
SCHUMACHER CR	Mason Lake	Mason	SPANGLE CR	Latah Cr	Spokane
SCOTTY CR	Peshastin Cr	Chelan	SPEARS CR	Siler Cr	Lewis
SEASTROM CR	Pacific Ocean	Grays Harbor	SPEILEI CR	Lewis R	Cowlitz
SECOND CR	Chumstick Cr	Chelan	SPENCER CR	Dabop Bay	Jefferson
SELAH CR	Yakima R	Yakima	SPOKANE R	Columbia R	Spokane
SEVENTEEN MILE CR	San Poil R	Ferry	SPRING CR	Ef Lewis R	Clark
SHADOW CR	Tanoum Cr	Kittitas	SPRING CR	Cle Elum Lake	Kittitas
SHANGHAI CR	Fourth Plain Cr	Clark	SPRING CR	L Klickitat R	Klickitat
SHASER CR	Peshastin Cr	Chelan	SPRING(ARMSTRONG)	L Spokane R	Spokane
SHEEP CR	Columbia R	Stevens	SPRING CR	Dry Cr	Walla Walla
SHEEP CANYON CR	Klickitat R	Klickitat	SPRING CR	Simcoe Cr	Yakima
SHELL CR	Puget Sound	Snohomish	SPRING CR	Kalama R	Cowlitz
SHERMAN CR	Columbia R	Ferry	SPRINGBROOK CR	Green R	King
SHERMAN CR	Tilton R	Lewis	SPRINGHOOL CR	Trout Cr	Pend Oreille
SHERWOOD (DEADMAN)	Kettle R	Ferry	SPURGEON CR	Deschutes R	Thurston
SHERWOOD CR	Cases Inlet	Mason	SQUALICUM CR	Bellingham Bay	Whatcom
SHERWOOD(E BRIDGE)	Colville R	Stevens	SQUAW CR	Methow R	Okanogan
SHUKSAN CR	Baker Cr	Whatcom	SQUAW (BERRY) CR	Rock Cr	Skamania
SIEBERT CR	Juan de Fuca Str	Clallam	SQUAW CR	Columbia R	Stevens
SILVER CANYON CR	Klickitat R	Klickitat	SQUAW CR	L Pend Oreille R	Stevens
SILVER CR	Entiat R	Chelan	SQUAW CR	Johnson Cr	Whatcom
SILVER CR	San Poil R	Ferry	SQUILLCHUCK CR	Columbia R	Chelan
SILVER CR	Yakima R	Kittitas	SQUIRE CR	Nf Stillaguam. R	Snohomish
SILVER CR	Cowlitz R	Lewis	STAFFORD CR	Grays Harbor	Grays Harbor
SILVER CR	Friday Cr	Skagit	STAFFORD CR	Nf Teanaway R	Kittitas
SILVER CR	Nf Deep Cr	Stevens	STAHL CR	Mill Cr	Lewis
SILVER CR	Bellingham Bay	Whatcom	ST CLOUD CR	Columbia R	Skamania
SILVER CR	Humphries Cr	Whatcom	STEELE CR	Port Orchard Bay	Kitsap
SILVER SPRINGS	Hammersley Inlet	Mason	STEHEKIN R	Lake Chelan	Chelan
SIMCOE CR	Toppenish Cr	Yakima	STEMILT CR	Columbia R	Chelan
SIMILKAMEEN R	Okanogan R	Okanogan	STEPTOE C R	Snake R	Whitman
SINLAHEKIN CR	Similkameen R	Okanogan	STEVENS CR	Humptulips R	Grays Harbor
SIOUXON CR	Lewis R	Clark	STEVENS CR	Latah Cr	Spokane
SIWASH CR	Okanogan R	Okanogan	STEVENS LAKE IN.	Stevens Lake	Snohomish
SIX PRONG CR	Alder Cr	Klickitat	STEVENS LAKE OUT.	Pilchuck R	Snohomish
SKAGIT R	Puget Sound	Whatcom	STILL CR	Wf Satsop R	Grays Harbor
SKAMOKAWA CR	Columbia R	Wahkiakum	STILLAGUAMISH R	Puget Sound	Snohomish
SKATE CR	Cowlitz R	Lewis	STILLAGUAMISH R, Nf	Stillaguamish R	Snohomish
SKINNEY CR	Chiwaukum Cr	Chelan	STILLAGUAMISH R. Sf	Stillaguamish R	Snohomish
SKOKOMISH R	Hood Canal	Mason	STILLWATER CR	Olequa Cr	Lewis
SKOKOMISH R, Nf	Skokomish R	Mason	STILLWATER CR	Snoqualmie R	King
SKOKOMISH R, Sf	Skokomish R	Mason	STONE (RITZ) CR	Walla Walla R	Walla Walla
SKOOKUM CR	Totten Inlet	Mason	STORMY CR	Entiat R	Chelan
SKOOKUM CR	Pend Oreille R	Pend Oreille	ST PETERS CR	Curlew Cr	Ferry
SKOOKUM CR, Nf	Skookum Cr	Pend Orellle	STRANGER CR	ColumblaR	Ferry
SKOOKU M CR, Sf	Skookum Cr	Pend Oreille	STRANGER CR	ColvilleR	Stevens
SKOOKUM CR	Sf Nooksack R	Whatcom	STRINGER CR	Willapa R	Pacific
SKOOKUMCHUCK R	Chehalis R	Lewis/Thurs.	STROM BERG CANY. CR	Chumstick Cr	Chelan
SKUNK CR	Cook Cr	Grays Harbor	STOSSEL CR	Snoqualmie R	King
SKUNK CR	Twisp Cr	Okanogan	STUART CR	Drays Cr	Cowlitz
SKUNK CABBAGE CR	San Poil R	Ferry	STUCK R (White)	Puyallup R	Pierce
SKYKOMISH R	Snohomish R	Snohomish	STUMP CR	Colville R	Stevens
SKYKOMISH R Sf	Snohomish R	King	SUIATTLE R	Sauk R	Snohomish
SKYKOMISH R Nf	Skykomish R	Snohomish	SULFUR R	Suiattle R	Snohomish
SLASLOPOLIS CR	Hood Canal	Mason	SULLIVAN CR	Port Orchard Bay	Kitsap
SLATE CR	Twisp R	Okanogan	SULLIVAN CR	Pend Oreille R	PendOreille
SLATE CR	Pend Oreille R	Pend Oreille	SULPHUR CR	White R	King
SLIDE CR	Colville R	Stevens	SULPHUR(RIFFLE) CR	Cowlitz R	Lewis
SMALL CR	San Poil R	Ferry	SULTAN R	Skykomish R	Snohomish
SMALLE CR	Pend Oreille R	Pend Oreille	SUMAS R	Fraser R	Whatcom
SMALLE CR, Ef	Smalle Cr	PendOreille	SUMMER CR	Kalama R	Cowlitz

STREAM	TRIBUTARY TO	COUNTY
SUMMIT CR	Ohanapecosh R	Lewis
SUMMIT CR	LoupLoup Cr	Okanogan
SUMMIT CR	Sol Duc R	Clallam
SUNDAY CR	Green R	King
SUNDS CR	Hood Canal	Mason
SUNITSCH CANY.CR	Chumstick Cr	Chelan
SURVEYORS CR	Klickitat R	Yakima
SUSIE CR	Lyre R	Clallam
SWAKANE CR	ColumbiaR	Chelan
SWALE CR	Klickitat R	Klickitat
SWAMP CR	Coweman R	Cowlitz
SWAMP CR	Yakima R	Kittitas
SWAMP CR	Cowlitz R	Lewis
SWAMP CR	Sammamish R	Snohomish
SWAMP CR	Chamokane Cr	Stevens
SWAMP CR	Klickitat R	Yakima
SWAMP CR	Naches R	Yakima
SWAMPY CR	Lewis R	Skamania
SWAUK CR	Yakima R	Kittitas
SWEAT CR	Wf Granite Cr	Okanogan
SWEAT CR	Summit Cr	Okanogan
SWEET CR	Pend Oreille R	Pend Oreille
SWIFT CR	Lewis R	Skamania
SWIFT CR	McLanes Cr	Thurston
SYLVIA CR	Wynoochee R	Grays Harbor
SYLVIA CR	Sol Duc R	Clallam
SYLVIA CR	Kalama R	Cowlitz

T

STREAM	TRIBUTARY TO	COUNTY
TACOMA CR	Queets R	Jefferson
TACOMA CR	Pend Oreille R	Pend Oreille
TAHUYA R	Hood Canal	Mason
TALLANT CR	Okanogan R	Okanogan
TANEUM CR	Yakima R	Kittitas
TANWAX CR	Nisqually R	Pierce
TARBOO CR	Hood Canal	Jefferson
TATE CR	Nf Snoqualmie R	King
TAYLOR CR	Carbon R	Pierce
TEANAWAY R	Yakima R	Kittitas
TELEPHONE CR	Yakima R	Kittitas
TENAS CR	Suiattle R	Skagit
TENAS MARY CR	Kettle R	Fenry
TEN MILE CR	Snake R	Asotin
TEN MILE CR	Nooskack R	Whatcom
TEN OCLOCK CR	Quinault R	Grays Harbor
TEXAS CR	Methow R	Okanogan
THIRTEEN MILE CR	San Poil R	Ferry
THIRTY MILE CR	San Poil R	Ferry
THOMASON CR	Colville R	Stevens
THORN CR	Pine Cr	Whitman
THORNTON CR	LakeWashington	King
THREE FORKS CR	Mill Cr	Stevens
THREE MILE CR	Pend Oreille R	Pend Oreille
THUNDER CR	Skagit R	Whatcom
TIETON R	Naches R	Yakima
TILTON R	Cowlitz R	Lewis
TOAD CR	Squalicum Cr	Whatcom
TOATS COULEE CR	Sinlahekin Cr	Okanogan
TOKUL CR	Snoqualmie R	King
TOLT R	Snoqualmie R	King
TONASKET CR	Curlew Cr	Ferry
TONASKET CR	Okanogan R	Okanogan
TONATA CR	Kettle R	Ferry
TOPPENISH CR	Yakima R	Yakima
TORBEL CR	Colville R	Stevens
TORODA CR	Kettle R	Okanogan
TOUCHET R	Walla Walla R	WallaW./Col
TOULOU CR	Kettle R	Stevens
TOUTLE R	Cowlitz R	Cowlitz/Skam.
TRAPPER CR	L Muddy Cr	Yakima
TRIMBLE CR	Pend Oreille R	Pend Oreille
TRONSON CR	Peshastin Cr	Chelan
TROUT CR	Curlew Lake	Ferry
TROUT CR	White Salmon R	Klickitat
TROUT (TURNER) CR	Toroda Cr	Okanogan
TROUT CR	Horseshoe Lake	Pend Oreille
TROUT CR	Wind R	Skamania
TROUT CR	Cottonwood Cr	Stevens
TROUT CR	Nf Deep Cr	Stevens
TSHLETSHY CR	Queets R	Jefferson

STREAM	TRIBUTARY TO	COUNTY
TUCANNON R	Snake R	Columbia
TUCK CR	Snoqualmie R	King
TUCKER CR	Yakima R	Kittitas
TUM TUM CR	Cedar R	Clark
TUMWATER CR	Port Angeles Har.	Clallam
TUNK CR	Okanogan R	Okanogan
TURNER CR	Hood Canal	Jefferson
TURNER (TROUT) CR	Toroda Cr	Okanogan
TUTTLE CR	North R	Grays Harbor
TWELVE MILE CR	Colville R	Stevens
TWENTY-ONE MILE CR	San Poil R	Ferry
TWENTY-THREE MILE CR	San Poil R	Ferry
TWENTY-FIVE MILE CR	Lake Chelan	Chelan
TWENTY-FIVE MILE CR	San Poil R	Ferry
TWENTY-FIVE MILE CR	Ohop Cr	Pierce
TWIN CR	Chiwawa R	Chelan
TWISP R	Methow R	Okanogan
TYE R	Sf Skykomish R	King

U

STREAM	TRIBUTARY TO	COUNTY
UDEN CR	Cowlitz R	Lewis
UMBRELLA CR	Ozette R	Clallam
UMTANUM CR	Yakima R	Kittitas
UNION CR	American R	Yakima
UNION CR	Palouse R	Whitman
UNION R	Hood Canal	Kitsap/Mason
UNION FLAT CR	Palouse R	Whitman
UPPER CASCAD E CR	White R	Pierce

V

STREAM	TRIBUTARY TO	COUNTY
VALLEY CR	L Washington	King
VALLEY CR	Port Angeles Har.	Clallam
VANCE CR	Sf Skokomish R	Mason
VAN HORN CR	White R	Pierce
VAN ORMAN CR	Chehalis R	Lewis
VASA PARK CR	L Washington	King
VAUGHN CR	Toroda Cr	Okanogan
VESTA CR	North R	Grays Harbor
VOGEL CR	Washougal R	Skamania
VOIGHTS CR	Carbon R	Pierce

W

STREAM	TRIBUTARY TO	COUNTY
WAATCH R	Pacific Ocean	Clallam
WADDLES CR	Black R	Thurston
WADO CR	Colville R	Stevens
WAITS CR	Colville R	Stevens
WAKOTICKEH CR	Hood Canal	Mason
WALKER CR	Meadow Cr	Okanogan
WALLACE R	Skykomish R	Snohomish
WALLA WALLA R	Coumbla R	Walla Walla
WAPATO CR	Commence.Bay	Pierce
WAR CR	Twisp R	Okanogan
WARBLE (WEBB) CR	Ef Lewis R	Clark
WARM SPRINGS	Caribou Cr	Kittitas
WARM SPRGS CANY.	Wenatchee R	Chelan
WASHOUGAL R	Columbia R	Clark/Skam.
WASHOUGAL R, Nf	Washougal R	Skamania
WASSUN CR	Rock Cr	Whitman
WAUGH (CORUS) CR	Columbia R	Stevens
WAWAWAI CR	Snake R	Whitman
WEAVER CR	Salmon Cr	Clark
WEAVER CR	Purdy Cr	Mason
WEBB (WARBLE) CR	Ef Lewis R	Clark
WISER LAKE OUTLET	Nooksack R	Whatcom
WELCH CR	Columbia R	Lincoln
WENAS CR	Yakima R	Yakima
WENATCHEE R	ColumbiaR	Chelan
WEST DOOR CR	Kettle R	Ferry
WEST TWIN CR	White R	King
WHIPPLE CR	Lake R	Clark
WHISKEY CR	Juan de Fuca Str	Clallam
WHISKEY CR	Touchet R	Columbia
WHISTLING CR	Twisp R	Okanogan
WHITAKER CR	Klickitat R	Klickitat
WHITE CR	Ennis Cr	Clallam
WHITE R	LakeWenatchee	Chelan
WHITE R	Stuck&PuyallupR	King/Pierce

STREAM	TRIBUTARY TO	COUNTY
WHITECHUCK R	Sauk R	Snohomish
WHITEHALL CR	Samish Bay	Skagiit
WHITE HORSE CR	Harvey Cr	Stevens
WHITE SALMON R	Columbia R	Klicklt./Skam.
WHITESTONE R	Rat Lake	Okanogan
WHITESTONE LK OUT.	Okanogan R	Okanogan
WILDCAT CR	Cloquallum Cr	Grays Harbor
WILDCAT CR	Tieton R	Yakima
WILDCAT CR	Chico Cr	Kltsap
WILD HORSE CR	Kalama R	Cowlitz
WILD ROSE CR	Dragoon Cr	Spokane
WILDESON(GALE) CR	S Prairie Cr	Pierce
WILLABY CR	Lake Quinault	Grays Harbor
WILLAPA R	Willapa Bay	Paclfic
WILLAPA R, Sf	Willapa R	Pacllic
WILLIAMS CR	Rock Cr	Grays Harbor
WILLIAMS (LION) CR	Swauk Cr	Kittltas
WILLIAMS CR	Nf Nemah R	Paclfic
WILLOW CR	Chiwawa R	Chelan
WILLOW CR	Newaukum R	Lewis
WILLOW CR	Mill Cr	Stevens
WILLOW CR	Palouse R	Whitman
WILSON CR	Port Orchard Bay	Kltsap
WILSON CR	Yakima R	Kittitas
WILSON CR	Fairchild Cr	Pacific
WILSON CR	L White Salmon R	Skamania
WINCHESTER CR	Kalispel Lake	Pend Orellle
WIND R	Columbia R	Skamania
WINSTON CR	Cowlitz R	Lewis
WISON CR	Soleduck R	Clallam
WISHKAH R	Grays Harbor	Grays Harbor
WOLF CR	Wf Methow R	Okanogan
WOLFE CR	Lake Keechelus	Kittitas

STREAM	TRIBUTARY TO	COUNTY
WOL FR ED(McLEOD) CR	Pend Oreille R	Pend Oreill e
WOOD CR	Sultan R	Snohomish
WOODARD CR	Henderson Inlet	Thurston
WOODCOCK CR	Dungeness R	Clallam
WOODLAND CR	Chehalis R	Grays Harbor
WOODLAND(HIMES) CR	South Bay	Thurston
WOODS CR	Skykomish R	Snohomlsh
WOODWARD CR	Columbia R	Skamania
WOOLFORD CR	Kalama R	Cowlitz
WORKMAN CR	Chehalis R	Grays Harbor
WRIGHT CR	Sinclair Inlet	Kitsap
WRIGHT CR	Union R	Kitsap
WRIGHTS CR	Colville R	Stevens
WYNOOCHEE R	Chehalis R	Grays Harbor

X

	TRIBUTARY TO	COUNTY
X CR	Van Winkle Cr	Grays Harbor

Y

	TRIBUTARY TO	COUNTY
YACOLT CR	Lewis R	Clark
YAKIMA R	Columbia R	Benton/Yak/ Kitt
YELLOW JACKET	Cispus R	Lewis
YELLOWHAWK CP	Walla Walla P	Walla Walla
YELM CR	Nisqually R	Thurston
YODER CR	Renshaw Cr	Pend Oreille

Z

	TRIBUTARY TO	COUNTY
ZIEGLER CR	Lake Quinault	Grays Harbor

Index

A

ABERDEEN LAKE 102
ABERNATHY CREEK 68
ADMIRALTY BAY POND 109
AENEAS LAKE 179
AGENCY CREEK 48
AHTANUM CREEK 283
AIRPLANE LAKE 38
ALASKA LAKE 144, 148
ALBACORE TUNA 18
ALDER CREEK 68, 191, 213
ALDER LAKE 156, 160, 202, 259
ALDRIDGE LAKE 171
ALDWELL LAKE 48
ALICE LAKE 117
ALKALI FLAT CREEK 280
ALKALI LAKE 88
ALLEN BANK 312
ALLEN LAKE 293
ALPOWA CREEK 33, 85
ALTA LAKE 179
AMBER LAKE 248
AMERICAN LAKE 202
AMERICAN RIVER 283
AMERICAN SHAD 21
AMES LAKE 117
ANCIENT LAKES 88
ANDERSON ISLAND 311
ANDERSON LAKE 111
ANDREWS CREEK 179
ANGELINE LAKE 119, 121
ANGLE LAKE 117
ANN LAKE 271
ANTILON LAKE 38
APPLE 289
ARKANSAS CREEK 68
ARMSTRONG LAKE 171, 232
ARROWHEAD LAKE 213
ART LAKE 156
ASHES LAKE 222
ASHLAND LAKES 232
ASOTIN CREEK 33
ASPEN LAKE 283
ATHEARNS PONDS 271
ATLANTIC SALMON 20
AUGUSTA LAKE 38
AZURITE LAKE 122

B

BACHELOR CREEK 283
BACHELOR SLOUGH 57
BACON CREEK 213, 271, 299
BADGER LAKE 248
BAGLEY LAKES 271
BAILEY LAKE 248
BAINBRIDGE ISLAND LAKE 140
BAINBRIDGE ISLAND POND 140
BAKER LAKE 144, 271, 275, 277
BAKER POND 85
BAKER RIVER 299
BAKER RIVER UPPER 271
BALD HILLS LAKE 259
BALLINGER LAKE 232

BANDANA LAKE 232
BANKS LAKE 88
BARCLAY LAKE 232
BARNABY CREEK 78
BARNES CREEK 304
BARNES LAKE 260
BARNSLEY LAKE 179
BARRETT CREEK 271
BARRETT LAKE 271, 278
BARTON CREEK BEAVER
    PONDS 283
BASIN LAKE 213, 283
BASS LAKE 117, 222, 260
BATH LAKE 232
BATHTUB LAKE 171
BATTALION LAKE 38
BATTLE GROUND LAKE 57
BAY LAKE 204
BAYLEY LAKE 253
BEAD LAKE 195, 196, 199
BEAR CREEK
    71, 85, 118, 213, 222
BEAR LAKE
    118, 133, 140, 213, 222,
    232, 233, 249, 283
BEAR PARK LAKE 293
BEAR RIVER 191
BEARPAW MT. LAKES 272
BEAVER 65, 137, 158
BEAVER CREEK 102, 204
BEAVER LAKE 48, 117, 213, 214
BEAVER LAKES 118, 179
BEAVER PLANT LAKE 233
BECKLER RIVER 118, 233
BEDA LAKE 88
BEE TREE LAKE. 157
BEECHER LAKE 233
BEEHIVE LAKE 44
BEEHIVE RESERVOIR 39
BENBOW LAKES 204
BENCH LAKE 283, 293
BENGSTON LAKE 118
BENJAMIN LAKE 253
BENNETTSEN LAKE 177
BENNINGTON LAKE (MILL
    CREEK RESERVOIR) 267
BENSON LAKE 171
BERDEEN LAKE 299
BERGLUND LAKE 284
BERTHA MAY LAKES 157
BERTRAND CREEK 272
BETH LAKE 179
BEVERLY 150
BEVIS LAKE 233
BIG BEEF CREEK 140
BIG CREEK 118, 157, 222
BIG FOUR 65
BIG HEART 122
BIG JIM LAKES 39
BIG LAKE 213
BIG RIVER 48
BIG SHEEP CREEK 253
BIG TREE CREEK 57

BIGELOW LAKE 260
BILLY CLAPP LAKE 88
BINGHAM CREEK 171
BIRD CREEK 152
BIRD LAKE 284
BISER POND 171
BITTER LAKE 118
BITTER LAKES 233
BLACK CRAPPIE 11
BLACK CREEK 102
BLACK DIAMOND LAKE 118
BLACK LAKE
    39, 118, 179, 191, 254, 260
BLACK LAKE DITCH CREEK 260
BLACK LAKES 29
BLACK PINE LAKE 179
BLACK RIVER 102, 260
BLACKMANS LAKE 233
BLACKSLOUGH POND 171
BLACKSMITH LAKE 171
BLACKWOOD LAKE 304
BLAKE 326
BLAKE ISLAND 317
BLAKES PONDS 48
BLANCA LAKE 233
BLANCHARD CREEK 249
BLANKENSHIP 289
BLANKENSHIP LAKES 284
BLAZER LAKE 125
BLOCKHOUSE CREEK 152
BLOODGOOD CREEK 153
BLUE 65
BLUE CATFISH 12
BLUE LAKE
    68, 89, 157, 222, 272, 284
BLUE LAKE (SINLAHEKIN) 179
BLUE LAKE(WANNACUT) 179
BLUE LAKES 222, 233
BLUE SHARKS 15
BLUFF LAKE 157, 222
BLUM LAKES 272
BLYTHE 89
BOARDMAN LAKE 233
BOBBY LAKE 92
BOGACHIEL 326
BOGACHIEL LAKE 304
BOGACHIEL RIVER
    48, 304, 332
BONAPARTE LAKE 179, 184
BONNER LAKE 180
BONNEY LAKE 204
BONNIE LAKE 249
BOREN LAKE 118
BORST LAKE 157
BOSWORTH LAKE 233
BOULDER CREEK
    39, 78, 180, 233, 301, 304
BOULDER LAKE 213, 304
BOUNDARY LAKE 195
BOUNDARY RESERVOIR 196
BOURGEA LAKE 78
BOWMAN CREEK 153
BOWMAN LAKE 204

BOX CANYON LAKE 144
BOX CANYON RESERVOIR 196
BOX LAKE 238
BOYLE 118
BOYLE LAKE 125
BRADER LAKE 222
BRADLEY POND 204
BREAKER LAKE 191
BREWSTER LAKE 118
BRIDGE CREEK 39, 301
BRIDGES LAKE 118
BROOK LAKE (AKA STRATFORD) 89
BROOK TROUT 8
BROOKS SLOUGH 265
BROWN TROUT 8
BROWN'S LAKE 112, 254
BRYANT LAKE 233
BUCK CREEK 233
BUCK CREEK BEAVER PONDS 157
BUCK LAKE 140, 171, 177, 180
BUCKING HORSE CREEK 304
BUCKSKIN LAKE 180
BUESCH LAKE 159
BUFFALO LAKE 180
BULL TROUT 9
BULLAR LAKE 213
BULLFROG POND 144
BULLHEAD CATFISH 12
BUMPING LAKE 284
BUMPING RIVER 284
BUNCH LAKE 304
BURBANK SLOUGH. 267
BURBOT 12
BURIEN LAKE 119
BURKE LAKE 89
BURLEY CREEK 141
BURNT BRIDGE CREEK 57
BURNT FORK CREEK 64
BUSH POINT 313
BUTTE CREEK 64
BUTTE LAKES 29
BUTTER CREEK 157
BUZZARD LAKE 180
BYRON PONDS 284

C

CABEZON 16
CABIN CREEK 144
CADY LAKE 78, 171, 177
CAIN LAKE 272
CALAWAH RIVER 49, 305, 332
CALDWELL LAKE 196
CALICHE LAKES 89
CALIFORNIA CREEK 272
CALLIGAN CREEK 119
CALLIGAN LAKE 119
CAMP CREEK BEAVER PONDS 272
CAMP GRANDE 109
CAMP LAKE 83
CAMP POND 171
CAMPBELL LAKE 29, 57, 180, 182, 213, 214
CANAAN LAKE 39
CANAL 89
CANARY ROCKFISH 15
CANNERY LAKE 213
CANNON RIVER 333
CANVASBACK LAKE 57
CANYON CREEK 57, 62, 157, 191, 234, 272, 326
CANYON LAKE 234, 272
CAP SANTE MARINA 217
CAPITOL LAKE 332

CARBON RIVER 204, 293
CAREYS LAKE 213
CARIBOU CREEK 144
CARL LAKE 196
CARLISLE LAKE 157
CARLISLE LAKES 102
CARLTON CREEK. 157
CARNEY LAKE 204
CAROLE LAKE 128
CAROLINE LAKE 119
CAROLINE LAKES 39
CARP LAKE 154
CARSON LAKE 171
CARTER LAKE 204
CARTY LAKE 57
CASCADE 89
CASCADE LAKE 210
CASCADE RIVER 213, 214, 300, 326
CASES POND 191
CASEY POND 267
CASKEY LAKE 213
CASSIDY LAKE 234
CASTLE CREEK 68
CASTLE LAKE 68, 89
CASTOR LAKE 180
CAT CREEK 305
CAVANAUGH LAKE 214, 217
CAVANAUGH LAKE (LITTLE) 234
CAVELERO'S BEACH 109
CEDAR CREEK 58, 102
CEDAR LAKE 254, 273, 305
CEDAR LAKES 289
CEDAR PONDS 234
CEDAR RIVER 119, 191
CEHALIS RIVER 332
CEPTIONPASS 313
CHAIN LAKE 196, 234
CHAMBERLAIN LAKE 153
CHAMBERS CREEK 204
CHAMBERS LAKE 157, 204, 260
CHAMOKANE CREEK 254
CHANNEL CATFISH 12
CHAPLAIN LAKE 234
CHAPLAIN POND 234
CHAPMAN LAKE 249
CHARLENE LAKE 83
CHARLIE FORK CREEK 34
CHARLIE LAKES 119
CHEHALIS RIVER 102, 157
CHEHALIS RIVER POTHOLES, PONDS 103
CHELAN LAKE 39, 301
CHELATCHIE CREEK 58
CHENOIS CREEK 103
CHENUIS LAKE 294
CHERRY CREEK 119
CHERRY LAKE 119
CHESTER MORSE 119
CHETWOOD LAKE 119, 120
CHETWOOT 122
CHEWELAH CREEK 254
CHEWUCH RIVER (AKA CHEWACK) 180
CHIKAMIN LAKE 144
CHILIWIST CREEK 181
CHILLIWACK RIVER 299
CHIMICUM CREEK 112
CHINOOK CREEK 294
CHINOOK SALMON 19
CHITWOOD LAKE 235
CHIWAUKUM CREEK 39
CHIWAUKUM LAKE 40
CHIWAWA RIVER 40
CHOPAKA LAKE 181
CHORAL LAKE 40
CHUKAR LAKE 89

CHUM SALMON 20
CICERO POND 235
CISPUS RIVER 157
CISPUS River 61
CLALLAM RIVER 49
CLAM LAKE 191
CLARA LAKE. 171
CLARICE LAKE 126
CLARK POND 83
CLARKS CREEK 204
CLE ELUM LAKE 144
CLE ELUM RIVER 144
CLEAR 222
CLEAR CREEK 235, 285
CLEAR CREEK, 227
CLEAR FORK 157
CLEAR LAKE 40, 204, 213, 214, 223, 249, 260, 261, 285
CLEARWATER 326
CLEARWATER CREEK 227, 273
CLEARWATER RIVER 112, 205, 332
CLEMENTINE LAKE 89
CLEVELAND LAKE 119
CLIFF 89
CLIFF LAKE 214
CLINE SPIT 49
CLOQUALLUM CREEK 103
COAL CREEK 68, 119, 158
COAL CREEK SLOUGHS 68
COAL LAKE 235
COCHRAN LAKE 235
COFFEE POT LAKE 167, 168
COFFIN LAKE 254
COHO SALMON 19
COLCHUCK LAKE 40
COLDWATER CREEK 68
COLDWATER LAKE 68
COLE CREEK 145
COLEMAN CREEK 145
COLLINS LAKE 171
COLUMBIA 326
COLUMBIA PARK FAMILY FISHING POND 36
COLUMBIA RIVER 36, 40, 58, 75, 89, 153, 191, 223, 332
COLUMBIA RIVER BARS 69, 265
COLVILLE RIVER 254
COMCOMLY LAKE 223
COMMENCEMENT BAY 312
COMPANY CREEK 40
CONCONULLY LAKE 183
CONCONULLY LAKE, UPPER, (AKA SALMON LAKE) 182
CONCONULLY RESERVOIR 187
CONEY LAKE 235
CONGER PONDS 196
CONNER LAKE 235
CONNERS LAKE 182
CONRAD LAKES 285
CONSTANCE LAKE 305
COOK CREEK 103
COOKE CREEK 145
COOKS LAKE 196
COON LAKE 302
COOPER LAKE 145
COOPERS POTHOLE 260
COPALIS RIVER 103
COPPEI CREEK 267
COPPER 122
COPPER CREEK 58, 235
COPPER LAKE 182, 273, 299
CORA LAKE 158
CORNET BAY STATE PARK 110
CORRAL 89

CORRAL LAKE 90
CORTRIGHT CREEK 159
COTTAGE LAKE 119
COTTONWOOD CREEK
    34, 254, 280
COTTONWOOD LAKE 148
COTTONWOOD LAKES 145
COUGAR CREEK 69
COUGAR LAKE 119, 182
COUGAR LAKES 285
COULTER CREEK 141, 171
COUNCIL LAKE 223
COUPEVILLE WATERFRONT 110
COURTHOUSE POND 191
COVINGSTON CREEK 120
COW CREEK 29
COW LAKE 29
COWBELL LAKE 235
COWEEMAN LAKE 69
COWEEMAN RIVER 69
COWICHE CREEK 285
COWLITZ RIVER
    61, 69, 158, 326, 332
CRAB CREEK 29, 90
CRABAPPLE LAKE 235
CRAG LAKES 285
CRAMER LAKE 285
CRANBERRY LAKE 110, 191
CRANBERRY LAKE (LITTLE) 214
CRANE LAKE 30
CRATER LAKE 90, 120, 171, 182
CRATER SLOUGH 90
CRAWFISH LAKE 182
CRAWFORD LAKE 120
CREEK LAKE 43, 160
CRESCENT BAY LAKE 90
CRESCENT LAKE
    49, 196, 198, 205, 235
CROCKER LAKE 112
CROOKED CREEK 64, 85
CROSSE LAKE 307
CROW CREEK 287
CROW CREEK LAKE 287
CRUMBACHER LAKE 183
CRYSTAL LAKE 89, 239
CRYSTAL LAKES 294
CUB CREEK 183
CUB LAKE 214
CULTUS CREEK 223
CULTUS LAKE 223
CUMMINGS CREEK 64
CUP 89
CURL 65
CURLEW LAKE 78, 338
CURLEW POND 268
CURLEY CREEK 141
CUSHMAN LAKE 171
CUTTHROAT LAKE, 183
CUTTHROAT LAKES 235
CUTTHROAT TROUT 7
CYCLONE LAKE 214, 219

D

DAGGER LAKE 234, 300
DAKOTA CREEK 273
DALLAS AND PARTRIDGE
    BANKS 314
DALLES LAKES 205
DALTON LAKE 83
DAM POND 64
DAMFINO LAKES 272
DAMON LAKE 103
DAN CREEK 235
DANCING 289

DAVIS LAKE 80, 159, 183, 197
DAVIS SLOUGH 214
DAY CREEK 214
DAY LAKE 214
DAYTON JUVENILE POND 64
DE ROUX CREEKS 150
DEAD LAKE 58
DEADMAN CREEK 80, 85
DEADMAN LAKE 30
DEADWOOD LAKES 294
DECEPTION CREEK 159
DECKER CREEK 103, 172
DECOURSEY POND 205
DEE LAKE 223
DEEP CREEK 120
DEEP CREEK-WEST TWIN
    RIVERS 49
DEEP LAKE
    90, 120, 121, 145, 223, 260
DEEP RIVER 265
DEER 65, 222
DEER CREEK 70
DEER LAKE
    110, 133, 168, 172, 191, 223, 255
DEER LAKES 145, 305
DELAMETER 68
DELAZINE CREEK 103
DENMARK POND 145
DENNY CREEK 120
DERRY LAKE 120
DESCHUTES RIVER 261
DESIRE LAKE 121
DEVEREAUX LAKE 172
DEVILS LAKE 214, 235, 236
DEVIL'S LAKE 112
DEVILS WASHBASIN LAKE 285
DEWATTO CREEK 332
DEWATTO RIVER 173
DEWEY LAKES 283, 294
DIABLO LAKE 273, 300
DIAMOND LAKE 145, 197, 235
DIBBLE LAKE 183
DICKEY RIVER 49
DIOBSUD LAKES 273
DISCOVERY LAKES 103
DOG LAKE 285
DOLLAR LAKES 235
DOLLOFF LAKE 121
DOLLY VARDEN 9
DOMKE LAKE 40
DONALD LAKE 40, 41
DOREEN LAKE 273
DOROTHY LAKE 121, 128, 133
DOSEWALLIPS RIVER
    112, 305, 332
DOT 89
DOUBLE BLUFF 313
DOUGLAS CREEK 76
DOUGLAS LAKE 255
DOWNEY LAKE 236
DOWNS LAKE 249
DRANO LAKE 332
DREAM LAKE 121, 126
DRUNKEN CHARLIE LAKE 121
DRY CREEK 268
DRY FALLS LAKE 90
DRYBED LAKES 173
DUCK 160
DUCK LAKE 104, 183, 184
DUCKABUSH RIVER
    113, 305, 332
DUFFY CREEK 236
DUFFY LAKE 183
DUFFY LAKES 236
DUGUALLA BAY LAKE 110
DUMBBELL LAKE 285
DUMBBELL LAKE. 159

DUMBELL 289
DUNGENESS RIVER
    49, 326, 332
DUNGENESS SPIT 49, 314
DUSTY LAKE 91
DUWAMISH HEAD-ELLIOTT BAY
    312
DUWAMISH RIVER 121, 332

E

EAGLE LAKES 306
EAST CANYON CREEK 224
EAST FORK LEWIS 326
EAST LAKE 205
EAST SOUND 314
EASTON LAKE 145
EASTON PONDS 145
EATON CREEK 261
EATONVILLE POND 205, 261
EBEY LAKE 236
ECHO LAKE 121, 205, 236
EDDS LAKE 121
EDIZ HOOK 314
EDMONDS 317
EDMONDS-POINT WELLS 313
EDNA LAKE 41
EDUCKET CREEK 49
EGG LAKE 210
EIGHT MILE CREEK 183
EIGHT MILE LAKE 40, 41
EILEEN LAKE 41
ELAIDE LAKE 293, 295
ELBOW LAKE
    80, 216, 255, 261, 273
ELEANOR LAKE 294
ELK 222, 225
ELK CREEK 70, 159
ELK CREEKS 72
ELK LAKE 224, 229, 306
ELK LAKES 173
ELK RIVER 104
ELL LAKE 183
ELLEN LAKE 80
ELOCHOMAN RIVER 265
ELOIKA LAKE 198, 249
ELSEY LAKE 41
ELTON LAKE NORTH 285
ELWHA RIVER 49, 306, 326
ELY LAKE 307
EMERALD LAKE 236
EMERALD LAKES 80
EMERALD PARK CREEK 40
EMMA LAKE 83
EMPIRE LAKES 80
ENCHANTMENT LAKES 41
ENJAR LAKE 214
ENTIAT RIVER 41
EPHRATA LAKE 91
EPHRATA PARK POND 91
ERICKSON LAKE 173
ERIE LAKE 213, 214
ETHEL LAKE 41, 295
EUNICE LAKE 222, 224
EVAN 233
EVAN LAKE 233, 236
EVANS, GOLF COURSE,
    SILCOTT PONDS 34
EVERETT LAKE 214
EVERGREEN RESERVOIR 338
EVERGREEN RESERVOIR 91

F

FAILOR LAKE 104
FAIRVIEW LAKE 141

FALCON LAKES 91
FALL CREEK 191
FALLS CREEK 224
FALLS LAKE 214, 216
FAN LAKE 197
FARGHER POND 58
FAWN LAKE 70, 183, 229
FAWN LAKES 225
FAZON LAKE 273
FENNER LAKE 285
FENWICK LAKE 121
FERGUSON PONDS 273
FERRY LAKE 80
FIDALGO 217
FIDALGO BAY 217
FIFTEEN LAKE 261
FIFTH PLAIN CREEK 58
FINNEL LAKE 30
FINNEY CREEK 214
FIO RITO LAKES NORTH AND
    SOUTH 145
FISH CREEK 41
FISH HOOK POND 268
FISH LAKE
    41, 46, 80, 121, 146, 179,
    183, 187, 224, 249, 285
FISHTRAP CREEK 273
FISHTRAP LAKE 168
FIVE MILE LAKE 121
FLAPJACK LAKES 306
FLAT LAKE 91
FLATIRON LAKE 286
FLORA LAKE 41, 141
FLORENCE LAKE 205
FLOWING LAKE 236
FLUME CREEK PONDS 215
FLY CREEK 58
FLY LAKE 215
FONTAL LAKE 236
FORBES LAKE 173
FORDE LAKE 183
FOREST 225
FOREST LAKE 205, 224
FORLORN LAKES 224
FORT CANBY LAKE 192
FORTSON MILL POND 236
FOSS LAKES (W. FK) 121
FOSS RIVER 122
FOSTER CREEK 76
FOUNDATION CREEK 283
FOUNTAIN LAKE 273
FOURTH OF JULY LAKE 30
FOX ISLAND 311
FRAGRANCE LAKE 273
FRANKLIN D. ROOSEVELT LAKE
    LOWER 168, 255
FRANZ LAKE 224
FRATER LAKE 197
FREEWAY LAKE 285
FRENCH CABIN CREEK 146
FRENCH CREEK 184, 236
FRENCH LAKE 226
FRESHWATER LAKE 192
FRIDAY CREEK 215
FROG LAKE 224
FROSTY MEADOW CREEK 80
FRY COVE 261
FRY LAKE 184
FRYING PAN 289
FRYING PAN LAKE 159
FUDGE POINT STATE PARK 173
FULTON CREEK BEAVER PONDS
    113

G

G CREEK 304
GALENA CHAIN LAKES 274
GARRISON CREEK 268

GEDNEY ISLAND 317
GEE CREEK 58
GEE POINT LAKE 215
GEHRKE LAKE 261
GELES LAKE 304
GEM LAKE 135
GENEVA LAKE 122
GEORGE LAKE 94, 294
GEORGE POND 205
GERMANY CREEK 70
GHOST LAKE 224, 229
GIBBS LAKE 113
GIFFIN LAKE 286, 287
GIG HARBOR 205
GILCHRIST POND 280
GILES LAKE 192
GILLETTE LAKE 224
GISSBERG PONDS 237
GLACIER CREEK. 159
GLACIER LAKE 136, 146, 159
GLADYS LAKE 306
GLASSES LAKE 41
GLOYD SEEPS CREEK 91
GLUD PONDS 141
GOAT CREEK 159
GOAT LAKE 237, 274
GOAT LAKE. 159
GOAT RANCH LAKE 173
GOBAR 72
GOBAR CREEK 70
GOBLIN CREEK 237
GODKIN CREEK 306
GOLD CREEK 146, 184
GOLD LAKE 146
GOLD LAKES 184
GOLDEN LAKES 294
GOLDENEYE LAKE 91
GOLDSBOROUGH CREEK 173
GOODELL CREEK 274
GOODMAN CREEK 113
GOODWIN LAKE 237, 242
GOOSE CREEK 197
GOOSE LAKE
    160, 184, 192, 224
GOOSE LAKES 91
GORGE LAKE 274, 277, 300
GOSS LAKE 110
GRAHAM-MORRIS POND 286
GRAND CREEK 306
GRAND LAKE (ETTA) 306
GRANDE RONDE RIVER 34
GRANDY LAKE 215
GRANGER LAKE 286
GRANITE CREEK 122, 197, 274
GRANITE LAKES 122, 215
GRANT LAKE 225
GRASS LAKE 173, 261
GRASS PICKEREL 13
GRAVEL PIT PONDS 110
GRAVELLY LAKE 205
GRAVES CREEK 306
GRAY WOLF RIVER 306
GRAYLING 9
GRAYS HARBOR 104
Grays Harbor 108
GRAYS RIVER 266
GRAYWOLF RIVER 50
GREEN 326
GREEN (DUWAMISH) RIVER 122
GREEN LAKE
    30, 58, 122, 184, 274, 286, 295,
    299, 338
GREEN PARK LAKES 295
GREEN RIVER 70, 332
GREENLEAF LAKE 225
GREENWATER LAKES 123, 205
GREENWATER RIVER 123, 209
GREIDER LAKES 237

GRIFFIN FORK 65
GRIMES LAKE 76
GRIMM CREEK 160
GRISDALE POND 104
GROTTO LAKE 123
GUEMES CHANNEL 314
GULCH LAKES 237

H

HALCYON LAKE 237
HALFMOON 30
HALFMOON LAKE 179, 197
HALIBUT 13
HALL LAKE 237
HALLER LAKE 123
HALLIN LAKE 30
HAMILTON CREEK 225
HAMMA HAMMA RIVER 173, 332
HAMPTON LAKES 91
HANAFORD LAKE 225
HANCOCK LAKE 123, 128
HANFORD LAKE 229
HANKS LAKE 173
HANNAFORD CREEK 160
HANNAN LAKE 236, 237, 238
HANSEN CREEK 123
HANSON LAKE 237
HANSON'S PONDS 146
HAPPY LAKE 306
HART LAKE 307
HARTS LAKE 205, 208
HARVEY CREEK 197
HAT ISLAND 313
HATCH LAKE 256
HATCHERY CREEK 71, 91
HATCHERY LAKE 173
HAVEN LAKE 173, 176, 177
HAWK CREEK 168
HAWKINS LAKE 215, 218
HAYES RIVER 306
HAYS CREEK 30
HEADGATE POND 34
HEART 89
HEART LAKE 92, 215
HEART LAKES 124
HEATHER LAKE 41
HEATHER LAKE. 237
HELENA LAKE. 237
HELL LAKE 286
HEMLOCK LAKE 225, 229
HEMPLE LAKE 237
HERMAN LAKE 30
HERRON LAKE 205
HERRON LAKES 92
HESS LAKE 184
HESTER LAKE 124
HEWITT LAKE 261
HICKS LAKE 261
HIDDEN LAKE 295, 300
HIDDEN LAKES 225
HILL LAKE 286
HILLE LAKE 205
HILT LAKE. 215
HOFFSTADT CREEK 71
HOG CANYON LAKE 249
HOH LAKE 91, 307
HOH RIVER 113, 307, 326, 332
HOKO RIVER 50
HOLM LAKE 124
HOLMES LAKE 110
HOLOMAN LAKE 124
HOPE ISLAND 313
HOPE LAKE 43
HOQUIAM RIVER 104, 332
HORSE THIEF LAKE 153

HORSESHOE LAKE
71, 113, 141, 160, 184, 198, 206, 225, 250
HORSESHOE POND 286
HORSESHOE SLOUGH 124
HOURGLASS LAKE 92
HOWARD LAKE 237
HOWE CREEK 113
HOWELL LAKE 171
HOZOMEEN LAKE 274
HUCKLEBERRY CREEK 295
HUDSON CREEK 146
HUGHES LAKE 237
HUGO LAKE 160
HULL LAKE 124
HUMMEL LAKE 210
HUMPTULIPS RIVER 105
HUNTER BAY 210
HUNTERS CREEK 256
HUTCHINSON 30
HUTCHINSON CREEK 274
HYAS LAKE 146

I

I-82 PONDS 286
ICEHOUSE LAKE 226
ICICLE CREEK 43
ILLINOIS CREEK 134
INDEPENDENCE LAKE 235, 237
INDIAN 150
INDIAN CREEK 168
INDIAN DAN LAKE 184
INDIAN HEAVEN LAKES 226
IONE MILL POND 198
IRON CREEK 160
ISABEL LAKE 237
ISABELLA LAKE 129, 173
ISLAND LAKE
124, 141, 174, 192
ISSAQUAH CREEK 124
ITSAMI LEDGE 317
ITSWOOT LAKE 214

J

JACKPOT LAKE. 160
JAMES LAKE 295
JAMESON LAKE 77
JANICKE SLOUGH 124
JANUS LAKE 237
JASON LAKES 40
JAY LAKE 238
JEFFERSON LAKES 173
JENKINS CREEK 124
JERRY LAKE 274
JESS LAKE 160
JEWITT CREEK 153
JIGGS LAKE 174
JIM CREEK 65
JOAN LAKE 238
JOE CREEK 105
JOE LAKE 146
JOHN WAYNE MARINA 50
JOHNS RIVER 105
JOHN'S RIVER 332
JOHNSON CREEK 160, 274
JOHNSON POINT 311
JONES LAKE 124
JORDAN CREEK 214, 216
JORDAN LAKES 216
JORGENSON LAKE 274
JOSEPH CREEK 34
JOSEPHINE LAKE 206
JOSEPHINE LAKES 216
JOY LAKE 124
JUANITA LAKE 125

JUDSON LAKE 274
JUDY LAKE 128
JUG LAKE 160, 289
JULIA LAKE 238
JUMPOFF JOE LAKE 256
JUNE LAKE 92
JUNGLE 150
JUPITER LAKES 114

K

KACHESS LAKE 146
KACHESS RIVER 147
KAHLOTUS LAKE 83
KALALOCH CREEK 114
KALAMA 326
KALAMA RIVER 71, 332
KAPOWSIN LAKE 206
KATHLEEN LAKE 125
KEECHELUS LAKE 147
KELCEMA LAKE 238
KELLOGG LAKE 238
KELP GREENLING 16
KENDALL LAKE 274
KENDALL PEAK LAKES 147
KENNEDY CREEK 261
KENWORTHY LAKE 295
KEOUGH LAKES 256
KERRS LAKE 125
KETCHUM LAKE 238
KETTLE RIVER 80, 256
KIDNEY LAKE 179, 226
KILLARNEY LAKE 125
KILLEBREW LAKE 210
KIMBALL CREEK 119
KING LAKE 43, 238
KINGS LAKE 125, 198
KI LAKE 238
KLAUS 118
KLAUS LAKE 125
KLEMENTS MILL POND 238
KLICKITAT 326
KLICKITAT RIVER 153
KLICKITAT RIVER (Upper) 286
KLINELINE POND 58, 62
KLONAQUA LAKES 43
KLONES LAKES 105
KNOWLTON CREEK 72
KNUPPENBURG LAKE 160
KOENEMAN LAKE 141
KOKANEE LAKE 174
KOKANEE LAKE (LOWER
CUSHMAN) 172
KOKANEE SALMON 8
KOTSUCK CREEK 295
KRAMER PONDS 286
KREGER'S LAKE 206
KRESS LAKE 72
KROOZE LAKE 238
KULLA KULLA LAKE 125
KUTSKO POINT 313
KWADDIS LAKE 226

L

LA FLEUR LAKE 80
LA RUSH LAKE 216
LACAMAS CREEK 58, 160
LACAMAS LAKE 59
LACONNER 217
LAKE ALDWELL 50
LAKE BALLINGER 237
LAKE CRESCENT 305
LAKE GENEVA 125
LAKE GOODWIN 235
LAKE KILLARNEY 122
LAKE MILLS 50
LAKE OF THE WOODS 198

LAKE QUINAULT 107
LAKE RIVER 60
LAKE ROOSEVELT 256, 258
LAKE SAMMAMISH 332
LAKE TAPPS 338
LAKE TROUT 9
LAKE WASHINGTON 332
LAKE WENATCHEE 46
LAKEVIEW PEAK LAKE 72
LANCASTER LAKE 60
LANGENDORFER LAKE 125
LANGLOIS LAKE 125
LAPUSH 50
LARGEMOUTH BASS 10
LARSEN LAKE 125
LARSON LAKES 226
LAURA 147
LAVA LAKES 226
LAVENDER LAKE 147
LAWRENCE LAKE 261
LEAD KING LAKES 198
LEADBETTER LAKE 198
LEADER LAKE 184
LEECH LAKE 286
LELAND CREEK 114
LELAND LAKE 114
LEMAH LAKE 147
LEMEI 222
LEMEI LAKE 226
LEMNA LAKE 92
LENA CREEK 174
LENA LAKES 114, 309
LENICE LAKE 90, 92
LENNOX CREEK 125, 134
LENORE LAKE 92
LEO LAKE 197, 198
LEOTA LAKE 126
LEWIS 326
LEWIS CREEK 65
LEWIS RIVER 73, 332
LEWIS RIVER EAST FORK 60
LEWIS RIVER MAIN STEM 60
LEWIS RIVER NORTH FORK
60, 226
LIBERTY LAKE 250
LICHTENWASSER LAKE 43
LILLIAN LAKE 146
LILLIAN LAKES 147
LILLIAN RIVER 307
LILLIWAUP CREEK 174
LILLIWAUP SWAMP 174
LILLIWAUP/HOODSPORT 313
LILLY LAKE 206
LILY LAKE
43, 158, 160, 216, 227, 286
LIME LAKE 238
LIMERICK LAKE 174
LINCOLN CREEK 160
LIND COULEE WASTEWAY 93
LINDA LAKE 30
LING COD 16
LITSCHKE LAKE 192
LITTLE ASHES LAKE 222
LITTLE CANYON CREEK 274
LITTLE CAVANAUGH LAKE 238
LITTLE CHAMBERS LAKE 260
LITTLE CHILLIWACK RIVER 299
LITTLE COUGAR 120, 285
LITTLE GEE 215
LITTLE HANK 173
LITTLE HART LAKE 205
LITTLE HATCH LAKE 256
LITTLE HEART 122, 124
LITTLE HESTER 124
LITTLE KACHESS 147
LITTLE KALAMA 72

LITTLE KLICKITAT 154
LITTLE LOST LAKE 198
LITTLE MAIN LAKES 226
LITTLE MASHEL 206
LITTLE MASON 125, 126
LITTLE MYRTLE LAKE 2800 feet
  S. of Big Myrtle. Lake 128
LITTLE NACHES RIVER 286
LITTLE NISQUALLY RIVER 160
LITTLE PEND OREILLE LAKES
  256, 257
LITTLE PEND OREILLE RIVER
  256
LITTLE PIERRE LAKE 258
LITTLE RIVER 307
LITTLE SNOW LAKE 159, 164
LITTLE SPOKANE RIVER
  198, 250
LITTLE SUNDAY 136
LITTLE TWIN LAKE 184
LITTLE WENATCHEE RIVER
  43, 46
LITTLE WHITE SALMON (DRANO
  LAKE) 326
LITTLE WIND RIVER 227
LIZARD LAKE 50, 216
LOCH KATRINE 136
LOCKE LAKE 154
LODGE LAKE 126
LOIS LAKE 261
LOMA LAKE 238
LONE LAKE 110
LONE TREE LAKE 160
LONESOME LAKE 209
LONG ALEC CREEK 80
LONG JOHN 289
LONG JOHN LAKE 287
LONG LAKE
  80, 93, 99, 141, 161, 165,
  183, 250, 256, 261
LONGS POND 261
LOOMIS LAKE 192
LOON LAKE 256
LOOP LAKE 126
LOST CREEK 184, 198
LOST HAT LAKE 161
LOST LAKE
  44, 61, 114, 147, 158, 162, 174, 184,
  192, 198, 227, 239, 274, 287, 295
LOST LAKE. 239
LOST RIVER 307
LOUIS LAKE 184
LOUISE LAKE 206, 216, 295
LOWER GOOSE 91
LOWER GRANITE DAM
  RESERVOIR 280
LOWER GRANITE LAKE 137
LOWER GREEN 184
LOWER LENA 309
LOWER PTARMIGAN 129
LOWER RIVORD 238
LOWER WILDCAT 139
LUCERNE LAKE 198
LUCERNE—PIPE LAKES 126
LUDLOW CREEK 114
LUDLOW LAKE 114
LUDVICK LAKE 141
LUGENBEAL SPRINGS CREEK
  30
LUNKER LAKES 128
LYLE LAKE 30
LYMAN LAKE 184
LYNCH LAKE 126
LYNX CREEK 80
LYRE RIVER 50

M_____

MAD RIVER 43
MAGGIE LAKE 174
MAJOR CREEK 154
MAL LAKE 287
MALACHITE 122
MALACHITE LAKE 126
MALLARD LAKE 93
MALONEY LAKES 126
MANASTASH LAKE 147
MARCH POINT 217
MARCO POLO LAKE 94
MARGARET AND MARY LAKES
  307
MARGARET LAKE 126, 238
MARIE LAKE 126
MARJORIE LAKE 295
MARMES POND 84
MARMOT LAKE 126, 307
MARPLE LAKE. 184
MARSH LAKE 295
MARSHALL LAKE 198
MARTEN LAKE 126, 275
MARTHA LAKE 94
MARTHA LAKE (ALDERWOOD
  MANOR) 239
MARTHA LAKE (WARM BEACH).
  239
MARTHA LAKE(LITTLE) 239
MARTIN CREEK 126
MARTIN LAKE 216
MARYHILL POND 154
MASHEL RIVER 206
MASON LAKE
  125, 126, 174, 177
MATTOON LAKE 148
MAUD LAKE 127
MAY CREEK 239
MAYFIELD LAKE 161, 338
MCALESTER LAKE 302
MCALLISTER CREEK 202, 261
MCBRIDE LAKE 73
MCCABE POND 148
MCCOY LAKE 257
MCDANIEL LAKE 287
MCDONALD LAKE 127
MCDOWELL LAKE 257
MCGINNIS LAKE 185
MCLANE'S CREEK 262
MCLEOD LAKE 127
MCMANNAMAN LAKE 30
MCMURRAY LAKE 216, 219
MCNARY POOL 268
MEADOW 94
MEADOW CREEK 44, 227
MEADOW LAKE
  44, 198, 239, 240
MEADOWBROOK SLOUGH 127
MEDICAL LAKE 250
MELAKWA LAKE 120
MELAKWA LAKES 127
MELBOURNE LAKE 174
MENZEL LAKES 240
MERCER CREEK 148
MERIDIAN LAKE 127
MERON CREEK 305
MERRILL LAKE 73
MERRITT LAKE 44
MERRY 92
MERRY LAKE 90, 94
MERWIN RESERVOIR 61, 338
MESA LAKE 84
META LAKE 227
METAN LAKE 240
METCALF LAKE 128
METCALF SLOUGH 127

METHOW RIVER 185
MICHAEL LAKE 148
MILK CREEK 148, 287
MILK CREEK POND 148
MILK LAKE 309
MILK LAKE. 148
MILL CREEK
  50, 73, 154, 192, 198, 257, 268
MILL CREEK POND 105
MILLER LAKE 280
MILLER MARSH 174
MILLER RIVER 128
MILLS LAKE 307
MINERAL CREEK 147, 162
MINERAL LAKE 162
MINK LAKE 307
MINKLER LAKE 216
MINTER CREEK 311
MIRROR 147
MIRROR LAKE
  44, 94, 145, 148, 275
MISERY POINT 313, 317
MISQUITO PASS 314
MISSION BAR 313
MISSION CREEK 44
MISSION LAKE 141
MISSION POND 141
MITCHELL POND 37
MOCCASIN LAKE 185
MOCLIPS RIVER 105
MOLSON LAKE 185
MONEYSMITH LAKE 128
MONOGRAM LAKE 300
MONOHAN 68
MONTE CRISTO LAKE 240
MOOLOCK LAKE 128
MOOSE LAKE 307
MORGAN 30
MORGAN LAKE 287
MORGE LAKES 206
MORSE CREEK 51
MORTON LAKE 128
MOSELY LAKES 227
MOSES LAKE 94
MOSQUITO CREEK 114
MOSQUITO LAKE 275
MOSQUITO LAKES. 227
MOSS LAKE 128, 162
MOUND POND 37
MOUNT ADAMS POND 154
MOUNTAIN LAKE 210
MOUSE LAKE 227
MOWICH LAKE 295
MOWICH RIVER 296
MPANY CREEK 302
MPTULIPS RIVER 332
MUCK CREEK 206
MUD CREEK 268
MUD LAKE
  61, 81, 128, 162, 206, 216,
  275, 287
MUDDY RIVER 227
MUDGETT LAKE 257
MUNN LAKE 262, 263
MURPHY LAKES 128
MUSKEGON LAKE 198
MYRON LAKE 287
MYRTLE LAKE 44, 128
MYSTIC LAKE 199, 296

N_____

NACHES RIVER 287
NADEAU 128
NAHWATZEL LAKE 174
NANEUM CREEK 148
NANEUM POND 148

NASELLE RIVER 192, 332
NASON CREEK 44
NATIONAL MILL POND 206
NEAH BAY 51, 314
NEMAH RIVER 192
NEORI LAKE 216
NEWAUKUM CREEK 128
NEWAUKUM LAKE 162
NEWAUKUM LAKES 162
NEWAUKUM RIVER 162
NEWMAN LAKE 250, 338
NILE CREEK. 288
NILE LAKE 199
NISQUALLY RIVER 296, 333
NISQUALLY LAKE 206
NISQUALLY RIVER 162
NISQUALLY RIVER 206
NO NAME CREEK 234
NO NAME LAKE 199, 200
NOISY CREEK 275
NOOKACHAMPS CREEK 216
NOOKSACK RIVER
   275, 299, 326, 333
NOOKSACK RIVER MIDDLE
   FORK 275
NOOKSACK RIVER NORTH
   FORK 275
NOOKSACK RIVER SOUTH
   FORK 216, 275
NORDRUM BASIN LAKES 128
NORTH BAY 175
NORTH ELTON POND 288
NORTH FORK LEWIS 326
NORTH FORK SAUK 241
NORTH FORK SKYKOMISH 326
NORTH FORK STILLAGUAMISH
   326
NORTH FORK TOUTLE 74
NORTH JETTY 104
NORTH LAKE 128, 240
NORTH NORTH WINDMILL 100
NORTH ORCAS ISLANDNORTH
   ORCAS ISLAND 314
NORTH RIVER 105, 193, 333
NORTH SILVER 250
NORTH SKOOKUM 200
NORTH WILLOW 100
NORTH WINDMILL 100
NORTHERN PIKE 13
NORTHERN PIKEMINNOW 13
NORTHRUP LAKE 95
NORTHWESTERN LAKE
   154, 227
NUNNALLY LAKE 90, 92, 95

O

OAK BAY/LIPLIP POINT 313
OAK CREEK 288
OBSCURITY LAKE 227
OCEAN SHORES BEACH,
   NORTH JETTY 106
ODELL CREEK 299
OFFUT LAKE 262
OHANAPECOSH RIVER 296
OHOP LAKE 206
OKANOGAN RIVER. 185
OLALLIE LAKE 125, 228
OLIVER LAKE 110, 295
OLSON LAKE 240
OMAK CREEK 185
OMAK LAKE 184, 185
ONAMAC POINT 317
ORCHARD POND 65
ORR'S POND 110
OSBORN LAKE 174
OSOYOOS LAKE 186

OSTRANDER CREEK 73
OTTER 122, 289
OTTER LAKE 288
OUTLET CREEK 154
OVAL LAKES 183, 186
OVER LAKE 294
OZETTE LAKE 51

P

P. J. LAKE 307
PACIFIC BEACHES 106
PACIFIC COD 17
PACIFIC LAKE 168
PACKWOOD LAKE 162
PADDEN LAKE 275
PADILLA 217
PALIS RIVER 332
PALISADES LAKES 296
PALIX RIVER 193
PALMER 37
PALMER LAKE 186, 187
PALOUSE RIVER 30, 280
PAMPA POND 281
PANHANDLE LAKE 175, 228
PANTHER CREEK 228
PANTHER LAKE
   129, 141, 175, 240
PARA-JUVENILE LAKE 95
PARADISE LAKES 129
PARADISE RIVER 296
PARK LAKE 89, 95
PARK LAKES 148
PARK LAKES, 147
PARKER LAKE 199
PASS LAKE 216, 235, 240
PATAHA CREEK 86
PATIT CREEK 65
PATTERSON LAKE 186
PATTISON LAKE 261
PATTISON LAKE. 262
PEACH LAKE 240
PEAR AND APPLE LAKES 288
PEAR LAKE 289
PEARRYGIN LAKE 186
PEEK-A-BOO LAKE 240
PELTON CREEK 307
PENAWAWA CREEK 281
PEND OREILLE RIVER 199
PENNY CREEK AND PONDS 114
PEPOON LAKE 257
PERCH 17
PERCH LAKE 95
PERCIVAL CREEK 262
PERCIVAL LAKE 262
PESHASTIN CREEK 44
PETE LAKE 148
PETERSON LAKE 129
PHANTOM LAKE 129
PHEBE LAKE 217
PHELAN LAKE 257
PHILLIPA LAKE 129
PHILLIPS LAKE 175, 257
PICNIC POINT POND 240
PIERRE LAKE 255, 258
PILCHUCK CREEK 217, 240
PILCHUCK RIVER 240
PILLAR 289
PILLAR LAKE 95
PILLAR POINT 51, 314
PINE CREEK 227
PINE LAKE 129, 276
PINES LAKE 30
PINK SALMON 19
PINNACLE LAKE 240

PIT LAKE 95
PIT PONDS. 37
PITCHER MT. LAKE 207
PLACER LAKE 288
PLACID LAKE 228
PLEASANT LAKE 51
PLUMMER LAKE 162
POINT DEFIANCE 207, 311
POINT HEYER 317
POINT JEFFERSON 312
POINT LAWRENCE 314
POINT NO POINT 313
PONDILLA LAKE 110
POPE LAKES 106
PORT ANGELES 51
PORT TOWNSEND 313
PORTER CREEK 106
POSSESSION POINT 317
POSSESSION POINT/BAR 312
POST OFFICE LAKE. 61
POTHOLE LAKE 154
POTTER LAKE 258
POTTERS POND 253
POULSBO 142
POWER LAKE 199
POWERLINE CROSSING 37
POWERLINE LAKE 84
POWERLINE POND 240
PRAIRIE CREEK 106
PRAIRIE LAKES 217
PRATT LAKE 125
PRATT RIVER 129
PRESTON MILL PONDS 129
PRICE LAKE 176
PRIEST POINT PARK 262
PRIEST RAPIDS RESERVOIR 96
PRIEST RIVER 199
PRINCE CREEK 44
PROCTOR CREEK 240
PROCTOR LAKE 186
PTARMIGAN LAKE 129
PUGET SOUND 130, 240
PUYALLUP RIVER 207, 333
PYSHT MILL POND 51
PYSHT RIVER 52

Q

QUAIL LAKE 30
QUARRY LAKE 268
QUARTZ CREEK 162
QUEETS 326
QUEETS RIVER 114, 308
QUEETS RIVER 333
QUILCENE RIVER 114, 333
QUILLAYUTE RIVER 52, 333
QUINAULT LAKE 106
QUINAULT RIVER
   106, 114, 308, 333
QUINAULT RIVER NORTH FORK
   308
QUINCY LAKE 96

R

RABBIT LAKES 147
RACEHORSE CREEK 276
RACHEL LAKE 148
RADAR PONDS 193
RAFT RIVER 106
RAGING RIVER 130
RAILROAD POND 84
RAINBOW 65
RAINBOW CREEK 44, 65, 302
RAINBOW LAKE 96, 125

RAINBOW TROUT 7
RAINIER SCHOOL POND 207
RAMON LAKES 186
RAPID RIVER 233, 241
RAPJOHN LAKE 207
RAT LAKE 186
RATTLESNAKE CREEK
  35, 154, 288
RATTLESNAKE LAKE 130
RAVENSDALE CREEK 130
RAVENSDALE LAKE 130
REBECCA LAKE 185
RED CREEK 130
RED ROCK LAKE 96
REDROCK LAKE 338
REFLECTION LAKE 296, 308
REICHEL LAKE 262
REID SLOUGH 130
REMMEL LAKE 187
RENDSLAND CREEK 176
RENNER LAKE 81
RETREAT LAKE 130
RIALTO-RUBY BEACHES 52
RIDGE LAKE 148
RIFFE LAKE 163
RILEY LAKE 241
RIMROCK LAKE 288
RIPARIAN POND 281
RIPLEY CREEK 114
ROBBINS LAKE 176
ROBINSON CREEK 65
ROCK BASS 12
ROCK CREEK
  31, 62, 119, 130, 154
ROCK ISLAND PONDS 77
ROCK LAKE
  44, 128, 130, 228, 281
ROCK LAKES 187
ROCK RABBIT LAKES 147
ROCKFISH 15
ROCKY CREEK 276
ROCKY FORD CREEK 95, 96
ROCKY LAKE 258
ROESIGER LAKE 241
ROOT LAKE 288
ROSE LAKE 176
ROSES LAKE 44
ROSS LAKE 276, 301
ROSS POINT 142
ROTARY LAKE 288
ROUND LAKE
  59, 62, 81, 96, 130, 187, 241
ROWEL LAKE 187
ROWLAND LAKE 155
ROY LAKE 208
ROYAL CREEK 308
ROYAL LAKE 31, 308
RUBY CREEK 199
RUE CREEK 193
RUFUS WOODS RESERVOIR
  75, 77
RUGGS LAKE 241
RUSHING WATER CREEK 295
RUTHERFORD SLOUGH 130
RYAN LAKE 228

S

SACAJAWEA LAKE 73
SACHEEN LAKE 199
SAGE LAKES 96
SAIL RIVER 52
SALMO RIVER 200
SALMON CREEK
  60, 62, 164, 187, 193
SALMON LAKE 187
SALMON RIVER 114, 308
SALTWATER 211, 217

SALTWATER FISHING 277
SAMISH 217
SAMISH LAKE 215, 277
SAMISH RIVER 217, 277, 333
SAMMAMISH (SLOUGH) RIVER
  131
SAMMAMISH LAKE 130
SAMMAMISH RIVER 333
SAN POIL RIVER 81, 187
SAND LAKE 96
SANDSTONE LAKE 289
SANDY SHORE LAKE 115
SARDINE LAKE 226
SARGE HUBBARD PARK POND
  289
SASSE LAKE 187
SATSOP LAKES 107
SATSOP RIVER 107, 108, 333
SATUS CREEK 289
SAUK LAKE 218
SAUK RIVER 326
SAUK RIVER LOWER 218
SAUK RIVER UPPER 241
SAWYER LAKE 131
SCANEWA LAKE 164
SCHAEFER LAKE 44
SCHALLOW POND 187
SCHEELITE LAKE 187
SCHUTES RIVER 332
SCOOTENEY RESERVOIR 84
SCOTT LAKE 262
SCOUT LAKE 123, 142, 308
SCRABBLE LAKE 242
SCRIBER LAKE 242
SCULPINS 17
SECOND LAKE 133
SECUALLITCHEW LAKE 208
SEEP LAKES 97
SEKIU 314
SEKIU (CLALLAM BAY) 52
SEKIU RIVER 53
SELAH CREEK 289
SEQUIM BAY 53, 314
SERENE LAKE 242
SEVEN LAKES BASIN 309
SHADOW LAKE 133
SHADY LAKE 133
SHANGHAI CREEK 62
SHANNON LAKE
  213, 214, 218, 220, 272
SHARKS 15
SHAW LAKE 242
SHEEP CREEK. 258
SHEEPHERDER LAKE 289
SHELF LAKE 218
SHELLROCK 289
SHERMAN CREEK 81, 168
SHERMAN LAKE 81
SHILSHOLE BAY 312
SHINE CREEK 115
SHINER 30
SHOE LAKE 177
SHOE LAKE. 176
SHOECRAFT LAKE 242
SHOVEL LAKE 228
SHOVELER LAKE 99
SHUKSAN LAKE 277
SHYE LAKE 107
SIDLEY LAKE 185, 187
SIKES LAKE 133
SILENT LAKE 115
SILER POND 164
SILVER CREEK 164, 242, 281
SILVER LAKE
  74, 110, 187, 206, 208, 242,
  246, 250, 277
SILVER LAKES 115

SIMILKAMEEN RIVER 187
SIMMONS LAKE 262
SIMPSON LAKE 176
SIMPSON LAKES 80
SINLAHEKIN CREEK 187
SIOUXON CREEK 62
SIXTEEN LAKE 218
SKAGIT 217, 326
SKAGIT RIVER 218, 301, 333
SKAGIT RIVER UPPER 277
SKAMOKAWA CREEK 266
SKARO LAKE 219
SKATE CREEK 164
SKATES 14
SKATING LAKE 193
SKOKOMISH RIVER 176, 333
SKOKOMISH RIVER NORTH
  FORK 309
SKOOKUM CREEK 277
SKOOKUM LAKES 200
SKOOKUMCHUCK RESERVOIR
  164
SKOOKUMCHUCK RIVER
  164, 262
SKYKOMISH 326
SKYKOMISH RIVER 333
SKYKOMISH RIVER (MAIN) 242
SKYKOMISH RIVER NORTH
  FORK 243
SKYKOMISH RIVER SOUTH
  FORK 133, 243
SKYLINE LAKE 133
SKYLINE MARINA 217
SLATE CREEK 200
SLIDE LAKE 214, 219
SMALLMOUTH BASS 11
SMC 128
SMELLING LAKE 243
SMELTS 21
SMITH CREEK 164, 193, 227
SMITH LAKE 262, 309
SNAKE RIVER
  35, 65, 84, 86, 268, 333
SNELL LAKE 208
SNOHOMISH RIVER 243, 333
SNOHOMISH RIVER SYSTEM
  326
SNOQUALMIE LAKE 133
SNOQUALMIE RIVER 326, 333
SNOQUALMIE RIVER MAIN 133
SNOQUALMIE RIVER MIDDLE
  FORK 134
SNOQUALMIE RIVER SOUTH
  FORK 134
SNOW 289
SNOW CREEK 115, 135
SNOW KING LAKE 219
SNOW LAKE 135, 164, 228, 293
SNOWPLOW LAKE 289
SNOWSLIDE LAKE 244
SOCKEYE SALMON 20
SODA LAKE 99
SOL DUC 53, 326
SOL DUC RIVER 309, 333
SOLES 14
SOOES CREEK 53
SOOES RIVER 53
SOOS CREEK 135
SOUPHOLE LAKE 135
SOURCE LAKE 135
SOUTH LEWIS COUNTY PARK
  338
SOUTH BEND MILL POND 194
SOUTH COUNTY PONDS 263
SOUTH CREEK 188
SOUTH FORK SAUK 242
SOUTH FORK SKYKOMISH 326

SOUTH FORK TOUTLE 74
SOUTH JETTY 104, 108
SOUTH LAKE 244
SOUTH LEWIS COUNTY PARK
   POND 165
SOUTH PRAIRIE CREEK. 208
SOUTH PRAIRIE LAKE 228
SOUTHWICK LAKE 262
SPADA LAKE 244
SPADE 150
SPADE LAKE 148
SPANAWAY LAKE 208
SPEARFISH LAKE 155
SPECTACLE LAKE 188, 189
SPENCER LAKE 175, 176
SPIDER LAKE 176
SPIRIT LAKE 74, 228
SPOKANE LAKE 250
SPOKANE RIVER 250
SPOOK LAKE 135
SPORTSMAN'S LAKE 211
SPRAGUE LAKE 31, 169
SPRING 65, 89
SPRING CREEK 94, 155
SPRING LAKE 135, 188
SPRING LAKES 99
SPRINGER LAKE 263
SPRINGSTEEN LAKE 219
SQUALICUM LAKE 277
SQUARE LAKE 142
SQUAW LAKE 149
SQUAXIN ISLAND 311
SQUILCHUCK CREEK 45
SQUIRE CREEK 245
ST CLAIR LAKE 261
ST. CLAIR LAKE 263
ST. HELEN'S LAKE 228
ST. JOHN LAKE 165
STAFFORD CREEKS 150
STAN COFFIN LAKE 99
STANDBY LAKE 172, 176
STAR LAKE 135
STARRY FLOUNDERS 14
STARVATION LAKE 258
STARZMAN LAKES 188
STEAMBOAT LAKE 228
STEEL LAKE 135
STEELHEAD 18
STEHEKIN RIVER 45, 302
STEILACOOM LAKE 208
STEVENS CREEK 296
STEVENS LAKE 176, 188, 245
STICKNEY LAKE 245
STICKNEY SLOUGH 135
STILLAGUAMISH RIVER
   245, 326, 333
STILLAGUAMISH RIVER NORTH
   FORK 245
STILLAGUAMISH RIVER SOUTH
   FORK 246
STIRRUP LAKE 149
STLER CREEK 308
STONE LAKE 246
STONES THROW LAKE 147
STORM LAKE 246
STOSSEL CREEK 135
STOSSEL LAKE 136
STRATFORD LAKE 99
STRAWBERRY LAKE 224, 229
STUCK RIVER 208
STUMP LAKE 107, 176
STURGEON 21
SUGARLOAF LAKE 188
SUIATTLE RIVER 219
SULLIVAN LAKE 198, 200
SULLIVAN MILL POND 200
SULTAN RIVER 246

SUMAS RIVER 277
SUMMIT CHIEF LAKE 149
SUMMIT CREEK 165
SUMMIT LAKE
   188, 207, 258, 261, 263
SUMNER LAKE 219
SUNDAY CREEK 136
SUNDAY LAKE 136, 246
SUNDOWN LAKE 309
SUNFISH 11
SUNRISE LAKE 296
SUNSET LAKE 208, 246
SURPRISE LAKE 136, 208, 289
SURPRISE LAKES 227, 229
SURVEYORS LAKE 136
SUSAN LAKE 99, 263
SUTHERLAND LAKE 53
SWAMP LAKE 285, 289
SWAN LAKE 82, 147, 149
SWANS MILL POND 136
SWARTZ LAKE. 246
SWAUK CREEK 149
SWIFT CREEK 277
SWIFT POWER CANAL 229
SWIFT RESERVOIR 227, 229
SWIMMING DEER LAKE 45
SWINOMISH CHANNEL 217
SWITCH POND 37
SWOFFORD POND 165
SYLVIA LAKE 107, 136

T

TACOMA CREEK 200
T'AHL LAKE 136
TAHOMA CREEK 296
TAHUYA LAKE 142
TAHUYA RIVER 177, 333
TAKHLAKH LAKE 223, 225, 229
TALAPUS LAKE 125, 136
TANEUM CREEK 149
TANEUM LAKE 149
TANWAX LAKE 208
TAPE LAKE 194
TAPPS LAKE 208
TARBOO CREEK 115
TARBOO LAKE 115
TATE CREEK 136
TATOOSH CREEK 296
TATOOSH LAKES 165
TAYLOR RIVER 136
TAYLOR RIVER TAYLOR RIVER
   134
TEAL LAKE 115
TEAL LAKES 99
TEE 176
TEE LAKE 176, 177
TEMPLE POND 246
TEN CREEKS 137
TEN LAKE 219
TENMILE CREEK 35, 278
TENNANT LAKE 278
TERRACE LAKE 150
TERRACE LAKES 136
TERRELL LAKE 278
TEXAS PONDS 219
THIRTYSIX LAKE 246
THOMAS LAKE 229, 246
THOMPSON LAKE 136
THORNDYKE CREEK 115
THORNTON LAKE 300
THORNTON LAKES 278
THORP LAKE 150
THREAD LAKE 32
THREE FINGER CHAIN BEAVER
   PONDS 142

THREE LAKE 45
THUNDER CREEK 219, 278
THUNDER LAKE 278
TICK LAKE 99
TIETON RIVER 289
TIGER LAKE 142, 177
TIGER MUSKIE 13
TIGER TROUT 8
TILTON RIVER 165
TINKER LAKE 194
TIPSOO LAKE 297
TOAD LAKE 278
TOKUL CREEK 133, 137
TOLIVA SHOAL 317
TOLIVIA SHOAL 311
TOLT RIVER 137, 333
TOM CREEK 309
TOMTIT LAKE 234, 246
TOMYHOI LAKE 278
TONATA CREEK 82
TOP LAKE 45, 137
TORODA CREEK 82, 188
TOUCHET RIVER 65, 269
TOUTLE RIVER 74, 333
TOWNSEND CREEK 115
TRADEDOLLAR LAKE 229
TRADITION LAKE 137
TRAIL LAKE 99
TRAILS END LAKE 263
TRAILS END LAKE (AKA
   PRICKETT) 177
TRAP CREEK 194
TRAP LAKE 45
TRAPPER LAKE 45, 300
TRASK LAKE 177
TRIPLET LAKES 302
TROSPER LAKE 264
TROUT CREEK 229
TROUT LAKE
   45, 82, 122, 138, 198, 200,
   224, 246
TROUT LAKE CREEK 155, 229
TSHLETSHY CREEK 309
TUCANNON LAKES 65
TUCANNON RIVER 66, 86
TUCQUALA LAKE 150
TULE LAKE 168, 208
TUNNEL LAKE 229
TUPSO LAKE 220
TURNER LAKE 188
TWANOH STATE PARK 177
TWELVE LAKE 138
TWENTY TWO LAKE 246
TWENTY-FIVE MILE CREEK
   39, 45
TWILIGHT LAKE 145
TWIN LAKE 254
TWIN LAKE, UPPER 115
TWIN LAKES
   82, 150, 169, 177, 186, 188,
   211, 247, 258
TWIN RIVERS 55
TWIN SISTERS LAKES 289
TWISP RIVER 188
TYE RIVER 138

U

UNDI LAKE 55
UNION FLAT CREEK 281
UNION LAKE 138
UNION RIVER 177
UNION RIVER 333
UNION/TAHUYA 313
UPPER BOARDMAN LAKE 235
UPPER CONCONULLY LAKE 188